Social Network Data Analytics

Charu C. Aggarwal
Editor

Social Network Data Analytics

Springer

Editor
Charu C. Aggarwal
IBM Thomas J. Watson Research Center
19 Skyline Drive
Hawthorne, NY 10532, USA
charu@us.ibm.com

ISBN 978-1-4419-8461-6 e-ISBN 978-1-4419-8462-3
DOI 10.1007/978-1-4419-8462-3
Springer New York Dordrecht Heidelberg London

Library of Congress Control Number: 2011922836

Printed on acid-free paper

Springer is part of Springer Science+Business Media (www.springer.com)

Contents

Preface	xiii
1	
An Introduction to Social Network Data Analytics	1
Charu C. Aggarwal	
1. Introduction	1
2. Online Social Networks: Research Issues	5
3. Research Topics in Social Networks	8
4. Conclusions and Future Directions	13
References	14
2	
Statistical Properties of Social Networks	17
Mary McGlohon, Leman Akoglu and Christos Faloutsos	
1. Preliminaries	19
1.1 Definitions	19
1.2 Data description	24
2. Static Properties	26
2.1 Static Unweighted Graphs	26
2.2 Static Weighted Graphs	27
3. Dynamic Properties	32
3.1 Dynamic Unweighted Graphs	32
3.2 Dynamic Weighted Graphs	36
4. Conclusion	39
References	40
3	
Random Walks in Social Networks and their Applications: A Survey	43
Purnamrita Sarkar and Andrew W. Moore	
1. Introduction	43
2. Random Walks on Graphs: Background	45
2.1 Random Walk based Proximity Measures	46
2.2 Other Graph-based Proximity Measures	52
2.3 Graph-theoretic Measures for Semi-supervised Learning	53
2.4 Clustering with random walk based measures	56
3. Related Work: Algorithms	57
3.1 Algorithms for Hitting and Commute Times	58
3.2 Algorithms for Computing Personalized Pagerank and Simrank	60

3.3 Algorithms for Computing Harmonic Functions 63
4. Related Work: Applications 63
4.1 Application in Computer Vision 64
4.2 Text Analysis 64
4.3 Collaborative Filtering 65
4.4 Combating Webspam 66
5. Related Work: Evaluation and datasets 66
5.1 Evaluation: Link Prediction 66
5.2 Publicly Available Data Sources 68
6. Conclusion and Future Work 69
References 71

4
Community Discovery in Social Networks: Applications, Methods and Emerging Trends 79
S. Parthasarathy, Y. Ruan and V. Satuluri
1. Introduction 80
2. Communities in Context 82
3. Core Methods 84
3.1 Quality Functions 85
3.2 The Kernighan-Lin(KL) algorithm 86
3.3 Agglomerative/Divisive Algorithms 87
3.4 Spectral Algorithms 89
3.5 Multi-level Graph Partitioning 90
3.6 Markov Clustering 91
3.7 Other Approaches 92
4. Emerging Fields and Problems 95
4.1 Community Discovery in Dynamic Networks 95
4.2 Community Discovery in Heterogeneous Networks 97
4.3 Community Discovery in Directed Networks 98
4.4 Coupling Content and Relationship Information for Community Discovery 100
5. Crosscutting Issues and Concluding Remarks 102
References 104

5
Node Classification in Social Networks 115
Smriti Bhagat, Graham Cormode and S. Muthukrishnan
1. Introduction 116
2. Problem Formulation 119
2.1 Representing data as a graph 119
2.2 The Node Classification Problem 123
3. Methods using Local Classifiers 124
3.1 Iterative Classification Method 125
4. Random Walk based Methods 127
4.1 Label Propagation 129
4.2 Graph Regularization 132
4.3 Adsorption 134
5. Applying Node Classification to Large Social Networks 136
5.1 Basic Approaches 137
5.2 Second-order Methods 137
5.3 Implementation within Map-Reduce 138

6. Related approaches 139
6.1 Inference using Graphical Models 139
6.2 Metric labeling 140
6.3 Spectral Partitioning 141
6.4 Graph Clustering 142
7. Variations on Node Classification 142
7.1 Dissimilarity in Labels 142
7.2 Edge Labeling 143
7.3 Label Summarization 144
8. Concluding Remarks 144
8.1 Future Directions and Challenges 145
8.2 Further Reading 146
References 146

6
Evolution in Social Networks: A Survey 149
Myra Spiliopoulou
1. Introduction 149
2. Framework 151
2.1 Modeling a Network across the Time Axis 151
2.2 Evolution across Four Dimensions 152
3. Challenges of Social Network Streams 154
4. Incremental Mining for Community Tracing 156
5. Tracing Smoothly Evolving Communities 160
5.1 Temporal Smoothness for Clusters 160
5.2 Dynamic Probabilistic Models 162
6. Laws of Evolution in Social Networks 167
7. Conclusion 169
References 170

7
A Survey of Models and Algorithms for Social Influence Analysis 177
Jimeng Sun and Jie Tang
1. Introduction 177
2. Influence Related Statistics 178
2.1 Edge Measures 178
2.2 Node Measures 180
3. Social Similarity and Influence 183
3.1 Homophily 183
3.2 Existential Test for Social Influence 188
3.3 Influence and Actions 189
3.4 Influence and Interaction 195
4. Influence Maximization in Viral Marketing 200
4.1 Influence Maximization 200
4.2 Other Applications 206
5. Conclusion 208
References 209

8
A Survey of Algorithms and Systems for Expert Location in Social Networks 215
Theodoros Lappas, Kun Liu and Evimaria Terzi
1. Introduction 216

2. Definitions and Notation 217
3. Expert Location without Graph Constraints 219
3.1 Language Models for Document Information Retrieval 219
3.2 Language Models for Expert Location 220
3.3 Further Reading 221
4. Expert Location with Score Propagation 221
4.1 The PageRank Algorithm 222
4.2 HITS Algorithm 223
4.3 Expert Score Propagation 224
4.4 Further Reading 226
5. Expert Team Formation 227
5.1 Metrics 227
5.2 Forming Teams of Experts 228
5.3 Further Reading 232
6. Other Related Approaches 232
6.1 Agent-based Approach 233
6.2 Influence Maximization 233
7. Expert Location Systems 235
8. Conclusions 235
References 236

9
A Survey of Link Prediction in Social Networks 243
Mohammad Al Hasan and Mohammed J. Zaki
1. Introduction 244
2. Background 245
3. Feature based Link Prediction 246
3.1 Feature Set Construction 247
3.2 Classification Models 253
4. Bayesian Probabilistic Models 259
4.1 Link Prediction by Local Probabilistic Models 259
4.2 Network Evolution based Probabilistic Model 261
4.3 Hierarchical Probabilistic Model 263
5. Probabilistic Relational Models 264
5.1 Relational Bayesian Network 266
5.2 Relational Markov Network 266
6. Linear Algebraic Methods 267
7. Recent development and Future Works 269
References 270

10
Privacy in Social Networks: A Survey 277
Elena Zheleva and Lise Getoor
1. Introduction 277
2. Privacy breaches in social networks 280
2.1 Identity disclosure 281
2.2 Attribute disclosure 282
2.3 Social link disclosure 283
2.4 Affiliation link disclosure 284
3. Privacy definitions for publishing data 286
3.1 k-anonymity 288

3.2 l-diversity and t-closeness 290
3.3 Differential privacy 291
4. Privacy-preserving mechanisms 292
4.1 Privacy mechanisms for social networks 292
4.2 Privacy mechanisms for affiliation networks 297
4.3 Privacy mechanisms for social and affiliation networks 300
5. Related literature 302
6. Conclusion 302
References 303

11
Visualizing Social Networks 307
Carlos D. Correa and Kwan-Liu Ma
1. Introduction 307
2. A Taxonomy of Visualizations 309
2.1 Structural Visualization 309
2.2 Semantic and Temporal Visualization 313
2.3 Statistical Visualization 315
3. The Convergence of Visualization, Interaction and Analytics 316
3.1 Structural and Semantic Filtering with Ontologies 319
3.2 Centrality-based Visual Discovery and Exploration 319
4. Summary 322
References 323

12
Data Mining in Social Media 327
Geoffrey Barbier and Huan Liu
1. Introduction 327
2. Data Mining in a Nutshell 328
3. Social Media 330
4. Motivations for Data Mining in Social Media 332
5. Data Mining Methods for Social Media 333
5.1 Data Representation 334
5.2 Data Mining - A Process 335
5.3 Social Networking Sites: Illustrative Examples 336
5.4 The Blogosphere: Illustrative Examples 340
6. Related Efforts 344
6.1 Ethnography and Netnography 344
6.2 Event Maps 345
7. Conclusions 345
References 347

13
Text Mining in Social Networks 353
Charu C. Aggarwal and Haixun Wang
1. Introduction 354
2. Keyword Search 356
2.1 Query Semantics and Answer Ranking 357
2.2 Keyword search over XML and relational data 358
2.3 Keyword search over graph data 360
3. Classification Algorithms 366

4. Clustering Algorithms 369
5. Transfer Learning in Heterogeneous Networks 371
6. Conclusions and Summary 373
References 374

14
Integrating Sensors and Social Networks 379
Charu C. Aggarwal and Tarek Abdelzaher
1. Introduction 379
2. Sensors and Social Networks: Technological Enablers 383
3. Dynamic Modeling of Social Networks 385
4. System Design and Architectural Challenges 387
4.1 Privacy-preserving data collection 388
4.2 Generalized Model Construction 389
4.3 Real-time Decision Services 389
4.4 Recruitment Issues 390
4.5 Other Architectural Challenges 390
5. Database Representation: Issues and Challenges 391
6. Privacy Issues 399
7. Sensors and Social Networks: Applications 402
7.1 The Google Latitude Application 402
7.2 The Citysense and Macrosense Applications 403
7.3 Green GPS 404
7.4 Microsoft SensorMap 405
7.5 Animal and Object Tracking Applications 405
7.6 Participatory Sensing for Real-Time Services 406
8. Future Challenges and Research Directions 407
References 407

15
Multimedia Information Networks in Social Media 413
Liangliang Cao, GuoJun Qi, Shen-Fu Tsai, Min-Hsuan Tsai, Andrey Del Pozo, Thomas S. Huang, Xuemei Zhang and Suk Hwan Lim
1. Introduction 414
2. Links from Semantics: Ontology-based Learning 415
3. Links from Community Media 416
3.1 Retrieval Systems for Community Media 417
3.2 Recommendation Systems for Community Media 418
4. Network of Personal Photo Albums 420
4.1 Actor-Centric Nature of Personal Collections 420
4.2 Quality Issues in Personal Collections 421
4.3 Time and Location Themes in Personal Collections 422
4.4 Content Overlap in Personal Collections 422
5. Network of Geographical Information 423
5.1 Semantic Annotation 425
5.2 Geographical Estimation 425
5.3 Other Applications 426
6. Inference Methods 427
6.1 Discriminative vs. Generative Models 427
6.2 Graph-based Inference: Ranking, Clustering and Semi-supervised Learning 428

6.3 Online Learning 429
7. Discussion of Data Sets and Industrial Systems 432
8. Discussion of Future Directions 434
8.1 Content-based Recommendation and Advertisements 434
8.2 Multimedia Information Networks via Cloud Computing 434
References 436

16
An Overview of Social Tagging and Applications 447
Manish Gupta, Rui Li, Zhijun Yin and Jiawei Han
1. Introduction 448
1.1 Problems with Metadata Generation and Fixed Taxonomies 449
1.2 Folksonomies as a Solution 449
1.3 Outline 450
2. Tags: Why and What? 451
2.1 Different User Tagging Motivations 451
2.2 Kinds of Tags 452
2.3 Categorizers Versus Describers 453
2.4 Linguistic Classification of Tags 454
2.5 Game-based Tagging 455
3. Tag Generation Models 455
3.1 Polya Urn Generation Model 456
3.2 Language Model 458
3.3 Other Influence Factors 459
4. Tagging System Design 460
5. Tag analysis 462
5.1 Tagging Distributions 463
5.2 Identifying Tag Semantics 464
5.3 Tags Versus Keywords 466
6. Visualization of Tags 467
6.1 Tag Clouds for Browsing/Search 468
6.2 Tag Selection for Tag Clouds 468
6.3 Tag Hierarchy Generation 469
6.4 Tag Clouds Display Format 470
6.5 Tag Evolution Visualization 470
6.6 Popular Tag Cloud Demos 471
7. Tag Recommendations 472
7.1 Using Tag Quality 472
7.2 Using Tag Co-occurrences 473
7.3 Using Mutual Information between Words, Documents and Tags 474
7.4 Using Object Features 474
8. Applications of Tags 475
8.1 Indexing 475
8.2 Search 475
8.3 Taxonomy Generation 480
8.4 Public Library Cataloging 481
8.5 Clustering and Classification 482
8.6 Social Interesting Discovery 483
8.7 Enhanced Browsing 484
9. Integration 485

9.1 Integration using Tag Co-occurrence Analysis and Clustering 485
9.2 TAGMAS: Federated Tagging System 486
9.3 Correlating User Profiles from Different Folksonomies 487
10. Tagging problems 488
10.1 Spamming 488
10.2 Canonicalization and Ambiguities 489
10.3 Other Problems 490
11. Conclusion and Future Directions 490
11.1 Analysis 491
11.2 Improving System Design 491
11.3 Personalized Tag Recommendations 491
11.4 More Applications 492
11.5 Dealing With Problems 492
References 492

Index 499

Preface

Social networks have been studied fairly extensively over two decades in the general context of analyzing interactions between people, and determining the important structural patterns in such interactions. The trends in recent years have focussed on *online* social networks, in which the social network is enabled as an *internet application.* Some examples of such networks are *Facebook*, *LinkedIn* and *MySpace*. Such social networks have rapidly grown in popularity, because they are no longer constrained by the geographical limitations of a conventional social network in which interactions are defined in more conventional way such as face-to-face meetings, or personal friendships.

The infrastructure which is built around social networks can support a rich variety of data analytic applications such as search, text analysis, image analysis, and sensor applications. Furthermore, the analysis and evolution of the structure of the social network is also an interesting problem in of itself. While some of these problems are also encountered in the more conventional notion of social networks, many of the problems which relate to the data-analytic aspects of social networks are relevant only in the context of online social networks. Furthermore, online social networks allow for more efficient data collection on a large scale, and therefore, the computational challenges are far more significant.

A number of books have been written in recent years on the topic of social networks, though most of these books focus on the non-technological aspect, and consider social networks more generally in the context of relationships between individuals. Therefore, these books mostly focus on the social, structural, and cognitive aspects of the social network, and do not focus on the unique issues which arise in the context of the interplay between the structural and data-centric aspects of the network. For example, an online social network may contain various kinds of contents or media such as text, images, blogs or web pages. The ability to mine these rich sources of information in the context of a social network provides an unprecedented challenge and also an opportunity to determine useful and actionable information in a wide variety of fields such as marketing, social sciences, and defense. The volume of the data available is also a challenge in many cases because of storage and efficiency constraints. This book provides a first comprehensive compendium on recent research on the *data-centric aspect* of social networks.

Research in the field of online social networks has seen a revival in the last ten years. The research in the field is now reaching a level of maturity where it is useful to create an organized set of chapters which describe the recent advancements in this field. This book contains a set of survey chapters on the different data analytic issues in online social networks. The chapters describe the different facets of the field in a comprehensive way. This creates an organized description of the significant body of research in the important and emerging field of online social networks.

Chapter 1

AN INTRODUCTION TO SOCIAL NETWORK DATA ANALYTICS

Charu C. Aggarwal
IBM T. J. Watson Research Center
Hawthorne, NY 10532
charu@us.ibm.com

Abstract The advent of online social networks has been one of the most exciting events in this decade. Many popular online social networks such as *Twitter*, *LinkedIn*, and *Facebook* have become increasingly popular. In addition, a number of multimedia networks such as *Flickr* have also seen an increasing level of popularity in recent years. Many such social networks are extremely rich in content, and they typically contain a tremendous amount of *content* and *linkage* data which can be leveraged for analysis. The linkage data is essentially the graph structure of the social network and the communications between entities; whereas the content data contains the text, images and other multimedia data in the network. The richness of this network provides unprecedented opportunities for data analytics in the context of social networks. This book provides a *data-centric view* of *online* social networks; a topic which has been missing from much of the literature. This chapter provides an overview of the key topics in this field, and their coverage in this book.

Keywords: Social Networks, Data Mining

1. Introduction

This chapter will provide an introduction of the topic of social networks, and the broad organization of this book. Social networks have become very popular in recent years because of the increasing proliferation and affordability of internet enabled devices such as personal computers, mobile devices and other more recent hardware innovations such as internet tablets. This is evidenced by the burgeoning popularity of many online social networks such as *Twitter*,

Facebook and *LinkedIn*. Such social networks have lead to a tremendous explosion of network-centric data in a wide variety of scenarios. Social networks can be defined either in the context of systems such as *Facebook* which are explicitly designed for social interactions, or in terms of other sites such as *Flickr* which are designed for a different service such as content sharing, but which also allow an extensive level of social interaction.

In general, a social network is defined as a network of *interactions* or *relationships*, where the nodes consist of actors, and the edges consist of the relationships or interactions between these actors. A generalization of the idea of social networks is that of *information networks*, in which the nodes could comprise *either* actors or *entities*, and the edges denote the relationships between them. Clearly, the concept of social networks is not restricted to the specific case of an internet-based social network such as *Facebook*; the problem of social networking has been studied often in the field of sociology in terms of generic interactions between any group of actors. Such interactions may be in any conventional or non-conventional form, whether they be face-to-face interactions, telecommunication interactions, email interactions or postal mail interactions.

The conventional studies on social network analysis have generally not focussed on *online interactions*, and have historically preceded the advent and popularity of computers or the internet. A classic example of this is the study of Milgram [18] in the sixties (well before the invention of the internet), who hypothesized the likelihood that any pair of actors on the planet are separated by at most six degrees of separation. While such hypotheses have largely remained conjectures over the last few decades, the development of online social networks has made it possible to test such hypotheses at least in an online setting. This is also referred to as the *small world* phenomenon. This phenomenon was tested in the context of MSN messenger data, and it was shown in [16] that the average path length between two MSN messenger users is 6.6. This can be considered a verification of the widely known rule of "six degrees of separation" in (generic) social networks. Such examples are by no means unique; a wide variety of online data is now available which has been used to verify the truth of a host of other conjectures such[1] as that of *shrinking diameters*[15] or *preferential attachment*. In general, *the availability of massive amounts of data in an online setting has given a new impetus towards a scientific and statistically robust study of the field of social networks.*

[1]The shrinking diameter conjecture hypothesizes that the diameters of social networks shrink in spite of the addition of new nodes, because of an increase in the density of the underlying edges. The preferential attachment conjecture hypothesizes that new nodes and edges in the social networks are more likely to be attached to the dense regions of the network.

This data-centric impetus has lead to a significant amount of research, which has been unique in its statistical and computational focus in analyzing large amounts of online social network data. In many cases, the underlying insights are applicable to the conventional social network setting as well. Before discussing the research topics in more detail, we will briefly enumerate the different settings for social network analysis, and specifically distinguish between the conventional and non-conventional scenarios. Specifically, these different settings are as follows:

- The most classical definition of a social network is one which is based purely on human interactions. This is the classical study of social networks in the field of sociology. These studies have traditionally been conducted with painstaking and laborious methods for measuring interactions between entities by collecting the actual data about human interactions manually. An example is the six-degrees-of-separation experiment by Milgram [18], who used postal mail between participants in order to test whether two arbitrary actors could be connected by a chain of 6 edges with the use of locally chosen forwards of the mail. Such experiments are often hard to conduct in a completely satisfactory way, because the actors in such experiments may have response rates which cannot be cleanly modeled in terms of social interaction behavior. An example is the case of the Milgram experiment, in which the results have often been questioned [14] because of the low forward rate of the letters which never reached the target. Furthermore, such social experiments are often biased towards high status targets in order to ensure likelihood of logical forwards. However, these results have eventually been accepted at least from a qualitative perspective, even though the rule of six degrees may not be precisely correct, depending upon the nature of the network which is being studied. Nevertheless, the "small world phenomenon" definitely seems to be correct, since the diameters of most such networks are relatively small.

  The social analysis of such networks has also been modeled in the field of cognitive science, where the cognitive aspects of such interactions are utilized for analytical purposes. Much of the research in the traditional field of social networks has been conducted from this perspective. A number of books [7, 24, 25] provide an understanding of this perspective. However, this work does not discuss the data-centric issues which are common to *online and internet-enabled* social networks.

- A number of technological enablers such as telecommunications, electronic mail, and electronic chat messengers (such as Skype, Google Talk or MSN Messenger), can be considered an indirect form of social networks, because they are naturally modeled as communications between different actors. One advantage of such applications is that the traces of the communication data are often available (subject to some privacy controls). This data can be used for extensive analysis of such social networks. Some examples are the extensive analysis on the Enron email data set [28], or the recent verification of the six degrees of separation conjecture in the context of the MSN messenger data in [16].

- In recent years, a number of sites have arisen explicitly in order to model the interactions between different actors. Some examples of such social networks are *Facebook*, *MySpace*, or *LinkedIn*. In addition, sites which are used for sharing online media content, such as *Flickr*, *Youtube* or *delicious*, can also be considered indirect forms of social networks, because they allow an extensive level of user interaction. In these cases, the interaction is centered around a specific service such as content-sharing; yet many fundamental principles of social networking apply. We note that such social networks are extremely *rich*, in that they contain a tremendous amount of content such as text, images, audio or video. Such content can be leveraged for a wide variety of purposes. In particular, the interaction between the links and content has provided impetus to a wide variety of mining applications. In addition, social media outlets provide a number of unique ways for users to interact with one another such as posting blogs, or tagging each other's images. Which such forms of interaction are indirect, they provide rich *content-based* knowledge which can be exploited for mining purposes. In recent years, it has even become possible to integrate *real-time sensor-based content* into dynamic social networks. This is because of the development of sensors, accelerometers, mobile devices and other GPS-enabled devices, which can be used in a social setting for providing a dynamic and interactive experience.

- Finally, a number of social networks can also be constructed from specific kinds of interactions in different communities. A classical example would be the scientific community in which bibliographic networks can be constructed from either co-authorship or citation data. These can be used in conjunction with the content of the publications in order to derive interesting trends and patterns about the underlying papers. We note that much of the analysis for the first case above applies to this as well, though a lot of data and content is available because of the way in which such documents networks are archived. A number of document collections and bibliographic networks are archived explicitly, and they can be used in conjunction with more principled data-centric techniques, because of the content which is available along with such networks.

While the results of this book may be applicable to all the different kinds of social networks, the specific focus is on the data-centric issues which arise in the context of online social networks. It is also important to understand that an online social network can be defined much more generally than an online site such as *Facebook*, *Twitter* or *LinkedIn* which are formally advertised as social networking sites. In fact, *any web-site or application which provides a social experience in the form of user-interactions* can be considered to be a form of social network. For example, media-sharing sites such as *Flickr*, *Youtube*, or *delicious* are formally not considered social networks; yet they allow for social interactions in the context of information exchange about the content being shared. Similarly, many mobile, web, and internet-driven chat applications also have social aspects embedded in them. Furthermore, many mobile applications such as *Google Latitude* allow the implicit embedding of sensor or GPS information, and this is used in order to enable user interactions. These are all novel forms of social networks, each of which brings with it a set of unique challenges for the purpose of analysis. Therefore, our definition of social networks is fairly broad, and many chapters will study aspects which are relevant to these alternative forms of social networks.

This chapter is organized as follows. In the next section, we discuss the main thrusts in the field of social networks. In section 3, we discuss the organization of the book and their relationships to these different thrusts. In section 4, we present the conclusions and related directions in the field.

2. Online Social Networks: Research Issues

The field of online social networks has seen a rapid revival in recent years. A key aspect of many of the online social networks is that they are *rich in data*, and provide unprecedented challenges and opportunities from the perspective of knowledge discovery and data mining. There are two primary kinds of data which are often analyzed in the context of social networks:

- **Linkage-based and Structural Analysis:** In linkage-based and structural analysis, we construct an analysis of the linkage behavior of the network in order to determine important nodes, communities, links, and evolving regions of the network. Such analysis provides a good overview of the global evolution behavior of the underlying network.

- **Adding Content-based Analysis:** Many social networks such as *Flickr*, *Message Networks*, and *Youtube* contain a tremendous amount of content which can be leveraged in order to improve the quality of the analysis. For example, a photograph sharing site such as *Flickr* contains a tremendous amount of text and image information in the form of user-tags and images. Similarly, blog networks, email networks and message boards contain text content which are linked to one another. It has been observed that combining content-based analysis with linkage-based analysis provides more effective results in a wide variety of applications. For example, communities which are designed with text-content are much richer in terms of carrying information about the topical expertise of the underlying community.

The other main differences which arises in the context of social network algorithms is that between *dynamic analysis* and *static analysis*. In the case of static analysis, we assume that the social network changes slowly over time, and we perform an analysis of the whole network in batch mode over particular snapshots. Such is often the case for many networks such as bibliographic networks in which the new events in the network may happen only slowly over time. On the other hand, in the case of many networks such as instant messaging networks, interactions are continuously received over time at very large rate, which may lead to network streams. The analysis of such networks is much more challenging, and is a subject of recent research [2–5]. The temporal aspect of networks often arises in the context of dynamic and evolving scenarios. Many interesting temporal characteristics of networks can be determined such as evolving communities, interactions between entities and temporal events in the underlying network.

Dynamic networks also arise in the context of *mobile applications*, in which moving entities constantly interact with one another. Such dynamic networks arise in the context of moving entities which interact with one another over time. For example, many mobile phones are equipped with GPS receivers, which are exploited by the applications on these phones. A classical example of such an application is the *Google Latitude* application which is capable of keeping track of the locations of different users, and issuing alerts when a given user is in the vicinity. Such dynamic social networks can be modeled as dynamic graphs for which the edges change constantly over time. Such dynamic graphs lead to massive challenges in processing because of the extremely large number of connections between the entities which may need to be tracked simultaneously. In such cases, graph stream mining applications are required in order to perform effective online analysis. Such applications are typically required to be able to summarize the network structure of the data in real time and utilize it for a variety of mining applications. Some recent advances in this direction are discussed in [1, 3].

A number of important problems arise in the context of structural analysis of social networks. An important line of research is to try to understand and model the nature of very large online networks. For example, the verification of the *small world phenomenon*, *preferential attachment*, and other general structural dynamics has been a topic of great interest in recent years. Since a significantly larger amount of data is available for the case of online social networks, the verification of such structural properties is much more robust in terms of statistical significance. For the first time, it has actually become possible to study these classical conjectures in the context of massive amounts of data.

The most well known structural problem in the context of social networks is that of *community detection*. The problem of community detection is closely related to the problem of finding structurally related groups in the network. These structurally related groups are referred to as *communities*. Some well known methods for community detection are discussed in [8, 9, 11, 19]. The problem of community detection arises both in a static setting in which the network changes slowly over time, as well as a dynamic setting in which the network structure evolves rapidly. While these problems have been studied in the traditional literature in the context of the problem of graph partitioning [11], social networks are significantly larger in size. Furthermore, a significant amount of content may be available for improving the effectiveness of community discovery. Such challenges are unique to the online scenario, and has lead to the development of a significant number of interesting algorithms.

Social networks can be viewed as a structure which enables the dissemination of information. This is direct corollary of its enabling of social interactions among individuals. The *analysis of the dynamics of such interaction* is a challenging problem in the field of social networks. For example, important news is propagated through the network with the use of the interactions between the different entities. A well known model for influence propagation may be found in [20]. The problem of influence analysis is very relevant in the context of social networks, especially in the context of determining the most influential members of the social network, who are most likely to propagate their influence to other entities in the social network [12]. The most influential members in the social network may be determined using flow models as in [12], or by using page rank style methods which determine the most well connected entities in the social network.

Finally, an important class of techniques is that of inferring links which are not yet known in the social networks. This problem is referred to as that of *link inference* [17]. The link prediction problem is useful for determining important *future* linkages in the underlying social network. Such future linkages provide an idea of the future relationships or missing relationships in the social network. Link prediction is also useful in a number of*adversarial applications* in which one does not fully know the linkages in an enemy or terrorist network, and uses automated data mining techniques in order to estimate the underlying links.

Many of the above mentioned applications can be greatly improved with the use of content information. For example, content can be associated with nodes in the community, which has been shown to greatly improve the quality of the clusters in the underlying network [26]. This is because the content information in different parts of the network is often closely related to its structure; the combination of the two can provide useful information which cannot be obtained from either as a single entity. It has also been observed [10] that the use of content information can also improve the qualitative results on problems such as link inference. In general, the incorporation of content can improve the end result of a wide variety of inference problems in social and information networks. In the case of photograph and video sharing web sites such as *Flickr* and *YouTube*, the content can be very rich and can contain data of different types, such as text, audio or video. Such heterogeneous data requires the design of methods which can learn and analyze data with heterogeneous feature spaces. In some cases, it is also useful to design methods which can transfer knowledge from one space to another. This has lead to an increasing interest in the field of *transfer learning* which uses the implicit links creates by users (such as tags) in order to transfer knowledge [27] from one space to another. Such methods can be particularly useful when a significant amount of content is available for learning in some spaces, but only a scan amount of content is available for learning in others. In the next section, we will discuss how the different chapters of this book are organized in the context of the afore-mentioned topics.

3. Research Topics in Social Networks

This book is organized into several chapters based on the topics discussed above. This chapter will discuss the different topics in detail and their relationship to the corresponding chapters. The discussion of these topics in this section is organized in approximate order of the corresponding chapters. The broad organization of the chapters is as follows:

- The first set of chapters are based on structural analysis of social networks. These include methods for statistical analysis of networks, community detection, classification, evolution analysis, privacy-preserving data mining, link inference and visualization.

- The second set of chapter are focussed on content-based mining issues in social networks. We have included chapters on several different kinds of content: (a) General data mining with arbitrary kinds of data (b) Text mining in social networks (b) Multimedia mining in social networks (d) Sensor and stream mining in social networks.

  We discuss how these different kinds of content can be leveraged in order to make interesting and valuable inferences in social networks. The richness of the underlying content results in a number of interesting inferences which are not possible with the use of purely structural methods.

Next, we will discuss the individual chapters in the book in detail, and how they relate to the above themes:

Statistical Analysis of Social Networks: The work of Milgram [18] laid the foundation for a more extensive analysis of the structural properties of large scale networks. In chapter 2, we study the important statistical properties of "typical" social networks. Some interesting questions which are examined in the chapter are to explore how typical social networks look like, on a large scale. The connectivity behavior of the nodes is examined to see if most nodes have few connections, with several "hubs" or whether the degrees are more evenly distributed. The clustering behavior of the nodes in typical social networks is examined. Another issue which is examined are the typical temporal characteristics of social networks. For example, it is examined how the structure varies as the network grows. As the network evolves over time, new entities may be added to the network, though certain graph properties may continue to be retained in spite of this. The behavior and distribution of the connected components of the graph is also examined.

Random Walks and their Applications in Social Networks: Ranking is one of the most well known methods in web search. Starting with the well known page-rank algorithm [6] for ranking web documents, the broad principle can also be applied for searching and ranking entities and actors in social networks. The page-rank algorithm uses random walk techniques for the ranking process. The idea is that a random walk approach is used on the network in order to estimate the probability of visiting each node. This probability is estimated as the *page rank*. Clearly, nodes which are structurally well connected have a higher page-rank, and are also naturally of greater importance. Random walk techniques can also be used in order to personalize the page-rank computation process, by biasing the ranking towards particular kinds of nodes. In chapter 3, we present methods for leveraging random walk techniques for a variety of ranking applications in social networks.

Community Detection in Social Networks: One of the most important problems in the context of social network analysis is that of community detection. The community detection problem is closely related to that of clustering, and it attempts to determine regions of the network, which are dense in terms of the linkage behavior. The topic is related to the generic problem of graph-partitioning [13] which partitions the network into dense regions based on the linkage behavior. However, social networks are usually dynamic, and this leads to some unique issues from a community detection point of view. In some cases, it is also possible to integrate the content behavior into the community detection process. In such cases, the content may be leveraged in order to determine groups of actors with similar interests. Chapter 4 provides an overview of some of the important algorithms on the problem of community detection.

Node Classification in Social Networks: In many applications, some of the nodes in the social network may be labeled, and it may be desirable to use the attribute and structural information in the social network in order to propagate these labels. For example, in in a marketing application, certain nodes may be known to be interested in a particular product, and it may be desirable to use the attribute and structural information in the network in order to learn other nodes which may also be interested in the same product. Social networks also contain rich information about the content and structure of the network, which may be leveraged for this purpose. For example, when two nodes in a social network are linked together, it is likely that the node labels are correlated as well. Therefore, the linkage structure can be used in order to *propagate* the labels among the different nodes. Content and attributes can be used in order to further improve the quality of classification. Chapter 5 discusses a variety of methods for link-based node classification in social networks.

Evolution in Dynamic Social Networks: Social Networks are inherently dynamic entities; new members join them, old members stop participating, new links emerge as new contacts are built, and old links become obsolete as the members stop interacting with one other. This leads to changes in the structure of the social network as a whole and of the communities in it. Two important questions arise in this context: (a) What are the laws which govern long term changes in the social network over time, which are frequently observed over large classes of social networks? (b) How does a community inside a social platform evolve over time? What changes can occur, and how do we capture and present them?
Chapter 6 elaborates on these questions in more detail. Advances associated with the first set of questions are studied in Chapter 2, and to a lesser extent in Chapter 6. Advances on the second question are studied in Chapter 6, where the main focus is on evolution in social networks.

Social Influence Analysis: Since social networks are primarily designed on the basis of the interactions between the different participants, it is natural that such interactions may lead to the different actors influencing one another in terms of their behavior. A classic example of this would be a viral marketing application in which we utilize the messages between interconnected participants in a social network in order to propagate the information across different parts of the network. A number of natural questions arise in this context:
(a) How do we model the nature of the influence across actors?
(b) How do we model the spread of influence?

(c) Who are the most influential actors for influence spread?
Chapter 7 studies these issues in considerable depth and provides a deep understanding of the nature of influence analysis in social networks.

Expert Discovery in Networks: Social networks can be used as a tool in order to identify experts for a particular task. For example, given the activities of candidates within a context (*e.g.*, authoring a document, answering a question), we first describe methods for evaluating the level of expertise for each of them. Often, experts are organized in networks that correspond to social networks or organizational structures of companies. Many complex tasks often require the collective expertise of more than one expert. In such cases, it is more realistic to require a team of experts that can collaborate towards a common goal. Chapter 8 discusses methods for determining teams of experts which can perform particular tasks.

Link Prediction in Social Networks: Much of the research in mining social networks is focussed on *using the links* in order to derive interesting information about the social network such as the underlying communities, or labeling the nodes with class labels. However, in most social networking applications, the links are dynamic, and may change considerably over time. For example, in a social network, friendship links are continuously created over time. Therefore, a natural question is to determine or predict future links in the social network. The prediction process may use either the structure of the network or the attribute-information at the different nodes. A variety of structural and relational models have been proposed in the literature for link prediction [17, 21–23]. Chapter 9 provides a detailed survey of such methods.

Privacy in Social Networks: Social networks contain a tremendous information about the individual in terms of their interests, demographic information, friendship link information, and other attributes. This can lead to disclosure of different kinds of information in the social network, such as identity disclosure, attribute disclosure, and linkage information disclosure. Chapter 10 discusses a detailed survey of privacy mechanisms in social networks in context of different kinds of models and different kinds of information which can be disclosed.

Visualizing Social Networks: As social networks become larger and more complex, reasoning about social dynamics via simple statistics is cumbersome, and not very intuitive. Visualization provides a natural way to summarize the information in order to make it much easier to understand. Recent years have witnessed a convergence of social network analytics and visualization, coupled with interaction, that is changing the way analysts understand and characterize social networks. In chapter 11, the main goal of visualization is discussed in the context of user understanding and interaction. The chapter also examines how different metaphors are aimed towards elucidating different aspects of social networks, such as structure and semantics. A number of methods are described, where analytics and visualization are interwoven towards providing a better comprehension of social structure and dynamics.

Data Mining in Social Media: Social Media provides a wealth of social network data, which can be mined in order to discover useful business applications. Data mining techniques provide researchers and practitioners the tools needed to analyze large, complex, and frequently changing social media data. An overview on the topic of data mining in social media is provided in Chapter 12. This chapter introduces the basics of data mining in the context of social media, and discusses how to mine social media data. The chapter also highlights a number of illustrative examples with an emphasis on social networking sites and blogs.

Text Mining in Social Networks: Social networks contain a lot of text in the nodes in various forms. For example, social networks may contain links to posts, blogs or other news articles. In some cases, users may tag one another, which is also a form of text data on the links. The use of content can greatly enhance the quality of the inferences which may be made in the context of graphs and social networks. In chapter 13, we present methods for using text mining techniques in social networks in the context of a variety of problems such as clustering and classification.

Integrating Sensors and Social Networks: Many mobile phones provide the ability for actors to interact with one another dynamically, and in real time depending upon their location and status. Such applications also result in the generation of massive streams in real time, which can be used to make inferences about one another, or about the aggregate properties of the objects which are being tracked. Since location information is private, this also naturally leads to a number of privacy concerns from a processing perspective. Chapter 14 discusses such methods for incorporating sensor data as an integral part of social network data analytics.

Multimedia Information Network Analysis in Social Media: Many forms of media sharing sites such as *Flickr* and *Youtube* provide the ability to share media. Such shared media are often used in conjunction with the interactions of different users, such as the placing of tags or comments on the different images. Such rich context-based information networks can be mined for a wide variety of applications by leveraging the combination of user tags and image data in the mining and retrieval process. Chapter 15 discusses methods for mining multimedia information networks with social media.

Social Tagging: Much of the interaction between users and social networks occurs in the form of *tagging*, in which users attach short descriptions to different objects in the social network, such as images, text, video or other multimedia data. Chapter 16 provides a detailed survey of various aspects of tagging. The chapter discusses properties of tag streams, tagging models, tag semantics, generating recommendations using tags, visualizations of tags, applications of tags, integration of different tagging systems and problems associated with tagging usage. Many interesting issues are discussed, such as the reason why people tag, what influences the choice of tags, how to model the tagging process, kinds of tags, different power laws observed in tagging domain, how tags are created and how to choose the right tags for recommendation.

4. Conclusions and Future Directions

This book is primarily focussed on providing readers with an introduction to the area of social networks. The broad area is so vast, that it is probably not possible to cover it comprehensively in a single book. The problem of social network data analytics is still in its infancy; there is a tremendous amount of work to be done, particularly in the area of content-based and temporal social networks. Some key research directions for the future are as follows:

- **Content-based Analysis:** Much of the past research in this area has been based on *structural analysis* of social networks. Such analysis primarily uses linkage structure only in order to infer interesting characteristics of the underlying network. Some recent research [26] has shown that the inclusion of content information can yield valuable insights about the underlying social network. For example, the content at a given node may provide more information about the expertise and interests of the corresponding actor.

- **Temporal Analysis:** Most of the research in social networks is based on static networks. However, a number of recent studies [8, 9, 11] have shown that the incorporation of temporal evolution into network analysis significantly improves the quality of the results. Therefore, a significant amount of work remains to be done on dynamic analysis of social networks which evolve rapidly over time.

- **Adversarial Networks:** In adversarial networks, it is desirable to determine the analytical structure of a network in which the actors in the network are adversaries, and the relationships among the different adversaries may not be fully known. For example, terrorist networks would be a typical adversarial network to a law enforcement agency. Such networks are far more challenging because the links may not be known a-priori, but may need to be inferred in many cases. Such inferred links may need to be used for analytical purposes.

In addition, we expect that it will be increasingly important to analyze networks in the context of heterogeneous data, in which the links are of different types and correspond to different kinds of relationships between the actors. A generalization of the concept of social networks is that of *information networks*, in which the nodes could be either actors of entities, and the edges correspond to logical relations among these entities. Such networks are also heterogeneous, and therefore it is increasingly important to design tools and techniques which can effectively analyze heterogeneous networks.

References

[1] C. C. Aggarwal, H. Wang. Managing and Mining Graph Data, *Springer*, 2010.

[2] C. C. Aggarwal. P. Yu. Online Analysis of Community Evolution over Data Streams, *SIAM Conference on Data Mining*, 2005.

[3] C. C. Aggarwal, Y. Zhao, P. Yu. On Clustering Graph Streams, *SIAM Conference on Data Mining*, 2010.

[4] C. C. Aggarwal, Y. Li, P. Yu, R. Jin. On Dense Pattern Mining in Graph Streams, *VLDB Conference*, 2010.

[5] C. C. Aggarwal, Y. Zhao, P. Yu. Outlier Detection in Graph Streams, *ICDE Conference*, 2011.

[6] S. Brin, L. Page. The Anatomy of a Large Scale Hypertextual Search Engine, *WWW Conference*, 1998.

[7] P. J. Carrington, J. Scott, S. Wasserman. *Models and Methods in Social Network Analysis (Structural Analysis in the Social Sciences)*, Cambridge University Press, 2005.

[8] D. Chakrabarti, R. Kumar, A. Tomkins. Evolutionary Clustering, *ACM KDD Conference*, 2000.

[9] Y. Chi, X. Song, D. Zhou, K. Hino, B. L. Tseng. Evolutionary spectral clustering by incorporating temporal smoothness. *KDD Conference*, 2007.

[10] L. Getoor, N. Friedman, D. Koller, and B. Taskar. Learning probabilistic models of relational structure. In *ICML*, pages 170–177, 2001.

[11] Y.-R. Lin, Y. Chi, S. Zhu, H. Sundaram, B. L. Tseng. FacetNet: A framework for analyzing communities and their evolutions in dynamic networks. *WWW Conference*, 2008.

[12] D. Kempe, J. Kleinberg, E. Tardos. Maximizing the Spread of Infuence in a Social Network, *ACM KDD Conference*, 2003.

[13] B. W. Kernighan, S. Lin, An efficient heuristic procedure for partitioning graphs, *Bell System Technical Journal*, 1970.

[14] J. Kleinberg. Complex Networks and Decentralized Search Algorithms, *Proceedings of the International Congress on Mathematics*, 2006.

[15] J. Leskovec, J. Kleinberg, C. Faloutsos. Graphs over time: Densification laws, shrinking diameters and possible explanations. *ACM KDD Conference*, 2005.

[16] J. Leskovec, E. Horvitz. Planetary-Scale Views on a Large Instant-Messaging Network, *WWW Conference*, 2008.

[17] D. Liben-Nowell and J. Kleinberg. The link prediction problem for social networks. In *LinkKDD*, 2004.

[18] S. Milgram. The Small World Problem, *Psychology Today*, 1967.

[19] M. Newman. Finding community structure in networks using the eigenvectors of matrices. *Physical Review E*, 2006.

[20] M. E. J. Newman. The spread of epidemic disease on networks, *Phys. Rev*. E 66, 016128, 2002.

[21] B. Taskar, P. Abbeel, and D. Koller. Discriminative probabilistic models for relational data. *UAI*, pages 485–492, 2002.

[22] B. Taskar, M. F. Wong, P. Abbeel, and D. Koller. Link prediction in relational data. *NIPS*, 2003.

[23] C. Wang, V. Satuluri, and S. Parthasarathy. Local probabilistic models for link prediction. *ICDM*, pages 322–331, 2007.

[24] S. Wasserman, K. Faust. *Social Network Analysis: Methods and Applications (Structural Analysis in the Social Sciences)*, Cambridge University Press, 1994.

[25] D. J. Watts. Six Degrees: The Science of a Connected Age, *W. W. Norton and Company*, 2004.

[26] Y. Zhou, H. Cheng, and J. X. Yu. Graph clustering based on structural/attribute similarities. *PVLDB*, 2(1):718–729, 2009.

[27] Y. Zhu, S. J. Pan, Y. Chen, G.-R. Xue, Q. Yang, Y. Yu. Heterogeneous Transfer Learning for Image Classification. *AAAI*, 2010.

[28] http://www.cs.cmu.edu/˜enron

Chapter 2

STATISTICAL PROPERTIES OF SOCIAL NETWORKS

Mary McGlohon
School of Computer Science
Carnegie Mellon University
mmcgloho@cs.cmu.edu

Leman Akoglu
School of Computer Science
Carnegie Mellon University
lakoglu@cs.cmu.edu

Christos Faloutsos
School of Computer Science
Carnegie Mellon University
christos@cs.cmu.edu

Abstract In this chapter we describe patterns that occur in the structure of social networks, represented as graphs. We describe two main classes of properties, static properties, or properties describing the structure of snapshots of graphs; and dynamic properties, properties describing how the structure evolves over time. These properties may be for unweighted or weighted graphs, where weights may represent multi-edges (e.g. multiple phone calls from one person to another), or edge weights (e.g. monetary amounts between a donor and a recipient in a political donation network).

Keywords: Power laws, network structure, weighted graphs

What do social networks look like on a global scale? How do they evolve over time? How do the different components of an entire network form? What happens when we take into account multiple edges and weighted edges? Can we identify certain patterns regarding these weights?

There has been extensive work focusing on static static snapshots of graphs, where fascinating properties have been discovered, the most striking ones being the 'small-world' phenomenon [38] (also known as 'six degrees of separation' [24]) and the power-law degree distributions [3, 12]. Time-evolving graphs have attracted attention only recently, where even more fascinating properties have been discovered, like *shrinking* diameters, and the so-called *densification power law* [18]. Moreover, we find interesting properties in terms of *multiple* edges between nodes, or edge weights.

In this chapter we will describe some of the most important properties apparent in social networks, with a particular emphasis on dynamic properties, and some of the newer findings with respect to edge weights.

The questions of interest are:

- *What do social networks look like, on a large scale?* Do most nodes have few connections, with several "hubs" or is the distribution more stable? What sort of clustering behavior occurs?
- *How do networks behave over time?* Does the structure vary as the network grows? In what fashion do new entities enter a network? Does the network retain certain graph properties as it grows and evolves? Does the graph undergo a "phase transition", in which its behavior suddenly changes?
- *How do the non-giant weakly connected components behave over time?* One might argue that they grow, as new nodes are being added; and their size would probably remain a fixed fraction of the size of the GCC. Someone else might counter-argue that they shrink, and they eventually get absorbed into the GCC. What is happening, in real graphs?
- *What distributions and patterns do weighted graphs maintain?* How does the distribution of weights change over time– do we also observe a densification of weights as well as single-edges? How does the distribution of weights relate to the degree distribution? Is the addition of weight bursty over time, or is it uniform?

Answering these questions is important to understand how natural graphs evolve, and to (a) spot anomalous graphs and sub-graphs; (b) answer questions about entities in a network and what-if scenarios; and (c) discard unrealistic graph generators.

Let's elaborate on each of the above applications: Spotting anomalies is vital for determining abuse of social and computer networks, such as link-spamming in a web graph, fraudulent reputation building in e-auction systems [29], detection of dwindling/abnormal social sub-groups in a social-networking site like Yahoo-360 (`360.yahoo.com`), Facebook (`www.facebook.com`) and LinkedIn

Symbol	Description
$\mathcal{G}$	Graph representation of datasets
$\mathcal{V}$	Set of nodes for graph $\mathcal{G}$
$\mathcal{E}$	Set of edges for graph $\mathcal{G}$
N	Number of nodes, or $\|\mathcal{V}\|$
E	Number of edges, or $\|\mathcal{E}\|$
$e_{i,j}$	Edge between node i and node j
$w_{i,j}$	Weight on edge $e_{i,j}$
w_i	Weight of node i (sum of weights of incident edges)
$\mathbf{A}$	0-1 Adjacency matrix of the unweighted graph
$\mathbf{A}_w$	Real-value adjacency matrix of the weighted graph
$a_{i,j}$	Entry in matrix $\mathbf{A}$
λ_1	Principal eigenvalue of unweighted graph
$\lambda_{1,w}$	Principal eigenvalue of weighted graph

Table 2.1. Table of Notations.

(`www.linkedin.com`), and network intrusion detection [17]. Analyzing network properties is also useful for identifying authorities and search algorithms [7, 9, 16], for discovering the "network value" of customers for using viral marketing [30], or to improve recommendation systems [5]. What-if scenarios are vital for extrapolation, provisioning and algorithm design: For example if we expect that the number of links will double within the next year, we should provision for the appropriate hardware to store and process the upcoming queries.

The rest of this chapter will examine both the static and dynamic properties, for weighted and unweighted graphs. However, before delving into these static and dynamic properties, we will next establish some terms and definitions we will use in the rest of the chapter.

1. Preliminaries

We will first provide some basic definitions and terms we will use, and then present some particular data sets we will reference. A full list of symbols can be shown in Table 2.1.

1.1 Definitions

1.1.1 Graphs. We can represent a social network as a *graph*. For the rest of the chapter we will use *network* and *graph* interchangeably.

A static, unweighted graph G consists of a set of nodes $\mathcal{V}$ and a set of edges $\mathcal{E}$: $G = (\mathcal{V}, \mathcal{E})$. We represent the sizes of $\mathcal{V}$ and $\mathcal{E}$ as N and E. A graph may be *directed* or *undirected*– for instance, a phone call may be from one party to another, and will have a directed edge, or a mutual friendship may be represented as an undirected edge. Most properties we examine will be on undirected graphs.

Graphs may also be *weighted*, where there may be multiple edges occurring between two nodes (e.g. repeated phone calls) or specific edge weights (e.g. monetary amounts for transactions). In a weighted graph $\mathcal{G}$, let $e_{i,j}$ be the edge between node i and node j. We shall refer to these two nodes as the *'neighboring nodes'* or *'incident nodes'* of edge $e_{i,j}$. Let $w_{i,j}$ be the weight on edge $e_{i,j}$. The *total weight* w_i of node i is defined as the sum of weights of all its incident edges, that is $w_i = \sum_{k=1}^{d_i} w_{i,k}$, where d_i denotes its degree. As we show later, there is a relation between a given edge weight $w_{i,j}$ and the weights of its neighboring nodes w_i and w_j.

Finally, graphs may be *unipartite* or *multipartite*. Most social networks one thinks of are unipartite– people in a group, papers in a citation network, etc. However, there may also be multipartite– that is, there are multiple classes of nodes and edges are only drawn between nodes of different classes. Bipartite graphs, like the movie-actor graph of IMDB, consist of disjoint sets of nodes $\mathcal{V}_1$ and $\mathcal{V}_2$, say, for authors and movies, with no edges among nodes of the same type.

We can represent a graph either visually, or with an *adjacency matrix* **A**, where nodes are in rows and columns, and numbers in the matrix indicate the existence of edges. For unweighted graphs, all entries are 0 or 1; for weighted graphs the adjacency matrix contains the values of the weights. Figure 2.1 shows examples of graphs and their adjacency matrices.

We next introduce other important concepts we use in analyzing these graphs.

1.1.2 Components. Another interesting property of a graph is its *component distribution*. We refer to a *connected component* in a graph as a set of nodes and edges where there exists a path between any two nodes in the set. (For directed graphs, this would be a *weakly connected component*, where a *strongly connected component* requires a directed path between any given two nodes in a set.) We find that in real graphs over time, a giant connected component (GCC) forms. However, it is also of interest to study the smaller components– when do they choose to join the GCC, and what size do they reach before doing so?

In our observations we will focus on the size of the second- and third- largest components. We will also look at the large scale distribution of all component sizes, and how that distribution changes over time. Not surprisingly, components of $rank \geq 2$ form a power law.

1.1.3 Diameter and Effective Diameter. We may want to answer the questions: How does the largest connected component of a real graph evolve over time? Do we start with one large CC, that keeps on growing? We propose to use the *diameter-plot* of the graph, that is, its diameter, over time, to answer these questions. For a given (static) graph, its *diameter* is defined as

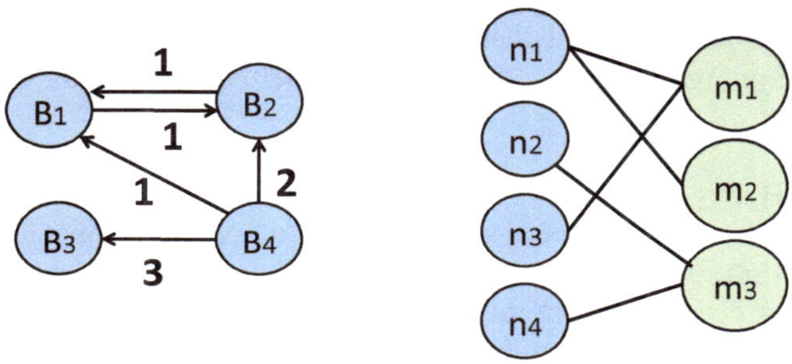

	B1	B2	B3	B4
B1	0	1	0	0
B2	1	0	0	0
B3	0	0	0	0
B4	1	2	3	0

	n1	n2	n3	n4
m1	1	0	1	0
m2	1	0	0	0
m3	0	1	0	1

Figure 2.1. Illustrations of example graphs. On the left is a unipartite, directed, weighted graph and the corresponding adjacency matrix. On the right is an undirected, bipartite graph and the corresponding adjacency matrix.

the maximum *distance* between any two nodes, where distance is the minimum number of hops (i.e., edges that must be traversed) on the path from one node to another, ignoring directionality. Calculating graph diameter is $O(N^2)$. Therefore, we choose to estimate the graph diameter by sampling nodes from the giant component. For $s = \{1, 2, ..., S\}$, we choose two nodes at random and calculate the distance (using breadth-first search). We then choose to record the 90 percentile value of distances, so we take the $.9S$ largest recorded value. The distance operation is $O(dk)$, where d is the graph diameter and k the maximum degree of any node– on average this is a much smaller cost. Intuitively, the diameter represents how much of a "small world" the graph is– how quickly one can get from one "end" of the graph to another. This is described in [35]. We use sampling to estimate the diameter; alternative methods would include ANF [28].

1.1.4 Heavy-tailed Distributions. While the Gaussian distribution is common in nature, there are many cases where the probability of events far to the right of the mean is significantly higher than in Gaussians. In the Internet, for example, most routers have a very low degree (perhaps "home" routers), while a few routers have extremely high degree (perhaps the "core" routers of the Internet backbone) [12] Heavy-tailed distributions attempt to model this. They are known as "heavy-tailed" because, while traditional exponential distributions have bounded variance (large deviations from the mean become nearly impossible), $p(x)$ decays polynomially quickly instead of exponentially as $x \to \infty$, creating a "fat tail" for extreme values on the PDF plot.

One of the more well-known heavy-tailed distributions is the power law distribution. Two variables x and y are related by a power law when:

$$y(x) = Ax^{-\gamma} \tag{2.1}$$

where A and γ are positive constants. The constant γ is often called the power law exponent.

A random variable is distributed according to a power law when the probability density function (pdf) is given by:

$$p(x) = Ax^{-\gamma}, \quad \gamma > 1, x \geq x_{min} \tag{2.2}$$

The extra $\gamma > 1$ requirement ensures that $p(x)$ can be normalized. Power laws with $\gamma < 1$ rarely occur in nature, if ever [26].

Skewed distributions, such as power laws, occur very often in real-world graphs, as we will discuss. Figures 2.2(a) and 2.2(b) show two examples of power laws.

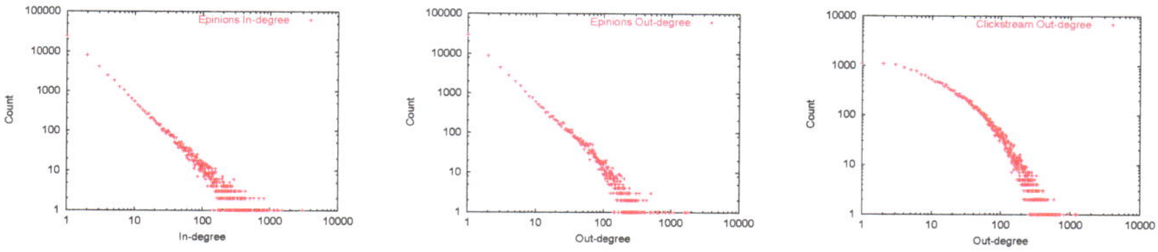

(a) Epinions In-degree (b) Epinions Out-degree (c) Clickstream Out-degree

Figure 2.2. Power laws and deviations: Plots (a) and (b) show the in-degree and out-degree distributions on a log-log scale for the *Epinions* graph (an online social network of $75,888$ people and $508,960$ edges [11]). Both follow power-laws. In contrast, plot (c) shows the out-degree distribution of a *Clickstream* graph (a bipartite graph of users and the websites they surf [25]), which deviates from the power-law pattern.

While power laws appear in a large number of graphs, deviations from a pure power law are sometimes observed. Two of the more common deviations are exponential cutoffs and lognormals.

Sometimes, the distribution looks like a power law over the lower range of values along the x-axis, but decays very fast for higher values. Often, this decay is exponential, and this is usually called an exponential cutoff:

$$y(x = k) \propto e^{-k/\kappa} k^{-\gamma} \tag{2.3}$$

where $e^{-k/\kappa}$ is the exponential cutoff term and $k^{-\gamma}$ is the power law term.

Similar distributions were studied by Bi et al. [6], who found that a discrete truncated lognormal (called the Discrete Gaussian Exponential or "DGX" by the authors) gives a very good fit. A lognormal is a distribution whose logarithm is a Gaussian; it looks like a truncated parabola in log-log scales. The DGX distribution has been used to fit the degree distribution of a bipartite "clickstream" graph linking websites and users (Figure 2.2(c)), telecommunications and other data.

Methods for fitting heavy-tailed distributions are described in [26, 10].

1.1.5 Burstiness and Entropy Plots. Human activity, including weight additions in graphs, is often bursty. If that the traffic is *self-similar*, then we can measure the burstiness, using the intrinsic, or *fractal* dimension of the cloud of timestamps of edge-additions (or weight-additions). Let $\Delta W(t)$ be the total weight of edges that were added during the t-th interval, e.g., the total network flow on day t, among all the machines we are observing.

Among the many methods that measure self-similarity (Hurst exponent, etc. [31]), we choose the *entropy plot* [37], which plots the entropy $H(r)$ versus the resolution r. The resolution is the scale, that is, at resolution r, we divide our time interval into 2^r equal sub-intervals, sum the weight-additions

$\Delta W(t)$ in each sub-interval k ($k = 1 \ldots 2^r$), normalize into fractions p_k ($= \Delta W(t)/W_{total}$), and compute the Shannon entropy of the sequence p_k: $H(r) = -\sum_k p_k \log_2 p_k$. If the plot $H(r)$ is linear in some range of resolutions, the corresponding time sequence is said to be *fractal* in that range, and the slope of the plot is defined as the *intrinsic* (or *fractal*) dimension D of the time sequence. Notice that a uniform weight-addition distribution yields D=1; a lower value of D corresponds to a more bursty time sequence like a Cantor dust [31], with a single burst having the lowest D=0: the intrinsic dimension of a point. Also notice that a variation of the 80-20 model, the so called 'b-model' [37], generates such self-similar traffic.

We studied several large real-world weighted graphs described in detail in Table 2.2. In particular, *BlogNet* contains blog-to-blog links, *NetworkTraffic* records IP-source/IP-destination pairs, along with the number of packets sent. Bipartite networks *Auth-Conf*, *Keyw-Conf*, and *Auth-Keyw* are from DBLP, representing submission records of authors to conferences with specified keywords. *CampaignOrg* is from the US FEC, a public record of donations between political candidates and organizations.

For *NetworkTraffic* and *CampaignOrg* datasets, the weights on the edges are actual weights representing number of packets and donation amounts. For the remaining datasets, the edge weights are simply the number of occurences of the edges. For instance, if author i submits a paper to conference j for the first time, the weight $w_{i,j}$ of edge $e_{i,j}$ is set to 1. If author i later submits another paper to the same conference, the edge weight becomes 2.

A complete list of the symbols used throughout text is listed in Table 2.1.

1.2 Data description

We will illustrate some properties described in this chapter on different real-world social networks. These are described in detail in Table 2.2. This includes both bipartite and unipartite, and weighted and unweighted graphs.

Several of our graphs had no obvious weighting scheme: for example, a single paper or patent will cite another only a single time. The graphs that did have weights are also further divided into two schemes, *multi-edges* and *edge-weights*. In the edge-weights scheme, there is an obvious weight on edges, such as amounts in campaign donations, or packet-counts in network traffic. For multi-edges, weights are added if there is more than one interaction between two nodes. For instance, if a blog cites another blog at a given time, its weight is 1. If it cites the blog again later, the weight becomes 2.

The datasets are gathered from publicly available data. *NIPS*[1], *Arxiv* and *Patent* [19] are academic paper or patent citation graphs with no weighting

[1] www.cs.toronto.edu/~roweis/data.html

Name	**Weights**	$\lvert N \rvert$,$\lvert E \rvert$,time	**Description**
PostNet	Unweighted	250K, 218K, 80 d.	Blog post citation network
NIPS	Unweighted	2K, 3K, 13 yr.	Paper citation network
Arxiv	Unweighted	30K, 60K, 13 yr.	Paper citation network
Patent	Unweighted	4M, 8M, 17 yr.	Patent citation network
IMDB	Unweighted	757K, 2M, 114 yr.	Bipartite actor-movie network
Netflix	Unweighted	125K, 14M, 72 mo.	Bipartite user-movie ratings
BlogNet	Multi-edges	60K, 125K, 80 d.	Social network of blogs based on citations
Auth-Conf	Multi-edges	17K, 22K, 25 yr.	Bipartite DBLP Author-to-Conference associations
Key-Conf	Multi-edges	10K, 23K, 25 yr.	Bipartite DBLP Keyword-to-Conference associations
Auth-Key	Multi-edges	27K, 189K, 25 yr.	Bipartite DBLP Author-to-Keyword associations
CampOrg	Edge-weights (Amounts)	23K, 877K, 28 yr.	Bipartite U.S. electoral campaign donations from organizations to candidates (available from FEC)
CampIndiv	Edge-weights (Amounts)	6M, 10M, 22 yr.	Bipartite election donations from individuals to organizations

Table 2.2. The datasets referred to in this chapter.

scheme. *IMDB* indicates movie-actor information, where an edge occurs if an actor participates in a movie [3]. *Netflix* is the dataset from the Netflix Prize competition[2], with user-movie links (we ignored the ratings); we also noticed that it only contained users with 100 or more ratings. *BlogNet* and *PostNet* are two representations of the same data, hyperlinks between blog posts [21]. in *PostNet* nodes represent individual posts, while in *BlogNet* each node represents a blog. Essentially, *PostNet* is a paper citation network while *BlogNet* is an author citation network (which contains multi-edges).

Auth-Conf, *Key-Conf*, and *Auth-Key* are all from DBLP [3], with the obvious meanings. *CampOrg* and *CampIndiv* are bipartite graphs from U.S. Federal Election Commission, recording donation amounts from organizations to political candidates and individuals to organizations [4].

In all the above cases, we assume that edges are never deleted, because edge deletion never explicitly appeared in these datasets.

[2] `www.netflixprize.com`
[3] `dblp.uni-trier.de/xml/`
[4] `www.cs.cmu.edu/~mmcgloho/fec/data/ fec_data.html`

2. Static Properties

We next review *static* properties of social graphs. While all networks we examine are evolving over time, there are properties that are measured at single points in time, that is, static snapshots of the graphs. For the purposes of organization we will further divide these properties into those applying to unweighted graphs and to weighted graphs.

2.1 Static Unweighted Graphs

Here, we present the 'laws' that apply to static snapshots of real graphs without considering the weights on the edges. Those include the patterns in degree distributions, the number of hops pairs of nodes can reach each other, local number of triangles, eigenvalues and communities. Next, we describe the related patterns in more detail.

2.1.1 S-1: Heavy-tailed Degree Distribution. The degree distribution of many real graphs obey a power law of the form $f(d) \propto d^{-\alpha}$, with the exponent $\alpha > 0$, and $f(d)$ being the fraction of nodes with degree d. Such power-law relations as well as many more have been reported in [8, 12, 15, 26]. Intuitively, power-law-like distributions for degrees state that there exist many low degree nodes, whereas only a few high degree nodes in real graphs.

2.1.2 S-2: Small Diameter. One of the most striking patterns that real-world graphs have is a small diameter, which is also known as the 'small-world phenomenon' or the 'six degrees of separation'.

For a given static graph, its diameter is defined as the maximum *distance* between any two nodes, where distance is the minimum number of hops (i.e., edges that must be traversed) on the path from one node to another, usually ignoring directionality. Intuitively, the diameter represents how much of a "small world" the graph is– how quickly one can get from one "end" of the graph to another.

Many real graphs were found to exhibit surprisingly small diameters– for example, 19 for the Web [2], and the well-known "six-degrees of separation" in social networks [4]. It has also been observed that the diameter spikes at the 'gelling point' [22].

Since the diameter is defined as the *maximum*-length shortest path between all possible pairs, it can easily be highjacked by long chains. Therefore, often the *effective diameter* is used as a more robust metric, which is the 90-percentile of the pairwise distances among all reachable pairs of nodes. In other words, the *effective diameter* is the minimum number of hops in which some fraction (usually 90%) of all connected node pairs can be reached [34].

Computing all-pairs-shortest-path lengths is practically intractable for very large graphs. The exact algorithm is prohibitively expensive (at least $O(N^2)$); while one can use sampling to estimate it, alternative methods would include ANF [28].

2.1.3 S-3: Triangle Power Law (TPL).

The number of triangles Δ and the number of nodes that participate in Δ number of triangles should follow a power-law in the form of $f(\Delta) \propto \Delta^{\sigma}$, with the exponent $\sigma < 0$ [36]. The TPL intuitively states that while many nodes have only a few triangles in their neighborhoods, a few nodes participate in many number of triangles with their neighbors. The local number of triangles is related to the clustering coefficient of graphs.

2.1.4 S-4: Eigenvalue Power Law (EPL).

Siganos et.al. [33] examined the spectrum of the adjacency matrix of the AS Internet topology and reported that the 20 or so largest eigenvalues of the Internet graph are power-law distributed. Michail and Papadimitriou [23] later provided an explanation for the 'Eigenvalue Power Law', showing that it is a consequence of the 'Degree Power Law'.

2.1.5 S-5: Community Structure.

Real-world graphs are found to exhibit a modular structure, with nodes forming groups, and possibly groups within groups [13, 14, 32]. In a modular graph, the nodes form communities where groups of nodes in the same community are tighter connected to each other than to those nodes outside the community. In [27], Newman and Girvan provide a quantitative measure for such a structure, called *modularity*.

2.2 Static Weighted Graphs

Here we try to find patterns that weighted graphs obey. In this section we consider graphs to be directed (and impose a single direction in bipartite graphs), as this will be an important consideration on the weights. The dataset consist of quadruples: (IP-source, IP-destination, timestamp, number-of-packets), where timestamp is in increments of, say, 30 minutes. Thus, we have multi-edges, as well as total weight for each (source, destination) pair. Let $W(t)$ be the total weight up to time t (ie., the grand total of all exchanged packets across all pairs), $E(t)$ the number of distinct edges up to time t, and $E_d(t)$ the number of multi-edges (the d subscript stands for *duplicate* edges), up to time t.

We present three "laws" that our datasets seem to follow: The first is the "weight power law" (WPL) correlating the total weight, the total number of edges and the total number of multi-edges, over time. THe second is the "edge weights power law", the same law as applied to individual nodes. The third is the "snapshot power law" (SPL), correlating the in-degree with the in-weight, and the out-degree with the out-weight, for all the nodes of a graph, at a given time-stamp.

2.2.1 SW-1: Weight Power Law (WPL).

As defined above, suppose we have $E(t)$ total unique edges up to time t (ie., count of pairs that know each other) and $W(t)$ being the total count of packets up to time t. Is there a relationship between $W(t)$ and $E(t)$? If every pair generated k packets, the relationships would be linear: if the count of pairs double, the packet count would double, too. This is reasonable, but it doesn't happen! In reality, the packet count over-doubles, following the "WPL" below. We shall refer to this phenomenon as the "*fortification effect*": more edges in the graph imply super-linearly higher total weight.

OBSERVATION 2.1 (WEIGHT POWER LAW (WPL)) *Let $E(t)$, $W(t)$ be the number of edges and total weight of a graph, at time t. They, they follow a power law*

$$W(t) = E(t)^w$$

where w is the weight *exponent. Power-laws also link the number of nodes $N(t)$, and the number of multi-edges $E_d(t)$, to $E(t)$, with exponents n and $dupE$, respectively.*

The weight exponent w ranges from 1.01 to 1.5 for the real graphs we have studied. The highest value corresponds to campaign donations: super-active organizations that support many campaigns also tend to spend even more money per campaign than the less active organizations. For bipartite graphs, we show the $nsrc$, $ndst$ exponents for the source and destination nodes (which also follow power laws: $N_{src}(t) = E(t)^{nsrc}$ and similarly for $N_{dst}(t)$).

Fig. 2.5 shows all these quantities, versus $E(t)$, for several datasets. The plots are all in log-log scales, and straight lines fit well. We report the slopes in Table 2.

2.2.2 SW-2: Edge Weights Power Law.

We observe that the weight of a given edge and weights of its neighboring two nodes are correlated. Our observation is similar to Newton's Gravitational Law stating that the gravitational force between two point masses is proportional to the product of the masses.

OBSERVATION 2.2 (EDGE WEIGHTS POWER LAW(EWPL)) *Given a real-world graph $\mathcal{G}$, 'communication' defined as the weight of the link between two given nodes has a power law relation with the weights of the nodes. In particular, given an edge $e_{i,j}$ with weight $w_{i,j}$ and its two neighbor nodes i*

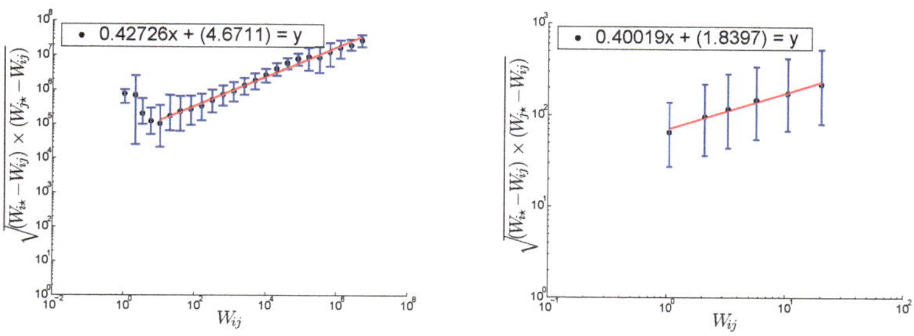

(a) Committee - Candidate (b) Blog Network

Figure 2.3. Illustration of the EWPL. Given the weight of a particular edge in the final snapshot of real graphs (x-axis), the multiplication of total weights(y-axis) of the edges incident to two neighboring nodes follow a power law. A line can be fit to the median values after logarithmic binning on the x-axis. Upper and lower bars indicate 75% and 25% of the data, respectively.

and j with weights w_i and w_j, respectively,

$$w_{i,j} \propto \left(\sqrt{(w_i - w_{i,j}) * (w_j - w_{i,j})}\right)^{\gamma}$$

We report corresponding experimental findings in Fig. 3.

2.2.3 SW-3: Snapshot Power Laws (SPL).

What about a static snapshot of a graph? If node i has out-degree out_i, what can we say about its out-weight $outw_i$? It turns out that there is a "fortification effect" here, too, resulting in more power laws, both for out-degrees/out-weights as well as for in-degrees/in-weights.

Specifically, at a given point in time, we plot the scatterplot of the in/out weight versus the in/out degree, for all the nodes in the graph, at a given time snapshot. An example of such a plot is in Fig. 2.4 (c) and (d). Here, every point represents a node and the x and y coordinates are its degree and total weight, respectively. To achieve a good fit, we bucketize the x axis with logarithmic binning [26], and, for each bin, we compute the median y.

We observed that the median values of weights versus mid-points of the intervals follow a power law for all datasets studied. Formally, the "Snapshot Power Law" is:

OBSERVATION 2.3 (SNAPSHOT POWER LAW (SPL)) *Consider the i-th node of a weighted graph, at time t, and let out_i, $outw_i$ be its out-degree and out-weight. Then*

$$outw_i \propto out_i^{ow}$$

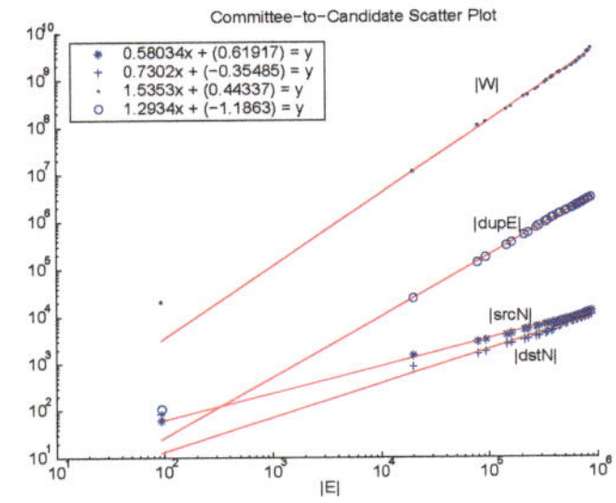

(a) WPL plot

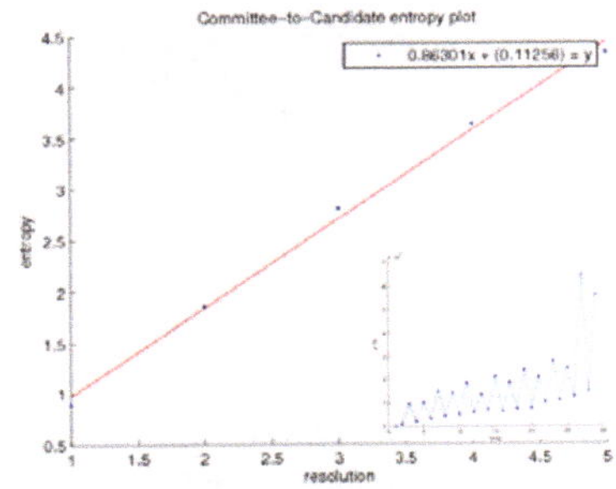

(b) entropy plot

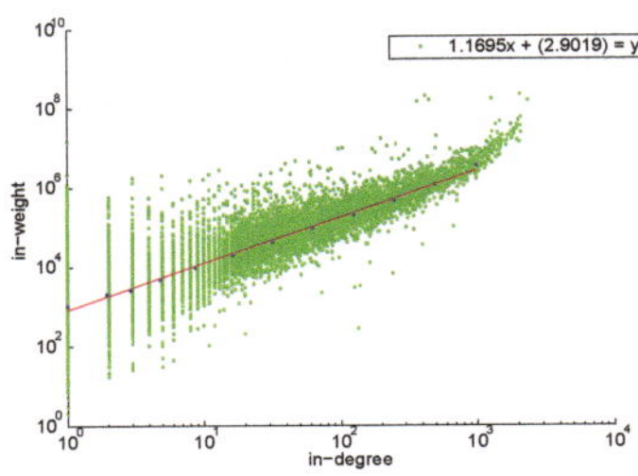

(c) inD-inW snapshot

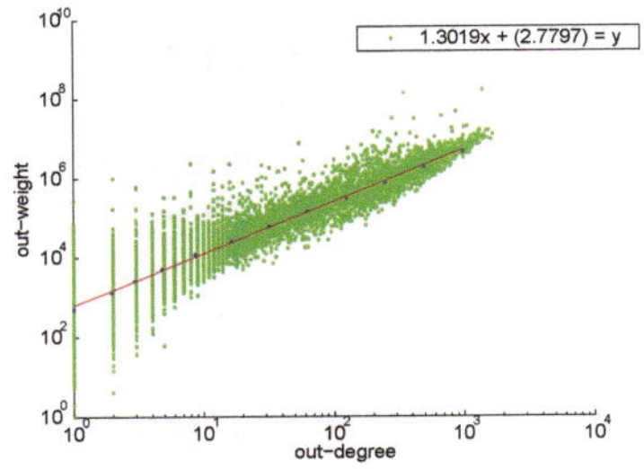

(d) outD-outW snapshot

Figure 2.4. Weight properties of *CampOrg* donations: (a) shows all the power laws as well as the WPL; the slope in (b) is ~ 0.86 indicating bursty weight additions over time; (c) and (d) have slopes > 1 ("fortification effect"), that is, that the more campaigns an organization supports, the superlinearly-more money it donates, and similarly, the more donations a candidate gets, the more average amount-per-donation is received. Inset plots on (c) and (d) show iw and ow versus time. Note they are very stable over time.

where ow is the out-weight-exponent *of the SPL. Similarly, for the in-degree, with in-weight-exponent iw.*

We studied the snapshot plots for several time-stamps (for brevity, we only report the slopes for the final timestamp in Table 2 for all the datasets we studied). We observed that SPL exponents of a graph over time remains almost constant. In Fig. 2.4 (c) ((d)), the inset plot shows how the $iw(ow)$ exponent changes over time (years) for the *CampOrg* dataset. We notice that iw and ow take values in the range [0.9-1.2] and [0.95-1.35], respectively. That is:

OBSERVATION 2.4 (PERSISTENCE OF SNAPSHOT POWER LAW) *The in- and out-exponents iw and ow of the SPL remain about constant, over time.*

Looking at Table 2, we observe that all SPL exponents are > 1, which imply a "*fortification effect*" with super-linear growth.

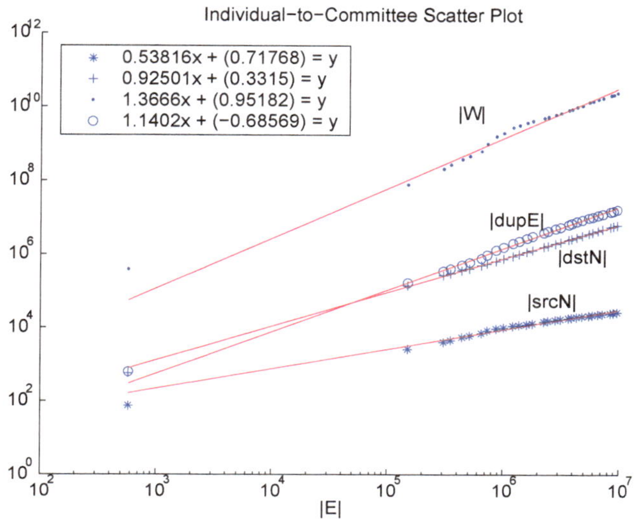

(a) *CampIndiv* WPLs

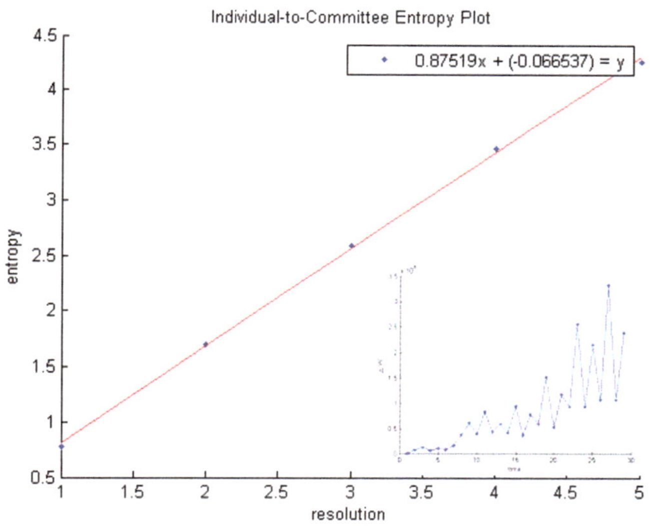

(b) *CampIndiv* entropy

Figure 2.5. Properties of weighted networks. Top: weight power laws for *CampIndiv*(W, E_d, N; vs E). The slopes for weight W and multi-edges E_d are above 1, indicating "fortification". Bottom: entropy plots for weight addition. Slope away from 1 indicates burstiness (eg., 0.88 for *CampIndiv*) The inset plot shows the corresponding time sequence ΔW versus time.

	w	*nsrc*	*ndst*	*dupE*	*iw*	*ow*	*fd*
CampOrg	1.53	0.58	0.73	1.29	1.16	1.30	0.86
CampIndiv	1.36	0.53	0.92	1.14	1.05	1.48	0.87
BlogNet	1.03	0.79	NA	NA	1.01	1.10	0.96
Auth-Key	1.01	0.90	0.70	NA	1.01	1.04	0.95
Auth-Conf	1.08	0.96	0.48	NA	1.04	1.81	0.96
Key-Conf	1.22	0.85	0.54	NA	1.26	2.14	0.95

Table 2.3. **Power law exponents for all the weighted datasets we studied: The x-axis being the number of non-duplicate edges E, *w*: WPL exponent, *nsrc, ndst*: WPL exponent for source and destination nodes respectively (if the graph is unipartite, then *nsrc* is the number of all nodes), *dupE*: exponent for multi-edges, *iw, ow*: SPL exponents for indegree and outdegree of nodes, respectively. Exponents above 1 indicate fortification/superlinear growth. Last column, *fd*: slope of the entropy plots, or information fractal dimension. Lower fd means more burstiness.**

3. Dynamic Properties

We next present several *dynamic* properties. These are typically studied by looking at a *series* of static snapshots and seeing how measurements of these snapshots compare. Like the static properties we presented previously, we also divide these into properties that take into account weights and those that don't.

3.1 Dynamic Unweighted Graphs

The patterns in dynamic time-evolving graphs that do not consider edge weights include the shrinking diameter property, the densification law, oscillating around a constant size secondary largest connected components, the largest eigenvalue law and the bursty and self-similar edge additions over time. We next describe these laws in detail.

3.1.1 D-1: Shrinking Diameter. Leskovec. et al. [18] showed that not only is the diameter of real graphs small, but it also *shrinks* and then *stabilizes* over time [18]. This pattern can be attributed to the 'gelling point' and the 'densification' in real graphs both of which are described in the following sections. Briefly, at the 'gelling point' many small disconnected components merge and form the largest connected component in the graph. This can be thought as the 'coalescence' of the graph at which point the diameter 'spikes'. Afterwards, with the addition of new edges the diameter keeps shrinking until it reaches an equilibrium.

3.1.2 D-2: Densification Power Law (DPL). Time-evolving graphs follow the 'Densification Power Law' with the equation $E(t) \propto N(t)^{\beta}$, at all time ticks t [18], where β is the densification exponent, and $E(t)$ and $N(t)$ are the number of edges and nodes at time t, respectively.

All our real graphs we studied obeyed the DPL, with exponents between 1.03 and 1.7. The power-law exponent being greater than 1 indicates a super-linearity between the number of nodes and the number of edges in real graphs. That is, it indicates that for example when the number of nodes N in a graph doubles, the number of edges E more than doubles– hence the densification. It also explains away the shrinking diameter phenomenon observed in real graphs described earlier. We will attempt to reproduce this property in a generative model later in this chapter.

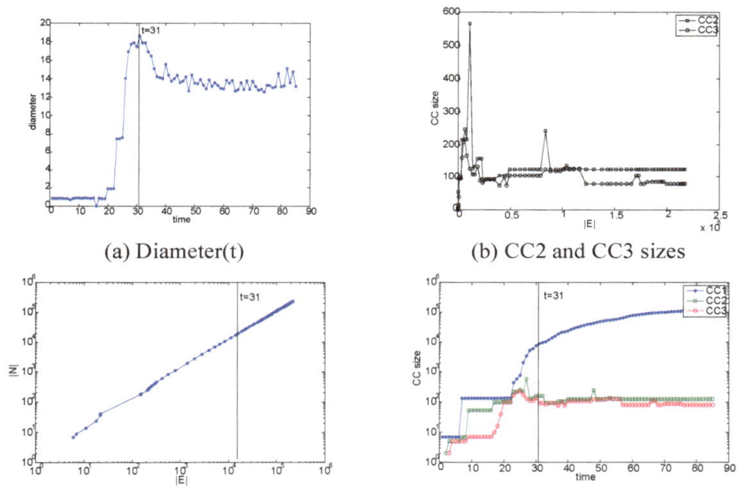

(a) Diameter(t) (b) CC2 and CC3 sizes

(c) N(t) vs E(t) (d) GCC, CC2, and CC3 (log-lin)

Figure 2.6. Properties of *PostNet* network. Notice that we experience an early gelling point at (a) (diameter versus time), stabilization/oscillation of the NLCC sizes in (b) (size of 2nd and 3rd CC, versus time). The vertical line marks the gelling point. Part (c) gives $N(t)$ vs $E(t)$ in log-log scales - the good linear fit agrees with the Densification Power Law. Part (d): component size (in log), vs time - the GCC is included, and it clearly dominates the rest, after the gelling point.

3.1.3 D-3: Diameter-plot and Gelling point.

Studying the effective diameter of the graphs, we notice that there is often a point in time when the diameter spikes. Before that point, the graph is more or less in an establishment period, typically consisting of a collection of small, disconnected components. This "*gelling point*" seems to also be the time where the GCC "takes off". After the gelling point, the graph obeys the expected rules, such as the densification power law; its diameter decreases or stabilizes; the giant connected component keeps growing, absorbing the vast majority of the newcomer nodes.

OBSERVATION 2.5 (GELLING POINT) *Real graphs exhibit a gelling point, at which the diameter spikes and (several) disconnected components gel into a giant component.*

In most of these graphs, both unipartite and bipartite, there are clear gelling points. For example, in *NIPS* the diameter spikes at $t = 8$ years, which is a reasonable time for an academic community to gel. In some networks, we only see one side of the spike, due to massive network size (*Patent*).

We show full results for *PostNet* in Fig. 2.6, including the diameter plot (Fig. 2.6(a)), sizes of the NLCCs (Fig. 2.6(b)), densification plot (Fig. 2.6(c)), and the sizes of the three largest connected components in log-linear scale, to observe how the GCC dominates the others (Fig. 2.6(d)). Results from other networks are similar, and are shown in condensed form for space (Fig. 2.7 for unipartite graphs, and Fig. 2.8 for bipartite graphs). The left column shows the diameter plots, and the right column shows the NLCCs, which we describe next.

3.1.4 D-4: Constant/Oscillating NLCCs. We particularly studied the second and the third connected component over time. We notice that, after the gelling point, the sizes of these components *oscillate* over time. Further investigation shows that the oscillation may be explained as follows: newcomer nodes typically link to the GCC; very few of the newcomers link to the 2nd (or 3rd) CC, helping them to grow slowly; in very rare cases, a newcomer links both to an NLCC, as well as the GCC, thus leading to the absorption of the NLCC into the GCC. It is exactly at these times that we have a drop in the size of the 2nd CC: Note that edges are not removed, thus, what is reported as the size of the 2nd CC is actually the size of yesterday's 3rd CC, causing the apparent "oscillation".

An unexpected (to us, at least) observation is that the largest size these components can get seems to be a constant. This is counter-intuitive – based on random graph theory, we would expect the size of the NLCCs to grow with increasing N. Using scale-free arguments, we would expect the NLCCs to have size that would be a (small, but constant) fraction of the size of the GCC – to our surprise, this *never* happened, on any of the real graphs we tried. If some underlying growth does exist, it was small enough to be impossible to observe throughout the (often lengthy) time in the datasets.

The second columns of Fig. 2.7 and Fig. 2.8 show the NLCC sizes versus time. Notice that, after the "gelling" point (marked with a vertical line), they all oscillate about constant value (different for each network). The only extreme cases are datasets with unusually high connectivity. For example, *Netflix*has

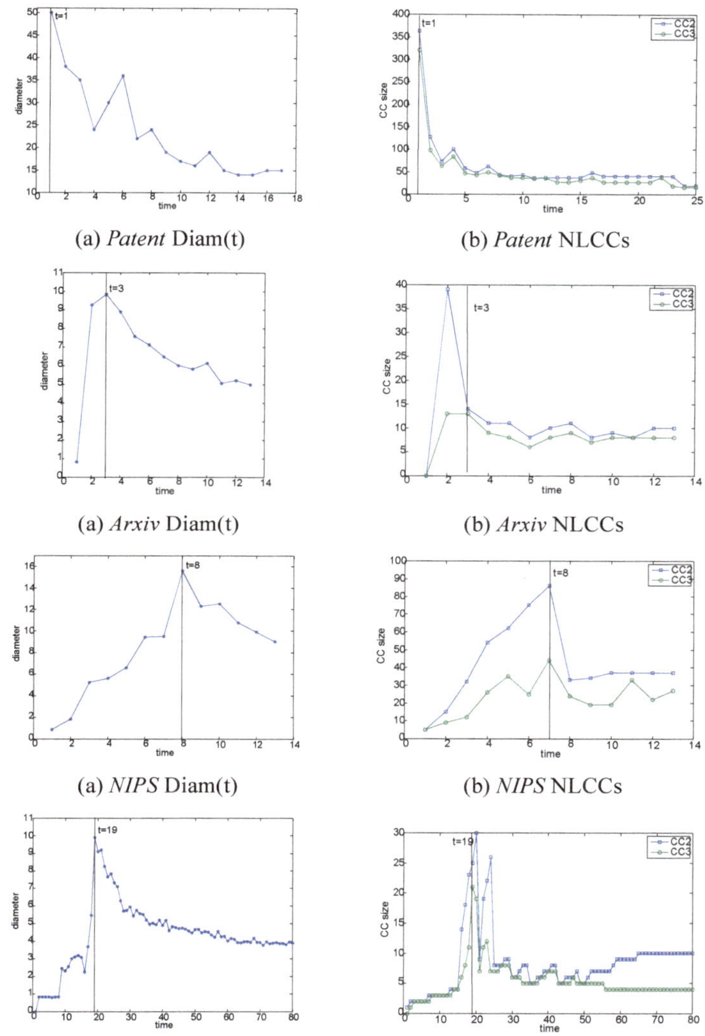

(a) *Patent* Diam(t) (b) *Patent* NLCCs

(a) *Arxiv* Diam(t) (b) *Arxiv* NLCCs

(a) *NIPS* Diam(t) (b) *NIPS* NLCCs

(a) *BlogNet* Diam(t) (b) *BlogNet* NLCCs

Figure 2.7. Properties of other unipartite networks. Diameter plot (left column), and NLCCs over time (right); vertical line marks the gelling point. All datasets exhibit an early gelling point, and stabilization of the NLCCs.

very small NLCCs. This may be explained by the fact the dataset is masked, omitting users with less than a hundred ratings (possibly to further protect the privacy of the encrypted user-ids). Therefore, the graph has abnormally high connectivity.

OBSERVATION 2.6 (OSCILLATING NLCCS) *After the gelling point, the secondary and tertiary connected components remain of approximately constant size, with small oscillations.*

3.1.5 D-5: LPL: Principal eigenvalue over time.

Plotting the largest (principal) eigenvalue of the 0-1 adjacency matrix **A** of our datasets over time, we notice that the principal eigenvalue grows following a power law with increasing number of edges. This observation is true especially after the *gelling point*. The 'gelling point' is defined to be the point at which a giant connected component (GCC) appears in real-world graphs - after this point, properties such as densification and shrinking diameter become increasingly evident. See [18] for details.

OBSERVATION 2.7 (λ_1 POWER LAW (LPL)) *In real graphs, the principal eigenvalue $\lambda_1(t)$ and the number of edges $E(t)$ over time follow a power law with exponent less than 0.5, especially after the 'gelling point'. That is,*

$$\lambda_1(t) \propto E(t)^{\alpha},\ \alpha \leq 0.5$$

We report the power law exponents in Fig. 2.9. Note that we fit the given lines *after* the gelling point which is shown by a vertical line for each dataset. Notice that the given slopes are less than 0.5, with the exception of the *CampaignOrg* dataset, with slope ≈ 0.53. This result is in agreement with graph theory. See [1] for details.

3.2 Dynamic Weighted Graphs

3.2.1 DW-1: Bursty/self-similar weight additions.

We tracked how much weight a graph puts on at each time interval and looking at the entropy plots, we observed that the weight additions over time show self-similarity. For those weighted graphs where the edge weight is defined as the number of reoccurrences of that edge, the slope of the entropy plot was greater than 0.95, pointing out uniformity. On the other hand, for those graphs where weight is not in terms of multiple edges but some other feature of the dataset such as the amount of donations for the FEC dataset, we observed that weight additions are more bursty, the slope being as low as 0.6 for the Network Traffic dataset. Fig. 2.5 (b) column shows the entropy plots for the weighted datasets we studied. ΔW values over time are also shown in insets at the bottom right corner of each figure.

OBSERVATION 2.8 (BURSTY/SELF-SIMILAR WEIGHT ADDITIONS) *In all our graphs, the addition of weight ($\Delta W(t)$) was self-similar, with fractal dimension ranging from $\approx$1 (smooth/uniform), down to 0.6 (bursty).*

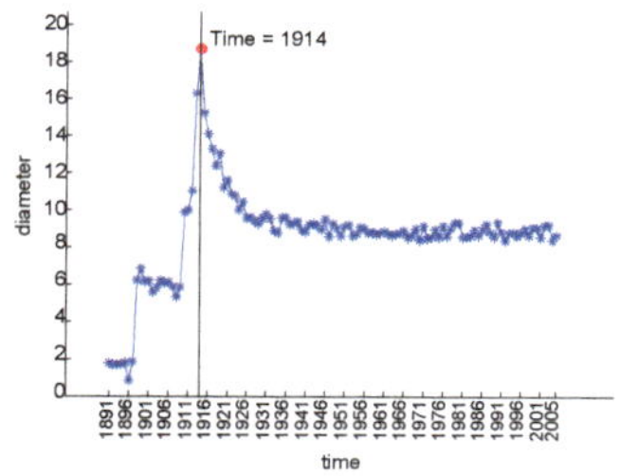

(a) *IMDB* Diam(t)

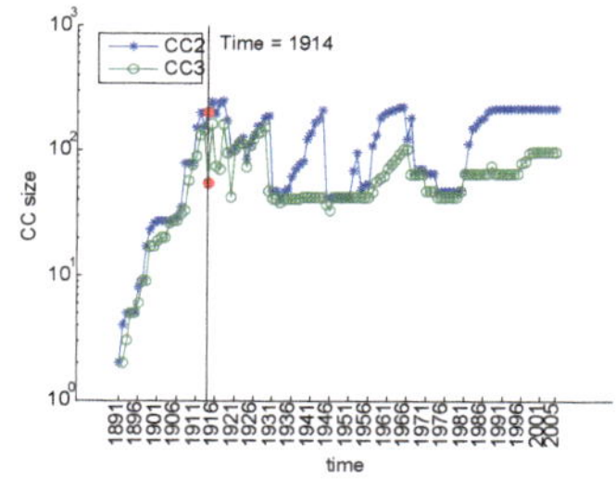

(b) *IMDB* NLCCs

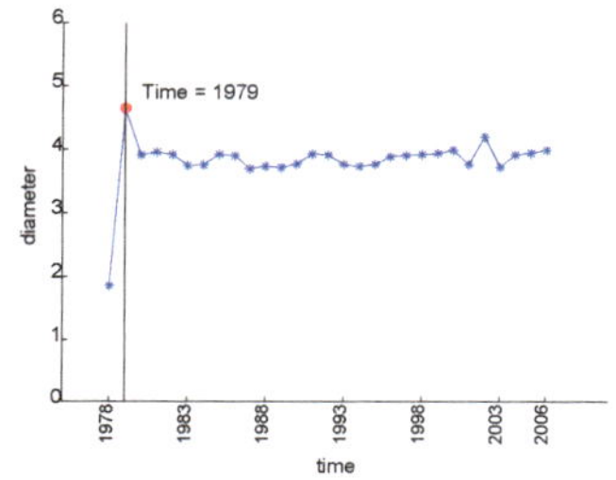

(c) *CampOrg* Diam(t)

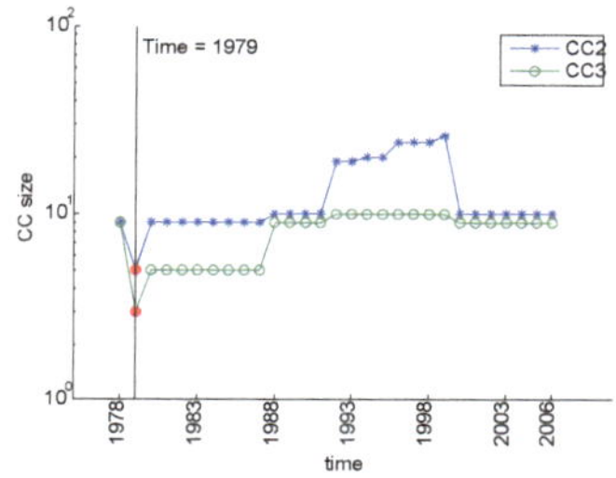

(d) *CampOrg* NLCCs

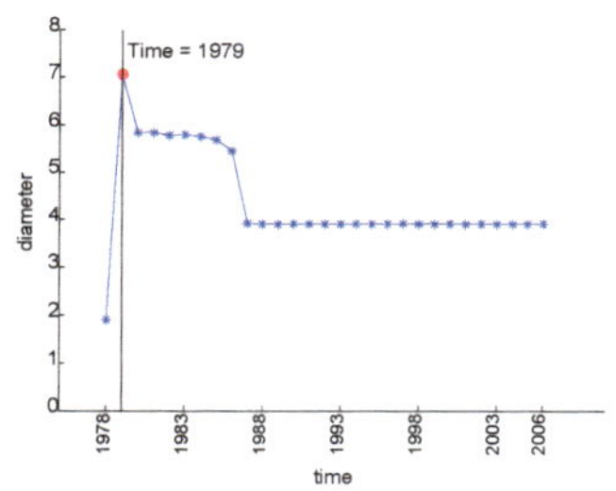

(e) *CampIndiv* Diam(t)

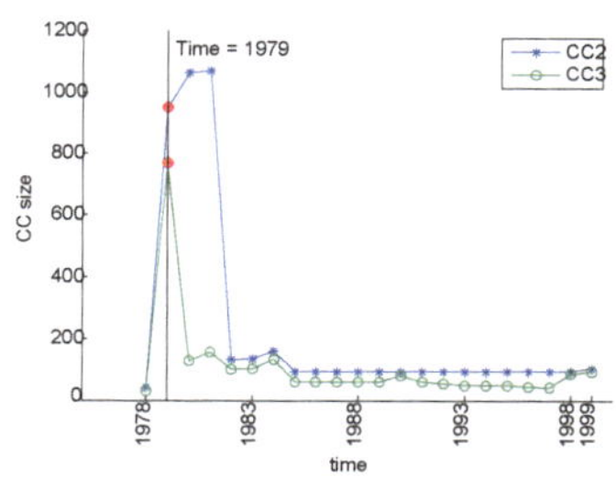

(f) *CampIndiv* NLCCs

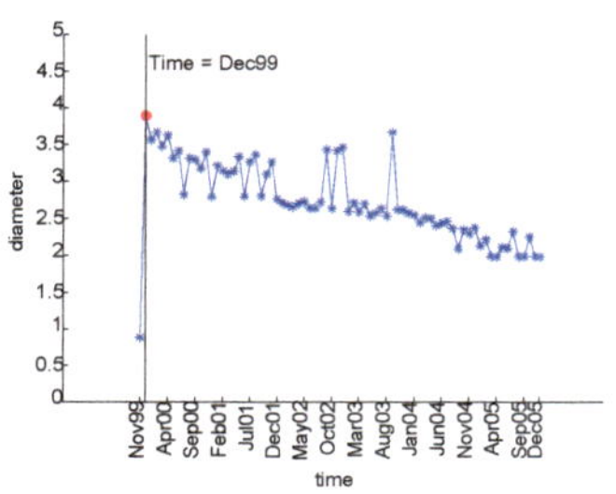

(g) *Netflix* Diam(t)

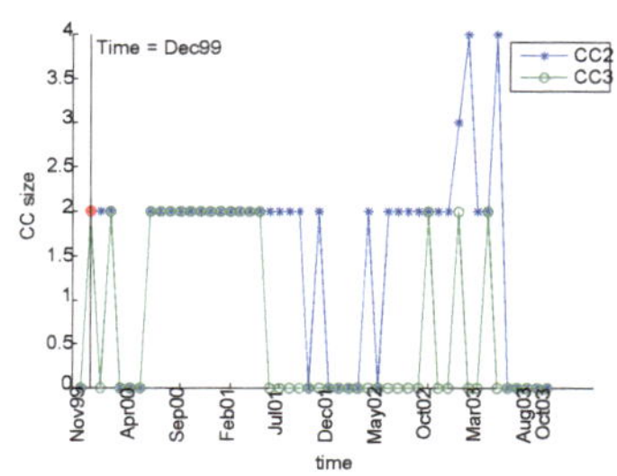

(h) *Netflix* NLCCs

Figure 2.8. Properties of bipartite networks. Diameter plot (left column), and NLCCs over time (right), with vertical line marking the gelling point. Again, all datasets exhibit an early gelling point, and stabilization of the NLCCs. *Netflix* has strange behavior because it is masked (see text).

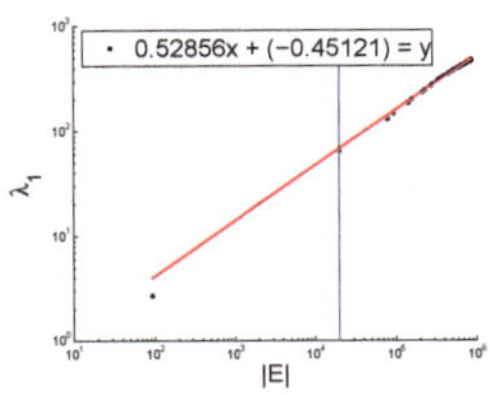

(a) Committee - Candidate

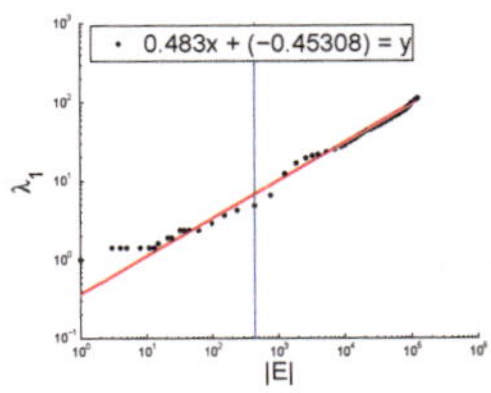

(b) Blog Network

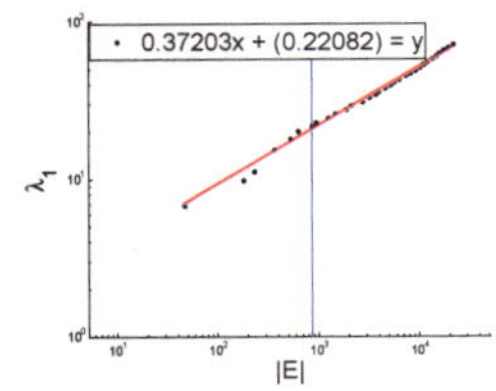

(c) Author - Conference

Figure 2.9. Illustration of the LPL. 1st eigenvalue $\lambda_1(t)$ of the *0-1* adjacency matrix $\mathbf{A}$ versus number of edges $E(t)$ over time. The vertical lines indicate the gelling point.

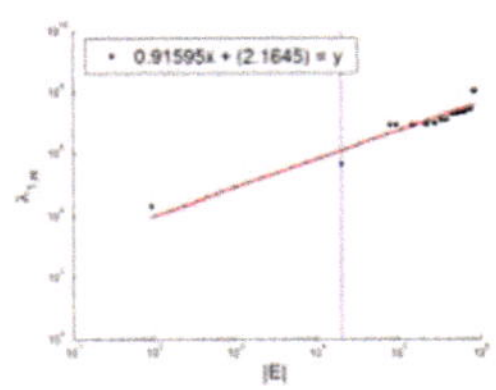

(a) Committee - Candidate

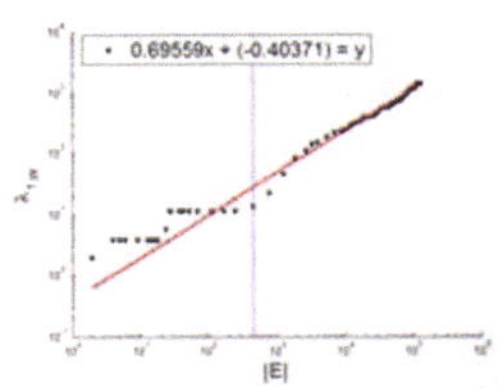

(b) Blog Network

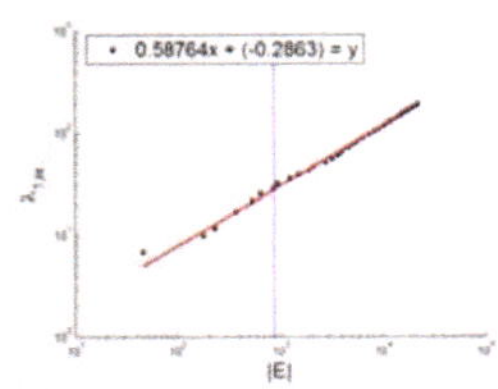

(c) Author - Conference

Figure 2.10. Illustration of the LWPL. 1st eigenvalue $\lambda_{1,w}(t)$ of the *weighted* adjacency matrix $\mathbf{A}_w$ versus number of edges $E(t)$ over time. The vertical lines indicate the gelling point.

3.2.2 DW-2: LWPL: Weighted principal eigenvalue over time. Given that unweighted (0-1) graphs follow the λ_1 Power Law, one may ask if there is a corresponding law for weighted graphs. To this end, we also compute the largest eigenvalue $\lambda_{1,w}$ of the *weighted* adjacency matrix $\mathbf{A}_w$. The entries $w_{i,j}$ of $\mathbf{A}_w$ now represent the actual edge weight between node i and j. We notice that $\lambda_{1,w}$ increases with increasing number of edges following a power law with a higher exponent than that of its λ_1 Power Law. We show the experimental results in Fig. 2.10.

OBSERVATION 2.9 ($\lambda_{1,w}$ POWER LAW (LWPL)) *Weighted real graphs exhibit a power law for the largest eigenvalue of the weighted adjacency matrix $\lambda_{1,w}(t)$ and the number of edges $E(t)$ over time. That is,*

$$\lambda_{1,w}(t) \propto E(t)^{\beta}$$

In our experiments, the exponent β ranged from 0.5 to 1.6.

4. Conclusion

We believe that the *Butterfly* model and the observation of constant NLCC's will shed light upon other research in the area, such as a recent, counter-intuitive discovery [20]: the GCC of several real graphs has *no* good cuts, so graph partitioning and clustering algorithms cannot help identify communities because no clear communities exist.

We have described the following static patterns:

- *Heavy-tailed degree distribution*, with a few "hubs" and most nodes having few neighbors.
- *Small diameter* and *community structure*– nodes form clusters, and it takes few "hops" to get between any two nodes in the network.
- Several power laws: *Triangle Power Law* and *Eigenalue Power Law* for unweighted graphs, and the *Weight Power Law*, *Edge Weights Power Law*, and *Snapshot Power Laws* for weighted graphs.

We have also described the following dynamic patterns:

- *Shrinking diameter* and *densification*– the "world gets smaller" as more nodes are added– increasingly more edges are added which causes the diameter to shrink. There is also a *gelling point* at which this occurs.
- *Constant-size smaller components* The large component takes off in size, but the others will not grow beyond a certain point before joining it.
- Several other power laws: *LPL*, or principal eigenvalue over time (both weighted and unweighted), and *bursty weight additions*.

These patterns are helpful to spot anomalous graphs and sub-graphs, and answer questions about entities in a network and what-if scenarios. Let's elaborate on each of the above applications: Spotting anomalies is vital for determining abuse of social and computer networks, such as link-spamming in a web graph, fraudulent reputation building in e-auction systems [29], detection of dwindling/abnormal social sub-groups in a social-networking site like Yahoo-360 (`360.yahoo.com`), Facebook (`www.facebook.com`) and LinkedIn (`www.linkedin.com`), and network intrusion detection [17]. Analyzing network properties is also useful for identifying authorities and search algorithms [7, 9, 16], for discovering the "network value" of customers for using viral marketing [30], or to improve recommendation systems [5]. What-if scenarios are vital for extrapolation, provisioning and algorithm design: For example if we expect that the number of links will double within the next year, we should provision for the appropriate hardware to store and process the upcoming queries.

References

[1] L. Akoglu, M. McGlohon, and C. Faloutsos. RTM: Laws and a recursive generator for weighted time-evolving graphs. *Carnegie Mellon University Technical Report*, Oct, 2008.

[2] Reka Albert, Hawoong Jeong, and Albert-Laszlo Barabasi. Diameter of the world wide web. *Nature*, (401):130–131, 1999.

[3] A. L. Barabasi and R. Albert. Emergence of scaling in random networks. *Science*, 286(5439):509–512, October 1999.

[4] Albert-Laszlo Barabasi. *Linked: How Everything Is Connected to Everything Else and What It Means for Business, Science, and Everyday Life.* Plume Books, April 2003.

[5] Robert Bell, Yehuda Koren, and Chris Volinsky. Modeling relationships at multiple scales to improve accuracy of large recommender systems. In *KDD '07: Proceedings of the 13th ACM SIGKDD international conference on Knowledge discovery and data mining*, pages 95–104, New York, NY, USA, 2007. ACM.

[6] Zhiqiang Bi, Christos Faloutsos, and Filip Korn. The DGX distribution for mining massive, skewed data. In *KDD*, pages 17–26, ACMA, 2001. ACM.

[7] Allan Borodin, Gareth O. Roberts, Jeffrey S. Rosenthal, and Panayiotis Tsaparas. Link analysis ranking: algorithms, theory, and experiments. *ACM Trans. Inter. Tech.*, 5(1):231–297, 2005.

[8] Deepayan Chakrabarti, Yiping Zhan, and Christos Faloutsos. R-MAT: A recursive model for graph mining. *SIAM Int. Conf. on Data Mining*, April 2004.

[9] Soumen Chakrabarti, Byron E. Dom, S. Ravi Kumar, Prabhakar Raghavan, Sridhar Rajagopalan, Andrew Tomkins, David Gibson, and Jon Kleinberg. Mining the web's link structure. *Computer*, 32(8):60–67, 1999.

[10] Aaron Clauset, Cosma R. Shalizi, and M. E. J. Newman. Power-law distributions in empirical data. *SIAM Review*, 51(4):661+, Feb 2009.

[11] Pedro Domingos and Matt Richardson. Mining the network value of customers. *KDD*, pages 57–66, 2001.

[12] Michalis Faloutsos, Petros Faloutsos, and Christos Faloutsos. On power-law relationships of the internet topology. *SIGCOMM*, pages 251–262, Aug-Sept. 1999.

[13] Gary Flake, Steve Lawrence, C. Lee Giles, and Frans Coetzee. Self-organization and identification of web communities. *IEEE Computer*, 35(3), March 2002.

[14] Michelle Girvan and M. E. J. Newman. Community structure in social and biological networks. *PNAS*, 99:7821, 2002.

[15] Jon M. Kleinberg, Ravi Kumar, Prabhakar Raghavan, Sridhar Rajagopalan, and Andrew S. Tomkins. The Web as a graph: Measurements, models and methods. *Lecture Notes in Computer Science*, 1627:1–17, 1999.

[16] Ravi Kumar, Prabhakar Raghavan, Sridhar Rajagopalan, and Andrew Tomkins. Core algorithms in the clever system. *ACM Trans. Inter. Tech.*, 6(2):131–152, 2006.

[17] Aleksandar Lazarevic, Levent Ertöz, Vipin Kumar, Aysel Ozgur, and Jaideep Srivastava. A comparative study of anomaly detection schemes in network intrusion detection. In *Proceedings of the Third SIAM International Conference on Data Mining*, 2003.

[18] Jure Leskovec, Jon Kleinberg, and Christos Faloutsos. Graphs over time: densification laws, shrinking diameters and possible explanations. In *Proc. of ACM SIGKDD*, pages 177–187, Chicago, Illinois, USA, 2005. ACM Press.

[19] Jure Leskovec, Jon Kleinberg, and Christos Faloutsos. Graphs over time: densification laws, shrinking diameters and possible explanations. In *KDD '05: Proceeding of the eleventh ACM SIGKDD international conference on Knowledge discovery in data mining*, pages 177–187, New York, NY, USA, 2005. ACM Press.

[20] Jure Leskovec, Kevin Lang, Anirban Dasgupta, and Michael Mahoney. Community structure in real graphs: The “negative dimensionality" paradox. In *International World Wide Web Conference*, 2008.

[21] Jure Leskovec, Mary Mcglohon, Christos Faloutsos, Natalie Glance, and Matthew Hurst. Cascading behavior in large blog graphs: Patterns and a model. In *Society of Applied and Industrial Mathematics: Data Mining (SDM07)*, 2007.

[22] Mary Mcglohon, Leman Akoglu, and Christos Faloutsos. Weighted graphs and disconnected components: Patterns and a generator. In *ACM Special Interest Group on Knowledge Discovery and Data Mining (SIGKDD)*, August 2008.

[23] M. Mihail and C. Papadimitriou. The eigenvalue power law, 2002.

[24] S. Milgram. The small-world problem. *Psychology Today*, 2:60–67, 1967.

[25] Alan L. Montgomery and Christos Faloutsos. Identifying web browsing trends and patterns. *IEEE Computer*, 34(7):94–95, July 2001.

[26] M. E. J. Newman. Power laws, pareto distributions and zipf's law. *Contemporary Physics*, 46, 2005.

[27] M. E. J. Newman and M. Girvan. Finding and evaluating community structure in networks. *Physical Review E*, 69:026113, 2004.

[28] C. R. Palmer, P. B. Gibbons, and C. Faloutsos. Anf: A fast and scalable tool for data mining in massive graphs. In *SIGKDD*, Edmonton, AB, Canada, 2002.

[29] Shashank Pandit, Duen H. Chau, Samuel Wang, and Christos Faloutsos. Netprobe: a fast and scalable system for fraud detection in online auction networks. In *WWW '07: Proceedings of the 16th international conference on World Wide Web*, pages 201–210, New York, NY, USA, 2007.

[30] M. Richardson and P. Domingos. Mining knowledge-sharing sites for viral marketing, 2002.

[31] Manfred Schroeder. *Fractals, Chaos, Power Laws: Minutes from an Infinite Paradise*. W.H. Freeman and Company, New York, 1991.

[32] Michael F. Schwartz and David C. M. Wood. Discovering shared interests among people using graph analysis of global electronic mail traffic. *Communications of the ACM*, 36:78–89, 1992.

[33] G. Siganos, M. Faloutsos, P. Faloutsos, and C. Faloutsos. Power laws and the AS-level internet topology, 2003.

[34] G. Siganos, S. L. Tauro, and M. Faloutsos. Jellyfish: a conceptual model for the as internet topology. *Journal of Communications and Networks*, 2006.

[35] SL Tauro, C. Palmer, G. Siganos, and M. Faloutsos. A simple conceptual model for the Internet topology. 2001.

[36] Charalampos E. Tsourakakis. Fast counting of triangles in large real networks without counting: Algorithms and laws. In *ICDM*, 2008.

[37] Mengzhi Wang, Tara Madhyastha, Ngai Hang Chang, Spiros Papadimitriou, and Christos Faloutsos. Data mining meets performance evaluation: Fast algorithms for modeling bursty traffic. *ICDE*, February 2002.

[38] Duncan J. Watts and Steven H. Strogatz. Collective dynamics of 'small-world' networks. *Nature*, (393):440–442, 1998.

Chapter 3

RANDOM WALKS IN SOCIAL NETWORKS AND THEIR APPLICATIONS: A SURVEY

Purnamrita Sarkar
Machine Learning Department
Carnegie Mellon University
psarkar@cs.cmu.edu

Andrew W. Moore
Google, Inc.
awm@google.com

Abstract A wide variety of interesting real world applications, e.g. friend suggestion in social networks, keyword search in databases, web-spam detection etc. can be framed as ranking entities in a graph. In order to obtain ranking we need a graph-theoretic measure of similarity. Ideally this should capture the information hidden in the graph structure. For example, two entities are similar, if there are lots of short paths between them. Random walks have proven to be a simple, yet powerful mathematical tool for extracting information from the ensemble of paths between entities in a graph. Since real world graphs are enormous and complex, ranking using random walks is still an active area of research. The research in this area spans from new applications to novel algorithms and mathematical analysis, bringing together ideas from different branches of statistics, mathematics and computer science. In this book chapter, we describe different random walk based proximity measures, their applications, and existing algorithms for computing them.

Keywords: random walks, proximity measures, hitting times, personalized pagerank, link prediction

1. Introduction

Link prediction in social networks, personalized graph search techniques, spam detection in the World Wide Web and collaborative filtering in recommender networks are important practical problems that greatly rely on graph theoretic measures of similarity. All these problems can be framed as ranking entities in a graph.

Take for example online social networks, where an important application is to suggest friends to a newcomer. Another example is movie and music recommendation systems (*Netflix, Last.fm*), where an user is suggested new movies and music based on his or her ratings so far. The graph in this case is a bipartite network between users and items, and an edge can be weighted by the rating given by the user to the item. Keyword search in large publication databases leads to another interesting problem setting, where the database can be seen as an entity-relation graph between papers, authors and words. The goal is to find papers which are "contextually" similar to the query submitted by the user.

The underlying question in all these problems is: given a node in a graph, which other nodes are most similar to this node. Ideally we would like this proximity measure to capture the graph structure such as having many common neighbors or having several short paths between two nodes.

Real world graphs are huge, complex and continuously evolving over time. Therefore it is important to find meaningful proximity measures, and design fast space-efficient algorithms to compute them.

A widely popular approach in graph-mining and machine learning literature is to compute proximity between nodes by using random walks on graphs: diffusion of information from one node to another. This chapter will be focused on these measures: the intuition behind their usefulness and effective algorithms to compute them, and important real-world problems where they have been applied.

Random walks provide a simple framework for unifying the information from ensembles of paths between two nodes. The ensemble of paths between two nodes is an essential ingredient of many popular measures such as personalized pagerank [37], hitting and commute times [4], Katz measure [46], harmonic functions [84]. Personalized page-rank vectors (PPV) have been used for keyword search in databases [9] and entity-relation graphs [18]. Hitting and commute times have been shown to be empirically effective for query suggestion [55], ranking in recommender networks [14] and image segmentation problems [64]. In [39] the authors show how to use hitting times for designing provably manipulation resistant reputation systems. Harmonic functions have been used for automated image-segmentation and coloring [52, 33], and document classification [84].

Naive computation of these measures usually requires $O(n^3)$ time, which is prohibitive for real world large graphs. Fast approximation algorithms for computing these bring together ideas from scientific computing, databases and graph theory. These algorithms span from clever offline preprocessing [40, 28,

74], fast online computation of sparse support of these measures [10, 70, 66] to hybrid algorithms which use best of both worlds [18]. In section 3 we would discuss these algorithms, study their interconnections, and see how they fit into the big picture.

Here is the organization: we will discuss two main aspects of random walk-based graph mining problems. First we will discuss different proximity measures arising from a random walk in section 2. Section 3 consists of some popular algorithms for computing different proximity measures. We show real-world applications of these measures in section 4, and conclude with experimental evaluation techniques and data-sources in section 5.

2. Random Walks on Graphs: Background

In this section we introduce some basic concepts of random walks on graphs. A graph $G = (V, E)$ is defined as a set of vertices V and edges E. The ij^{th} entry of the adjacency matrix A is nonnegative and denotes the weight on edge i, j, and is zero if the edge does not exist. In unweighted graphs the weight of any edge is 1, whereas in a weighted graph it can be any positive number. D is an $n \times n$ diagonal matrix, where $D_{ii} = \sum_j A_{ij}$. We will denote D_{ii} by the degree $d(i)$ of node i from now on. The Laplacian L of G is defined as $D - A$. This is used widely in machine learning algorithms as a regularizer ([73, 86]). For undirected[1] graphs, L is positive semi-definite, since for any vector $\boldsymbol{g}$, $\boldsymbol{g}^T L \boldsymbol{g}$ equals $\sum_{i,j \in E} (g(i) - g(j))^2$.

$P = p_{ij}, i, j \in V$ denotes the transition probability matrix, so that $P_{ij} = A_{ij}/D_{ii}$ if $(i, j) \in E$ and zero otherwise. A random walk on this graph is a Markov chain ([4]) with transition probabilities specified by this matrix. For an undirected graph, A is symmetric and L is symmetric positive semi-definite. We will denote the set of neighbors of a node i by $\mathcal{N}(i)$. For an unweighted graph, $d(i)$ is simply the size of this neighborhood. For a directed graph, the set of nodes having an edge to node i is denoted by $I(i)$, and the indegree is denoted by $d^-(i)$. Similarly the set of out-neighbors is denoted by $O(i)$, and the outdegree is denoted by $d^+(i)$. Both in and outdegree are weighted for weighted graphs.

In a random walk, if node v_0 is chosen from a distribution x_0, then the distributions $x_0, x_1, ..$ are in general different from one another. However if $x_t = x_{t+1}$, then we say that x_t is the stationary distribution for the graph. According to the Perron-Frobenius theorem, there exists a unique stationary distribution, if P is irreducible and aperiodic. For graphs that are undirected, non-bipartite and connected (both irreducible and aperiodic) the stationary distribution is proportional to the degree distribution.

[1] Laplacian matrices for directed graphs have been proposed in [21].

2.1 Random Walk based Proximity Measures

Now we will briefly describe popular random walk based similarity measures, e.g. personalized pagerank, hitting and commute times, simrank, etc. We will first discuss a few query-independent and broad topic based search algorithms, more specifically pagerank, HITS and its variants including SALSA. Note that the primary focus of this chapter is to give a comprehensive survey of random walk based proximity measures, and hence we will not discuss fast algorithms for computing pagerank, HITS or SALSA in section 3. We will briefly mention some algorithms for making SALSA and HITS faster after introducing them. An excellent study of pagerank can be found in [50].

Query independent search and broad topic search. Pagerank [15] is a widely known tool for ranking web-pages. If the world-wide-web is considered as a graph then the pagerank is defined as the distribution that satisfies the following linear equation (3.1):

$$\mathbf{v} = (1-\alpha)P^T\mathbf{v} + \frac{\alpha}{n}\mathbf{1} \tag{3.1}$$

α is the probability of restarting the random walk at a given step. Note that the α restart factor plays a very important role. The Perron-Frobenius theorem indicates that a stochastic matrix P has a unique principal eigenvector iff it is irreducible and aperiodic. The random restart assures that, since under this model 1) all nodes are reachable from all other nodes, and 2) the Markov chain is aperiodic. Also the restart probability makes the second largest eigenvalue to be upper bounded by α [45].

Pagerank does not provide topic-specific search results. In [47] the authors introduced the idea of Hubs and Authorities (HITS) for distilling search results for a broad topic. The key intuition behind the HITS algorithm is that the useful web-pages for searching a broad topic are generally of two types: the authorities and the hubs. The authorities are pages which are good sources of information about a given topic, whereas a hub is one which provides pointers to many authorities. Given a topic, first the authors find a subgraph of the web A. This subgraph ideally should be small, should consist of pages relevant to the given query and should contain most of the authoritative pages. The authors obtain this subgraph by expanding a root set of nodes "along the links that enter and leave it". The details can be found in the paper. The root set consists of the top k search results for the given query from a standard text-based search engine. Given this subgraph, the idea is to assign two numbers to a node: a hub-score and an authority score. A node is a good hub if it points to many good authorities, whereas a node is a good authority if many good hubs point to it. This leads to iterating over two vectors $\boldsymbol{h}$ and $\boldsymbol{a}$, namely:

$$\boldsymbol{a}(i) \leftarrow \sum_{j:j \in I(i)} \boldsymbol{h}(j) \tag{3.2}$$

$$\boldsymbol{h}(i) \leftarrow \sum_{j:j \in O(i)} \boldsymbol{a}(j) \tag{3.3}$$

Both these vectors are normalized to have unit length (the squares of the entries sum to 1). The last two equations can also be written as follows. Let A be the un-weighted adjacency matrix of the subgraph.

$$\boldsymbol{a} = A^T \boldsymbol{h} \qquad\qquad \boldsymbol{h} = A\boldsymbol{a}$$

The above equation simply means that $\boldsymbol{h}$ converges to the principal eigenvector of AA^T, whereas $\boldsymbol{a}$ converges to the principal eigenvector of $A^T A$. As mentioned in [51], the matrix AA^T can be described as the bibliographic coupling matrix. This is because, the $\{i,j\}^{th}$ entry of the matrix AA^T is given by $\sum_k A(i,k)A(j,k)$, which is simply the number of nodes both i and j point to. On the other hand, $A^T A$ can be thought of as the co-citation matrix, i.e. the $\{i,j\}^{th}$ entry is given by $\sum_k A(k,i)A(k,j)$, i.e. the number of nodes which point to both i and j.

There has been algorithms which use the same idea as in HITS but alter the recurrence relation. The main idea behind these is to emphasize the higher authority-scores more while computing the hub scores. These algorithms can be divided in roughly two kinds: the authority threshold ($AT(k)$) and the $Norm(p)$ families[2]. In [13] the authors restrict the sum in eq (3.3) to the k largest authority scores, while keeping eq (3.2) intact. The underlying intuition is that a good hub should point to at least k good authorities. When k is the maximum out-degree, this algorithm is identical to HITS. The $Norm(p)$ family uses a smoother way to scale the authority weights. The p-norm of the authority weights vector is used in eq (3.3), while keeping eq 3.2 intact. A similar approach was used in [30]. When p is 1 this is the HITS algorithm. The MAX algorithm is a special case of the $AT(k)$ family (for $k = 1$), and the $Norm(p)$ family (when $p = \infty$). An in-depth study of this special case (MAX) of these two families is provided in [80].

SALSA [51] combines the idea of a random surfer from pagerank with hubs and authorities from HITS. The idea is to conceptually build an undirected bipartite graph, with two sides containing hubs and authorities. A node i can be both a hub ($h(i)$) and an authority ($a(i)$). A link is added between nodes

[2]We use the same names as mentioned in [80].

$h(i)$ and $a(j)$, if there is link $i \rightarrow j$ in the original subgraph. The nodes and links are constrained to a part of the web-graph relevant to the query, built in a manner similar to HITS. Two Markov chains are considered, s.t. one step of each consists of traversing two links in a row. This way each walk visits nodes only on one side of the bipartite graph. The stationary distributions of these walks are used as the hub and authority scores for the original subgraph.

It can be shown that these vectors are simply principal eigenvectors of $A_r A_c^T$ and $A_c^T A_r$ (instead of the matrices AA^T and $A^T A$ as in HITS). A_r is the row normalized version of A whereas A_c is the column normalized version of A. Let D_+ be the diagonal matrix of out-degrees, and D_- be the diagonal in-degree matrix. A_r is simply $D_+^{-1}A$, and A_c is AD_-^{-1}. Matrix $A_r A_c^T$ is equal to $D_+^{-1}AD_-^{-1}A^T$. Denote this as $D_+^{-1}\mathcal{H}$, where[3] $\mathcal{H}$ equals $AD_-^{-1}A^T$. The $\{i,j\}^{th}$ entry of this matrix is given by $\sum_k A(i,k)A(j,k)/d^-(k)$. Note that this is the number of nodes both i and j point to, as in AA^T, except each *common* neighbor is inversely weighted by its indegree. Here is an intuitive reason why this kind of weighting is useful. Consider two pairs of papers in a citation network. The first pair, i and j, both point to a very highly cited paper (high indegree), whereas the second pair, i' and j', both point to a rather obscure paper (low indegree). In this case, i' and j' are much more likely to be contextually similar than i and j.

Also, since the ith row of matrix $\mathcal{H}$ sums to $d^+(i)$, the matrix $A_r A_c^T$ is a stochastic matrix (each row sums to 1). As $\mathcal{H}$ is undirected, when it is connected, the principal eigenvector of the probability transition matrix resulting from it is proportional to the degree distribution of this modified adjacency matrix, in this case, the out-degrees. The case of a number of connected components is described in [51]. Similarly, it can be shown that the principal eigenvector of $A_c^T A_r$, also a stochastic matrix, is the in-degree distribution.

Thus, the construction of SALSA simply means that high indegree nodes *in the topic-specific subgraph* are good authorities, whereas high out-degree nodes *in the topic-specific subgraph* are good hubs. This is surprising, since earlier it has been pointed out that ranking simply with respect to (w.r.t) in-degrees on the entire WWW graph is not adequate [47].In [51] the authors point out that this conflict results from better techniques for assembling a topic-specific WWW subgraph. These techniques augment the original subgraph-expansion [47] with link-filtering schemes to remove noisy links, and use simple heuristics to assign weights to links, so that weighted indegree or out-degrees can be computed.

One problem with the HITS ranking is the sensitivity to the tightly knit communities, coined as the TKC effect. This happens when a small tightly-

[3] The matrix AA^T is denoted by H in [51].

knit community of nodes rank highly, although they are not most authoritative. Using a combinatorial construction and examples of search results from the web graph, it has been demonstrated that SALSA is less vulnerable to the TKC effect than HITS [51].

Note that neighborhood construction is key to both HITS, MAX and SALSA, and is a major computational bottleneck at query time. In [58] the authors show how to precompute score maps for web-pages in order to drastically lower query latency. Later consistent unbiased sampling [17] and bloom filters [11] have been used for approximating neighborhood graphs [59].

Personalized Pagerank. PageRank gives a democratic view of the respective importance of the webpages. However by using a non-uniform restart probability density we can create a personalized view of the relative importance of the nodes. The basic idea is to start a random walk from a node i; at any step the walk moves randomly to a neighbor of the current node with probability $1 - \alpha$, and is reset to the start node i with probability α. The stationary distribution of this process is the personalized pagerank w.r.t node i. As a result, the stationary distribution is localized around the start node. This was also called "rooted pagerank" in [53].

If we generalize the start node i to a start distribution $\boldsymbol{r}$, the personalization vector will be given by:

$$\mathbf{v} = (1 - \alpha)P^T\mathbf{v} + \alpha\boldsymbol{r} \tag{3.4}$$

In order to obtain personalization w.r.t node i, the restart distribution $\boldsymbol{r}$ is set to a vector where the ith entry is set to 1, and all other entries are set to 0. $P^T\boldsymbol{v}$ is the distribution after one step of random walk from $\boldsymbol{v}$. The above definition implies that personalized pagerank can be computed by solving a large linear system involving the transition matrix P.

While most algorithms use personalized pagerank as a measure of similarity between two nodes, in [81] the authors presented a setting where the restart distribution is learnt using quadratic programming from ordinal preferences provided by an administrator. The authors presented a scalable optimization problem by reducing the number of parameters by clustering the WWW graph.

Simrank. Simrank is a proximity measure defined in [41], which is based on the intuition that two nodes are similar if they share many neighbors. The recursive definition of simrank is given by

$$s(a, b) = \frac{\gamma}{|I(a)||I(b)|} \sum_{i \in I(a), j \in I(b)} s(i, j) \tag{3.5}$$

If two random surfers start two simultaneous backward walks from nodes a and b, then this quantity can be interpreted as the expectation of γ^{ℓ}, where ℓ equals the time when those two walks meet.

Hitting and Commute time. The hitting time ([4]) between nodes i and j is defined as the expected number of steps in a random walk starting from node i before node j is visited for the first time. H is an $n \times n$ matrix. Recursively h_{ij} can be written as

$$h_{ij} = \begin{cases} 1 + \sum_k p_{ik} h_{kj} & \text{If } i \neq j \\ 0 & \text{If } i = j \end{cases} \tag{3.6}$$

The hitting time can also be interpreted as weighted path-length from node i to node j, i.e. $h_{ij} = \sum_{path(i,j)} |path(i,j)| P(path(i,j))$. Hitting times are not symmetric even for undirected graphs. This can be seen by considering an undirected star graph with a central node with large degree, which is connected to many nodes with degree one. The central node has high hitting time to all of its neighbors, since there are many different destinations of a random walk. On the other hand, the degree-1 neighbors have a small hitting time ($= 1$) to the central node. Hitting times also follow the triangle inequality ([54]).

Commute time between a pair of nodes is defined as $c_{ij} = h_{ij} + h_{ji}$. We will now show some surprising properties of commute times for undirected graphs. For undirected graphs[4] there is a direct analogy of hitting and commute times with electrical networks ([25]). Consider an undirected graph. Now think of each edge as a resistor with conductance A_{ij}. In this setting, the commute time can be shown ([20]) to be equal to the effective resistance between two nodes up to a multiplicative constant.

Let $vol(G)$ denote the volume of the graph. This is defined as the sum of degrees of all nodes, which also equals twice the number of edges in an undirected graph. If $d(i)$ amount of current is injected at node $i, \forall i$, and $vol(G)$ amount of current is withdrawn from node j, let the voltage at of node i be $\psi(i)$. Now, the voltage at node i w.r.t node j is denoted by $\psi(i,j)$. This is essentially $\psi(i) - \psi(j)$. Using Kirchhoff's law we can write:

$$d(i) = \sum_{k \in \mathcal{N}(i)} (\psi(i,j) - \psi(k,j))$$

Using algebraic manipulation we have:

$$\psi(i,j) = \begin{cases} 1 + \sum_{k \in \mathcal{N}(i)} \dfrac{\psi(k,j)}{d(i)} & \text{If } i \neq j \\ 0 & \text{Otherwise} \end{cases} \tag{3.7}$$

[4] A detailed discussion of hitting and commute times in directed graphs can be found in [12].

Note that this linear system is identical to the definition of hitting time from i to j (eq. 3.6) and hence hitting time from i to j is identical to the voltage at node i w.r.t j. The above can be written as a solution to the following linear system:

$$L\boldsymbol{\psi} = \boldsymbol{y} \tag{3.8}$$

$\boldsymbol{y}$ is the vector of currents injected in the system, in particular, $y(x) = d(x)$, $\forall x \neq j$ and for node j, $y(j) = d(j) - vol(G)$. Note that, if $\boldsymbol{\psi}$ is a solution to eq. 3.8 then any vector obtained by shifting each entry of it by a fixed constant is also a solution. The intuition behind this is that, the currents in the system only depend on the difference in the voltages between two nodes, not the respective values. Hence, if all voltages are shifted by a constant, the currents will stay the same. More concretely, this happens because L is not full rank: one of its eigenvectors, the all ones vector, has eigenvalue zero. Hence, it is not invertible. This is why the Moore-Penrose pseudo-inverse, denoted by L^+, is used ([29]). This matrix, i.e. L^+, can also be written as $(L - \frac{1}{n}\mathbf{1}\mathbf{1}^T)^{-1} + \frac{1}{n}\mathbf{1}\mathbf{1}^T$ ([29, 88]).

Hence from eq. 3.8, we have:

$$\boldsymbol{\psi} - \mathbf{1}\frac{\mathbf{1}^T\boldsymbol{\psi}}{n} = L^+\boldsymbol{y} \tag{3.9}$$

The second term on the L.H.S is simply the constant vector, where each entry equals $\frac{\mathbf{1}^T\boldsymbol{\psi}}{n}$, i.e. the mean of $\boldsymbol{\psi}$. Since the hitting time measures the voltage difference, this mean shifting does not matter, i.e. $H(i,j) = \psi(i,j) = \psi(i) - \psi(j) = (\boldsymbol{e_i} - \boldsymbol{e_j})^T L^+ \boldsymbol{y}$.

Now consider the system where $vol(G)$ current is withdrawn from i and $d(x)$ amount is injected at all nodes x. Now the voltage drop at j w.r.t i will be $h_{ji} = (\boldsymbol{e_j} - \boldsymbol{e_i})^T L^+ \boldsymbol{y'}$, where $\boldsymbol{y'}$ is the new current vector with $\boldsymbol{y}(x) = d(x), \forall x \neq i$ and for node i, $y(i) = d(i) - vol(G)$. Note that $\boldsymbol{y} - \boldsymbol{y'} = vol(G)(\boldsymbol{e_i} - \boldsymbol{e_j})$. Hence, $c_{ij} = h_{ij} + h_{ji}$ is given by,

$$c_{ij} = vol(G)(\boldsymbol{e_i} - \boldsymbol{e_j})^T L^+ (\boldsymbol{e_i} - \boldsymbol{e_j}) \tag{3.10}$$

This also gives us some intuition about the effectiveness of commute time as a proximity measure. First, if the effective resistance between two nodes is small, then it is easier for information to diffuse from one node to the other. Second, since electrical properties of networks do not change much by adding or removing a few edges, hitting and commute times should be robust to small perturbation in datasets ([25]).

From eq. (3.10) we see that L^+ maps each vertex of a graph to a Euclidian space $i \mapsto \boldsymbol{x_i}$, where $\boldsymbol{x_i} = (L^+)^{\frac{1}{2}}\boldsymbol{e_i}$. This is how in undirected graphs pairwise commute time can be expressed as the squared Euclidian distance in the transformed space (eq. 3.11).

$$\begin{aligned} c_{ij} &= vol(G)(l^+_{ii} + l^+_{jj} - 2l^+_{ij}) \\ &= vol(G)(\boldsymbol{e_i} - \boldsymbol{e_j})^T L^+(\boldsymbol{e_i} - \boldsymbol{e_j}) \end{aligned} \tag{3.11}$$

Let us now look at the entries of L^+ in terms of these position vectors. The ij^{th} entry $l^+_{ij} = \boldsymbol{x_i}^T \boldsymbol{x_j}$, denotes the dot-product between the position vectors of vertex i and j. The diagonal element l^+_{ii} denotes the squared length of the position vector of i. The cosine similarity ([14]) between two nodes is defined as $l^+_{ij}/\sqrt{l^+_{ii}l^+_{jj}}$. We discuss different ways of computing the above quantities in section 3.

More random-walk based proximity measures. A discounted version of escape probability from node i to node j (probability to hit node j before coming back to node i in a random walk started from node i) has been used for computing connection subgraphs in [26]. A connection subgraph is a small subgraph of the original network which best captures the relationship between two query nodes. Escape probabilities have also been used to compute *direction aware proximity* in graphs [78]. Koren et al. use cycle-free escape probability from i to j (probability that a random walk started at i will reach j without visiting any node more than once) for computing connection subgraphs for a group of nodes in [48].

2.2 Other Graph-based Proximity Measures

In their detailed empirical study of different graph-based proximity measures for link-prediction tasks [53] have used the Katz score, number of common neighbors and Jaccard score. The authors also presented higher-level *meta* approaches for link prediction which use the above measures as a basic component. These approaches included low rank approximations of the adjacency matrix, unseen bigrams from language modeling, and clustering.

Katz Score. [46] had designed a similarity measure based on ensemble of paths between two nodes.

$$Katz(i,j) = \sum_{\ell=1}^{\infty} \beta^{\ell}.A^{\ell}(i,j)$$

Note that $A^{\ell}(i,j)$ is simply the number of paths of length ℓ from i to j. Hence the matrix of scores can be written as $(I - \beta A)^{-1} - I$. In order to compute the Katz score from a given query node, one needs to solve a linear system over the adjacency matrix. For very small β the Katz score mostly returns nodes with many common neighbors with the query node, whereas larger values of beta allows one to examine longer paths. Also, the weighted version (which takes into account weights of edges in the graph) of the Katz score was introduced in [53].

Common Neighbors, Adamic/Adar and Jaccard Coefficient. Recall that in an undirected graph, we define the set of neighbors of node i by $\mathcal{N}(i)$. Then the number of common neighbors of nodes i and j is given by $|\mathcal{N}(i) \cap \mathcal{N}(j)|$. If two nodes have a large number of common neighbors they are more likely to share a link in the future. This leads to the use of number of common neighbors as a pairwise proximity measure.

The Adamic/Adar score [1] is similar to this, except the high degree common neighbors are weighed less. The Adamic/Adar score is defined as:

$$\texttt{Adamic/Adar}(i, j) = \sum_{k \in \mathcal{N}(i) \cap \mathcal{N}(j)} \frac{1}{\log |\mathcal{N}(k)|} \tag{3.12}$$

The intuition behind this score is that, a popular common interest, gives less evidence of a strong tie between two people. For example, many people subscribe to the New York Times. But a few subscribe to the Journal of Neurosurgery. Hence, it is much more likely that two people share similar interests if they both subscribe to the second journal in place of the first.

The Jaccard coefficient computes the probability that two nodes i and j will have a common neighbor k, given k is a neighbor of either i or j.

$$J(i, j) = \frac{|\mathcal{N}(i) \cap \mathcal{N}(j)|}{|\mathcal{N}(i) \cup \mathcal{N}(j)|} \tag{3.13}$$

The matrix of Jaccard coefficients can be shown to be positive definite [32].

Often the Jaccard coefficient is used to compute document similarity in information retrieval [65]. Note that for the bag of words model, computing this score between two documents can be expensive. An efficient randomized algorithm (shingles) for computing this was introduced by [16]. The idea is to represent a document by a set of subsequences of words using a moving window of length ℓ. Now these sequences are hashed to integers, and then the smallest k of these are used to form a sketch of each document. Now the Jaccard score is computed based on this new sketch of a document. The authors show that an unbiased estimate of the Jaccard score can be computed by comparing these sketches.

2.3 Graph-theoretic Measures for Semi-supervised Learning

While random-walks have been used to compute proximity measures between two nodes in a graph or global or topic-specific importance of nodes, they also provide a natural framework to include negative information. The question we ask for obtaining nearest neighbors is: which nodes are close or relevant to this query node? In semi-supervised learning we ask, given a graph where a few nodes are labeled relevant (positive) and irrelevant (negative) which nodes are more similar to the relevant ones than the irrelevant ones. We will now formalize this idea.

Consider a partially labeled dataset with l labeled data-points denoted by $\{(\boldsymbol{x}_1, y_1), \ldots, (\boldsymbol{x}_l, y_l), \boldsymbol{x}_{l+1}, \ldots, \boldsymbol{x}_n\}$. The goal is to classify the unlabeled points, from the labeled examples. Often labels are available for a small fraction of dataset, since labeling might require human intervention. Szummer et al. [76] represent a data-point using random walks on the graph built from this dataset. For node k the authors compute the probability that a random walk started at node i, conditioned on the fact that it ended at k after t steps ($P_{0|t}(i|k)$). This distribution in terms of the start distribution over all nodes is the new representation of node k. This probability can be computed from the standard t-step probability of reaching k from i using Bayes rule. The intuition is that two datapoints are similar under this notion if they have similar start distributions. Now the classification rule is to assign to an unlabeled node k the class c, which maximizes $\sum_i P_{0|t}(i|k)P(y = c|i)$. The parameters $P(y|i)$ are the hidden class distribution over the nodes, and are estimated by maximizing likelihood via Expectation Maximization, or maximizing margin of classification. The parameter t is crucial for this algorithm and is chosen so that the average margin per class is maximized. The authors also propose heuristics for estimating *adaptive time scales* for different nodes.

Zhu et al. [84] use another graph theoretic approach for semi-supervised learning. Given labeled and unlabeled data-points as nodes in a graph, the main goal is to exploit the graph structure to label the unlabeled examples using the few labeled ones. The authors introduce the harmonic function, which is based on the intuition that nodes *close* in the graph have similar labels. A harmonic function is defined as $f : V \rightarrow \mathcal{R}$ which has fixed values at the given labeled points and is smooth over the graph topology. More specifically the harmonic property means that the function value at an unlabeled node is the average of function values at the neighbors. Let U denote the set of unlabeled nodes in the graph. Now the harmonic property can be mathematically expressed as follows:

$$f(i) = \frac{\sum_j A_{ij} f(j)}{d(i)}, i \in U$$

Let's assume that for the labeled nodes we assign $f(i) = 1$, if i has label 1, and 0 otherwise. This can also be expressed as $f = Pf$. We now divide P into four blocks by grouping the labeled and unlabeled points together. f is grouped into

f_u (unlabeled) and f_l (labeled nodes with fixed values). This gives:

$$f_u = (I - P_{uu})^{-1} P_{ul} f_l \quad (3.14)$$

The above function represents the probability of hitting a label '1' before a label '0'. This can be easily generalized to multi-class classification setting, using a one vs. all encoding of labels. Harmonic functions can also be thought of as the voltage at all nodes in a electrical network, where the positive nodes are connected to a unit voltage external source and the negative nodes are grounded (zero voltage).

Relationship between harmonic functions, escape probabilities and commute times. We have shown that commute times, escape probabilities and harmonic functions are widely used for proximity computation and semi-supervised learning. The harmonic function f with boundary conditions $f(s) = 1$ and $f(t) = 0$ at node i, computes the probability that a random walk from node i will hit s before t. The escape probability from s to t [25] ($P_{esc}(s,t)$) is defined as the probability of reaching t before returning to s in a random walk stated at s. Hence $P_{esc}(s,t) = 1 - \sum_i P(s,i) f(i)$. This can be seen as the escape probability equals the probability of visiting a neighbor i, and from there reaching t before returning to s. However the latter has probability $1 - f(i)$, by definition of harmonic functions.

As mentioned earlier, harmonic functions can also be thought of as the voltage at node i resulting from connecting node s to a unit voltage source, and node t to a zero voltage source. Now we will see the relationship of escape probabilities and harmonic functions with commute time. Let the total current drawn by node s from the outside source be I_s. Using Kirchhoff's law this quantity is $\sum_i A_{s,i}(1 - f(i))$, where $C_{s,i}$ is the conductance or weight of the edge $\{s,i\}$, since $f(s) = 1$. This is simply $d(s) \sum_i P(s,i)(1 - f(i))$, which is simply the degree of node s times the escape probability from s to t. Hence the effective conductance between nodes s and t for a unit voltage drop is $d(s) P_{esc}(s,t)$. Recall that the effective conductance between nodes s and t is the reciprocal of the effective resistance between nodes s and t, which is proportional to the commute time between nodes s and t.

Using the Laplacian for Graph Regularization. Most semi-supervised algorithms are variations of learning a function over a graph. The goal is to optimize the function over the labeled nodes, and enforce smoothness over the graph topology via regularization. Zhu et al. [86] provide an excellent survey which unifies different semi-supervised learning algorithms under this framework. The authors discuss a number of algorithms and show the different choice of the loss function and the regularizer. A number of these algorithms use the graph Laplacian L, or the normalized graph Laplacian $D^{-1/2} L D^{-1/2}$

for regularizing the function. This, (e.g. in [84]) sometimes leads to a function closely related to a random walk on the underlying graph. Agarwal et al. [2] connect the Laplacian regularization framework with random walk based measures (e.g. personalized pagerank) and provide generalization guarantees for the latter in directed graphs.

2.4 Clustering with random walk based measures

Random walks provide a natural way of examining the graph structure. It is popular for clustering applications as well. Spectral clustering [60] is a body of algorithms that clusters datapoints $\boldsymbol{x_i}$ using eigenvectors of a matrix derived from the affinity matrix A constructed from the data. Each datapoint is associated to a node in a graph. The weight on a link between two nodes i and j, i.e. A_{ij}, is obtained from a measure of similarity between the two datapoints. One widely used edge weighting scheme transforms the Euclidian distance between the datapoints, i.e. $A_{ij} = \exp(\|\boldsymbol{x_i} - \boldsymbol{x_j}\|^2/\sigma^2)$, where σ is a free parameter.

Meila et al. [56] provide a random-walk based probabilistic interpretation of spectral clustering algorithms including Normalized Cut [72]. Building the affinity matrix poses an important algorithmic question, which has not yet been studied extensively. The choice of σ is crucial. Zhu et al. [86] describe different techniques for building graphs and estimating σ.

Global graph clustering using random walks. Saerens et al. [64] exploit equation (3.11) to embed a graph and provide distances between any pair of nodes. In [83] the authors replace traditional shortest-path distances between nodes in a graph by hitting and commute times and show that standard clustering algorithms (e.g. K-means) produce much better results when applied to these re-weighted graphs. These techniques exploit the fact that commute times are robust to noise and provide a finer measure of cluster cohesion than simple use of edge weight. Harel et al. [36] present a general framework for using random walk based measures as *separating operators* which can be repeatedly applied to reveal cluster structure at different scales of granularity. The authors propose using t step probabilities, escape probabilities and other variants to obtain edge separation. The authors show how to use these operators as a primitive for other high level clustering algorithms like multi-level and agglomerative clustering. In a similar sprit, Azran et al. [8] use different powers of the transition matrix P to obtain clustering of the data. The authors estimate the number of steps and the number of clusters by optimizing spectral properties of P.

Local Graph Clustering. Random walks provide a natural way of clustering a graph. If a cluster has relatively fewer number of cross-edges compared to number of edges inside, then a random walk will tend to stay inside that cluster. Recently there has been interesting theoretical work [75, 5] for using random walk based approaches for computing good quality local graph partitions (cluster) near a given seed node. The main intuition is that a random walk started inside a good cluster will mostly stay inside the cluster. Cluster-quality is measured by its conductance, which is defined as follows: For a subset of S of all nodes V, let $\Phi_V(S)$ denote conductance of S, and $vol(S) = \sum_{i \in S} d(i)$. As in [75], conductance is defined as:

$$\Phi_V(S) = \frac{E(S, V \setminus S)}{min(vol(S), vol(V \setminus S))} \tag{3.15}$$

A good-quality cluster has small conductance, resulting from a small number of cross-edges compared to the total number of edges. The smaller the conductance, the better the cluster quality. Hence 0 is perfect score, for a disconnected partition, whereas 1 is the worst score for having a cluster with no intra-cluster edges. Conductance of a graph is defined as the minimum conductance of all subsets S of the set of nodes V.

The formal algorithm to compute a low conductance local partition near a seed node is given in [75]. The algorithm propagates probability mass from the seed node and at any step rounds the small probabilities, leading to a sparse representation of the probability distribution. Now a local cluster is obtained by making a sweep over this probability distribution. The running time is nearly linear in the size of the cluster it outputs. [5] improve upon the above result by computing local cuts from personalized pagerank vectors from the predefined seed nodes. The authors also generalized their result to strongly connected directed graphs in a subsequent paper [6].

So far we have introduced different random-walk based proximity measures, and looked at how they are related to each other. The rest of this chapter will be divided into three parts. First we will discuss the existing algorithms for fast computation of different random walk based proximity measures introduced in the last section. Then we will describe different applications of these measures. Finally we will conclude with experimental evaluation of these measures, and some sources of publicly available networks.

3. Related Work: Algorithms

In this section, we will describe the popular algorithms designed for computing the proximity measures described in section 2. Katz, personalized pagerank, hitting times, simrank etc. can each be computed as a fixed point of a recursive definition. This can be computed either by computing the solution to a linear system, by clever dynamic programming approaches, or by efficient sampling algorithms. We will briefly describe some of these approaches. Some of the dynamic programming approaches are local in nature, i.e. given a query node, the algorithm only examines a local neighborhood of the graph. Some of these approaches are well-suited for external memory graphs, i.e. for graphs which are too big to fit into main memory.

3.1 Algorithms for Hitting and Commute Times

Most clustering applications based on commute times either require extensive computation to produce pairwise proximity measures, or employ heuristics for restricting the computation to subgraphs. Some authors avoid cubic computation by using sparse matrix manipulation techniques. Saerens et al. [64] compute the trailing eigenvectors of L to reconstruct L^+. This requires solving for the eigenvectors corresponding to the smallest eigenvalues of L, which requires significant pre-computation and can be expensive for very large graphs.

Brand et al. [14] compute sub-matrices of the hitting time and commute time matrices H and C by iterative sparse matrix multiplications. Note that computing the ith row of C, i.e. $C(i,*)$ or the cosine-similarities of all j with i requires $L^+_{jj}, \forall j$. The exact value of L^+_{jj} requires solving linear systems of equations for all other rows of L^+. The authors state that for large Markov chains the square of the inverse stationary distribution of j is a close constant factor approximation to L^+_{jj}; however no approximation guarantee is provided. In short, it is only tractable to compute these measures on graphs with a few thousand nodes for most purposes. Also these techniques are not applicable to a directed graph.

Spielman at al. [74] have designed a fast algorithm for computing pairwise commute times within a constant factor approximation. The idea is to use the Johnson-Lindenstrauss lemma [43] in conjunction with a nearly linear time solver [75] to compute a $n \times \log n/\epsilon^2$ matrix of random projections in $\tilde{O}(m)$ time, ϵ being the approximation error and m the number of edges. At query time the commute time can be computed by computing the Euclidian distance between two points in $O(\log n)$ time.

Mei et al. [55] compute hitting time by iterating over the dynamic programming step for a fixed number of times. This leads to the *truncated* hitting time. In order to scale the search, the authors do a depth-first search from a query node and stop expansion when the subgraph exceeds a predefined number. Now the iterative algorithm is applied to this subgraph, and the query nodes are ranked based on hitting time. The problem with this approach is that there is no formal guarantee that the algorithm will not miss a potential nearest neighbor.

A formal approach of computing nearest neighbors in truncated hitting time to a node by doing neighborhood expansion can be found in [66]. The goal is to compute k ϵ-approximate nearest neighbors of query nodes s within T-

truncated hitting time τ. The main idea is to expand a neighborhood around the given query node, and stop when all nodes outside the neighborhood can be proven to be "un-interesting". The key is to obtain provable lower and upper bounds on the truncated hitting time from the nodes inside the current neighborhood to the query. These bounds enable the authors to expand the neighborhood in an adaptive fashion, i.e. include "potential" nearest neighbors. As the neighborhood is expanded these bounds become tighter. For all nodes outside the neighborhood the authors maintain a global lower bound on hitting time to the query node. The expansion is stopped when this bound exceeds τ; this guarantees that the hitting times of nodes outside the current neighborhood is larger than τ, and hence uninteresting.

Note that although it is easy to compute hitting time *to a node* by using dynamic programming, it is hard to use dynamic programming for computing hitting time *from a node*. The reason is: by definition of hitting times, i.e. expected time to hit a node *for the first time*, it is hard to define a problem based on smaller subproblems. We will show this using two examples:

$$P^t(i,j) = \sum_k P(i,k)P^{t-1}(k,j) \tag{3.16}$$

$$P^t(i,j) = \sum_k P^{t-1}(i,k)P(k,j) \tag{3.17}$$

Consider the t step probability of reaching node j from node i. Using eq. 3.16 we can compute t step probabilities from all nodes to node j, whereas eq. 3.17 can be iterated to compute t-step probabilities from node i to all other nodes. If we could write hitting time from node i using

$$h^t(i,j) \stackrel{?}{=} \sum_k h^{t-1}(i,k)P(k,j)$$

we would be able to use dynamic programming to compute hitting time from i to all other nodes. However this is not true, since $h^{t-1}(i,k)$ consists of paths through j, whereas $h^t(i,j)$ is defined to look at paths that stop at j. Sampling provides a useful approach for computing *truncated* hitting time from a node. The idea is simple: sample M random walks from the query node. Now look at the first occurrence time $X^t(i,k)$ of the nodes k which have been encountered during the random walk. Hitting time is given by $\sum_t min\{X^t(i,k),T\}/M$. Sarkar et al. [69] provide sample complexity bounds for this and use this in conjunction with a neighborhood expansion scheme to compute nearest neighbors in commute time from a node with high probability.

3.2 Algorithms for Computing Personalized Pagerank and Simrank

Personalized pagerank vectors (PPV) are often used to measure the proximity between two nodes in a network. Although it was first introduced in early 2000, fast algorithms for computing it is still an active area of research. It has been proven [40] that the PPV from a set of webpages can be computed by linearly combining those for each individual webpage in the set. The problem is that it is hard to store all possible personalization vectors or compute the personalized pagerank vector at query time because of the sheer size of the internet graph. We will briefly sketch a few well-known algorithms here.

Haveliwala et al. [37] divide the web-corpora into k (16) topics. The personalized pagerank for each topic (a collection of pages from the Open Directory) is pre-computed offline and stored. At runtime a user-query is transformed into a probability distribution on these basis topics. The resulting personalized pagerank for the query is now a linear combination of the topics, weighted by the probability distribution of the query over the topics.

Jeh et al. [40] assume that the preferences of personalized search, i.e. restart distributions are restricted to a set of important pages, denoted by the "hubs". Hence the size of this set determines the degree of personalization. The authors pick the 1000 to $100,000$ top pagerank pages as the "hub" set. If the hub vectors can be pre-computed and stored, it would be easy to linearly combine these vectors at query time to obtain different personalizations. If this set is too large, it becomes computationally expensive to compute the personalization vectors for each hub-node. In order to achieve higher degrees of personalization, the authors make the key observation that these vectors share common components, which can be pre-computed, stored and combined at query time. The two major components are the partial vectors and the hub skeleton. A hub-skeleton vector corresponding to a hub-node i measures the influence of node i on all other nodes via paths through the set of hub nodes, whereas the partial vector for node i is a result of the paths which do not go via H. If the hub nodes are chosen such that most paths in the graph go via them, then for many pairs i, j, the partial vector will be very sparse. The authors show how to compute these hub-skeletons and partial vectors via dynamic programming, so that redundant computation can be avoided.

Fogaras et al. [28] achieve full personalization by simulating random walks. Personalized pagerank from i to j can also be defined as the probability that a random walk of length L started at node i will stop at node j, where ℓ is chosen from the geometric distribution with parameter α, i.e. $P(\ell = t) = \alpha(1-\alpha)^{t-1}$. This leads to a simple estimation procedure: simulate M random walks from i, such that after each step the walk continues with probability $1 - \alpha$ and stops with probability α. The fraction of times the walk ends in j gives an estimate of $PPV(i,j)$. The authors also provide lower bounds on the size of a database needed for achieving approximate answers to different queries with high probability, e.g. query if a personalized pagerank value is positive, compare values at two nodes, compute an approximation of a PPV value, etc. The interesting observation is that if one wants to obtain full personalization the lower bound on database size is $O(n^2)$; However allowing a small probability of error and approximation can let one have database size linear in the number of vertices. The sampling algorithm in fact achieves this lower bound. The authors show how to compute "fingerprints" of random walks from each node efficiently for external memory graphs. A fingerprint is a compact version of a random walk: it just stores the start and end vertices of the walk so far. By sequentially passing through two files, one with the edges (sorted lexicographically by source), and the other with the current fingerprints (sorted lexicographically by the end-node), one can generate the fingerprint for the next time-step efficiently.

Fogaras et al. [27] use the sampling algorithm to give the first scalable algorithm for computing simrank. The authors first show how to estimate simrank values by generating independent backward random walks of a fixed length from every node. It is simple to estimate the simrank between two nodes from the first meeting time of pairwise walks from two nodes. However storing a number of fixed length random walks from each node in a graph can be prohibitive for a web-scale graph. The authors use coalesced random walks, which save both time and space-complexity. The authors also show how to represent a set of *coalesced* reverse random walks compactly. The key is to store the minimal information such that just the first meeting times for a pair of walks can be reconstructed without reconstructing the entire path. This reduces the storage complexity from fixed-length walks to one integer per node in the graph.

Sarlós et al. [70] improve upon the sampling algorithm in [28] by introducing rounding and sketching based deterministic algorithms which reduces the approximation error significantly. Instead of using a power method approach to compute personalized pagerank *from a node*, Sarlós et al. use dynamic programming to compute personalized pagerank *to a node* (similar to [40]). At any iteration of the dynamic programming, the authors round the small pagerank values to zero, and show that this rounding scheme leads to sparse supports for personalized pagerank while leading to a small approximation error. The authors also point out that in a power method approach, at a high in-degree node the errors from the in-neighbors add up and lead to large approximation error (proportional to the indegree). However, a dynamic programming approach computes an *average* over the pagerank values of the out-neighbors of a node and hence does not amplify error. The space-requirement of the deterministic rounding algorithm is improved further by using Count-Min sketches [23] to represent the intermediate sparse distributions. The authors also show that similar rounding ideas can be used to compute simrank, by reducing it to personalized pagerank.

The previously mentioned algorithms compute partial personalized pagerank vectors offline and combine them at query time. Berkhin et al. [10] propose a simple but novel "Bookmark Coloring Algorithm" (BCA) for computing sparse personalized pagerank from any given node. Personalized pagerank can be thought of as the stationary distribution of a random process where every node retains α fraction of its color (probability) and distributes the rest along its out-neighbors. The process starts by injecting unit color (probability) to the node, w.r.t which we want to personalize the measure. A matrix multiplication step in personalized pagerank, as in eq. (3.4) achieves exactly this, where at any node the contribution of its in-neighbors are added. BCA can be thought of as an adaptive version of the matrix multiplication, where only the large probability masses are propagated. The authors achieve this by maintaining a queue with the personalized pagerank values. At any step the queue is popped to find the largest $\{i,w\}$ pair, where i is the node with w amount of residual probability. The personalized pagerank vector is updated by adding α fraction of w to entry i, whereas the entries $\{j, (1-\alpha)/d^+(i)\}$ for all outgoing neighbors of j are enqueued in Q. The propagating of probability stops when the amount falls below a pre-specified small threshold ϵ.

This algorithm is formally analyzed in [5]. The authors improve the time complexity of BCA algorithm by eliminating the queue, and propagating any probability that is above ϵ. Theoretical guarantees are provided for both approximation error and runtime. The key intuition is to express the personalized pagerank as the sum of the approximate pagerank and the personalized pagerank with the start distribution of the residual probability vector (values stored in the queue in case of BCA). With ϵ as the threshold the approximation error simply involves the personalized pagerank w.r.t a residual vector whose largest entry is ϵ. The authors use this approximate pagerank vector to compute a local graph partition around the start node, and provide theoretical guarantees about the quality of the partition. Note that personalized pagerank computed using these approaches may have large accumulated approximation error at high-indegree nodes.

Chakrabarti et al. [18] show how to compute approximate personalized pagerank vectors using clever neighborhood expansion schemes which would drastically reduce the amount of off-line storage and computation. The motivation of the HubRank algorithm comes from using PPV for context-sensitive keyword search in entity-relation graphs. Since the vocabulary is huge, it is often prohibitive to cache PPV for every word. At query time the vectors for different query words are combined to compute ranking for a multi-word query. For using personalized pagerank in this setting Balmin et al. [9] rounded the personalized pagerank values in order to save space. However this can adversely affect the ranking accuracy of multi-word queries. In order to reduce this storage requirement, HubRank only stores Monte-Carlo fingerprints (defined in [28]) of a set of words and other entity nodes (e.g. papers or authors), by examining query logs. Given a query, the algorithm identifies a small *active* subgraph whose personalized pagerank values must be computed. Then the pagerank values are computed only on this subgraph by loading in bordering nodes of this subgraph for whom random walk fingerprints were already stored.

3.3 Algorithms for Computing Harmonic Functions

Zhu et al. [86] present a thorough survey of algorithms for semi-supervised learning algorithms. We will briefly describe a few of them, which use random walk based measures. The key to computing a harmonic function is to compute the solution to the linear system in eq. (3.14). A detailed comparison among the label propagation, loopy belief propagation, and conjugate gradient approaches is provided in [85]. Label propagation simply uses the basic definition of harmonic functions, i.e. the function value at an unlabeled node is the mean of the function value at its neighbors. The harmonic values can be viewed as the mean values of the marginal probabilities of the unlabeled nodes; this is why loopy belief propagation can be used for computing these. It was shown that loopy belief propagation and preconditioned conjugate gradient often converge faster than the other algorithms. Label propagation is the simplest among all these approaches, and also the slowest.

In [87] the authors combine the idea of learning mixture models with regularizing the function over the graph topology. The solution to the resulting *Harmonic Mixture Model* involves a much smaller "backbone" graph, where the nodes are merged into super-nodes using the mixture components. For example, if one obtains hard clustering, then all points in one mixture component are merged into one super-node representing that component. This considerably reduces the cost of solving the linear system. Sarkar et al. [68] use a truncated version of harmonic functions to rerank search results after incorporating user feedback. The authors give a neighborhood expansion scheme to quickly identify the top ranking nodes (w.r.t harmonic function values), where the labels on a few nodes are provided by the users through an interactive setting. Azran et al. [7] compute harmonic functions by computing the eigen-decomposition of a *Rendezvous* graph, where the labeled nodes are converted into sink nodes.

4. Related Work: Applications

The random walks approach has been highly successful in social network analysis [46] and computer vision [31, 62], personalized graph search [40,

37, 28], keyword search in database graphs [9, 18], detecting spam [35, 82]. Here we briefly describe some of these applications.

4.1 Application in Computer Vision

A common technique in computer vision is to use a graph-representation of an image frame, where two neighboring pixels share a strong connection if they have similar color, intensity or texture.

Gorelick et al. [31] use the average hitting time of a random walk from an object boundary to characterize object shape from silhouettes. Grady et al. [34] introduced a novel graph clustering algorithm which was shown to have an interpretation in terms of random walks. Hitting times from all nodes to a designated node were thresholded to produce partitions with various beneficial theoretical properties. Qiu et al have used commute times clustering for robust multibody motion tracking in [63] and image segmentation [62].

Harmonic functions have been used for colorizing images [52], and for automated image-segmentation [33]. The colorization application involves adding color to a monochrome image or movie. An artist annotates the image with a few colored scribbles and the indicated color is propagated to produce a fully colored image. This can be viewed as a multi-class classification problem when the class (color) information is available for only a few pixels. The segmentation example uses user-defined labels for different segments and quickly propagates the information to produce high-quality segmentation of the image. All of the above examples rely on the same intuition: neighboring nodes in a graph should have similar labels.

4.2 Text Analysis

A collection of documents can be represented in graph in many different ways based on the available information. We will describe a few popular approaches. Zhu et al. [84] build a sparse graph using feature similarity between pairs of documents, and then a subset of labels are used to compute the harmonic function for document classification.

Another way to build a graph from documents in a publication database, is to build an entity-relation graph from authors and papers, where papers are connected via citations and co-authors. The *ObjectRank* algorithm in [9] computes personalized pagerank for keyword-specific ranking in such a graph built from a publication database. For keyword search surfers start random walks from different entities containing that word. Any surfer either moves randomly to a neighboring node or jumps back to a node containing the keyword. The final ranking is done based on the resulting probability distribution on the objects in the database. In essence the personalized pagerank for each word is computed and stored offline, and at query time combined linearly to generate keyword-specific ranking. Chakrabarti et al. [18] also use the same graph representation.

Mei et al. [55] use hitting times for query suggestion. The authors build a bipartite graph of query words and URLs, such that a query is connected to a URL if the user clicked on the URL when the query was submitted to the URL. Note that one can consider the Markov chain over this bipartite graph or construct a Markov chain between the query nodes, by using the shared URLs between two query nodes. For a given query q the top k query nodes in hitting time q are suggested as alternate queries. Lafferty et al. [49] build a bipartite graph out of words and documents, and use the top ranked words in personalized pagerank from a query for query expansion. This model is augmented with external information in [22]. Besides the linkage information inherent in co-occurring terms, the authors formed the links based on external information, like synonymy, stemming, word-association and morphology relations etc. Also their random walk consists of three stages: early, middle and final to emphasize the relationships differently at different stages of the walk, e.g. the co-occurrence relation could be weighted more in the early stage, whereas links from synonymy are weighed more highly in later steps.

Minkov et al. [57] build an entity relation graph from email data, where the entities and relations are extracted from the inherent *who-sent-whom* social network, content of the emails and the time-stamps. The authors use random walks with restart for contextual search and name disambiguation in this graph. The probabilities obtained from the random walk are augmented with global features to obtain better predictive performance. In a Markov chain where the states correspond to words, Toutanova et al. [79] focus on learning the transition probabilities of the chain to obtain better word dependency distributions. The authors define a number of different link types as the basic transition distribution. Each link type has a corresponding probability transition matrix. Learning these basic parameters reduces computational complexity, and also allows the authors to learn complex random walk models. In [3] Agarwal et al. show how to compute the parameters of a random walk on a entity relation graph by including relevance feedback. The authors bring together the idea of generalizing the Markov chain model to network flow models [77] and maximum margin optimization to learn rankings [42].

4.3 Collaborative Filtering

Hitting and commute times have been successfully used for collaborative filtering. Brand et al. [14] use different measures resulting from random walks on undirected graphs to recommend products to users based on their purchase history. The authors give empirical evidence of the fact that these measures are often small if one of the nodes has a high degree.It is also shown empirically that the cosine similarity (defined in section 2) does not have this problem since the effect of individual popularity is normalized out. Fouss et al. [29] use hitting and commute times for recommending movies in the MovieLens dataset and show that these perform much better than shortest path on link prediction tasks.

4.4 Combating Webspam

There have been a number of learning algorithms to aid spam detection in the web, which is an extremely important task. These algorithms can be roughly divided into two classes: content-based methods, and graph based approaches. The content-based approaches [61] focus on the content of the webpage, e.g. number of words in the page and page title, amount of anchor text, fraction of visible content etc. to separate a spam-page from a non-spam page.

Graph-based algorithms look at the link structure of the web to classify web-spam. We will briefly discuss two of these. TrustRank [35] uses a similar idea as personalized pagerank computation . The restart distribution contains the web-pages which are known to be not spammy.

Harmonic ranking has been successfully used for spam detection by [44]. The authors build an anchor set of nodes, and compute a harmonic function with restart. For the good anchor nodes the authors use the harmonic ranking where as for the bad anchors they use a forward-propagation from the anchor set to identify other nodes with similar labels. Note that the authors only used the harmonic rank with a homogeneous anchor set.

5. Related Work: Evaluation and datasets

In this section, we will briefly describe a widely used metric for evaluating proximity measures, namely, link prediction. Then we will give a few pointers to publicly available datasets which have been used by some of the publications mentioned in this chapter.

5.1 Evaluation: Link Prediction

While there has been a large body of work for modeling pairwise proximity in network data, evaluating the different measures is often hard. Although anecdotal evidence can be used to present nice properties of a measure, they hardly provide a solid ground for believing in the performance of a given measure. One option is to conduct a user study, which is time consuming and might suffer from selection bias. The other option which has been adopted by many authors is to obtain quantitative scores via link-prediction. Given a snapshot of a social network, the link prediction problem seeks this answer: which new connections among entities are likely to occur in the future?

In general there are a few ways of conducting link prediction experiments. These are:

1. Randomly hold out a links of the graph. *Rank all non-existing links* based on a given proximity measure, and see what fraction of the top k links were originally held out.

2. Randomly hold out a links of the graph. *For every node* compute k nearest neighbors based on a given proximity measure, and see what fraction of these nodes were originally held out.

3. For every node, hold out a few links randomly and compute nearest neighbors for prediction. Add these links back, and repeat the process.

4. If time information for the data is available, divide the time-steps into training and test parts, and compute the ranking based on the older training data, which is used to predict the future links in the test set. For example, one might want to predict, which two actors who had never worked together prior to 2005 will work together in 2010?

Obviously, it is important to rank only the candidate nodes/edges. For example if a node has only one neighbor, its link is not a candidate for removal. In fact one can pick a parameter to decide if a link is candidate for being held out. For example, if the source and destination nodes have degree higher than κ, we consider it for deletion. Liben-Nowell et al. [53] use two parameters κ_{test} and $\kappa_{training}$. They divide the time period into $< t_0, t_0', t_1, t_1' >$. Now the data in the period $< t_0, t_0' >$ is used as training data, whereas $< t_1, t_1' >$ is used as the test data. A node which has at least $\kappa_{training}$ edges in the training data and κ_{test} edges in the test data is a candidate node for link prediction (i.e. some edges from it can be held out).

Liben-Nowell et al. [53] also investigate different proximity measures between nodes in a graph for link prediction. While this gives a comprehensive and quantitative platform for evaluating the goodness of different proximity measures, this also can give analytical intuitions about the evolution of real world graphs. Now we will present a few empirical observations from ([53], [14] and [66]).

A surprising result by [53] is that simple measures like number of common neighbors, and Adamic Adar often perform as accurately as more complicated measures which take into account longer paths. Recall that the Adamic Adar score (eq. 3.12) weighs the contribution of high degree common neighbors less than low degree ones. It outperforms number of common neighbors in a number of datasets.

The authors showed that the hitting and commute times suffer from their sensitivity to long paths. The most effective measure was shown to be the Katz measure [46], with a small discount factor. Also, [14] shows that hitting and commute times tend to give high rank to high degree nodes, which hurt their predictive performance. This, along with the fact that Katz score performs well with a small discount factor provide strong evidence of the fact that focusing on shorter paths, as in personalized pagerank, simrank, truncated/discounted hitting and commute times can increase predictive performance of a measure.

Another observation from [53], [14] and [66] is that shortest path performs very poorly compared to measures which look at ensemble of paths (note that number of common neighbors and Adamic/Adar also look at ensemble of length 2 paths).

5.2 Publicly Available Data Sources

In section 4 we have given a few ways of building a graph from publication databases, email data and images. Here is a brief description of the sources of these publicly available datasets.

1 MovieLens data: bipartite graph of movies and users. (`http://www.grouplens.org/node/73`). This was used in [14, 29] etc.

2 Netflix data: bipartite graph of movies and users, available from the Netflix challenge.

3 Citeseer data: can be used to build co-authorship networks and Entity-relation graphs. Maintained by Prof. C. Lee. Giles (`http://clgiles.ist.psu.edu/`). This was used in [18, 66, 69] etc.

4 The DBLP dataset: can be used to build co-authorship networks and Entity-relation graphs. (`http://dblp.uni-trier.de/xml/`). Different versions of the dataset was used in [9, 68].

5 A variety of social networks are available at `http://snap.stanford.edu/data/`. Collected and maintained by Dr. Jure Leskovec. These include online social networks like LiveJournal, email communication datasets, citation and co-authorship networks, web-graphs, peer to peer datasets, blog data, the Epinions dataset etc. Smaller versions of Arxiv publication networks were used in [53].

6 A large collection of Web spam datasets are posted in `http://barcelona.research.yahoo.net/webspam/`.

7 A large collection of web sites can be found under the Stanford WebBase project [38] `http://diglib.stanford.edu:8091/~testbed/doc2/WebBase/`. Different snapshots of the web available from this project were used in [37, 40, 28, 70].

8 A large web-corpus was released for searching for related entities and properties of a given entity in the Entity Track in the Text Retrieval Conference (TREC) 2009.
`http://ilps.science.uva.nl/trec-entity/`.

9 Manually hand-labeled segmentations of images are available in:
`http://www.eecs.berkeley.edu/Research/Projects/CS/vision/bsds/`.

10 Document and hand written digit data-sets used for graph-based semi-supervised learning are available in Prof. Xiaojin Xhu's webpage:
`http://pages.cs.wisc.edu/~jerryzhu/publications.html`.

11 More datasets on handwritten digits, 20 Newsgroups, and publications in the Neural Information Processing System (NIPS) conference are available in Prof. Sam Roweis's webpage:
(`http://cs.nyu.edu/~roweis/data.html`).

6. Conclusion and Future Work

In this chapter, we have built the necessary background for understanding random walk based measures of proximity; studied popular proximity measures, fast algorithms for computing them, and real world applications. The last few sections lead to a challenging and interesting array of questions which involve machine learning with very large graphs. For example: how to design infrastructure to enable end-users with off-the-shelf computing units use the existing algorithms? How does one identify the right measure for a given learning task? In settings where human intervention is needed to make an informed decision, how can we minimize it as much as possible? Is there a relationship between random walks on graphs and regularized approaches to graph-based semi-supervised learning? We can answer these questions by unifying our knowledge in diverse areas like graph theory, data mining, information theory and database systems.

Often fast search algorithms make an inherent assumption: the graph can be fit into main memory. Consider the setting where the graph is too large to be memory-resident. Searching personal information networks [19], which requires integrating the users personal information with information from the Web, often needs to be performed on the user's own machine for preserving privacy [24]. For general purpose user-end machines we need memory-efficient fast algorithms. There has been some work to design algorithms on external memory graphs: Fogaras et al. [28] show how to precompute random walks from all nodes in external memory graphs. Das Sarma et al. [71] design streaming algorithms for sampling short random walks from a given query node using a few passes. Sarkar et al. [67] show how to use a clustered representation of disk-resident graphs for computing nearest neighbors using random walk-based proximity measures. One of the important future directions is to characterize the tradeoffs and limitations of algorithms in this external-memory setting.

Personalized search being the holy grail, algorithms for re-ranking and ranking refinement which incorporate user-feedback are gaining popularity. Under this setting the user is asked to label a set of results. Ideally we would want to exploit this feedback loop the most. This brings us to graph-based active and semi-supervised learning problems.

Zhu et al. [86] showed that there is a relationship between the popular regularization framework of semi-supervised learning on graphs with random walk based measures. Agarwal et al. [2] explore this connection for obtaining generalization guarantees for popular random walk based measures. It would be interesting to explore this direction more.

As mentioned in section 5, it is common practice to empirically evaluate different proximity measures using link prediction tasks. Previous empirical studies indicate that different proximity measures perform differently on different tasks on different graphs. However there has not been any theoretical work on *why some measures work better than others*. This is discussed in detail in [53], where the properties of different graphs are studied to better explain the behavior of different measures on different tasks. The answer to this would have a tremendous impact on our intuition about real world graphs, and would enable automatic identification of the right measure for a task at hand on a given graph. It would also save end-users the trouble to understand and compute every metric separately for a task.

Identifying nearest neighbors in graphs is a key ingredient in a diverse set of applications, starting from finding friends on a social network like Face-book to suggesting movies or music in recommender systems; from viral marketing to image-segmentation; from intelligence analysis to context-based keyword search in databases. Random walks provide a popular, intuitive and mathematically principled framework for computing the underlying measure of "nearness" or proximity. A deep understanding of the behavior of these measures holds the key to efficiently utilizing the massive source of networked data that is being generated from corporate and public sources every day.

Acknowledgements

The authors will like to thank Geoffrey Gordon for his valuable comments and suggestions on this chapter. Also, the material relating graph Laplacians to hitting and commute times have been largely inspired by Gary Miller's class on "Spectral Graph Theory and Scientific Computing" at Carnegie Mellon.

References

[1] Lada A. Adamic and Eytan Adar. Friends and neighbors on the web. *Social Networks*, 25, 2003.

[2] Alekh Agarwal and Soumen Chakrabarti. Learning random walks to rank nodes in graphs. In *ICML '07: Proceedings of the 24th international conference on Machine learning*, 2007.

[3] Alekh Agarwal, Soumen Chakrabarti, and Sunny Aggarwal. Learning to rank networked entities. In *KDD '06: Proceedings of the 12th ACM SIGKDD international conference on Knowledge discovery and data mining*, 2006.

[4] David Aldous and James Allen Fill. *Reversible Markov Chains*. 2001.

[5] Reid Andersen, Fan Chung, and Kevin Lang. Local graph partitioning using pagerank vectors. In *FOCS*, 2006. ISBN 0-7695-2720-5.

[6] Reid Andersen, Fan Chung, and Kevin Lang. Local Partitioning for Directed Graphs Using PageRank. *Algorithms and Models for the Web-Graph*, 2006.

[7] Arik Azran. The rendezvous algorithm: multiclass semi-supervised learning with markov random walks. In *ICML '07: Proceedings of the 24th international conference on Machine learning*, 2007.

[8] Arik Azran and Zoubin Ghahramani. A new approach to data driven clustering. In *ICML '06: Proceedings of the 23rd international conference on Machine learning*, 2006.

[9] A. Balmin, V. Hristidis, and Y. Papakonstantinou. ObjectRank: Authority-based keyword search in databases. In *VLDB*, 2004.

[10] P. Berkhin. Bookmark-Coloring Algorithm for Personalized PageRank Computing. *Internet Mathematics*, 2006.

[11] Burton H. Bloom. Space/time trade-offs in hash coding with allowable errors. *Commun. ACM*, 13(7), 1970.

[12] D. Boley, G. Ranjan, and Z. Zhang. Commute times for a directed graph using an asymmetric Laplacian. Technical report:10-005, University of Minnesota, 2010.

[13] Allan Borodin, Gareth O. Roberts, Jeffrey S. Rosenthal, and Panayiotis Tsaparas. Finding authorities and hubs from link structures on the world wide web. In *WWW '01: Proceedings of the 10th international conference on World Wide Web*, pages 415–429, New York, NY, USA, 2001. ACM. ISBN 1-58113-348-0.

[14] M. Brand. A Random Walks Perspective on Maximizing Satisfaction and Profit. In *SIAM '05*, 2005.

[15] S. Brin and L. Page. The anatomy of a large-scale hypertextual web search engine. In *Proc. WWW*, 1998.

[16] Andrei Z. Broder. On the resemblance and containment of documents. In *In Compression and Complexity of Sequences (SEQUENCES'97)*, pages 21–29. IEEE Computer Society, 1997.

[17] Andrei Z. Broder, Moses Charikar, Alan M. Frieze, and Michael Mitzenmacher. Min-wise independent permutations (extended abstract). In *STOC '98: Proceedings of the thirtieth annual ACM symposium on Theory of computing*, 1998.

[18] Soumen Chakrabarti. Dynamic personalized pagerank in entity-relation graphs. In *Proc. WWW*, New York, NY, USA, 2007.

[19] Soumen Chakrabarti, Jeetendra Mirchandani, and Arnab Nandi. Spin: searching personal information networks. In *SIGIR '05: Proceedings of the 28th annual international ACM SIGIR conference on Research and development in information retrieval*, 2005.

[20] A. K. Chandra, P. Raghavan, W. L. Ruzzo, and R. Smolensky. The electrical resistance of a graph captures its commute and cover times. In *STOC*, pages 574–586, 1989.

[21] Fan Chung. Laplacians and the cheeger inequality for directed graphs. *Annals of Combinatorics*, 2005.

[22] K. Collins-Thompson and J. Callan. Query expansion using random walk models. In *CIKM '05: Proceedings of the 14th ACM international conference on Information and knowledge management*, 2005.

[23] Graham Cormode and S. Muthukrishnan. An improved data stream summary: the count-min sketch and its applications. *J. Algorithms*, 55(1): 58–75, 2005.

[24] Bhavana Bharat Dalvi, Meghana Kshirsagar, and S. Sudarshan. Keyword search on external memory data graphs. *Proc. VLDB Endow.*, 1(1):1189–1204, 2008.

[25] P. G. Doyle and J. L. Snell. *Random Walks and Electric Networks.* The Mathematical Assoc. of America., 1984.

[26] Christos Faloutsos, Kevin S. McCurley, and Andrew Tomkins. Fast discovery of connection subgraphs. In *KDD '04: Proceedings of the tenth ACM SIGKDD international conference on Knowledge discovery and data mining*, 2004.

[27] D. Fogaras and B. Racz. Scaling link-based similarity search. In *Proceedings of the 14th Int'l World Wide Web Conference*, 2005.

[28] D. Fogaras, B. Rcz, K. Csalogány, and Tamás Sarlós. Towards scaling fully personalized pagerank: Algorithms, lower bounds, and experiments. *Internet Mathematics*, 2004.

[29] Francois Fouss, Alain Pirotte, Jean michel Renders, and Marco Saerens. A novel way of computing dissimilarities between nodes of a graph, with application to collaborative filtering. In *ECML workshop on Statistical Approaches for Web Mining*, 2004.

[30] David Gibson, Jon Kleinberg, and Prabhakar Raghavan. Clustering categorical data: an approach based on dynamical systems. *The VLDB Journal*, 8(3-4), 2000.

[31] L. Gorelick, M. Galun, E. Sharon, R. Basri, and A. Brandt. Shape representation and classification using the poisson equation. In *CVPR*, 2004.

[32] J.C. Gower. A general coefficient of similarity and some of its properties. *Biometrics*, 27:857–871, 1971.

[33] Leo Grady. Random walks for image segmentation. *IEEE Transactions on Pattern Analysis and Machine Intelligence*, 28(11):1768–1783, 2006. ISSN 0162-8828.

[34] Leo Grady and Eric L. Schwartz. Isoperimetric graph partitioning for data clustering and image segmentation. In *IEEE PAMI*, 2006.

[35] Zoltan Gyongyi, Hector Garcia-Molina, and Jan Pedersen. Combating web spam with trustrank. In *VLDB'2004: Proceedings of the Thirtieth international conference on Very large data bases*. VLDB Endowment, 2004.

[36] David Harel and Yehuda Koren. On clustering using random walks. In *Foundations of Software Technology and Theoretical Computer Science 2245*. Springer-Verlag, 2001.

[37] T. Haveliwala. Topic-sensitive pagerank. In *Proceedings of the Eleventh International World Wide Web Conference*, 2002.

[38] Jun Hirai, Sriram Raghavan, Hector Garcia-molina, and Andreas Paepcke. Webbase : A repository of web pages. In *In Proceedings of the Ninth International World Wide Web Conference*, 2000.

[39] John Hopcroft and Daniel Sheldon. Manipulation-resistant reputations using hitting time. Technical report, Cornell University, 2007.

[40] G. Jeh and J. Widom. Scaling personalized web search. In *Stanford University Technical Report*, 2002.

[41] Glen Jeh and Jennifer Widom. Simrank: A measure if structural-context similarity. In *ACM SIGKDD*, 2002.

[42] Thorsten Joachims. Optimizing search engines using clickthrough data. In *KDD '02: Proceedings of the eighth ACM SIGKDD international conference on Knowledge discovery and data mining*, 2002.

[43] W. Johnson and J. Lindenstrauss. Extensions of lipschitz maps into a hilbert space. *Contemporary Mathematics*, 26:189–206, 1984.

[44] Amruta Joshi, Ravi Kumar, Benjamin Reed, and Andrew Tomkins. Anchor-based proximity measures. In *WWW '07: Proceedings of the 16th international conference on World Wide Web*, 2007.

[45] Sepandar D. Kamvar, Taher H. Haveliwala, Christopher D. Manning, and Gene H. Golub. Extrapolation methods for accelerating pagerank computations. In *WWW '03: Proceedings of the 12th international conference on World Wide Web*, 2003.

[46] L. Katz. A new status index derived from sociometric analysis. In *Psychometrika*, 1953.

[47] Jon M. Kleinberg. Authoritative sources in a hyperlinked environment. *J. ACM*, 46(5), 1999.

[48] Yehuda Koren, Stephen C. North, and Chris Volinsky. Measuring and extracting proximity in networks. In *KDD '06: Proceedings of the 12th ACM SIGKDD international conference on Knowledge discovery and data mining*, 2006.

[49] John Lafferty and Chengxiang Zhai. Document language models, query models, and risk minimization for information retrieval. In *SIGIR '01: Proceedings of the 24th annual international ACM SIGIR conference on Research and development in information retrieval*, 2001.

[50] Amy N. Langville and Carl D. Meyer. Deeper inside pagerank. 2003.

[51] R. Lempel and S. Moran. Salsa: the stochastic approach for link-structure analysis. *ACM Trans. Inf. Syst.*, 19(2), 2001.

[52] Anat Levin, Dani Lischinski, and Yair Weiss. Colorization using optimization. *ACM Transactions on Graphics*, 23:689–694, 2004.

[53] David Liben-Nowell and Jon Kleinberg. The link prediction problem for social networks. In *CIKM '03*, 2003.

[54] Laszlo Lovasz. Random walks on graphs: a survey. 1996.

[55] Qiaozhu Mei, Dengyong Zhou, and Kenneth Church. Query suggestion using hitting time. In *CIKM '08*, pages 469–478, New York, NY, USA, 2008. ACM. ISBN 978-1-59593-991-3.

[56] Marina Meila and Jianbo Shi. A random walks view of spectral segmentation. In *AISTATS*, 2001.

[57] Einat Minkov, William W. Cohen, and Andrew Y. Ng. Contextual search and name disambiguation in email using graphs. In *SIGIR '06*, 2006.

[58] Marc Najork and Nick Craswell. Efficient and effective link analysis with precomputed SALSA maps. In *CIKM '08: Proceeding of the 17th ACM conference on Information and knowledge management*, 2008.

[59] Marc Najork, Sreenivas Gollapudi, and Rina Panigrahy. Less is more: sampling the neighborhood graph makes SALSA better and faster. In

WSDM '09: Proceedings of the Second ACM International Conference on Web Search and Data Mining, 2009.

[60] A. Ng, M. Jordan, and Y. Weiss. On spectral clustering: Analysis and an algorithm. In *Advances in Neural Information Processing Systems*, 2001.

[61] Alexandros Ntoulas, Marc Najork, Mark Manasse, and Dennis Fetterly. Detecting spam web pages through content analysis. In *WWW '06: Proceedings of the 15th international conference on World Wide Web*, 2006.

[62] Huaijun Qiu and Edwin R. Hancock. Image segmentation using commute times. In *Proc. BMVC*, 2005.

[63] Huaijun Qiu and Edwin R. Hancock. Robust multi-body motion tracking using commute time clustering. In *ECCV'06*, 2006.

[64] M. Saerens, F. Fouss, L. Yen, and P. Dupont. The principal component analysis of a graph and its relationships to spectral clustering, 2004.

[65] Gerard Salton and Michael J. McGill. *Introduction to Modern Information Retrieval*. McGraw-Hill, Inc., New York, NY, USA, 1986. ISBN 0070544840.

[66] Purnamrita Sarkar and Andrew Moore. A tractable approach to finding closest truncated-commute-time neighbors in large graphs. In *Proc. UAI*, 2007.

[67] Purnamrita Sarkar and Andrew Moore. Fast nearest-neighbor search in disk-resident graphs. Technical report, Machine Learning Department, Carnegie Mellon University, 2010.

[68] Purnamrita Sarkar and Andrew W. Moore. Fast dynamic reranking in large graphs. In *International World Wide Web Conference*, 2009.

[69] Purnamrita Sarkar, Andrew W. Moore, and Amit Prakash. Fast incremental proximity search in large graphs. In *Proceedings of the 25th International Conference on Machine Learning*, 2008.

[70] Tamas Sarlos, Andras A. Benczur, Karoly Csalogany, Daniel Fogaras, and Balazs Racz. To randomize or not to randomize: space optimal summaries for hyperlink analysis. In *WWW*, 2006.

[71] Atish Das Sarma, Sreenivas Gollapudi, and Rina Panigrahy. Estimating pagerank on graph streams. In *PODS*, 2008.

[72] Jianbo Shi and Jitendra Malik. Normalized cuts and image segmentation. In *CVPR '97: Proceedings of the 1997 Conference on Computer Vision and Pattern Recognition (CVPR '97)*, 1997.

[73] A. Smola and R. Kondor. Kernels and regularization on graphs. In Springer Verlag, editor, *Learning Theory and Kernel Machines*, 2003.

[74] D. Spielman and N. Srivastava. Graph sparsification by effective resistances. In *Proceedings of the STOC'08*, 2008.

[75] D. Spielman and S. Teng. Nearly-linear time algorithms for graph partitioning, graph sparsification, and solving linear systems. In *Proceedings of the STOC'04*, 2004.

[76] Martin Szummer and Tommi Jaakkola. Partially labeled classification with markov random walks. In *Advances in Neural Information Processing Systems*, volume 14, 2001.

[77] John A. Tomlin. A new paradigm for ranking pages on the world wide web. In *WWW '03: Proceedings of the 12th international conference on World Wide Web*, 2003.

[78] Hanghang Tong, Yehuda Koren, and Christos Faloutsos. Fast direction-aware proximity for graph mining. In *ACM SIGKDD, Proceeding of the Internation Conference on Knowledge Discovery and Data Mining*, 2007.

[79] Kristina Toutanova, Christopher D. Manning, and Andrew Y. Ng. Learning random walk models for inducing word dependency distributions. In *ICML '04: Proceedings of the twenty-first international conference on Machine learning*, 2004.

[80] Panayiotis Tsaparas. Using non-linear dynamical systems for web searching and ranking. In *PODS '04: Proceedings of the twenty-third ACM SIGMOD-SIGACT-SIGART symposium on Principles of database systems*, 2004.

[81] Ah Chung Tsoi, Gianni Morini, Franco Scarselli, Markus Hagenbuchner, and Marco Maggini. Adaptive ranking of web pages. In *WWW '03: Proceedings of the 12th international conference on World Wide Web*, 2003.

[82] Baoning Wu and Kumar Chellapilla. Extracting link spam using biased random walks from spam seed sets. In *WWW*, 2007.

[83] L. Yen, L. Vanvyve, D. Wouters, F. Fouss, F. Verleysen, and M. Saerens. Clustering using a random-walk based distance measure. In *ESANN 2005*, pages 317–324, 2005.

[84] X. Zhu, Z. Ghahramani, and J. Lafferty. Semi-supervised learning using gaussian fields and harmonic functions. In *ICML, volume 20*, 2003.

[85] Xiaojin Zhu. *Semi-supervised learning with graphs*. PhD thesis, Carnegie Mellon University, Pittsburgh, PA, USA, 2005. Chair-Lafferty, John and Chair-Rosenfeld, Ronald.

[86] Xiaojin Zhu. Semi-supervised learning literature survey, 2006.

[87] Xiaojin Zhu and John Lafferty. Harmonic mixtures: combining mixture models and graph-based methods for inductive and scalable semi-supervised learning. In *ICML '05: Proceedings of the 22nd international conference on Machine learning*, 2005.

[88] C. Rao and S. Mitra. *Generalized inverse of matrices and its applications*. John Wiley and Sons, 1971.

Chapter 4

COMMUNITY DISCOVERY IN SOCIAL NETWORKS: APPLICATIONS, METHODS AND EMERGING TRENDS

S. Parthasarathy
The Ohio State University
2015 Neil Ave, DL395, Columbus, OH
srini@cse.ohio-state.edu

Y. Ruan
The Ohio State University
2015 Neil Ave, DL395, Columbus, OH
ruan@cse.ohio-state.edu

V. Satuluri
The Ohio State University
2015 Neil Ave, DL395, Columbus, OH
satuluri@cse.ohio-state.edu

Abstract Data sets originating from many different real world domains can be represented in the form of interaction networks in a very natural, concise and meaningful fashion. This is particularly true in the social context, especially given recent advances in Internet technologies and Web 2.0 applications leading to a diverse range of evolving social networks. Analysis of such networks can result in the discovery of important patterns and potentially shed light on important properties governing the growth of such networks.

It has been shown that most of these networks exhibit strong modular nature or community structure. An important research agenda thus is to identify communities of interest and study their behavior over time. Given the importance of this problem there has been significant activity within this field particularly over the last few years. In this article we survey the landscape and attempt to characterize the principle methods for community discovery (and related variants) and identify current and emerging trends as well as crosscutting research issues within this dynamic field.

Keywords: Graph Mining, Community Discovery, Social Networks

1. Introduction

Many real world problems can be effectively modeled as complex relationship networks where nodes represent entities of interest and edges mimic the interactions or relationships among them. Fueled by technological advances and inspired by empirical analysis, the number of such problems and the diversity of domains from which they arise – biological [47, 86, 98, 114, 118], clinical [9, 30], ecological [14, 33, 68, 69, 97], engineering [1, 75, 122], linguistic [46], scientific [29, 42, 71, 99], social [72, 91, 113, 121, 124], technological [4, 34, 37, 87, 92], to name a few – is growing steadily.

It has recently been observed that while such networks arise in a host of diverse arenas they often share important common concepts or themes. The study of such complex relationship networks, recently referred to as *network science*, can provide insight into their structures, properties and emergent behaviors [11, 12, 41, 77]. Of particular interest here are rigorous methods for uncovering and understanding important network or sub-network (community) structures and motifs at multiple topological and temporal scales as noted in a recent government report [17]. Extracting such community structure and leveraging them for predicting the emergent, critical, and causal nature of such networks in a dynamic setting is of growing importance.

Extracting such structure is indeed a grand challenge. First, the topological properties of such networks coupled with an uncertain setting [5, 102], often limit the applicability of existing off-the-shelf techniques [9]. Second, the requirements imposed by directed and dynamic [1] networks require research into appropriate solutions. Finally, underpinning all of these challenges is the issue of scalability. Many of the problems we consider require us to deal with problems of immense size and scale where graphs may involve millions of nodes and billions of edges[48].

In this chapter we limit our discussion primarily to the problem of community detection within social networks (albeit a lot of what we will discuss may apply naturally to other domains as well). We begin by discussing why

[1] By *dynamic*, here we refer to any network that changes. This includes not only time-varying networks, but also networks that change due to external factors (e.g. networks that change due to trust issues and source credibility issues, such as intelligence networks).

community discovery in such networks is useful in Section 2. In other words what are the actionable patterns[82] or tools one can derive from such an analysis on social networks. Sample applications abound ranging from the study of intelligence reports to the social behavior of Zebras and Dolphins, from the collaborative nature of physical and computer scientists, to the often cited Karate Club social network, from well established communities in Facebook to the role of communities in Twitter networks for emergency management. We discuss these issues in Section 2.

In Section 3 we discuss the core methods for community discovery proposed in the literature to date. We discuss hierarchical algorithms (agglomerative or divisive) that are popular within the Physics community [78]. The advantages of such algorithms lie in their intuitive simplicity but as noted elsewhere [24] they often do not scale well to large networks. We take a close look at the related literature in graph partitioning, starting with the early work by Kernighan and Lin, as well as more recent multi-level graph partitioning algorithms such as Metis [51], Graclus and MLR-MCL[93]. These are highly scalable and have been used in studies of some of the biggest graph datasets [61, 93]. Spectral methods that target weighted cuts [96] form an important class of algorithms that can be used for community discovery, and are shown to be qualitatively very effective in the social network context. Recent advances in this domain have targeted large scale networks (e.g. local spectral clustering) and these will be discussed as well. To this mix of graph clustering and community discovery algorithms one can also include Markov Clustering (MCL), a graph clustering algorithm based on (stochastic) flow simulation [115]. MCL has drawn limited attention from the broader network science, web science, and data mining communities primarily because it does not scale very well even to moderate sized graphs [24], and other limitations. However, recent advances have suggested effective ways to redress these limitations while retaining its advantages[93, 95]. In addition to the above recent research has suggested the use of hybrid algorithms (e.g. Metis+MQI) and the notion of different kinds of community structures (e.g. whiskers and viewpoint neighborhoods), and we will discuss these in Section 3 as well.

In Section 4 we will primarily discuss relatively new domains within social network analysis where community discovery can play an important role as we move forward. Particular attention here will be paid to work on community discovery in heterogeneous social networks (e.g. Flickr where links may correspond to common tags, similar images, or similar user profiles), community discovery in dynamic social networks (community evolution, dispersion, merging[9]), community discovery in directed social networks (e.g. Twitter), and community discovery that combines content and network information in a natural manner (e.g. topic driven community discovery, social media analytics etc.). In Section 5, we conclude with a discussion of cross cutting research issues that relate to the current state-of-art in this area.

2. Communities in Context

In this section we will discuss the role(s) of community discovery in social network analysis. Specifically we will discuss end applications and contextual benefits from both a scientific as well as actionable perspective.

Social community analysis has been the focus of many studies over the past eighty years[121]. One of the earliest studies in this context include work by Rice on the analysis of communities of individuals based on their political biases and voting patterns[89]. A much more recent study along similar lines but focusing on the network structure of political blogs was discussed by Adamic and Glance[2]. Homans was the first to show that social groups could be revealed by suitably rearranging the rows and the columns of matrices describing social ties, until they take an approximate block-diagonal form[44]. In fact this idea still serves as the basic tool for visualizing social community structure and more generally clustering structure[110]. Weiss and Jacobson examined work groups within a government agency[123]. A central theme of their work was the identification of bridging nodes and using such nodes to separate out community structure. In fact this work can be thought of as an early version of the notion of betweenness centrality popularized by Newman[76]. The karate club study by anthropologist Zachary, is a well-known graph regularly commonly used as a benchmark to test community detection algorithms[126]. It consists of 34 vertices, the members of a karate club in the United States, who were observed during a period of three years and it includes a well known community fission instance and thus the subject of many studies. Another study by Bech and Atalay analyzed the social network of loans among financial institutions to understand how interactions among multiple communities affect the health of the system as a whole[15]. A large majority of these studies focused on simply understanding the underpinning social structure and its evolution (for instance in the karate club data the underlying cause of the fission in the community structure resulting from a difference of opinion between two members of the club).

In addition to the study of human social networks zoologists and biologists have also begun to study the social behavior of other animals and sea creatures. Lusseau in a land mark study examined the behavior of 62 bottlenose dolphins off the coast of New Zealand[65]. This study looked at the social behavior of 62 dolphins and edges were set between animals that were seen together more often than expected by random chance. Lusseau notes the cohesive and cliquish structure of the resulting graph suggesting that the social behavior of such marine mammals is often quite marked. More recently an interdisciplinary team comprising zoologists and computer scientists have studied the social behavior of zebras[109]. Insights ranging from the identification of influential herd leaders within communities, and the evolutionary behavior of the resulting social network of zebras have led to a significantly increased understanding of how these animals communicate and socialize to survive.

Since the advent of the Internet and more recently the World Wide Web a number of applications of community discovery have arisen. In the World Wide Web context a common application of community discovery is in the context of proxy caches[103]. A grouping of web clients who have similar interests and are geographically near each other may enable them to be served by a dedicated proxy server. Another example from the same domain is to identify communities within the hyperlinked structure of the web. Such communities may help in the detection of link farms[21, 40]. Similarly in the E-commerce domain the grouping together of customers with similar buying profiles enables more personalized recommendation engines[88]. In a completely different arena, community discovery in mobile ad-hoc networks can enable efficient message routing and posting[104]. In this context it is important to distinguish core members of the community from members on the border (analogous to edge routers).

Recently there has been a tremendous thrust in the use of community discovery techniques for analyzing online social media data[73]. The user-generated content explosion on Web 2.0 applications such as Twitter, Facebook, review blogs, micro-blogs and various multimedia sharing sites such as Flickr, presents many opportunities for both facilitators and users. For facilitators, this user-generated content is a rich source of implicit consumer feedback. For users the ability to sense and respond interactively and to be able to leverage the wisdom of the crowds (or communities) can be extremely fruitful and useful. It is becoming increasingly clear that a unified approach to analysis combining content information with network analysis is necessary to make headway into this arena.

The above examples show that community discovery in social or socio-technical networks is at the heart of various research agendas. We are now in a position to discuss some of the implications of this technique. At the most fundamental level, community discovery (either in a static or evolutionary context) can facilitate and aid in our understanding of a social system. Much like the role of clustering and community discovery can be thought of as clustering on graphs, community discovery allows us to summarize the interactions within a network concisely, enabling a richer understanding of the underlying social phenomenon. Beyond this basic understanding of the network and how it evolves[9], community discovery can also lend itself to actionable pattern discovery. Identification of influential nodes, or sub-communities within a broader community can be used for viral marketing[32, 53, 59], churn prediction within telecommunication networks[90] and ratings predictions[56]. We will conclude this section with an example of how community discovery can be useful for organizational entities.

Von Hayek, one of the leading economists of the twentieth century, when discussing a competitive market mechanism, articulated the important fact that the minds of millions of people is not available to any central body or any group of decision-makers who have to determine prices, employment, production, and investment policies[116]. He further argued that an increase in decentralization was an essential component to rational decision-making by organizations in a complex society. The ideas he expounded have broad utility beyond the context he was considering. Emergency management is an analogous example of a large and complex socio-technical system, where many people distributed in space and time may potentially harness the power of modern social information technologies to coordinate activities of many in order to accomplish a complex task. In this context recent work by Palen and Liu [80] makes a strong case for the value of understanding the dynamic of social networking and specifically community structure, in relation to managing and mitigating the impact of disasters.

3. Core Methods

Informally, a community in a network is a group of nodes with greater ties internally than to the rest of the network. This intuitive definition has been formalized in a number of competing ways, usually by way of a quality function, which quantifies the goodness of a given division of the network into communities. Some of these quality metrics, such as Normalized Cuts [96] and Modularity [78] are more popular than others, but none has gained universal acceptance since no single metric is applicable in all situations. Several such metrics are discussed in Section 3.1.

Algorithms for community discovery vary on a number of important dimensions, including their approach to the problem as well as their performance characteristics. An important dimension on which algorithms vary in their approaches is whether or not they explicitly optimize a specific quality metric. Spectral methods, the Kernighan-Lin algorithm and flow-based postprocessing are all examples of algorithms which explicitly try to optimize a specific quality metric, while other algorithms, such as Markov Clustering (MCL) and clustering via shingling do not do so. Another dimension on which algorithms vary is in how (or even whether) they let the user control the granularity of the division of the network into communities. Some algorithms (such as spectral methods) are mainly meant for bi-partitioning the network, but this can be used to recursively subdivide the network into as many communities as desired. Other algorithms such as agglomerative clustering or MCL allow the user to indirectly control the granularity of the output communities through certain parameters. Still other algorithms, such as certain algorithms optimizing the Modularity function, do not allow (or require) the user to control the output number of communities at all. Another important characteristic differentiating community discovery algorithms is the importance they attach to a balanced division of the network - while metrics such as the KL objective function explicitly encourage balanced division, other metrics capture balance only implicitly or not at all. Coming to performance characteristics, algorithms also vary in their scalability to big networks, with multi-level clustering algorithms such as Metis, MLR-MCL and Graclus and local clustering algorithms scaling better than many other approaches.

3.1 Quality Functions

A variety of quality functions or measures have been proposed in the literature to capture the goodness of a division of a graph into clusters. In what follows, A denotes the adjacency matrix of the network or graph, with $A(i, j)$ representing the edge weight or affinity between nodes i and j, and V denotes the vertex or node set of the graph or network.

The normalized cut of a group of vertices $S \subset V$ is defined as[96, 67]

$$Ncut(S) = \frac{\sum_{i \in S, j \in \bar{S}} A(i,j)}{\sum_{i \in S} degree(i)} + \frac{\sum_{i \in S, j \in \bar{S}} A(i,j)}{\sum_{j \in \bar{S}} degree(j)} \tag{4.1}$$

In words, the normalized cut of a group of nodes S is the sum of weights of the edges that connect S to the rest of the graph, normalized by the total edge weight of S and that of the rest of the graph $\bar{S}$. Intuitively, groups with low normalized cut make for good communities, as they are well connected amongst themselves but are sparsely connected to the rest of the graph.

The *conductance* of a group of vertices $S \subset V$ is closely related and is defined as [50]

$$Conductance(S) = \frac{\sum_{i \in S, j \in \bar{S}} A(i,j)}{\min(\sum_{i \in S} degree(i), \sum_{i \in \bar{S}} degree(i))} \tag{4.2}$$

The normalized cut (or conductance) of a division of the graph into k clusters $V_1, \ldots, V_k$ is the sum of the normalized cuts (or conductances) of each of the clusters $V_i \{i = 1, \ldots, k\}$ [31].

The *Kernighan-Lin (KL) objective* looks to minimize the edge cut (or the sum of the inter-cluster edge weights) under the constraint that all clusters be of the same size (making the simplifying assumption that the size of the network is a multiple of the number of clusters):

$$KLObj(V_1, \ldots, V_k) = \sum_{i \neq j} A(V_i, V_j) \text{subject to} |V_1| = |V_2| = \ldots = |V_k| \tag{4.3}$$

Here $A(V_i, V_j)$ denotes the sum of edge affinities between vertices in V_i and V_j, i.e. $A(V_i, V_j) = \sum_{u \in V_i, v \in V_j} A(u, v)$

Modularity [78] has recently become quite popular as a way to measure the goodness of a clustering of a graph. One of the advantages of modularity is that it is independent of the number of clusters that the graph is divided into. The intuition behind the definition of modularity is that the farther the subgraph corresponding to each community is from a random subgraph (i.e. the null model), the better or more significant the discovered community structure is. The modularity Q for a division of the graph into k clusters $\{V_1, \ldots, V_k\}$ is given by:

$$Q = \sum_{c=1}^{k} \left[\frac{A(V_i, V_i)}{m} - \left(\frac{degree(V_i)}{2m} \right)^2 \right] \tag{4.4}$$

In the above, the V_is are the clusters, m is the number of edges in the graph and $degree(V_i)$ is the total degree of the cluster V_i. For each cluster, we take the difference between the fraction of edges internal to that cluster and the fraction of edges that would be expected to be inside a random cluster with the same total degree.

Optimizing any of these objective functions is NP-hard [39, 96, 18].

3.2 The Kernighan-Lin(KL) algorithm

The KL algorithm [54] is one of the classic graph partitioning algorithms which optimizes the KL objective function i.e. minimize the edge cut while keeping the cluster sizes balanced (see Equation 4.3. The algorithm is iterative in nature and starts with an initial bipartition of the graph. At each iteration, the algorithm searches for a subset of vertices from each part of the graph such that swapping them will lead to a reduction in the edge cut. The identification of such subsets is via a greedy procedure. The *gain* g_v of a vertex v is the reduction in edge-cut if vertex v is moved from its current partition to the other partition. The KL algorithm repeatedly selects from the larger partition the vertex with the largest gain and moves it to the other partition; a vertex is not considered for moving again if it has already been moved in the current iteration. After a vertex has been moved, the gains for its neighboring vertices will be updated in order to reflect the new assignment of vertices to partitions. While each iteration in the original KL algorithm [54] had a complexity of $O(|E| \log |E|)$, Fiduccia and Mattheyses improved it to $O(|E|)$ per iteration using appropriate data structures. This algorithm can be extended to multi-way partitions by improving each pair of partitions in the multi-way partition in the above described way.

3.3 Agglomerative/Divisive Algorithms

Agglomerative algorithms begin with each node in the social network in its own community, and at each step merge communities that are deemed to be sufficiently similar, continuing until either the desired number of communities is obtained or the remaining communities are found to be too dissimilar to merge any further. Divisive algorithms operate in reverse; they begin with the entire network as one community, and at each step, choose a certain community and split it into two parts. Both kinds of hierarchical clustering algorithms often output a *dendrogram* which is a binary tree , where the leaves are nodes of the network, and each internal node is a community. In the case of divisive algorithms, a parent-child relationship indicates that the community represented by the parent node was divided to obtain the communities represented by the child nodes. In the case of agglomerative algorithms, a parent-child relationship in the dendrogram indicates that the communities represented by the child nodes were agglomerated (or merged) to obtain the community represented by the parent node.

Girvan and Newman's divisive algorithm: Newman and Girvan [78] proposed a divisive algorithm for community discovery, using ideas of *edge betweenness*. Edge betweenness measures are defined in a way that edges with high betweenness scores are more likely to be the edges that connect different communities. That is, inter-community edges are designed to have higher edge betweenness scores than intra-community edges do. Hence, by identifying and discarding such edges with high betweenness scores, one can disconnect the social network into its constituent communities.

Shortest path betweenness is one example of an edge betweenness measure: the intuitive idea here is that since there will only be a few inter-community edges, shortest paths between nodes that belong to different communities will be constrained to pass through those few inter-community edges. Also enumerated are two other examples of edge betweenness. In the definition of *random-walk betweenness*, the choice of path connecting any two nodes is the result of random walk instead of geodesic as in the case of *shortest path*. The *current-flow betweenness* definition is motivated by the circuit theory. First the network is virtually transformed into a resistance network where each edge is replaced by a unit resistance and two nodes are chosen as unit current source and sink. Then the betweenness of each edge is computed as the sum of absolute values of the currents flowing on it with all possible selections of node pairs.

The general form of their algorithms is as follows:

1 Calculate betweenness score for all edges in the network using any measure.

2 Find the edge with the highest score and remove it from the network.

3 Recalculate betweenness for all remaining edges.

4 Repeat from step 2.

The above procedure is continued until a sufficiently small number of communities are obtained, and a hierarchical nesting of the communities is also obtained as a natural by-product. On the contrary to the speculation that different measures of edge betweenness may lead to diverged community structures, the experiment showed that the exact betweenness measure used is not so crucial. As long as the recalculation step is executed, the results by different measures only differ from each other slightly. The motivation for the recalculation step is as follows: if the edge betweenness scores are only calculated once and edges are then removed by the decreasing order of scores, these scores won't get updated and no longer reflect the new network structure after edge removals. Therefore, recalculation is in fact the most critical step in the algorithm to achieve satisfactory results. The main disadvantage of this approach is the high computational cost: simply computing the betweenness for all edges takes $O(|V||E|)$ time, and the entire algorithm requires $O(|V|^3)$ time.

Newman's greedy optimization of modularity: Newman [74] proposed a greedy agglomerative clustering algorithm for optimizing modularity. The basic idea of the algorithm is that at each stage, groups of vertices are successively merged to form larger communities such that the modularity of the resulting division of the network increases after each merge. At the start, each node in the network is in its own community, and at each step one chooses the two communities whose merger leads to the biggest increase in the modularity. We only need to consider those communities which share at least one edge, since merging communities which do not share any edges cannot result in an increase in modularity - hence this step takes $O(|E|)$ time. An additional data structure which maintains the fraction of shared edges between each pair of communities in the current partition is also maintained, and updating this data structure takes worst-case $O(|V|)$ time. There are a total of $|V| - 1$ iterations (i.e. mergers), hence the algorithm requires $O(|V|^2)$ time. Clauset et al. [29] later improved the complexity of this algorithm by the use of efficient data structures such as max-heaps, with the final complexity coming to $O(|E| d \log |V|)$, where d is the depth of the dendrogram describing the successive partitions found during the execution of the algorithm.

3.4 Spectral Algorithms

Spectral algorithms are among the classic methods for clustering and community discovery. Spectral methods generally refer to algorithms that assign nodes to communities based on the eigenvectors of matrices, such as the adjacency matrix of the network itself or other related matrices. The top k eigenvectors define an embedding of the nodes of the network as points in a k-dimensional space, and one can subsequently use classical data clustering techniques such as K-means clustering to derive the final assignment of nodes to clusters [117]. The main idea behind spectral clustering is that the low-dimensional representation, induced by the top eigenvectors, exposes the cluster structure in the original graph with greater clarity. From an alternative perspective, spectral clustering can be shown to solve real relaxations of different weighted graph cut problems, including the normalized cut defined above [117, 96].

The main matrix that is used in spectral clustering applications is the Laplacian matrix $\mathcal{L}$. If A is the adjacency matrix of the network, and D is the diagonal matrix with the degrees of the nodes along the diagonal, then the unnormalized Laplacian L is given as $L = D - A$. The Laplacian (or the normalized Laplacian) $\mathcal{L}$ is given by $\mathcal{L} = D^{-1/2}(D - A)D^{-1/2} = I - D^{-1/2}AD^{-1/2}$. It can be verified that both L and $\mathcal{L}$ are symmetric and positive definite, and therefore have real and positive eigenvalues [27, 117]. The Laplacian has 0 as an eigenvalue with multiplicity equal to the number of connected components in the graph. The eigenvector corresponding to the smallest non-zero eigenvalue of $\mathcal{L}$ is known as the Fiedler vector [35], and usually forms the basis for bi-partitioning the graph.

The main disadvantage of spectral algorithms lies in their computational complexity. Most modern implementations for eigenvector computation use iterative algorithms such as the Lanczos algorithm, where at each stage a series of matrix vector multiplications are performed to obtain successive approximations to the eigenvector currently being computed. The complexity for computing the top eigenvector is $O(kM(m))$, where k is the number of matrix-vector multiplications and $M(m)$ is the complexity of each such multiplication, dependent primarily on the number of non-zeros m in the matrix. k depends on the specific properties of the matrix at hand - such as the spectral gap i.e. the difference between the current eigenvalue and the next eigenvalue; the smaller this gap, the more number of matrix-vector multiplications are required for convergence. In practice, spectral clustering is hard to scale up to networks with more than tens of thousands of vertices without employing parallel algorithms.

Dhillon et al. [31] showed that the weighted cut measures such as normalized cut that are often optimized using spectral clustering can also be optimized using an equivalent weighted kernel k-means algorithm. This is the core idea behind their algorithm **Graclus**, which can cluster graphs at a comparable quality to spectral clustering without paying the same computational cost, since k-means is much faster compared to eigenvector computation.

3.5 Multi-level Graph Partitioning

Multi-level methods provide a powerful framework for fast and high-quality graph partitioning, and in fact have been used for solving a variety of other problems as well [112]. The main idea here is to shrink or coarsen the input graph successively so as to obtain a small graph, partition this small graph and then successively project this partition back up to the original graph, refining the partition at each step along the way. Multi-level graph partitioning methods include multi-level spectral clustering [13], **Metis** (which optimizes the KL objective function) [51], **Graclus** (which optimizes normalized cuts and other weighted cuts) [31] and **MLR-MCL** [93] (further discussed in Section 3.6).

The main components of a multi-level graph partitioning strategy are:

1 **Coarsening**. The goal here is to produce a smaller graph that is similar to the original graph. This step may be applied repeatedly to obtain a graph that is small enough to be partitioned quickly and with high-quality. A popular coarsening strategy is to first construct a *matching* on the graph, where a matching is defined as a set of edges no two of which are incident on the same vertex. For each edge in the matching, the vertices at the ends of the edge are collapsed together and are represented by a single node in the coarsened graph. Coarsening can be performed very quickly using simple randomized strategies [51].

2 **Initial partitioning**. In this step, a partitioning of the coarsest graph is performed. Since the graph at this stage is small enough, one may use strategies like spectral partitioning which are slow but are known to give high quality partitions.

3 **Uncoarsening**. In this phase, the partition on the current graph is used to initialize a partition on the finer (bigger) graph. The finer connectivity structure of the graph revealed by the uncoarsening is used to refine the partition, usually by performing local search. This step is continued until we arrive at the original input graph.

At a finer level, Metis uses a variant of the KL algorithm in its uncoarsening phase to refine the partition obtained from previous steps. Graclus, on the other hand, uses weighted kernel k-means for refining the partition.

3.6 Markov Clustering

Stijn van Dongen's Markov Clustering algorithm (MCL) clusters graphs via manipulation of the stochastic matrix or transition probability matrix corresponding to the graph [115]. In what follows, the transition probability between two nodes is also referred to as *stochastic flow*. The MCL process consists of two operations on stochastic matrices, *Expand* and *Inflate*. *Expand(M)* is simply $M * M$, and *Inflate*(M, r) raises each entry in the matrix M to the inflation parameter r (> 1, and typically set to 2) followed by re-normalizing the columns to sum to 1. These two operators are applied in alternation iteratively until convergence, starting with the initial transition probability matrix.

The *expand* step spreads the stochastic flow out of a vertex to potentially new vertices and also enhances the stochastic flow to those vertices which are reachable by multiple paths. This has the effect of enhancing within-cluster stochastic flows as there are more paths between two nodes that are in the same cluster than between those in different clusters. The inflation step introduces a non-linearity into the process, with the purpose of strengthening intra-cluster stochastic flow and weakening inter-cluster stochastic flow. The process as a whole sets up a positive feedback loop that forces all the nodes within a tightly-linked group of nodes to stochastically flow to one "attractor" node within the group, allowing us to identify the group.

MCL has received a lot of attention in the bioinformatics field, with multiple researchers finding it to be very effective at clustering biological interaction networks ([20, 62]). However, MCL has two major shortcomings [93]. First, MCL is slow, since the Expand step, which involves matrix-matrix multiplication, is very time consuming in the first few iterations when many entries in the stochastic flow matrix have not been pruned out. Second, MCL tends to produce imbalanced clustering, usually by producing a large number of very small clusters (singleton clusters or clusters with only 2 or 3 nodes), or by producing one very big cluster, or by doing both at the same time.

Recent Variants of MCL: Recently, Regularized MCL and Multi-level Regularized MCL (MLR-MCL) [93, 95] have been proposed that fix the above two weaknesses of poor scalability and imbalanced clustering. Regularized MCL ensures that the stochastic flows of neighboring nodes are taken into account when updating the stochastic flows of each node by replacing the *Expand* step of MCL with a *Regularize* step, which is $M := M * M_G$, where M_G is the original stochastic (transition) matrix corresponding to the graph. Other regularization matrices instead of M_G are also explored in [95] with the intention of reducing the imbalance in the sizes of output clusters. Multi-level Regularized MCL (MLR-MCL) embeds Regularized MCL in a multi-level framework, with the algorithm working its way up the chain of coarsened graphs of the input graph, and projecting intermediate results from the smaller graph onto the next bigger graph. MLR-MCL achieves state-of-the-art scalability since the initial iterations of the algorithm, which are the most expensive in the total computation, are performed on the smallest graphs, and the matrices are sparse enough at the biggest graphs to enable fast multiplication.

3.7 Other Approaches

Local Graph Clustering: A *local algorithm* is one that finds a solution containing or near a given vertex (or vertices) without looking at the whole graph. Local algorithms are interesting in the context of large graphs since their time complexity depends on the size of the solution rather than the size of the graph to a large extent. (Although if the clusters need to cover the whole graph, then it is not possible to be independent of the size of the graph.) The main intuition is that random walks simulated from inside a group of internally well-connected nodes will not mix well enough/soon enough, as the cluster boundary acts a bottleneck that prevents the probability from seeping out of the cluster easily. Low-probability vertices are removed at each step to keep the complexity of the algorithm tractable.

Spielman and Teng [101, 100] described the first such local clustering algorithm using random walks. Let $p_{t,v}$ be the probability distribution of the t-step random walk starting at v. ($p_{t,v}$ is truncated i.e. low probability entries are set to zero, in order to avoid exploring too much of the graph.) For each t, let π be the permutation on the vertices of the graph that indicates the sorted order of the degree-normalized probabilities i.e.

$$\frac{p_t(\pi(i))}{d(\pi(i))} \geq \frac{p_t(\pi(i+1))}{d(\pi(i+1))} \tag{4.5}$$

The sweep sets $S_1^t, S_2^t, \ldots, S_n^t$ are defined as $S_j^t = \{\pi(1), \ldots, \pi(j)\}$. Let ψ_V be the final stationary distribution of the random walk (all random walks within a component converge to the same stationary distribution.) The main theoretical result exploited says that the difference between $p^t(S_j^t)$ and $\psi_V(S_j^t)$ is either small, or there exists a cut with low conductance among the sweep sets. Therefore by checking the conductance of the sweep sets S_j^t at each time step t, we discover clusters of low conductance.

Andersen and Lang [7] extended this work to handle seed sets (instead of just a seed vertex). On real datasets such as web graph, IMDB graph etc. they select a random subset of nodes belonging to a known community and show that the local clustering approach is able to recover the original community.

Andersen et al. [6] improved upon Spielman and Teng's algorithm by simulating random walks with restarts (i.e. Personalized PageRank), instead of just plain random walks. The notion of sweep sets for probability distributions, obtained by sorting the degree-normalized probabilities, is the same.

The theoretical results here involve pagerank vectors though; if there is a set of vertices whose probability in the pagerank vector is significantly greater than their probability in the general stationary distribution, then some sweep set of the pagerank vector has low conductance. They show that they can compute an approximate page rank vector in time depending only on the error of the approximation and the truncation threshold (and not on the graph size). Once the approximate pagerank vector is computed, conductances of successive sweep sets are calculated to discover a set of vertices with low conductance.

Flow-Based Post-Processing for Improving Community Detection: We will discuss how algorithms for computing the maximum flow in flow networks can be used to post-process or improve existing partitions of the graph. Flake et al. [36] proposed to discover web communities by using a focused crawler to first obtain a coarse or approximate community and then set up a max-flow/min-cut problem whose solution can be used to obtain the actual set of pages that belong to the same community. Lang and Rao [57] discuss a strategy for improving the conductance of any arbitrary bipartition or cut of the graph. Given a cut of the graph $(S, \bar{S})$, their algorithm finds the best improvement among all cuts $(S', \bar{S'})$ such that S' is a strict subset of S. Their main approach is to construct a new instance of a max-flow problem, such that the solution to this problem (which can be found in polynomial time) can be used to find the set S' with the lowest conductance among all subsets of S. They refer to their method as MQI (Max-Flow Quotient-Cut Improvement). They use Metis+MQI to recursively bi-partition the input graph; at each step they bi-partition using Metis first and then improve the partition using MQI and repeat the process on the individual partitions. Anderson and Lang [7] find that MQI can improve the partitions found by local clustering as well.

Community Discovery via Shingling: Broder et al. [19] introduced the idea of clustering web documents through the use of *shingles* and fingerprints (also denoted as *sketches*). In short, a length-s *shingle* is s of all parts of the object. For example, a length-s shingle of a graph node contains s outgoing links of the node; a length-s shingle of a document is a contiguous subsequence of length s of the document. Meanwhile, a *sketch* is a constant-size subset of all shingles with a specific length, with the remarkable property that the similarity between sets of two objects' sketches approximates the similarity between the objects themselves (here the definition of similarity being used is Jaccard similarity, i.e. $sim(A, B) = |A \cap B|/|A \cup B|$. This property makes sketch an object's fingerprint.

Gibson et al. [40] attempt to extract dense communities from large-scale graphs via a recursive application of shingling. In this algorithm, the first-level shingling is performed on each graph node using its outgoing links. That is, each node v is associated with a sketch of c_1 shingles, each of which stands for s_1 nodes selected from all nodes that v points to. Then an inverted index is built, containing each first-level shingle and a list of all nodes that the shingle is associated with. The second-level shingling function is then performed on each first-level shingle, producing second-level shingles (also called meta-shingles) and sketches. Two first-level shingles are considered as relevant if they share at least one meta-shingle in common, and the interpretation is that these two shingles are associated with some common nodes. If a new graph is constructed in such a way that nodes stand for first-level shingles and edges indicate the above-defined relation, then clusters of first-level shingles correspond to connect components in this new graph. Finally, communities can be extracted by mapping first-level shingles clusters back to original nodes plus including associated common meta-shingles. This algorithm is inherently applicable to both bipartite and directed graph, and can also be extended to the case of undirected graph. It is also very efficient in terms of both memory usage and running time, thus can handle graph of billions of edges.

Alternative Definitions of Communities: At the start of this section, we informally defined a community as a subset of nodes well connected internally and weakly connected to the rest of the graph. We now look at additional notions of communities which are either different from this definition or are refinements of this idea for a particular context.

Asur and Parthasarathy [10] recently introduced the idea of *viewpoint neighborhoods*, which are groups of nodes that are salient or influential from the viewpoint of a single node (or subset of nodes) in the network. Thus a viewpoint neighborhood may be seen as a cluster or community of nodes that is local to the node (or subset of nodes) that is being analyzed. The same paper also proposes algorithms for extraction of viewpoint neighborhoods using activation spread models that are general enough to incorporate different notions of salience or influence. Viewpoint analysis of graphs provides us a novel analytic and conceptual tool for understanding large networks at a fine scale.

Leskovec et al. [60] find that in a wide variety of real-world networks, some of the best communities, according to the measure of conductance (see Equation 4.2) , are groups of nodes that are connected to the rest of the graph by only one edge. They refer to such communities as *whiskers* (with groups of nodes that are connected by 2 edges called *2-whiskers* etc.) They postulate a core-and-whiskers model for the structure of networks, where most networks consist of a core part of the network surrounded by whiskers which are often connected to the rest of the network by only one or two edges. The whiskers of a network may either represent patterns that are useful within the context of the domain or may be considered noise which is to be removed while preprocessing the network.

4. Emerging Fields and Problems

In this section we attempt to identify recent research trends within the domain of community discovery in social networks. Given the relatively preliminary nature of the work presented in this section our objective here is to identify and discuss exemplar efforts rather than provide a comprehensive survey of all results in each sub-area.

4.1 Community Discovery in Dynamic Networks

Most of the community discovery algorithms discussed in Section 3 were designed with the implicit assumption that the underlying network is unchanging. In most real social networks however, the networks themselves as well as the communities and their members evolve over time. Some of the questions consequently raised are: How should community discovery algorithms be modified to take into account the dynamic and temporally evolving nature of social networks? How do communities get formed? How persistent and stable are communities and their members? How do they evolve over time? In this section, we introduce the reader to the slew of recent work that addresses these questions.

Asur et al.[9] presented an an event-based approach for understanding the evolution of communities and their members over time. The key ideas brought forth by this work is a structured way to reason about how communities and individual elements within such networks evolve over time and what are the critical events that characterize their behavior. Events involving communities include *continue, κ-merge, κ-split, form* and *dissolve*, and events involving individuals include *appear, disappear* and *join*. The authors demonstrate how behavioral indices such as stability and influence as well as a diffusion model can be efficiently composed from the events detected by their framework and can be used to effectively analyze real-life evolving networks in an incremental fashion. Their model can also be used to predict future community behavior (e.g. collaboration between groups). Also it can help identifying nodes with interests (e.g. sociable or influential users). Furthermore, semantic content can be integrated in the model naturally.

Recently, much research effort has gone into the question of designing community discovery algorithms for dynamic networks. The simple approach of treating treating each network snapshot as an independent network and applying a conventional community discovery algorithm may result in undesirable fluctuations of community memberships from one snapshot to the next. Consider an extreme example from [25], where there exist two orthogonal splits (A and B) on a data set. A performs slightly better on odd-numbered days, while B is a little superior on even-numbered days. Taking the optimal split every day results in radical change in the obtained communities from day to day, and therefore it may be better to sacrifice some optimality and instead adopt a consistent split (either A or B) on all days.

Initial approaches to tackle this problem focused on constructing temporal slices of the network and then relied on community discovery on each slice to detect temporal changes to community structure between consecutive slices. For example, Berger-Wolf and Saia[16] took partitions of individuals at each time-stamp as input, trying to find a *metagroup* that contains a sequence of groups which are similar to each other. Definitions of three extreme meta-groups (namely most persistent metagroup, most stable metagroup and largest metagroup) were given, and the extraction algorithms were discussed. Tantipathananandh et al. [111] studied the problem of identifying the "true" community affiliations of the individuals in a dynamic network, given the affiliations of the individuals in each timeslice. They formulate this as a combinatorial optimization problem and show that the problem is NP-hard. Consequently they solve the problem using a combination of approximate greedy heuristics and dynamic programming.

An alternative approach to dynamic analysis of networks is to take a holistic view of the community discovery across time-slices, by constraining the network division in a time-slice to not be too divergent from the network divisions of the previous time-slices. Chakrabarti et al.[25] were among the first to work on this problem and referred to it as evolutionary clustering. The most essential contribution of it is, instead of first extracting communities on each network snapshots and then finding connections among communities in different snapshots, it considers *snapshot quality* (how well the clustering at certain time C_t represents the data at t) and *history cost* (how different is the clustering C_t from clustering C_{t-1}) as a whole. In this way, community structure and its evolution are studied at the same time. Furthermore, it allows the compromise between these two parts by linear combination of snapshot quality and history cost. They also adapted agglomerative hierarchical clustering and k-means clustering for this framework.

Sun et al.[106] present an alternative approach to clustering time-evolving graphs using the *Minimum Description Length* (MDL) principle. Here, graphs of consecutive timestamps are grouped into graph stream segments, and these segments are divided by change-points. These change-points indeed indicate points of drastic discontinuities in the network structure. The total cost of graph stream encoding is then defined as $C = \sum_s C^{(s)}$, where $C^{(s)}$ is the encoding cost for s-th graph stream segment. The segment encoding cost, $C^{(s)}$ is again a sum of the segment length, the graph encoding cost and the partition encoding cost. Unfortunately, minimizing total cost was proved NP-hard, leading to a greedy algorithm based on alternating minimizations called GraphScope. Basically it deals with when to start a new graph stream segment and how to find well-formed communities among all snapshots in a single segment. One of GraphScope's advantages is that it doesn't require any parameter as input.

Chi et al.[26] extended spectral clustering to a dynamic network setting. They proposed two frameworks, named *preserving cluster quality* (PCQ) and *preserving cluster membership* (PCM) respectively, to measure the temporal/history cost. The former metric is interested in how well the partition at time t (C_t) performs on the data at time $t-1$, while latter cares how similar the two consecutive partitions (C_t and C_{t-1}) are. This framework also allows variation in cluster numbers as well as insertion and removal of nodes.

Lin et al.[63] proposed *FacetNet* for dynamic community discovery through the use of probabilistic community membership models. The advantage of such probabilistic models is the ability to assign each individuals to multiple communities with a weight indicating the degree of membership for each community. They used KL-divergence to measure the snapshot quality and history cost respectively. It was proved in[64] that when certain assumptions hold, optimization of total cost is equivalent to maximization of the log-likelihood function $L(U_t) = \log P(W_t|U_t) + \log P(U_t|U_{t-1})$, where W_t is the data at time t, and U_t the cover at t.

Kim and Han[55] revisited the cost function used in existing research and found that temporal smoothing at the clustering level can degrade the performance because of the need to adjust the clustering result iteratively. Their remedy was to *push down* the cost to each pair of nodes, get a temporal-smoothed version of pair-wise node distance and then conduct density-based clustering on this new distance metric. To deal with the problem that the number of communities change over time, greedy local clustering mapping based on mutual information was performed. By doing so, the model can account for the arbitrary creation/dissolution as well as growing/shrinking of a community over time.

4.2 Community Discovery in Heterogeneous Networks

Most conventional algorithms assume the existence of a homogeneous network where nodes and edges are of the same type. In the real world, however, we often have to deal with heterogeneous social networks, where the nodes are of different kinds, edges are of dissimilar types (e.g. relationships based upon various communication methods[43]) or even both of them at the same time[108]. Consider an IMDB network, where the entities may be of multiple types such as movies, directors, actors and the relationships may also be of different types such as acted-in, directed-by, co-acted-in and so on. Such diversity presents both an opportunity and challenge, since there may exist valuable information to be gained from recognizing the heterogeneity in the network and yet it is not obvious how to appropriately handle nodes and edges that belong to different types.

Guy et al.[43] designed the SONAR API, aiming at aggregating social network information from emails, instant messaging, organization charts, blogs and so on. They experimented with different weighted combination of these information sources and subsequently performed the task of user recommendation based on the outcome network. It was reported that recommendation based on aggregated network had a better performance than that based on any of the input networks. However, they did not discuss how to find the best combination scheme.

Cai et al.[23] looked into the problem of finding the best linear combination of different source networks. Their main idea is to first build a target network, with associated adjacency matrix $\tilde{M}$, and regress it on the source networks M_i.

$$\mathbf{a}^{opt} = \arg\min_{\mathbf{a}} \|\tilde{M} - \sum_{i=1}^{n} a_i M_i\|^2 \tag{4.6}$$

The a_is are the coefficients for the corresponding source networks. However, since we rarely know the full target network, the authors assume that the user provides only a few example target relationships, and derive a linear programming formulation that efficiently solves the linear regression problem.

The NetClus algorithm introduced by Sun et al.[108] dealt with clustering networks with *star network* schema. In the star network, each record is actually a compound of a single *target type* and several *attribute types*. The decision of cluster assignment is made by ranking the posterior probabilities resulting from a generative model. This ranking-assignment process is then iterated until convergence. By taking advantage of the ranking distribution for each type of objects (e.g. conference, author and topic), importance/influence ranking in each type can be retrieved as well as communities themselves. Therefore the results become more meaningful and interpretable. The usage of this algorithm, however, is limited by its ability to process only networks with *star network* schema. Similarly, the RankClus algorithm[107] is only designed to deal with bi-type network, where the network's vertex set have two types of vertices.

Finally, we also mention that ensemble clustering [105, 8] - an approach where the results of multiple clusterings are combined - is also a potential solution for clustering heterogeneous networks.

4.3 Community Discovery in Directed Networks

Community discovery has generally concerned itself with undirected networks; however the networks from a number of important domains are essentially directed, e.g. networks of web pages, research papers and Twitter users.

Simply ignoring directionality when analyzing such networks, as has been implicitly done in many studies, both ignores the additional information in the directionality as well as can lead to false conclusions. For this reason, there has recently been some work on community discovery for directed networks.

Many researchers have extended existing objective functions for community discovery from undirected networks (see Section 3.1) to take into account directionality. Using the random-walks interpretation of Normalized Cuts [67], multiple researchers have defined a directed version of Normalized Cuts. Let P be the transition matrix of a random walk on the directed graph, with π being its associated stationary distribution vector (e.g. PageRank vector) satisfying $\pi P = \pi$. The (directed) Normalized Cut for a group $S \subset V$ is given as [127, 28, 45, 66]:

$$Ncut_{dir}(S) = \frac{\sum_{i \in S, j \in \bar{S}} \pi(i) P(i,j)}{\sum_{i \in S} \pi(i)} + \frac{\sum_{j \in \bar{S}, i \in S} \pi(j) P(j,i)}{\sum_{j \in \bar{S}} \pi(j)} \tag{4.7}$$

The above objective function is often minimized using spectral clustering - this time by post-processing the top eigenvectors of the directed Laplacian, defined as [127, 28, 45, 66] (P and Π are defined as above):

$$\mathcal{L} = I - \frac{\Pi^{1/2} P \Pi^{-1/2} + \Pi^{-1/2} P' \Pi^{1/2}}{2} \tag{4.8}$$

Leicht and Newman[58] introduced the directed version of modularity[78] as follows:

$$Q = \frac{1}{m} \sum_{ij} [A_{ij} - \frac{k_i^{in} k_j^{out}}{m}] \delta_{c_i, c_j} \tag{4.9}$$

where k_i^{in} is the in-degree of node i, and k_j^{out} the out-degree of j. To fit the new metric into spectral optimization method proposed in[77] where a large community is bisected at each step, the definition of modularity matrix $\mathbf{B}$ is modified as $B_{ij} = A_{ij} - \frac{k_i^{in} k_j^{out}}{m}$. Furthermore, the modularity function is rewritten as

$$Q = \frac{1}{4m} \mathbf{s}^T (\mathbf{B} + \mathbf{B}^T) s \tag{4.10}$$

since $\mathbf{B}$ alone may not be symmetric. However, the algorithm may still suffer from the resolution problem, as pointed out by Fortunato and Barthélemy[38].

Satuluri and Parthasarathy [94] argue that a clustering with low directed normalized cut or high directed modularity is often not the most meaningful way to cluster directed graphs. In particular, such objective functions still favor clusters with high inter-connectivity, while inter-connectivity is not necessary for a group of vertices to form a meaningful cluster in directed networks [94]. They argue instead for a more general framework where we first convert the input directed graph into a weighted, undirected graph using a (symmetric) similarity measure for the vertices of the directed graph. They find that a similarity measure that uses in-link and out-link similarity while also discounting common links to highly connected nodes is more effective than existing approaches at discovering communities from directed networks.

4.4 Coupling Content and Relationship Information for Community Discovery

Although relationship information of social networks has been extensively investigated, the work of incorporating content and relationship information to facilitate community discovery has not been thoroughly studied yet. In fact this problem is at the heart of recent efforts to analyze social media. Relationship information can be viewed as a plain graph with vertices and edges, while content information are properties attached to these graph elements. Content may exist in the form of text, images, or even geographical locations. With the availability of content information, it is expected that the extracted communities are not only topologically well-connected, but also semantically coherent and meaningful. Consider the email communication network where sender-recipient communication can be modeled as user relationship. Then a spammer account will have a large amount of connections with others and thus be regarded as the center of a new community, which is useless in most cases. The importance of utilizing content information can be clearly perceived from this simple example. Although in previous studies many datasets also contain rich contents, they are merely used to infer user relationships (e.g. establish a link between two authors of a research paper), not to contribute to community extraction.

Content information may be in the forms of user profile or user-created material, in which case they are associated with vertices. Content may also be associated with edges in the network, as we will see in some literatures discusses below. In some cases, it's more intuitive to use "attribute" instead of "content", thus they are used interchangeably in the following context. The problem of interest is: how can communities be found, using both relationship and content information?

First introduced are three approaches using Bayesian generative models, aiming to incorporating textual contents. The Group-Topic model proposed by Wang et al.[120] is an extension of the stochastic blockstructures model [79], where both relations and their attributes are considered. Here, an entity is related with another if they behave the same way on an event, and texts associated with the event are this relationship's attributes. Furthermore, each event corresponds to one of the T latent topics. Therefore, the group membership of an entity is no longer constant, but changes over different topics. This blueprint of directed probabilistic model guides the discovery of groups by topics, and vice-versa.

Zhou et al.[128] introduce the notion of a *semantic community* and two corresponding Community-User-Topic (CUT) models. Their objective is to extract semantic communities from communication documents. In the CUT_1 model, the distribution of topics is conditioned on users, who are, in turn, conditioned on communities. This algorithm is similar to conventional community discovery algorithms, in the sense that a community is still defined as no more than a group of users. On the contrary, the CUT_2 model let communities decide topics and topics decide users, assuming a tighter connection between community and topic. As the experiments report, CUT_2 model finds higher-quality semantic communities, and is computationally more efficient than CUT_1.

Pathak et al.[84] presented the Community-Author-Recipient-Topic (CART) model in a setting of email communication networks, assuming that the discussion among users within a community is relevant to these users as well as the community. The model constrains all users involved and topics discussed in the email conversation to belong to a single community, while same users and topics in different conversations can be assigned to different communities. Compared with previous models including CUT models, this model is argued to emphasize more on how topics and relationships *jointly* affect community structure. Yet, all these three methods suffer from a common disadvantage: inference of the generative model using Gibbs sampling may converge slowly, thus the running time may be a problem in practice, especially for large-scale datasets.

The problem of Connected *X* Clusters (*CXC*) introduced by Moser et al.[70] was inspired by traditional graph clustering. While the algorithm still assumes that each cluster is compact and distinctive from neighboring ones (by using content information), the idea of *community* is enforced by requiring each cluster to be *internally connected* (by using relationship information). They also formally derived the number of initial centroids such that each true cluster is represented by at least one initial cluster atom (the smallest building component in the algorithm), at certain pre-defined confidence level. The proposed algorithm (called *JointClust*) is essentially a agglomerative clustering method. It first determines cluster atoms based on the number of initial centroids. In the second phase, it merges cluster atoms in a bottom-up fashion based on the *joint Silhouette coefficient*, an extension of traditional Silhouette coefficient [52]. This algorithm does not require pre-specified cluster number. It, however, still takes as a parameter the minimum size of each cluster.

Negoescu and Gatica-Perez[73] proposed an algorithm to identify communities of groups on Flickr, an image-sharing website. In the context of this algorithm, groups refer to self-organized sets of Flickr users, and are the elements of the final communities that we are looking for. Therefore, a community is also referred to as a *hypergroup*. The procedure is to first abstract each group into a bag-of-tags model, where tags come from the group's images and can be regarded as contents generated by the group. Then latent Dirichlet allocation *LDA* method is applied, giving distribution of latent topics over each group. Several similarity measures can be exploited to build the similarity matrix for groups, and the original problem is cast to a clustering problem on similarity matrix. Although it's not discussed in the paper, this algorithm is applicable to finding communities of users. Again, efficiency may be a potential concern, which is intrinsic to all latent-topic-based approaches.

5. Crosscutting Issues and Concluding Remarks

In this article we surveyed the principal results on community discovery within social networks. We first examined the contexts and use-case scenarios for community discovery within various social settings. We next took a look at the core methods developed to extract community structure from large networks ranging from the traditional to the current state-of-the-art. Subsequently we focused on recent and emerging strands of research that is gaining traction within this community. Below we briefly highlight four cross-cutting research themes that are likely to play a significant role as we move forward within this field. Note, that this is by no means a comprehensive list of cross-cutting issues but highlight some of the key challenges and opportunities within the field.

- Scalable Algorithms: With the size and scale of networks and information involved researchers are increasingly turning to scalable, parallel and distributed algorithms for community discovery within social networks. At the algorithmic level multi-level algorithms relying on graph coarsening and refinement offer potential [51, 31, 93]. Architecture conscious algorithms on the GPU and multi-cores offer another orthogonal approach [22, 83] as do streaming algorithms[3]. Given the recent trend towards cloud computing, researchers are beginning to investigate algorithms for community discovery on platforms such as Hadoop [81, 48, 49].

- Visualization of Communities and their Evolution: Visualizing large complex networks and honing in on important topological characteristics is a grand challenge since one often runs out of pixel space especially when attempting to characterize the behavior of billion node networks. This area, particularly in the context of community discovery within social networks has seen limited research thus far [119, 125, 21, 85]. Moving forward we envision multiple roles for visualization in this context. First as a front end to display dynamic (sub-)networks (details-on-demand) housed within the warehouse (e.g. visualizing a trust network). Second, as a mechanism to help understand and drive the analysis process. Third, as a means to validate and lend transparency to the discovery process. An important challenge here is to determine how dynamic information is to be modeled and visualized effectively and efficiently.

- Incorporating Domain Knowledge:It has been our observation that often we as data mining researchers tend to under-utilize available domain information during the pattern discovery or model building process. In fact data mining researchers often specifically omit important domain knowledge from the training phase as it then allows them a means to independently confirm the utility of the proposed methods during validation and testing. While useful, such a methodology often limits scientific advances within the domain. We believe a fresh look at how domain knowledge can be embedded in existing approaches and better testing and validation methodologies in close conjunction with domain experts must be designed (see for example work in the field of Bioinformatics). It is our hypothesis that domain knowledge is often too valuable a resource to simply ignore during the discovery phase as it can be an effective means to prune and guide the search for interesting patterns.

- Ranking and Summarization: While ranking and summarizing patterns has been the subject of much research in the data mining community the role of such methods in this community has been much less researched. As networks become larger and particularly with an increasing focus on dynamic networks identifying a hierarchy of patterns from most important to least important becomes crucial to help domain experts focus on the key insights to be drawn from the analysis. Leveraging domain information (as noted above) will be crucial for this endeavor.

In conclusion we would like to add that the field of community discovery in networks (particularly social) is still fairly new with a number of open and exciting problems ranging from the theoretical to the empirical and covering a gamut of core research areas both within computer science and across disciplines. Given the dynamic nature of the field and the broad interest across multiple disciplines we expect to see many more exciting results on this topic in the future.

5.0.1 Acknowledgments. This work is supported in part by the following grants: NSF CAREER IIS-0347662, CCF-0702587, IIS-0917070. The authors would also like to thank Charu Aggarwal and the anonymous reviewers for useful comments for improving this article.

References

[1] J. Abello, P. Pardalos, and MGC Resende. On maximum clique problems in very large graphs. In *External memory algorithms*, pages 119–130. American Mathematical Society, 1999.

[2] L.A. Adamic and N. Glance. The political blogosphere and the 2004 US election: divided they blog. In *Proceedings of the 3rd international workshop on Link discovery*, page 43. ACM, 2005.

[3] Charu C. Aggarwal, Yuchen Zhao, and Philip S. Yu. On clustering graph streams. In *SDM*, pages 478–489, 2010.

[4] R. Albert, H. Jeong, and A.L. Barabási. Diameter of the World-Wide Web. *Nature*, 401(6749):130–131, 1999.

[5] P. Aloy and R.B. Russell. The third dimension for protein interactions and complexes. *Trends in biochemical sciences*, 27(12):633–638, 2002.

[6] R. Andersen, F. Chung, and K. Lang. Local graph partitioning using pagerank vectors. In *FOCS '06: Proceedings of the 47th Annual IEEE Symposium on Foundations of Computer Science*, pages 475–486, Washington, DC, USA, 2006. IEEE Computer Society.

[7] R. Andersen and K.J. Lang. Communities from seed sets. In *WWW '06: Proceedings of the 15th international conference on World Wide Web*, page 232. ACM, 2006.

[8] S. Asur, S. Parthasarathy, and D. Ucar. An ensemble approach for clustering scalefree graphs. In *LinkKDD workshop*, 2006.

[9] S. Asur, S. Parthasarathy, and D. Ucar. An event-based framework for characterizing the evolutionary behavior of interaction graphs. In *KDD '07: Proceedings of the 13th ACM SIGKDD international conference on Knowledge discovery and data mining*, pages 913–921, New York, NY, USA, 2007. ACM.

[10] Sitaram Asur and Srinivasan Parthasarathy. A viewpoint-based approach for interaction graph analysis. In *KDD '09: Proceedings of the 15th ACM SIGKDD international conference on Knowledge discovery and data mining*, pages 79–88, New York, NY, USA, 2009. ACM.

[11] A.L. Barabási and E. Bonabeau. Scale-free networks. *Scientific American*, 288(5):60, 2003.

[12] A.L. Barabási and RE Crandall. Linked: The new science of networks. *American journal of Physics*, 71:409, 2003.

[13] S.T. Barnard and H.D. Simon. Fast multilevel implementation of recursive spectral bisection for partitioning unstructured problems. *Concurrency Practice and Experience*, 6(2):101–118, 1994.

[14] J. Bascompte, P. Jordano, C.J. Melián, and J.M. Olesen. The nested assembly of plant–animal mutualistic networks. *Proceedings of the National Academy of Sciences of the United States of America*, 100(16):9383, 2003.

[15] M.L. Bech and E. Atalay. The topology of the federal funds market. *Working Paper Series*, 2008.

[16] T.Y. Berger-Wolf and J. Saia. A framework for analysis of dynamic social networks. In *KDD '06: Proceedings of the 12th ACM SIGKDD international conference on Knowledge discovery and data mining*, page 528. ACM, 2006.

[17] Board on Army Science and Technology. *Strategy for an Army Center for Network Science, Technology, and Experim entation.* The National Academies Press, 2007.

[18] U. Brandes, D. Delling, M. Gaertler, R. Gorke, M. Hoefer, Z. Nikoloski, and D. Wagner. On finding graph clusterings with maximum modularity. In *Graph-Theoretic Concepts in Computer Science*, pages 121–132. Springer, 2007.

[19] A.Z. Broder, S.C. Glassman, M.S. Manasse, and G. Zweig. Syntactic clustering of the web. *Computer Networks and ISDN Systems*, 29(8-13):1157–1166, 1997.

[20] S. Brohee and J. Van Helden. Evaluation of clustering algorithms for protein-protein interaction networks. *BMC bioinformatics*, 7(1):488, 2006.

[21] G. Buehrer and K. Chellapilla. A scalable pattern mining approach to web graph compression with communities. In *WSDM '08: Proceedings of the international conference on Web search and web data mining*, pages 95–106, New York, NY, USA, 2008. ACM.

[22] G. Buehrer, S. Parthasarathy, and M. Goyder. Data mining on the cell broadband engine. In *Proceedings of the 22nd annual international conference on Supercomputing*, pages 26–35. ACM, 2008.

[23] D. Cai, Z. Shao, X. He, X. Yan, and J. Han. Mining hidden community in heterogeneous social networks. In *Proceedings of the 3rd international workshop on Link discovery*, page 65. ACM, 2005.

[24] D. Chakrabarti and C. Faloutsos. Graph mining: Laws, generators, and algorithms. *ACM Comput. Surv.*, 38(1):2, 2006.

[25] D. Chakrabarti, R. Kumar, and A. Tomkins. Evolutionary clustering. In *KDD '06: Proceedings of the 12th ACM SIGKDD international conference on Knowledge discovery and data mining*, pages 554–560. ACM New York, NY, USA, 2006.

[26] Y. Chi, X. Song, K. Hino, and B.L. Tseng. Evolutionary spectral clustering by incorporating temporal smoothness, October 18 2007. US Patent App. 11/874,395.

[27] F. Chung. Spectral graph theory. *CBMS Regional Conference Series in Mathematics*, 1997.

[28] F. Chung. Laplacians and the Cheeger inequality for directed graphs. *Annals of Combinatorics*, 9(1):1–19, 2005.

[29] A. Clauset, M.E.J. Newman, and C. Moore. Finding community structure in very large networks. *Physical Review E*, 70(6):66111, 2004.

[30] R. DerSimonian and N. Laird. Meta-analysis in clinical trials* 1. *Controlled clinical trials*, 7(3):177–188, 1986.

[31] I.S. Dhillon, Y. Guan, and B. Kulis. Weighted Graph Cuts without Eigenvectors: A Multilevel Approach. *IEEE Trans. Pattern Anal. Mach. Intell.*, 29(11):1944–1957, 2007.

[32] P. Domingos and M. Richardson. Mining the network value of customers. In *KDD '01: Proceedings of the seventh ACM SIGKDD international conference on Knowledge discovery and data mining*, pages 57–66. ACM, 2001.

[33] J.A. Dunne, R.J. Williams, and N.D. Martinez. Network structure and biodiversity loss in food webs: robustness increases with connectance. *Ecology Letters*, 5(4):558–567, 2002.

[34] M. Faloutsos, P. Faloutsos, and C. Faloutsos. On power-law relationships of the internet topology. In *Proceedings of the conference on Applications, technologies, architectures, and protocols for computer communication*, page 262. ACM, 1999.

[35] M. Fiedler. Algebraic connectivity of graphs. *Czechoslovak Mathematical Journal*, 23(2):298–305, 1973.

[36] G.W. Flake, S. Lawrence, and C.L. Giles. Efficient identification of web communities. In *KDD '00: Proceedings of the sixth ACM SIGKDD international conference on Knowledge discovery and data mining*, page 160. ACM, 2000.

[37] G.W. Flake, S. Lawrence, C.L. Giles, and F.M. Coetzee. Self-organization of the web and identification of communities. *Communities*, 35(3):66–71, 2002.

[38] S. Fortunato and M. Barthélemy. Resolution limit in community detection. *Proceedings of the National Academy of Sciences*, 104(1):36, 2007.

[39] M.R. Garey and L. Johnson. Some simplified NP-complete graph problems. *Theoretical computer science*, 1(3):237–267, 1976.

[40] D. Gibson, R. Kumar, and A. Tomkins. Discovering Large Dense Subgraphs in Massive Graphs. In *VLDB '05: Proceedings of the 31st International Conference on Very Large Data Bases, Trondheim, Norway, August 30-September 2, 2005*, page 721. ACM, 2005.

[41] M. Girvan and M.E.J. Newman. Community structure in social and biological networks. *Proceedings of the National Academy of Sciences*, 99(12):7821, 2002.

[42] W. Glanzel and A. Schubert. Analysing scientific networks through coauthorship. *Handbook of quantitative science and technology research*, pages 257–276, 2004.

[43] I. Guy, M. Jacovi, E. Shahar, N. Meshulam, V. Soroka, and S. Farrell. Harvesting with SONAR: the value of aggregating social network information. In *Proceeding of the twenty-sixth annual SIGCHI conference on Human factors in computing systems*, pages 1017–1026. ACM, 2008.

[44] G. C. Homans. *The Human Group*. New York: Harcourt, Brace, 1950.

[45] J. Huang, T. Zhu, and D. Schuurmans. Web communities identification from random walks. *Lecture Notes in Computer Science*, 4213:187, 2006.

[46] R.F. i Cancho. The small world of human language. *Proceedings of the Royal Society B: Biological Sciences*, 268(1482):2261–2265, 2001.

[47] H. Jeong, S.P. Mason, A.L. Barabási, and Z.N. Oltvai. Lethality and centrality in protein networks. *Nature*, 411(6833):41–42, 2001.

[48] U. Kang, C. Tsourakakis, A.P. Appel, C. Faloutsos, and J. Leskovec. Radius plots for mining tera-byte scale graphs: Algorithms, patterns, and observations. In *SIAM International Conference on Data Mining*, 2010.

[49] U Kang, C.E Tsourakakis, and C. Faloutsos. Pegasus: Mining peta-scale graphs. *Knowledge and Information Systems*, 2010.

[50] R. Kannan, S. Vempala, and A. Veta. On clusterings-good, bad and spectral. In *FOCS '00*, page 367. IEEE Computer Society, 2000.

[51] G. Karypis and V. Kumar. A fast and high quality multilevel scheme for partitioning irregular graphs. *SIAM Journal on Scientific Computing*, 20, 1999.

[52] L. Kaufman and PJ Rousseeuw. Finding groups in data; an introduction to cluster analysis. *Wiley Series in Probability and Mathematical Statistics. Applied Probability and Statistics Section (EUA).*, 1990.

[53] D. Kempe, J. Kleinberg, and É. Tardos. Maximizing the spread of influence through a social network. In *KDD '03: Proceedings of the ninth ACM SIGKDD international conference on Knowledge discovery and data mining*, pages 137–146, New York, NY, USA, 2003. ACM.

[54] B. Kernighan and S. Lin. An Efficient Heuristic Procedure for partitioning graphs. *The Bell System Technical J.*, 49, 1970.

[55] M.S. Kim and J. Han. A particle-and-density based evolutionary clustering method for dynamic networks. *Proceedings of the VLDB Endowment*, 2(1):622–633, 2009.

[56] Y. Koren. The BellKor Solution to the Netflix Grand Prize. *KorBell Team's Report to Netflix*, 2009.

[57] K. Lang and S. Rao. A flow-based method for improving the expansion or conductance of graph cuts. *Lecture notes in computer science*, pages 325–337, 2004.

[58] E.A. Leicht and M.E.J. Newman. Community structure in directed networks. *Physical review letters*, 100(11):118703, 2008.

[59] J. Leskovec, L.A. Adamic, and B.A. Huberman. The dynamics of viral marketing. *ACM Transactions on the Web (TWEB)*, 1(1):5, 2007.

[60] J. Leskovec, K.J. Lang, A. Dasgupta, and M.W. Mahoney. Community Structure in Large Networks: Natural Cluster Sizes and the Absence of Large Well-Defined Clusters. *CoRR*, abs/0810.1355, 2008.

[61] J. Leskovec, K.J. Lang, A. Dasgupta, and M.W. Mahoney. Statistical properties of community structure in large social and information networks. In *WWW '08*, pages 695–704, New York, NY, USA, 2008. ACM.

[62] L. Li, C.J. Stoeckert, and D.S. Roos. OrthoMCL: identification of ortholog groups for eukaryotic genomes. *Genome Res*, 13(9):2178–2189, September 2003.

[63] Y.R. Lin, Y. Chi, S. Zhu, H. Sundaram, and B.L. Tseng. Facetnet: a framework for analyzing communities and their evolutions in dynamic networks. In *WWW '08: Proceeding of the 17th international conference on World Wide Web*, pages 685–694, New York, NY, USA, 2008. ACM.

[64] Y.R. Lin, Y. Chi, S. Zhu, H. Sundaram, and B.L. Tseng. Analyzing communities and their evolutions in dynamic social networks. *ACM Transactions on Knowledge Discovery from Data (TKDD)*, 3(2):1–31, 2009.

[65] D. Lusseau. The emergent properties of a dolphin social network. *Proceedings of the Royal Society of London. Series B: Biological Sciences*, 270(Suppl 2):S186, 2003.

[66] M. Meila and W. Pentney. Clustering by weighted cuts in directed graphs. In *Proceedings of the 7th SIAM International Conference on Data Mining*, pages 135–144. Citeseer, 2007.

[67] M. Meila and J. Shi. A random walks view of spectral segmentation. *AI and Statistics (AISTATS)*, 2001, 2001.

[68] J. Memmott, N.M. Waser, and M.V. Price. Tolerance of pollination networks to species extinctions. *Proceedings of the Royal Society of London. Series B: Biological Sciences*, 271(1557):2605, 2004.

[69] J.M. Montoya et al. Small world patterns in food webs. *Journal of theoretical biology*, 214(3):405–412, 2002.

[70] F. Moser, R. Ge, and M. Ester. Joint cluster analysis of attribute and relationship data withouta-priori specification of the number of clusters. In *KDD '07: Proceedings of the 13th ACM SIGKDD international conference on Knowledge discovery and data mining*, pages 510–519. ACM New York, NY, USA, 2007.

[71] F. Murray. Innovation as co-evolution of scientific and technological networks: exploring tissue engineering. *Research Policy*, 31(8-9):1389–1403, 2002.

[72] S.F. Nadel. The Theory of Social Structure. *London: Cohen and West*, 1957.

[73] R.A. Negoescu, B. Adams, D. Phung, S. Venkatesh, and D. Gatica-Perez. Flickr hypergroups. In *Proceedings of the seventeen ACM international conference on Multimedia*, pages 813–816. ACM, 2009.

[74] M. E. J. Newman. Fast algorithm for detecting community structure in networks. *Physical Review E*, 69(6):066133, 2004.

[75] M.E.J. Newman. Assortative mixing in networks. *Physical Review Letters*, 89(20):208701, 2002.

[76] M.E.J. Newman. A measure of betweenness centrality based on random walks. *Social networks*, 27(1):39–54, 2005.

[77] M.E.J. Newman. Modularity and community structure in networks. *Proceedings of the National Academy of Sciences*, 103(23):8577, 2006.

[78] M.E.J. Newman and M. Girvan. Finding and evaluating community structure in networks. *Phys. Rev. E*, 69(2):026113, Feb 2004.

[79] K. Nowicki and T.A.B. Snijders. Estimation and prediction for stochastic blockstructures. *Journal of the American Statistical Association*, 96(455):1077–1087, 2001.

[80] L. Palen and S.B. Liu. Citizen communications in crisis: anticipating a future of ICT-supported public participation. In *Proceedings of the SIGCHI conference on Human factors in computing systems*, page 736. ACM, 2007.

[81] S. Papadimitriou and J. Sun. Disco: Distributed co-clustering with Map-Reduce: A case study towards petabyte-scale end-to-end mining. In *Eighth IEEE International Conference on Data Mining, 2008. ICDM'08*, pages 512–521, 2008.

[82] S. Parthasarathy. Data mining at the crossroads: successes, failures and learning from them. In *KDD '07: Proceedings of the 13th ACM SIGKDD international conference on Knowledge discovery and data mining*, page 1055. ACM, 2007.

[83] S. Parthasarathy, S. Tatikonda, G. Buehrer, and A. Ghoting. *Next Generation of Data Mining*, chapter Architecture Conscious Data Mining: Current Directions and Future Outlook, pages 261–280. Chapman and Hall/CRC, 2008.

[84] N. Pathak, C. DeLong, A. Banerjee, and K. Erickson. Social topic models for community extraction. In *The 2nd SNA-KDD Workshop*, volume 8, 2008.

[85] A. Perer and B. Shneiderman. Balancing systematic and flexible exploration of social networks. *IEEE Transactions on Visualization and Computer Graphics*, pages 693–700, 2006.

[86] J. Podani, Z.N. Oltvai, H. Jeong, B. Tombor, A.L. Barabási, and E. Szathmary. Comparable system-level organization of Archaea and Eukaryotes. *Nature genetics*, 29(1):54–56, 2001.

[87] P. Raghavan. Social networks: from the Web to the enterprise. *IEEE Internet Computing*, 6(1):91–94, 2002.

[88] P.K. Reddy, M. Kitsuregawa, P. Sreekanth, and S.S. Rao. A graph based approach to extract a neighborhood customer community for collaborative filtering. In *Databases in networked information systems: second international workshop, DNIS 2002, Aizu, Japan, December 16-18, 2002: proceedings*, page 188. Springer-Verlag New York Inc, 2002.

[89] S.A. Rice. The identification of blocs in small political bodies. *The American Political Science Review*, 21(3):619–627, 1927.

[90] Y. Richter, E. Yom-Tov, and N. Slonim. Predicting customer churn in mobile networks through analysis of social groups. In *Proceedings of the 2010 SIAM International Conference on Data Mining*, 2010.

[91] E.M. Rogers. *Diffusion of innovations*. Free Pr, 1995.

[92] E.M. Rogers and D.L. Kincaid. *Communication networks: Toward a new paradigm for research*. Free Pr, 1981.

[93] V. Satuluri and S. Parthasarathy. Scalable graph clustering using stochastic flows: applications to community discovery. In *KDD '09*, pages 737–746, New York, NY, USA, 2009. ACM.

[94] V. Satuluri and S. Parthasarathy. Symmetrizations for clustering directed graphs. In *Workshop on Mining and Learning with Graphs, MLG 2010*, 2010. Also available as technical report from `ftp://ftp.cse.ohio-state.edu/pub/tech-report/2010/TR12.pdf`.

[95] V. Satuluri, S. Parthasarathy, and D. Ucar. Markov Clustering of Protein Interaction Networks with Improved Balance and Scalability. In *Proceedings of the ACM Conference on Bioinformatics and Computational Biology*, 2010.

[96] J. Shi and J. Malik. Normalized Cuts and Image Segmentation. *IEEE Transactions on Pattern Analysis and Machine Intelligence*, 22(8):888–905, 2000.

[97] R.V. Solé and M. Montoya. Complexity and fragility in ecological networks. *Proceedings of the Royal Society of London. Series B: Biological Sciences*, 268(1480):2039, 2001.

[98] R.V. Solé and R. Pastor-Satorras. Complex networks in genomics and proteomics. *Handbook of Graphs and Networks*, pages 147–169, 2002.

[99] E.D. Sontag. Structure and stability of certain chemical networks andapplications to the kinetic proofreading model of T-cell receptor signal-transduction. *IEEE transactions on automatic control*, 46(7):1028–1047, 2001.

[100] D.A. Spielman and N. Srivastava. Graph sparsification by effective resistances. In *STOC '08: Proceedings of the 40th annual ACM symposium on Theory of computing*, pages 563–568, New York, NY, USA, 2008. ACM.

[101] D.A. Spielman and S.H. Teng. Nearly-linear time algorithms for graph partitioning, graph sparsification, and solving linear systems. In *Proceedings of the thirty-sixth annual ACM symposium on Theory of computing*, pages 81–90. ACM New York, NY, USA, 2004.

[102] E. Sprinzak, S. Sattath, and H. Margalit. How reliable are experimental protein-protein interaction data? *Journal of molecular biology*, 327(5):919–923, 2003.

[103] J. Srivastava, R. Cooley, M. Deshpande, and P.N. Tan. Web usage mining: Discovery and applications of usage patterns from web data. *ACM SIGKDD Explorations Newsletter*, 1(2):23, 2000.

[104] M. Steenstrup. Cluster-based networks. In *Ad hoc networking*, page 138. Addison-Wesley Longman Publishing Co., Inc., 2001.

[105] A. Strehl and J. Ghosh. Cluster ensembles—a knowledge reuse framework for combining multiple partitions. *The Journal of Machine Learning Research*, 3:583–617, 2003.

[106] J. Sun, C. Faloutsos, S. Papadimitriou, and P.S. Yu. Graphscope: parameter-free mining of large time-evolving graphs. In *KDD '07: Proceedings of the 13th ACM SIGKDD international conference on Knowledge discovery and data mining*, pages 687–696. ACM New York, NY, USA, 2007.

[107] Y. Sun, J. Han, P. Zhao, Z. Yin, H. Cheng, and T. Wu. RankClus: integrating clustering with ranking for heterogeneous information network analysis. In *Proceedings of the 12th International Conference on Extending Database Technology: Advances in Database Technology*, pages 565–576. ACM, 2009.

[108] Y. Sun, Y. Yu, and J. Han. Ranking-based clustering of heterogeneous information networks with star network schema. In *KDD '09: Proceedings of the 15th ACM SIGKDD international conference on Knowledge discovery and data mining*, pages 797–806. ACM, 2009.

[109] S.R. Sundaresan, I.R. Fischhoff, J. Dushoff, and D.I. Rubenstein. Network metrics reveal differences in social organization between two fission–fusion species, Grevy's zebra and onager. *Oecologia*, 151(1):140–149, 2007.

[110] P.N. Tan, M. Steinbach, and V. Kumar. *Introduction to data mining*. Pearson Addison Wesley Boston, 2006.

[111] C. Tantipathananandh, T. Berger-Wolf, and D. Kempe. A framework for community identification in dynamic social networks. In *KDD '07: Proceedings of the 13th ACM SIGKDD international conference on Knowledge discovery and data mining*, page 726. ACM, 2007.

[112] S.H. Teng. Coarsening, sampling, and smoothing: Elements of the multilevel method. *Algorithms for Parallel Processing*, 105:247–276, 1999.

[113] N.M. Tichy, M.L. Tushman, and C. Fombrun. Social network analysis for organizations. *Academy of Management Review*, 4(4):507–519, 1979.

[114] P. Uetz, L. Giot, G. Cagney, T.A. Mansfield, R.S. Judson, J.R. Knight, V. Lockshon, D. a nd Narayan, M. Srinivasan, P. Pochart, et al. A comprehensive analysis of protein–protein interactions in Saccharomyces cerevisiae. *Nature*, 403(6770):623–627, 2000.

[115] S. Van Dongen. *Graph Clustering by Flow Simulation*. PhD thesis, University of Utrecht, 2000.

[116] F.A. Von Hayek. The use of knowledge in society. *American Economic Review*, 35(4):519–530, 1945.

[117] U. Von Luxburg. A tutorial on spectral clustering. *Statistics and Computing*, 17(4):395–416, 2007.

[118] A. Wagner and D.A. Fell. The small world inside large metabolic networks. *Proceedings of the Royal Society of London. Series B: Biological Sciences*, 268(1478):1803, 2001.

[119] N. Wang, S. Parthasarathy, K.L. Tan, and A.K.H. Tung. CSV: visualizing and mining cohesive subgraphs. In *Proceedings of the 2008 ACM SIGMOD international conference on Management of data*, pages 445–458. ACM, 2008.

[120] X. Wang, N. Mohanty, and A. McCallum. Group and topic discovery from relations and their attributes. *Advances in Neural Information Processing Systems*, 18:1449, 2006.

[121] S. Wasserman and K. Faust. *Social network analysis: Methods and applications*. Cambridge Univ Pr, 1994.

[122] D.J. Watts. *Small worlds: the dynamics of networks between order and randomness*. Princeton Univ Press, 2003.

[123] R.S. Weiss and E. Jacobson. A method for the analysis of the structure of complex organizations. *American Sociological Review*, 20(6):661–668, 1955.

[124] J. Xu and H. Chen. Criminal network analysis and visualization. *Commun. ACM*, 48(6):100–107, 2005.

[125] X. Yang, S. Asur, S. Parthasarathy, and S. Mehta. A visual-analytic toolkit for dynamic interaction graphs. In *Proceeding of the 14th ACM SIGKDD international conference on Knowledge discovery and data mining*, pages 1016–1024. ACM, 2008.

[126] W.W. Zachary. An information flow model for conflict and fission in small groups. *Journal of Anthropological Research*, 33(4):452–473, 1977.

[127] D. Zhou, J. Huang, and B. Scholkopf. Learning from labeled and unlabeled data on a directed graph. In *ICML '05*, pages 1036–1043, 2005.

[128] D. Zhou, E. Manavoglu, J. Li, C.L. Giles, and H. Zha. Probabilistic models for discovering e-communities. In *WWW '06: Proceedings of the 15th international conference on World Wide Web*, page 182. ACM, 2006.

Chapter 5

NODE CLASSIFICATION IN SOCIAL NETWORKS

Smriti Bhagat
Rutgers University
smbhagat@cs.rutgers.edu

Graham Cormode
AT&T Labs–Research
graham@research.att.com

S. Muthukrishnan
Rutgers University
muthu@cs.rutgers.edu

Abstract When dealing with large graphs, such as those that arise in the context of online social networks, a subset of nodes may be labeled. These labels can indicate demographic values, interest, beliefs or other characteristics of the nodes (users). A core problem is to use this information to extend the labeling so that all nodes are assigned a label (or labels).

In this chapter, we survey classification techniques that have been proposed for this problem. We consider two broad categories: methods based on iterative application of traditional classifiers using graph information as features, and methods which propagate the existing labels via random walks. We adopt a common perspective on these methods to highlight the similarities between different approaches within and across the two categories. We also describe some extensions and related directions to the central problem of node classification.

Keywords: Node classification, Graph labeling, Semi-supervised learning, Iterative methods

1. Introduction

The emergence of online social networks (OSNs) in the past decade has led to a vast increase in the volume of information about individuals, their activities, connections amongst individuals or groups, and their opinions and thoughts. A large part of this data can be modeled as *labels* associated with individuals, which are in turn represented as nodes within a graph or graph-like structure. These labels come in many forms: demographic labels, such as age, gender and location; labels which represent political or religious beliefs; labels that encode interests, hobbies, and affiliations; and many other possible characteristics capturing aspects of an individual's preferences or behavior. The labels typically appear on the user's profile within the network, or attached to other objects in the network (photos, videos etc.).

There are many new applications that can make use of these kinds of labels:

- Suggesting new connections or contacts to individuals, based on finding others with similar interests, demographics, or experiences.
- Recommendation systems to suggest objects (music, movies, activities) based on the interests of other individuals with overlapping characteristics.
- Question answering systems which direct questions to those with most relevant experience to a given question.
- Advertising systems which show advertisements to those individuals most likely to be interested and receptive to advertising on a particular topic.
- Sociological study of communities, such as the extent to which communities form around particular interests or affiliations.
- Epidemiological study of how ideas and "memes" spread through communities over time.

Of course, these are just a few examples of the many different ways social network data is of interest to businesses, researchers, and operators of social networks. They have in common the aspect that knowing labels for individuals is a key element of each application.

In an ideal world (as far as these applications are concerned), every user within a social network is associated with all and only the labels that are relevant to them. But in the real world, this is far from the case. While many users choose labels to apply to themselves, these labels can be misleading, inappropriate, outdated, or partial. This is for a variety of reasons: users may fail to update or add new labels as time progresses, letting their profile information grow "stale"; out of concerns for privacy, users may omit or distort information about themselves; users may simply forget or neglect to include information about their most important activities and interests; and some users simply delight in listing wantonly misleading information to amuse themselves and those who know them. Such distortions are prevalent, although not overwhelmingly so [18]. The consequence of this noise is to reduce the effectiveness of methods for the applications listed above. In particular, the most pressing problem is the absence of labels in certain categories (such as demographics or interests), which can make it impossible to provide useful suggestions or recommendations to that user.

The Node Classification Problem. This leads to the central problem of interest in this chapter: given a social network (or more generally, any network structure) with labels on some nodes, how to provide a high quality labeling for every node? We refer to this as the "node classification problem", with the understanding that the basic problem can be abstracted as providing a labeling for nodes in a graph structure. Variations on this problem might work over generalized graph structures, such as hypergraphs, graphs with weighted, labeled, or timestamped edges, multiple edges between nodes, and so on.

A first approach to this problem is to engage experts to provide labels on nodes, based on additional data about the corresponding individuals and their connections. Or individuals can be incentivized to provide accurate labels, via financial or other inducements. Indeed, historically this is exactly what sociologists have done when studying social groups of the order of tens to a hundred nodes, for example [35]. But this approach does not scale when confronted with networks containing hundreds of thousands to millions of individuals. While it may be feasible to rely on a moderate number of expert labeled nodes, or even a large fraction of "noisy" self-labeled nodes, this is very far from the goal of all nodes perfectly labeled.

Instead, we consider methods which use the information already encoded in the partially labeled graph to help us predict labels. This is based on the paradigm of machine learning and classification. In other words, we aim to train a classifier based on the examples of nodes that are labeled so we can apply it to the unlabeled nodes to predict labels for them (and also to nodes that have some labels to augment or replace their current labels). However, there are several aspects of this setting which make it somewhat different to the traditional model of classification, as will become apparent.

As is usual in machine learning, we first have to identify some "features" of nodes that can be used to guide the classification. The obvious features are properties of the node itself: information that may be known for all (or most) nodes, such as age, location, and some other existing nodes. But the presence of an explicit link structure makes the node classification problem different from traditional machine learning classification tasks, where objects being classified are considered independent. In contrast to the traditional setting, we can define additional features, based on adjacency or proximity in the graph. A first set of features are based on simple graph properties: the degree (number of neighbors) of the node; the neighborhood size reachable within two or three steps; the number of shortest paths that traverse through the node, and so on. But perhaps more interesting are features derived from properties of the nearby nodes: the *labels* of the neighbors form a canonical feature in this setting.

One may ask why the labels of neighboring nodes should be useful in predicting the label of a node. Certainly, if the edges between nodes were completely arbitrarily generated, there would not be much information to glean. But in social networks, links between nodes are far from arbitrary, and typically indicate some form of a relationship between the individuals that the nodes represent. In particular, a link can indicate some degree of similarity between the linked individuals: certainly not exact duplication, but sufficient to be a useful input into a learning algorithm.

Formally, the social sciences identify two important phenomena that can apply in online social networks:

- **homophily**, also known informally as "birds of a feather", is when a link between individuals (such as friendship or other social connection) is correlated with those individuals being similar in nature. For example, friends often tend to be similar in characteristics like age, social background, and education level.

- **co-citation regularity** is a related concept, which holds when similar individuals tend to refer or connect to the same things. For example, when two individuals have similar tastes in music, literature or fashion, co-citation regularity suggests that they may be similar in other ways or have other common interests.

If one can argue that either of these phenomena apply in a network of interest, then it suggests that information about nodes with short graph distance, or with similar attributes, may be useful in helping to classify a node of interest.

A secondary aspect of the graph setting is that the classification process can be iterative. That is, we may be faced with a node such that we initially have very little information about the node or its neighborhood. However, after an initial application of classification, we may know have a richer set of (putative) information about the neighborhood, giving more of a basis to label the node in question. In other words, the classification process can spread information to new places in the graph, and feed into the features that we use for classification. The classification continues to be iterated until it converges, or a fixed number of iterations have taken place. This iterative approach stands in contrast to the traditional model of classification, where the feature set is given at the start, and does not alter. The use of the graph edges to spread the labeling can be thought of as a special case of semi-supervised learning (where both labeled and unlabeled examples are used to build the classifier).

Chapter Outline. In this chapter we survey techniques that have been proposed to address the problem of node classification. We consider two broad classes of approaches.

In the first, we try to build on the vast knowledge of methods to solve the traditional classification problem. In other words, we define a method to generate vectors of features for each node (such as labels from neighboring nodes), and then apply a "local classifier" such as Naive Bayes, decision trees and so on to to generate the labeling. As indicated above, this approach can be *iterative*: after a first round of classification, by training on the newly labeled examples.

Many other techniques have been suggested that more directly use the structure of the graph to aid in the labeling task. We take a unifying approach, and observe that it is possible to view many of these methods as performing *random walks* over the network to determine a labeling function. We thus refer to these as random walk based methods, and compare them in a common framework. This helps to identify similarities and highlight differences between these techniques. In particular, we see that all methods can be described via similar iterative matrix formulations, and that they are also closely related to iterative approaches with simple classifiers.

Based on this taxonomy of methods, we proceed as follows: in Section 2 we formalize the notions of graphs and labelings, and more precisely define the node classification problem over these structures. Given these definitions, we present methods for this problem in the graph domain. Then Section 3 describes the (iterative) local classifier method, while Section 4 explains how many methods can be viewed as random walks. We present additional details on applying the methods to large social networks in Section 5. Sections 6 and 7 discuss other approaches and related problems respectively, and we give concluding remarks in Section 8.

2. Problem Formulation

In this section, we discuss how online social networks (or more generally other networks) can be represented as (weighted) graphs. We then present the formal definition of the node classification problem.

2.1 Representing data as a graph

We consider data from social networks such as Facebook and LinkedIn, as well as other online networks for content access and sharing, such as Netflix,

YouTube and Flickr. As is standard in this area, we choose to represent these networks as graphs of nodes connected by edges. In our setting, we consider graphs of the form $G(V, E, W)$ from this data, where V is the set of n nodes, E is the set of edges and W is the edge weight matrix. We also let $\mathcal{Y}$ be a set of m labels that can be applied to nodes of the graph.

Given a network such as those above, there are typically many choices of how to perform this modeling, depending on which features are captured by the model and which are overlooked. The question of modeling network data is a topic worthy of study on its own. Likewise, the question of how this data is collected and prepared (via random sampling, crawling, or activity monitoring) is beyond the scope of this survey; rather, for this presentation we assume that the data is readily available in the desired graph model. For clarity, we provide some illustrative examples of how (social) network data may be captured by a variety of choices of graph models:

EXAMPLE 5.1 *Consider Facebook as an example of a modern, complex social network. Users of Facebook have the option of entering a variety of personal and demographic information into their Facebook profile. In addition, two Facebook users may interact by (mutually) listing each other as friends, sending a message, posting on a wall, engaging in an IM chat, and so on. We can create a graph representation of the Facebook social network in the form* $G(V, E, W)$, *where*

- *Nodes V: The set of nodes V represents users of Facebook.*

- *Edges E: An edge $(i, j) \in E$ between two nodes v_i, v_j could represent a variety of possibilities: a relationship (friendship, sibling, partner), an interaction (wall post, private message, group message), or an activity (tagging in a photo, playing games). To make this example concrete, consider only edges which represent declared "friendships".*

- *Node Labels $\mathcal{Y}$: The set of labels at a node may include the user's demographics (age, location, gender, occupation), interests (hobbies, movies, books, music) etc. Various restrictions may apply to some labels: a user is allowed to declare only one age and gender, whereas they can be a fan of an almost unlimited number of bands.*

- *Edge Weights W: The weight w_{ij} on an edge between nodes v_i, v_j can be used to indicate the strength of the connection. In our example, it may be a function of interactions among users, e.g., the number of messages exchanged, number of common friends etc.; or it may simply be set to 1 throughout when the link is present.*

EXAMPLE 5.2 *As an example of a different kind of a network, consider the video sharing website, YouTube. Let graph $G(V, E, W)$ represent the YouTube user network, where*

- *Nodes V: A node $v_i \in V$ represents a user.*
- *Edges E: An edge $(i, j) \in E$ between two nodes v_i, v_j could be an explicit link denoting subscription or friend relation; alternately, it could be a derived link where v_i, v_j are connected if the corresponding users have co-viewed more than a certain number of videos.*
- *Node Labels $\mathcal{Y}$: The set of labels at a node may include the user's demographics (age, location, gender, occupation), interests (hobbies, movies, books, music), a list of recommended videos extracted from the site, and so on.*
- *Edge Weights W: The weight on an edge could indicate the strength of the similarity by recording the number of co-viewed videos.*

EXAMPLE 5.3 *Using the same YouTube data, one can derive a quite different graph $G(V, E, W)$, where*

- *Nodes V: A node $v \in V$ represents a video.*
- *Edges E: An edge $(i, j) \in E$ between two nodes v_i, v_j may represent that the corresponding videos are present in certain number of playlists or have been co-viewed by a certain number of people.*
- *Node Labels $\mathcal{Y}$: The set of labels at a node may be the tags or categories assigned to the video, the number of times viewed, time of upload, owner, ratings etc.*
- *Edge Weights W: The weight on an edge may denote the number of users who co-viewed the videos.*

The graphs abstracted in each example vary not only in the semantics of nodes, edges and labels but also in graph properties such as directionality, symmetry and weight. For instance, the friend interactions in Facebook and YouTube are reciprocal, hence a graph G where edges represent friendship relationship is *undirected*, i.e. it has a *symmetric* adjacency matrix. On the other hand, a graph where an edge represents a subscription in YouTube or a wall post in Facebook, is directed. Further, depending on the availability of interaction information, the graph may be *unweighted*, and all edges treated uniformly.

Inducing a graph. In some applications, the input may be a set of objects with no explicit link structure, for instance, a set of images from Flickr. We may choose to *induce* a graph structure for the objects, based on the principles of homophily or co-citation regularity: we should link entities which have similar characteristics (homophily) or which refer to the same objects (co-citation regularity).

Applying these principles, several choices of how to induce graphs have been advocated in the literature, including:

- Materializing the fully connected graph on V where each edge (i, j) is weighted by a suitable distance metric based on the similarity between v_i and v_j. A special case is the exp-weighted graph where the weight on an edge (i, j) is given by:

$$w_{ij} = \exp(-\frac{\|v_i - v_j\|^2}{2\sigma^2}) \tag{5.1}$$

  Here, nodes in V are interpreted as points in a geometric space (such as Euclidean space) and σ^2 represents a normalizing constant, which is the the variance of all points.

- Given a node v_i, let $NN(v_i)$ denote the set of k nearest neighbors, i.e. the k other nodes which are closest based on some measure of distance: this could be cosine or euclidean distance based on the features of the nodes. The k Nearest Neighbor (kNN) graph then has an edge between a pair of nodes v_i, v_j if $v_j \in NN(v_i)$. A kNN graph is by definition a directed graph with each node having outdegree k. An undirected, symmetric kNN graph can be defined where nodes v_i, v_j are connected if $v_i \in NN(v_j) \wedge v_j \in NN(v_i)$, possibly resulting in nodes having degree less than k.

- The ε-weighted graph is where only the subset of edges with weight greater than a threshold ε from the fully connected graph are included.

The methods we describe do not make many assumptions about the nature of the graph or the edge weight distribution, beyond the fact that the weights on edges are assumed to be non-negative and $w_{ij} = 0$ if $(i, j) \notin E$.

Types of Labels. Users of social networks often reveal only partial information about themselves. For instance, only a subset of users reveal their age or location on Facebook. Therefore, the graph abstracted from user-generated data has labels on only a subset of nodes. The labels on nodes can be of different types:

- binary: only two possible values are allowed (gender is often restricted to male or female); equivalently, a label may only appear in the positive form ("smoker") and its absence is assumed to indicate the negative form ("non-smoker").

- numeric: the label takes a numeric value (age, number of views), Only values in some range may be allowed (age restricted to 0-120), or the range may be "bucketized" (age is 0-17; 18-35; 36-50, 50+).
- categorical: the label may be restricted to a set of specified categories (such as for interests, occupation).
- free-text: users may enter arbitrary text to identify the labels that apply to the node (as in listing favorite bands, or tags that apply to a photograph).

Some datasets have many labels in many categories (such as age, gender, location, and interests in a Facebook dataset), while in some cases there may be only a single label recorded (e.g. the only profile information available about a user in Netflix is location). Some label types allow a single value (users may declare only a single age), while others allow many values (users may list many differing tags for a photograph). For node classification, our goal is typically to provide values of a single label type, even though we may have information about other label types to use as features: our goal may be to predict age of Facebook users, given (partial) information about other users' age, sex and location.

In some cases, there may be weights associated with labels. For instance, the video sharing service Hulu displays the number of times each tag was assigned to a video. When normalized, the label-weight vector at each node can be thought of as providing confidence scores, or in some cases as probabilities for different labels. This can arise even when the original data does not exhibit weights: when labels are imputed, these may be given lower confidence scores than labels that were present in the original data. Depending on the dataset, some labels may be known for all nodes (e.g., the number of videos posted by a user on YouTube), and can be used as additional features for inferring the missing values of other labels.

2.2 The Node Classification Problem

We can now formally define the node classification problem.

Problem Statement. We are given a graph $G(V, E, W)$ with a subset of nodes $V_l \subset V$ labeled, where V is the set of n nodes in the graph (possibly augmented with other features), and $V_u = V \setminus V_l$ is the set of unlabeled nodes. Here W is the weight matrix, and E is the set of edges. Let $\mathcal{Y}$ be the set of m possible labels, and $Y_l = \{y_1, y_2, \ldots, y_l\}$ be the initial labels on nodes in the set V_l. The task is to infer labels $\tilde{Y}$ on all nodes V of the graph.

Preliminaries and Definitions. Let V_l be the set of l initially labeled nodes and V_u the set of $n - l$ unlabeled nodes such that $V = V_l \cup V_u$. We assume the nodes are ordered such that the first l nodes are initially labeled and the remaining nodes are unlabeled so that $V = \{v_1, \ldots, v_l, v_{l+1}, \ldots, v_n\}$. An edge $(i,j) \in E$ between nodes v_i and v_j has weight w_{ij}. A transition matrix T is computed by row normalizing the weight matrix W as:

$$T = D^{-1}W$$

where D is a diagonal matrix $D = \text{diag}(d_i)$ and $d_i = \sum_j w_{ij}$. The *unnormalized graph Laplacian* of the graph is defined as: $L = D - W$, and the *normalized graph Laplacian* as: $\mathcal{L} = D^{-1/2}LD^{-1/2}$. If W is symmetric, then both these Laplacians are positive semi-definite matrices.

Let $Y_l = \{y_1, y_2, \ldots, y_l\}$ be the initial labels from the label set $\mathcal{Y}$, on nodes in the set V_l. The label y_i on node v_i may be a binary label, a single label or a multi-label. For binary classification, we may distinguish the presence of a label as $y_i \in \{-1, 1\}$ if $v_i \in V_l$ and 0 otherwise to indicate the absence of a label. For a single label classification, y_i can take values from $\mathcal{Y}$, the range of possible values of that label. Finally, for a multi-class classification, y_i denotes a probability distribution over $\mathcal{Y}$, where $\mathcal{Y}$ is the set of possible labels. For any label $c \in \mathcal{Y}$, $y_i[c]$ is the probability of labeling node v_i with label c. Here, Y_l is a matrix of size $l \times m$. We denote the initial label matrix of size $n \times m$ as Y, such that it has the first l rows as Y_l for labeled nodes and zeros in the next $n - l$ rows representing unlabeled nodes.

The output of the node classification problem is labels $\tilde{Y}$ on all nodes in V. A slightly different problem is to determine the labels on only the unlabeled nodes (i.e., $\tilde{Y}_u$ for nodes in V_u), and assume that the labels on the nodes in V_l are fixed. Another variant is to learn a labeling function f which is used to determine the label on the nodes of the graph.

3. Methods using Local Classifiers

In the following sections we describe the different approaches to solve the node classification problem and its variations. We start by describing a class of iterative methods that use local neighborhood information to generate features that are used to learn local classifiers.

These iterative methods are based on building feature vectors for nodes from the information known about them and their neighborhood (immediately adjacent or nearby nodes). These feature vectors are then used along with the known class values Y_l, to build an instance of a local classifier such as Naive Bayes, Decision Trees etc. for inferring the labels on nodes in V_u.

Algorithm 1 ICA(V, E, W, Y_l)

Compute Φ^1 from V, E, W, Y_l
Train classifier using Φ_l
for $t \leftarrow 1$ **to** τ **do**
  Apply classifier to Φ_u^t to compute Y_u^t
  Update Φ_u^t
$\tilde{Y} \leftarrow Y^\tau$
return $\tilde{Y}$

3.1 Iterative Classification Method

This notion of iteratively building a classifier is quite natural and has appeared several times in the literature. Here, we follow the outline of Neville and Jensen [26].

Input. As with traditional classification problems, a set of attributes may be known for each node $v_i \in V$. These attributes form a part of the feature vector for that node and are known as *node features*. Consider the YouTube graph from Example 5.3: attributes such as the number of times a video is viewed, the time of upload, rating etc. are node features that are known for each video.

What makes classification of graph data different is the presence of links between objects (nodes) being classified. The information about the neighborhood of each object is captured by *link features*, such as the (multi)set of tags on videos. Typically, link features are presented to the classifier as aggregate statistics derived from the labels on nodes in the neighborhood. A popular choice for computing a link feature is the frequency with which a particular label is present in the neighborhood. For instance, for a video v_i in the YouTube graph, the number of times the label *music* appears in the nodes adjacent to v_i is a link feature. If the graph is directed, the link features may be computed separately for incoming and outgoing links. The features may also include graph properties, such as node degrees and connectivity information.

Iterative Framework. Let Φ denote the matrix of feature vectors for all nodes in V, where the i-th row of Φ represents the feature vector ϕ_i for node v_i. The feature vector ϕ_i may be composed of both the node and link features; these are not treated differently within the vector. Let Φ_l and Φ_u denote the feature vectors for labeled and unlabeled nodes respectively. Algorithm 1 presents the Iterative Classification Algorithm (ICA) framework for classifying nodes in a graph. An initial classifier is trained using Φ_l and the given node labels Y_l. In the first iteration, the trained classifier is applied to Φ_u to compute the new labeling Y_u^1. For any node v_i, some previously unlabeled nodes in the

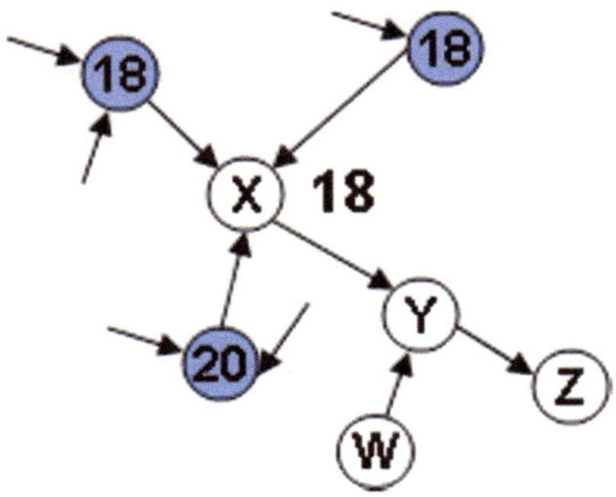

(a) Step 1

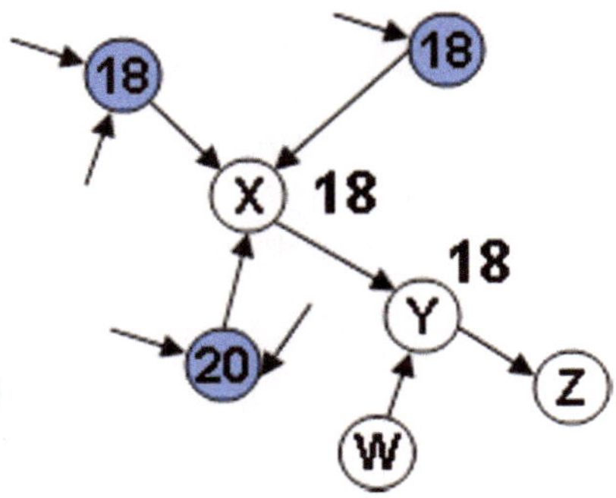

(b) Step 2

Figure 5.1. Two steps of a local iterative approach to node classification

neighborhood of v_i now have labels from Y_u^1. Since link features are computed using the labels in the neighborhood, after applying the classifier once, the values of these features can change. It therefore makes sense to iterate the ICA process. In the tth iteration, the procedure builds a new feature vector Φ^t based on Φ_l and Y_u^{t-1}, and then applies the classifier to produce new labels Y_u^t. Optionally, we may choose to retrain the classifier at each step, over the current set of labels and features.

If node features are not known, the inference is based only on link features. In such a case, if a node has no labeled node in its neighborhood, it is remains unlabeled in the first iteration. As the algorithm proceeds, more nodes are labeled. Thus, the total number of iterations τ should be sufficiently large to at least allow all nodes to receive labels. One possibility is to run the iteration until "stability" is achieved, that is, until no label changes in an iteration—but for arbitrary local classifiers there is no guarantee that stability will be reached. Instead, we may choose to iterate for fixed number of iterations that is considered large enough, or until some large fraction of node labels do not change in an iteration.

Figure 5.1 shows two steps of local iteration on a simple graph. Here, shaded nodes are initially labeled. In this example, the first stage labels node X with the label '18'. Based on this new link feature, in the second iteration this label is propagated to node Y. Additional iterations will propagate the labeling further.

A consequence of basing the labeling solely on the labels of other nodes (a common characteristic of many of the methods we describe in this chapter) is that if the graph contains isolated components that do not have a single labeled node, then all nodes in that component will remain unlabeled, no matter how many iterations are applied.

Instances of the Iterative Framework. Neville *et al.* originally used a Naive Bayes classifier to infer labels in their instantiation of the ICA framework [26]. A strategy they found useful was to sort the predicted class labels in descending order of their associated probability and retain only the top-k labels, thus removing the less confident possibilities. Since then, ICA has been applied to graph data from different domains, with a variety of classifiers. For example, Lu and Getoor [20] applied logistic regression to classify linked documents.

An important special case is the method of Macskassy and Provost [21], who used a simpler classification method based on taking a weighted average of the class probabilities in the neighborhood (effectively "voting" on the label to assign). This classifier is based on a direct application of homophily (the premise that nodes link to other nodes with similar labels), and uses the immediate neighborhood of a node for classification. Bhagat *et al.* [5] proposed a method that considers the labeled nodes in the entire graph. This can be viewed as an instance of ICA using a nearest neighbor classifier to find a labeled node that is most similar to an unlabeled node being classified. It is based on co-citation regularity, the premise that nodes with similar neighborhoods have similar labels. These two simple methods (voting and nearest neighbor) are shown to be surprisingly effective on social network data, achieving quite high accuracy (70-90% on certain demographic labels) from relatively little local information [5].

One of the seminal works on classification of linked documents was by Chakrabarti *et al.* [8]. Their method used features from neighboring documents to aid the classification, which can be viewed as an instance of ICA on a graph formed by documents. Their experiments showed a significant improvement when using link features over just using the text at each node.

4. Random Walk based Methods

The next set of methods we discuss are based on propagating the labels by performing random walks on the graph. These are often thought of as semi-supervised learning or transductive learning methods and can be shown to be equivalent to learning a global labeling function over the graph with provable convergence guarantees. Unlike the iterative methods described so far that rely on computing link features to encode the information in the neighborhood, these methods more explicitly use the link structure for labeling nodes. However, we will see that there are strong connections between random walk and iterative methods.

The idea underlying the random walk methods is as follows: the probability of labeling a node $v_i \in V$ with label $c \in \mathcal{Y}$ is the total probability that a random walk starting at v_i will end at a node labeled c. The various methods proposed in the literature differ in their definition of the random walk used for labeling. For this to provide a complete labeling, the graph G is often assumed to be *label connected* [2]. That is, it is possible to reach a labeled node from any unlabeled node in finite number of steps.

The random walk is defined by a transition matrix P, so that the walk proceeds from node v_i to node v_j with probability p_{ij}, the (i, j)-th entry of P. For this to be well defined, we require $0 \le p_{ij} \le 1$ and $\sum_j p_{ij} = 1$. The matrix P also encodes the *absorbing states* of the random walk. These are nodes where the state remains the same with probability 1, so there is zero probability of leaving the node, i.e., if a random walk reaches such a node, it ends there. Let $p_{ij}^{(t)}$ be the probability of reaching node v_j after t steps of a random walk that started at node v_i, and let P^t denote the corresponding matrix at time t. For $t \to \infty$, the entry p_{ij} of matrix P^∞ represents the probability of the walk that starts at node v_i is at node v_j as the length of the walk tends to infinity. That is, if the *start distribution* is e_i, the vector with 1 at the i-th position and zeros elsewhere, a random walk on G with transition matrix P will converge to a stationary distribution which is the i-th row of the matrix P^∞. We will often be able to show a closed-form expression for P^∞ as a function of P.

Labeling. The walk is typically defined over nodes of the graph, and this is used to define a labeling. The probability of label $c \in \mathcal{Y}$ being assigned to node v_i is computed as the total probability of reaching nodes labeled c on convergence, starting at v_i. More precisely,

$$\tilde{y}_i[c] = \sum_{j|v_j \in V_l} p_{ij}^\infty y_j[c] \tag{5.2}$$

where the input label y_j at $v_j \in V_l$ is assumed to be a probability distribution over labels. If the graph is label connected, as $t \to \infty$ the probability of reaching a labeled node is 1, so it follows that the output labeling $\tilde{y}_i$ at node $v_i \in V$ is also a probability distribution with

$$\sum_{c \in \mathcal{Y}} \sum_{j|v_j \in V_l} p_{ij}^\infty y_j[c] = 1.$$

If the output is required to be a single label on each node, then the most probable label can be assigned to each node, i.e.

$$\tilde{y}_i = \arg\max_{c \in \mathcal{Y}} \sum_{j; y_j = c} p_{ij}^\infty.$$

Recall that Y is the matrix that records the label distribution for each labeled node, and 0 for unlabeled nodes. Consequently, the matrix equation for node classification using random walks can be written as:

$$\tilde{Y} = P^{\infty} Y \tag{5.3}$$

When Y represents a matrix of probability distributions over the label set, then the result can be scaled to ensure that the output is a probability distribution as: $\tilde{Y} = N^{-1} P^{\infty} Y$, where N^{-1} is a diagonal normalization matrix, defined as $N_{ii} = \sum_{j=1}^{m} (P^{\infty} Y)_{ij}$. We next consider various methods based on random walks in detail. Given a description of a random walk, we aim to find a description of the stationary distribution P^{∞}, from which the labeling follows using the above equations.

4.1 Label Propagation

The node classification method of Zhu *et al.* [38] was proposed in the context of semi-supervised learning, where a symmetric weight matrix W is constructed using Equation (5.1). More generally, we consider it to take as input a graph $G(V, E, W)$, from which we derive the matrix $T = D^{-1}W$. Nodes V_l have initial labels Y_l from the label set $\mathcal{Y}$.

Random Walk Formulation. The random walk at node v_i picks an (outgoing) edge with probability proportional to the edge weight, if v_i is unlabeled; however, if v_i is labeled, the walk always loops to v_i. Therefore the nodes in V_l are absorbing states, i.e. they are treated as if they have no outgoing edges, and thus their labels do not change. Since we have ordered the nodes so that the labeled nodes are indexed before the unlabeled nodes, we can write the transition matrix P as a block matrix,

$$P = \begin{pmatrix} P_{ll} & P_{lu} \\ P_{ul} & P_{uu} \end{pmatrix} = \begin{pmatrix} I & 0 \\ P_{ul} & P_{uu} \end{pmatrix} \tag{5.4}$$

where the matrix P_{ll} corresponds to the block of probabilities corresponding to transitions from a labeled node to another labeled node, and so on. Recall that a random walk that reaches a labeled node ends there, thus P_{ll} reduces to I and P_{lu} is a matrix of all zeros. In other words, the transition matrix P can be defined as $P_i = (D^{-1}W)_i$ if $i \in V_u$, else $P_i = e_i$ if $i \in V_l$.

Now, computing the matrix $\lim_{t \to \infty} P^t$, we obtain

$$P^{\infty} = \begin{pmatrix} I & 0 \\ (I - P_{uu})^{-1} P_{ul} & P_{uu}^{\infty} \end{pmatrix}. \tag{5.5}$$

For a graph in which every connected component has a labeled node, each entry of matrix P_{uu} is less than 1. So $P_{uu}^{\infty} = 0$, and P_{ul}^{∞} is a distribution over labeled nodes. By combining Equations (5.3) and (5.5), the labels on unlabeled nodes can be computed as

Algorithm 2 LP-ZHU(Y, P)

$Y^0 \leftarrow Y$
$t \leftarrow 1$
repeat
  $Y^t \leftarrow PY^{t-1}$
  $Y_l^t \leftarrow Y_l$
until convergence to Y^∞
$\tilde{Y} \leftarrow Y^\infty$ **return** $\tilde{Y}$

$$\tilde{Y}_u = (I - P_{uu})^{-1} P_{ul} Y_l \tag{5.6}$$

This provides a precise characterization of how the labels on nodes are computed, and can be applied directly when P_{uu} is small enough to invert directly. The solution is valid only when $(I - P_{uu})^{-1}$ is non-singular, which is true for all label connected graphs.

Observe that if the labeled nodes were not defined to be absorbing states, a random walk over G would converge to a stationary distribution that is independent of the starting point (and hence would not be meaningful for the purpose of labeling). Szummer and Jaakkola [31] considered the variation where the labeled nodes are not forced to be absorbing states. In their definition, they perform random walks for t steps. Such methods depend critically on the parameter t: it is easy to see that the extreme case $t = 1$ gives exactly the local voting scheme of Macskassy and Provost executed for a single iteration, while we argued that allowing t to grow too large, the process mixes, and is independent of the starting location. In experiments, Szummer and Jaakola found small constant values of t to be effective, around $t = 8$ on a dataset with a few thousand examples.

Iterative Formulation. We now show that this random walk is equivalent to a simple iterative algorithm in the limit. Consider an iterative algorithm where each node is assigned a label distribution (or a null distribution) in each step. In step t, each unlabeled node takes the set of distributions of its neighbors from step $t-1$, and takes their mean as its label distribution for step t. The labels of the labeled nodes V_l are not changed. This is essentially the iterative algorithm of Macskassy and Provost [21] described above. The initial label distributions are given by Y. We can observe that each iterative step has the effect of multiplying the previous distribution by P, the block matrix defined above. This is illustrated in Algorithm 2.

The tth iteration of the algorithm sets

$$Y_u^t = P_{ul} Y_l + P_{uu} Y_u^{t-1},$$

which can be rewritten as

$$Y_u^t = \sum_{i=1}^{t} P_{uu}^{i-1} P_{ul} Y_l + P_{uu}^t Y_u.$$

On convergence, we get

$$\tilde{Y}_u = \lim_{t \to \infty} Y^t = (I - P_{uu})^{-1} P_{ul} Y_l.$$

In other words, this iterative algorithm converges to the same labeling as the random walk just described.

Thus, node classification performed by the iterative Algorithm 2 is the same as solving the matrix equation (5.6). Other equivalences can be shown: for an input graph G which has a symmetric weight matrix W and binary labels $\mathcal{Y} = \{0, 1\}$ on nodes, Zhu *et al.* show that labeling using equation (5.6) is equivalent to computing $\tilde{Y}$ using the value of a minimum energy harmonic function $f : V \to \mathbb{R}$ [38].

Rendezvous approach to Label Propagation. Azran [2] showed a different analysis of the label propagation random walk that more strongly uses the assumption that the graph is label connected. Since G is label connected, the probability of moving from one unlabeled node to another after an infinite number of steps is 0, i.e., P_{uu}^{∞} is a zero matrix. Therefore, the limiting matrix P^{∞} has the form:

$$P^{\infty} = \begin{pmatrix} I & 0 \\ (P^{\infty})_{ul} & 0 \end{pmatrix} \tag{5.7}$$

Let $P = S\Lambda S^{-1}$ and $P^{\infty} = S\Lambda^{\infty} S^{-1}$, where S is the matrix of left eigenvectors of P and Λ is the diagonal matrix of eigenvalues. Azran showed that the structure of P and P^{∞} is such that the l leading eigenvalues of both are 1. All other eigenvalues of P have magnitude less than 1, and so are negligible for P^{∞}. Thus, to compute P^{∞}, it is sufficient to compute the l leading eigenvectors of P. Further, the transition matrix defined in Equation (5.7) can be computed as:

$$(P^{\infty})_{ij} = \frac{s_{ij}}{s_{jj}} \tag{5.8}$$

where i, j are indices for unlabeled and labeled nodes respectively. That is, the equation holds for $l + 1 \leq i \leq n$ and $1 \leq j \leq l$. As before, the labels on unlabeled nodes can then be computed using Equation (5.2).

In many applications, the number of unlabeled nodes is typically much larger than the number of labeled nodes. Thus, while inverting the matrix $(I - P_{uu})$ from the label propagation method would be too expensive, computing the l principal eigenvectors of P may be cheaper.

Algorithm 3 LP-ZHOU(Y, α, T)

$t \leftarrow 1$
$Y^0 \leftarrow Y$
repeat
  $Y^t \leftarrow \alpha T Y^{t-1} + (1-\alpha) Y^0$
until convergence to Y^∞
for each $i \in V$ **do**
  $c = \arg\max_{j \in \mathcal{Y}} y_i^\infty[j]$
  $\tilde{y}_i[c] = 1$
return $\tilde{Y}$

4.2 Graph Regularization

The graph regularization method introduced by Zhou *et al.* [36] differs from label propagation in a key way: the labels on nodes in V_l are allowed to change during label propagation. The initial labels are represented by a binary $n \times m$ matrix Y such that $y_i[c] = 1$ if node v_i has label $c \in \mathcal{Y}$, and each node has at most one label.

We first describe the method in terms of a random walk starting from a node v_i. Now the random walk at every node proceeds to a neighbor with probability α (whether or not the node is unlabeled) but, with probability $1-\alpha$ the walk jumps back to v_i, the starting node. Here, $1-\alpha$ can be thought of a "reset probability". In matrix form, the t-step transition probability Q^t can be written as

$$Q^t = \alpha T Q^{t-1} + (1-\alpha) I.$$

This random walk has been well studied in other contexts—in particular, it corresponds to the "personalized page rank", introduced by Jeh and Widom [14] It can be shown to converge, to the stationary distribution

$$Q^\infty = (1-\alpha)(I - \alpha T)^{-1}.$$

Further, the corresponding label distribution can be computed as

$$\tilde{Y} = Q^\infty Y = (1-\alpha)(I - \alpha T)^{-1} Y.$$

Iterative Formulation. As in the previous case, this can also be seen as implementing a simple iterative method: at each step, the label distribution of node i is computed as an α fraction of the sum of label distributions of its neighbors from the previous step, plus a $1-\alpha$ fraction of its initial label distribution. This is illustrated in Algorithm 3. One can verify that this formulation leads to the same solution, i.e. the final label distribution is given by

$$\tilde{Y} = Y^{\infty} = (1-\alpha)(I-\alpha T)^{-1}Y \tag{5.9}$$

which can be scaled up appropriately (via a diagonal normalization matrix) so there is a probability distribution over labels.

Regularization Framework. Zhou *et al.* considered several variations of this method, based on replacing P with related matrices. In particular, they suggest the symmetrically normalizing W via the diagonal matrix of row sums D as, $\mathcal{P} = D^{-1/2}WD^{-1/2}$. $\mathcal{P}$ can also be written in terms of the normalized Laplacian as $\mathcal{P} = I - \mathcal{L}$. This is no longer a stochastic matrix, since the rows do not yield probability distributions. Nevertheless, we can still apply this as a generalized random walk/iterative method by computing $Y^t = \alpha \mathcal{P} Q^{t-1}Y + (1-\alpha)Y$, which converges to $Q^{\infty} = (1-\alpha)(I-\alpha\mathcal{P})^{-1}Y$.

The choice of $\mathcal{P}$ can be seen as arising naturally from some requirements on the labeling. Two such requirements are: (1) the difference between initial and output labels on labeled nodes should be small; and (2) the difference in the labels of neighbors (especially those with large edge weight) should be small, i.e., neighbors should have similar labels.

The task of finding a labeling which satisfies these two conditions can be formulated as an optimization problem to find a function $\tilde{f}$ that minimizes the above two conditions. This process is known as "regularization". Formally, define

$$\tilde{f} = \arg\min_{f} \frac{\mu}{2}\|f - Y\|^2 + f^T \mathcal{L} f,$$

for a parameter $\mu > 0$. The first term measures the difference between the labeling given by the labeling function and the original labeling Y, to capture (1). The second term uses the Laplacian $\mathcal{L}$ (which is related to the gradient of the function) to measure the smoothness of the labeling function, to capture (2). The parameter μ then controls the tradeoff between these two terms. Thus, solving for $\tilde{f}$ is intended to satisfy both the requirements. Rewriting this minimization in terms of the Euclidean norm results in

$$\min_{f} \frac{1}{2} \sum_{i,j=1}^{n} w_{ij} \left\| \frac{f_i}{\sqrt{d_i}} - \frac{f_j}{\sqrt{d_j}} \right\|^2 + \frac{\mu}{2}\|f - Y\|^2 \tag{5.10}$$

Differentiating and equating to zero, we get

$$\tilde{f} - D^{-1/2}WD^{-1/2}\tilde{f} + \mu(\tilde{f} - Y) = 0$$

$$(1+\mu)\tilde{f} - \mathcal{P}\tilde{f} = \mu Y$$

Solving for $\tilde{f}$ and setting $\alpha = \frac{1}{1+\mu}$, we have

$$\tilde{f} = (1 - \alpha)(I - \alpha\mathcal{P})^{-1}Y \tag{5.11}$$

Notice that if we defined the transition matrix Q in terms $\mathcal{P}$ instead of T, or iterated over $\mathcal{P}$ instead of T, the solution on convergence would match Equation (5.9). In other words, we can argue that this solution is a natural consequence of the formalization of the two requirements (1) and (2). It is possible to motivate other node classification algorithms based on similar optimization criteria. The survey of Bengio *et al.* [4] has more details on this perspective.

4.3 Adsorption

The "adsorption" method, proposed by Baluja *et al.* [3] is also based on iteratively averaging the labels from neighbors, in common with the previous algorithms studied. However, this method incorporates some additional features and parameters, so it can be seen as a generalization of other methods.

Adsorption takes as input a directed graph G with weight matrix W. The initial labels are represented as $Y = \{y_1, y_2, \ldots, y_n\}$ such that y_i is the probability distribution over labels $\mathcal{Y}$ if node $v_i \in V_l$, and is zero if node $v_i \in V_u$. As with graph regularization, adsorption does not keep the labels on nodes in V_l fixed, but instead lets them be set by the labeling process. In order to maintain and propagate the initial labeling, adsorption creates a *shadow* vertex $\tilde{v}_i$ for each labeled node $v_i \in V_l$ such that $\tilde{v}_i$ has a single incoming edge to v_i, and no outgoing edges. In other words, the shadow vertex is an absorbing state when we view the algorithm as a random walk. Then, the label distribution y_i is moved from v_i to the corresponding shadow vertex $\tilde{v}_i$, so initially v_i is treated as unlabeled. The set of shadow vertices is $\tilde{V} = \{\tilde{v}_i | v_i \in V_l\}$.

The weight on the edge from a vertex to its shadow is a parameter that can be adjusted. That is, it can be set so that the random walk has a probability $1 - \alpha_i$ of transitioning from vertex v_i to its shadow $\tilde{v}_i$ and terminating. This *injection probability* was set to be a constant such as $\frac{1}{4}$ for all labeled nodes (and 1 for all unlabeled nodes) in the initial experimental study [3].

Random Walk Formulation. Based on this augmented set of nodes and labels, the Adsorption method defines additional matrices. First, A captures the injection probabilities from each node v_i: A is the $n \times n$ diagonal matrix $A = \text{diag}(\alpha_1, \alpha_2, \ldots, \alpha_l, 1, \ldots, 1)$ where $1 - \alpha_i$ is the (injection) probability that a random walk currently at v_i transitions to the shadow vertex $\tilde{v}_i$ and terminates. Hence α_i is the probability that the walk continues to a different neighbor vertex.

A transition matrix T encodes the probability that the walk transitions from v_i to each of its non-shadow neighbors, so $T = D^{-1}W$ as before. Consequently the transitions among the non-shadow vertices are given by (AT), while the transitions to shadow vertices are given by the first l columns of

$(I - A)$, which we denote as $(I - A)_{(l)}$. Putting these pieces together, we obtain an overall transition matrix R over the set of $l + n$ nodes $\tilde{V} \cup V$ as:

$$R = \begin{pmatrix} I & 0 \\ (I - A)_{(l)} & AT \end{pmatrix} \tag{5.12}$$

The first l columns of R represent the transition probabilities to $\tilde{V}$, and the next n columns give the transition probabilities to (within) V. The $(l + i)$-th row of R gives the probability of starting at node v_i for $1 \leq i \leq n$, and moving to the other nodes of the graph in one step. We can compute R^t to give the t-step transition probabilities. Assuming that the graph is label connected, and since $0 \leq \alpha_i \leq 1$ and T is a row stochastic matrix, as $t \to \infty$ we get

$$R^{\infty} = \begin{pmatrix} I & 0 \\ (I - AT)^{-1}(I - A)_{(l)} & 0 \end{pmatrix} \tag{5.13}$$

Let Y_s be the matrix of labels on shadow vertices, i.e, the labels that were originally associated with nodes in V_l, then the matrix of initial labels is defined as: $\bar{Y}^0 = \begin{pmatrix} Y_s \\ 0 \end{pmatrix}$. Then the labeling at step t is $\bar{Y}^t = R^{t-1}\bar{Y}^0$, and as $t \to \infty$,

$$\bar{Y}^{\infty} = R^{\infty}\bar{Y}^0 = \begin{pmatrix} Y_s \\ (I - AT)^{-1}(I - A)_{(l)}Y_s \end{pmatrix} \tag{5.14}$$

It can be verified that $\bar{Y}^{\infty}$ from Equation (5.14) is an eigenvector of R with eigenvalue 1. The output as defined by Equation (5.14) is also a linear combination of the initial labels. Since R and its powers are row stochastic matrices, and the initial labels are probability distributions, the output at each node is guaranteed to be probability distribution over labels. The resulting labeling can be rewritten in terms of the original graph (without shadow vertices) as:

$$\tilde{Y} = (I - AT)^{-1}(I - A)_{(l)}Y_l \tag{5.15}$$

Iterative Formulation. We now describe a local averaging method that is equivalent to the random walk method described above. Consider the graph G and weight matrix W as above, but with the directionality of all edges reversed. At each iteration, the algorithm computes the label distribution at node v_i as a weighted sum of the labels in the neighborhood, and the node's initial labeling, the weight being given by α_i. Formally, at the t-th iteration, for a node $v_i \in V$, the label distribution is computed as

$$y_i^t = \alpha_i \sum_j p_{ji} y_j^{t-1} + (1 - \alpha_i) y_i^0 \tag{5.16}$$

Rewriting Equation (5.16) as a matrix equation, with $Y^0 = \begin{pmatrix} Y_l \\ 0 \end{pmatrix}$, and $A = \text{diag}(\alpha_1, \alpha_2, \ldots, \alpha_l, 1, \ldots, 1)$ as before,

$$\begin{aligned} Y^t &= ATY^{t-1} + (I - A)Y^0 \\ &= (AT)^{t-1}Y^0 + \sum_{i=0}^{t-1}(AT)^i(I - A)Y^0 \end{aligned}$$

We know that $0 \leq \alpha_i \leq 1$, and T is a stochastic matrix, thus as $t \to \infty$, we reach

$$\tilde{Y} = Y^\infty = (I - AT)^{-1}(I - A)Y^0 \tag{5.17}$$

Connection to other methods. Observe that Equations (5.17) and (5.15) can be made to agree, since Y^0 has first l rows non-zero and remaining u rows as zeros. In particular, (5.9) can be obtained from (5.17) by setting $A_{ii} = \alpha$ for all i. In other words, the graph regularization method can be viewed as a special case of adsorption. This can be seen by comparing the description of the iterative formulations of both, and observing that both rely on averaging neighborhoods with the original label of a node. However, the definition of adsorption prefers to set α_i to be 1 for unlabeled nodes, to ensure that the final labeling is directly a probability distribution over labels without rescaling.

A second equivalence is achieved by setting $\alpha_i = 0$ for all (initially) labeled nodes. This has the effect of making them absorbing (any random walk which reaches them halts there with probability 1) and so we obtain the original label propagation algorithm again. This analysis shows that the adsorption method unifies the previous random walk methods.

5. Applying Node Classification to Large Social Networks

Our motivation for node classification comes from social networks. These networks can have millions of nodes and billions of edges, and the label set may consist of thousands of labels, e.g., the set of all tags on videos in YouTube. As we have indicated in our discussion, it be very computationally expensive to directly apply some of the methods described to datasets of this size. In particular, several methods are described in terms of finding the solution to a set of matrix equations. For example, in the random walk based method by Zhou *et al.*, using Equation (5.9) requires inverting a matrix of size $n \times n$, where n is the number of nodes in the graph. In general, inverting this matrix takes time $O(n^3)$, although for sparse matrices methods from numerical analysis aim to compute the inverse (approximately) more quickly [12]. Similarly, the method by Azran *et al.* requires computing the l leading eigenvectors of an $n \times n$ matrix, which can be done in time $O(n^2)$ for a sparse matrix. When n is large, costs that are significantly superlinear in n are not feasible, and we look for more scalable solutions.

5.1 Basic Approaches

When matrix inversion is not practical, there are several alternate approaches to finding the stationary distribution of the random walks we consider:

Iteration. When the number of labels $m \ll n$, it can be more efficient to work with the iterative form of the random walk, applied to Y. That is, rather than compute the $(n \times n)$ stationary distribution via P^∞, instead compute the $(n \times m)$ stationary distribution of label probabilities Y^∞. This in turn is computed by iterating to compute $Y^1, Y^2, \ldots$. In the limit, this converges to Y^∞.

In practice, we may not run this procedure to convergence, but rather for a sufficiently large fixed number of iterations, or until the difference $\|Y_u^t - Y_u^{t-1}\|$ is sufficiently small. Such power iteration methods are known to converge exponentially quickly (i.e. the difference $\|Y_u^t - Y_u^\infty\|$ decreases by a constant factor each iteration) [17]. Hence only a constant number of steps is needed to reach a close enough approximation—of the order of tens to a hundred iterations.

Random Walk Simulation. An alternative approach is to directly simulate r random walks that begin at v_i for some number of steps, and use the distribution of the end point of these random walks as a surrogate for the stationary distribution. In some situations, such as where the graph is too large to represent as a matrix and compute matrix multiplications with, it may be more efficient to instead simulate random walks, which just require to access the adjacency lists of visited nodes, to pick the next node. This has been applied when the data is too large to store in memory [28].

5.2 Second-order Methods

When the classification method can be formalized as a matrix iteration, as in the random walk methods, then there have been many approaches suggested to reducing the number of iterations needed before the process converges. The main idea behind these *second-order methods* is that the update performed at each iteration is adjusted by the update performed at the previous iteration. These methods have been shown to converge more rapidly than simple iterations (referred to as *first-order methods*) for applications such as load balancing [24] and multi-commodity flow [25]. For node classifica-

Algorithm 4 MAP(Key v_i, Value y_i^{t-1})

Data: P
for each $v_j \in V|(i,j) \in E$ **do**
  emit $(v_j, (y_i^{t-1}, p_{ij}))$

Algorithm 5 REDUCE(Key v_j, ValueIterator $labelWt$)

$vec_{1\times m} \leftarrow 0$
for each $(label, wt) \in labelWt$ **do**
  $vec[label]$ += wt
$y_j^t \leftarrow \arg\max(vec)$
emit (v_j, y_j^t)

tion, a first order iteration of the form $Y^{t+1} = PY^t$ can be reformulated as $Y^{t+1} = \beta PY^t + (1-\beta)Y^{t-1}$ to yield a second-order method. Here, β is a parameter weighting the current update. Second order methods have been shown to converge faster for $1 \leq \beta \leq 2$.

5.3 Implementation within Map-Reduce

The Map-Reduce framework [9] is a popular programming model that facilitates distributing computation over a cluster of machines for data-intensive tasks. Applications in this framework are implemented via two operations (1) Map: input represented as key/value pairs is processed to generate intermediate key/value pairs, and (2) Reduce: all intermediate pairs associated with the same key are collected and aggregated. The system takes care of allocating map and reduce tasks to different machines, which can operate in parallel.

This framework is particularly powerful for cases when the data being processed is so large that it does not fit on one machine, but must be stored in a distributed file system, as may be the case for social network data. We observe that all of the methods discussed so far fit well into the map-reduce model: both local iterative methods and random walk methods can be implemented so that each node collects information about its neighbors (map), and applies some process to compute its new label distribution (reduce).

We illustrate the power of Map-Reduce to distribute computations over large social networks with an example implementation of iterative graph labeling methods. Consider a simple instance of the ICA method, where the classifier is based on weighted voting on labels in the neighborhood, as described in [5]. More specifically, at each iteration of the method, the label assigned to a node is the weighted vote of labels on its neighbors. This can be thought of as an iterative message passing scheme, where each node passes its current label (weighted by the edge weight) as a message to each neighbor. Then, each node collects the messages received from its neighbors and combines then to compute its label, in this case using a voting function.

This process fits neatly into the Map-Reduce setting. Algorithms 4 and 5 describe the Map and Reduce operations performed at each iteration of node classification. As described in Section 2, P is the normalized weight matrix and Y is a vector of initial labels, so that y_i is a single label initially assigned to node v_i, and y_i^t is the label at the t-th iteration. vec is a temporary vector to aggregate the weight received for each label. The Map function implements the message passing, where each node v_i sends a message (y_i^{t-1}, p_{ij}) at iteration t. The Reduce function receives the messages as $labelWt$ and aggregates them to infer the label y_j^t at a node v_j at iteration t.

Likewise, many other iterative algorithms for node classification can be implemented in Map-Reduce. One round of Map-Reduce computes each iteration (equivalently, computes the product of a matrix and a vector). Thus only a moderate number of rounds are required to converge on the solution.

6. Related approaches

In this section, we survey some of the other approaches to the node classification problem.

6.1 Inference using Graphical Models

The area of Statistical Relational Learning (SRL) has emerged over the last decade. SRL is generally concerned with creating models of data which fully describes the correlations between the different objects that are described by the data. It therefore encompasses node classification as a central problem. Another example of a problem in SRL is edge prediction: creating a model which can be used to predict which new edges are likely to be formed in a graph.

Among many approaches proposed within the SRL framework, two that have been directly applied to the node classification problem are Probabilistic Relational Models (PRMs) [10, 33] and Relational Markov Network Models (RMNs) [32]. Essentially, the two approaches learn a probabilistic graph model to represent the relational (graph) data. The model used is a Bayesian network (directed) for PRMs and a Markov network (undirected) for RMNs. The learnt models are then used to perform inference or labeling over the graphs.

Formally, the nodes V in the given graph G are represented by random variables X which can take values from the set $\mathcal{Y}$. Let X_l denote the observed random variables associated with labeled nodes and X_u be the unobserved variables for the unlabeled nodes. The task is to determine the joint probability distribution $P(X_u|X_l)$, i.e., the probability distribution over the labels for each unobserved variable (unlabeled node), given the observed variables (labeled nodes), and use it for inference.

In PRMs, each random variable x_i representing node v_i is associated with a conditional probability distribution $\mathbb{P}(x_i|\text{parents}(x_i))$, where $\text{parents}(x_i)$ is the set of label assignments on nodes that have an outgoing edge to node v_i. In the case of RMNs, a pairwise Markov Random Field (MRF) is defined over the graph that is parametrized by a set of arbitrary non-negative functions known as clique potentials.

These relational models are represented by a joint probability distribution of label assignments over nodes of the graph. This stands in contrast to methods such as random walks for graph labeling, which do not make these models for the label of a node explicit, but rather which use an implicit model to compute the labeling. To use a relational model for node classification, we must compute the marginal probability distribution for each node. However, this is not a simple task, since there are correlations (mutual dependencies) between the distributions on the nodes, and so there is no compact closed form for these marginals.

A popular choice for approximate inference in relational models is loopy belief propagation (LBP). LBP is an iterative message passing algorithm, where a message sent from node v_i to v_j is the belief of v_i on what the value of v_j should be. Pragmatically, this seems similar in spirit to the iterative methods which pass messages in the form of distributions of label values. LBP does not guarantee convergence except for special cases such as when the graphical model is a tree. Nevertheless, it has been found to work well in practice [34].

6.2 Metric labeling

There has been much other work on the problem of labeling objects when there are some relationships known between them. A central example is the work by Kleinberg and Tardos [15] that describes the problem of *Metric Labeling*. Here, there is a collection of objects with pairwise relationships between them (so relationships can be modeled as a graph). Each object also has an initial label (for example, this could be a user's declared age in a setting where many users do not reveal their true demographics). There are therefore two forces at work in the labeling: to pick labels which are consistent with the assigned labels of neighboring objects (due to implicit assumption of homophily), and to pick labels which are consistent with the initial labels. Kleinberg and Tardos formalize this problem by defining two functions, the first defined over (initial label, assigned label) pairs, and the second defined over (assigned label, neighbor's assigned label) pairs.

This then naturally defines an optimization problem over graphs: given the initial labeling of nodes, the edges, and the two cost functions, choose a labeling with minimum cost summed over all nodes and edges. Using the language of combinatorial optimization, this becomes a well-defined optimization problem, since every assignment has an associated cost: therefore, there must exist some assignment(s) with minimum cost. Kleinberg and Tardos are able to give guaranteed *approximations* to this problem: they show an algorithm to find an assignment whose cost is more expensive than the optimal one by a factor that is at most logarithmic in the number of labels. The approach relies on solving a carefully defined linear program, and arguing that rounding the fractional solution gives a good approximation to the original problem.

Applying this approach to the node classification problem is possible, but requires some effort. First, one needs to choose appropriate metrics over labels, and to extend these to capture the case of missing labels (which should not be penalized excessively by the metric over neighbors). Second, for graphs of social networks, it is necessary to solve a linear program defined over all the edges and nodes in the graph, which may stretch the limits of modern solvers.

6.3 Spectral Partitioning

A different approach studied by McSherry [23] is to use spectral methods (study of eigenvalues and eigenvectors) to recover a labeling. For the analysis, the graph is assumed to have been produced by a random process. Each of the n nodes in V has a (secret) initial label from the m possibilities. It is assumed that edges are created by a random process: let Q be an $m \times m$ matrix where q_{ij} denotes the probability of including an edge between a node with label i and node with label j for $i, j < m$. In this model, the given graph G is drawn from the distribution implied by the hidden labels and Q. Computing the maximum-likelihood labeling is NP-hard in this setting, so McSherry presents an algorithm based on random partitioning and projections to infer the true labeling on the nodes of the graph with high probability.

Sidiropoulos (in the survey of Aggarwal *et al.* [1] points out that in most cases, it is not realistic to consider connections between all pairs of objects in the generative model. Hence the distribution of graphs considered by McSherry does not correspond to typical social network graphs. To better model such graphs, they consider a slightly modified model where for a given graph H, each edge e of H is *removed* with probability $1 - q_{ij}$, where i, j are labels on the endpoints of e and Q is the $m \times m$ matrix of probabilities as before. Sidiropoulos argues that for arbitrary graphs H, it is not possible to recover almost all labels with high probability, but that simple algorithms may still recover a constant fraction of labels.

6.4 Graph Clustering

A set of approaches proposed for node classification are based on partitioning the nodes into clusters and assigning the same label to the nodes in the cluster. Blum and Chawla [7] assume that the weights on edges of the graph denote similarity between the associated nodes. Thus, a high edge weight means the nodes are very similar. A binary classification problem is solved by finding a "mincut": a partition of the nodes to minimize the number of edges crossing the cut. The intuition is that placing highly connected nodes in the same class will separate the nodes labeled "positive" from the "negative" ones. Such problems can be solved in polynomial time using classical max-flow algorithms. This approach is motivated by observing that on certain cases, finding the minimum cut produces the smallest classification error.

Similar ideas are used by Shi and Malik [30], who propose a graph partitioning method for image segmentation. An image is represented as a graph, where a node represented a pixel in the image and the weight on an edge between two nodes represented the similarity between the pixel features (brightness, color etc.). After normalizing the edge weights, it is shown that the solution is equivalent to computing the second smallest eigenvector of a suitable matrix defined using the graph laplacian.

A recently proposed method by Zhou *et al.* [37] considers partitioning a graph based on both structural and attribute similarity of nodes of the graph. To combine the contribution of both types of feature, Zhou *et al.* define an *attribute augmented graph*, where new nodes are introduced for each attribute value. An edge is created between an existing node v_i and an attribute node if v_i has the corresponding attribute. To compute similarity between nodes, a distance measure based on a random walk is computed over the augmented graph, as in Section 4. However, rather than assign labels directly from the distribution of nodes reached, the method clusters nodes based on the random walk distance of pairs of nodes, via a method such as k-Medoids. Thus each cluster is assumed to consist of nodes that have similar labels: empirically, this was used to cluster (label) blogs based on political leaning, and researchers based on their research topic.

7. Variations on Node Classification

In this section, we identify a few generalizations of the graph labeling problem and methods which have been proposed for them.

7.1 Dissimilarity in Labels

Goldberg *et al.* [11] make the observation that nodes may link to each other even if they do not have similar labels. Consider the graph in Example 5.2, where an edge represents two videos that are often co-viewed. These videos may represent the two sides of a polarized debate, so the co-viewing relation could indicate that the videos are *dissimilar*, not similar. This can be formalized by allowing two types of edge, indicating either affinity or disagreement. Goldberg *et al.*assume that the type of each edge is known. For the case of binary labels, the goal is to find a function f which maps nodes to either the +1 class or the -1 class. This is formalized as trying to minimize the following cost function:

$$\sum_{i,j} w_{ij}(f(v_i) - s_{ij} f(v_j))^2$$

where s_{ij} is 1 if edge (i, j) is a similarity edge and -1 otherwise and w_{ij} is the edge weight as before. This minimization requires solving a quadratic program to find f to label the graph. It can be extended to the multi-class setting by introducing a labeling function f_k for each class. Such programs can be solved for a moderate number of examples (hundreds to thousands) but may not scale to huge graphs.

7.2 Edge Labeling

Thus far in our discussion of node classification, we have assumed the weight matrix W is known, or can be computed directly from node attribute similarity. But in fact the problem of computing edge weights can be abstracted as a problem in itself, to infer labels on edges of a graph. The simplest case is the binary classification problem to label the edges as positive or negative. For instance, in a network of blogs, a user may connect to users with whom they either (broadly) agree or disagree. Leskovec *et al.* [19] study the problem of classifying edges as positive and negative through the lens of two theories from social science literature: Balance and Status. The balance theory is based on notions such as “the friend of my friend is my friend”, “the enemy of my friend is my enemy” etc. to balance the signs on edges within a triad. The status theory asserts that a positive (negative) edge from v_i to v_j indicates that the v_i believes that v_j has a higher (lower) status that v_i. Given two edges connecting three users, both models can predict the sign of the third edge, but disagree on some cases. Analyzing real data shows that balance tends to model the case of undirected edges, while status better captures the directed case.

Goyal *et al.* [13] studied a problem of edge labeling with applications such as viral marketing, where it is useful to know the influence that a user has on his neighbors. The problem is formulated as that of inferring a weight $0 \leq w_{ij} \leq 1$ on each edge (i, j), termed as an influence probability. Specifically, influence is measured in terms of actions performed by neighbors of a user after the user has performed those actions. The authors present static and time-dependent models for learning edge weights.

Krushevskaja and Muthukrishnan [16] formulate a more general edge labeling problem, for arbitrary sets of possible edge labels. Formally, given a graph $G(V, E)$ with nodes V and edges E, a subset of the edges $E_l \subset E$ are labeled. A label y_i on edge $e_i \in E_l$ is a probability distribution over the label set $\mathcal{Y}$. The goal is to label all edges in the graph. As an example, consider a social network graph, with users represented by nodes and interactions between users represented by edges in the graph. The set of labels consists of types of interactions such as email, public post, tag in a photo, and video message. A subset of edges are labeled with a probability distribution over the label set. The probability associated with a label, say *email*, at any edge is the likelihood of the corresponding pair of users interacting by email. Krushevskaja and Muthukrishnan study two algorithms for the edge labeling problem, one in which edge labeling is reduced to node labeling on a line graph, and the other is a direct random walk based approach to edge labeling.

7.3 Label Summarization

In applications involving user generated data, such as tagging videos in YouTube (Example 5.3), a classification algorithm might choose a non-zero probability for a large number of labels on a given node. Simply picking the most likely few labels is not optimal: the chosen tags may be redundant, picking synonyms and omitting ones which better capture the content. A secondary concern is that computing the final label distribution is more costly if the algorithm has to store a complete label distribution for each node at each intermediate step. Given this motivation, Bhagat *et al.* [6] formulate a space-constrained variant of the graph labeling problem, where each node has space to store at most k labels and associated weights. That is, given a partially labeled graph, the goal is to output a label summary of size k at each node.

The simplest approach to solving the space-constrained labeling problem is to perform one of the node classification methods discussed earlier, and to prune each computed distribution to have only k labels. A more sophisticated approach is to summarize label distributions using the semantic relationship among labels, modeled as a hierarchy over the label set. Now the goal is to choose k appropriate labels from the hierarchy to best represent the computed distribution at each step. Such algorithms can run in small space, requiring space proportional to the number of labels in the neighborhood at any node.

8. Concluding Remarks

The problem of node classification has been defined and addressed in many works over the last 15 years, prompted by the growth of large networks such as the web, social networks, and other social media. In this chapter, we have surveyed the main lines of work, based on iterative methods and random walks, as well as several variations. When viewed from the right perspective, there is a surprising commonality between many methods: the methods discussed in Section 4, and several of the methods in Section 3 can all be seen as generating the labeling from the occupancy probabilities of a random walk over the graph. The universality of this concept, which may not have been obvious from the original papers, can be motivated from both linear algebraic and optimization considerations.

8.1 Future Directions and Challenges

Having surveyed so many approaches to this problem, we step back to ask the question, "Given a partially labeled graph, do we know how to classify the other nodes?". The short answer to this question is "no". Partly this is because the problem is underspecified: unless we make strong assumptions about the process that generates a true but hidden labeling, we are unable to prove any theorems which quantify the quality of any inferred labeling. So, as with other problems in the machine learning world, we should seek to evaluate solutions, by withholding some known labels and comparing the imputed labels on these nodes. Here, we enounter two limitations in the current literature. Firstly, some proposed methods do not scale up to the large graphs that result from the motivating social network setting, and have only been tested on graphs of a few thousand nodes or not at all. Secondly, for those techniques which do scale, there has been little attempt to compare multiple methods on the same baseline. A step in the right direction is the work of Macskassy and Provost [22], which compares multiple methods on relatively small data sets (hundreds to thousands of nodes).

Given these shortcomings, we identify the following challenges for the area:

- The random walk and iterative approaches have the advantage of being easy to implement and distribute via Map-Reduce. A next step is to provide baseline implementations of several of these methods, and to evaluate them across a common test set of large graphs derived from social networks to compare the behavior.

- Other methods suggested based on classical graph algorithms, combinatorial optimization, and spectral properties have not yet been tested on the large graphs which arise in from social networks. A natural next step is to understand how well approaches such as metric labeling, spectral partitioning and inference perform at this task, in terms of both accuracy and scalability. In particular, can they be implemented within the Map-Reduce framework?

- The complex models which arise from relational learning are typically solved by approximate message passing algorithms such as loopy belief propagation. Are there special cases of these models for which the LBP solution coincides with a known iterative algorithm? This would show a novel connection between these approaches.

- It is open to see if new algorithms can be developed which combine aspects from multiple different labeling methods to achieve a labeling which is better than that from any individual method (i.e. hybrid algorithms).
- Many methods are motivated based on hypotheses about what links are present: homophily, co-citation regularity, balance, status etc. To what extent can these hypotheses be tested within large scale data?

8.2 Further Reading

Several other sources have discussed different aspects of the graph labeling problem and its generalizations. As mentioned in Section 4.2, the survey by Bengio *et al.* [4] relates the semi-supervised learning methods in the context of optimizing a quadratic cost function.

The survey of Sen *et al.* [29] compares various node classification methods including ICA and relational learning method RMN that uses LBP. They empirically compare the methods on document classification tasks and show that the simple ICA method is the most efficient. The authors note that although in some experiments LBP had better labeling accuracy than ICA, but learning the parameters for the method is not trivial. Macskassy and Provost [22] survey different approaches, and give empirical comparisons on some web-based data sets. The tutorial of Neville and Provost [27] presents the machine learning perspective, and has slides and a reading list available.

Acknowledgments

The work of the first and third authors is supported by NSF grant 0916782.

References

[1] G. Aggarwal, N. Ailon, F. Constantin, E. Even-Dar, J. Feldman, G. Frahling, M. R. Henzinger, S. Muthukrishnan, N. Nisan, M. Pal, M. Sandler, and A. Sidiropoulos. Theory research at google. *ACM SIGACT News archive*, 39, 2008.

[2] A. Azran. The rendezvous algorithm: Multiclass semi-supervised learning with markov random walks. In *ICML*, 2007.

[3] S. Baluja, R. Seth, D. Sivakumar, Y. Jing, J. Yagnik, S. Kumar, D. Ravichandran, and M. Aly. Video suggestion and discovery for youtube: Taking random walks through the view graph. In *WWW*, 2008.

[4] Y. Bengio, O. Delalleau, and N. Le Roux. Label propagation and quadratic criterion. In O. Chapelle, B. Scholkopf, and A. Zien, editors, *Semi-Supervised Learning*, pages 193–216. MIT Press, 2006.

[5] S. Bhagat, G. Cormode, and I. Rozenbaum. Applying link-based classification to label blogs. In *Joint 9th WEBKDD and 1st SNA-KDD Workshop*, 2007.

[6] S. Bhagat, S. Muthukrishnan, and D. Sivakumar. Hierarchical probabilistic node labeling, 2010. Manuscript.

[7] A. Blum and S. Chawla. Learning from labeled and unlabeled data using graph mincuts. In *ICML*, 2001.

[8] S. Chakrabarti, B. Dom, and P. Indyk. Enhanced hypertext categorization using hyperlinks. In *ACM SIGMOD*, 1998.

[9] J. Dean and S. Ghemawat. Mapreduce: Simplified data processing on large clusters. In *OSDI*, 2004.

[10] N. Friedman, L. Getoor, D. Koller, and A. Pfeffer. Learning probabilistic relational models. In *IJCAI*, 1999.

[11] A. B. Goldberg, X. Zhu, and S. Wright. Dissimilarity in graph-based semisupervised classification. In *Eleventh International Conference on Artificial Intelligence and Statistics (AISTATS)*, 2007.

[12] G. H. Golub and C. F. Van Loan. *Matrix computations (3rd ed.)*. Johns Hopkins University Press, 1996.

[13] A. Goyal, F. Bonchi, and L. V. S. Lakshmanan. Learning influence probabilities in social networks. In *WSDM*, 2010.

[14] G. Jeh and J. Widom. Scaling personalized web search. In *WWW*, 2003.

[15] J. Kleinberg and E. Tardos. Approximation algorithms for classification problems with pairwise relationships: Metric labeling and markov random fields. In *FOCS*, 1999.

[16] D. Krushevskaja and S. Muthukrishnan. Inferring multi-labels on relationships, 2010. Manuscript.

[17] A. N. Langville and C. D. Meyer. The use of linear algebra by web search engines. *IMAGE Newsletter*, 33:2–6, December 2004.

[18] A. Lenhart and M. Madden. Teens, privacy and online social networks. `http://www.pewinternet.org/Reports/2007/Teens-Privacy-and-Online-Social-Networks.aspx`, 2007.

[19] J. Leskovec, D. Huttenlocher, and J. Kleinberg. Predicting positive and negative links in online social networks. In *WWW*, 2010.

[20] Q. Lu and L. Getoor. Link-based classification. In *ICML*, 2003.

[21] S. A. Macskassy and F. Provost. A simple relational classifier. In *MRDM Workshop, SIGKDD*, 2003.

[22] Sofus A. Macskassy and Foster Provost. Classification in networked data: A toolkit and a univariate case study. *Journal of Machine Learning*, 8:935–983, May 2007.

[23] F. McSherry. Spectral partitioning of random graphs. In *FOCS*, 2001.

[24] S. Muthukrishnan, B. Ghosh, and M. H. Schultz. First- and second-order diffusive methods for rapid, coarse, distributed load balancing. *Theory Comput. Syst.*, 31(4), 1998.

[25] S. Muthukrishnan and T. Suel. Second-order methods for distributed approximate single- and multicommodity flow. In *RANDOM*, 1998.

[26] J. Neville and D. Jensen. Iterative classification in relational data. In *Workshop on Learning Statistical Models from Relational Data, AAAI*, 2000.

[27] J. Neville and F. Provost. Predictive modeling with social networks. `http://www.cs.purdue.edu/homes/neville/courses/icwsm09-tutorial.html`, 2009.

[28] A. D. Sarma, S. Gollapudi, and R. Panigrahy. Estimating pagerank on graph streams. In *PODS*, 2008.

[29] P. Sen, G. M. Namata, M. Bilgic, L. Getoor, B. Gallagher, and T. Eliassi-Rad. Collective classification in network data. *AI Magazine*, 29(3):93–106, 2008.

[30] J. Shi and J. Malik. Normalized cuts and image segmentation. In *IEEE Transactions on Pattern Analysis and Machine Intelligence*, 1997.

[31] M. Szummer and T. Jaakkola. Partially labeled classification with markov random walks. In *NIPS*, 2001.

[32] B. Taskar, P. Abbeel, and D. Koller. Discriminative probabilistic models for relational data. In *UAI*, 2002.

[33] B. Taskar, E. Segal, and D. Koller. Probabilistic classification and clustering in relational data. In *IJCAI*, 2001.

[34] J. S. Yedidia, W. T. Freeman, and Y. Weiss. Constructing free-energy approximations and generalized belief propagation algorithms. In *IEEE Transactions on Information Theory*, 2005.

[35] W. W. Zachary. An information flow model for conflict and fission in small groups. *Journal of Anthropological Research*, 33:452–473, 1977.

[36] D. Zhou, O. Bousquet, T. N. Lal, J. Weston, and B. Scholkopf. Learning with local and global consistency. In *NIPS*, 2004.

[37] Y. Zhou, H. Cheng, and J. X. Yu. Graph clustering based on structural/attribute similarities. In *VLDB*, 2009.

[38] X. Zhu, Z. Ghahramani, and J. Lafferty. Semi-supervised learning using Gaussian fields and harmonic functions. In *ICML*, 2003.

Chapter 6

EVOLUTION IN SOCIAL NETWORKS: A SURVEY

Myra Spiliopoulou
Otto-von-Guericke-University Magdeburg
Magdeburg, Germany
myra@iti.cs.uni-magdeburg.de

Abstract There is much research on social network analysis but only recently did scholars turn their attention to the volatility of social networks. An abundance of questions emerged. How does a social network evolve – can we find laws and derive models that explain its evolution? How do communities emerge in a social network and how do they expand or shrink? What *is* a community in an evolving network – can we claim that two communities seen at two distinct timepoints are the same one, even if they have next to no members in common? Research advances have different perspectives: some scholars focus on how evolution manifests itself in a social network, while others investigate how individual communities evolve as new members join and old ones become inactive. There are methods for discovering communities and capturing their changes in time, and methods that consider a community as a smoothly evolving constellation and thus build and adapt models upon that premise. This survey organizes advances on evolution in social networks into a common framework and gives an overview of these different perspectives.

Keywords: Dynamic social networks, social network evolution, community evolution, stream clustering, incremental tensor-based clustering, dynamic probabilistic models

1. Introduction

Evolution in social networks is a research domain of some intricacy. Understanding the evolution of social communities is an appealing subject, but the evolution of the social networks themselves is a distinct, no less captivating problem. The underpinnings of social network evolution are to be found in modeling and studying evolving graphs. In contrast, an evolving community is not necessarily part of an evolving graph: many scholars rather perceive a community as a group of individuals that have some features in common. These different perceptions have lead to different methods for the study of community evolution and to different definitions of the concept "evolving community". This study is a survey of the advances on understanding and on predicting the evolution of social constellations, sometimes called social networks, other times called communities and often modeled as graphs.

Informally, evolution refers to a change that manifests itself across the time axis. In the field of *Knowledge Discovery from Data*, there is a distinction between mining static data and mining a data stream. The stream paradigm of computation dictates that instances arrive in sequential order and each instance is seen only once [22]. Stream mining algorithms must solve the challenge of adapting a model over the new data under resource constraints. Some stream mining algorithms focus on monitoring model evolution, i.e. understanding how the model changes. Stream mining algorithms that adapt or monitor evolving communities are obviously within the scope of our survey, albeit graph stream mining is not. The reader is referred to [49] for an overview of stream algorithms on graphs. Further, an in-depth discussion on laws explaining (dynamic) graphs can be found in [9].

In his report on community detection in graphs [18], Fortunato devotes the small chapter 13 to the "Detection of Dynamic Communities" [18] and elaborates on the works of [36, 5, 42, 10, 11, 28] (in order of appearance), methods that the reader will also find in the next pages. Since the survey starting below is devoted solely to evolution, the emphasis is on placing these and many other methods in a comprehensive framework, stressing their commonalities and their differences *in objectives, assumptions, methodology and perspective*.

The survey is organized as follows. In Section 2, we take the stream paradigm of computation as basis for the study of social network dynamics. We organize research advances on social network evolution across different dimensions that capture the perspective taken and the axioms defined in the individual studies. We distinguish between methods that study community evolution in a social network (Sections 3-5) and methods that use all temporal data to derive a single static model that captures the dynamics of the network (Section 6).

Section 3 identifies challenges on community evolution. We identify two main threads in this topic. Communities can be perceived as clusters built at each timepoint: analysis of community evolution involves tracing the same community/cluster at consecutive timepoints and identifying changes. Research advances in this thread are discussed in Section 4. But communities can also be perceived as *smoothly* evolving constellations: community monitoring then involves learning models that adapt smoothly from one timepoint to the next. We elaborate on this thread in Section 5. In Section 6, we discuss examples of evolutionary methods that build one model of social network dynamics, exploiting all data within a given time horizon. The last section concludes this chapter with a discussion of open issues on community evolution.

2. Framework

The activities of the participants of a social network constitute a stream. We therefore use the stream model of computation [22] to describe an evolving social network across the time axis, albeit this representation is not always supported by current algorithms for dynamic social networks. We then identify different perspectives for the study of evolution on a social network. This leads, in section 2.2, to the multi-dimensional framework of this survey.

2.1 Modeling a Network across the Time Axis

A social network is a graph $G(V, E)$ where V is the set of nodes and V is the set of edges. For our purposes, we study the graph across the time axis and assume a series of discrete timepoints $t_1, \ldots, t_{n-1}, t_n, \ldots$. At timepoint t_i we observe the graph instance $G(V_i, E_i)$ which we will also denote as G_i. The most obvious changes that may occur between two timepoints t_{i-1} and t_i are the addition of edges, i.e. $E_i \supset E_{i-1}$, and the appearance of additional nodes, i.e. $V_i \supset V_{i-1}$.

We can postulate that timepoint t_i is the moment at which a new node or a new edge has been recorded. This corresponds to the stream model of computation (cf. [22]): the stream is a sequence of records $x_1, \ldots, x_i, \ldots, x_n, \ldots$, arriving in increasing order of the index i, where x_i may be a new node or a new edge. Alternatively, we may opt for a discretization of the time axis into intervals of equal length, e.g. years, days or seconds, or into record buckets of equal size.

The objective of a stream mining algorithm is to maintain an up-to-date model of the data. This translates into adapting the model learned to the currently visible records. These may be all the records seen thus far. However, for many types of analysis, e.g. for the identification of influential nodes or for understanding how communities grow and shrink, it is also reasonable to "forget" some graph elements. In stream mining, this is typically modeled by a *sliding window*: only records within the window are considered for model adaptation. There are several elaborate algorithms that assign weights to the records inside the time window, e.g. [34], and for filling the time window with the records expected to be most representative [7].

Modeling the activities in a dynamic social network as a stream of arriving events allows us to abstract the joint task of community discovery and community evolution monitoring as follows: one model M_i is built at each timepoint i and adapted at the next timepoint into model M_{i+1} using the contents of the time window. The methods we discuss in Sections 3-5 adhere to this abstract task description, while the methods in Section 6 do not. This is not coincidence: the stream model of computation allows us to distinguish between two fundamentally different threads in the study of dynamic social networks. They constitute the first dimension of our multi-dimensional framework below.

The stream model of computation has been designed for less complex data than found in a social network. While the activities recorded in the social network constitute streams (e.g. user postings, uploading of resources, exchange of messages), the entities themselves (users, resources, tags etc) are rather stationary. We come again to this issue in Section 3, when we discuss challenges on community evolution.

2.2 Evolution across Four Dimensions

We organize the advances on evolution in a multi-dimensional framework. We identify four dimensions that are associated to knowledge discovery in social networks and elaborate on their interplay in the context of evolution.

Dimension 1: Dealing with Time. We identify two different threads of research on the analysis of dynamic social networks. Both threads consider the temporal information about the social network for model learning, but they exploit the temporal data differently and, ultimately, deliver different types of knowledge about network dynamics.

Methods of the first thread learn *a single model* that captures the dynamics of the network by exploiting information on how the network has changed from one timepoint to the next. These methods observe the temporal data as a time series that has a beginning and an end. Advances in this thread include[19, 25, 27, 45, 26], many of the methods are of evolutionary nature. The model they learn provides insights on how the network has evolved, and can also be used for prediction on how it will change in the future, provided that the process which generated the data is stationary. Hence, such a model delivers *laws* on the evolution of the network, given its past data.

Methods of the second thread learn one model at each timepoint and adapt it to the data arriving at the next timepoint. Although some early examples [46, 2, 37] are contemporary or even older than the first thread, the popularity of this thread has grown more recently.These methods observe the temporal data as an endless stream. They deliver insights on how each community evolves, and mostly assume a non-stationary data generating process.

The differences between the two threads are fundamental in many aspects. *The object of study* for the first thread is a time series, for the second one it is a stream. From the algorithmic perspective, the methods of the first thread can exploit *all* information available about the network and use data structures that accommodate this information in an efficient way, e.g. using a matrix of interactions among network members. Methods of the second thread cannot know how the network will grow and how many entities will show up at each timepoint, so they must resort to structures that can adapt to an evolving network size. But foremostly, the two threads differ in their *objective* (see Dimension 2 below): while the second thread monitors communities, the first thread derives laws of evolution that govern all communities in a given network.

Dimension 2: Objective of Study. One of the most appealing objectives at the eve of the Social Web was understanding how social networks are formed and how they evolve. This is pursued mainly within the first research thread of Dimension 1, which seeks to find *laws* of evolution that explain the dynamics of the large social networks we see in the Web. A prominent example is the work of Leskovec et al. in [26].

The design of methods that monitor the evolution of communities within a social network is a different task. The goal of community evolution monitoring is pursued by algorithms that derive and adapt models over a stream of user interactions or user postings. The underpinnings come from two domains: stream clustering (see e.g. [1, 22]) and dynamic probabilistic modeling (see e.g. [37]). The use of methods from two domains is reflected in the definition of the term "community", as discussed in Dimension 3 below.

Dimension 3: Definition of a Community. A community may be defined by structure, e.g. communities as cliques. Alternatively, it may be defined by proximity or similarity of members, whereupon many authors assume that nodes are proximal if they are linked, while others assume that nodes are similar if they have similar semantics.

The first research thread under Dimension 1 considers both communities by structure (cliques or less restrictive geometric structures) and communities as groups of proximal nodes in a graph. The second research thread under Dimension 1 further distinguishes among crisp communities (a node belongs to exactly one community at any time), as e.g. in [2], or soft communities (a node belongs to a community with some probability or possibility, or a node is described by each latent community with some probability), e.g. in [37, 36].

In the context of community evolution, the definition depends strongly on the underlying model of computation: if stream clustering is used, then communities are crisp clusters; if fuzzy clustering is used, then communities are fuzzy clusters; if dynamic probabilistic modeling is used (e.g. in [37]), then communities are latent variables that describe each data instance with a specific likelihood, thus allowing an instance to be member of many communities.

Dimension 4: Evolution as Objective vs Assumption. The first category encompasses methods that discretize the time axis to study how communities have changed from one timepoint to the next. The second category encompasses methods that make the assumption of smooth evolution across time and learn community models that preserve temporal smoothness.

We organize the studies across the first, second and forth dimensions in the framework depicted in Figure 6.1. We focus on community evolution hereafter, i.e. on the second thread of Dimension 1 (left box of the figure), and return to laws on evolution in Section 6.

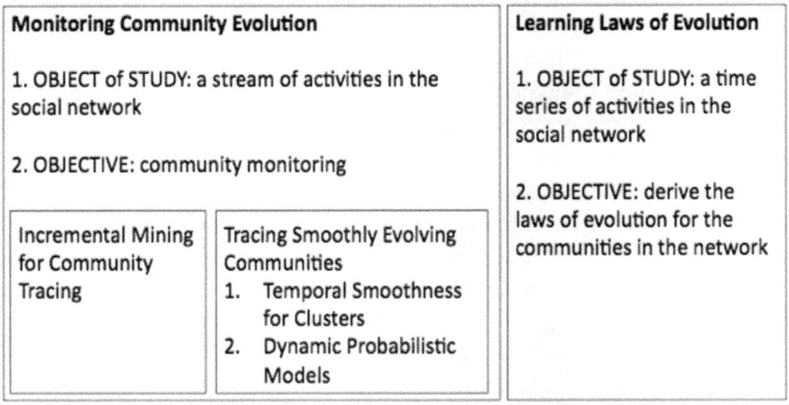

Figure 6.1. A framework for social network evolution

As we see in the left box of the figure, community evolution is governed by Dimension 4. We discuss methods that observe a community as a crisp cluster in Subsection 4, and methods based on dynamic topic modeling and assuming temporal smoothness in Subsection 5. The main objective (Dimension 2) is model adaptation, although we will see some methods that compare models in Subsection 4. Different definitions of a community (Dimension 3) can be found in all sections.

3. Challenges of Social Network Streams

Intuitively, the activities among the members of a social network can be conceived as a stream: an interaction between two network members is an event that is seen and forgotten, as postulated by the stream paradigm [22]. However, the activities of a social network members constitute more than one streams: in the Web 2.0, people contribute resources to a social platform *and* annotate resources with tags. Albeit one may decide to perceive the stream of resource contributions and the stream of tag postings as independent, it is obvious that the two streams are interrelated. In the static case, the ternary relationship among tags, resources and users has been already recognized as beneficial for model learning, at least in the context of recommendation systems (see e.g. [44]). The importance of the temporal dimension for the formulation of reliable recommendations (cf. [24]) indicates that this ternary relationship is also important when observing communities over time. Hence, *community monitoring involves multiple, interrelated streams (challenge C1).*

It is obvious that the recorded activities of social network members constitute the basis for community discovery. However, these activities involve semantically rich entities [1], the information of which contributes further insights into community formation and evolution. For example, the semantics of documents uploaded in a folksonomy do influence the likelihood that a particular user reads them, as well as the likelihood of choosing a particular tag for them. Some social platforms possess further information about their users, such as gender, demographics and affinities towards specific product properties. The incorporation of such information into the model learning process is important for both the static and the dynamic case. Hence, *community monitoring requires taking account of the information on the data entities in each of the streams involved (C2).*

A remarkable difference between conventional stream mining and community stream mining concerns the *permanence* of the entities involved. Individual activities, such as resource uploads or tag postings may be perceived like conventional stream elements: they are observed and may then be forgotten. In contrast, the users, the uploaded resources and the posted tags may not be forgotten: they are elements of the social network and influence its further evolution. Do then users (as well as tags and resources) constitute a stream of particular nature? In [39], such entities are termed *perennial objects* and are characterized by following properties: (i) new ones may show up at any time, while (ii) existing ones may or may not be forgotten [38], (iii) they evolve over time [40], and (iv) they are fed with data from the streams associated with them [39].

Although the cited studies on perennial objects do not focus on social network analysis[2], it is easy to see that *community monitoring involves entities that have the properties of perennial objects (C3)*: (C3.i) new users join the social platform at any time, new resources are uploaded and new tags are recorded; (C3.ii) existing entries might be forgotten if they are inactive for a long time, but any user may become active again after a dormant period, any half-forgotten resource may attract people's interest and any tag may exhibit periods of heavy use and periods of oblivion. Further, (C3.iii) users may exhibit changes in their properties; a customer may start preferring different products from before, an author may shift in her research subjects, and a user may contribute different types of resources in the summer than in the winter.

Hence, community stream mining involves learning on and monitoring of perennial objects that arrive in a stream-like manner but may not be forgot-

[1] Lin et al. [28] introduced the term "facet" for each type of entity appearing in a social network.

[2] The example application and test dataset in [38–40] come from Customer Relationship Management.

ten; such an entity is associated with more than one, interrelated conventional streams, and may change its properties over time. This has side-effects on the data representation used for the evolving social network. If a graph representation is used, then it is necessary that the graph involves different types of nodes, that new nodes be added, and that a node (as well as an edge) have properties that themselves change from one moment to the next. if a tensor representation is used, then the dimensionality of the tensor must be allowed to change with time. For both representations, model adaptation further requires defining a data ageing function and dealing with streams of different speeds.

In the following, we discuss advances on tracing communities upon a stream of social network activities and point out to what extend they address the aforementioned challenges.

4. Incremental Mining for Community Tracing

In incremental clustering and in stream clustering, a cluster built at some point of time evolves as new data arrive and old data are forgotten. In community stream mining, one could also observe a community as a cluster, however one would require some insights about the evolution of each *specific* community/cluster. One research thread focusses on tracing the same community at different timepoints, while another thread learns communities across time while ensuring *temporal smoothness*. We discuss the first thread here and the second one in Section5.

The early work of Toyoda and Kitsuregawa [46] contains a framework for different types of transitions that a community can experience, namely growing, shrinking, emerging, dissolving and splitting, as well as metrics for those transitions; these metrics are based on community membership. Their method has not been designed for community monitoring over a stream, and the term "community" is perhaps less appropriate from the current point of view: a community is a set of URLs from a Web archive, where a URL is linked to others by a HITS-like method. Nonetheless, [46] is one of the earliest methods that categorize and monitor community transitions.

The work of Aggarwal and Yu on community evolution adheres to the stream paradigm, while allowing for an offline exploratory component [2]. The method builds upon the distinction between online and offline components [1], the online component being responsible for summarizing the information in the stream and building micro-clusters, while the offline component is invoked by the user for different time frames and delivers the final clusters from the micro-clusters. Aggarwal and Yu propose three community transitions, namely expansion, contraction and no change (stable state), based on the interaction level among the member entities. For community clustering, they summarize the arriving interactions online, thereby taking the recency of interactions into account in a weighting scheme, and then allowing the generation of graphs over the user-specified time horizon(s).

For the detection of evolving communities and the characterization of the transitions that have taken place, Aggarwal and Yu point out that some edges in the interaction graph indicate intensified interaction (positive edges), while other edges are negative, denoting less interaction than before. The proposed algorithm for the offline component starts with a set of seeds (centroids), to which further nodes are assigned, and then partitions the interaction graph in such a way that partitions contain edges with similar kind of evolution (mostly positive edges, mostly negative edges or neither). Remarkable in this method is that the nature of the interaction (increasing or decreasing) drives the partitioning process [2], without making assumptions on the smoothness of the evolution (as done by the methods in section 5).

A distinction between positive and negative changes in community evolution is also reported in [15], who propose DENGRAPH, an incremental variation of DBSCAN for a graph of interactions. Similarly to IncrementalDBSCAN [12], DENGRAPH has not been designed for a fast stream, but is in principle appropriate for stream clustering, if coupled with a mechanism that adds new data and forgets old entries. For each snapshot of interactions, DENGRAPH computes the proximity between entities (interacting users), thereby forgetting very old interactions and taking new ones into account. The former are negative changes and lead potentially to community splits, shrinking or disappearance, while the latter are positive changes that may lead to community growth, to emerging communities or to community fusion [15].

While the methods in [2, 15] adapt communities, the methods CoDYM [14], GraphScope [42] and TimeFall [17] are oriented towards comparison of communities detected at different timepoints, and support visualization of their evolution. Visualization is also the focus of ContexTour [30], which is based on the assumption of smooth community evolution (cf. Section 5 below).

The approach of Falkowski et al. has a static and a dynamic part [13, 14, 16]. The static component is based on the hierarchical divisive clustering algorithm of Girvan and Newman: the algorithm computes the edge betweenness of nodes [20] and gradually eliminates edges (interactions), thus building a dendrogram of clusters/communities that are increasingly tight towards the leaf nodes. The quality measure proposed in [35] is used to identify the best level for cutting the dendrogram. The static component in [13] applies this algorithm upon the graph of interactions, as recorded within the current time window: interactions that have moved outside the window are forgotten, and hence nodes may become disconnected, while new connections may emerge.

The dynamic component of [13, 16] is responsible for matching communities detected at proximal timepoints. To this purpose, the framework MONIC for the comparison of clusters built at different timepoints [41] is being applied: two communities are considered "same" (or very similar) if their overlap in members exceeds a threshold; they are then linked with an undirected edge. The result is a temporal graph, having as nodes the communities found at different timepoints. The hierarchical divisive clustering algorithm of Girvan and Newman is again invoked for this graph, delivering persistent communities and studying the evolution of volatile ones over the stream. Measures on the stability, density and cohesion of communities across the time axis, as well as visualization aids for an a posteriori inspection of a computed temporal graph have been presented in [14].

GraphScope [42] analyzes a stream of bipartite graphs with three objectives. (i) Split the stream into *graph stream segments*, i.e. subsequences of graphs, such that the end of each segment marks a *change point* in the evolution of the studied social network. (ii) Partition the contents of each graph stream segment (two types of entities) in such a way that the resulting models are good. (iii) Achieve the first two objectives without the need for user-defined parameters. The method builds upon incremental tensor-based clustering [43]: the bipartite graphs are modeled on a 2-mode tensor, assuming m source nodes (first mode) and n destination nodes (second mode); these numbers remain constant with time, i.e. all entities involved in the stream are known in advance.

The core idea of GraphScope is lossless encoding [42]. If a graph stream segment is given and a partitioning has been learnt for it, then the *cost* of this segment can be computed as the cost of describing/transmitting the partitions and the subgraphs (per mode) in each partition. A good partitioning is one that can be losslessly compressed at low cost. If the number of partitions per mode were known, the task would be rather simple, but the third objective of GraphScope disallows input parameters. Therefore, GraphScope performs a local search, starting with a number of partitions for the 1st and the 2nd mode, checking if cost improvements can be achieved by changing the number of partitions in the 1st mode, while taking into account the influence of a change upon the partitioning of the 2nd mode.

Similarly, a good segmentation of the stream is one that minimizes the sum of the costs of transmitting the individual segments. Since a segment consists of graphs recorded at adjacent timepoints, and since any two adjacent graphs are expected to differ only in some edges, a good segmentation is one that starts a new segment, i.e. introduces a *change point*, only if the arriving graph is too different from the previous one. Equivalently, a good segmentation keeps the arriving graph in the current segment as long as a cost benefit is achieved by doing so. An extensive study with different real datasets of various sizes shows that the communities and change points found by GraphScope are reasonable: they either agree with prior knowledge on the data (e.g. the change points in the ENRON dataset agree with known relevant events) or they allow for a straightforward semantic interpretation (e.g. entities that share the same values for a small number of properties) [42].

Ferlez et al. also study the evolution of communities learned as clusters over bipartite graphs, but with emphasis on visualization [17]. Graph clustering takes place at discrete timepoints; then their algorithm *TimeFall* compares the models learned at different timepoints. For this comparison, a community is expressed as a set of words, e.g. the words describing a user profile. This somehow limits the approach to networks where nodes can be described as word vectors. However, it allows the use of the powerful Minimum Description Length criterion for community matching. Matched communities are linked into a temporal graph that is pictorially perceived as a *time waterfall*, hence the name "TimeFall" for the algorithm [17].

The methods discussed thus far assume that a network participant is associated with one community only. Palla et al. study the evolution of overlapping communities, i.e. of social groups that may share members at each timepoint [36]. For the discovery of overlapping communities, they apply the Clique Percolation Method (CPM) at each timepoint. CPM defines "a community [...] as a union of all k-cliques (complete sub-graphs of size k) that can be reached from each other through a series of adjacent k-cliques (where adjacency means sharing k-1 nodes)" and ensures following key features: "(i) [community] members can be reached through well connected subsets of nodes, and (ii) the communities may overlap (share nodes with each other)", as summarized in the section *METHODS*, resp. in the second page of [36].

To match communities found in adjacent timepoints $t, t+1$, Palla et al. take the union of the edges in the networks G at t and G' at $t+1$, and apply CPM over the joing graph. They point out that a community from either t or $t+1$ would be "contained in exactly one community of the joint graph .... Thus, the communities in the joint graph provide a natural connection between the communities at t and at $t+1$" [36].

Taking this matching algorithm as basis, Palla et al. model community dynamics by first enumerating the basic events that a community may experience (emerge, disappear, merge with another, get split), and then identifying two core characteristics of a community – its size and its age (in timepoints). They examine the interplay between community size, stability (which they call "stationarity") and lifetime (i.e. the age a community reaches before it dies out), and show that there are significant differences in the evolution of large vs small communities in the (two) inspected networks [36].

In the extended version of their KDD 2007 paper [5], Asur et al. also start their study of community dynamics by designing an event-based model [6]. This model encompasses events that a community may experience from one timepoint to the next, and also the events that an individual may encounter. This second category contains the events "join" (individual joins community) and "leave", and the events "appear" (a new individual enters the scene) and "disappear". For this model, Asur et al. propose an event detection algorithm and a set of indices which quantify the behavior of nodes and communities [6]. The stability index measures the extend to which a node interacts with the same nodes in a time interval, while the sociability index counts the interactions of a node in an interval. The popularity index counts the number of nodes that joined a community/cluster in a time period and subtracts those that have left the community. Particularly interesting is their "influence index": it attempts to capture the influence of a node x on the evolution of a cluster by identifying the nodes that join or leave a cluster together with x. Of course, identifying these nodes (and demonstrating causality) is far from trivial; Asur et al. propose heuristics to detect the influential nodes in the data [6].

With respect to the challenges listed in section 3, we see that all methods discussed here focus on analyzing one stream (challenge C1). GraphScope [42] has the potential of analyzing multiple streams, but the issue of stream synchronization is not addressed. Properties of the network members and of the entities (e.g. resources, tags) these members act upon (challenge C2) are not considered by the above methods. The methods in [2, 15] and CoDym [13, 16] allow for the addition of new network members (C3.i) and for forgetting new ones (C3.ii), while Asur et al. explicitly address both challenges in their event model [6].

The tensor-based methods [42, 17] assume a fixed number of nodes for each entity type in the bipartite graph, i.e. all nodes must be known in advance. Node addition in incremental tensor mining leads to a fundamental problem, for which heuristic solutions have been proposed; this issue is discussed in Section 5.1 below.

5. Tracing Smoothly Evolving Communities

The methods of Section 4 *trace* communities over time and can depict how each community evolves. A different perspective to the community evolution problem is that of incorporating assumptions on how communities evolve into the learning process. More precisely, let us assume that communities are smoothly evolving constellations of interacting entities. Then community learning over time translates into finding a sequence of models [10], or into dynamically learning and adapting a probabilistic model [37], such that the model valid at each timepoint is of good quality and has evolved more or less smoothly from the previous model.

5.1 Temporal Smoothness for Clusters

Chakrabarti et al. capture continuity with respect to the previously learned model through the notion of *temporal smoothness*, which they incorporate into the objective function to be optimized during learning [10]. In particular, they propose two aspects of model quality or, equivalently, model cost: *snapshot cost* captures the quality of the clustering learned at each time interval, while *temporal cost* measures the (dis-)similarity of a clustering learned at a particular timepoint to the clustering learned at the previous timepoint [10]. Then, cluster monitoring translates to the optimization problem of finding a sequence of models that minimizes the overall cost, where the cost of model ξ_t to be learned from the entity similarity matrix M_t valid at timepoint t is

$$Cost(\xi_t, M_t) = snapshotCost(\xi_t, M_t) + \beta \times temporalCost(\xi_{t-1}, \xi_t) \quad (6.1)$$

The matrix M_t is computed by considering (i) local similarity of entities, where "local" refers to the current snapshot of the underlying bipartite graph, as well as (ii) "temporal similarity", which reflects similarity with entities at earlier moments. This approach assumes that entities (users) found to be similar in the past are likely to be still similar.

The "change parameter" β expresses the importance of *temporal smoothness* between the old model ξ_{t-1} and the new one ξ_t relatively to the quality of the new model. This parameter ranges between zero and one, hence the cost function can be tuned to force smoothness (β is close to one) or rather allow for shifts (β is close to zero).

Chi et al. took over this idea for community monitoring over time [11], slightly remodeled the cost function to allow for tuning the impact of the snapshot cost explicitly:

$$Cost(\xi_t, M_t) = \alpha \times snapshotCost(\xi_t, M_t) + \beta \times temporalCost(\xi_{t-1}, \xi_t) \quad (6.2)$$

and made several extensions to the original approach of [10]. First, they proposed two ways of modeling temporal smoothness (equivalently, temporal cost): (a) preservation of cluster membership at timepoint t, by measuring the overlap between the cluster members at t vs the previous timepoint $t-1$, and (b) preservation of cluster quality at t, by measuring the degradation of the quality of the clusters found in $t-1$ towards the new clustering. Further, they did not only consider K-Means as in [10], but also spectral clustering over bipartite graphs. The implementation of each component of the cost function depends obviously on the choice of clustering algorithm. For K-means, the snapshot cost of model ξ_t at t is expressed as the sum of square errors $SSE(\xi_t, t)$; preservation of cluster quality from $t-1$ to t is the SSE of the clusters in ξ_t towards the centers they had at $t-1$ and normalized by the cluster cardinalities in $t-1$; preservation of cluster membership from ξ_{t-1} to ξ_t is computed as:

$$PCM(\xi_{t-1}, \xi_t) = -\sum_{X \in \xi_{t-1}} \sum_{Y \in \xi_t} \frac{|X \cap Y|}{]X| \times |Y|} \quad (6.3)$$

while the corresponding functions for spectral clustering are aiming to minimize the normalized cut or the negation of the average association between subsets of graph nodes.

The core approach of Chakrabarti et al. [10] and Chi et al. [11] is designed for a graph that has a fixed, a priori known, number of nodes. As already mentioned in section 3 (challenges C3.i, C3.ii), the social network may grow by new individuals at any time, while the information on old, inactive individuals may need to be forgotten.

The addition of new graph nodes leads to the following problem. All computations in [10, 11] are performed upon a matrix that contains derived similarities for each pair of graph nodes; when new nodes arrive, similarities to old nodes must be derived to fill the matrix, but there are no data to derive them from. Chi et al. propose heuristics for filling the matrix, namely to derive average values from the data seen thus far [11]. In contrast, forgetting old individuals is less of a challenge: the matrix rows and columns can be simply eliminated [11]. Hence, methods building upon the approach of Chi et al. [11], such as [28, 31, 30] discussed below, implicitly possess a heuristic solution to challenges C3.i and C3.ii on adding and deleting nodes.

5.2 Dynamic Probabilistic Models

Model adaptation under the assumption of smooth evolution is intensively studied with probabilistic learning methods. A field where these methods are being successfully applied for years is text stream mining, under the name *dynamic topic modeling*, see e.g.[23, 33, 32, 8, 47, 4, 21] (in chronological order).

The transition from clustering to probabilistic modeling implies a change on what a community *is*. For the methods discussed thus far, a community is a cluster of proximal entities, where proximity may be modeled as similarity in behavior, similarity in ground properties or both. If probabilistic modeling is used instead, then it is assumed that the data generating process is *described* by a number of latent variables. Then, the behavior of each entity is described/determined by each latent variable to a different degree (contribution), while all contributions add to 1. If the latent variables are called "communities", as e.g. in [28, 31], then a community determines each activity observed at each timepoint with some probability (the variable's contribution to this activity). These latent variables describe the stream(s) of activities rather than the (stream of) entities, and thus do not determine the addition or removal of network nodes, nor do they correspond to communities of entities.

5.2.1 Discovering and Monitoring Latent Communities. Sarkar and Moore exploit the power of dynamic probabilistic modeling for community evolution in [37]. They study a social network of interacting entities, i.e. a single stream of interaction data, and investigate the evolution of social relationships among entities, under two assumptions. First, "entities can move in latent space between time steps, but large moves are improbable"; second, a "standard Markov assumption [is done, namely that] latent locations at time $t + 1$ are conditionally independent of all previous locations given latent locations at time t and that the observed graph at time t is conditionally independent of all other positions and graphs, given the locations at time t ([37]: section 1).

The first assumption in [37] means that the contribution of a latent variable to a given entity's interaction behavior may change from one timepoint to the next but not drastically. As an informal example, assume that there are three hidden variables and that an entity x is described by them with probabilities p_1, p_2, p_3 (adding to 1) at timepoint t; at the next timepoint, any of these probabilities may change but, the more drastic a change, the less likely it is. If one observes these latent variables as communities [28, 31], then the above assumption means that the influence of each community on an entity's behavior is unlikely to drop or increase dramatically from one timepoint to the next.

The Dynamic Social Network in Latent Space Model (DSNL) of Sarkar and More consists of an observation model and a transition model [37]. The observation part encompasses a likelihood score function that "measures how well the model explains pairs of entities who are actually connected in the training graph as well as those that are not" ([37]: section 2.1). Entities are allowed to vary their "sociability" and linking probabilities are weighted (a kernel function is used). The core idea is that the sociability of an entity is a radius in the latent space, in the sense that the entity will link with all entities that are within its radius with a high probability, and with further entities with a (constant) probability ρ that corresponds to noise. The transition part penalizes drastic changes of the current model towards the previous one.

There is a correspondence to the snapshot cost and the temporal cost proposed for clusters in later years [10, 11]: the early method of Sarkar and Moore targets quality of the probabilistic model at each timepoint (snapshot quality) and minimal perturbation between timepoints (temporal smoothness). With respect to both objectives, Sarkar and Moore pay particular attention in avoiding local minima. Their method is indeed shown to perform very well for synthetic and real networks, including two networks from Citeseer, the largest containing more than 11,000 nodes [37].

Dynamic topic modeling for community monitoring is used in the method FacetNet, presented in [28]. FacetNet builds upon the evolutionary clustering criterion of [10, 11]. The cost of deviating from temporal smoothness is modeled using Kubler-Leibler divergence. According to the probabilistic learning paradigm, a community is a latent variable, and each node is described by all communities - with different probabilities. Hence, a node participates to each community to some extend. Community evolution is then captured by building an *Evolution Net*, the nodes of which are the communities at distinct timepoints and an edge between a community c at t and a community c' at $t' > t$ is the probability of reaching c' from c. There is some similarity of this temporal graph to the one proposed in [14], where the overlap between community members is used to compute the edges. However, the Evolution Net is conceptually much closer to the temporal graph proposed by Mei and Zhai for topic evolution [32], because a topic is defined as a latent variable and dynamic topic modeling is performed. The addition of nodes (challenge C3.i of Section 3) is addressed heuristically (as in [11]) by filling the missing rows and columns with values derived under assumptions on the contribution of each community to the newly arriving nodes.

Further community monitoring advances that build upon the core idea of dynamic topic modeling include [48, 29, 31]. The *Dynamic Stochastic Block Model* of Yang et al. uses Bayesian inference with Gibbs sampling to optimize the posterior probabilities at each step [48]. In advances for dynamic topic modeling (on text streams), it is usual to model the problem of deriving the a posteriori probabilities as a Maximum A Posteriori (MAP) estimation problem that can be solved with Expectation Maximization. Yang et al. rather use a probabilistic simulated annealing algorithm [48], while the extension of FacetNet by Lin et al. [31] reformulates the original community learning problem of [28], so that EM can be used for MAP estimation.

ContexTour [30] visualizes evolving communities, building upon the methods in [28, 29, 31]. The core ideas are (i) the selection of important entities within each mode, (ii) the generation of different, context-specific views, where a view corresponds to a mode, and (iii) the automatic identification of the number of communities at each timepoint, using the soft modularity principle [28]. The method allows the observer to see community splits, merges and other transitions, as well as the content of each community around its most important entities.

5.2.2 Dealing with Assumptions on the Data Generating Process.

One of the challenging issues in (dynamic) probabilistic modeling is assessing the number of latent variables K. A further associated challenge is to decide whether the number of latent variables that describe the observed process should be assumed constant over time or should be allowed to vary.

For FacetNet [28], Lin et al. derive the number of latent variables at each timepoint. To do so, they extend the concept of modularity [35], which may be used to assess the number of crisp communities, into *soft modularity* for overlapping communities [28]. Then, if the number of latent variables is allowed to change from timepoint $t - 1$ to t, the cost function is aligned [3] to prevent too strong a difference between the old model and the new one [28].

A further challenge is to design a mathematically and statistically appropriate model of temporal smoothness. As we have seen, smooth evolution is a core assumption for the methods in Section 5. This assumption can be used to *drive the learning process*, i.e. to learn models that are structurally close to those of the previous timepoint(s). Ahmed and Xing [3] rather model temporal smoothness as a penalty in the loss function and allow it to be traded off with data fitness (cf. perspective taken in clustering under the assumption of temporal smoothness, Section 5.1, Eq. 6.2). This allows for a proper exploitation of prior knowledge about the dynamics of the social network. As the authors point out (page 11879ff), methods that take smooth evolution as a precondition "may run into difficulties" in "cases where more turbulent dynamics (e.g. sudden jumps) drives graph evolution." They have applied their method TESLA on the voting record of the U.S. Senate Network for the period 2005-2006 and have exemplarily highlighted the evolution in the voting behavior of three senators.

In contrast to [3], Zhou et al. [50] stick to the assumption of temporal smoothness and seek for a *non-parametric* method that can learn a sequence of graph models from the smoothly evolving distribution. They model the interplay between model quality and smoothness by two risk functions, one capturing model persistency and the other capturing *sparsistency* (as the size of the symmetric difference between two sets of edges). Then, they prove that if the covariance changes smoothly over time, then their method (based on kernel regression) delivers good estimates of the covariance matrix at each point.

The approaches in [50, 3] demonstrate how background knowledge can be exploited in a proper and transparent way to model community evolution. If the assumption of temporal smoothness is known to hold, then Zhou et al. [50] deliver a non-parametric estimator with provably good performance on sparse graphs. If it is not known whether the assumption holds, but tuning of the hyperparameters from a reasonable number of samples is possible, then Ahmed and Xing [3] show that the original problem translates into a convex optimization problem with a smooth objective and linear constraint functions, for which solvers are already available.

An assumption that is rather rarely addressed in studies of social network dynamics concerns the number of nodes. A priori knowledge about all nodes in the network is a core premise in [37, 3] who consider both the presence and the absence of links, and model the emergence of new links as time pro-

---

[3] As the authors state, "instead of regularizing the community structure itself, we regularize the marginal distribution induced by the community structure at time t $(\dots)$ so that it is not too far away from that at time $t-1$ $(\dots)$.

gresses. This assumption is justified in a retrospective analysis of a network's evolution; as a matter of fact, Ahmed and Xing use the expression "recovering time-varying networks" (also in the title of [3]) that reflects the intention of understanding a network a posteriori. In contrast, for studies intending to understand how communities evolve at each timepoint, given a stream of activities, this assumption is unrealistic. As already noted in Section 5.1, approaches like [28, 31, 30] that build upon the method of [11] have a heuristic for node insertion and deletion.

5.2.3 Extending the Notion of Community. The method MetaFac of Lin et al. [31], a followup of FacetNet [28], goes beyond the bipartite graph representation of social data. The authors point out that social networks have many different types of resources and allow for different actions on each one, e.g. uploading pictures and tagging them, uploading, sharing, tagging and commenting stories; some social sites allow users to interact with each other directly, while others do not. Hence, Lin et al. propose the notion of *multi-relational hypergraph (metagraph)* with *hyperedges* that capture the interaction among two or more *facets*, i.e. entities of one or more types [31]. For example, assigning a tag to a picture is a 3-way relation involving the facets "user", "picture", "tag", while assigning a tag to a document involves the facet "document" instead of "picture". It is of course still possible to observe documents and pictures as resources, but the new concept allows to deal with the fact that documents may be associated with different properties (title, author, content) than pictures. Thus, MetaFac addresses challenge C2 (section 3) on the need to take information on each of the entities involved in the social network into account when learning.

For model learning, Lin et al. identify three issues to be dealt with (cf. [31], section 4): "(1) how to represent multi-relational social data (...), (2) how to reveal the latent communities consistently across multiple relations, and (3) how to track the communities over time (...)." Multi-relational social data are modeled in the metagraph that is implemented with multiple tensors, and a new factorization is proposed for it. Objective of the MetaFac factorization is to output a core tensor [4] and as many factors as there are facets, so that the approximate reconstruction of a tensor from the core tensor and some factor(s) is consistent with the reconstruction of each other tensor that involves one or more of these factors. The approximation cost for one tensor is modeled as Kubler-Leibler divergence, and the *consistency* is pursued by minimizing the aggregated cost of all approximations. As in [28], KL-divergence is used to express temporal smoothness [10], or, more precisely, the cost of deviating from the previously learned model.

[4] The length of the core tensor is the number of latent communities and must be specified in advance.

5.2.4 Complexity.

A challenging issue of (dynamic) probabilistic modeling concerns execution time, because the complexity is quadratic to the number of *nodes*, if no optimizations are undertaken. The approach of Sarkar and Moore achieves $O(nlogn)$ complexity, where n is the number of nodes [37]. For the Citeseer subnetwork of 9,364 nodes (studied in 6 time slots), the recorded processing time was 3.5 hours, increasing to 4.5 hours for the Citeseer subnetwork of 11,218 entities that were more densely connected; for studied networks with up to 7000 edges, the reported time per iteration increased linearly to around 0.15 of a second and the number of iterations needed until convergence was almost constant between 600 and 800, implying a total processing time of less than 2 minutes [37].

While [37, 3] focus on reducing the complexity with respect to the number of nodes, other methods in the domain study the complexity with respect to the number of edges. For FacetNet [28], the complexity of each iteration (updating the model) is $O(N)$, where N is the number of *edges* in the snapshot graph. The incremental algorithm of Yang et al. exploits data sparsity and also achieves a complexity linear to the number of edges, if the network is sparse [48].

Unfortunately, the results of [37, 3] and [28, 48] are not comparable to each other. First, the methods in [37, 3] capture both the presence *and* the absence of edges, hence they *must* refer to the number of entities in the network, while [28, 48] can focus on the edges of the snapshot graph only. Second, FacetNet studies bipartite graphs [28], while [37, 3] concentrate on graphs of direct interactions between entities, hence the graphs are not of the same nature. The structure of the networks studied by FacetNet is not detailed in [28], but one may assume that the 7000 edges reported in [28] originate from much less than the 9,000 entities studied in [37]. In any case, the absolute numbers reported in [28] are very encouraging [5].

6. Laws of Evolution in Social Networks

In Section 2, we have pointed to a thread of research that aims to discover *laws* that govern the evolution of all communities inside a social network (cf. Figure 6.1, right side). Research advances in this thread include [19, 25, 27, 45, 26].

Some of the approaches in this thread use evolutionary algorithms, e.g. [45, 26], so they seem very close to the approaches discussed in the two previous sections. However, algorithms that seek for laws of evolution derive a single model, not a sequence of models (nor a mechanism that adapts a model from one timepoint to the next). Second, these algorithms assume availability of *all*

[5] Yang et al. do not evaluate on execution time [48].

time stamped data, i.e. treat the information on the social network as a time series rather than a stream. In contrast, the incremental algorithms ofSsection 4 and the adaptive methods of Section 5 treat the data as a stream on which the earlier model must be adapted at each time point. As a side-effect, algorithms that derive one model of a social network's dynamics can assume that all nodes (network participants) are known in advance, while the algorithms of the two previous sections must deal with newly arriving nodes (cf. challence C3.i of section 3). In the following, we discuss two evolutionary algorithms of this research thread.

In [26], Leskovec et al. study evolving social networks within a time horizon. Their approach is evolutionary in the sense that they let the four real networks under study grow edge-by-edge and then test how given models fit them, i.e. predict well the next event on the network. Hence, the (single) learned model can predict how the network will evolve, whether a community in it will decay or grow, given the events seen in the past (and assuming that the data generating process is not changing). Remarkable for this method is that it has been applied to large and popular networks (Flickr, Delicious, Answers, LinkedIn) and thus delivers insights on the laws governing the evolution of each one.

Tantipathananandh et al. express the problem of *community identification* in dynamic social networks as a graph coloring problem[45]. Their approach is based on a set of assumptions about community membership, and thus, implicitly, about what a community *is*. Briefly, their assumptions are that (i) communities are distinct and well-separated entities, (ii) an individual is member of exactly one community at each moment, (iii) moves rarely from one community to another, and (iv) such movements are towards a rather small number of target communities. Further, (v) an individual expresses its presence within the own community often and is much less present with members outside that community. Hence, a community is a rather stable constellation that binds its members - this binding is expressed as the community color. Accordingly, there are different forms of cost associated with the migration from one community to another: cost incurs when an individual changes color and when the individual is present/active but not with other individuals of the same color; the more colors an individual changes, the higher the associated cost. Hence, the objective of community mining is to find a *community interpretation* that minimizes cost. Tantipathananandh et al. show that this problem is NP-hard but an approximate solution can be achieved with dynamic programming [45]. As with the previous method, the result is one model of the social network, which should be re-learned if new data arrive.

Ultimately, the difference between the methods in this research thread and those in the previous two sections is one of perspective. If the dynamic social network should be analyzed retrospectively, then it is possible (and reasonable) to exploit *all* temporal data and treat them as a multivariate time series. The methods we have focussed in this survey are rather those that treat the activities in the dynamic social network as an ongoing stream, and thus never have access to all data.

7. Conclusion

The field of social network analysis is intensively studied and the subject of community evolution gained momentum in the last years. Powerful methods are being developed. Their focus is on capturing the multifaceted nature of online social platforms, on detecting changes in community structure and on expressing these changes in a comprehensible way. Despite the intensity of research, many open issues remain, while new ones emerge together with the latest research results.

An open issue of increasing importance is *validation*. There is an abundance of real datasets with publicly available data from social platforms, but there is no ground truth in them. Hence, verifying that the communities discovered by a learning algorithm are indeed the real ones becomes a challenge by itself; verifying that the community evolution patterns detected are the true ones is even more difficult. The pragmatic alternative pursued by many studies is to show that the evolution patterns found are realistic, i.e. they conform to prior knowledge or can be verified by inspection of the underlying data (see e.g. experiments on real datasets in [31, 42, 14]). This approach is reasonable but does not generalize well. First, an algorithm finds more evolving communities in a large network than an expert can inspect. Second, some evolving communities are easier to verify than others: it is easy to monitor a community associated with a prominent person or a popular product, but very difficult to find an explanation behind each change in one of the many communities of anonymous and not very active users inside a social platform. A solution may be the imputation of transparently specified evolution patterns in real data.

A further issue that emerged through the proliferation of many innovative methods is *comparability*. Many methods turn to be incomparable with respect to their goals, as the earlier mentioned approaches of Sarkar and Moore [37] and [28], where dynamic probabilistic modeling is used upon the same data but with different objectives. Nonetheless, it should be possible to compare algorithms on their scalability towards number of nodes, network density or different distributions of edges. The absence of even synthetic benchmarks has lead to handcrafted experiments that are not always described in full detail. Hence, there is need for data generators that can express the characteristics of a real evolving social network.

Online social networks can have millions of nodes, but the distribution of activity among the network members follows Zipf's law. For incremental tensor-based methods, this implies that huge initial tensors must be built at each timepoint and that sophisticated heuristics (as in [11, 28]) are needed to fill the entries for new nodes with imputed average values of some reliability. The sheer number of such nodes makes it likely that the derived values may affect the model. Even if there are no side-effects on the quality of the learned model, there are effects on execution time and storage demand. There is need for *economical* or even *parsimonious* use of resources when adapting models upon sparse graphs. How this can be achieved with incremental methods that process matrices or tensors is still an open issue, but there are solutions at least in the area of dynamic topic modeling for text streams (see e.g. the methods [4, 21] which use an evolving subset of the complete feature space).

The need for huge initial tensors emerges from the fact that social network members, resources, tags and other entities encountered in a social platform are *perennial objects* with inherent properties that can be exploited for learning but may change in time. The challenges listed in Section 3 on synchronizing and processing multiple streams of activities associated with such objects are not yet covered by existing methods.

Presently, research on community evolution is driven by the need for powerful methods that can extract good models from the data. The exploitation of these models in applications is less investigated. For example, it is known that communities have influential members and that communities influence their members. Such facts are important for recommendation engines. But how to incorporate knowledge about community evolution on the ranking of entities recommended to a community member? And how do recommendations on entities inside a social platform affect community formation and evolution? How to select the most relevant community for an individual given the individual's current preferences and context, and how to adapt this selection as communities and individuals change with time? The coupling of community evolution methods with advances in potential application domains can motivate application owners to provide benchmark data, can deliver validation frameworks and promote comparability, and can stimulate the formulation of further research questions.

References

[1] C. Aggarwal, J. Han, J. Wang, and P. Yu. A framework for clustering evolving data streams. In *29th Int. Conf. on Very Large Data Bases (VLDB'03)*, Berlin, Germany, 2003.

[2] Charu Aggarwal and Philip Yu. Online analysis of community evolution in data streams. In *Proc. of SIAM Int. Conf. on Data Mining (SDM'05)*, 2005.

[3] Amr Ahmed and Eric Xing. Recovering time-varying networks of dependencies in social and biological studies. *PNAS*, 106:11878–1188, July 2009.

[4] L. AlSumait, Daniel Barbara, and Carlotta Domeniconi. On-line LDA: Adaptive topic models for mining text streams with applications to topic detection and tracking. In *Proc. of 2008 IEEE Conf. on Data Mining (ICDM'08)*, pages 373–382, Pisa, Italy, Dec. 2008. IEEE.

[5] Sitaram Asur, Srinivasan Parthasarathy, and Duygu Ucar. An event-based framework for characterizing the evolutionary behavior of interaction graphs. In *Proceedings of the 13th ACM SIGKDD international conference on Knowledge discovery and data mining (KDD'07)*, pages 913–921, New York, NY, USA, 2007. ACM.

[6] Sitaram Asur, Srinivasan Parthasarathy, and Duygu Ucar. An event-based framework for characterizing the evolutionary behavior of interaction graphs. *ACM Trans. Knowl. Discov. Data*, 3(4):1–36, 2009.

[7] Albert Bifet and Ricard Gavaldá. Learning from time-changing data with adaptive windowing. In *SIAM Int. Conf. on Data Mining (SDM'07)*, 2007.

[8] David M. Blei and John D. Lafferty. Dynamic topic models. In *Proc. of 23rd Int. Conf. on Machine Learning (ICML'06)*, Pittsburgh, PA, 2006.

[9] Deepayan Chakrabarti, Christos Faloutsos, and Mary McGlohon. Graph mining: Laws and generators. In Charu Aggarwal and Haixun Wang, editors, *Managing and Mining Graph Data*, pages 67–121. 2010.

[10] Deepayan Chakrabarti, Ravi Kumar, and Andrew Tomkins. Evolutionary clustering. In *Proceedings of 12th ACM SIGKDD Int. Conf (KDD'06)*, pages 554–560, Philadelphia, PA, Aug. 2006. ACM.

[11] Yun Chi, Xiaodan Song, Dengyong Zhou, Koji Hino, and Belle Tseng. Evolutionary spectral clustering by incorporating temporal smoothness. In *Proceedings of 13th ACM SIGKDD Int. Conf (KDD'07)*, San Jose, CA, Aug. 2007. ACM.

[12] Martin Ester, Hans-Peter Kriegel, Jörg Sander, Michael Wimmer, and Xiaowei Xu. Incremental Clustering for Mining in a Data Warehousing Environment. In *Proceedings of the 24th International Conference on Very Large Data Bases*, pages 323–333, New York City, New York, USA, August 1998. Morgan Kaufmann.

[13] Tanja Falkowski, Jörg Bartelheimer, and Myra Spiliopoulou. Community dynamics mining. In *Proc. of 14th European Conf. on Information Systems (ECIS'2006)*, Göteborg, SWEDEN, June 2006.

[14] Tanja Falkowski, Jörg Bartelheimer, and Myra Spiliopoulou. Mining and visualizing the evolution of subgroups in social networks. In *WI '06: Pro-*

ceedings of the 2006 IEEE/WIC/ACM International Conference on Web Intelligence, pages 52–58, Washington, DC, USA, 2006. IEEE Computer Society.

[15] Tanja Falkowski, Anja Barth, and Myra Spiliopoulou. Studying community dynamics with an incremental graph mining algorithm. In *Proc. of the 14th Americas Conference on Information Systems*, Toronto, Canada, Aug. 2008.

[16] Tanja Falkowski and Myra Spiliopoulou. Users in volatile communities: Studying active participation and community evolution. In C. Conati, K. McCoy, and G. Paliouras, editors, *Proceedings of User Modeling 2007 - LNAI 4511*, pages 57–66. Springer, 2007.

[17] Jure Ferlez, Christos Faloutsos, Jure Leskovec, Dunja Mladenic, and Marko Grobelnik. Monitoring network evolution using MDL. In *Proceedings of IEEE Int. Conf. on Data Engineering (ICDE'08)*. IEEE, 2008.

[18] Santo Fortunato. Community detection in graphs. *Physics Report*, 486:75–174, Feb. 2010.

[19] David Gibson, Ravi Kumar, and Andrew Tomkins. Discovering large dense subgraphs in massive graphs. In *31st Int. Conf. on Very Large Data Bases (VLDBâĂŹ05)*, pages 721–732, Trondheim, Norway, 2005.

[20] M. Girvan and M.E.J. Newman. Community structure in social and biological networks. *PNAS*, 99(12):7821–7826, 2002.

[21] Andre Gohr, Alexander Hinneburg, Rene Schult, and Myra Spiliopoulou. Topic evolution in a stream of documents. In *SIAM Data Mining Conf. (SDM'09)*, pages 378–385, Reno, CA, Apr.-May 2009.

[22] S. Guha, A. Meyerson, N. Mishra, R. Motwani, and L. O'Callaghan. Clustering data streams: Theory and practice. *IEEE Trans. of Knowledge and Data Eng.*, 15(3):515–528, 2003.

[23] Ata Kabán and Mark Girolami. A dynamic probabilistic model to visualise topic evolution in text streams. *Journal of Intelligent Information Systems*, 18(2/3):107–125, 2002.

[24] Yehuda Koren. Collaborative filtering with temporal dynamics. *Communications of ACM*, 53(4):89–97, 2010.

[25] Ravi Kumar, Jasmine Novak, and Andrew Tomkins. Structure and evolution of online social networks. In *Proceedings of 12th ACM SIGKDD Int. Conf (KDD'06)*, Philadelphia, PA, Aug. 2006. ACM.

[26] Jure Leskovec, Lars Backstrom, Ravi Kumar, and Andrew Tomkins. Microscopic evolution of social networks. In *Proceedings of 14th ACM SIGKDD Int. Conf (KDD'08)*, Las Vegas, Nevada, Aug. 2007. ACM.

[27] Jure Leskovec and Christos Faloutsos. Sampling from large graphs. In *Proceedings of 12th ACM SIGKDD Int. Conf (KDD'06)*, Philadelphia, PA, Aug. 2006. ACM.

[28] Yu-Ru Lin, Yun Chi, Shenghuo Zhu, Hari Sundaram, and Belle Tseng. FacetNet: A framework for analyzing communities and their evolutions in dynamic networks. In *Proceedings of World Wide Web Int. Conf. (WWW'08)*, pages 685–694, Beijing, China, Apr. 2008. ACM.

[29] Yu-Ru Lin, Yun Chi, Shenghuo Zhu, Hari Sundaram, and Belle Tseng. Analyzing communities and their evolutions in dynamic social networks. *ACM Transactions on Knowledge Discovery from Data*, 3(2), 2009.

[30] Yu-Ru Lin, Jimeng Sun, Nanl Cao, and Shixia Liu. ContexTour: Contextual contour visual analysis on dynamic multi-relational clustering. In *Proceedings of SIAM Data Mining Conf. (SDM'10)*, pages 418–429. SIAM, Apr. 2010.

[31] Yu-Ru Lin, Jimeng Sun, Paul Castro, Ravi Konuru, Hari Sundaram, and Aisling Kelliher. MetaFac: Community discovery via relational hypergraph factorization. In *Proceedings of 16th ACM SIGKDD Int. Conf. (KDD'09)*, Paris, France, June-July 2009. ACM.

[32] Qiaozhu Mei and ChengXiang Zhai. Discovering Evolutionary Theme Patterns from Text - An Exploration of Temporal Text Mining. In *Proc. of 11th ACM SIGKDD Int. Conf. on Knowledge Discovery and Data Mining (KDD'05)*, pages 198–207, Chicago, IL, Aug. 2005. ACM Press.

[33] Satoshi Moringa and Kenji Yamanichi. Tracking Dynamics of Topic Trends Using a Finite Mixture Model. In *Proc.of 10th ACM SIGKDD Int. Conf. on Knowledge Discovery and Data Mining (KDD'04)*, pages 811–816, Seattle, Washington, Aug. 2004. ACM Press.

[34] Olfa Nasraoui, Cesar Cardona-Uribe, and CArsols Rojas-Coronel. Tecno-Streams: Tracking evolving clusters in noisy data streams with an scalable immune system learning method. In *Proc. IEEE Int. Conf. on Data Mining (ICDM'03)*, Melbourne, Australia, 2003.

[35] M.E.J. Newman and M. Girvan. Finding and evaluating community structure in networks. *Physical Review*, E69(026113), 2004.

[36] Gergely Palla, Albert-László Barabási, and Tamás Vicske. Quantifying social group evolution. *Nature*, 446(7136):664–667, Apr. 2007.

[37] Purnamrita Sarkar and Andrew W. Moore. Dynamic social network analysis using latent space models. *SIGKDD Explorations Newsletter*, 7(2):31–40, 2005.

[38] Zaigham Faraz Siddiqui and Myra Spiliopoulou. Combining multiple interrelated streams for incremental clustering. In *Proceedings of 21st*

International Conference on Scientific and Statistical Database Management, SSDBM '09, pages 535–552, New Orleans, May 2009.

[39] Zaigham Faraz Siddiqui and Myra Spiliopoulou. Stream clustering of growing objects. In *Proceedings of Discovery Science '09*, Oporto, Portugal, Oct. 2009.

[40] Zaigham Faraz Siddiqui and Myra Spiliopoulou. Tree induction over a stream of perennial objects (to be published in july 2010). In *Proc of 22nd International Conference on Scientific and Statistical Database Management, SSDBM '10*. Springer-Verlag, 2010.

[41] Myra Spiliopoulou, Irene Ntoutsi, Yannis Theodoridis, and Rene Schult. Monic – modeling and monitoring cluster transitions. In *Proc. of 12th ACM SIGKDD Int. Conf. on Knowledge Discovery and Data Mining (KDD'06)*, pages 706–711, Philadelphia, USA, Aug. 2006. ACM.

[42] Jimeng Sun, Christos Faloutsos, S. Papadimitriou, and Philip Yu. Graph-Scope: Parameter-free mining of large time-evolving graphs. In *Proceedings of 13th ACM SIGKDD Int. Conf (KDD'07)*, pages 687–696, San Jose, CA, Aug. 2007. ACM.

[43] Jimeng Sun, D. Tao, and Christos Faloutsos. Beyond streams and graphs: Dynamic tensor analysis. In *Proceedings of 12th ACM SIGKDD Int. Conf (KDD'06)*, Philadelphia, PA, Aug. 2006. ACM.

[44] Panagiotis Symeonidis, Alexandros Nanopoulos, and Yannis Manolopoulos. A unified framework for providing recommendations in social tagging systems based on ternary semantic analysis. *IEEE Transactions on Knowledge and Data Engineering*, 22(2):179–192, Feb. 2010.

[45] Chayant Tantipathananandh, Tanya Berger-Wolf, and David Kempe. A framework for community identification in dynamic social networks. In *KDD '07: Proceedings of the 13th ACM SIGKDD international conference on Knowledge discovery and data mining*, pages 717–726, New York, NY, USA, 2007. ACM.

[46] Masashi Toyoda and Masaru Kitsuregawa. Extracting evolution of web communities from a series of web archives. In *Proc. of the 14th ACM Conference on Hypertext and Hypermedia (HYPERTEXT '03)*, pages 28–37, Nottingham, UK, 2003. ACM.

[47] Xuerui Wang and Andrew McCallum. Topics over time: a non-Markov continuous-time model of topical trends. In *Proceedings of 12th ACM SIGKDD Int. Conf (KDD'06)*, pages 424–433, Philadelphia, PA, Aug. 2006. ACM.

[48] Tianbao Yang, Yun Chi, Shenguo Zhu, Yihong Gong, and Rong Jin. A bayesian approach toward finding communities and their evolutions in

dynamic social networks. In *SIAM Int. Conf. on Data Mining (SDM'09)*, pages 990–1001, Reno, CA, Apr.-May 2009.

[49] Jian Zhang. A survey on streaming algorithms for massive graphs. In Charu Aggarwal and Haixun Wang, editors, *Managing and Mining Graph Data*, pages 391–418. 2010.

[50] Shuheng Zhou, John Lafferty, and Larry Wasserman. Time varying undirected graphs. *Machine Learning*, 80:295–319, 2010. DOI: 10.1007/s10994-010-5180-0.

Chapter 7

A SURVEY OF MODELS AND ALGORITHMS FOR SOCIAL INFLUENCE ANALYSIS

Jimeng Sun
IBM TJ Watson Research Center, USA
jimeng@us.ibm.com

Jie Tang
Tsinghua University, China
jietang@tsinghua.edu.cn

Abstract Social influence is the behavioral change of a person because of the perceived relationship with other people, organizations and society in general. Social influence has been a widely accepted phenomenon in social networks for decades. Many applications have been built based around the implicit notation of social influence between people, such as marketing, advertisement and recommendations. With the exponential growth of online social network services such as Facebook and Twitter, social influence can for the first time be measured over a large population. In this chapter, we survey the research on social influence analysis with a focus on the computational aspects. First, we present statistical measurements related to social influence. Second, we describe the literature on social similarity and influences. Third, we present the research on social influence maximization which has many practical applications including marketing and advertisement.

Keywords: Social network analysis, Social influence analysis, Network centrality, Influence maximization

1. Introduction

Social influence refers to the behavioral change of individuals affected by others in a network. Social influence is an intuitive and well-accepted phenomenon in social networks[22]. The strength of social influence depends on many factors such as the strength of relationships between people in the networks, the network distance between users, temporal effects, characteristics of networks and individuals in the network. In this chapter, we focus on computational aspect of social influence analysis and describe the measures and algorithms related to it. More specifically, we aim at qualitatively or quantitatively measuring the influence levels of nodes and edges in the network.

This chapter is organized as follows. First, we present standard measures and concepts of social networks in section 2. These measures are those of centrality, closeness and betweenness, and are fundamentally related to the concept of social influence in terms of the structural effects of different edges and nodes. These measures are also fundamental concepts about social network analysis. In section 2, we present the qualitative and quantitative social influence analysis and applications. This has been well studied in sociology research. Much of the work focuses on differentiating social correlation and social influence. Many qualitative models and tests have been proposed to explain social phenomena in social networks. However, most studies are limited to smaller scale data sets and macro-level observation, partly because of the lack of high-quality longitudinal data on social networks. In section 4, we survey influence maximization techniques, which go beyond simple statistic measures such as centrality. We also present several applications of influence maximization. These include methods for predicting customer behavior and online advertising through viral marketing. The conclusions are presented in section 5.

2. Influence Related Statistics

A social network is modeled as a graph $G = \{V, E\}$, where V is the set of nodes, and E is the set of edges. As is the convention, the links correspond to actors (people) and the links correspond to social relationships. At the local level, social influence is a directional effect from node A to node B, and is related to the edge strength from A to B. On a global level, some nodes can have intrinsically higher influence than others due to network structure. These global measures are often associated with nodes in the network rather than edges. We next present the concepts and measures at a local and global level respectively.

2.1 Edge Measures

Edge measures relate the influence-based concepts and measures on a pair of nodes. Such measures explain simple influence-related processes and interactions between individual nodes.

Tie strength. According to Granovetter's seminal work [32], the tie strength between two nodes depends on the overlap of their neighborhoods. In particular, the more common neighbors that a pair of nodes A and B may have, the stronger the tie between them. If the overlap of neighborhoods between A and B is large, we consider A and B to have a strong tie. Otherwise, they are considered to have a weak tie. We formally define the strength $S(A, B)$ in terms of their Jaccard coefficient.

$$S(A, B) = \frac{|n_A \cap n_B|}{|n_A \cup n_B|}$$

Here, n_A and n_B indicate the neighborhoods of A and B, respectively. Sometimes, the tie strength is defined under a different name called embeddedness. The embeddedness of an edge is high if two nodes incident on the edge have a high overlap of neighborhoods. When two individuals are connected by an embedded edge, it makes it easier for them to trust one another, because it is easier to find out dishonest behavior through mutual friends [33]. On the other end, when embeddedness is zero, two end nodes have no mutual friends. Therefore, it is riskier for them to trust each other because there are no mutual friends for behavioral verification.

A corollary from this tie strength is the hypothesis of *triadic closure*. This relates to the nature of the ties between sets of three actors A, B, and C. If strong ties connect A to B and A to C, then B and C are likely to be connected by a strong tie as well. Conversely, if A-B and A-C are weak ties, B and C are less likely to have a strong tie. Triadic closure is measured by the clustering coefficient of the network[35, 67]. The clustering coefficient of a node A is defined as the probability that two randomly selected friends of A are friends with each other. In other words, it is the fraction of pairs of friends of A that are linked to one another. This is naturally related to the problem of triangle counting in a network. Let n_Δ be the number of triangles in the network and $|E|$ be the number of edges. The clustering coefficient is formally defined as follows:

$$C = \frac{6n_\Delta}{|E|}$$

The naive way of counting the number of triangles n_Δ is expensive. An interesting connection between n_Δ and the eigenvalues of the network was discovered by Tsourakakis [66]. This work shows that n_Δ is approximately equal to the third-moment of the eigenvalues (or $\sum \lambda_i^3$, where λ_i is the ith eigenvalue). Given the skewed distribution of eigenvalues, the triangle counts can be approximated by computing the third moment of only a small number of the top eigenvalues. This also provides an efficient way for computing the clustering coefficient, because the top few eigenvalues can be computed more efficiently than the exhaustive determination of all the eigenvalues.

Weak ties. When the overlap of the neighborhoods of A and B is small, the connection A-B is considered to be a weak tie. When there is no overlap, the connection A-B is a local bridge [32]. In the extreme case, the removal of A-B may result in the disconnection of the connected component containing A and B. In such a case, the connection A-B may be considered a global bridge. It may be argued that in real networks, global bridges occur rarely as compared to local bridges. However, the effect of local and global bridges is quite similar.

Edge Betweenness. Another important measure is the edge betweenness, which measures the total amount of flow across the edge. Here, we assume that the information flow between A and B are evenly distributed on the shortest paths between A and B. Freeman [27, 28] first articulated the concept of betweenness in the context of sociology. One application of edge betweenness is that of graph partitioning. The idea is to gradually remove edges of high betweenness scores to turn the network into a hierarchy of disconnected components. These disconnected components will be the clusters of nodes in the network. More detailed studies on clustering methods are presented in the work by Girvan and Newman [29].

2.2 Node Measures

Node-based centrality is defined in order to measure the importance of a node in the network. Centrality has attracted a lot of attention as a tool for studying social networks [28, 9]. A node with high centrality score is usually considered more highly influential than other nodes in the network. Many centrality measures have been proposed based on the precise definition of influence. The main principle in categorizing the centrality measures is the type of random walk computation involved. In particular, centrality measures can be grouped into two categories: *radial* and *medial* measures [9]. Radial measures assess random walks that start or end from a given node. On the other hand, medial measures assess random walks that pass through a given node. The radial measures are further categorized into *volume* measures and *length* measures based on the type of random walks. Volume measures fix the length of walks and find the volume (or number) of the walks limited by the length. Length measures fix the volume of the target nodes and find the length of walks to reach the target volume. Next, we introduce some popular centrality measures based on these categories.

Degree. The first group of the centrality measures is that of the radial and volume-based measures. The simplest and most popular measure in this category is that of degree centrality. Let A be the adjacency matrix of a network, and $deg(i)$ be the degree of node i. The degree centrality c_i^{DEG} of node i is defined to be the degree of the node:

$$c_i^{DEG} = deg(i).$$

One way of interpreting the degree centrality is that it counts the number of paths of length 1 that starts from a node. A natural generalization from this perspective is the $K - path$ centrality which is the number of paths of length at most k that start from a node.

Another class of measures are based on the diffusion behavior in the network. The Katz centrality [40] counts the number of walks starting from a node, while penalizing longer walks. More formally, the Katz centrality c_i^{KATZ} of node i is defined as follows:

$$c_i^{KATZ} = e_i^T (\sum_{j=1}^{\infty} (\beta A)^j) \mathbf{1}$$

Here, e_i is a column vector whose ith element is 1, and all other elements are 0. The value of β is a positive penalty constant between 0 and 1.

A slight variation of the Katz measure is the Bonacich centrality [8] which allows for negative values of β. The Bonacich centrality c_i^{BON} of node i is defined as follows:

$$c_i^{BON} = e_i^T (\frac{1}{\beta} \sum_{j=1}^{\infty} (\beta A)^j) \mathbf{1}$$

Here the negative weight allows to subtract the even-numbered walks from the odd-numbered walks which have an interpretation in exchange networks [9]. The Katz and the Bonacich centralities are special cases of the Hubbell centrality [37]. The Hubbell centrality c_i^{HUB} of node i is defined to be

$$c_i^{HUB} = e_i^T (\sum_{j=0}^{\infty} X^j) \mathbf{y}$$

Here, X is a matrix and y is a vector. It can be shown that $X = \beta A$ and $y = \beta A \mathbf{1}$ lead to the Katz centrality, and $X = \beta A$ and $y = A\mathbf{1}$ lead to the Bonacich centrality. The eigenvector centrality [7], the principal eigenvector of the matrix A, is related to the Katz centrality: the eigenvector centrality is the limit of the Katz centrality as β approaches $\frac{1}{\lambda}$ from below [9].

Closeness. The second group of the centrality measures is that of radial and length based measures. Unlike the volume based measures, the length based measures count the length of the walks. The most popular centrality measure in this group is the Freeman's closeness centrality [28]. It measures the centrality by computing the average of the shortest distances to all other nodes. Then, the closeness centrality c_i^{CLO} of node i is defined as follows:

$$c_i^{CLO} = e_i^T S \mathbf{1}.$$

Here S be the matrix whose (i, j)th element contains the length of the shortest path from node i to j and $\mathbf{1}$ is the all one vector.

Node Betweenness. As is the case for edges of high betweenness, nodes of high betweenness occupy critical positions in the network structure, and are therefore able to play critical roles. This is often enabled by a large amount of flow, which is carried by nodes which occupy a position at the interface of tightly-knit groups. Such nodes are considered to have high betweenness. The concept of betweenness is related to nodes that span *structural holes* in a social network. We will discuss more on this point slightly later.

Another popular group of the centrality measures is that of *medial* measures. It is called 'medial' since all the walks *passing through* a node are considered. The most well-known centrality in this group is the Freeman's betweenness centrality [27]. It measures how much a given node lies in the shortest paths of other nodes. The betweenness centrality c_i^{BET} of node i is defined as follows:

$$c_i^{BET} = \sum_{j,k} \frac{b_{jik}}{b_{jk}}$$

Here b_{jk} is the number of shortest paths from node j to k, and b_{jik} be the number of shortest paths from node j to k that pass through node i.

The naive algorithm for computing the betweenness involves all-pair shortest paths. This requires $\Theta(n^3)$ time and $\Theta(n^2)$ storage. Brandes [10] designed a faster algorithm with the use of n single-source-shortest-path algorithms. This requires $O(n+m)$ space and runs in $O(nm)$ and $O(nm+n^2 \log n)$ time, where n is the number of nodes and m is the number of edges.

Newman [52] proposed an alternative betweenness centrality measure based on random walks on the graph. The main idea is that instead of considering shortest paths, it considers all possible walks and computes the betweenness from these different walks. Then, the Newman's betweenness centrality c_i^{NBE} of node i is defined as follows:

$$c_i^{NBE} = \sum_{j \neq i \neq k} R_{jk}^{(i)}.$$

Here $R^{(i)}$ be the matrix whose (j,k)th element $R_{jk}^{(i)}$ contains the probability of a random walk from j to k, which contains i as an intermediate node.

Structural holes. In a network, we call a node a structural hole if it is connected to multiple local bridges. A canonical example is that an actor's success within a social network[1] often depends on their access to local bridges [12]. By removing such an actor, an "empty space" will occur in the network. This is referred to as a *structural hole*. The actor who serves as a structural hole

[1]This analogously refers to a person's success within a company or organization.

can interconnect information originating from multiple noninteracting parties. Therefore, this actor is structurally important to the connectivity of diverse regions of the network. Another interesting point is that the interests of the actor representing a structural hole and of the organization may not be aligned. For the organization, accelerating the information flow between groups could be beneficial, which requires building of bridges. However, this building of bridges would come at the expense of structural hole's latent power of regulating information flow at the boundaries of these groups.

3. Social Similarity and Influence

A central problem for social influence is to understand the interplay between similarity and social ties [20]. A lot of research has tried to identify influence and correlation in social networks from many different aspects: social similarity and influence [2, 20]; marketing through social influence [21, 55], influence maximization [41]; social influence model and practice through conformity, compliance and obedience [18, 24], and social influence in virtual worlds [23, 5].

3.1 Homophily

Homophily [43] is one of the most fundamental characteristics of social networks. This suggests that an actor in the social network tends to be similar to their connected neighbors or "friends". This is a natural result, because the friends or neighbors of a given actor in the social network are not a random sample of the underlying population. The neighbors of a given actor in the social network are often similar to that actor along many different dimensions including racial and ethnic dimensions, age, their occupations, and their interests and beliefs. McPherson et al. [48] provide an extensive review of research in the long and rich history on homophily. Singla et al. [60] has conducted a large-scale experiment of homophily on real social networks, which includes data from user interactions in the MSN Messenger network and a subset of Microsoft Web search data collected in the summer of 2006. They observe that the similarities between friends is significantly larger than a random pairwise sample, especially in attributes such as age, location and query category. This experiment confirms the existence of homophily at a global scale in large online social networks.

The phenomenon of homophily can originate from many different mechanisms:

- *Social influence:* This indicates that people tend to follow the behaviors of their friends. The social influence effect leads people to adopt behaviors exhibited by their neighbors.

- *Selection:* This indicates that people tend to create relationships with other people who are already similar to them;
- *Confounding variables:* Other unknown variables exist, which may cause friends to behave similarly with one another.

These three factors are often intertwined in real social networks, and the overall effect is to provide a strong support for the homophily phenomenon. Intuitively, the effects of selection and social influence lead to different applications in mining social network data. In particular, recommendation systems are based on the selection/social similarity, while viral marketing [21, 55] is based on social influence. To model these different factors, several models have been proposed [36, 20].

Generative models for selection and influence. Holme and Newman [36] proposed a generative model to balance the effects of selection and influence. The idea is to initially place the M edges of the network uniformly at random between vertex pairs, and also assign opinions to vertices uniformly at random. With this initialization, an influence- and selection-based dynamic is simulated. Each step of the simulation either moves an edge to lie between two individuals whose opinions agree (selection process), or we change the opinion of an individual to agree with one of their neighbors (influence process). The results of their simulation confirmed that the selection tend to generate a large number of small clusters, while social influence will generate large coherent clusters. Thus, this interesting model suggests that these two factors both support clusters in the network, though the nature of such clusters is quite different.

Every vertex in the Holme-Newman model [36] at a given time can only have one opinion. This may be an oversimplification of real social networks. To address this limitation, Crandall et al. [20] introduced multi-dimensional opinion vectors to better model complex social networks. In particular, they assumed that there is a set of m possible activities in the social network. Each node v at time t has an m-dimensional vector $v(t)$, where the ith coordinate of $v(t)$ represents the extent to which person v is engaging in activity i. They use cosine similarity to compute the similarity between two people. Similar to the Holme-Newman model, Crandall et al. also propose a more comprehensive generative model which samples a person's activities based on their own history, their neighbors' history, and a background distribution. Crandall's model is arguably more powerful, but also requires more parameters. Therefore more data is required in order to learn the parameters. Finally, they applied their model and conducted a predictive modeling study on wikipedia and live journal datasets. The benefit of the proposed similarity model are still inconclusive.

Quantifying influence and selection. Subsequent to the work in [20], Scripps et al. [58] proposed the formal computational definitions of selection and influence. We formally define selection and influence as follows:

$$Selection = \frac{p(a_{ij}^t = 1 | a_{ij}^{t-1} = 0, \langle \mathbf{x}_i^{t-1}, \mathbf{x}_j^{t-1} \rangle > \epsilon)}{p(a_{ij}^t = 1 | a_{ij}^{t-1} = 0)}$$

Here, the denominator is the conditional probability that an unlinked pair will become linked and the numerator is the same probability for unlinked pairs whose similarity exceeds the threshold ϵ. Values greater than one indicate the presence of selection.

$$Influence = \frac{p(\langle \mathbf{x}_i^t, \mathbf{x}_j^{tT} \rangle > \langle \mathbf{x}_i^{t-1}, \mathbf{x}_j^{t-1} \rangle | a_{ij}^{t-1} = 0, a_{ij}^t = 1)}{p(\langle \mathbf{x}_i^t, \mathbf{x}_j^t \rangle > \langle \mathbf{x}_i^{t-1}, \mathbf{x}_j^{t-1} \rangle | a_{ij}^{t-1} = 0)}$$

Here, the numerator is the conditional probability that similarity increases from time $t-1$ to t between two nodes that became linked at time t and the denominator is the probability that the similarity increases from time $t-1$ to t between two nodes that were not linked at time $t-1$. As with selection, values greater than one indicate the presence of influence.

Based on this definition, Scripps et al. [58] present a matrix alignment framework by incorporating the temporal information to learn the weight of different attributes for establishing relationships between users. This can be done by optimizing (minimizing) the following objective function:

$$\min_W \sum_{t=1}^{T} \| A^t - X^{t-1} W X^{(t-1)\top} \|_F^2 \tag{7.1}$$

where the diagonal elements of W correspond to the vector of weights of attributes and $\|\cdot\|_F$ denotes the Frobenius norm. Solving the objective function (Eq. 7.1) is equivalent to the problem of finding the weights of different attributes associated with users. A distortion distance function is used to measure the degree of influence and selection.

The above method can be used to analyze influence and selection. However, it does not differentiate the influence from different angles (topics). Several theories in sociology [32, 42] show that the effect of the social influence from different angles (topics) may be different. This can be easily understood by observing different social phenomenon for different angles. For example, colleagues have strong influence on an actor's work, whereas friends have strong influence on an actor's daily life. Thus, there are several challenging problems in terms of differentiating the social influences from different angles (topics). A number of key questions arise in this context. (a) How do we quantify the strength of those social influences? (b) How do we construct a model and estimate the model parameters for real large networks?

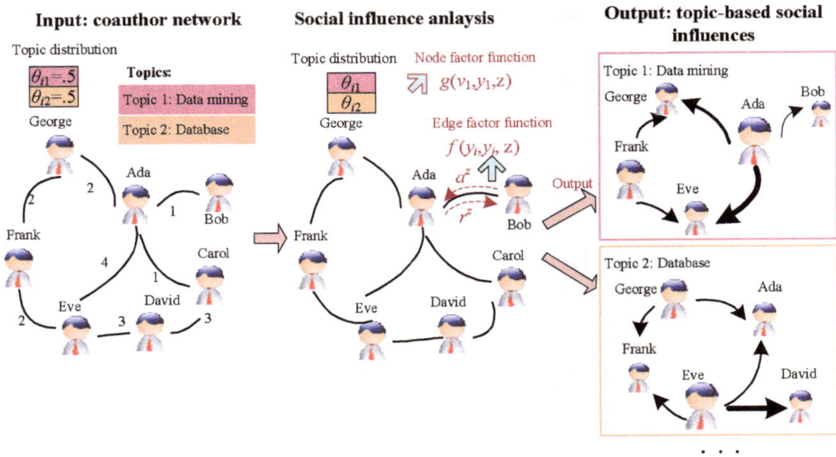

Topic-level Social influence Analysis on Co-author Network.

The motivation can be further explained using Example Figure 3.1.0.0. The left figure illustrates the input, which is a co-author network of 7 researchers, and the topic distribution of each researcher. For example, George has the same probability (.5) on both topics, "data mining" and "database"; The right figure shows the output of our social influence analysis: two social influence graphs, one for each topic, where the arrows indicate the direction and strength. We see that Ada is the key person on "data mining", while Eve is the key person on "databases". Thus, the goal is to effectively and efficiently obtain the social influence graphs for real and large networks.

To address this problem, Tang et al. [63] propose a Topical Factor Graph (TFG) model to formalize the topic-level social influence analysis into a unified graphical model, and present Topical Affinity Propagation (TAP) for model learning. In particular, the goal of the model is to simultaneously capture the user topical distributions (or user interests), similarity between users, and network structure. Figure 7.1 shows the graphical structure of the proposed model. The TFG model has a set of observed variables $\{v_i\}_{i=1}^N$ and a set of hidden vectors $\{\mathbf{y}_i\}_{i=1}^N$, which correspond to the N nodes in the input network.

The hidden vector $\mathbf{y}_i \in \{1, \ldots, N\}^T$ models the topic-level influence from other nodes to node v_i. Each element y_i^z takes the value from the set $\{1, \ldots, N\}$, and represents the node that has the highest probability to influence node v_i on topic z.

For example, Figure 7.1 shows a simple example of an TFG. The observed data consists of four nodes $\{v_1, \ldots, v_4\}$, which have corresponding hidden vectors $\mathbf{Y} = \{\mathbf{y}_1, \ldots, \mathbf{y}_4\}$. The edges between the hidden nodes indicate the

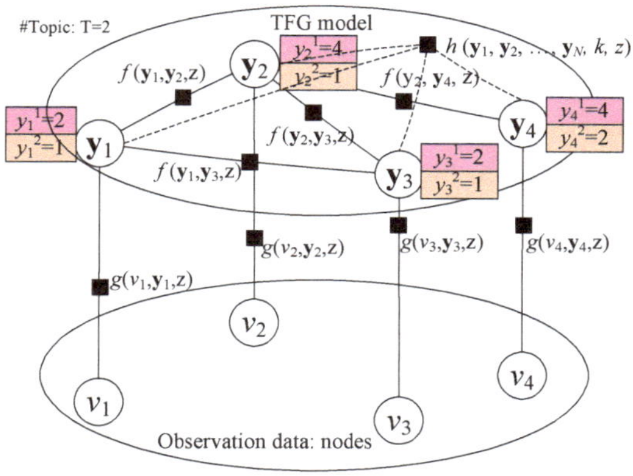

Figure 7.1. Graphical representation of the topical factor graph model. $\{v_1 \dots v_4\}$ are observable nodes in the social network; $\{y1 \dots y_4\}$ are hidden vectors defined on all nodes, with each element representing which node has the highest probability to influence the corresponding node; $g(.)$ represents a feature function defined on a node, $f(.)$ represents a feature function defined on an edge; and $h(.)$ represents a global feature function defined for each node, i.e. $k \in \{1 \dots N\}$.

four social relationships in the original network (or edges in the original network).

Three types of feature functions are defined in order to capture the network information: node feature function $g(v_i, \mathbf{y}_i, z)$, edge feature function $f(\mathbf{y}_i, \mathbf{y}_j, z)$, and global feature function $h(\mathbf{y}_1, \dots, \mathbf{y}_N, k, z)$.

The node feature function g describes the local information on nodes (e.g., attributes associated with users or topical distribution of users). The edge feature function f describes the correlation between users via the edge on the graph model, and the global feature function captures constraints defined on the network. Based on the formulation, an objective function is defined by maximizing the likelihood of the observation.

$$P(\mathbf{v}, \mathbf{Y}) = \frac{1}{Z} \prod_{k=1}^{N} \prod_{z=1}^{T} h(\mathbf{y}_1, \dots, \mathbf{y}_N, k, z)$$

$$\prod_{i=1}^{N} \prod_{z=1}^{T} g(v_i, \mathbf{y}_i, z) \prod_{e_{kl} \in E} \prod_{z=1}^{T} f(\mathbf{y}_k, \mathbf{y}_l, z) \tag{7.2}$$

Here, Z is a normalizing factor; $\mathbf{v} = [v_1, \dots, v_N]$ and $\mathbf{Y} = [\mathbf{y}_1, \dots, \mathbf{y}_N]$ corresponds to all observed and hidden variables, respectively. The feature function f, g, and h can be defined in multiple different ways. For example, in the work described in [63], f is defined with binary values in order to capture the existence of the edge between two users; the node feature function g is defined according to the similarity of two users on a topic; and the global feature function h is defined as a constraint.

Based on this formulation, the task of social influence is cast as that of identifying the node which has the highest probability to influence another node on a specific topic along with the edge. This is the same as that of maximizing the likelihood function $P(\mathbf{v}, \mathbf{Y})$.

3.2 Existential Test for Social Influence

Anagnostopoulos et al. [2] try to differentiate social influence from homophily or confounding variables by proposing the shuffle test and edge reversal test. The idea of shuffle test is that if social influence does not play a role, even though an agent's probability of activation could depend on her friends, the timing of such an activation should be independent of the timing of other agents. Therefore, the data distribution and characteristics will not change even if the exact time of occurrence is shuffled around. The idea of edge-reversal test is that other forms of social correlation (than social influence) are only based on the fact that two friends often share common characteristics or are affected by the same external variables and are independent of which of these two individuals has named the other as a friend. Thus, reversing the edges will not change our estimate of the social correlation significantly. On the other hand, social influence spreads in the direction specified by the edges of the graph, and hence reversing the edges should intuitively change the estimate of the correlation. Anagnostopoulos and et al. [2] test their models using tagging data from Flickr and validate social influence as a source of correlation between the actions of individuals with social ties.

The proposed tests in [2] assume a static network, which is true in many real social networks. LaFond and Neville [25] propose a different randomization test with the use of a relational autoregression model. More specifically, they propose to model the social network as a time-evolving graph $G_t = (V, E_t)$ where V is the set of all nodes, E_t is the set of all edges at time t. Besides G_t, the nodes have some attribute at time t denoted by X_t. The main idea is that selection and social influence can be differentiated through the autocorrelation between X_t and G_t . On the one hand, the selection process can be represented as a causal relationship from X_{t-1} to G_t, which means the node attributes at time $t-1$, i.e., X_{t-1}, determines the social network at G_t. On the other hand, the social influence can be represented as the causal relation from G_{t-1} to X_t, which means the social network at time t, i.e., G_t, determines the node attributes at time t, i.e., X_t .

Aral et al. [3] propose a diffusion model for differentiating selection and social influence. In particular, their intuition is that although the diffusion patterns created by peer influence-driven contagions and homophilous diffusion are similar, the effects are likely to result in significantly different dynamics. Influence-driven contagions are self-reinforcing and display rapid, exponential, and less predictable diffusion as they evolve, whereas selection-driven diffusion processes are governed by the distributions of characteristics over nodes. In [3], they develop a matched sample estimation framework to distinguish influence and homophily effects in dynamic networks.

Social influence in Healthcare. Christakis and Fowler studied the effect of social influence on health related issues including alcohol consumption [56], obesity [16], smoking [17], trouble sleep [49], loneliness [13], happiness [26]. In these studies, they use longitudinal data covering roughly 12,000 people and correlate health status and social network structure over a 32-year period. They found that clusters of nodes with similar health status in the network. In another word, people tend to be more similar in health status to their friends than in a random graph. The main focus of all these studies is to explain why homophily of health status is present. The analysis in Christakis and Fowler argues that, even accounting for effects of selection and confounding variables, there is significant evidence for social influence as well. The evidence suggests that health status can be influenced by the health status of the neighbors. For example, their obesity study [16] suggests that obesity may exhibit some amount of "contagion" in the social network. Although people do not necessarily catch it as the way one catches the flu, it can spread through the underlying social network via the mechanism of social influence. Similar observations of their study on alcohol consumption[56] discover that clusters of drinkers and abstainers were present in the network at all time points, and the clusters extended to 3 degrees of separation through the social network. These clusters were not only due to selective formation of social ties among drinkers but also seem to reflect social influence. Changes in the alcohol consumption behavior of a person's social network had a statistically significant effect on that person's subsequent alcohol consumption behavior. The behaviors of immediate neighbors and co-workers were not significantly associated with a person's drinking behavior, but the behavior of relatives and friends was.

3.3 Influence and Actions

Influence is usually reflected in changes in social action patterns (user behavior) in the social network. Recent work [31, 68] has studied the problem of learning the influence degree from historical user actions, while some other work [58, 64] investigates how social actions evolve in the context of the network, and how such actions are affected by social influence factors. Before introducing these methods, we will first define the time-varying attribute augmented networks with user actions:

DEFINITION 7.1 ***Time-varying attribute-action augmented network**: The time-varying attribute-action augmented network is denoted as $G^t = (V^t, E^t, X^t, Y^t)$, wheren V^t is the set of users and E^t is the set of links between users at time t, X^t represents the attribute matrix of all users in the network at time t and Y^t represents the set of actions of all users at time t.*

For all actions, they define a set of action tuples as $\mathbf{Y} = (v, y, t)$, where $v \in V^t, t \in 1, \cdots, T$, and $y \in Y^t$.

Learning influence probabilities Goyal et al. [31] study the problem of learning the influence degrees (called probabilities) from a historic log of user actions. They present the concept of user influential probability and action influential probability. The assumption is that if user v_i performs an action y at time t and later ($t' > t$) his friend v_j also perform the action, then there is an influence from v_i on v_j. The goal of learning influence probabilities [31] is find a (static of dynamic) model to best capture the user influence and action influence information in the network. They give a general user influential probability and action influential probability definitions as follows:

- User Influence Probability

$$infl(v_i) = \frac{|\{y|\exists v, \Delta t : prop(a, v_i, v_j, \Delta t) \wedge 0 \leq \Delta t|}{Y_{v_i}}$$

- Action Influence Probability

$$infl(y) = \frac{|\{v_i|\exists v_j, \Delta t : prop(a, v_j, v_i, \Delta t) \wedge 0 \leq \Delta t\}|}{\text{number of users performing } y}$$

where $\Delta t = t_j - t_i$ represents the difference between the time when user v_j performing the action and the time when user v_i performing the action, given $e_{ij} = 1$; $prop(a, v_i, v_j, \Delta t)$ represents the action propagation score.

Goyal et al. [31] propose three methods in order to approximate the action propagation $prop(a, v_i, v_j, \Delta t)$: 1) static model (based on Bernoulli distribution, Jaccard Index, and Partial Credits), 2) Continuous Time (CT) Model, and 3) Discrete Time (DT) Model. The model can be learned with a two-stage algorithm. Finally, the learned influence probabilities have been applied to action prediction and the experiments show that the Continuous Time (CT) model can achieve a better performance than other models on the Flickr social network with the action of "joining a group".

Social action tracking The main advantage of methods proposed in [31] is that the model is scalable and it is effective for a large social network. One

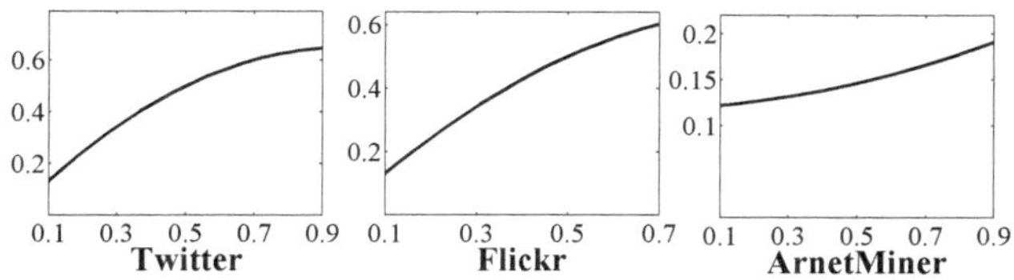

Figure 7.2. Social influence. The x-axis stands for the percentage of one's friends who perform an action at $t-1$ and the y-axis represents the likelihood that the user also performs the action at t.

limitation is that it ignores the correlation between user actions, and it also does not consider the attributes associated with each user node.

To address this problem, Tan et al. [62] propose the social action tracking problem. This problem discusses how to simultaneously model the social network structure, user attributes and user actions over time. They perform an analysis on three real social networks: Twitter[2], Flickr[3], and Arnetminer[4]. On Twitter, the action is defined as whether a user discusses the topic "Haiti Earthquake" on his microblogs (tweets). On Flickr, the action is defined as whether a user adds a photo to his favorite list. In the case of Arnetminer, the action is defined as whether a researcher publishes a paper on a specific conference (or journal). The analysis includes three aspects: (1) social influence; (2) time-dependency of user actions; (3) action correlation between users. Figure 7.2 [62] shows the effect of social influence. We see that with the percentage of one's friends performing an action increasing, the likelihood that the user also performs the action is increased. For example, when the percentage of one's friends discussing "Haiti Earthquake" on their tweets increases the likelihood that the user herself posts tweets about "Haiti Earthquake" is also increased significantly. Figure 7.3 illustrates how a user's action is dependent on his historic behaviors. It can be seen that a strong time-dependency exists for users' actions. For instance, on Twitter, averagely users who posted tweets about "Haiti Earthquake" will have a much higher probability (+20 to 40%) to post tweets on this topic than those who never discussed this topic on their blogs. Figure 7.4 shows the correlation between users' actions at the same timestamp. An interesting phenomenon is that friends may perform an action at the same time. For example, on Twitter, two friends have a higher probability (+19.6%) to discuss the "Haiti Earthquake" than two users randomly chosen from the network.

[2]http://www.twitter.com, a microblogging system.
[3]http://www.flickr.com, a photo sharing system.
[4]http://arnetminer.org, an academic search system.

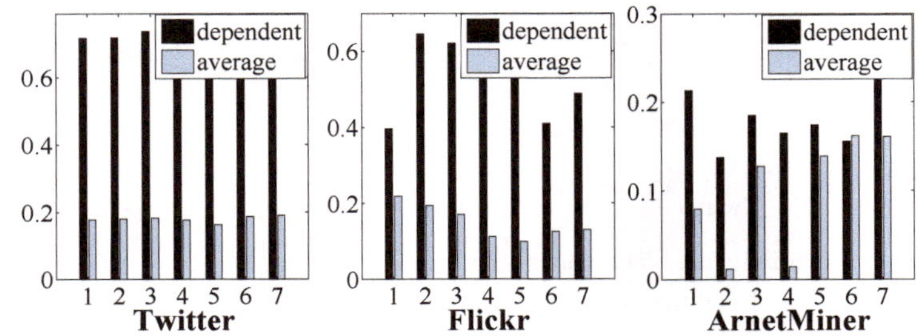

Figure 7.3. Time-dependency of user actions. The x-axis stands for different timestamps. "dependent" denotes the likelihood that a user performs an action which was previously performed by herself; "average" represents the likelihood that a user performs the action.

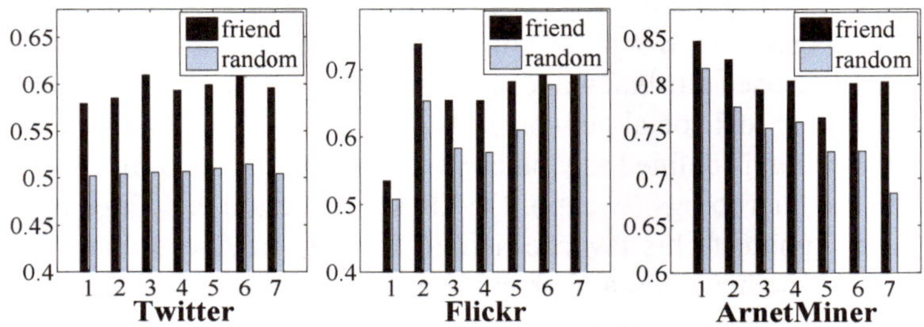

Figure 7.4. Action correlation. The x-axis stands for different time windows. "friend" denotes the likelihood that two friends perform an action together; "random" represents the likelihood that two random users perform the action together.

In order to model and track social influence and user actions, Tan et al. [62] propose a Noise-Tolerant Time-varying Factor Graph Model (NTT-FGM), which is based on three intuitions:

1 User actions at time t are influenced by their friends' historic actions (time $< t$).

2 User actions at time t are usually dependent on their previous actions.

3 User actions at a same time t have a (strong) correlation.

Moreover, the discrete variable y_i^t only models the user action at a coarse level, but cannot describe the intention of the user to perform an action. Directly modeling the social action Y would inevitably introduce noise into the model. A continuous variable for modeling the *action bias* is favorable. Thus, the concept of latent action state is presented:

DEFINITION 7.2 ***Latent action state**: For each user action y_i^t, we define a (continuous) latent state $z_i^t \in [0, 1]$, which corresponds to a combination of*

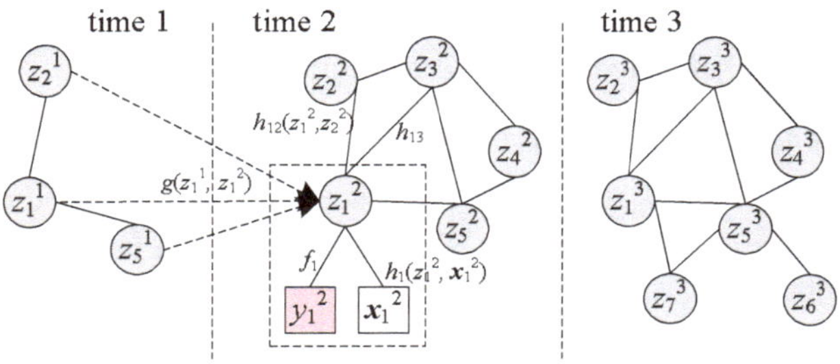

Figure 7.5. Graphical representation of the NTT-FGM model. Each circle stands for a user's latent action state z_i^t at time t in the network, which is used to characterize the intention degree of the user to perform the action; the latent state is associated with the action y_i^t, a vector of attributes $\mathbf{x}_i^t$, and depends on friends' historic actions $\mathbf{z}_{\sim v_i}^{t-1}$ and correlates with friends' actions $\mathbf{z}_{\sim v_i}^t$ at time t; $g(.)$ denotes a factor function to represent the friends' influence on a user's action; $h_i(.)$ represents a factor defined on user v_i's attributes; and $h_{ij}(.)$ represents a factor to capture the correlation between users' actions.

the observed action y_i and a possible bias, to describe the actual intensity of the intention of the user to perform the action.

Figure 7.5 shows the graphical structure of the NTT-FGM model. An action of user v_i at time t, i.e., y_i^t is modeled by using a (continuous) latent action state z_i^t, which is dependent on friends' historic actions $\mathbf{z}_{\sim v_i}^{t-1}$ (where $\sim v_i$ represents friends of user v_i in the network), users' action correlation $\mathbf{z}_{\sim v_i}^t$, and users' attributes $\mathbf{x}_i^t$. Specifically, in the NTT-FGM model, each discrete action is mapped into the latent state space and the action bias is modeled using a factor function. For example, for $y_i^t = 1$, a small value of its corresponding z_i^t suggests that a user v_i has a low intention to perform the action, thus a large action bias $|y_i^t - z_i^t|$. Next, influence between users is modeled using the latent states based on the same assumption: latent states of user actions at time t are conditionally independent of all the previous states given the latent states at time $t-1$. Finally, the correlation between actions is also modeled in the latent state space. A Markov random field is defined to model the dependency (correlation) among the continuous latent states.

Thus, given a series of attribute-augmented networks denoted by $\mathbf{G} = \{G^t = (V^t, E^t, X^t, Y^t)\}$, where $t \in \{1, \cdots, T\}$ and $V = V^1 \cup V^2 \cup \ldots \cup V^T, |V| = N$, the joint distribution over the actions $\mathbf{Y}$ given $\mathbf{G}$ can be written as follows:

$$p(\mathbf{Y}|\mathbf{G}) = \prod_{t=1}^{T} \prod_{i=1}^{N} f(y_i^t|z_i^t) f(z_i^t|\mathbf{z}_{\sim v_i}^{t-1}) f(z_i^t|\mathbf{z}_{\sim v_i}^t, \mathbf{x}_i^t) \tag{7.3}$$

where notation $\sim v_i$ represents neighbors of v_i in the social network. The joint probability has three types of factor functions:

- Action bias factor: $f(y_i^t|z_i^t)$ represents the posterior probability of user v_i's action y_i at time t given the continuous latent state z_i^t;
- Influence factor: $f(z_i^t|\mathbf{z}_{\sim v_i}^{t-1})$ reflects friends' influence on user v_i's action at time t;
- Correlation factor: $f(z_i^t|\mathbf{z}_{\sim v_i}^t, \mathbf{x}_i^t)$ denotes the correlation between users' action at time t.

The three factors can be instantiated in different ways, reflecting the prior knowledge for different applications. Finally, in the work [62], all the three factor function are defined by quadratic functions due to two reasons: the quadratic function is integrable and it offer the possibility to design an exact solution to solve the objective function (joint probability). Finally, the model is learned using an EM-style algorithm and for scale up to large-scale data sets, a distributed learning algorithm has been designed based on the MPI (Message Passing Interface).

Mixture model for user actions Manavoglu et al. [47] propose a mixture-model based approach for learning individualized behavior (action) models for Web users where a behavior model is a probabilistic model describing which actions the user will perform in the future.

They first build a global behavior model for the entire population and then personalize this global model for the existing users by assigning each user individual component weights for the mixture model, and then use these individual weights to group the users into behavior model clusters. Finally they show that the clusters generated in this manner are interpretable and able to represent dominant behavior patterns.

They claim that they are able to eliminate one of the biggest problems of personalization, which is the lack of sufficient information about each individual. This is achieved by starting with a global model and optimizing the weights for each individual with respect to the amount of data available for him or her.

Specifically, for each action in a user session, the history $H(U)$ is defined by the ordered sequence of actions, which have been observed so far. Their behavior model for individual U is a model, that predicts the next action A^{next} given the history $H(U)$. Therefore the problem is to infer this model, $P(A^{next}|H(U), Data)$, for each individual given the training data. For example, the Markov model is often used for such problems.

In the first stage, they use a global mixture model to capture the ordered sequence of actions for an individual U as follows:

$$P(A^{next}|H(U), Data) = \sum_{k=1}^{N_c} \alpha_k P(A^{next}|H(U), Data, k) \quad (7.4)$$

Here the prior probability of cluster k is denoted by α_k, and therefore we have $\sum_{k=1}^{N_c} \alpha_k = 1$. The distribution for the k-th component is denoted by the notation $P(A^{next}|H(U), Data, k)$. For the global model, the different α_k take on the same values across all the users.

There are two ways to model the cluster-specific distributions: a first order Markov model and the maximum entropy model. Regarding the Markov model, we can use the following way to model the k-th cluster distribution

$$P(A^{next}|H(U), Data, k) \propto \theta_{0,k} \prod_{h=1}^{|H(U)|} \theta_{h \to (h+1),k} \tag{7.5}$$

where $\theta_{0,k}$ is the probability of observing $H(U)_0$ as the first action in the history, and $\theta_{h \to (h+1),k}$ is the probability of observing a transition from action number h to action number $h+1$ in the history.

In the second stage, we personalize the mixture model by using individual cluster probabilities, $\alpha_{U,k}$'s, for each user as follows:

$$P_U(A^{next}|H(U), Data) = \sum_{k=1}^{N_c} \alpha_{U,k} P(A^{next}|H(U), Data, k) \tag{7.6}$$

where $\sum_{k=1}^{N_c} \alpha_{U,k} = 1$. The component distribution, $P(A^{next}|H(U), Data, k)$, is the same as in global mixture model: either maximum entropy or Markov model, which is fixed across all users.

An EM-style algorithm is utilized to estimate the model parameters.

3.4 Influence and Interaction

Besides the attribute and user actions, influence can be also reflected by the interactions between users. Typically, online communities contain ancillary interaction information about users. For example, a Facebook user has a Wall page, where her friends can post messages. Based on the messages posted on the Wall, one can infer which friends are close and which are acquaintances only. Similarly, one can use follower and following members on Twitter to infer the strength of a relationship.

Xiang et al [68] propose a latent variable model to infer relationship strength based on profile similarity and interaction activity, with the goal of automatically distinguishing strong relation- ships from weak ones. The model attempts to represent the intrinsic causality of social interactions via statistical dependencies. It distinguishes interaction activity from user profile data, and integrates two types of information by considering the relationship strength to

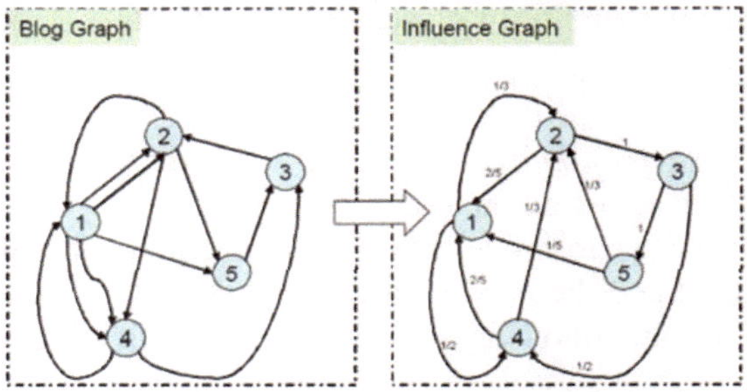

Figure 7.6. From blog graph to influence graph

be the hidden effect of user profile similarities, as well as the hidden cause of the interactions between users.

The input to the problem can be considered an attribute-augmented network $G = (V, E, X)$ with interaction information $\mathbf{m}_{ij} \subset M$ between users, where $\mathbf{m}_{ij}$ is a set of different interactions between users v_i and v_j. The model also uses continuous latent variable z, but for each link rather than action. The latent variable can be further treated as the strength of the social influence.

There are some methods aiming to model social influence using a link analysis method. The basic idea is similar to the concept of random walks. Java et al. [39] employ such a method to model the influence in online social networks.

Figure 7.6 shows the conversion of a blog network into an influence graph. A link from u to v indicates that u is influenced by v. The edges in the influence graph are the reverse of the blog graph to indicate this influence. Multiple edges indicate stronger influence and are weighted higher. In the influence graph, the direction of edges is opposite as the blog graph. The influence weight $W_{u,v}$ can be computed by the following expression:

$$W_{u,v} = \frac{C_{u,v}}{d_v}$$

Based on the influence graph, they proposed several typical applications, such as spam detection and node selection. The classical PageRank and HITS algorithms can also be employed here.

3.4.1 Influence and Friendship Drift. Sarkar et al. [57] study the problem of friendships drifting over time. They explore two aspects of social network modeling by the use of a latent space model. First, they generalize a static model of relationships into a dynamic model that accounts for friendships drifting over time. Second, they show how to make it tractable to learn such models from data, even as the number of entities n gets large. The generalized model associates each entity with a point in p-dimensional Euclidean latent space. The points can move as time progresses but large moves in latent space are improbable. Observed links between entities are more likely if the entities are close in latent space. They show how to make such a model tractable (sub-quadratic in the number of entities) by the use of the following characteristics (a) appropriate kernel functions for similarity in latent space; (b) the use of low dimensional KD-trees; (c) a new efficient dynamic adaptation of multidimensional scaling for a first pass of approximate projection of entities into latent space; and (d) an efficient conjugate gradient update rule for non-linear local optimization in which amortized time per entity during an update is O($logn$). They use both synthetic and real data on up to 11,000 entities which indicate near-linear scaling in computation time and improved performance over four alternative approaches. We also illustrate the system operating on twelve years of NIPS co-authorship data.

3.4.2 Influence and Autocorrelation. Autocorrelation refers to correlation between values of the same variable (e.g., action or attribute) associated with linked nodes (users) [51]. More formally, autocorrelation in social networks, and in particular for influence analysis, can be defined with respect to a set of linked users $e_{ij} = 1, e_{ij} \in E$ and an attribute matrix X associated with these uses, as the correlation between the values of X on these instance pairs.

Neville et al. provide an overview of research on autocorrelation in a number of fields with an emphasis on implications for relational learning, and outline a number of challenges and opportunities for model learning and inference [51]. Social phenomena such as social influence, diffusion processes, and the principle of homophily give rise to autocorrelated observations as well, through their influence on social interactions that govern the data generation process.

Another related topic is referred to as collective behavior in social networks. Essentially, collective behavior modeling is to understand the behavior correlation in the social network. For this purpose, much work has been done. For example, Tang and Liu [65] aim to predict collective behaviors in social media. In particular, they try to answer the question: given information about some individuals, how can we infer the behavior of unobserved individuals in the same network?

They attempt to utilize the behavior correlation presented in a social network to predict the collective behavior in social media. The input of their problem is the same as Definition 7.1. They propose a framework called *SocDim* [64], which is composed of two steps, which are those of social dimension extraction and discriminative learning respectively. In the instantiation of the framework *SocDim*, modularity maximization is adopted to extract social dimensions. There are several concerns about the scalability of *SocDim*:

- The social dimensions extracted according to modularity maximization are dense.

- The modularity maximization requires the computation of the top eigenvectors of a modularity matrix which will become a daunting task when the network scales to millions of node.
- Networks in social media tend to evolve which entails efficient update of the model for collective behavior prediction.

3.4.3 Influence and Grouping Behavior. Grouping behavior, e.g., user's participation behavior into a forum, is an important action in the social network. The point of influence and grouping behavior is to study how different factors influence the dynamics of grouping behaviors.

Shi et al. investigated the user participation behavior in diverse online forums [59]. In that paper, they are mainly focused on three central questions:

1 What are the factors in online forums that potentially influence people's behavior in joining communities and what is the corresponding impact?

2 What are the relationships between these factors, i.e. which ones are more effective in predicting the user joining behavior, and which ones carry supplementary information?

3 What are the similarities and differences of user grouping behavior in forums of different types (such as news forums versus technology forums)?

In order to answer the first question, they analyze four features that can usually be obtained from a forum dataset:

1 *Friends of Reply Relationship.* Use this feature to describe how users are influenced by the numbers of neighbors with whom they have ever had any reply relationship.

2 *Community Sizes.* Use community size as the measurement to quantify the 'popularity' of information.

3 *Average Ratings of Top Posts.* Aside from the popularity of information, we are also interested in how the authority or interestingness of information impacts user behavior.

4 *Similarities of Users.* This is the only feature with dependency: if two users are 'similar' in a certain way, what is the correlation of the sets of communities they join?

Their first discovery is that, despite the relative randomness, the diffusion curve of influence from users of reply relationships has very similar diffusion patterns. However, the reasons that people are linked together are very different. They also investigate the influence of the features associated with communities, which include the size of communities and the authority or the interestingness of the information in the communities. They find that their corresponding information diffusion curves show some strong regularities of user joining behavior as well, and these curves are very different from those of reply relationships. Furthermore, we analyze the effects of similarity of users on the communities they join, and find two users who communicate more frequently or have more common friends are more likely to be in the same set of communities.

In order to answer the second question, we construct a bipartite graph, whose two sets of nodes are users and communities, to encompass all the features and their relationships in this problem. Based on the bipartite graph, we build a bipartite Markov Random Field (BiMRF) model to quantitatively evaluate how much each feature affects the grouping behavior in online forums, as well as their relationships with each other. BiMRF is a Markov random graph with edges and two-stars as its configuration, and incorporates the node-level features we have described as in a social selection model. The most significant advantage of using the BiMRF model is that it can explicitly incorporate the dependency between different users' joining behavior, i.e., how a user's joining behavior is affected by her friends' joining behavior. The results of this quantitative analysis shows that different features have different effectiveness of prediction in news forums versus technology forums.

Backstrom et al. [4] also explore a large corpus of thriving online communities. These groups vary widely in size, moderation and privacy, and cover an equally diverse set of subject matter. They present a number of descriptive statistics of these groups. Using metadata from groups, members, and individual messages, they identify users who post and are replied-to frequently by multiple group members. They classify these high-engagement users based on the longevity of their engagements. Their results show that users who will go on to become long-lived, highly-engaged user experience significantly better treatment than other users from the moment they join the group, well before there is an opportunity for them to develop a long-standing relationship with members of the group. They also present a simple model explaining long-term heavy engagement as a combination of user-dependent and group dependent factors. Using this model as an analytical tool, they show that properties of the user alone are sufficient to explain 95% of all memberships, but introducing a small amount of group-specific information dramatically improves our ability to model users belonging to multiple groups.

4. Influence Maximization in Viral Marketing

Social influence analysis has various real-world applications. Influence maximization in viral marketing is an example of such an important application. In this section, we will introduce the problem of influence maximization and review recent research progress. We will also introduce relevant work on representative user and expert discovery.

4.1 Influence Maximization

The problem of influence maximization can be traced back to the research on "word-of-mouth" and "viral marketing" [6, 11, 21, 38, 46, 55]. The problem of often motivated by the determination of potential customers for marketing purposes. The goal is to minimize marketing cost and more generally to maximize profit. For example, a company may wish to market a new product through the natural "word of mouth" effect arising from the interactions in a social network. The goal is to get a small number of influential users to adopt the product, and subsequently trigger a large cascade of further adoptions. In order to achieve this goal, we need a measure to quantify the intrinsic characteristics of the user (e.g., the expected profit from the user) and the user network value (e.g., the expected profit from users that may be influenced by the user). Previously, the problem has mainly been studied in marketing decision or business management. Domingos and Richardson [21] formulated this problem as a ranking problem using a Markov random field model. They further present an efficient algorithm to learn the model [55]. However, the method models the marketing decision process in a "black box". How users influence each other once a set of users have been marketed (selected), how they will influence their neighbors and how the diffusion process will continue are problems which are still not fully solved. Kempe et al. [41] took the first step to formally define the process in two diffusion models and theoretically proved that the optimization problem of selecting the most influential nodes in the two models is NP-hard. They have developed an algorithm to solve the models with approximation guarantees. The efficiency and scalability of the algorithm has been further improved in recent years [14, 15]. We will skip the work in marketing or business and focus on the formulation of the problem and model learning.

4.1.1 Diffusion Influence Model. There are quite a few classical models of this problem. Here, we review some of them. For ease in explanation, we associate each user with a status: active or inactive. Then, the status of the chosen set of users to market (also referred to as "seed nodes") is viewed as active, while the other users are viewed as inactive. The problem of influence maximization is studied with the use of this status-based dynamic. Initially

all users are considered inactive. Then, the chosen users are activated, who may further influence their friends (neighbor nodes) to be active as well. The simplest model is to quantify the influence of each node with some heuristics. Some examples are as follows:
1) High-degree heuristic. It chooses the seed nodes according to their degree d_v. The strategy is very simple but also natural because the nodes with more neighbors would arguably tend to impose more influence upon its direct neighbors. This consideration of high-degree nodes is also known in the sociology literature as "degree centrality".
2) Low-distance Heuristic. Another commonly used influence measure in sociology is distance centrality, which considers the nodes with the shortest paths to other nodes as be seed nodes. This strategy is based on the intuition that individuals are more likely to be influenced by those who are closely related to them [26].
3) Degree discount heuristic. The general idea of this approach is that if u has been selected as a seed, then when considering selecting v as a new seed based on its degree, we should not count the edge $\overrightarrow{vu}$ towards its degree. This is referred to as SingleDiscount. More specifically, for a node v with d_v neighbors of which t_v are selected as seeds already, we should discount v's degree by $2t_v + (d_v - t_v)\, t_v p$.
4) Linear threshold model. In this family of models, whether a given node v will be active can be based on an arbitrary monotone function of the set of neighbors of v that are already active. We associate a monotone threshold function f_v which maps subsets of v's neighbors to real numbers in $[0, 1]$. Then, each node v is given a threshold θ_v, and v will turn active in step t if$f_v(S) > \theta_v$, where S is the set of neighbors of v that are active in step $t - 1$.

Specifically, in [41] the threshold function $f_v(S)$ is instantiated as $f_v\,(S) = \sum_{u \in S} b_{v.u}$ where $b_{v.u}$ can be seen as a fixed weight, subject to the following constraint:

$$\sum_{u neighbors of v} b_{v,u} \leq 1$$

5) General cascade model. We first define an incremental function $p_v(u, S) \in [0, 1]$ as the success probability of user u activating user v, i.e., user u tries to activate v and finally succeeds, where S is those of v's neighbors that have already attempted but failed to make v active. A special version of this model used in [41] is called Independent Cascade Model in which $p_v(u, S)$ is a constant, meaning that whether v is to be active does not depend on the order v's neighbors try to activate it. A special case of the Independent Cascade Model is the weighted cascade model, where each edge from node u to v is assigned probability $1/d_v$ of activating v.

One challenging problem in the diffusion influence model is the evaluation of its effectiveness and efficiency. From the theoretical perspective, Kempe et al. [41] prove that the optimization of their two proposed models, i.e., linear threshold model and general cascade model is NP-hard. Their proposed approximation algorithms can also theoretically guarantee that the influence spread is within $(1 - 1/e)$ of the optimal influence spread. From an empirical perspective, Kempe et al. [41] show that their proposed models can outperform the traditional heuristics in terms of the maximization of social influences. Recent research mainly focuses on the improvement of the efficiency of the algorithm. For example, Leskovec et al. [44] present an optimization strategy referred to as "Cost-Effective Lazy Forward" or "CELF", which could accelerate the procedure by up to 700 times with no worse effectiveness. Chen et al. [14] further improve the efficiency by employing a new heuristics and in [15] they extend the algorithm to handle large-scale data sets. Another problem is the evaluation of the effectiveness of the models for influence maximization. Some recent work has been proposed in [21] and [55], though these methods are designed only for small data sets. It is still a challenging problem to extend these methods to large data sets.

4.1.2 Learning to Predict Customers. Viral Marketing aims to increase brand awareness and marketer revenue with the help of social networks and social influence. Direct marketing is an important application, which attempts to market only to a select set of potentially profitable customers. Previously, the problem was mainly addressed by constructing a model that predicts a customer's response from their past buying behavior and any available demographic information [45]. When applied successfully, this approach can significantly increase profits [53]. One limitation of the approach is that it treats each customer independently of other customers in terms of their actions. In reality, a person's decision to buy a product is often influenced by their friends and acquaintances. It is not desirable to ignore such a networking influence, because it can lead to severely suboptimal decisions.

We will first introduce a model that tries to combine the network value with customer intrinsic value [21]. Here, the intrinsic value represents attributes (e.g., customer behavior history) that are directly associated with a customer. Such attributes might affect the likelihood of the customer to buy the product, while the network value represents the social network (e.g., customers' friends), which may influence the customer's buying decision.

The basic idea here is to formalize the social network as Markov random fields, where each customer's probability of buying is modeled as a function of both the intrinsic desirability of the product for the customer and the influence of other customers. Formally, the input can be defined as: consider a social network $G = (V, E)$, with n potential customers and their relationships recorded in E, and let $\mathbf{x}_i$ indicate the attributes associated with each customer v_i. We assign a boolean variable y_i to each customer that takes the value 1 if the customer v_i buys the product being marketed, and 0 otherwise. Further let NB^i be the neighbors of v_i in the social network and z_i be a variable representing the marketing action that is taken for customer v_i. z_i can boolean variable, with $z_i = 1$ if the customer is selected to market (e.g., be offered a free product), and $z_i = 0$ otherwise. Alternatively, z_i could be a continuous variable indicating a discount offered to the customer. Given this, we can define the marketing process for customer v_i in a Markov random field as follows:

$$\begin{aligned} P(y_i|\mathbf{y}_{NB^i}, \mathbf{x}_i, \mathbf{z}) &= \textstyle\sum_{C(NB^i)} P(y_i, \mathbf{y}_{NB^i}|\mathbf{x}_i, \mathbf{z}) \\ &= \textstyle\sum_{C(NB^i)} P(y_i|\mathbf{y}_{NB^i}, \mathbf{x}_i, \mathbf{z}) P(\mathbf{y}_{NB^i}|\mathbf{X}, \mathbf{z}) \end{aligned} \quad (7.7)$$

where $C(NB^i)$ is the set of all possible configuration of the neighbors of v_i; and $\mathbf{X}$ represent attributes of all customers. To estimate $P(\mathbf{y}_{NB^i}|\mathbf{X}, \mathbf{z})$, Domingos and Richardson [21] employ the maximum entropy estimation to approximate the probability based on the independent assumption, i.e.,

$$P(\mathbf{y}_{NB^i}|\mathbf{X}, \mathbf{z}) = \prod_{v_j \in NB^i} P(y_j|\mathbf{X}, \mathbf{z}) \quad (7.8)$$

The marketing action z is modeled as a Boolean variable. The cost of marketing to a customer is further considered in the Markov model. Let r_0 be the revenue from selling the product to the customer if no marketing action is performed, and r_1 be the revenue if marketing is performed. The cost can be considered as offering a discount to the marketed customer. Thus the expected lift in profit from marketing to customer v_i in isolation (without influence) can be defined as follows:

$$ELP_i^{\,1}(Y, z) = r_1 P(y_i = 1|Y, f_i^{\,1}(M)) - r_0 P(y_i = 1|Y, f_i^{\,0}(z)) - c \quad (7.9)$$

where $f_i^{\,1}(z_i)$ be the result of setting z_i to 1 and leaving the rest of $\mathbf{z}$ unchanged, and similarly for $f_i^0(z_i)$.

Thus the global lift in profit for a particular choice $\mathbf{z}$:

$$ELP_i^{\,1}(Y, \mathbf{z}) = \sum_{i=1}^{n} [r_i P(X_i = 1|Y, \mathbf{z}) - r_0 P(X_i = 1|Y, z_0) - c_i]$$

A customer's total value is the global lift in profit from marketing to him

$$ELP(Y, f_i^{\,1}(z_i)) - ELP(Y, f_i^{\,0}(z_i))$$

and his network value is the difference between his total and intrinsic values. The model can be also adjusted to a continuous version with no qualitative difference.

In marketing context, the goal for modeling the value of a customer is to find the **z** that can maximize the lift in profit. Richardson and Domingos propose several approximation algorithms in [21] to solve this problem. They make further contributions to this field in their later paper [55] by showing a tractable way to calculate the optimum value of M by directly solving the equation:

$$r\Delta_i(Y)\frac{d\Delta P_i(z,Y)}{dz} = \frac{dc(z)}{dz}$$

Here z denotes the market action. The network effect $\Delta_i(Y) = \sum_{j=1}^{n} w_{ji}\Delta_j(Y)$ is the total increase in probability of purchasing in the network (including y_i) that results from a unit change in $P_0(y_i)$ when w_{ji} indicates how much v_j can influence v_i. The value of $\Delta P_i(z,Y)$ denotes the immediate change in customer v_i's probability of purchasing when he is subjected to by the marketing action z. This value is given by the following expression:

$$\Delta P_i(z,Y) = \beta_i\left[P_0(X_i = 1|Y, M_i = z) - P_0(X_i = 1|Y, M_i = 0)\right] \quad (7.10)$$

Some other work aims to find the optimal marketing strategy by directly maximizing the revenue rather than social influence. An example of this approach is the work discussed in [34]. The basic idea is as follows. A customer who owns a product can have an impact on potential buyers, and therefore it is important to decide the sequence of marketing, as well as the particular price to to be offered to different buyers. Thus a simple marketing strategy, called influence-and-exploit strategy is introduced. This strategy consists of an influence step and an exploit step. In the influence step, the seller starts by giving some products for free to some specially chosen customers who are deemed the most influential. In the exploit step, the seller tries to sell products to the remaining customers at a fixed optimal price. Hartline et al. [34] also proved that the influence-and-exploit method works as a reasonable approximation of the NP-hard problem of finding the optimal marketing strategy.

4.1.3 Maximizing the Spread of Influence. Kempe et al. [41] proposed the linear threshold model and the independent cascade model. The optimal solution to either model is NP-hard. The solution here is to use a submodular function to approximate the influence function. Submodular functions have a number of very nice tractability properties in terms of the design of approximation algorithms. One important property that is used in the approach is as follows. Given a function f that is submodular, taking only non-negative values, then we have

$$f(S \cup \{v\}) \geq f(S)$$

for all elements v and sets S. Thus, the problem can be transformed into finding a k-element set S for which $f(S)$ is maximized. The problem, can be solved using a greedy hill-climbing algorithm which approximates the optimal solution within a factor of $(1 - 1/e)$. The following theorem formally defines the problem.

THEOREM 7.3 *[19, 50] For a non-negative, monotone submodular function f, let S be a set of size k obtained by selecting elements one at a time, each time choosing an element that provides the largest marginal increase in the function value. Let $S^\star$ be a set that maximizes the value of f over all k-element sets. Then $f(S) \geq (1 - 1/e) \cdot f(S^\star)$; in other words, S provides a $(1 - 1/e)$-approximation.*

The model can be further extended to assume that each node v has an associated non-negative weight w_v, which can be used to capture the human prior knowledge to the task at hand, e.g., how important it is that v be activated in the final outcome.

To adapt the model to a more realistic scenario, we may have a number of m of different marketing actions M_i available, each of which may affect some subset of nodes by increasing their probabilities of becoming active; however, different nodes may respond to marketing actions in different ways. Thus a more general model can considered [41]. More specifically, we can introduce investment t_i for each marketing action M_i. Thus the goal is to reach a maximum profit lift while the total investments do not exceed the budget. A marketing strategy is then an m-dimensional vector $\mathbf{t}$ of investments. The probability that node v will become active is determined by the strategy and denoted by $h_v(\mathbf{t})$. By assuming that the function is non-decreasing and satisfies the "diminishing returns" property for all $t \geq t'$ and $a \geq 0$:

$$h_v(t + a) - h_v(t) \leq h_v(t' + a) - h_v(t') \tag{7.11}$$

Satisfying the above inequality corresponds to an interesting marketing intuition: the marketing action would be more effective when the targeted individual is less "marketing-saturated" at that point. Finally, the objective of the model is to maximize the expected size of the final active set. Given an initial set A and let the expected size of the final active set is $\sigma(A)$, then the expected revenue of the marketing strategy $\mathbf{t}$ can be defined as:

$$g(\mathbf{t}) = \sum_{A \subset V} \sigma(A) \cdot \prod_{v \in A} h_v(t) \cdot \prod_{u \in V - A} (1 - h_u(\mathbf{t})) \tag{7.12}$$

We note that if A be the active set of nodes, then the inactive set of nodes is denoted by $V-A$. We can use the submodular property in order to optimize the function corresponding to the revenue of the marketing strategy. We can design a greedy hill-climbing algorithm, which can still guarantee an approximation within a constant factor. A proof of this result may be found in [41].

4.2 Other Applications

4.2.1 Online Advertising. Social influence analysis techniques can also be leveraged for online advertising. For example, the work in [54] proposes methods for identifying brand-specific audiences without utilizing the user private information. The proposed method takes advantage of the notion of "seed nodes", which can specifically indicate the users (or browsers) who exhibit brand affinity. Yet another term "brand proximity" is a distance measure between candidate nodes and the seed nodes. For each browser b_i we use $\overrightarrow{\phi}_{b_i} = [\phi^1{}_{b_i}, \phi^2{}_{b_i}, ..., \phi^P{}_{b_i}]$ to denote the effect of the P proximity measures. Then we can discover the best audiences for marketing by ranking the candidate nodes b_i with respect to $\overrightarrow{\phi}_{b_i}$ based on some monotonic function $score(b_i) = f_i(\overrightarrow{\phi}_{b_i} \cdot \overrightarrow{I}_q)$. The selection vector $\overrightarrow{I}_q = [0, ..., 1, ..., 0]$ holds a 1 in the q-th row. The proximity measures P can be chosen from a pool. Finally, the authors show that the quasi-social network extracted from the data corresponds well with a real social network. This means that the modeled "friends" on the virtual network accurately reflect the relationships between friends or relatives in the real world.

Another tractable approach for viral marketing is through frequent pattern mining, which is studied by Goyal et al. in [30].Their research focuses on the actions performed by the users, under the assumption that users can see their friends' actions. The authors formally define leaders in a social network, and introduce an efficient algorithm aiming at discovering the leaders. The basic formation of the problem is that actions take place in different time steps, and the actions which come up later could be influenced by the earlier taken actions. This is called the propagation of influence. The notion of leaders corresponds to people who can influence a sufficient number of people in the network with their actions for a long enough period of time. Aside from the normal leaders, there are other kinds of users who only influence a smaller subset of people. These users are called tribe leaders. The algorithm for finding leaders in a social network makes use of action logs, which sorts actions chronologically.

4.2.2 Influential Blog Discovery. In the web 2.0 era, people spend a significant amount of time on user-generated content web sites, a classic example of which are blog sites. People form an online social network by visiting other users' blog posts. Some of the blog users bring in new information, ideas, and opinions, and disseminate them down to the masses. This influences the opinions and decisions of others by word of mouth. This set of users are called opinion leaders.

In order to tackle this problem, we can first define the following properties for each blogger:

- **R**ecognition: An influential blog post is recognized by many people. This generally means that there are a lot of inlinks to the article.
- **A**ctivity generation: Blogs often have comments associated with them. A large number of comments indicates that the contents of the article encourages discussion. This indicates that the blog is influential.
- **Novelty**: Normally a novel blog is one that with less outgoing links.
- **E**loquence: Longer articles posted on blog sites tend to be more eloquent, and can thus be more influential.

The work in [1] presents a model which takes advantages of the above four properties to describe the influence flow in the influence-graph consisting of all the blogger pages. Basically, the influence flow probability is defined as follows:

$$InfluenceFlow(p) = w_{in} \sum_{m=1}^{|\iota|} I(p_m) - w_{out} \sum_{n=1}^{|\theta|} I(p_n) \tag{7.13}$$

w_{in} and w_{out} is the weight to describe the contribution of incoming and outgoing links. Finally, the influence of a blog is defined as:

$$I(p) = w(\lambda) \times (w_{com}\gamma_p + InfluenceFlow(p)) \tag{7.14}$$

where w_{com} denotes the weight that can be used to regulate the contribution of the number of comments (γ_p) towards the influence of the blog post p.

In another work [61], Song et al. associate a hidden node v_e to each node v to represent the source of the novel information in blog v. More specifically, let $Out(v)$ denote the set of blogs that v links to. The information novelty contribution of entry v_e is then calculated as:

$$Nov\left(v_e|Out(v_e)\right) = \min_{O_e \in Out(v_e)} Nov(v_e|O_e) \tag{7.15}$$

The information novelty provided by the hidden node of blog v is measured as the average of the novelty scores of the entries it contains.

$$Nov\,(v|Out(v)) = \frac{\sum\limits_{v_e \in V} (Nov\,(v_e|Out(v_e)))}{card\,(Set\,(v_e))} \tag{7.16}$$

where $card(\cdot)$ denotes total number of entries of interest in blog v. Then, the problem can be formulated as solving the InfluenceRank IR.

$$IR^T(I-(1-\beta)\alpha W-(1-\beta)\alpha a\cdot e^T) = (1-\beta)(1-\alpha)e^T+\beta.Nov^T \tag{7.17}$$

with $IR^T \cdot e = 1$.

As the InfluenceRank can be fitted in a random walk framework, α is the probability that the random walk follows a link. β reflects how significant the novelty is to the opinion leaders we expect to detect. e is the n-vector of all ones and a is the vector with components $a_i = 1$ if i-th row of W corresponds to a dangling node, and 0, otherwise, where W is the normalized adjacent matrix.

5. Conclusion

Social influence analysis aims at qualitatively and quantitatively measuring the influence of one person on others. As social networking becomes more prevalent in the activities of millions of people on a day-to-day basis, both research study and practical applications on social influence will continue to grow. Furthermore, the size of the networks on which the underlying applications need to be used also continues to grow over time. Therefore, effective and efficient social influence methods are in high demand.

In this chapter, we focus on the computational aspects of social influence analysis and describe different methods and algorithms for calculating social influence related measures. First, we cover the basic statistical measure of networks such as centrality, closeness and betweenness; second, we present the social influence and selection models. These covers the fundamental concepts on influence; third, we present the influence maximization and its application for viral marketing.

In the future, an important and challenging research area is to develop efficient, effective and quantifiable social influence mechanisms to enable various applications in social networks and social media. This area lies in the intersection of computer science, sociology, and physics. In particular, scalable and parallel data mining algorithms, and scalable database and web technology have been changing how sociologists approach this problem. Instead of building conceptual models and conducting small scale simulations and user studies, more and more people now rely on large-scale data mining algorithms to analyze social network data. This provides more realistic results for large-scale applications. This chapter provides an introduction of the problem space in social influence analysis. The area is still in its infancy, and we anticipate that more techniques will be developed for this problem in the future.

References

[1] N. Agarwal, H. Liu, L. Tang, and P. S. Yu. Identifying the influential bloggers in a community. In *Proceedings of the 1st ACM International Conference on Web Search and Data Mining (WSDM'08)*, pages 207–217, 2008.

[2] A. Anagnostopoulos, R. Kumar, and M. Mahdian. Influence and correlation in social networks. In *Proceeding of the 14th ACM SIGKDD international conference on Knowledge discovery and data mining (KDD'08)*, pages 7–15, 2008.

[3] S. Aral, L. Muchnika, and A. Sundararajan. Distinguishing influence-based contagion from homophily-driven diffusion in dynamic networks. *Proceedings of the National Academy of Sciences*, 106(51):21544–21549, 2009.

[4] L. Backstrom, R. Kumar, C. Marlow, J. Novak, and A. Tomkins. Preferential behavior in online groups. In *Proceedings of the international conference on Web search and web data mining (WSDM'08)*, pages 117–128, 2008.

[5] E. Bakshy, B. Karrer, and L. A. Adamic. Social influence and the diffusion of user-created content. In *EC '09: Proceedings of the tenth ACM conference on Electronic commerce*, pages 325–334, New York, NY, USA, 2009. ACM.

[6] F. M. Bass. A new product growth for model consumer durables. *Management Science*, 15(5):215–227, 1969.

[7] P. Bonacich. Factoring and weighting approaches to status scores and clique identification. *Journal of Mathematical Sociology*, 2:113–120, 1972.

[8] P. Bonacich. Power and centrality: a family of measures. *American Journal of Sociology*, 92:1170–1182, 1987.

[9] S. P. Borgatti and M. G. Everett. A graph-theoretic perspective on centrality. *Social Networks*, 2006.

[10] U. Brandes. A faster algorithm for betweenness centrality. *Journal of Mathematical Sociology*, 2001.

[11] J. J. Brown and P. H. Reingen. Social ties and word-of-mouth referral behavior. *The Journal of Consumer Research*, 14(3):350–362, 1987.

[12] R. S. Burt. *Structural holes: The social structure of competition.* Harvard University Press, Cambridge, MA, 1992.

[13] J. T. Cacioppo, J. H. Fowler, and N. A. Christakis. Alone in the Crowd: The Structure and Spread of Loneliness in a Large Social Network. *SSRN eLibrary*, 2008.

[14] W. Chen, Y. Wang, and S. Yang. Efficient influence maximization in social networks. In *Proceedings of the 15th ACM SIGKDD International Conference on Knowledge Discovery and Data Mining (SIGKDD'09)*, pages 199–207, 2009.

[15] W. Chen, Y. Wang, and S. Yang. Scalable influence maximization for prevalent viral marketing in large-scale social networks. In *Proceedings of the 16th ACM SIGKDD International Conference on Knowledge Discovery and Data Mining (SIGKDD'10)*, pages 807–816, 2010.

[16] N. A. Christakis and J. H. Fowler. The spread of obesity in a large social network over 32 years. *New England Journal of Medicine*, 357, 2007.

[17] N. A. Christakis and J. H. Fowler. The collective dynamics of smoking in a large social network. *N Engl J Med*, 358(21):2249–2258, May 2008.

[18] R. B. Cialdini and N. J. Goldstein. Social influence: compliance and conformity. *Annu Rev Psychol*, 55:591–621, 2004.

[19] G. Cornuejols, M. L. Fisher, and G. L. Nemhauser. Location of bank accounts to optimize float: An analytic study of exact and approximate algorithms. *Management Science*, 23(8):789–810, 1977.

[20] D. Crandall, D. Cosley, D. Huttenlocher, J. Kleinberg, and S. Suri. Feedback effects between similarity and social influence in online communities. In *Proceeding of the 14th ACM SIGKDD international conference on Knowledge discovery and data mining (KDD'08)*, pages 160–168, 2008.

[21] P. Domingos and M. Richardson. Mining the network value of customers. In *Proceedings of the seventh ACM SIGKDD international conference on Knowledge discovery and data mining (KDD'01)*, pages 57–66, 2001.

[22] D. Easley and J. Kleinberg. *Networks, Crowds, and Markets: Reasoning About a Highly Connected World.* Cambridge University Press, 2010.

[23] P. W. Eastwick and W. L. Gardner. Is it a game? evidence for social influence in the virtual world. *Social Influence*, 4(1):18–32, 2009.

[24] S. M. Elias and A. R. Pratkanis. Teaching social influence: Demonstrations and exercises from the discipline of social psychology. *Social Influence*, 1(2):147–162, 2006.

[25] T. L. Fond and J. Neville. Randomization tests for distinguishing social influence and homophily effects. In *Proceeding of the 19th international conference on World Wide Web (WWW'10)*, 2010.

[26] J. H. Fowler and N. A. Christakis. Dynamic Spread of Happiness in a Large Social Network: Longitudinal Analysis Over 20 Years in the Framingham Heart Study. *British Medical Journal, Vol. 3, January 2009*, 2008.

[27] L. C. Freeman. A set of measure of centrality based on betweenness. *Sociometry*, 40:35–41, 1977.

[28] L. C. Freeman. Centrality in social networks: Conceptual clarification. *Social Networks*, 1:215Ð239, 1979.

[29] M. Girvan and M. E. J. Newman. Community structure in social and biological networks. *Proceedings of the National Academy of Sciences of the United States of America*, 99(12):7821–7826, June 2002.

[30] A. Goyal, F. Bonchi, and L. V. Lakshmanan. Discovering leaders from community actions. In *Proceeding of the 17th ACM conference on Information and knowledge management (CIKM'08)*, pages 499–508, 2008.

[31] A. Goyal, F. Bonchi, and L. V. Lakshmanan. Learning influence probabilities in social networks. In *Proceedings of the 3st ACM International Conference on Web Search and Data Mining (WSDM'10)*, pages 207–217, 2010.

[32] M. Granovetter. The strength of weak ties. *American Journal of Sociology*, 78(6):1360–1380, 1973.

[33] M. Granovetter. Economic action and social structure: The problem of embeddedness. *American Journal of Sociology*, 91(3):481–510, 1985.

[34] J. Hartline, V. Mirrokni, and M. Sundararajan. Optimal marketing strategies over social networks. In *WWW '08: Proceeding of the 17th international conference on World Wide Web*, pages 189–198, New York, NY, USA, 2008. ACM.

[35] P. W. Holland and S. Leinhardt. Transitivity in structural models of small groups. *Small Group Research*, 2: pp. 107–124, 1971.

[36] P. Holme and M. E. J. Newman. Nonequilibrium phase transition in the coevolution of networks and opinions. *Physical Review*, 74(056108), 2006.

[37] C. Hubbell. An input-output approach to clique identification. *Sociometry*, 28:377–399, 1965.

[38] G. J., L. B., and M. E. Talk of the network: A complex systems look at the underlying process of word-of-mouth. *Marketing Letters*, 12:211–223(13), August 2001.

[39] A. Java, P. Kolari, T. Finin, and T. Oates. Modeling the spread of influence on the blogosphere. In *Proceeding of the 15th international conference on World Wide Web (WWW'06)*, 2006.

[40] L. Katz. A new index derived from sociometric data analysis. *Psychometrika*, 18:39–43, 1953.

[41] D. Kempe, J. Kleinberg, and E. Tardos. Maximizing the spread of influence through a social network. In *Proceedings of the ninth ACM SIGKDD international conference on Knowledge discovery and data mining (KDD'03)*, pages 137–146, 2003.

[42] D. Krackhardt. *The Strength of Strong ties: the importance of philos in networks and organization in Book of Nitin Nohria and Robert G. Eccles (Ed.), Networks and Organizations*. Cambridge, Harvard Business School Press, Hershey, USA, 1992.

[43] P. Lazarsfeld and R. K. Merton. Friendship as a social process: A substantive and methodological analysis. *Freedom and Control in Modern Society*, page 18Ð66, 1954.

[44] J. Leskovec, A. Krause, C. Guestrin, C. Faloutsos, J. VanBriesen, and N. Glance. Cost-effective outbreak detection in networks. In *Proceedings of the 13th ACM SIGKDD international conference on Knowledge discovery and data mining (KDD'07)*, pages 420–429, 2007.

[45] C. X. Ling and C. Li. Data mining for direct marketing: Problems and solutions. In *KDD'98*, pages 73–79, 1998.

[46] V. Mahajan, E. Muller, and F. M. Bass. New product diffusion models in marketing: A review and directions for research. *The Journal of Marketing*, 54(1):1–26, 1990.

[47] E. Manavoglu, D. Pavlov, and C. L. Giles. Probabilistic user behavior models. In *Proceedings of the Third IEEE International Conference on Data Mining (ICDM'03)*, page 203, Washington, DC, USA, 2003. IEEE Computer Society.

[48] M. McPherson, L. Smith-Lovin, and J. M. Cook. Birds of a feather: Homophily in social networks. *Annual Review of Sociology*, 27:415–444, 2001.

[49] S. C. Mednick, N. A. Christakis, and J. H. Fowler. The spread of sleep loss influences drug use in adolescent social networks. *PLoS ONE*, 5(3):e9775, 03 2010.

[50] G. L. Nemhauser, L. A. Wolsey, and M. L. Fisher. An analysis of approximations for maximizing submodular set functions. *Mathematical Programming*, 14(1):265–294, 1978.

[51] J. Neville, O. Simsek, and D. Jensen. Autocorrelation and relational learning: challenges and opportunities. In *Proceedings of the ICML-04 Workshop on Statistical Relational Learning*, 2004.

[52] M. E. J. Newman. A measure of betweenness centrality based on random walks. *Social Networks*, 2005.

[53] G. Piatetsky-Shapiro and B. M. Masand. Estimating campaign benefits and modeling lift. In *KDD'99*, pages 185–193, 1999.

[54] F. Provost, B. Dalessandro, R. Hook, X. Zhang, and A. Murray. Audience selection for on-line brand advertising: privacy-friendly social network targeting. In *KDD '09: Proceedings of the 15th ACM SIGKDD in-*

ternational conference on Knowledge discovery and data mining, pages 707–716, New York, NY, USA, 2009. ACM.

[55] M. Richardson and P. Domingos. Mining knowledge-sharing sites for viral marketing. In *Proceedings of the eighth ACM SIGKDD international conference on Knowledge discovery and data mining (KDD'02)*, pages 61–70, 2002.

[56] J. N. Rosenquist, J. Murabito, J. H. Fowler, and N. A. Christakis. The Spread of Alcohol Consumption Behavior in a Large Social Network. *Annals of Internal Medicine*, 152(7):426–433, 2010.

[57] P. Sarkar and A. W. Moore. Dynamic social network analysis using latent space models. *SIGKDD Explor. Newsl.*, 7(2):31–40, 2005.

[58] J. Scripps, P.-N. Tan, and A.-H. Esfahanian. Measuring the effects of preprocessing decisions and network forces in dynamic network analysis. In *Proceedings of the 15th ACM SIGKDD international conference on Knowledge discovery and data mining (KDD'09)*, pages 747–756, 2009.

[59] X. Shi, J. Zhu, R. Cai, and L. Zhang. User grouping behavior in online forums. In *Proceedings of the 15th ACM SIGKDD international conference on Knowledge discovery and data mining(KDD'09)*, pages 777–786, New York, NY, USA, 2009. ACM.

[60] P. Singla and M. Richardson. Yes, there is a correlation: - from social networks to personal behavior on the web. In *Proceeding of the 17th international conference on World Wide Web (WWW'08)*, pages 655–664, 2008.

[61] X. Song, Y. Chi, K. Hino, and B. L. Tseng. Identifying opinion leaders in the blogosphere. In *Proceedings of the 15th ACM international conference on Information and knowledge management (CIKM'06)*, pages 971–974, 2007.

[62] C. Tan, J. Tang, J. Sun, Q. Lin, and F. Wang. Social action tracking via noise tolerant time-varying factor graphs. In *Proceedings of the 16th ACM SIGKDD International Conference on Knowledge Discovery and Data Mining (SIGKDD'10)*, pages 807–816, 2010.

[63] J. Tang, J. Sun, C. Wang, and Z. Yang. Social influence analysis in large-scale networks. In *Proceedings of the 15th ACM SIGKDD International Conference on Knowledge Discovery and Data Mining (SIGKDD'09)*, pages 807–816, 2009.

[64] L. Tang and H. Liu. Relational learning via latent social dimensions. In *Proceedings of the 15th ACM SIGKDD international conference on Knowledge discovery and data mining (KDD'09)*, pages 817–826, 2009.

[65] L. Tang and H. Liu. Scalable learning of collective behavior based on sparse social dimensions. In *Proceeding of the 18th ACM conference*

on Information and knowledge management(CIKM'09), pages 1107–1116, New York, NY, USA, 2009. ACM.

[66] C. E. Tsourakakis. Fast counting of triangles in large real networks without counting: Algorithms and laws. In *Proceedings of the 8th IEEE International Conference on Data Mining (ICDM 2008)*, pages 608–617, 2008.

[67] D. J. Watts and S. H. Strogatz. Collective dynamics of 'small-world' networks. *Nature*, pages 440–442, Jun 1998.

[68] R. Xiang, J. Neville, and M. Rogati. Modeling relationship strength in online social networks. In *Proceeding of the 19th international conference on World Wide Web (WWW'10)*, pages 981–990, 2010.

Chapter 8

A SURVEY OF ALGORITHMS AND SYSTEMS FOR EXPERT LOCATION IN SOCIAL NETWORKS

Theodoros Lappas
University of California Riverside
tlappas@cs.ucr.edu

Kun Liu
Yahoo! Labs
kun@yahoo-inc.com

Evimaria Terzi
Boston University
evimaria@cs.bu.edu

Abstract Given a particular task and a set of candidates, one often wants to identify the right expert (or set of experts) that can perform the given task. We call this problem the *expert-location* problem and we survey its different aspects as they arise in practice. For example, given the activities of candidates within a context (*e.g.*, authoring a document, answering a question), we first describe methods for evaluating the level of expertise for each of them. Often, experts are organized in networks that correspond to social networks or organizational structures of companies. We next devote part of the chapter for describing algorithms that compute the expertise level of individuals by taking into account their position in such a network. Finally, complex tasks often require the collective expertise of more than one experts. In such cases, it is more realistic to require a team of experts that can collaborate towards a common goal. We describe algorithms that identify effective expert teams within a network of experts. The chapter is a survey of different algorithms for expertise evaluation and team identification. We highlight the basic algorithmic problems and give some indicative algorithms that have been developed in the literature. We conclude the chapter by providing a comprehensive overview of real-life systems for expert location.

Keywords: Expertise Location, Language Models, Ranking, Propagation, Team Formation

1. Introduction

The term expert is used to refer to a person/agent with a high degree of a skill or knowledge of a certain subject. Ideally, given a task at hand and a set of candidates, one wishes to to efficiently identify the right expert (or set of experts) that can perform the given task. We call this problem the *expert-location* problem. The abundance of data that monitors people's online presence and expertise imposes several challenges to the expert-location problem.

Consider, for example, data from a large enterprise that records the activity of employees within the organization (*e.g.*, documents, patents, emails). Given such a dataset, managers need to measure the degree of expertise of the employees with respect to different topics. Such knowledge allows managers to identify the right employees that could be valuable for a particular project. Therefore, an important aspect of expert location is finding out the expertise of different individuals from the available data. We call this problem *expert location without graph constraints*.

The data associated with different candidate experts can sometimes be missing or incomplete. In such scenarios, the connections of the various candidates within the organizational chart of the company can be useful in inferring expertise. For example, the data associated with a new employee who works in the GIS-information systems department of an IT company might provide little evidence that he is an expert in GIS systems. However, his connections with his colleagues that are indeed experts might prove useful in identifying the former as an expert in GIS as well. We call the problem of inferring the expertise of individuals using their connections with other experts as *expert location with score propagation*.

Elaborating on the example above, the success of a project depends not only on the expertise of people who are involved, but also on how effectively these people collaborate, communicate and work together as a team. Assume, for example, an IT project manager who wants to build a team of engineers skilled in the following areas: T={*algorithms, software engineering, distributed systems, web programming*}. Also, assume that there are five candidates, *{a, b, c, d, e}*, with the following backgrounds: X_a={*algorithms*}, X_b={*web programming*}, X_c={*software engineering, distributed systems*}, X_d={*software engineering*} and X_e={*software engineering, distributed systems, web programming*}. The relationships among these candidates are represented by the social network shown in Figure 8.1, where the existence of an edge between two nodes in G indicates that the corresponding persons can collaborate effectively.

Without considering how effectively these people can collaborate, the manager can select either $\mathcal{X}' = \{a, b, c\}$ or $\mathcal{X}'' = \{a, e\}$ – both these teams have the required skill set. However, the existence of graph G makes $\mathcal{X}' = \{a, b, c\}$

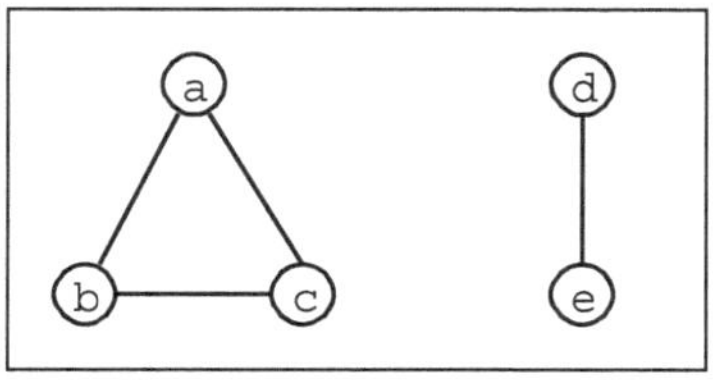

Figure 8.1. Network of connections between individuals in $\{a, b, c, d, e\}$.

a superior solution since the structure of G indicates that a and e cannot work together at all. We call the problem of identifying a team of experts that can communicate well the *expert team formation* problem.

The existence of a social network among individuals is quite common in real scenarios. In a company, the network may capture the hierarchical organization of the employees. In this case, the graph encodes the fact that people in the same group or department can communicate easier than people working in different divisions. In a research community, the network captures previous successful collaborations among scientists. Other examples of social networks between professionals include LinkedIn (`www.linkedin.com`), Xing (`www.xing.com`) and others.

In this chapter, we give an overview of the problems and algorithms for each of the above three scenarios, with a specific focus on the latter two. The rest of the chapter is organized as follows. Section 2 introduces the notations and problem definitions. Section 3 provides a brief overview of traditional expert-location solutions which do not consider any graph/network structures. Section 4 discusses how popular web page ranking algorithms (*e.g.*, PageRank [6], HITS [36]) and their variations can help identify experts on the network. Section 5 details the work on expert team formation – how to find a group experts who can collectively perform a task with minimum collaboration/communication cost in the network. Section 6 mentions several other relevant work that can be used for expert-location in the network. Section 7 provides a list of expert-location systems. Finally, we conclude this chapter in Section 8.

2. Definitions and Notation

For the rest of the discussion, we assume there exists a pool of n candidate experts $\mathcal{X} = \{x_1, ..., x_n\}$. Each candidate x_i has a set of skills, either explicitly or implicitly described by a feature vector $\vec{x}_i$. Each element in this vector is associated with a topic or term and the actual element value represents the strength of the expert with respect to a particular topic or term. For most of the cases, we further assume that these candidates are organized in a social graph

$G = (\mathcal{X}, E)$. This graph can represent the actual friendship relations, or it can indicate an organizational hierarchy on experts, or it can be constructed from email communication networks, co-authorship networks etc.

In its very basic form, the expert-location problem can be defined as follows:

DEFINITION 8.1 (EXPERT LOCATION WITHOUT GRAPH CONSTRAINTS) *Given a query $\mathcal{Q}$ that consists of a list of skills, identify a subset of candidates $\mathcal{X}' \subseteq \mathcal{X}$ who have the skills specified by the query.*

A large body of literature has treated this problem as an information-retrieval task. In this scenario, we are usually given a set of documents, a list of candidate names, and a set of topics, and the goal is to find experts from the candidates for each of the topics. Mathematically, one wants to estimate the probability of a candidate being an expert for a given query, *i.e.*, $P\{x_i|\mathcal{Q}\}$. The top k candidates with the highest probabilities are deemed the most probable experts for the given query. In Section 3, we will briefly introduce some of the representative work for this problem definition.

Link-analysis ranking has brought new perspectives in expertise-location problems. Popular webpage-ranking algorithms such as PageRank [6] and HITS [36] have been used to enhance the identification and ranking of experts. In this setting, a new class of expert-location problems has risen; those where the degree of expertise of a candidate depends on how well-connected this candidate is in a *(social) network* of experts. A generic definition of this class of problems is given below.

DEFINITION 8.2 (EXPERT LOC. WITH SCORE PROPAGATION) *Given a query $\mathcal{Q}$ that consists of a list of skills, and the social graph G, identify an initial subset of candidates $\mathcal{X}' \subseteq \mathcal{X}$ who have the skills specified by the query. Use the input graph among experts to propagate the initial expertise scores to rerank experts or to identify new experts.*

In Section 4, we will discuss how PageRank and HITS can help with this experts location problem.

With the proliferation of social networks, the focus has been geared towards leveraging social interactions to form teams of experts that can work together towards the successful completion of a project. This has brought up the *expert team formation* problem defined as follows:

DEFINITION 8.3 (EXPERT TEAM FORMATION) *Given a query $\mathcal{Q}$ that consists of a list of skills, and the social graph G, identify a subset of candidates $\mathcal{X}' \subseteq \mathcal{X}$ so that the chosen candidates cover the required skills and the collaboration/communication cost of $\mathcal{X}'$ is minimized. The collaboration/communication cost is defined over the input graph G.*

In Section 5, we will elaborate on the formal problem definitions and algorithms for this problem.

3. Expert Location without Graph Constraints

Traditional systems (without graph constraints) often use information retrieval techniques (*e.g.*, language models [47]) to discover expertise from a large collection of text corpus. The general idea is to estimate the probability that a candidate x_i could be an expert with respect to a given topic query $\mathcal{Q}$, *i.e.*, $p(x_i|\mathcal{Q})$. Using Bayes rule, we can obtain the following:

$$P(x_i|\mathcal{Q}) = \frac{P(\mathcal{Q}|x_i)P(x_i)}{P(\mathcal{Q})} \propto P(\mathcal{Q}|x_i)P(x_i). \tag{8.1}$$

In the above equation, $P(\mathcal{Q}|x_i)$ is the generating probability of query $\mathcal{Q}$ given candidate x_i and $P(x_i)$ indicates candidate x_i's general expertise, which is independent of the query. Often we can ignore $P(x_i)$ by assuming a uniform prior for all the candidates. Thus the focus is on how to compute $P(\mathcal{Q}|x_i)$ using, for example, language models. In the following subsections, we will first introduce languages models in the general context of information retrieval. Then we will describe several representative work using language models for expert location.

3.1 Language Models for Document Information Retrieval

In information retrieval, a language model [47] formulates the probability that a document is relevant to a query as follows:

$$P(d|\mathcal{Q}) \propto P(\mathcal{Q}|d)P(d). \tag{8.2}$$

Since we usually assume that terms contained in a query q are independent of each other, we have

$$P(\mathcal{Q}|d) = \prod_{t_i \in \mathcal{Q}} P(t_i|d), \tag{8.3}$$

where t_i is the i-th term in $\mathcal{Q}$ and $P(t_i|d)$ is the probability of term t_i under the term distribution for document d. The maximum likelihood estimate of the $P(t_i|d)$ with Dirichlet smoothing is:

$$P(t_i|d) = \lambda \cdot \frac{tf(t_i,d)}{|d|} + (1-\lambda) \cdot \frac{tf(t_i,D)}{|D|}, \text{ and } \lambda = \tfrac{|d|}{|d|+\mu}. \tag{8.4}$$

In the above equation, $|d|$ is the length of document d, $tf(t_i, d)$ is the term frequency of term t_i in d, $|D|$ is the number of documents in the text collection D, $tf(t_i, D)$ is the term frequency of term t_i in D, λ is a weighting parameter ranging in $[0, 1]$, and μ is another control parameter which is often the average document lengths in D. Next, we will see how the language models are used for solving the expert-location problem.

3.2 Language Models for Expert Location

Balog *et al.* [1] proposed two general strategies to expert location from a document collection. The first one, which we call *user profile-centric approach,* directly models a candidate's expertise based on the documents associated with this candidate. The second one, which we call *document-centric approach,* first locates document relevant to a topic query, and then finds the associated expert. Both follow the principle that the relevance of the textual context of a candidate with respect to a topical query adds up to the evidence of his expertise.

3.2.1 User Profile-centric Approach. This approach builds a model for each candidate x_i using the documents associated with him. Specifically, for each term t in the vocabulary, the model computes the probability of t given the candidate x_i, *i.e.*, $P(t|x_i)$. Following the independence assumption of terms in a query, $P(\mathcal{Q}|x_i)$ in Equation 8.1 can be calculated as follows:

$$P(\mathcal{Q}|x_i) = \prod_{t_i \in \mathcal{Q}} P(t_i|x_i) \tag{8.5}$$

$$= \prod_{t_i \in \mathcal{Q}} \left[\sum_{d_j \in D} P(t_i|d_j)P(d_j|x_i) \right]. \tag{8.6}$$

In the above equation, $P(t_i|d_j)$ can be obtained using Equation 8.4. $P(d_j|x_i)$ denotes the strength of the association between candidate x_i and document d_j. This association may capture various aspects of the relation between a candidate and a document. For instance, $P(d_j|x_i)$ may quantify the extent to which this candidate has contributed to the document. A simple example is to set $P(d_j|x_i) = 1$ if x_i is the co-author of d_j or 0 otherwise. We refer interested readers to Balog *et al.*'s work [1] for more details on how to build associations.

3.2.2 Document-centric Approach. This approach computes $P(\mathcal{Q}|x_i)$ by assuming conditional independence between the query $\mathcal{Q}$ and the candidate x_i as follows:

$$P(\mathcal{Q}|x_i) = \sum_{d_j \in D} P(\mathcal{Q}|d_j)P(d_j|x_i) \tag{8.7}$$

$$= \sum_{d_j \in D} \left[\prod_{t_i \in \mathcal{Q}} P(t_i|d_j) \right] P(d_j|x_i). \tag{8.8}$$

Following Equation 8.7, the probability of a query $\mathcal{Q}$ given a candidate x_i can be viewed as the following generative process: 1) for a given candidate x_i, select a document d_j with probability $P(d_j|x_i)$; and 2) with the selected document d_j, generate the query $\mathcal{Q}$ with probability $P(\mathcal{Q}|d_j)$. The most importance property of this model is that documents are viewed as "hidden variables", and they separate the query from the candidate so that candidate is not directly modeled.

3.3 Further Reading

The 2005 Text REtrieval Conference (TREC) provided a common platform in the Enterprise Search Track for researchers to empirically assess methods for expert location from large collections of text documents. Since then, a significant amount of work has been devoted to using language models for the problem. However, as the focus of this chapter is graphs and social networks, we will only briefly mention a few more representative work and refer interested readers to the references wherein for more details.

Zhang *et al.* [67] proposed to use Probabilistic Latent Semantic Analysis [29] to compute $P(\mathcal{Q}|d_j)$ in Equation 8.7. The idea is to add a hidden topic layer $\Theta = \{\theta_1, \theta_2, \dots, \theta_k\}$ between the document d_j and the query $\mathcal{Q}$: $P(\mathcal{Q}|d_j) = \sum_{m=1}^{k} P(\mathcal{Q}|\theta_m)P(\theta_m|d_j) = \sum_{m=1}^{k} \left[\prod_{t_i \in \mathcal{Q}} P(t_i|\theta_m)\right] P(\theta_m|d_j)$. Here $P(\theta_m|d_j)$ denotes the probability of generating a topic given a document, and $P(\mathcal{Q}|\theta_m)$ denotes the probability of generating the query given a topic. In this way, the model captures the semantic meaning of both document and query.

Dent *et al.* [14] proposed two improved language models for expert location on DBLP bibliography data. The first model adds documents weights to Equation 8.7, *i.e.*, $P(\mathcal{Q}|x_i) = \sum_{d_j \in D} w_{d_j} \left[\prod_{t_i \in \mathcal{Q}} P(t_i|d_j)\right] P(d_j|x_i)$. In their second model, the authors explicitly introduced latent topics θ_k between candidate x_i and query $\mathcal{Q}$ rather than implicitly using document d_j as the latent variable in Equation 8.7.

Cao *et al.* [8] developed a two-stage language model for the expert search competition in the Enterprise Track of TREC 2005. Specifically, their model is formulated as $P(x_i|\mathcal{Q}) = \sum_{d_j \in D} P(x_i, d_j|\mathcal{Q}) = \sum_{d_j \in D} P(d_j|\mathcal{Q})P(x_i|d_j, \mathcal{Q})$. In this equation, $P(d_j|\mathcal{Q})$ is the regular language model as described in Equation 8.2. $P(x_i|d_j, \mathcal{Q})$ characterizes the co-occurrence of the candidate and the topic terms in the document.

4. Expert Location with Score Propagation

A candidate's expertise can be often inferred or boosted by the skills of other people he is connected with. There is a natural connection between this concept and many popular webpage ranking algorithms such as PageRank [6] or HITS [36]. In this chapter, we discuss how these algorithms can be used for the expert location problem. At a high level, solutions in this category often embody a two-step process: 1) using language model or heuristic rules described in Section 3 to compute an initial expertise score for each candidate; and 2) using graph-based ranking algorithms to propagate scores computed in the first step and rerank experts. Candidates with no initial scores can also obtain a quantitative measurement of their expertise through the propagation. In the following, we first briefly describe the PageRank and HITS algorithms in order to provide some necessary background. We then discuss some representative work to better illustrate the ideas.

4.1 The PageRank Algorithm

PageRank models the probability that a web page will be visited by a random surfer. At each time step, the surfer proceeds from his current web page u to a randomly chosen web page v following one of two strategies: 1) When u does not have outlinks, the surfer jumps to an arbitrary page in the Web. 2) When u has outlinks, the surfer jumps to an arbitrary page in the Web with probability α, and a random page that u hyperlinks to with probability $1 - \alpha$. Here, α is a fixed parameter chosen in advance.

As the surfer continues this walk from page to page, some pages are visited more often than others. Intuitively, these are the pages with many incoming links from other frequently visited pages. The idea behind PageRank is that pages visited more often in this walk are more important. Using the theory of Markov chains [43], one may argue that, when the surfer follows the above combined process, the probability of him visiting a webpage u, denoted by $\pi(u)$, converges to a fixed, steady-state quantity. We call this probability $\pi(u)$ the PageRank of u.

Next, we briefly describe how $\pi(u)$ is computed in the context of Markov chains. There, each web page corresponds to one state; the transition probability represents the probability of a random surfer moving from one page to another. Let us use A to denote the adjacency matrix of the web graph with N pages/nodes. If there is a hyperlink from page i to j, then $A_{ij} = 1$, otherwise $A_{ij} = 0$. The transition probability matrix P that captures the move of the random surfer described above can be derived as follows:

1. If a row in A has no 1's, then replace each entry in this row by $\frac{1}{N}$.
2. If a row in A has at least one 1, divide each 1 in A by the number of 1's in its row.
3. Multiply the resulting entries from Step 1 and 2 by $1 - \alpha$.
4. Add $\frac{\alpha}{N}$ to every resulting entry from Step 3 to obtain P.

If we denote the probability distribution of the surfer's position at time t by an N-dimensional probability vector $\vec{\pi}_t = (\pi(1), \ldots, \pi(u), \ldots, \pi(N))$, then at time $t+1$ the distribution becomes $\vec{\pi}_t P$. The following theorem shows that this probability distribution converges to its steady-state.

THEOREM 8.4 *[43] For a Markov chain characterized by the transition probability P described above, there is a unique steady-state probability vector $\vec{\pi} = (\pi(1), \ldots, \pi(u), \ldots, \pi(N))$ such that if $\eta(u,t)$ is the number of visits to state u in t steps, then*

$$\lim_{t \to \infty} \frac{\eta(u,t)}{t} = \pi(u), \tag{8.9}$$

where $\pi(u) > 0$ is the steady-state probability for state u. This steady-state probability vector $\vec{\pi}$ corresponds to the principal left eigenvector of P with eigenvalue being equal to 1.

We call $\pi(u)$ the PageRank of the corresponding web page u. Following Theorem 8.4, we can compute $\vec{\pi}$ with the following standard eigenvalue/eigenvector equation.

$$\vec{\pi} P = 1\vec{\pi}. \tag{8.10}$$

Next we illustrate HITS, another important web page ranking algorithm that is often used for expert location.

4.2 HITS Algorithm

There are two types of web pages useful as results for broad-topic searches. A broad topic search is conceptually an informational query such as "KDD conference". In this case, the web page on `www.sigkdd.org` is an authoritative source for the query. We call such a page the *authority*. On the other hand, there are many other pages that contain lists of links to authoritative pages on a specific topic. We call such pages *hubs*. A good hub is one that points to many good authorities; a good authority page is one that is linked to by many good hubs. Therefore, each web page can be assigned two scores – an *authority score* and a *hub score*. This circular definition of hubs and authorities leads to an iterative computation of the scores.

Let $\vec{h}$ and $\vec{a}$ be the vector of hub and authority scores of all pages, respectively. Let A denote the adjacency matrix of the web graph. The entry A_{ij} is 1 if there is a hyperlink from page i to page j, and 0 otherwise. Then the hub and authority scores are updated as follows:

$$\begin{aligned} \vec{h} &\leftarrow A\vec{a} \\ \vec{a} &\leftarrow A^T\vec{h}, \end{aligned} \tag{8.11}$$

where A^T is the transpose of the matrix A. Now the left hand side of each line of Equation 8.11 is a vector that is the right hand side of the other line in

Equation 8.11. Substituting these into one another, we have

$$\begin{aligned} \vec{h} &\leftarrow AA^T\vec{h}, \\ \vec{a} &\leftarrow A^TA\vec{a}. \end{aligned} \tag{8.12}$$

Replacing $\leftarrow$ with $=$ and introducing eigenvalues, the first line of Eq. 8.12 becomes the equation for the eigenvectors of AA^T. The second becomes the equation for the eigenvectors of A^TA:

$$\begin{aligned} \vec{h} &= \frac{1}{\lambda_h} AA^T\vec{h}, \\ \vec{a} &= \frac{1}{\lambda_a} A^TA\vec{a}, \end{aligned}$$

where λ_h denotes the eigenvalue of AA^T and λ_a denotes the eigenvalue of A^TA. Thus, the hub and authority scores $\vec{h}$ and $\vec{a}$ correspond to the (principal) eigenvectors of AA^T and A^TA.

Having described the PageRank and HITS algorithms, we are ready to discuss how they are employed to solve the traditional expertise identification problem in the presence of networks.

4.3 Expert Score Propagation

A common way for people to find information within an organization is to ask other colleagues, following referrals until someone with the right information is found. Since this communication is often done through emails, Campbell *et al.* [7] and Dom *et al.* [15] utilized the email communication network to refine their expertise identification. In this network, each node corresponds to a person and each directed edge points from a sender to a receiver. Because our knowledge of expertise determines whom we want to send questions to, those who can provide high quality information about certain topics tend to receive more emails regarding those topics. Therefore, people who have received many email inquiries are defined as the *authorities* or *experts*, and people who are able to forward questions to many *experts* are defined as the *hubs*. Consequently, the *authority* score computed from the HITS algorithm on this network can be used to rank the individuals in the network.

Zhang *et al.* [68] employed both PageRank and HITS on community-based question-answering networks such as Yahoo! Answers and Google Groups. In these networks, a node represents a user and an edge is drawn from the user who made the initial post (or questions) to everyone who replied to it. A user A who replied to another user B's question often indicates that A has more knowledge on the subject than B. Additionally, if user B answered questions from C, then A's expertise score should be boosted because he can answer a question from someone who himself has a certain level of expertise. This simple idea leads to their PageRank-style algorithm:

ALGORITHM 1 *Assume user A has answered questions for users $U_1, \ldots, U_n$, then the expertise ranking score of A, denoted by $ER(A)$, is computed as follows:*

$$ER(A) = (1 - \alpha) + \alpha \left(\sum_{i=1}^{n} \frac{ER(U_i)}{C(U_i)} \right).$$

In the above equation, $C(U_i)$ is the total number of users who have helped U_i (recall that there is a edge from U_i to each of his helpers), and α is the damping factor which can be set between 0 and 1.

Loosely speaking, this score indicates the probability that a user will receive help requests from other regular users and experts in the network. The authors also used a similarly adaptation of the HITS algorithm. In their context, a good hub is a user who is helped by many experts. Similarly, a good authority (a.k.a. expert) is a user who helps many good hubs. The authority score computed by HITS is used to quantify the expertise of a user.

Zhang *et al.* [66] considered expertise location in academic collaboration networks. They first calculated the initial expert scores from the candidates' personal information using probabilistic information retrieval models. Then they used a belief propagation model [17] to update the scores. The intuition behind their propagation model is similar to what we have described in PageRank and HITS – if a person has tight connections with many other experts on a topic, then it is likely that this person is also an expert on that topic. This idea is captured in the following algorithm.

ALGORITHM 2 *The expert score of a user v_i, denoted by $s(v_i)$, is updated using the following rules:*

$$s(v_i)^{t+1} = s(v_i)^t + \sum_{v_j \in U} \sum_{e \in R_{ji}} w\left((v_j, v_i), e\right) s(v_j)^t.$$

In the above equation, $w\left((v_j, v_i), e\right)$ is the propagation coefficient and $e \in R_{ji}$ is one kind of relationship from person v_j to v_i. U denotes the set of neighbors to v_i and R_{ji} is the set of all relationships between v_j and v_i.

Karimzadehgan *et al.* [33] utilized the organizational hierarchy in an organization to tackle the expert finding problem. The basic observation is that those in close proximity to each other in the hierarchy tend to have similar topic knowledge. Consequently, propagating expertise scores among neighbors, (*e.g.*, managers, peers) in an organization would improve the retrieval performance. Their hierarchy-based algorithm works as follows. First, they build an expertise profile for each employee using the content of their emails. Second, they used language models to calculate for each employee an initial expertise score, denoted by $p(q|e_j)$, where q is the topic and e_j is the expertise profile of employee e_j. Finally, each employee's score is locally smoothed with their neighbors' scores using the following algorithm.

ALGORITHM 3 *Employee e_j's expertise score $p(q|e_j)$ on a given topic q is smoothed using the following equation:*

$$p_{smooth}(q|e_j) = \alpha p(q|e_j) + \frac{1-\alpha}{N_j}\sum_{i=1}^{N_j} p(q|e_i),$$

where α is weighting parameter and N_j is the number of neighbors for employee e_j. $p(q|e_j)$ and $p(q|e_i)$ are the initial scores for employee e_j and his neighbor e_i, respectively.

In their multi-step propagation algorithm, the scores are computed by considering all neighbors within 2-hops or 3-hops away from e_j.

4.4 Further Reading

Lu *et al.* [42] adopted the same propagation model used by Zhang *et al.* [66] in the context of user-interactive question answering (UIQA) networks. Jurczyk and Agichtein [32, 31] also leveraged HITS to estimate a user's authority score in an UIQA service. These solutions can be potentially used for ranking answers, finding experts, and detecting spam. Fu *et al.* [20] first selected a subset of top candidates according to their probability of being experts for a certain topic. Then they utilized propagation models on social networks to discover other potential experts. Jiao *et al.* [30] focused on discussion groups and modified PageRank algorithm to rerank experts. Seo and Croft [53] focused on the hierarchical structures of email and discussion threads, and devised a modified PageRank algorithm to rank experts.

Serdyukov *et al.* [54] studied topic-specific expertise graphs where both documents and candidate experts are vertices and the directed edges denote the authorship, organizational connections, or other rich interactions among documents and candidates. The authors considered the expert location as an infinite or an absorbing process of consulting with both documents and people. They proposed a multi-step relevance propagation models to solve the problem.

Some work has also been devoted to studying the expert location problem in evolving graphs. For instance, Li and Tang [41] developed a random walk model that incorporates the temporal information in a forward-and-backward propagation process. Berberich *et al.* [5] introduced T-Rank, a modified version of PageRank that considers the temporal freshness (*i.e.*, timestamps of the most recent updates) and activity (*i.e.*, update rates) of the nodes and edges in the graph.

5. Expert Team Formation

In this section, we discuss the *expert-team formation* problem in social networks. The objective is to find a group of experts in the network who can collectively perform a task in an effective manner.

Most of the formulations we discuss in this section consider each expert to be associated with a set of skills. These skills can be provided as part of the input or can be pre-computed using the approaches we discussed in Section 3 and 4. Apart from the skills, the communication/collaboration cost, *i.e.*, the overhead incurred when the team members work together, also plays an important role in the overall performance of the team. This cost is influenced by various factors including the personality of individual team members and their social connections. We begin with a brief introduction to some metrics that can be used to quantify these factors. We will provide formal definition of the cost when we discuss the concrete algorithms.

5.1 Metrics

Many methodologies have been developed to measure the personality of an individual. We summarize some of them below.

The *Myers-Briggs Type Indicator* (MBTI): MBTI is a frequently-employed personality assessment tool. It can help people to identify the sort of jobs where they would be "most comfortable and effective". According to Hammer and Huszczo [28], this metric can be used in improving and predicting team performance. Also, Chen and Lin in [11] used MBTI to evaluate candidates' interpersonal relationships as team members.

Herrmann Brain Dominance Instrument (HBDI): HBDI is another index that reflects individual's affinity for creativity, facts, form and feelings. Despite the fact that this metric has been used in several experimental settings [4], it appears that the obtained results are very often subjective. This has raised some questions related to the validity of the measure [21].

Kolbe Conative Index (KCI): KCI is a psychometric system that measures conation, *i.e.*, the way an individual instinctively approaches problem solving, arranges ideas or objects, and uses time or energy. This system was first presented by Kolbe [38, 37]. Several studies have shown that the KCI index is effective in predicting team's performance. For example, Fitzpatrick and Askin [18] used KCI to measure individuals' drive and temperament, which in turn reflects the quality of the team.

In addition to personality measurements, social metrics have also been studied. These metrics assess the impact of the network structure among the team members on the performance of the team. For example, Lappas *et al.* [40] focused on the social graph constructed by the team members. They used the diameter of the graph as well as the cost of the minimum spanning tree of the graph to measure the communication overhead of the team. Gaston *et al.* [24] also conducted an experimental study of how different graph structures among the individuals affect the performance of a team.

5.2 Forming Teams of Experts

In this section, we take Lappas *et al.*'s work [40] as an example to illustrate the computational aspects of expert team-formation process in a social network.

In their work, the authors assumed that there exists a pool of n experts $\mathcal{X} = \{1, \ldots, n\}$, where each expert i has a set of skills X_i. They also assumed that the experts are organized in a *weighted* and *undirected* social graph $G = (\mathcal{X}, E)$. The weights of the edges of G should be interpreted as follows: a low-weight edge between nodes i, j implies that expert i and expert j can collaborate and/or communicate more easily than two experts that are connected via a high-weight edge. These weights can be instantiated in different ways in different application domains. For example, in a company, the weight between two employees may correlate to the length of the path from one employee to another through the organizational chart. In a scientific research community, the weight between two scientists is related to the total number of publications they have coauthored. Interpersonal relationships among individuals as measured by the personality metrics described in the previous section can also be used to calculate the weights.

Given a task T that requires a set of skills, the goal is to find a set of individuals $\mathcal{X}' \subseteq \mathcal{X}$ that can successfully complete the task. In the formulation of the problem, individuals in $\mathcal{X}'$ are required to collectively have all the necessary skills to perform T, as well as be able to work effectively together as a team. Lappas *et al.* measured the effectiveness of collaboration using the notion of the *communication cost* incurred by the subgraph in G that involves only the team members $\mathcal{X}'$. We denote this subgraph as $G[\mathcal{X}']$. The formal problem definitions are the following.

PROBLEM 1 *[TEAM FORMATION] Given a set of n individuals denoted by $\mathcal{X} = \{1, \ldots, n\}$, a graph $G(\mathcal{X}, E)$, and task T, find $\mathcal{X}' \subseteq \mathcal{X}$, so that $(\cup_{i \in \mathcal{X}'} X_i) \cap T = T$, and the communication cost $\text{Cc}(\mathcal{X}')$ is minimized.*

In the above definition, $(\cup_{i \in \mathcal{X}'} X_i) \cap T = T$ means that the skills possessed by the team members in $\mathcal{X}'$ satisfy the requirement of the task T. The communication cost is purposefully left undefined though. Lappas *et al.* focused on two instantiations of the communication-cost function. The first communication cost is modeled as the *diameter* of the subgraph of G defined by the members of $\mathcal{X}'$. The second version the communication cost is measured as the cost of the *minimum spanning tree* that spans all the nodes in $\mathcal{X}'$.

Diameter (R)**:** Given graph $G(\mathcal{X}, E)$ and a set of individuals $\mathcal{X}' \subseteq \mathcal{X}$, we define the *diameter communication cost* of $\mathcal{X}'$, denoted by $\text{Cc-R}(\mathcal{X}')$, to be the diameter of the subgraph $G[\mathcal{X}']$. Recall that the diameter of a graph is the largest shortest path between any two nodes in the graph.

Minimum Spanning Tree (MST)**:** Given graph $G(\mathcal{X}, E)$ and $\mathcal{X}' \subseteq \mathcal{X}$, we define the MST *communication cost* of $\mathcal{X}'$, denoted by $\text{Cc-Mst}(\mathcal{X}')$, to be the cost of the *minimum spanning tree* on the subgraph $G[\mathcal{X}']$. Recall that the cost of a spanning tree is simply the sum of the weights of its edges.

The TEAM FORMATION problem with communication function CC-R is called the DIAMETER-TF problem. Similarly, the TEAM FORMATION problem with communication function CC-MST is called the MST-TF problem. The following result is true for the complexity of the two problems.

PROPOSITION 1 *([40]) Both the* DIAMETER-TF *and the* MST-TF *problems are NP-complete.*

For the DIAMETER-TF problem, Lappas *et al.* proposed the `RarestFirst` algorithm, with pseudocode described in Algorithm 6. First, for every skill a required by the task T, the algorithm computes $S(a)$, the support of a, which is the set of individuals in $\mathcal{X}$ that have this skill. Then, the algorithm picks the skill $a_{\text{rare}} \in T$ with the lowest-cardinality support $S(a_{\text{rare}})$. Note that at least one individual from the set $S(a_{\text{rare}})$ needs to be included in the solution. Among all candidates from the set $S(a_{\text{rare}})$, the algorithm picks the one that leads to the smallest diameter subgraph, when connected to its closest individual in all other support groups $S(a)$, $a \in T$ and $a \neq a_{\text{rare}}$.

To understand Algorithm 6, we first introduce some notations. For every two nodes $i, i' \in \mathcal{X}$, we define the distance function $d(i, i')$ to be the weight of the shortest path between i and i' in G. Note that this distance function between the nodes is a metric and thus satisfies the triangle inequality. For every pair of nodes, we use $Path(i, i')$ to represent the set of nodes that are along the shortest path from i to i'. We also define the distance between a node $i \in \mathcal{X}$ and a set of nodes $\mathcal{X}' \subseteq X$ to be $d(i, \mathcal{X}') = \min_{i' \in \mathcal{X}'} d(i, i')$. In this case, we use $Path(i, \mathcal{X}')$ to represent the set of nodes that are along the shortest path from i to the node $j = \arg\min_{i' \in \mathcal{X}'} d(i, i')$.

Armed with these notations, we can take a further look at Algorithm 6. In line 6, $d(i, S(a))$ is simply $\min_{i' \in S(a)} d(i, i')$. Also, *Path* $(i^*, S(a))$ in line

Algorithm 6 The `RarestFirst` algorithm for the DIAMETER-TF problem.

Input: Graph $G\,(\mathcal{X}, E)$; individuals' skill vectors $\{X_1, \ldots, X_n\}$ and task T.

Output: Team $\mathcal{X}' \subseteq \mathcal{X}$ and subgraph $G\,[\mathcal{X}']$.

1: **for** every $a \in T$ **do**

2: $\quad S(a) = \{i \mid a \in X_i\}$

3: $a_{rare} \leftarrow \arg\min_{a \in T} |S(a)|$

4: **for** every $i \in S\,(a_{rare})$ **do**

5: $\quad$ **for** $a \in T$ and $a \neq a_{rare}$ **do**

6: $\quad\quad R_{ia} \leftarrow d\big(i, S\,(a)\,\big)$

7: $\quad R_i \leftarrow \max_a R_{ia}$

8: $i^* \leftarrow \arg\min R_i$

9: $\mathcal{X}' = i^* \cup \{Path\,(i^*, S\,(a)) \mid a \in T\}$

9 refers to the set of nodes in the graph that are along the shortest path from i^* to i', where i' is such that $i' \in S(a)$ and $d\big(i^*, S\,(a)\,\big) = d(i^*, i')$. If all-pairs shortest path have been pre-computed, and hashtables are used for storing the skills of every individual, and a different set of hashtables are used for storing the individuals that posses a specific attribute, then, the running time of the `RarestFirst` algorithm is $\mathcal{O}\,(|S\,(a_{rare})| \times n)$. A worst-case analysis suggests that $|S\,(a_{rare})| = \mathcal{O}\,(n)$. Thus the worst-case running time of the `RarestFirst` is $\mathcal{O}\,\big(n^2\big)$. However, in practice, the running time of the algorithm is much less that this worst-case analysis suggests.

In fact, `RarestFirst` is a 2-approximation algorithm for the DIAMETER-TF problem. This is mostly due to the fact that the employed distance d is a metric. Therefore the following proposition is true.

PROPOSITION 2 *For any graph-distance function d that satisfies the triangle inequality, the* CC-R *cost of the solution $\mathcal{X}'$, given by* `RarestFirst` *for a given task, is at most twice the* CC-R *cost of the optimal solution $\mathcal{X}^*$. That is,* CC-R $(\mathcal{X}') \leq 2 \cdot$ CC-R $(\mathcal{X}^*)$.

For the MST-TF problem Lappas *et al.* proposed the `EnhancedSteiner` algorithm. This algorithm starts by first enhancing graph G with additional nodes and edges to form the *enhanced graph* H. Then, `SteinerTree` is evoked to solve the STEINER TREE problem (to be described later) on the enhanced graph H. The pseudocode describing this two steps of the algorithm is shown in Algorithm 7.

Let the task to be performed require k skills, *i.e.*, $T = \{a_1, \ldots, a_k\}$. Routine `EnhanceGraph` (line 1 of Algorithm 7) makes a linear pass over the graph G and enhances it as follows: an additional node Y_j is created for every skill $a_j \in T$. Each such new node Y_j is connected to a node $i \in \mathcal{X}$ if and only if

Algorithm 7 The EnhancedSteiner algorithm for the MST-TF problem.

Input: Graph $G(\mathcal{X}, E)$; individuals' skill vectors $\{X_1, \ldots, X_n\}$ and task T.

Output: Team $\mathcal{X}' \subseteq \mathcal{X}$ and subgraph $G[\mathcal{X}']$.

1: $H \leftarrow$ EnhanceGraph(G, T)

2: $\mathcal{X}_H \leftarrow$ SteinerTree$(H, \{Y_1, \ldots, Y_k\})$

3: $\mathcal{X}' \leftarrow \mathcal{X}_H \setminus \{Y_1, \ldots, Y_k\}$

$a_j \in X_i$ (node i has the skill a_j). The distance between node Y_j and nodes $i \in S(a_j)$ are set to be $d(Y_j, i) = D$ where D is a large real number, larger than the sum of all the pairwise distances of the nodes in the graph G. Finally, every node $i \in \mathcal{X}$ that has abilities X_i is replaced by a clique C_i of size $|X_i|$. Each node in the clique C_i should be considered as a copy of individual i that has only a single distinct skill from the set X_i. The distance between every two nodes in the clique C_i is set to zero. Each node in the clique C_i maintains all the existing connections of node i to the rest of the graph – including the connections to nodes $\{Y_1, \ldots, Y_k\}$.

The second step of the algorithm solves the STEINER TREE problem on the enhanced graph H. In the standard STEINER TREE problem, we are given an undirected graph with non-negative edge costs. The nodes of this graph are partitioned into two disjoint sets: the *required* and the *Steiner* nodes [61]. The STEINER TREE problem then asks for the minimum-cost tree in the input graph that contains all *required* nodes and any subset of the *Steiner* nodes. There exist many algorithms for solving this classic STEINER TREE problem. So we use SteinerTree to collectively refer to *any* algorithm for the problem. Lappas *et al.* used an approximation algorithm due to Takahashi and Matsuyama [57]. In line 2 of Algorithm 7, the SteinerTree takes as input the enhanced graph H, and the k required nodes $\{Y_1, \ldots, Y_k\}$, then it produces the set of nodes $\mathcal{X}_H$ that participate in the resulting Steiner tree.

In a final step (line 3 of Algorithm 7), the algorithm removes from set $\mathcal{X}_H$ the artificially added nodes $Y_1, \ldots, Y_k$ (and their incident edges) to obtain the final solution $\mathcal{X}'$. The overall running time of the EnhancedSteiner algorithm is $\mathcal{O}(k \times |E|)$.

The EnhancedSteiner algorithm is in fact motivated by the obvious similarity between the MST-TF problem and the GROUP STEINER TREE (GST) problem. In the GST problem the input again consists of an undirected graph, with non-negative edge weights and ℓ subsets of the vertex set V. These ℓ subsets are denoted by $g_1, \ldots, g_\ell \subseteq V$. The objective is to find the minimum cost subtree of the graph that contains at least one vertex from each subset g_i. If one thinks of every subset g_i as the set of nodes that have a particular skill, then the similarity between the MST-TF and the GST problems becomes apparent. Therefore, instead of the `EnhancedSteiner` algorithm any other (approximation) algorithm for the GST problem can also be used to solve the MST-TF problem. We have picked the `EnhancedSteiner` algorithm because it is simple, intuitive and works well in practice. The best approximation ratio achieved by an algorithm is $O(\log^3 n \log k)$ [22]. For a review of some recent approximation algorithms for the GST problem see [10, 16, 22] and references therein.

5.3 Further Reading

In the Operations Research community, the team-formation problem is often formulated as an integer linear programming problem (ILP). These formulations are then solved using standard combinatorial-optimization techniques such as simulated annealing [2], branch-and-cut [69] or genetic algorithms [63]. The common characteristic of all these studies is that the organizational or social bonds among individuals are ignored and the focus is on their matching experts skills with the task requirements.

In practice, team formation within large organizations relies on managerial decisions that are usually made in an ad-hoc manner. Managers tend to select persons they are acquainted with as project-team members without rigorous analysis. As part of the academic efforts to overcome these disadvantages, Tsai *et al.* [59] suggested a model that utilizes Taguchi's parameter design (`http://en.wikipedia.org/wiki/Taguchi_methods`) to form teams. This method has been shown to achieve robust performance as well as significantly reduce project cost and duration. Tseng *et al.* [60] suggested to use fuzzy set theory and grey decision theory to form a multi-functional team. Each member in the team is required to be competent in his/her work and also able to share responsibility with other members.

In the spirit of Lappas *et al.*, the social-network structure among individuals is taken into account in other team-formation methodologies. For example, Wi *et al.* [64] proposed a set of social-network measures for identifying the effectiveness of a team and proposed a genetic algorithm for finding a good team of experts. In another piece of work along these lines, Cheatham and Cleereman [9] used social-network information among individuals to construct teams of diverse individuals that share similar interests and aptitudes.

6. Other Related Approaches

In this section we briefly introduce several other approaches for expert location in networks. These approaches do not fall in the three scenarios we defined in Section 2. But they could be valuable additions to the existing expert location literature. The first one leverages multi-agent systems to discover

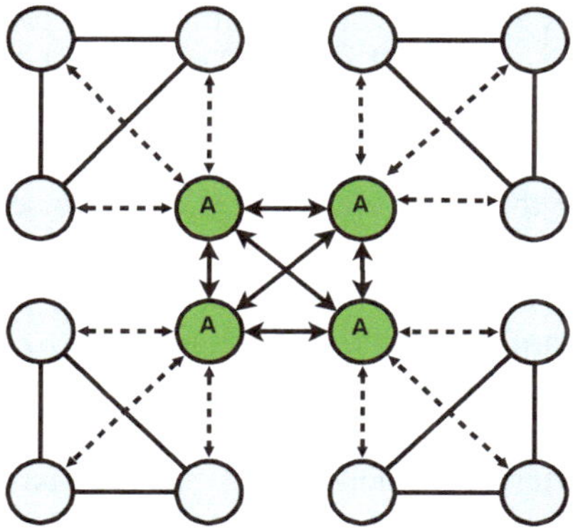

Figure 8.2. A sketch of an Agent-based referral system

experts; and the second one identifies the most influential nodes in a professional network and views those nodes as the experts.

6.1 Agent-based Approach

A large body of work solves the expert-location problem via the use of *referrals*. Such systems typically rely upon agents – autonomous entities who exchange information with others and locate the appropriate expert on a given topic. Figure 8.2 sketches the architecture of such a system with four agents (the dark nodes marked with letter A). Each user is assigned an agent to learn his preferences and expertise. Each agent interacts with a different part of the network, gathering information on the expertise of the nodes/users that it has access to. Once a user submits a request for an expert on a specific topic, his agent examines the local database first. If it cannot find the proper candidates, the agent forwards the request to other agents, and so on.

Some representative systems include the NetExpert system by Sanguesa and Pujol [51], the Referral Web by Kautz *et al.* [34], the Yenta system by Foner [19], and many others by Yu and Singh [65], Pujol *et al.* [48] and Pushpa *et al.* [49].

6.2 Influence Maximization

Another relevant problem is *influence maximization*, which has its roots in viral marketing [50]. The idea is as follows. Assume that we can estimate the extent to which individuals influence one another in a social network and we want to market a new product that we hope will be adopted by a large fraction of the network. We can select a few "influential" individuals and convince them to adopt the new product first. By doing so, we hope they can trigger a cascade of influence by which friends will recommend the product to other friends, and ultimately many people will try it. The goal of *influence maximization* is to identify such a small set of key individuals so that the expected number of individuals who will adopt the new product at the end of this process is maximized. Mapping this use case to the scenario of expert location, we can view those most influential nodes in a professional network (*e.g.*, academic network in a specific area) as the experts since their work/theories are widely adopted by other researchers in the same field.

There are two most widely studied models on how the adoption spreads through a social network: the *linear threshold model* and the *independent cascade model*. Granovetter and Schelling [27, 52] were among the first to propose models that uses node-specific thresholds. Many models of this type have been studied but the *linear threshold model* is one of the most important ones. In the model, a node v is influenced by his neighbor u according to a weight $w_{u,v}$ such that $\sum_{u \in \text{Neighbor of } v} w_{u,v} < 1$. The adoption process proceeds as follows. Each node v chooses a threshold θ_v uniformly at random from the interval $[0, 1]$. This threshold represents the weighted fraction of v's neighbors that must become active in order for v to become active. Here the "active" means the node adopts the product or new ideas and "inactive" means the node does not adopt the product or new ideas. Given a random choice of the thresholds, and an initial set of active nodes A_0 (with all other nodes inactive), the process unfolds deterministically in discrete steps. In step t, all nodes that were active in step $(t-1)$ remain active, and we activate any node v for which the total weight of his active neighbors is at least θ_v: $\sum_{u \in \text{Neighbor of } v} w_{u,v} \geq \theta_v$. Thus, the threshold θ_v represents the latent tendency of a node to adopt the product or new ideas when his neighbors do. The fact that these thresholds are randomly selected is meant to model our lack of knowledge of their true values.

The *independence cascade model* was originally investigated by Goldenberg, Libai, and Muller [25, 26]. The process proceeds in discrete steps with the following randomized rule. When node u first becomes active in step t, it is given a single chance to activate each of his inactive neighbor v. It succeeds with a probability $p_{u,v}$. If u succeeds, then v will become active in step $(t+1)$. However, no matter whether u succeeds or not, it cannot make any further attempts to active v in subsequent rounds. The process runs until no more activations are possible.

The optimization problem of selecting the most influential nodes with both models is NP-hard. Kempe [35] developed the first provable approximation guarantees for efficient algorithms. Using an analysis framework based on submodular functions, they showed that a natural greedy strategy obtains a solution that is provably within 63% of optimal for several classes of models. The authors also proposed a general framework that simultaneously includes both of these models as special cases. Many variations have been investigated since then. Due to page constraints, we are not able to enumerate all of them. We refer interested readers to Jon Kleinberg's publication list (`http://www.cs.cornell.edu/home/kleinber/`) for more details.

7. Expert Location Systems

The popularity of the expert-location problem in different contexts has lead to the implementation of many relevant systems. This section briefly overviews some of them. We also refer interested readers to MITRE (`http://www.mitre.org`)'s technical report [44] for the comparisons of several commercial tools.

A large body of traditional systems manage the skills of individuals in relational database systems. The database contains a set of expert "profiles" or backgrounds of individuals who are knowledgeable on particular topics. By searching the database, we can find certain experts or to match jobs with individual capabilities. Systems in this category include but are not limited to: the Searchable Answer Generating Environment(*SAGE*) and the *Expert Seeker* by Becerra-Fernandez [3]; the *CONNEX* by Hewlett-Packard; the *SPUD* system by Microsoft [13], and the *OntoProPer* by Sure *et al.* [56].

The Text REtrieval Conference (TREC) provided a common platform for researchers to empirically evaluate methods for expert location from large collections of text corpus. It has motivated a significant number of systems, most of which use variations of language models to build expert profiles and discover the right candidates. Interested readers are referred to Section 3 and TREC website (`http://trec.nist.gov/`) for more details.

As social networks become more popular, many systems start to utilize the connections among individuals to identify experts. A featured example is the *ArnetMiner* system developed by Tang *et al.* [58] for academic search. This system employs both language models and belief propagation models to rank experts. Given a topical query, the system returns a list of experts on this topic. The system also suggests the top conferences and papers on this topic. Other examples of systems that make use of the information encoded in an underlying social network include *Spree* by Metze *et al.* [46] and *Expertise Recommender* by McDonald *et al.* [45].

There exists another body of work built upon agent-based architecture to search experts. Such systems include the *ReferralWeb* [34], *Yenta* [19], *NetExpert* [51], *ContactFinder* [39], and the (unnamed) ones by Vivacqua [62], Crowder *et al.* [12], Garro and Palopoli [23] and Sugawara [55].

8. Conclusions

In this chapter, we surveyed three main aspects of the expert-location problem:

- Expert location without graph constraints: it focuses on identifying the degree of expertise of different individuals without graph/network constraints.
- Expert location with score propagation: it models the propagation of expertise among people in the network.
- Expert team formation: it considers the problem of identifying a group of experts that can collectively perform a given task while minimizing the communication/collaboratino cost incurred over the network.

We have also highlighted some existing expert-location systems. With the proliferation of expertise networks, *e.g.*, email communication network, user-interactive question answering network, organization hierarchy, social network, etc., we expect to see more intelligent and practical expert-location solutions that capture both individuals' skill sets as well as their social interactions to maximize the quality the search results.

References

[1] Krisztian Balog, Leif Azzopardi, and Maarten de Rijke. Formal models for expert finding in enterprise corpora. In *Proceedings of the 29th Annual International ACM SIGIR Conference on Research and Development in Information Retrieval (SIGIR'06)*, pages 43–50, 2006.

[2] Adil Baykasoglu, Turkay Dereli, and Sena Das. Project team selection using fuzzy optimization approach. *Cybernetics and Systems*, 38(2):155–185, 2007.

[3] Irma Becerra-Fernandez. The role of artificial intelligence technologies in the implementation of people-finder knowledge management systems. *Knowl.-Based Syst.*, 13(5):315–320, 2000.

[4] R. M. Belbin, B. Watson, and C. West. True colors. *People Management*, 3(5):34–38, 1997.

[5] Klaus Berberich, Michalis Vazirgiannis, and Gerhard Weikum. T-rank: Time-aware authority ranking. In *Algorithms and Models for the Web-Graph*, volume 3243/2004, pages 131–142. Springer Berlin / Heidelberg, 2004.

[6] Sergey Brin and Larry Page. The anatomy of a large-scale hypertextual web search engine. In *Proceedings of the 7th international conference on World Wide Web (WWW'98)*, pages 107–117, Brisbane, Australia, 1998.

[7] Christopher S. Campbell, Paul P. Maglio, Alex Cozzi, and Byron Dom. Expertise identification using email communications. In *Proceedings of the 12th International Conference on Information and Knowledge Management (CIKM'03)*, pages 528–531, New Orleans, LA, 2003.

[8] Yunbo Cao, Jingjing Liu, Shenghua Bao, Hang Li, and Nick Craswell. A two-stage model for expert search. Technical Report MSR-TR-2008-143, Microsoft Research, 2008.

[9] Michelle Cheatham and Kevin Cleereman. Application of social network analysis to collaborative team formation. In *Proceedings of the International Symposium on Collaborative Technologies and Systems*, pages 306–311, 2006.

[10] Chandra Chekuri, Guy Even, and Guy Kortsarz. A greedy approximation algorithm for the group steiner problem. *Discrete Applied Mathematics*, 154(1):15–34, 2006.

[11] Shi-Jie Chen and Li Lin. Modeling team member characteristics for the formation of a multifunctional team in concurrent engineering. *IEEE Transactions on Engineering Management*, 51(2):111–124, 2004.

[12] Richard Crowder, Gareth V. Hughes, and Wendy Hall. An agent based approach to finding expertise. In *PAKM '02: Proceedings of the 4th International Conference on Practical Aspects of Knowledge Management*, pages 179–188, London, UK, 2002. Springer-Verlag.

[13] Thomas H. Davenport. Knowledge management case study. http://www.itmweb.com/essay536.htm, 1997.

[14] Hongbo Deng, Irwin King, and Michael R. Lyu. Formal models for expert finding on dblp bibliography data. In *Proceedings of the 2008 Eighth IEEE International Conference on Data Mining (ICDM'08)*, pages 163–172, 2008.

[15] Byron Dom, Iris Eiron, Alex Cozzi, and Yi Zhang. Graph-based ranking algorithms for e-mail expertise analysis. In *Proceedings of the 8th ACM SIGMOD Workshop on Research Issues in Data Mining and Knowledge Discovery*, pages 42–48, San Diego, CA, 2003.

[16] C. W. Duin, A. Volgenant, and S. Vo. Solving group Steiner problems as Steiner problems. *European Journal of Operational Research*, 154(1):323–329, 2004.

[17] Pedro F. Felzenszwalb and Daniel P. Huttenlocher. Efficient belief propagation for early vision. *International Journal of Computer Vision*, 70(1):41–54, October 2006.

[18] Erin L. Fitzpatrick and Ronald G. Askin. Forming effective worker teams with multi-functional skill requirements. *Computers and Industrial Engineering*, 48(3):593–608, 2005.

[19] Leonard N. Foner. Yenta: A multi-agent, referral-based matchmaking system. In *Agents*, pages 301–307, 1997.

[20] Yupeng Fu, Rongjing Xiang, Yiqun Liu, Min Zhang, and Shaoping Ma. Finding experts using social network analysis. In *Proceedings of the*

IEEE/WIC/ACM International Conference on Web Intelligence, pages 77–80, 2007.

[21] A. Furnham, H. Steele, and D. Pendleton. A psychometric assesement of the belbin team-role self-perception inventory. *Journal of Occupational and Organizational Psychology*, 55:245–257, 1993.

[22] Naveen Garg, Goran Konjevod, and R. Ravi. A polylogarithmic approximation algorithm for the group steiner tree problem. In *Proceedings of the Ninth Annual ACM-SIAM Symposium on Discrete Algorithms*, 253–259, 1998.

[23] Alfredo Garro and Luigi Palopoli. An xml multi-agent system for e-learning and skill management. In *Agent Technologies, Infrastructures, Tools, and Applications for E-Services*, pages 283–294, 2002.

[24] Matthew E. Gaston, John Simmons, and Marie desJardins. Adapting network structures for efficient team formation. In *Proceedings of the AAAI Fall Symposium on Artificial Multi-agent Learning*, 2004.

[25] J. Goldenberg, B. Libai, and E. Muller. Talk of the network: A complex systems look at the underlying process of word-of-mouth. *Marketing Letters*, 12(3):211–223, 2001.

[26] J. Goldenberg, B. Libai, and E. Muller. Using complex systems analysis to advance marketing theory development. *Academy of Marketing Science Review*, 2001.

[27] M. Granovetter. Threshold models of collective behavior. *American Journal of Sociology*, 83(6):1420–1443, 1978.

[28] A.L. Hammer and G.E. Huszczo. *Teams*. Consulting Psychologists Press, 1996.

[29] Thomas Hofmann. Probabilistic latent semantic indexing. In *Proceedings of the Twenty-Second Annual International SIGIR Conference on Research and Development in Information Retrieval*, pages 50–57, 1999.

[30] Jian Jiao, Jun Yan, Haibei Zhao, and Weiguo Fan. Expertrank: An expert user ranking algorithm in online communities. In *Proceedings of the 2009 International Conference on New Trends in Information and Service Science*, pages 674–679, 2009.

[31] Pawel Jurczyk and Eugene Agichtein. Discovering authorities in question answer communities by using link analysis. In *Proceedings of the Sixteenth ACM Conference on Conference on Information and Knowledge Management (CIKM'07)*, pages 919–922, Lisbon, Portugal, 2007.

[32] Pawel Jurczyk and Eugene Agichtein. Hits on question answer portals: exploration of link analysis for author ranking. In *Proceedings of the 30th*

Annual International ACM SIGIR Conference on Research and Development in Information Retrieval (SIGIR'07), pages 845–846, Amsterdam, The Netherlands, 2007.

[33] Maryam Karimzadehgan, Ryen W. White, and Matthew Richardson. Enhancing expert finding using organizational hierarchies. In *Proceedings of the 31th European Conference on IR Research on Advances in Information Retrieval*, pages 177–188, Toulouse, France, 2009.

[34] Henry Kautz, Bart Selman, and Mehul Shah. Referral web: combining social networks and collaborative filtering. *Commun. ACM*, 40(3):63–65, 1997.

[35] David Kempe, Jon Kleinberg, and Éva Tardos. Maximizing the spread of influence through a social network. In *Proceedings of the Ninth ACM SIGKDD International Conference on Knowledge Discovery and Data Mining*, pages 137–146, Washington, DC, 2003.

[36] Jon M. Kleinberg. Authoritative sources in a hyperlinked environment. *Journal of the ACM (JACM)*, 46(5):604–632, 1999.

[37] Kathy Kolbe. *Pure Instinct*. Kolbe Corp, 1995.

[38] Kathy Kolbe. *The Conative Connection : Acting on Instinct*. Addison-Wesley, 1997.

[39] Bruce Krulwich and Chad Burkey. The contactfinder agent: Answering bulletin board questions with referrals. In *AAAI/IAAI, Vol. 1*, pages 10–15, 1996.

[40] Theodoros Lappas, Kun Liu, and Evimaria Terzi. Finding a team of experts in social networks. In *Proceedings of the 15th ACM SIGKDD International Conference on Knowledge Discovery and Data Mining (KDD'09)*, pages 467–476, Paris, France, 2009.

[41] Yize Li and Jie Tang. Expertise search in a time-varying social network. In *Proceedings of the 2008 The Ninth International Conference on Web-Age Information Management*, pages 293–300, 2008.

[42] Yao Lu, Xiaojun Quan, Xingliang Ni, Wenyin Liu, and Yinlong Xu. Latent link analysis for expert finding in user-interactive question answering services. In *2009 Fifth International Conference on Semantics, Knowledge and Grid*, pages 54–59, 2009.

[43] Christopher D. Manning, Prabhakar Raghavan, and Hinrich Schütze. *Introduction to Information Retrieval*, chapter 21, page 467. Cambridge University Press, 2008.

[44] M. T. Maybury. Expert finding systems. In *Technical Report MTR06B000040, MITRE Corporation*, 2006.

[45] David W. McDonald and Mark S. Ackerman. Expertise recommender: a flexible recommendation system and architecture. In *CSCW*, pages 231–240, 2000.

[46] Florian Metze, Christian Bauckhage, and Tansu Alpcan. The "spree" expert finding system. In *ICSC '07: Proceedings of the International Conference on Semantic Computing*, pages 551–558, Washington, DC, USA, 2007. IEEE Computer Society.

[47] Jay M. Ponte and W. Bruce Croft. A language modeling approach to information retrieval. In *Proceedings of the 21st Annual International ACM SIGIR Conference on Research and Development in Information Retrieval (SIGIR'98)*, pages 275–281, 1998.

[48] Josep M. Pujol, Ramon Sanguesa, and Jordi Delgado. Extracting reputation in multi agent systems by means of social network topology, 2002.

[49] S. Pushpa, K. S. Easwarakumar, Susan Elias, and Zakaria Maamar. Referral based expertise search system in a time evolving social network. In *COMPUTE '10: Proceedings of the Third Annual ACM Bangalore Conference*, pages 1–8, New York, NY, USA, 2010. ACM.

[50] Matthew Richardson and Pedro Domingos. Mining knowledge-sharing sites for viral marketing. In *Proceedings of the Eighth ACM SIGKDD International Conference on Knowledge Discovery and Data Mining*, pages 61–70, Edmonton, Alberta, Canada, 2002.

[51] R. Sangüesa and J.M. Pujol. Netexpert: A multiagent system for expertise location. In *Proceedings of the Workshop on Organizational Memories and Knowledge Management, International Joint Conference on Artificial Intelligence (IJCAI-01)*, pages 85–93, 2001.

[52] T. Schelling. *Micromotives and Macrobehavior*. Norton, 1978.

[53] Jangwon Seo and W. Bruce Croft. Thread-based expert finding. In *Workshop on Search in Social Media (SSM'09)*, Boston, MA, 2009.

[54] Pavel Serdyukov, Henning Rode, and Djoerd Hiemstra. Modeling multi-step relevance propagation for expert finding. In *Proceeding of the 17th ACM Conference on Information and Knowledge Management (CIKM'08)*, pages 1133–1142, Napa Valley, CA, 2008.

[55] Kenji Sugawara. Agent-based application for supporting job matchmaking for teleworkers. In *ICCI '03: Proceedings of the 2nd IEEE International Conference on Cognitive Informatics*, page 137, Washington, DC, USA, 2003. IEEE Computer Society.

[56] York Sure, Alexander Maedche, and Steffen Staab. Leveraging corporate skill knowledge - From ProPer to OntoProper. In D. Mahling and U. Reimer, editors, *Proceedings of the Third International Conference on*

Practical Aspects of Knowledge Management. Basel, Switzerland, October 30-31, 2000, 2000. http://www.research.swisslife.ch/pakm2000/.

[57] H. Takahashi and A. Matsuyama. An approximate solution for the Steiner problem in graphs. *Mathematica Japonica*, 24:573–577, 1980.

[58] Jie Tang, Jing Zhang, Limin Yao, Juanzi Li, Li Zhang, and Zhong Su. Arnetminer: extraction and mining of academic social networks. In *KDD*, pages 990–998, 2008.

[59] Hsien-Tang Tsai, Herbert Moskowitz, and Lai-Hsi Lee. Human resource selection for software development projects using taguchi's parameter design. *European Journal of Operational Research*, 151(1):167–180, 2003.

[60] Tzu-Liang Tseng, Chun-Che Huang, How-Wei Chu, and Roger R. Gung. Novel approach to multi-functional project team formation. *International Journal of Project Management*, 22(2):147–159, 2004.

[61] Vijay Vazirani. *Approximation Algorithms*. Springer, 2003.

[62] Adriana S. Vivacqua. Agents for expertise location. In *In Proc. 1999 AAAI Spring Symposium Workshop on Intelligent Agents in Cyberspace*, pages 9–13, 1999.

[63] Hyeongon Wi, Seungjin Oh, Jungtae Mun, and Mooyoung Jung. A team formation model based on knowledge and collaboration. *Expert Systems with Applications: An International Journal*, 36(5):9121–9134, 2009.

[64] Hyeongon Wi, Seungjin Oh, Jungtae Mun, and Mooyoung Jung. A team formation model based on knowledge and collaboration. *Expert Systems with Applications*, 36(5):9121–9134, 2009.

[65] Bin Yu and Munindar P. Singh. Searching social networks. Technical report, North Carolina State University at Raleigh, 2002.

[66] Jing Zhang, Jie Tang, , and Juanzi Li. Expert finding in a social network. In *Advances in Databases: Concepts, Systems and Applications*, volume 4443/2010, pages 1066–1069. Springer Berlin / Heidelberg, 2010.

[67] Jing Zhang, Jie Tang, Liu Liu, and Juanzi Li. A mixture model for expert finding. In *Advances in Knowledge Discovery and Data Mining*, pages 466–478, 2008.

[68] Jun Zhang, Mark S. Ackerman, and Lada Adamic. Expertise networks in online communities: structure and algorithms. In *Proceedings of the 16th International Conference on World Wide Web (WWW'07)*, pages 221–230, Banff, Alberta, Canada, 2007.

[69] Armen Zzkarian and Andrew Kusiak. Forming teams: an analytical approach. *IIE Transactions*, 31(1):85–97, 1999.

Chapter 9

A SURVEY OF LINK PREDICTION IN SOCIAL NETWORKS

Mohammad Al Hasan
Department of Computer and Information Science
Indiana University- Purdue University
Indianapolis, IN 46202
alhasan@cs.iupui.edu

Mohammed J. Zaki
Department of Computer Science, Rensselaer Polytechnic Institute
Troy, NY 12180
zaki@cs.rpi.edu

Abstract Link prediction is an important task for analying social networks which also has applications in other domains like, information retrieval, bioinformatics and e-commerce. There exist a variety of techniques for link prediction, ranging from feature-based classification and kernel-based method to matrix factorization and probabilistic graphical models. These methods differ from each other with respect to model complexity, prediction performance, scalability, and generalization ability. In this article, we survey some representative link prediction methods by categorizing them by the type of the models. We largely consider three types of models: first, the traditional (non-Bayesian) models which extract a set of features to train a binary classification model. Second, the probabilistic approaches which model the joint-probability among the entities in a network by Bayesian graphical models. And, finally the linear algebraic approach which computes the similarity between the nodes in a network by rank-reduced similarity matrices. We discuss various existing link prediction models that fall in these broad categories and analyze their strength and weakness. We conclude the survey with a discussion on recent developments and future research direction.

Keywords: Link prediction, network evolution model, social network analysis, probabilistic model, local probabilistic model

1. Introduction

Social networks are a popular way to model the interactions among the people in a group or community. They can be visualized as graphs, where a vertex corresponds to a person in some group and an edge represents some form of association between the corresponding persons. The associations are usually driven by mutual interests that are intrinsic to a group. However, social networks are very dynamic, since new edges and vertices are added to the graph over time. Understanding the dynamics that drive the evolution of social network is a complex problem due to a large number of variable parameters. But, a comparatively easier problem is to understand the association between two specific nodes. For instance, some of the interesting questions that can be posed are: How does the association pattern change over time? What are the factors that drive the associations? How is the association between two nodes affected by other nodes? The specific problem instance that we address in this article is to predict the likelihood of a future association between two nodes, knowing that there is no association between the nodes in the current state of the graph. This problem is commonly known as the *Link Prediction* problem.

More formally, the link prediction task can be formulated as followed (based upon the definition in Liben-Nowell and Kleinberg [36]): Given a social network $G(V, E)$ in which an edge $e = (u, v) \in E$ represents some form of interactions between its endpoints at a particular time $t(e)$. We can record multiple interactions by parallel edges or by using a complex timestamp for an edge. For time $t \leq t'$ we assume that $G[t,\ t']$ denotes the subgraph of G restricted to the the edges with time-stamps between t and t'. In a supervised training setup for link prediction, we can choose a training interval $[t_0,\ t_0']$ and a test interval $[t_1,\ t_1']$ where $t_0' < t_1$. Now the link prediction task is to output a list of edges not present in $G[t_0, t_0']$, but are predicted to appear in the network $G[t_1, t_1']$.

Link prediction is applicable to a wide variety of application areas. In the area of Internet and web science, it can be used in tasks like automatic web hyper-link creation [3] and web site hyper-link prediction [65]. In e-commerce, one of the most prominent usages of link prediction is to build recommendation systems [25, 37, 35]. It also has various applications in other scientific disciplines. For instance, in bibliography and library science, it can be used for de-duplication [39] and record linkage [4]; in Bioinformatics, it has been used in protein-protein interaction (PPI) prediction [6] or to annotate the PPI graph [18]. In security related applications, it can be used to identify hidden groups of terrorists and criminals. In many of the above applications, the graphs that we work on are not necessarily social network graphs, rather they can be Internet, information networks, biological entity networks, and so on.

In this article, we present a survey of existing approaches to link prediction, with focus mainly on social network graphs. We classify the extant approaches into several groups. One group of the algorithms computes a similarity score between a pair of nodes so that a supervised learning method can be employed. In this class we also include methods that use a kernel matrix, and then employ a maximum margin classifier. Another class of algorithms consists of those based on Bayesian probabilistic models, and probabilistic relational models. Beside these, there are algorithms that are based on graph evolution models or on linear algebraic formulations. Several methods span multiple classes in the above classification scheme. After a brief overview, we discuss each group of methods in more detail below.

2. Background

Liben-Nowell and Kleinberg [36] proposed one of the earliest link prediction models that works explicitly on a social network. Every vertex in the graph represents a person and an edge between two vertices represents the interaction between the persons. Multiplicity of interactions can be modeled explicitly by allowing parallel edges or by adopting a suitable weighting scheme for the edges. The learning paradigm in this setup typically extracts the similarity between a pair of vertices by various graph-based similarity metrics and uses the ranking on the similarity scores to predict the link between two vertices. They concentrated mostly on the performance of various graph-based similarity metrics for the link prediction task. Later, Hasan et. al. [22] extended this work in two ways. First, they showed that using external data outside the scope of graph topology can significantly improve the prediction result. Second, they used various similarity metric as features in a supervised learning setup where the link prediction problem is posed as a binary classification task. Since then, the supervised classification approach has been popular in various other works in link prediction [10, 58, 15].

The link prediction problem has also been studied previously in the context of relational data [53, 46, 47] and also in the Internet domain [50], where explicit graph representations were not used. The prediction system proposed in these works can accept any relational dataset, where the objects in the dataset are related to each other in any complex manners and the task of the system is to predict the *existence* and the *type* of links between a pair of objects in the dataset. Probabilistic relational models [21], graphical models [40], stochastic relational models [6, 61, 20], and different variants of these are the main modeling paradigm used in these works. The advantages of these approaches include the genericity and ease with which they can incorporate the attributes of the entities in the model. On the down side, they are usually complex, and have too many parameters, many of which may not be that intuitive to the user.

The research on social network evolution [7, 32, 34] closely resembles the link prediction problem. An evolution model predicts the future edges of a network, taking into account some well known attributes of social networks, such as the power law degree distribution [7] and the small world phenomenon [32]. This remains the main difference between evolution models and the link prediction models. The former concentrate on the global properties of the network and the latter model the local states of the network to predict the probability of the existence of a link between a specific pair of nodes in the network. Nevertheless, the ideas from these models have been instrumental for some research works [29] that directly addressed the task of link prediction.

One of the main challenges of link prediction concerns the evolution of Internet scale social networks like facebook, mySpace, flickr, and so on. These networks are huge in size and highly dynamic in nature for which earlier algorithms may not scale and adapt well—more direct approaches are required to address these limitations. For instance, Tylenda et. al. [56] shows that utilizing the time stamps of past interactions, which explicitly utilize the lineage of interactions, can significantly improve the link prediction performance. Recently, Song et. al. [52] used matrix factorization to estimate similarity between the nodes in a real life social network having approximately 2 millions nodes and 90 millions edges. Any traditional algorithm that aims to compute pair-wise similarities between vertices of such a big graph is doomed to fail. Recently, the matrix based factorization works have been extended to the more richer higher-order models such as tensors [1].

Having outlined the background methods, we now review the existing methods to link prediction. We begin with feature-based methods that construct pair-wise features to use in a classification task. Next we consider Bayesian approaches, followed by the probabilistic relational models. After reviewing methods based on linear algebra, we present some recent trends and directions for future work.

Notation. Typically, we will use small letters, like x, y, z to denote a node in a social network, the edges are represented by the letter e. For a node x, $\Gamma(x)$ represents the set of neighbors of x. $degree(x)$ is the size of the $\Gamma(x)$. We use the letter A for the adjacency matrix of the graph.

3. Feature based Link Prediction

We can model the link prediction problem as a *supervised classification* task, where each data point corresponds to a pair of vertices in the social network graph. To train the learning model, we can use the link information from the training interval ($[t_0,\ t_0']$). From this model, predictions of future links in the test interval ($[t_1,\ t_1']$) can be made. More formally, assume $u, v \in V$ are two vertices in the graph $G(V, E)$ and the label of the data point $\langle u, v \rangle$ is $y^{\langle u,v \rangle}$.

Note that we assume that the interactions between u and v are symmetric, so the pair $\langle u, v\rangle$ and $\langle v, u\rangle$ represent the same data point, hence, $y^{\langle u,v\rangle} = y^{\langle v,u\rangle}$. Now,

$$y^{\langle u,v\rangle} = \begin{cases} +1, & \text{if } \langle u, v\rangle \in E \\ -1, & \text{if } \langle u, v\rangle \notin E \end{cases}$$

Using the above labeling for a set of training data points, we build a classification model that can predict the unknown labels of a pair of vertices $\langle u, v\rangle$ where $\langle u, v\rangle \notin E$ in the graph $G[t_1, t_1']$.

This is a typical binary classification task and any of the popular supervised classification tools, such as naive Bayes, neural networks, support vector machines (SVM) and k nearest neighbors, can be used. But, the major challenge in this approach is to choose a set of features for the classification task. Next we will discuss the set of features that have been used successfully for supervised link prediction tasks.

3.1 Feature Set Construction

Choosing an appropriate feature set is the most critical part of any machine learning algorithm. For link prediction, each data point corresponds to a pair of vertices with the label denoting their link status, so the chosen features should represent some form of proximity between the pair of vertices. In existing research works on link prediction, majority of the features are extracted from the graph topology. Also, some works develop a feature set constructed from a graph evolution model. Besides these, the attributes of vertices and edges can also be very good features for many application domains.

The features that are based on graph topology are the most natural for link prediction. Here we call them graph-topological feature. In fact, many works [36, 29] on link prediction concentrated only on the graph topological feature-set. Typically, they compute the similarity based on the node neighborhoods or based on the ensembles of paths between a pair of nodes. The advantage of these features are that they are generic and are applicable for graphs from any domain. Thus, no domain knowledge is necessary to compute the values of these features from the social network. However, for large social networks, some of these features may be computationally expensive. Below we explain some of the popular graph topological features under two categories: (1) Node neighborhood based and (2) Path based. Majority of these features are adapted from [36, 22]. Following that we discuss a set of features that are extracted from the vertex or edge properties of the graph.

3.1.1 Node Neighborhood based Features.

Common Neighbors. For two nodes, x and y, the size of their common neighbors is defined as $|\Gamma(x) \cap \Gamma(y)|$. The idea of using the size of common neighbors is just an attestation to the network transitivity property. In simple words, it means that in social networks if vertex x is connected to vertex z and vertex y is connected to vertex z, then there is a heightened probability that vertex x will also be connected to vertex y. So, as the number of common neighbors grows higher, the chance that x and y will have a link between them increases. Newman [41] has computed this quantity in the context of collaboration networks to show that a positive correlation exists between the number of common neighbors of x and y at time t, and the probability that they will collaborate in the future.

Jaccard Coefficient. The common neighbors metric is not normalized, so one can use the Jaccard Coefficient, which normalizes the size of common neighbors as below:

$$\textbf{Jaccard-coefficient}(x,y) = \frac{|\Gamma(x) \cap \Gamma(y)|}{|\Gamma(x) \cup \Gamma(y)|} \tag{9.1}$$

Conceptually, it defines the probability that a common neighbor of a pair of vertices x and y would be selected if the selection is made randomly from the union of the neighbor-sets of x and y. So, for high number of common neighbors, the score would be higher. However, from the experimental results of four different collaboration networks, Liben-Nowell et. al. [36] showed that the performance of Jaccard coefficient is worse in comparison to the number of common neighbors.

Adamic/Adar. Adamic and Adar [2] proposed this score as a metric of similarity between two web pages. For a set of features z, it is defined as below.

$$\sum_{z\,:\,\text{feature shared by } x,y} \frac{1}{\log(frequency(z))} \tag{9.2}$$

For link prediction, [36] customized this metric as below, where the common neighbors are considered as features.

$$\textbf{adamic/adar}(x,y) = \sum_{z \in \Gamma(x) \cap \Gamma(y)} \frac{1}{\log |\Gamma(z)|} \tag{9.3}$$

In this way, Adamic/Adar weighs the common neighbors with smaller degree more heavily. From the reported results of the existing works on link prediction, Adamic/Adar works better than the previous two metrics.

3.1.2 Path based Features.

Shortest Path Distance. The fact that the friends of a friend can become a friend suggests that the path distance between two nodes in a social network can influence the formation of a link between them. The shorter the distance, the higher the chance that it could happen. But, also note that, due to the small world [59] phenomenon, mostly every pair of nodes is separated by a small number of vertices. So, this feature sometimes does not work that well. Hasan et. al. [22] found this feature to have an average rank of 4 among 9 features that they used in their work on link prediction in a biological co-authorship network. Similar finding of poor performance by this feature was also reported in [36].

Katz. Leo Katz proposed this metric in [31]. It is a variant of shortest path distance, but generally works better for link prediction. It directly sums over all the paths that exist between a pair of vertices x and y. But, to penalize the contribution of longer paths in the similarity computation it exponentially damps the contribution of a path by a factor of β^l, where l is the path length. The exact equation to compute the Katz value is as below:

$$\textbf{katz}(x,y) = \sum_{l=1}^{\infty} \beta^l \cdot |\text{paths}_{x,y}^{\langle l \rangle}| \tag{9.4}$$

where $|paths_{x,y}^{\langle l \rangle}|$ is the set of all paths of length l from x to y. Katz generally works much better than the shortest path since it is based on the ensemble of all paths between the nodes x and y. The parameter $\beta (\leq 1)$ can be used to regularize this feature. A small value of β considers only the shorter paths for which this feature very much behaves like features that are based on the node neighborhood. One problem with this feature is that it is computationally expensive. It can be shown that the Katz score between all the pairs of vertices can be computed by finding $(I - \beta A)^{-1} - I$, where A is the adjacency matrix and I is an identity matrix of proper size. This task has roughly cubic complexity which could be infeasible for large social networks.

Hitting Time. The concept of hitting time comes from random walks on a graph. For two vertices, x and y in a graph, the hitting time, $H_{x,y}$ defines the expected number of steps required for a random walk starting at x to reach y. Shorter hitting time denotes that the nodes are similar to each other, so they have a higher chance of linking in the future. Since this metric is not symmetric, for undirected graphs the commute time, $C_{x,y} = H_{x,y} + H_{y,x}$, can be used. The benefit of this metric is that it is easy to compute by performing some trial random walks. On the downside, its value can have high variance; hence, prediction by this feature can be poor [36]. For instance, the hitting time between x and y can be affected by a vertex z, which is far away from x and y; for instance, if z has high stationary probability, then it could be hard for a random walk to escape from the neighborhood of z. To protect against this problem we can use random walks with restart, where we periodically reset the random walk by returning to x with a fixed probability α in each step. Due to the scale free nature of a social network some of the vertices may have very high stationary probability (π) in a random walk; to safeguard against it, the hitting time can be normalized by multiplying it with the stationary probability of the respective node, as shown below:

$$\textbf{normalized-hitting-time}(x,y) = H_{x,y} \cdot \pi_y + H_{y,x} \cdot \pi_x \qquad (9.5)$$

Rooted Pagerank. Chung and Zhao [13] showed that the Pagerank [11] measures that is used for web-page ranking has inherent relationship with the hitting time. So, pagerank value can also be used as a feature for link prediction. However, since pagerank is an attribute of a single vertex, it requires to be modified so that it can represent a similarity between a pair of vertices x and y. The original definition of pagerank denotes the importance of a vertex under two assumptions: for some fixed probability α, a surfer at a web-page jumps to a random web-page with probability α and follows a linked hyperlink with probability $1 - \alpha$. Under this random walk, the importance of an web-page v is the expected sum of the importance of all the web-pages u that link to v. In random walk terminology, one can replace the term *importance* by the term *stationary distribution*. For link prediction, the random walk assumption of the original pagerank can be altered as below: similarity score between two vertices x and y can be measured as the stationary probability of y in a random walk that returns to x with probability $1 - \beta$ in each step, moving to a random neighbor with probability β. This metric is assymetric and can be made symmetric by summing with the counterpart where the role of x and y are reversed. In [36], it is named as *rooted pagerank*. The rooted pagerank between all node pairs (represented as RPR) can be derived as follows. Let D be a diagonal *degree matrix* with $D[i,i] = \sum_j A[i,j]$. Let, $N = D^{-1}A$ be the adjacency matrix with row sums normalized to 1. Then,

$$RPR = (1 - \beta)(I - \beta N)^{-1}$$

3.1.3 Features based on Vertex and Edge Attributes. Vertex and edge attributes play an important role for link prediction. Note that, in a social network the links are directly motivated by the utility of the individual representing the nodes and the utility is a function of vertex and edge attributes. Many studies [22, 15] showed that vertex or edge attributes as proximity features can significantly increase the performance of link prediction tasks. For example, Hasan et. al. [22] showed that for link prediction in a co-authorship social network, attributes such as the degree of overlap among the research keywords used by a pair of authors is the top ranked attribute for some datasets. Here the vertex attribute is the research keyword set and the assumption is that a pair of authors are close (in the sense of a social network) to each other, if their research work evolves around a larger set of common keywords. Similarly, the Katz metric computed the similarity between two web-pages by the degree to which they have a larger set of common words where the words in the web-page are the vertex attributes. The advantage of such a feature set is that it is generally cheap to compute. On the down-side, the features are very tightly tied with the domain, so, it requires good domain knowledge to identify them. Below, we will provide a generic approach to show how these features can be incorporated in a link prediction task.

Vertex Feature Aggregation. Once we identify an attribute a of a node in a social network, we need to devise some meaningful aggregation function, f. To compute the similarity value between the vertices x and y, f accepts the corresponding attribute values of these vertices to produce a similarity score. The choice of function entirely depends on the type of the attribute. In the followings we show two examples where we aggregated some local metric of a vertex.

- *Preferential Attachment Score:* The preferential attachment concept [8] is akin to the well known *rich gets richer* model. In short, it proposes that a vertex connect to other vertices in the network based on the probability of their degree. So, if we consider the neighborhood size as feature value, then multiplication can be an aggregation function, which is named as preferential attachment score:

$$\textbf{preferential attachment score}(x, y) = \Gamma(x) \,.\, \Gamma(y) \tag{9.6}$$

  Actually, the summation function can also be used to aggregate the feature values. In Hasan et. al. [22], the authors show that the summation of the neighbor-count of a pair of vertices is a very good attribute, which stands out as the second ranked feature in the link prediction task in a co-authorship network.

- *Clustering Coefficient Score:* Clustering coefficient of a vertex v is defined as below.

$$\textbf{clustering coef.}(v) = \frac{3 \times \#\text{ triangles adjacent to } u}{\#\text{ possible triples adjacent to } u} \tag{9.7}$$

  To compute a score for link prediction between the vertex x and y, one can sum or multiply the clustering coefficient score of x and y.

Kernel Feature Conjunction. In many domains, there could be numerous vertex attributes or the attributes could be complex or attribute values between a pair of instances may have no apparent match between them, hence direct application of aggregation function to each such attributes could be either cumbersome or misleading. In such a scenario, one can use pairwise kernel based feature conjunction [43, 9]. The basic idea is to obtain a kernel function that computes the similarity between two pairs of instances from the feature space which is expanded through Cartesian product. More details on this approach will be given below in Section 3.2.

Extended Graph Formulation. For a categorical vertex attribute, we can make an extended graph where the social network is extended by additional vertices where each additional vertex represents a specific attribute. The additional vertices can have a link among themselves based on co-existence of other similarity properties. Moreover, an original vertex can also be connected to an attribute vertex if that vertex shares that attribute value. This process can be repeated for any number of vertex attributes. Now, all the graph topological metrics can be deployed in the extended graph to compute a similarity score which considers both attributes and graph topology. For example, for link prediction in a co-authorship network, Hasan et. al. [22] considered an author-keyword extended graph where an additional vertex is added for each keyword. Each keyword node is connected to an author node, if that keyword is used by the authors in any of his papers. Moreover, two keywords that appear together in any paper are also connected by an edge. In this way, if two vertices do not have any matching values for an attribute, they can still be similar through the similarity link among the attributes values. Say, an author x is connected to a keyword node, named *machine learning* and the author y is connected to another keyword node, named *information retrieval* and if *machine learning* and *information retrieval* are connected to each other in this extended graph, attribute based similarity between node x and y can be inferred through the extended graph.

Generic SimRank. In the above extended graph, we use the concept that "two objects are similar if they are similar to two similar objects". Jeh and Widom [27] suggested a generic metric called *SimRank* which captures this notion recursively. The simRank score is the fixed point of the following recursive equation.

$$\textbf{simRank(x,y)} = \begin{cases} 1 & \text{if } x = y \\ \gamma \cdot \frac{\sum_{a \in \Gamma(x)} \sum_{b \in \Gamma(y)} simRank(a,b)}{|\Gamma(x)| \cdot |\Gamma(y)|} & \text{otherwise} \end{cases}$$

Note that, if we apply simRank in the extended graph, the similarity score considers both the graph topological and attribute based similarity.

3.2 Classification Models

There exist a plethora of classification models for supervised learning, such as decision trees, naive Bayes, neural networks, SVMs, k nearest neighbors, and ensemble methods like bagging and boosting. Also regression models like logistic regression can also be used for this task [38]. Although their performances are comparable, some usually work better than others for a specific data set or domain. In [22], the authors found that for a co-authorship social network, bagging and support vector machines have marginal competitive edge. However, learning a model for a link prediction task has some specific challenges that may make some models more attractive than others.

In this section we first discuss the specific challenges when modeling link prediction as a classification task. We then discuss supervised learning models that are custom-made to cope with some of these challenges.

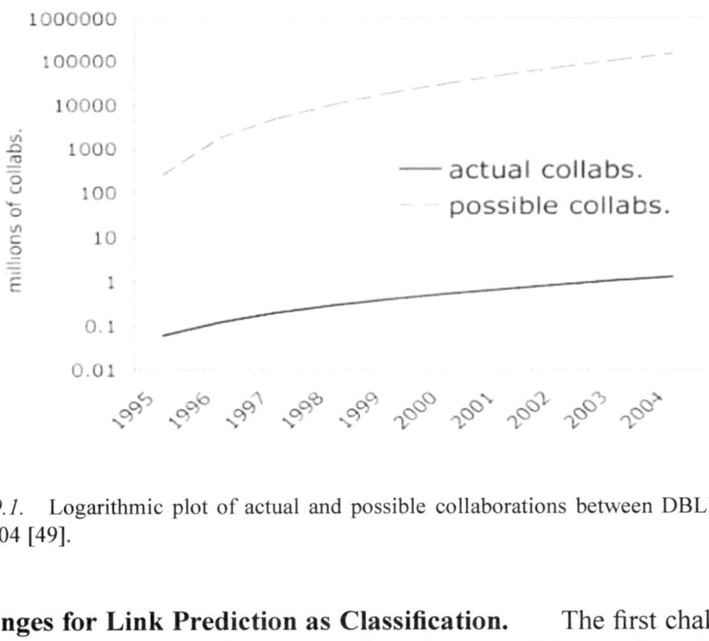

Figure 9.1. Logarithmic plot of actual and possible collaborations between DBLP authors, 1995-2004 [49].

Challenges for Link Prediction as Classification. The first challenge in supervised link prediction is extreme *class skewness*. The number of possible links is quadratic in the number of vertices in a social network, however the number of actual links (the edges in the graph) added to the graph is only a tiny fraction of this number. This results in large class skewness, causing training and inference to become difficult tasks. Hasan et. al. [22] reported very good performance of link prediction on DBLP and BIOBASE datasets, but they ignored the class distribution and reported cross validation performance from a dataset where the population is balanced. It is fair to say that the performance would drop (sometimes significantly) if the original class distribution were used. Rattigan an Jensen [49] studied this problem closely. As illustrated in Figure 9.1, they showed that in the DBLP dataset, in the year 2000, the ratio of actual and possible link is as low as 2×10^{-5}. So, in a uniformly sampled dataset with one million training instances, we can expect only 20 positive instances. Even worse, the ratio between the number of positive links and the number of possible links also slowly decreases over time, since the negative links grow quadratically whereas positive links grow only linearly with a new node. As reported in [49], for a period of 10 years, from 1995 to 2004 the number of authors in DBLP increased from 22 thousand to 286 thousand, thus the possible collaborations increased by a factor of 169, whereas the actual collaborations increased by only a factor of 21.

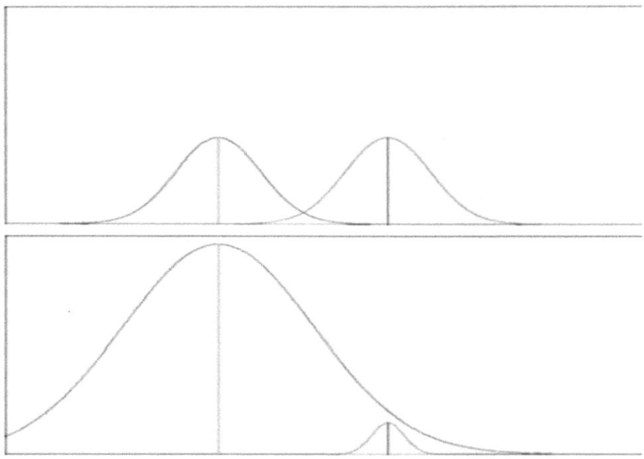

Figure 9.2. Schematic of the effect of large class skew on a model's ability to discriminate between classes. In first case (top), the two distributions are easily distinguished. In the second case (bottom), large class skew makes the discrimination really difficult. Image taken from [49].

The problem of class skew in supervised learning is well known in machine learning. The poor performance of a learning algorithm in this case results from both the variance in the models estimates and the imbalance in the class distribution. Even if a low proportion of negative instances have the predictor value similar to the positive instances, the model will end up with a large raw number of false positives. We borrowed the following schematic explanation (see Figure 9.2) from [49]. For a hypothetical dataset, let us consider a predictor s measured on the instance pairs. Also assume that the values of s are drawn from a normal distribution with different means for positive (linked) and negative (not-linked) object pairs. In presence of large class skew, the entirety of the positive class distribution is "swallowed" by the tail of the negative class, as shown in Figure 9.2.

To cope with class skew, existing research suggests several different approaches. These methods include the altering of the training sample by up-sampling or down-sampling [12], altering the learning method by making the process active [16] or cost-sensitive [28], and also more generally by treating the classifier score with different thresholds [48]. For kernel based classification, there exist some specific methods [63, 57] to cope with this problem. In general, learning from imbalanced datasets is a very important research consideration and we like to refer the reader to [60], which has a good discussion of various techniques to solve this.

The second challenge in supervised link prediction is model calibration [42], which is somewhat related to the class imbalance problem. However, model calibration is worth mentioning in its own merit because in the application domain of link prediction, calibrating the model is sometimes much more crucial than finding the right algorithm to build the classification model. Model calibration is the process to find the function that transforms the output score value of the model to a label. By varying (or biasing) the function we can control the ratio of false positive error and false negative error. In many application domains of link prediction, such as for detecting social network links in a terrorist network, the cost of missing a true link could be a catastrophic. One the other hand, in online social networks, recommending (predicting) a wrong link could be considered a more serious mistake than missing a true link. Based on these, the system designer needs to calibrate the model carefully. For some classifiers, calibration is very easy as the model predicts a score which can be thresholded to convert to a +1/-1 decision. For others, it may requires some alteration in the output of the model.

Another problem of link prediction is the training cost in terms of time complexity. Most of the social networks are large and also due to the class imbalances, a model's training dataset needs to consists of a large number of samples so that the rare cases [60] of the positive class are represented in the model. In such a scenario, classification cost may also become a consideration while choosing the model. For instance, running an SVM with millions of training instances could be quite costly in terms of time and resources, whereas Bayesian classification is comparably much cheaper.

Another important model consideration is the availability of dynamic updating options for the model. This is important for social networks because they are changing constantly and a trade off between completely rebuilding and updating the model may be worth considering. Recently, some models have been proposed that consider dynamic updates explicitly.

Above we also discussed how vertex attributes can be used for the task of link prediction. In supervised classification of link prediction, this is sometimes tricky because an instance in the training data represents a pair of vertices, rather than a single vertex. If the proposed model provides some options to map vertex attributes to pair attributes smoothly, that also makes the model an excellent choice for the link prediction task. Below we discuss a couple of supervised models that address some of the above limitations more explicitly.

3.2.1 Chance-Constrained with Second-Order Cone Programming. To explicitly handle imbalanced datasets, Doppa et. al. [15] proposed a second order cone programming (SOCP) formulation for the link prediction task. SOCP can be solved efficiently with methods for semi-definite programs, such as interior point methods. The complexity of SOCP is moderately higher than linear programs but they can be solved using general purpose SOCP solvers. The authors discussed two algorithms, named CBSOCP (Cluster-based SOCP formulation) and LBSOCP (Specified lower-bound SOCP).

In CBSOCP, the class conditional densities of positive and negative points are modeled as mixture models with component distribution having spherical covariances. If k_1 and k_2 denotes the number of components in the mixtures models for the positive and negative class, CBSOCP first finds k_1 positive clusters and k_2 negative clusters by estimating the second order moment (μ, σ^2) of all the clusters. Given these positive and negative clusters, it obtains a discriminating hyperplane ($w^T x - b = 0$), like in SVM, that separates the positive and negative clusters. The following two chance-constraints are used.

$$
\begin{aligned}
Pr(w^T X_i - b \geq 1) &\geq \eta_1 : \forall i \in \{1 \dots k_1\} \\
Pr(w^T X_j - b \leq -1) &\geq \eta_2 : \forall j \in \{1 \dots k_2\}
\end{aligned}
$$

Here X_i and X_j are random variables corresponding to the components of the mixture models for positive and negative classes, and η_1 and η_2 are the lower bound of the classification accuracy of these two classes. The chance-constraints can be replaced by deterministic constraints by using multinomial Chevyshev inequality (also known as Chevishev-Cantelli inequality) as below:

$$
\begin{array}{lll}
\min_{w,b,\xi_i} & \sum_{i=1}^{k} \xi_i & \\
\text{s.t.} & y_i(w^T \mu_i - b) \geq 1 - \xi_i + \kappa_1 \sigma_i W, & \forall i = 1, \dots, k_1 \\
 & y_j(w^T \mu_j - b) \geq 1 - \xi_j + \kappa_2 \sigma_j W, & \forall j = 1, \dots, k_2 \\
 & \xi_i \geq 0 & \forall i = 1, \dots, k_1 + k_2 \\
 & W \geq \|w\|_2 &
\end{array}
$$

where, $k = k_1 + k_2$, $\kappa_i = \sqrt{\frac{\eta_i}{1-\eta_i}}$ and W is a user-defined parameter which lower bounds the margin between the two classes. By solving the above SOCP problem, we get the optimum values of w and b, and a new data point x can be classified as $sign(w^T x - b)$.

LBSOCP imposes lower bounds on the desired accuracy in each class, thus controlling the false positive and false-negative rates. It considers the following formulation:

$$\begin{array}{ll} min_{w,b} & \frac{1}{2}\|w\|_2 \\ \text{s.t.} & Pr(X \in \mathcal{H}_2) \leq 1 - \eta_1 \\ & Pr(X \in \mathcal{H}_1) \leq 1 - \eta_2 \\ & X_1 \sim (\mu_1, \Sigma_1), X_2 \sim (\mu_2, \Sigma_2) \end{array}$$

where $\mathcal{H}_1$ and $\mathcal{H}_2$ denote the positive and negative half-spaces, respectively. The chance constraints specify that the probability that false-negative and false-positive rate should not exceed $1 - \eta_1$ and $1 - \eta_2$, respectively. Like before, using Chevyshev inequality, this can be formulated using a SOCP problem as below:

$$\begin{array}{ll} \min_{w,b,t} & t \\ \text{s.t.} & t \geq \|w\|_2 \\ & w^T\mu_1 - b \geq 1 + \kappa_1\|C_1^T w\|_2 \\ & b - w^T\mu_2 \geq 1 + \kappa_2\|C_2^T w\|_2 \end{array}$$

where, $\kappa_i = \sqrt{\frac{\eta_i}{1-\eta_i}}$, and C_1 and C_2 are square matrices such that $\Sigma_1 = C_1C_1^T$ and $\Sigma_2 = C_2C_2^T$. Note that such matrices exist since Σ_1 and Σ_2 are positive semi-definite. After solving this above problem, the optimal value of w and b can be obtained which can be used to classify new data point x as $sign(w^Tx - b)$.

The strength of above two SOCP formulations is that they allow an explicit mechanism to control the false positive and false negative in link prediction. So, they are well suited for the case of imbalanced classification. Also they are scalable. Authors in [15] show that they perform significantly better than a traditional SVM classifier.

3.2.2 Pairwise Kernel Approach. In Section 3.1, we discussed the pairwise kernel technique for automatically converting the vertex attributes to pair attributes; this technique has been used to build kernel based classifiers for link prediction [30]. The main objective is to build a pair-wise classifier [43, 30]. Standard binary classification problem aims to learn a function $f : V \rightarrow \{+1, -1\}$, where V indicates the set of all possible instances. On the other hand, in the (binary) pairwise classification, the goal is to learn a function $f : V^{(1)} \times V^{(2)} \rightarrow \{+1, -1\}$, where $V^{(1)}$ and $V^{(2)}$ are two sets of possible instances. There also exists a matrix $\mathbf{F}$ of size $|V^{(1)}| \times |V^{(2)}|$ whose elements are +1 (link exist) and -1 (link does not exist). For link prediction task, $V^{(1)} = V^{(2)} = V$ the vertex set of the social network $G(V, E)$ and the matrix $\mathbf{F}$ is just the adjacency matrix of the graph G. For pairwise classification using kernels, we also have two positive semi-definite kernel matrices, $\mathbf{K}^{(1)}$ and $\mathbf{K}^{(2)}$ for $V^{(1)}$ and $V^{(2)}$ respectively. For link prediction task, $\mathbf{K}^{(1)} = \mathbf{K}^{(2)} = \mathbf{K}$. $\mathbf{K}$ is a kernel matrix of size $|V| \times |V|$, in which each entry denotes the similarity between the corresponding pair of nodes in the social network. To compute $\mathbf{K}$, any function that maps a pair of nodes to a real number can be used as long as $\mathbf{K}$ remains semi-definite.

Generally, the assumption that drives pair-wise classification is that the similarity score between a pair of instances (an instance itself is a pair) is higher if the first elements from both the instances are similar and also the second elements from both the pairs are similar. So, if $v_{i_1}^{(1)}, v_{j_1}^{(1)} \in V^{(1)}$, $v_{i_2}^{(2)}, v_{j_2}^{(2)} \in V^{(2)}$ and $(v_{i_1}^{(1)}, v_{i_2}^{(2)})$ and $(v_{j_1}^{(1)}, v_{j_2}^{(2)})$ are similar, we expect $v_{i_1}^{(1)}$ and $v_{j_1}^{(1)}$ are similar and $v_{i_2}^{(2)}$ and $v_{j_2}^{(2)}$ are similar. To model this expectation in the kernel framework, [43] proposed to consider the pairwise similarity to be the product of two instance-wise similarities, i.e.,

$$k_{\otimes}((v_{i_1}^{(1)}, v_{i_2}^{(2)}), (v_{j_1}^{(1)}, v_{j_2}^{(2)})) = [\mathbf{K}^{(1)}]_{i_1,j_1} \, [\mathbf{K}^{(2)}]_{i_2,j_2}$$

Since the product of Mercer kernels is also a Mercer kernel [51], the above similarity measure is also a Mercer kernel if the element-wise kernels are Mercer kernels. Using the above formulation, the kernel for the pair-wise classifier is just the Kronecker product of the instance kernel matrices: $\mathbf{K}_{\otimes} = \mathbf{K}^{(1)} \otimes \mathbf{K}^{(2)}$. This pairwise kernel matrix can be interpreted as a weighted adjacency matrix of the Kronecker product graph [26] of the two graphs whose weighted adjacency matrices are the instance-wise kernel matrices. [30] named it as *Kronecker Kernel* and proposed an alternative that is based on Cartesian product graph, hence named *Cartesian kernel*. The difference between them is just the way how these two product graphs are formed. In case of Kronecker product, if $(v_{i_1}^{(1)}, v_{i_2}^{(2)})$ and $(v_{j_1}^{(1)}, v_{j_2}^{(2)})$ are node pairs in the product graph, there exist a link between the pair $v_{i_1}^{(1)}$ and $v_{j_1}^{(1)}$ and also a link between the pair $v_{i_2}^{(2)}$ and $v_{j_2}^{(2)}$. On the other hand, for the case of Cartesian product a link between these two pairs in the product graph exists if and only if $v_{i_1}^{(1)} = v_{j_1}^{(1)}$ in the first graph and there is a link between $v_{i_2}^{(2)}$ and $v_{j_2}^{(2)}$ in the second graph or a link exists between $v_{i_1}^{(1)}$ and $v_{j_1}^{(1)}$ in the first graph and $v_{i_2}^{(2)} = v_{j_2}^{(2)}$ in the second graph. Based on this, Cartesian kernel is defined as below:

$$k_{\otimes}((v_{i_1}^{(1)}, v_{i_2}^{(2)}), (v_{j_1}^{(1)}, v_{j_2}^{(2)})) = \delta(i_2 = j_2)[\mathbf{K}^{(1)}]_{i_1,j_1} + \delta(i_1 = j_1)[\mathbf{K}^{(2)}]_{i_2,j_2}$$

For link prediction on undirected graphs, both the instance matrices are the same and also the element pairs in an instance are exchangeable. The Kronecker kernel can be made symmetric as below:

$$k_{\otimes}^{\text{SYM}}((v_{i_1}, v_{i_2}), (v_{j_1}, v_{j_2})) = [\mathbf{K}]_{i_1,j_1} \, [\mathbf{K}]_{i_2,j_2} + [\mathbf{K}]_{i_1,j_2} \, [\mathbf{K}]_{i_2,j_1}$$

And for Cartesian kernel it is as shown below:

$$k_{\otimes}^{\text{SYM}}((v_{i_1}, v_{i_2}), (v_{j_1}, v_{j_2})) = \delta(i_2 = j_2)[\mathbf{K}]_{i_1,j_1} + \delta(i_1 = j_1)[\mathbf{K}]_{i_2,j_2} + \delta(i_2 = j_1)[\mathbf{K}]_{i_1,j_2} + \delta(i_1 = j_2)[\mathbf{K}]_{i_2,j_1}$$

The advantage of Cartesian kernel over the Kronecker kernel is that it has many more zero entries (an entry is zero if the two pairs do not share at least one instance). So, the training time is much faster. [30] showed via experiments that its performance is comparable with respect to the Kronecker kernel.

4. Bayesian Probabilistic Models

In this section, we will discuss supervised models that use Bayesian concepts. The main idea here is to obtain a posterior probability that denotes the chance of co-occurrence of the vertex pairs we are interested in. An advantage of such model is that the score itself can be used as a feature in classification, as we discussed in section 3.2. Contenders in this category are the algorithms proposed by Wang, Satuluri and Parthasarathy [58] and by Kashima and Abe [29]. The former uses a MRF based local probabilistic model and the later uses a parameterized probabilistic model. [58] also takes the output from the probabilistic method and uses it as a feature in a subsequent steps that employs several other features (Katz, vertex attribute similarity) to predict a binary value.

4.1 Link Prediction by Local Probabilistic Models

Wang et. al. [58] proposed a local probabilistic model for link prediction that uses Markov Random Field (MRF), an undirected graphical model. To predict the link between a pair of nodes x and y, it introduces the concept of *central neighborhood set*, which consists of other nodes that appear in the local neighborhood of x or y. Let $\{w, x, y, z\}$ be *one* such set, then the main objective of this model is to compute the joint probability $P(\{w, x, y, z\})$, which represents the probability of co-occurrence of the objects in this set. This probability can be marginalized (in this example, over all possible w and z) to find the co-occurrence probability between x and y. There can be many such central neighborhood sets (of varying size) for the pair x and y, which makes learning the marginal probability ($p(x, y)$) tricky. The authors exploited MRFs to solve the learning problem; their approach has three steps, as described below.

The first step is to find a collection of central neighborhood sets. Given two nodes x and y, their central neighborhood sets can be found in many ways. The most natural way is to find a shortest path between x and y and then all the nodes along this path can belong to one central neighborhood set. If there exist many shortest paths of the same length, all of them can be included in the collection. Finding shortest path of arbitrary length can be costly for very large graphs. So in [58] the authors only considered shortest paths up to length 4. Let us assume that the set Q contains all the objects that are present in any of the central neighborhood set.

The second step is to obtain the training data for the MRF model, which is taken from the event log of the social network. Typically a social network is formed by a chronological set of events where two or more actors in the network participate. In case of co-authorship network, co-authoring an article by two or more persons in the network is an event. Given an event-list, [58] forms a transaction dataset, where each transaction includes the set of actors participates in that event. On this dataset, they perform a variation of itemset mining, named non-derivable itemset mining, which outputs all the non-redundant itemsets (along with their frequencies) in the transaction data. This collection is further refined to include only those itemsets that contain only the objects belonging to the set Q. Assume this collection is the set $\mathcal{V}_Q$.

In the final step, an MRF model (say, M) is trained from the training data. This training process is translated to a maximum entropy optimization problem which is solved by *iterative scaling* algorithm. If $P_M(Q)$ is the probability distribution over the power set of Q, we have $\sum_{q \in \wp(Q)} P_M(q) = 1$, where $\wp(Q)$ denotes the power-set of Q. Each itemset along with its associated count in the set $\mathcal{V}_Q$ imposes a constraint on this distribution by specifying a value for that specific subset (of Q). Together, all these counts restrict the distribution to a feasible set of probability distributions, say $\mathcal{P}$. Since, the itemset counts come from empirical data, $\mathcal{P}$ is non-empty. But, the set of constraints coming through $\mathcal{V}_Q$ typically under-constrains the target distribution, for which we adopt the maximum entropy principle so that a unique (and unbiased) estimate of $P_M(Q)$ can be obtained from the feasible distribution set $\mathcal{P}$. Thus, we are trying to solve the following optimization problem,

$$P_M(Q) = \arg\max_{p \in \mathcal{P}} \ H(p)$$

where, $H(p) = -\sum_x p(x) \ \log p(x)$. The optimization problem is feasible and a unique target distribution exists only if the constraints are consistent (in this case, the frequency constraints are consistent since they are taken from the itemset support value). The solution has the following product form:

$$P_M(Q) = \mu_0 \prod_{j:V_j \in \mathcal{V}_Q} \mu_j^{I(\text{constraint } V_j \text{ satisfies})}$$

Here, $\mu_j : j \in \{1 \ldots |\mathcal{V}_Q|\}$ are parameters associated with each constraint, I is an indicator function which ensures that a constraint is considered in the model only if it is satisfied and μ_0 is a normalizing constant to ensure $\sum_{q \in \wp(Q)} P_M(q) = 1$. The value of the parameters can be obtained by an iterative scaling algorithm; for details, see [44].

Once the model $P_M(Q)$ is built, one can use inference to estimate the joint probability between the vertex x and y. The advantage of a local mode is that the number of variables in the set $\mathcal{V}_Q$ is small, so exact inference is feasible. [58] used the Junction Tree algorithm as an inference mechanism.

4.2 Network Evolution based Probabilistic Model

Kashima et. al. [29] proposed an interesting probabilistic model of network evolution which can be used for link prediction. The connection between these two problems is emphasized in [36] that we quote here: "*a network model is useful to the extent that it can support meaningful inference from observed network data*". Motivated from this statement, the authors in [29] showed that by having tunable parameters in an evolution model naturally gives rise to a learning algorithm for link prediction. First we discuss the network evolution model and later show how they use the model to perform link prediction.

The proposed evolution model considers only the topological (structural) properties of the network. For a graph $G(V, \phi)$, where V is the set of nodes and $\phi : V \times V \rightarrow [0, 1]$ is an edge label function, $\phi(x, y)$ denotes the probability that an edge exists between node x and y in G. In particular, $\phi(x, y) = 1$ denotes that an edge exists and $\phi(x, y) = 0$ denotes that an edge does not exist. $\phi^{(t)}$ denotes the edge label function at time t, which changes over time; further, the model is Markovian, i.e., $\phi^{(t+1)}$ depends only on $\phi^{(t)}$. In this model V remains fixed. The model evolves over the time as below: An edge label is copied from node l to node m randomly with probability w_{lm}. First, the model decides on l and m, then chooses an edge label uniformly from one of l's $|V| - 1$ edge labels (excluding $\phi(l, m)$) to copy as m's edge label. The model satisfies the following probability constraints.

$$\sum_{lm} w_{lm} = 1, \; w_{lm} > 0, w_{ll} = 0$$

The above idea closely resembles the transitivity property of social network – a friend of a friend becomes a friend. Through the edge label copying process, l can become friend of one of m's friend. The learning task in the above model is to compute the weights w_{ij} and the edge labels $\phi^{(t+1)}$ given the edge label $\phi^{(t)}$ from training dataset.

There are two possible ways for $\phi^{(t)}(i, j)$ to assume a particular edge label. The first is that node k copied one of its edge label to either node i or to node j. The other is that, copying happened elsewhere and $\phi^{(t+1)}(i, j) = \phi^{(t)}$. Following this, we have:

$$\begin{aligned}\phi^{(t+1)}(i,j) = \; & \frac{1}{|V|-1} \sum_{k \neq i,j} w_{kj} \phi^{(t)}(k,i) \, I\left(\phi^{(t)}(k,j) = 1\right) \\ & + \frac{1}{|V|-1} \sum_{k \neq i,j} w_{ki} \phi^{(t)}(k,j) \, I\left(\phi^{(t)}(k,i) = 1\right) \\ & + \left(1 - \frac{1}{|V|-1} \sum_{k \neq i,j} (w_{kj} + w_{ki})\right) \phi^{(t)}(i,j)\end{aligned} \tag{9.8}$$

Note that, for the case when the copy happens if k copies its label to node i, then k should already have an edge with j and if k copies its label to node j, it should already have an edge with i. This requirement is manifested by the indicator function I, which assumes a value 0 if the condition inside the parenthesis is not satisfied. By iterative application of this equation on the edge labels, the network structure evolves over time.

For the task of link prediction, the model considers that the current network is in an stationary state, i.e., $\phi^{(\infty)}(k,i) = \phi^{(t+1)}(k,i) = \phi^{(t)}(k,i)$; by plugging this assumption in Equation 9.8, we obtain the following equation

$$\phi^{(\infty)}(i,j) = \frac{\sum_{k \neq i,j} \left(w_{kj} \phi^{(\infty)}(k,i) + w_{ki} \phi^{(\infty)}(k,j)\right)}{\sum_{k \neq i,j} (w_{kj} + w_{ki})} \tag{9.9}$$

The log-likelihood for the edge label $\phi(i,j)$ can be written as

$$\begin{aligned}L_{ij} & = \phi^{(\infty)}(i,j) \log \frac{\sum_{k \neq i,j} \left(w_{kj} \phi^{(\infty)}(k,i) + w_{ki} \phi^{(\infty)}(k,j)\right)}{\sum_{k \neq i,j} (w_{kj} + w_{ki})} \\ & \left(1 - \phi^{(\infty)}(i,j)\right) \log \left(1 - \frac{\sum_{k \neq i,j} \left(w_{kj} \phi^{(\infty)}(k,i) + w_{ki} \phi^{(\infty)}(k,j)\right)}{\sum_{k \neq i,j} (w_{kj} + w_{ki})}\right)\end{aligned} \tag{9.10}$$

Total log-likelihood for the known edge labels is defined as:

$$L(W) = \sum_{(i,j) \in E^{\text{train}}} L_{ij} \tag{9.11}$$

Now, the parameter estimation process is mapped to the following constrained optimization problem:

$$\text{Maximize}_{w, \phi^{(\infty)}(i,j) \text{ for } (i,j) \in E^{\text{train}}} \; L(W)$$

s. t.

$$\phi^{(\infty)}(i,j) = \frac{\sum_{k \neq i,j} \left(w_{kj} \phi^{(\infty)}(k,i) + w_{ki} \phi^{(\infty)}(k,j)\right)}{\sum_{k \neq i,j} (w_{kj} + w_{ki})}, \forall (i,j) \in$$

$$E^{\text{train}}, \text{ and} \sum_{l,m} w_{lm} = 1, \;\; w_{lm} \geq 0$$

The above optimization problem can be solved by an Expectation Maximization type transductive learning; for details, see [29].

The benefit of this model is that it is very generic and can be applied to any social network. Further, the EM based learning yields an efficient algorithm. However, the performance of the algorithm entirely depends on the degree to which the network agree to the proposed graph evolution model.

4.3 Hierarchical Probabilistic Model

Clauset et. al. [14] proposed a probabilistic model which considers the hierarchical organization in the network, where vertices divide into groups that further subdivide into groups of groups and so forth over multiple scales. The model infers hierarchical structure from network data and can be used for prediction of missing links. It is proposed as a probabilistic model for hierarchical random graphs. The learning task is to use the observed network data to fit the most likely hierarchical structure through statistical inference – a combination of the maximum likelihood approach and a Monte Carlo sampling algorithm.

Let G be a graph with n vertices. A *dendogram* D is a binary tree with n leaves corresponding to the vertices of G. Each of the $n-1$ internal nodes of D corresponds to the group of vertices that are descended from it. A probability p_r is associated with each internal node r. Then, given two vertices i,j of G, the probability p_{ij} that they are connected by an edge is $p_{ij} = p_r$ where r is the lowest common ancestor in D. The combination, $(D, \{p_r\})$ of the dendogram and the set of probabilities then defines a *hierarchical random graph*.

The learning task is to find the hierarchical random graph or graphs that best fits the observed real world network data. Assuming all hierarchical graphs are *a priori* equally likely, the probability that a given model, $(D, \{p_r\})$ is the correct explanation of the data is, by Bayes theorem, proportional to the posterior probability or likelihood, $\mathcal{L}$ with which the model generates the observed network. The goal is to maximize $\mathcal{L}$.

Let E_r be the number of edges in G whose endpoints have r as their lowest common ancestor in D, and let L_r and R_r, respectively, be the numbers of leaves in the left and right subtrees rooted at r. Then, the likelihood of the hierarchical random graph is $\mathcal{L}(D, \{p_r\}) = \prod_{r \in D} p_r^{E_r}(1-p_r)^{L_r R_r - E_r}$, with the convention that $0^0 = 1$. If we fix the dendogram D, it is easy to find the probabilities $\{\bar{p}_r\}$ that maximize $\mathcal{L}(D, \{p_r\})$, which is:

$$\bar{p}_r = \frac{E_r}{L_r R_r} \tag{9.12}$$

the fraction of the potential edges between the two subtrees of r that actually appear in the graph G. The logarithm of the likelihood is:

$$\log \mathcal{L}(D) = -\sum_{r \in D} L_r R_r h(\bar{p}_r) \tag{9.13}$$

where, $h(p) = -p \log p - (1-p) \log(1-p)$. Note that each term $-L_r R_r h(\bar{p}_r)$ is maximized when $\bar{p}_r$ is close to 0 or close to 1. In other words, high-likelihood dendograms are those that partition the vertices into groups between which connections are either very common or very rare.

The choice among the dendograms are made by a Markov chain Monte Carlo sampling method with probabilities proportional to their likelihood. To create the Markov chain, the method first creates a set of transitions between possible dendograms through rearrangement. For rearrangement, the method chooses an internal node of a dendogram and then chooses uniformly among various configuration of the subtree at that node; for details, see [14]. Once the transition criteria is known the sampling process initiates a random walk. A new rearrangement is accepted according to the Metropolis-Hastings sampling rule, i.e., for a transition from a dendogram D to another rearranged dendogram D', the transition is accepted if $\Delta \log \mathcal{L} = \log \mathcal{L}(D') - \log \mathcal{L}(D)$ is nonnegative, otherwise it is accepted with a probability $\mathcal{L}(D')/\mathcal{L}(D)$. Authors proved that the random walk is ergodic and at stationary distribution the dendogram are sampled according to their probability of likelihood.

For the task of link prediction, a set of sample dendograms are obtained at regular intervals once the MCMC random walk reaches an equilibrium. Then, for the pair of vertices x and y for which no connection exists, the model computes a mean probability p_{xy} that they are connected by averaging over the corresponding probability p_{xy} in each of the sampled dendograms. For a binary decision, a model calibration can be made through a calibration dataset. The unique nature of the hierarchical random graph model is that it allows an hierarchy in the model. Also, it allows to sample over the set of hierarchical structures to obtain a consensus probability. On the downside, it may not be that accurate unless MCMC converges to the stationary distribution in a reasonable number of steps. Also for large graphs the entire process could be very costly.

5. Probabilistic Relational Models

In earlier sections, we discussed that the vertex attributes play a significant role in link prediction task. We also showed how different link prediction methods try to incorporate the vertex attributes in the prediction model to obtain better performance. However, in most of the cases, these approaches are not generic, and thus, are not applicable in all possible scenarios. Probabilistic Relational model (PRM) is a concrete modeling tool that provides a systematic way to incorporate both vertex and edge attributes to model the joint probability distribution of a set of entities and the links that associate them. The benefit of a PRM is that it considers the object-relational nature of structured data by capturing probabilistic interactions between entities and the links themselves. So, it is better than a flat model which discards such relational information. There are two pioneering approach of PRM, one based on Bayesian networks, which consider the relation links to be directed [21], and the other based on relational Markov networks, which consider the relation links to be undirected [53]. Though both are suitable for link prediction task, for most networks an undirected model seems to be more appropriate due to its flexibility.

As an example consider the link prediction problem in a co-authorship network. The only entities that other (non-relational) models consider is the *person*. However, in PRM we can mix heterogeneous entities in the model. So it is entirely possible to include other relevant objects in this model, such as *article*, *conferenceVenue*, and *institution*. Similar to a database schema, each of these objects can have attributes. For example, a person may have attributes like *name*, *affiliationInstitute*, *status* (whether (s)he is a student, an employee or a professor); an article may have *publicationYear*, *conferenceVenue*; an institute may have *location*, and a conference venue may have attributes like *ResearchKeywords* and so on. Then there can be relational links between these entities. Two person can be related by an *advisor/advisee* relationship. A person can be related to a paper by an *author* relationship. A paper can be related to a conference venue by *publish* relationship. In this way, the model can include a complete relational schema similar to an object relational database.

PRM was originally designed for the attribute prediction problem in relational data. For link prediction task, it was extended [21, 53] so that the links are first-class citizens in the model, so additional objects, named *link objects* are added in the relational schema. Any link object, l, is associated with a tuple of entity objects $(o_1, \ldots o_k)$ that participate in the relation (for most of the cases, links will be between a tuple of two entity objects). Following the example in the previous paragraph, one of the link object can be *advisor/advisee* object that relates two persons. The model also allows the link objects to have attributes. Now, consider a object named *potentialLink* that relates two persons. It has a binary attribute named *exist* which is *true* if there exists a link between the associated objects, and false otherwise. The link prediction task now reduces to the problem of predicting the existence attribute of these link objects.

In the training step of the model, a single probabilistic model is defined over the entire link graph, including both object labels and links between the objects. The model parameters are trained discriminatively, to maximize the probability of the (object) and the link labels given the known attributes. The learned model is then applied using probabilistic inference, to predict and classify links using observed attributes and links.

5.1 Relational Bayesian Network

A Relational Bayesian Network (RBN) is the relational counterpart of a Bayesian network (BN). Hence, the model graph of RBN $G_M^D = (V_M, E_M)$ is a directed acyclic graph with a set of conditional probability distribution (CPD) to represent a joint distribution over the attributes of the item types. Each CPD corresponding to an attribute X represents $P(X|pa(X))$, where $pa(X)$ are the parents of X in the network. In RBN, like BN, the joint probability distribution can be factorized according to the dependencies in the acyclic graph structure. RBN has closed-form parameter estimation techniques, which make the learning of the model parameters very efficient. The learning process is almost identical to BN. As for inference, RBN adopts belief propagation [21], which could perform poorly in many cases.

5.2 Relational Markov Network

Relational Markov Network (RMN) is the relational counterpart of undirected graphical models or Markov Networks [45]. Let V denotes a set of discrete random variables, and v is an instantiation of the variables in V. A Markov network for V defines a joint distribution over V through an undirected dependency network and a set of parameters. For a graph G, if $C(G)$ is the set of cliques (not necessarily maximal), the Markov network defines the distribution $p(v) = \frac{1}{Z}\prod_{c\in C(G)} \phi_c(v_c)$, where Z is the standard normalizing factor, v_c is the vertex set of the clique c, and ϕ_c is a clique potential function. RMN specifies the cliques using the notion of a *relational clique template*, which specifies tuples of variables in the instantiation using a relational query language.

Given a particular instantiation $\mathcal{I}$ of the schema, the RMN $\mathcal{M}$ produces an *unrolled* Markov network over the attributes of entities in $\mathcal{I}$ (see [55] for details). The cliques in the unrolled network are determined by the clique template C. There exists one clique for each $c \in C(\mathcal{I})$, and all of these cliques are associated with the same clique potential ϕ_C. Tasker et. al. [54] show how the parameters of a RMN over a fixed set of cliques can be learned from data. In a large network with a lot of relational attributes, the network is typically large, so exact inference is typically infeasible. So, like RBN, RMN also uses belief propagation for inference.

Besides the above two, their exists several other relational models that can be used for link prediction. These are several Bayesian relational models such as DAPER (Directed Acyclic Probabilistic Entity Relationship) [24], relational dependency network [23], parametric hierarchical Bayesian relational model [62], non-parametric hierarchical Bayesian relational model [61] and stochastic relational model [64]. For details on these, we encourage the readers to read the respective references.

6. Linear Algebraic Methods

Kunegis et. al. [33] proposed a very general method that generalizes several graph kernels and dimensionality reduction methods to solve the link prediction problem. This method is unique in the sense that it is the only method that proposes to learn a function F which works directly on the graph adjacency or the graph Laplacian matrix.

Let $\mathbf{A}$ and $\mathbf{B}$ be two adjacency matrices of the training and test set for the link prediction. We assume that they have the same vertex set. Now, consider a spectral transformation function F that maps $\mathbf{A}$ to $\mathbf{B}$ with minimal error given by the solution to the following optimization problem:

$$\begin{aligned} \min_F \quad & \| F(\mathbf{A}) - \mathbf{B}\|_F \\ s.t. \quad & F \in \mathcal{S} \end{aligned} \tag{9.14}$$

where $\| \, . \, \|_F$ *denotes the Frobenius norm.* Here, the constrain ensures that the function F belongs to the family of spectral transformation functions ($\mathcal{S}$). Given a symmetric matrix $\mathbf{A} = \mathbf{U\Lambda U}^T$, for such an F, we have $F(\mathbf{A}) = \mathbf{U}F(\mathbf{\Lambda})\mathbf{U}^T$, where $F(\mathbf{A})$ applies the corresponding function on reals to each eigenvalue separately. Note that the above formulation of link prediction is a form of transductive learning as the entire test data is available to learn the model parameters.

The optimization problem in (9.14) can be solved by computing the eigenvalue decomposition $\mathbf{A} = \mathbf{U\Lambda U}^T$ and using the fact that the Frobenius norm is invariant under multiplication by an orthogonal matrix

$$\begin{aligned} & \| F(\mathbf{A}) - \mathbf{B}\|_F \\ = \; & \| \mathbf{U}F(\mathbf{\Lambda})\mathbf{U}^T - \mathbf{B}\|_F \\ = \; & \| F(\mathbf{\Lambda}) - \mathbf{U}^T\mathbf{B}\mathbf{U}\|_F \end{aligned} \tag{9.15}$$

Since, the off-diagonal entries in the expression (9.15) are not dependent on the function F, the desired optimization function on the matrix can be transformed into an optimization function on real numbers as below:

$$\min_f \sum_i \left(f(\mathbf{\Lambda}_{ii}) - \mathbf{U}_{.i}^T\mathbf{B}\mathbf{U}_{.i}\right)^2 \tag{9.16}$$

So, the link prediction problem thus reduces to a one-dimensional least square curve fitting problem.

Now, the above general method can be used to fit many possible spectral transformation functions. In particular, we are looking for a function F that accepts a matrix and return another matrix which is suitable for link prediction, i.e., the entries in the returned matrix should encode the similarity between the corresponding vertex pairs. There are many graph kernels which can be used for the function F.

Exponential Kernel. For an adjacency matrix of an unweighted graph, $\mathbf{A}$, the powers, $\mathbf{A}^n$ denotes the number of paths of length n connecting all node pairs. On the basis that the nodes connected by many paths should be consider nearer to each other than nodes connected by few paths, a function F for link prediction can be as below:

$$F_P(\mathbf{A}) = \sum_{i=0}^{d} \alpha_i \mathbf{A}^i \tag{9.17}$$

The constant α_i should be decreasing as α grows larger to penalize longer paths. Now an exponential kernel can be expressed as below which models the above path counting.

$$exp(\alpha \mathbf{A}) = \sum_{i=0}^{\infty} \frac{\alpha^i}{i!} \mathbf{A}^i \tag{9.18}$$

Von-Neumann Kernel. It is defined similar to the exponential kernel

$$(\mathbf{I} - \alpha \mathbf{A})^{-1} = \sum_{i=0}^{\infty} \alpha^i \mathbf{A}^i \tag{9.19}$$

it also models a path counting kernel.

Laplacian kernels. The generic idea proposed in this method is not confined to use functions on adjacency matrix. In fact, one is also allowed to use functions that apply on the Laplacian matrix, $\mathbf{L}$ which is defined as $\mathbf{L} = \mathbf{D} - \mathbf{A}$, where $\mathbf{D}$ is the diagonal degree matrix. The normalized Laplacian matrix, $\mathcal{L}$ is defined as $\mathcal{L} = \mathbf{I} - \mathbf{D}^{-1/2}\mathbf{L}\mathbf{D}^{-1/2}$. While using Laplacian matrices, the entire formulation proposed in this method remains the same except that instead of an adjacency matrix we use a Laplacian matrix. Many graph kernels are defined on the Laplacian matrix. For example, by taking the Moore-Penrose pseudo-inverse of the Laplacian we can obtain the commute time kernel:

$$\begin{aligned} F_{COM}(\mathbf{L}) &= \mathbf{L}^+ \\ F_{COM}(\mathcal{L}) &= \mathcal{L}^+ \end{aligned}$$

by applying regualrization, we can obtain regularized commute time kernels:

$$F_{COMR}(\mathbf{L}) = (\mathbf{I}+\alpha\mathbf{L})^{-1}$$
$$F_{COMR}(\mathcal{L}) = (\mathbf{I}+\alpha\mathcal{L})^{-1}$$

We can also obtain heat diffusion kernels as below:

$$f_{HEAT}(\mathbf{L}) = exp(-\alpha\mathbf{L})$$
$$f_{HEAT}(\mathcal{L}) = exp(-\alpha\mathcal{L})$$

Link Prediction Function	Real Function
$F_P(\mathbf{A}) = \sum_{i=0}^{d} \alpha_i \mathbf{A}^i$	$f(x) = \sum_{i=0}^{d} \alpha_i x^i$
$F_{EXP}(\mathbf{A}) = \exp(\alpha\mathbf{A})$	$f(x) = e^{\alpha x}$
$F_{NEU}(\mathbf{A}) = ((I) - \alpha\mathbf{A})^{-1}$	$f(x) = \frac{1}{1-\alpha x}$
$F_{COM}(\mathbf{L}) = \mathbf{L}^+$	$f(x) = x^(- 1)$ when $x > 0$, $f(x) = 0$, otherwise
$F_{COMR}(\mathbf{L}) = ((I) + \alpha\mathbf{L})^{-1}$	$f(x) = \frac{1}{1+\alpha x}$
$F_{HEAT}(\mathbf{L}) = (exp)(-\alpha\mathbf{L})$	$f(x) = e^{-\alpha x}$

Table 9.1. One dimensional link prediction functions

For some of the above functions, the corresponding one dimensional function on reals is shown in Table 9.1.

The advantage of this method is its genericity and simplicity. The number of parameters to learn in this model is much less compared to many other models that we discussed. On the downside, this model cannot incorporate vertex based attributes. Morevoer, The computational cost of this method mostly depends on the cost of eigen-decomposition of **A**, which could be costly for large matrices. However, efficient methods for this task are available [19].

7. Recent development and Future Works

In recent years, the works on link prediction has evolved over various aspects. One of the main aspects among these is to consider the time in the model, which can be named as time-aware link prediciton [56, 5]. Some of the algorithms that we discussed in this survey can be extended to consider the temporal attribute of a link. For example, algorithms that perform supervised learning by using a set of features can directly consider the temporal properties in the feature value calculation. For instance, while computing Jaccard coefficient between two nodes, one can redefine the similariy metric so that recent association is weighted more than the past associations. But, the approach is somewhat ad-hoc because the desired (or optimal) temporal weighting mechanism is not available and for different metrics different weighting may apply. In case of relational model, we can always include time in the relational schema just as an edge attribute. However, in the context of link prediction, the model needs to accord special treatment for the time attribute, so that progression of the time can be captured in the model properly instead of just matching the time values. Tylenda et. al. [56] showed that considering the time stamp of the previous interactions significantly improves the accuracy of the link prediction model. Ahmed et. al. [5] proposed an scalable solution to a slightly different problem from link prediction, where they find how links in the network vary over time. They use a temporally smoothed l_1-regularized logistic regression formalism to solve this problem. Techniques like these can be borrowed to perform time-aware link prediction in a more principled manner.

Another important concern is the scalability of the proposed solutions for link prediction. Social networks are large and many of the proposed solutions, specifically, the probabilistic methods that consider the entire graph in one model is too large for most of the inference mechanisms to handle. Technique such as kernel based methods are also not scalable, because it is practically impossible to obtain a kernel matrix for such a large graph data. Note that a kernel matrix in this case is not of size $|V| \times |V|$, but of size $|V^2| \times |V^2|$. For most of the real-life social networks, $|V|$ is in the range of several millions to even billions, for which this approach is just not feasible. Even for the methods that perform feature based classification, computation of some of the features are very costly. Specially features such as Katz and rooted pagerank may require significant time to compute their values for a large number of vertex pairs. So, an approximate solution for these features can be a good research topic (see for example [52]).

Game theoretic concepts are very prominent in modeling various social problems, however these have surprisingly been ignored in the link prediction task. The closest work is the local connection game proposed by Fabrikant et. al.[17]. In this game the edges have constant cost and the players try to minimize their cost plus the sum of distances to all other pairs. However, such a local connection model may not be practical in the social network domain because the utility function partly considers a global objective which minimizes the distances to all pairs. So, it may not yield good result for the link prediction task. An interesting alteration to this model that considers the utility of a person in the network from more subjective viewpoint is worth considering.

Acknowledgments

This work was supported in part by NSF Grants EMT-0829835 and EIA-0103708, and NIH Grant 1R01EB0080161-01A1.

References

[1] Acar, Evrim, and Dunlavy, Daniel M., Kolda, Tamara G. (2009). *Link Prediction on Evolving Data Using Matrix and Tensor Factorizations*. In Pro-

ceedings of the Workshop on Large Scale Data Mining Theory and Applications. ICDM Workshops:262-269

[2] Adamic, Lada A. and Adar, Eytan. (2003). *Friends and neighbors on the web*. Social Networks, 25(3):211-230.

[3] Adafre, Sisay F., and Rijke, Maarten de. (2005). *Discovering missing links in Wikipedia*. LINK-KDD '05: Proceedings of the Third International Workshop on Link Discovery.

[4] Ahmed, Elmagarmid, and Ipeirotis, Panagiotis G., and Verykios, Vassilios. (2007) *Duplicate Record Detection: A Survey*. In IEEE Transactions on Knowledge and Data Engineering 19 (1):1âĂŞ16

[5] Ahmed, Amr, and Xing, Eric P. (2009). *Recovering time-varying network of dependencies in Social and biological studies*. PNAS 106(29):11878-11883.

[6] Airodi, Edoardo M., and Blei, David M., and Xing, Eric P., and Fienberg, Stephen E. (2006). *Mixed Membership stochastic block models for relational data, with applications to protein-protein interactions*. Proceedings of Ineterational Biometric Society-ENAR Annual Meetings.

[7] Barabasi, Albert-Laszlo, and Albert, Reka. (1999) *Emergence of Scaling in Random Networks*, Science, 286(5439):509.

[8] Barabasi, Albert-Laszlo, and Jeong, H., and Neda, Z. and Ravasz, E. (2002) *Evolution of the social network of scientific collaboration*. Physics A, 311(3-4):590-614.

[9] Basilico, J., and Hofmann, T. (2004) *Unifying Collaborative and Content-based filtering*. In Proceedings of European Conference on Machine Learning.

[10] Bilgic, Mustafa, and Namata, Galileo M., and Getoor, Lise. (2007). *Combining collective classification and link prediction*. In Proceedings of the Workshop on Mining Graphs and Complex Structures at ICDM Conference.

[11] Brin, Sergey, and Page, Lawrence. (1998). *The anatomy of a large-scale hypertextual Web search engine*. Computer Networks and ISDN Systems, 30(1-7):107-117.

[12] Chawla, Nitesh V, and Bowyer, Kevin W., and Hall, Lawrence O., and W. Kegelmeyer, Philip. (2002) *SMOTE: synthetic minority over-sampling technique*. Journal of Artificial Intelligence Research, 16(1):321-357.

[13] Chung, Fan, and Zhao, Wenbo, (2010). *PageRank and random walks on graphs*. Proceedings of the "Fete of Combinatorics" conference in honor of Lovasz.

[14] Clause, Aaron, and Moore, Christopher, and Newman, M. E. J. (2008). *Hierarchical structure and the prediction of missing links in network*. Nature 453:98-101.

[15] Doppa, Janardhan R., and Yu, Jun, and Tadepalli, Prasad, and Getoor, Lise. (2009). *Chance-Constrained Programs for Link Prediction*. In Proceedings of Workshop on Analyzing Networks and Learning with Graphs at NIPS Conference.

[16] Erketin, Syeda, and Huang, Jian, and Giles, Lee. (2007). *Active learning for Class imbalance problem*. In Proceedings of the 30th ACM SIGIR Conference.

[17] Fabrikant, Alex, and Luthra, Ankur, and Maneva, Elitza, and Papadimitriou, Christos H., and Shenker, Scott. (2003). *On a Network Creation Game*. In Proc. of the twenty-second annual symposium on principles of distributed computing, pp:347-351.

[18] Freschi, Valerio. (2009). *A Graph-based Semi-Supervised Algorithm for Protein Function Prediction from Interaction Maps*. In Learning and Intelligent Optimization, Lecture Notes in Computer Science, 5851:249-258

[19] Frieze, A, and Kannan, R., and Vempala, S. (1998) *Fast monte-carlo algorithms for finding low-rank approximations*. in Journal of the ACM (JACM), 51(6):1025âĂŞ1041.

[20] Fu, Wenjie, and Song, Le, and Xing, Eric P. (2009) . In Proc. of the 26th International Conference on Machine Learning.

[21] Getoor, Lise, and Friedman, Nir, and Koller, Dephne, and Taskar, Benjamin. (2002) *Learning Probabilistic Models of Link structure*. Journal of Machine Learning Research, 3:679-707.

[22] Hasan, Mohammad A., and Chaoji, Vineet, and Salem, Saeed and Zaki, Mohammed. (2006) *Link Prediction using Supervised Learning*. In Proceedings of SDM Workshop of Link Analysis, Counterterrorism and Security.

[23] Heckerman, David, and Chickering, David M., and Meek, Christopher, and Rounthwaite, Robert, and Kadie, Carl M. (2000) *Dependency Networks for inference, collaborative filtering, and data visualization*. Journal of Machine Learning Research, 1:49-75.

[24] Heckerman, David, and Meek, Christopher, and Koller, Daphne. (2004) *Probabilistic models for relational data*. Technical Report, Microsoft.

[25] Huang, Zan, and Li, Xin, and Chen Hsinchun. (2005) *Link Prediction approach to collaborative filtering*. Proceedings of the fifth ACM/IEEE Joint Conference on Digital Libraries.

[26] Imrich, W., Klavzar, S. (2000). *Product Graphs: Structure and Recognition*. Wiley.

[27] Jeh, Glen, and Widom, Jennifer. (2002) *SimRank: A measure of structural-context similarity*. In Proceedings of ACM SIGKDD International Conference of Knowledge Discovery and Data Mining.

[28] Karakoulas, Grigoris, and Shawe-Taylor, John. (1999). *Optimizing classifiers for imbalanced training sets*. Proceedings of NIPS, 253-259.

[29] Kashima, Hisashi, and Abe, Naoke. (2006) *A Parameterized Probabilistic Model of Network Evolution for Supervised Link Prediction*. ICDM '06: Proceedings of the Sixth IEEE International Conference on Data Mining. 340-349.

[30] Kashima, Hisashi, and Oyama, Satoshi, and Yamanishi, Yoshihiro, and Tsuda, Koji. (2009). *On Pairwise Kernels: An Efficient Alternative and Generalization Analysis*, Proceedings of the 13th Pacific-Asia Conference on Advances in Knowledge Discovery and Data Mining, pp.1030-1037.

[31] Katz, Leo. (1953) *A new status index derived from sociometric analysis*. Psychometrika, 18(1):39-43.

[32] Kleinberg, Jon M. (2000). *Navigation in a small world*. Nature 406, (845).

[33] Kunegis, Jerome, and Lommatzsch, Andreas. (2009) *Learning Spectral Graph Transformations for Link Prediction*. In Proceedings of the International Conference on Machine Learning, pp 561-568.

[34] Leskovec, Jure, and Kleinberg, Jon M, and Faloutsos, Christos. (2005). *Graphs over time:densification laws, shrinking diameters and possible explanations*. KDD '05: Proceedings of the Eleventh ACM SIGKDD International Conference on Knowledge Discovery in Data Mining.

[35] Li, Xin, Chen Hsinchun. (2009). *Recommendation as link prediction: a graph kernel-based machine learning approach*. Proceedings of the ninth ACM/IEEE Joint Conference on Digital Libraries.

[36] Liben-Nowell, David, and Kleinberg, Jon. (2007). *The Link Prediction Problem for Social Networks*. Journal of the American Society for Information Science and Technology, 58(7):1019-1031.

[37] Liu, Yan and Kou, Zhenzhen. (2007). *Predicting who rated what in large-scale datasets*. SIGKDD Exploration Newsletter, 9 (2).

[38] Madadhai, J., and Hutchins, J., and Smyth, P. (2005). *Prediction and Ranking algorithms for event-based Network Data*. SIGKDD Explorations Newsletter, 7(2):23-30.

[39] Malin, Bradley, and Airoldi, Edoardo, and Carley, Kathlee M. (2005). *A Network Analysis Model for Disambiguation of Names in Lists*. In Journal of Computational and Mathematical Organization Theory, 11(2):119-139.

[40] Nallapati, Ramesh, and Ahmed, Amr, and Xing, Eric P., and Cohen, William W. (2008). *Joint Latent Topic Models for Text and Citations*. In

Proc. of The Fourteen ACM SIGKDD International Conference on Knowledge Discovery and Data Mining.

[41] Newman, M. E. J. (2001). *Clustering and Preferential attachment in growing networks*. PHysical Review Letters E, 64(025102).

[42] Niculescu-Mizil, and Alexandru, and Caruana, Rich. (2005). *Predicting Good Probabilities with Supervised Learning*. International Conference on Machine Learning.

[43] Oyama, Satoshi, and Manning, Christopher D., (2004). *Using feature conjunctions across examples for learning pairwise classifiers*, In The Proc. of European Conference on Machine Learning, pp. 323-333.

[44] Pavlov, Dmitry, and Mannila, Heikki, and Smyth, Phadraic. (2009) *Beyond Independence: Probabilistic Models for Query Approximation on Binary Transaction Data*. University of California, Irvine Technical Report UCI-ICS-TR-01-09.

[45] Pearl, Judea. (1988). *Probabilistic Reasoning in Intelligent Systems*. Morgan Kaufmann, San Fransisco.

[46] Popescul, Alexandrin and Ungar, Lyle H. (2003). *Statistical Relational Learning for Link Prediction*. In Proceedings of Workshop on Learning Statistical Models from Relational Data at IJCAI Conference.

[47] Popescul, Alexandrin and Ungar, Lyle H. (2003). *Structural Logistic Regression for Link Analysis*. In Proceedings of Workshop on Multi-Relational Data Mining at KDD Conference.

[48] Provost, Foster, and Fawcell, Tom. (2001). *Robust Classification for Imprecise Environments*. Machine Learning, 42(3):203-231.

[49] Rattigan, Matthew J., and Jensen, David. (2005). *The case for anomalous link discovery*. SIGKDD Explorations Newsletter, 7 (2):41-47.

[50] Sarukkai, Ramesh R. (2000). *Link Prediction and Path Analysis using Markov Chain*. WWW '00: Proceedings of the Ninth World Wide Web Conference, 377-386.

[51] Shawe-taylor, J., and Cristianini, Nelo. (2004). *Kernel Methods for Pattern Analysis*. Cambridge University Press, NY.

[52] Song, Han H., and Cho Tae W., and Dave, Vacha, and Zhang, Yin, and Qiu, Lili. (2009). *Scalable proximity Estimation and Link Prediction in Online Social Networks*, IMC '09: In Proceedings of the Internet Measurement Conference.

[53] Tasker, Benjamin, and Wong, Ming F., and Abbeel, Pieter, and Koller, Daphne. (2003). Link Prediction in Relational Data. NIPS '03: In Proceedings of Neural Information Processing Systems.

[54] Tasker, Benjamin, and Abbeel, Pieter, and Koller, Daphne. (2002). Discriminative Probabilistic Models for Relational Data. In Proceedings of Uncertainty in Artificial Intelligence Conference.

[55] Taskar, Benjamin, and Abbeel, Pieter, and Wong, M.-F, and Koller, Daphne (2007). *Relational Markov Networks*. In L. Getoor and B. Taskar, editors, Introduction to Statistical Relational Learning.

[56] Tylenda, Tomasz, and Angelova, Ralitsa, and Bahadur, Srikanta. (2009). *Towards time-aware link prediction in evolving social network*. SNA-KDD '09: Proceedings of the third Workshop on Social Network Mining and Analysis.

[57] Campbell, Veropoulos, and Campbell, C.K., and Cristianini, N., *Controlling the sensitivity of support vector machines*. In: Dean, T. (Ed.), IJCAI: Proceedings of International Joint Conference on Artificial Intelligence. pp. 55-60.

[58] Wang, Chao, and Satuluri, Venu, and Parthasarathy, Srinivasan. (2007). *Local Probabilistic Models for Link Prediction*. ICDM '07: In Proceedings of International Conference on Data Mining.

[59] Watts, D, and Stogatz, S. (1998). *Small world*. Nature, 393:440-442.

[60] Weiss, Gary M. (2004) *Mining with rarity: a unifying framework*, In SIGKDD Explorations Newsletter, 6(1):7-19.

[61] Xu, Zhao, and Tresp, Volker, and Yu, Shipeng, and Yu, Kai. (2005). *Nonparametric Relational Learning for Social Network Analysis*. SNA-KDD '08: In Proceedings of the Second Workshop on Social Network Mining and Analysis.

[62] Xu, Zhao, and Tresp, Volker, and Yu, Kai and Kriegel, Hans-Peter. (2005). *Dirichlet Enhanced Relational Learning*. In Proceedings of International Conference on Machine Learning, pp 1004-1011.

[63] Yang, Chan-Yun, and Yang, Jr-Syu, and Wang Jian-Jun. (2009). *Margin Calibration in SVM class-imbalanced learning*, Neurocomputing, 73(1-3):397-411.

[64] Yu, Kai, and Chu, Wei, and Yu, Shipeng, and Tresp, Volker, and Xu, Zhao. (2006). *Stochastic relational models for discriminative link prediction*. In Proceedings of NIPS, pp-1553-1560

[65] Zhu, Jianhan, and Hong, Jun, and Hughes G. (2002). *Using Markov models for web site link prediction*. HYPERTEXT '02: Proceedings of the Thirteenth ACM Conference on Hypertext and Hypermedia.

Chapter 10

PRIVACY IN SOCIAL NETWORKS: A SURVEY

Elena Zheleva
Department of Computer Science
University of Maryland
College Park, MD 20742, USA
elena@cs.umd.edu

Lise Getoor
Department of Computer Science
University of Maryland
College Park, MD 20742, USA
getoor@cs.umd.edu

Abstract In this chapter, we survey the literature on privacy in social networks. We focus both on online social networks and online affiliation networks. We formally define the possible privacy breaches and describe the privacy attacks that have been studied. We present definitions of privacy in the context of anonymization together with existing anonymization techniques.

Keywords: privacy, social networks, anonymization, disclosure

1. Introduction

With the proliferation of online social networks, there has been increasing concern about the privacy of individuals participating in them. While disclosing information on the web is a voluntary activity on the part of the users, users are often unaware of who is able to access their data and how their data can potentially be used. Data privacy is defined as "freedom from unauthorized intrusion" [28]. However, what constitutes an unauthorized intrusion in social networks is an open question. Because privacy in social networks is a young field, in this chapter, we mainly aim at identifying the space of problems in this emerging area rather than proposing solutions. We present existing work when appropriate, but many of these problems have not yet been addressed in the research literature. One of the contributions of this chapter is in cataloging the different types of privacy disclosures in social networks. These are studied in the research literature but they are often not explicitly formalized.

We focus on two scenarios for privacy in social networks: privacy breaches and data anonymization. In the first scenario, an adversary is interested in learning the private information of an individual using publicly available social network data, possibly anonymized. In the second scenario, a data provider would like to release a social network dataset to researchers but preserve the privacy of its users. For this purpose, the data provider needs to provide a privacy mechanism, so that researchers can access the (possibly perturbed) data in a manner which does not compromise users' privacy. A common assumption in the data anonymization literature is that the data is described by a single table with attribute information for each of the entries. However, social network data can exhibit rich dependencies between entities which can be exploited for learning the private attributes of users, and we explore the consequences of this possibility.

In Section 2, we discuss the different types of privacy breaches: private information that can leak from a social network. We define the types of queries for each type of disclosure, and ways to measure the extent to which a disclosure has occurred in an online or anonymized social network. We are abstracting these definitions from the types of privacy breaches that have been studied in data anonymization. The definitions can be applied both in the anonymization scenario and in the scenario of an intrusion in an online social network. We also provide pointers to work which studies these privacy breaches in the context of anonymization. We present privacy definitions in Section 3 and privacy mechanisms for publishing social network data in Section 4.

In the context of this book chapter, when we refer to social networks, we generally mean online social networks. This includes online sites such as Facebook, Flickr, LinkedIn, etc., where individuals can link to, or "friend," each other, and which allow rich interactions such as joining communities or groups of interest, or participating in discussion forums. These sites often also include online services which allow users to create profiles and share their preferences and opinions about items, such as tagging articles and postings, commenting on photos, and rating movies, books or music. Thus, we view a social network as a multi-modal graph in which there are multiple kinds of entities, including people, groups, and items, but where at least one type is an individual and the links between individuals represent some sort of social tie. Each node of an individual has a profile, and profiles can have personal attributes, such as age, gender, political affiliation, etc. Our view is informed by the link mining and statistical relational learning research communities [22, 23], which study the mining of interconnected relational data.

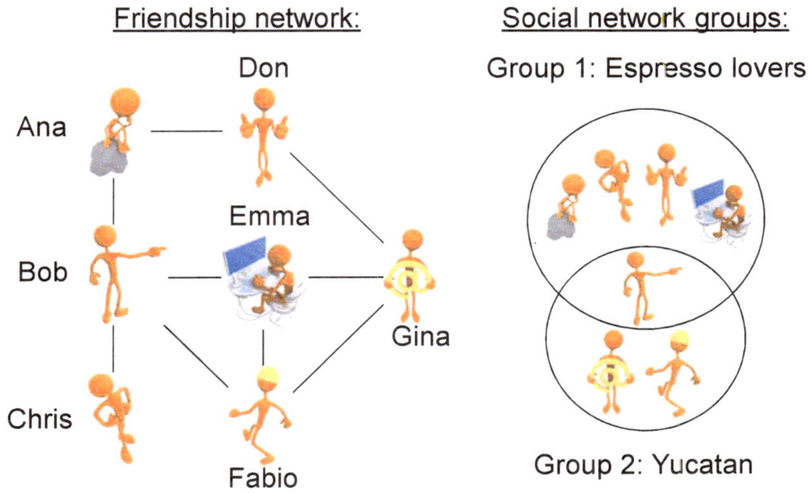

Figure 10.1. A toy social network.

We concentrate on networks which have two types of commonly occurring links - user-user links, and user-group links. More formally, we represent the social network as a graph $G = (V, E_v, H, E_h)$, where V is a set of n nodes which represent user profiles, such as the one in Figure 10.2. Each node can have a set of properties $v.A$. An edge $e_v(v_i, v_j) \in E_v$ is a *social link* and represents a relationship between the nodes v_i and v_j such as friendship. Relationships can be of different types (such as in a multiplex network), and there can be more than one relationship between a pair of users. We use H to denote both formal online groups and other online content for which users have preference, such as photos, movies, fan pages, etc. We refer to H as affiliation groups. An edge $e_h(v_i, h_j) \in E_h$ represents an *affiliation link* of the membership of node v_i to affiliation group h_j. Social links, affiliation links and groups also can have attributes, $e_v.A$, $e_h.A$ and $h.A$, respectively. We also define P to be a set of real-world entities which represent actual people.

As a running example, we consider the social network presented in Figure 10.1. It consists of seven profiles which describe a collection of individuals (Ana, Bob, Chris, Don, Emma, Fabio, and Gina), along with their friendship links and their affiliation groups of interest. Users are linked by a friendship link, and in this example they are reciprocal. There are two groups that users can participate in: the "Espresso lovers" affiliation group and the "Yucatan" affiliation group. These individuals also have personal attributes on their profiles: name, age, gender, zip code and political views (see Figure 10.5 on page 288). User-group affiliations can also be represented as a bipartite graph, such as the ones in Figure 10.6 (page 298) and Figure 10.7(a) (page 299).

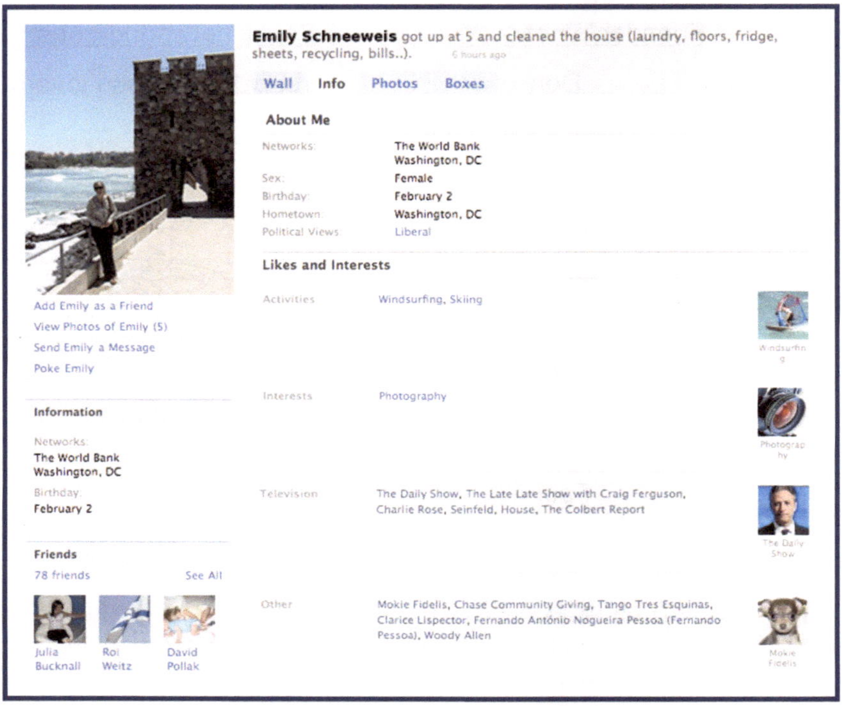

Figure 10.2. A hypothetical Facebook profile.

In this chapter, we focus on both privacy breaches in online social networks and privacy-preserving techniques for publishing social network data. In addition, there are other existing surveys on privacy preservation in social networks that focus on different aspects [12, 25, 34, 47, 52]. The surveys on privacy-preserving data publication for networks cover privacy attacks, edge modification, randomization and generalization privacy-preserving strategies for network structure [34, 47, 52] and richer graphs [47]. Clarkson et al. [12] discuss anonymization techniques which aim to prevent identity disclosure. The survey of Hay et al. [25] concentrates on privacy issues with network structure, and it covers attacks and their effectiveness, anonymization strategies, and differential privacy for private query answering.

2. Privacy breaches in social networks

When studying privacy, it is important to specify what defines a failure to preserve privacy. A *privacy breach* occurs when a piece of sensitive information about an individual is disclosed to an adversary, someone whose goal is to compromise privacy. Traditionally, two types of privacy breaches have been studied: *identity disclosure* and *attribute disclosure*. We discuss these two types in the context of social networks. We also present two more disclosure types, specific to network data: *social link disclosure* and *affiliation link disclosure*.

2.1 Identity disclosure

Identity disclosure occurs when an adversary is able to determine the mapping from a profile v in the social network to a specific real-world entity p. Before we are able to provide a formal definition of identity disclosure, let us consider three questions related to the identity of p in which an adversary may be interested.

DEFINITION 10.1 **Mapping query**. *In a set of individual profiles V in a social network G, find which profile v maps to a particular individual p. Return v.*

DEFINITION 10.2 **Existence query**. *For a particular individual p, find if this individual has a profile v in the network G. Return true or false.*

DEFINITION 10.3 **Co-reference resolution query**. *For two individual profiles v_i and v_j, find if they refer to the same individual p. Return true or false.*

A simple way of defining *identity disclosure* is to say that the adversary can answer the *mapping query* correctly and with full certainty. However, unless the adversary knows unique attributes of individual p that can be matched with the observed attributes of profiles in V, this is hard to achieve. One way of formalizing *identity disclosure* for an individual p is to assoicate a random variable $\hat{v}_p$ which ranges over the profiles in the network. We assume that the adversary has a way of computing the probability of each profile v_i belonging to individual p, $Pr(\hat{v}_p = v_i)$. In addition, we introduce a dummy profile v_{dummy} in the network which serves the purpose of absorbing the probability of individual p not having a profile in the network. We assume that p has exactly one profile, and the true profile of p in $V \cup \{v_{dummy}\}$ is v_*. We use the shorthand $Pr_p(v_i) = Pr(\hat{v}_p = v_i)$ to denote the probability that v_i corresponds to p; Pr_p provides a mapping $Pr_p : V \cup \{v_{dummy}\} \rightarrow \mathbb{R}$. We leave it open as to how the adversary constructs Pr_p. Then we can define *identity disclosure* as follows:

DEFINITION 10.4 **Identity disclosure with confidence** t. *In a set of individual profiles V in a social network G, identity disclosure occurs with confidence t when $Pr_p(v_*) \geq t$ and $v_* \neq v_{dummy}$.*

An alternative definition of *identity disclosure* considers that the possible values of v_i can be ranked according to their probabilities.

DEFINITION 10.5 **Identity disclosure with *top-k* confidence**. *In a set of individual profiles V in a social network G, identity disclosure occurs with* top-k *confidence when v_* appears in the top k profiles (or top p% $= k * 100/|V|$), in the list of profiles ranked by Pr_p from high to low.*

The majority of research in social network privacy has concentrated on identity disclosure [4, 8, 26, 27, 30, 35, 41, 45, 48, 51, 53]. We discuss it in more detail in Section 4.

2.2 Attribute disclosure

A common assumption in the privacy literature is that there are three types of possibly overlapping sets of personal attributes:

- Identifying attributes - attributes, such as social security number (SSN), which identify a person uniquely.
- Quasi-identifying attributes - a combination of attributes which can identify a person uniquely, such as name and address.
- Sensitive attributes - attributes that users may like to keep hidden from the public, such as politic affiliation and sexual orientation.

Attribute disclosure occurs when an adversary is able to determine the value of a sensitive user attribute, one that the user intended to stay private. This attribute can be an attribute of the node itself, the node's links or the node's affiliations. Without loss of generality, here we discuss the attributes of the node itself. Again, to make this definition more concrete, we assume that each sensitive attribute $v.a_s$ for profile v has an associated random variable $v.\hat{a}_s$ which ranges over the possible values for $v.a_s$. Let the true value of $v.a_s$ be $v.a_*$. We also assume that the adversary can map the set of possible sensitive attribute values to probabilities, $Pr_a(v.\hat{a}_s = v.a) : v.a \rightarrow \mathbb{R}$, for each possible value $v.a$. Note that this mapping can be different for each node/profile. Now, we can define attribute disclosure as follows:

DEFINITION 10.6 **Attribute disclosure with confidence** t. *For a profile v with a hidden attribute value $v.a_s = v.a_*$, attribute disclosure occurs with confidence t when $Pr_a(v.\hat{a}_s = v.a_*) \geq t$.*

Similarly to *identity disclosure*, there is an alternative definition of *attribute disclosure* which considers that the possible values of $v.A_s$ can be ranked according to their probabilities.

DEFINITION 10.7 **Attribute disclosure with *top-k* confidence**. *For a profile v with a hidden attribute value $v.a_s = v.a_*$, attribute disclosure occurs with* top-k *confidence when a_* appears in the top k values of the list of possible values ranked by their probabilities Pr_a.*

Clearly, if an adversary can see the identifying attributes in a social network, then answering the identity *mapping query* becomes trivial, and identity disclosure with confidence 1 can occur. For example, if a profile contains a SSN, then identifying the real person behind the profile is trivial since there is a one-to-one mapping between individuals and their social security numbers. Therefore, in order to prevent identity disclosure, the identifying attributes have to be removed from the profiles.

Sometimes, a combination of attributes, referred to as *quasi-identifying attributes*, can lead to identity disclosure. What constitutes *quasi-identifying attributes* depends on the context. For example, it has been observed that 87% of individuals in the U.S. Census from 1990 can be uniquely identified based on their date of birth, gender and zip code [43]. Another example of quasi-identifiers is a combination of a person's name and address.

Similarly, matching records from different datasets with quasi-identifying attributes can lead to further privacy breaches. This is known as a *linking attack.* If the identities of users in one dataset are known and the second dataset does not have the identities but it contains sensitive attributes, then the sensitive attributes of the users from the first dataset can be revealed. For example, matching health insurance records, in which the identifying information is removed, with public voter registration records can reveal sensitive health information about voters. Using this attack, Sweeney was able to identify the medical record of the governor of Massachusetts [43].

In the context of social and affiliation networks, there has not been much work on sensitive attribute disclosure. Most studies look at how attributes can be predicted [40, 33, 50], and very few on how they can be protected [8]. We discuss this work in more detail in Section 4.

2.3 Social link disclosure

Social link disclosure occurs when an adversary is able to find out about the existence of a sensitive relationship between two users, a relationship that these users would like to remain hidden from the public. Similarly to the previous types of disclosures, we assume that there is a random variable $\hat{e}_{i,j}$ associated with the link existence between two nodes v_i and v_j, and an adversary has a model for assigning a probability to $\hat{e}_{i,j}$, $Pr(\hat{e}_{i,j} = true) : e_{i,j} \rightarrow \mathbb{R}$.

DEFINITION 10.8 **Social link disclosure with confidence** t. *For two profiles v_i and v_j, a social link disclosure occurs with confidence t when $e_v(v_i, v_j) \in E_v$ and $Pr(\hat{e}_{i,j} = true) \geq t$.*

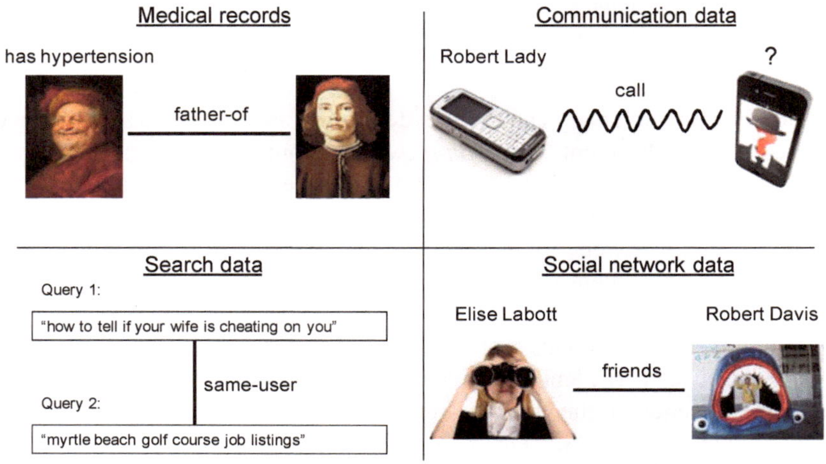

Figure 10.3. Sensitive link examples.

Note that since the link existence $\hat{e}_{i,j}$ has only two possible values, true and false, the *top-k* definition does not apply to social link disclosure.

Examples of sensitive relationships can be found in social networks, communication data, disease data and others. In social network data, based on the friendship relationships of a person and the public preferences of the friends such as political affiliation, it may be possible to infer the personal preferences of the person in question as well. In cell phone communication data, finding that an unknown individual has made phone calls to a cell phone number of a known organization can compromise the identity of the unknown individual. In hereditary disease data, knowing the family relationships between individuals who have been diagnosed with hereditary diseases and ones that have not, can help infer the probability of the healthy individuals to develop these diseases. Figure 10.3 presents a summary of these examples.

Researchers have studied attacks that expose sensitive links in social networks [4, 6, 31, 49]. Sensitive edge properties, such as link strength (or weight), have also been the focus of recent work [16, 37].

2.4 Affiliation link disclosure

Another type of privacy breach in relational data is *affiliation link disclosure* whether a person belongs to a particular affiliation group. Whether two users are affiliated with the same group can also be of sensitive nature. Sometimes, affiliation link disclosure can lead to attribute disclosure, social link disclosure, or identity disclosure. Thus, hiding affiliations is a key to preserving the privacy of individuals.

As before, we assume that there is a random variable $\hat{e}_{v,h}$ associated with the existence of an affiliation link between a profile v and a group h, and that an adversary has a way of computing the probability of $\hat{e}_{v,h}$, $Pr(\hat{e}_{v,h} = true) : e_{v,h} \rightarrow \mathbb{R}$.

DEFINITION 10.9 **Affiliation link disclosure with confidence** t. *For a profile v and an affiliation group h, an affiliation link disclosure occurs with confidence t when $e_h(v, h) \in E_h$ and $Pr(\hat{e}_{v,h} = true) \geq t$.*

One type of disclosure can lead to another type. For example, Wondracek et al. [45] show a de-identification attack in which affiliation link disclosure can lead to the identity disclosure of a supposedly anonymous Internet user. An adversary starts the attack by crawling a social networking website and collecting information about the online social group memberships of its users. It is assumed that the identities of the social network users are known. According to the collected data, each user who participates in at least one group has a group signature, which is the set of groups he belongs to. Then, the adversary applies a *history stealing attack* (for more details on the attack, see [45]) which collects the web browsing history of the target Internet user. By finding the group signatures of social network users which match the browsing history of the Internet user, the adversary is able to find a subset of potential social network users who may be the Internet user. In the last step of the attack, the adversary looks for a match between the id's of the potential users and the browsing history of the target individual, which can lead to de-identification of the Internet user.

Another example of affiliation link disclosure leading to identity disclosure is in search data. If we assume that users posing queries to a search engine are the individuals in the social network, and the search queries they pose are the affiliation groups, then disclosing the links between users and queries can help an adversary identify people in the network. Users interact with search engines in an uninhibited way and reveal a lot of personal information in the text of their queries. There was a scandal in 2006 when AOL, an Internet Service provider, released an "anonymized" sample of over half a million users and their queries posed to the AOL search engine. The release was well-intentioned and meant to boost search ranking research by supplementing it with real-world data. Each user was specified by a unique identifier, and each query contained information about the user identifier, search query, the website the user clicked on, the ranking of that website in the search results, and the timestamp of the query.

One of the problems with the released data was that even though it was in a table format (Table 10.1), its entries were not independent of each other. Shortly after the data release, New York Times reporters linked 454 search queries made by the same individual which gave away enough personal infor-

Table 10.1. A snapshot of the data released by AOL. Here, we are omitting the timestamps included in the data.

User ID	*Search query*	*Clicked website*	*Ranking*
4417749	clothes for age 60	http://www.news.cornell.edu	10
4417749	dog who urinate on everything	http://www.dogdayusa.com	6
4417749	landscapers in lilburn ga.		
4417749	pine straw in lilburn ga.	http://gwinnett-online.com	9
4417749	gwinnett county yellow pages	http://directory.respond.com	1
4417749	best retirement place in usa	http://www.amazon.com	7
4417749	mini strokes	http://www.ninds.nih.gov	1

mation to identify that individual – Thelma Arnold, a 62-year old widow from Lilburn, Georgia [5]. Her queries included names of people with the same last name as hers, information about retirement, her location, etc.

Affiliation link disclosure can also lead to attribute disclosure, as illustrated in a *guilt-by-association attack* [14]. This attack assumes that there are groups of users whose sensitive attribute values are the same, thus recovering the sensitive value of one user and the affiliation of another user to the group can help recover the sensitive value of the second user. This attack was used in the BitTorrent file-sharing network to discover the downloading habits of users [11]. Communities were detected based on social links, and monitoring only one user in each community was enough to infer the interests of the other people in the community. In this case the sensitive attribute that users would like to keep private is whether they violate copyrights. This attack has also been applied to identifying fraudulent callers in a phone network [14]. Cormode et al. [13] study data anonymization to prevent affiliation link disclosure. They refer to affiliation links as associations (see Section 4.2).

3. Privacy definitions for publishing data

The goal of data mining is discovering new and useful knowledge from data. Sometimes, the data contains sensitive information, and it needs to be sanitized before it is published publicly in order to address privacy concerns. Data sanitization is a complex problem in which hiding private information trades off with utility reduction. The goal of sanitization is to remove or perturb the attributes of the data which help an adversary infer sensitive information. The solution depends on the properties of the data and the notions of privacy and utility in the data.

Privacy preservation in the context of social network data is a relatively new research field. Rather than assuming data which is described by a single table of independent records with attribute information for each, it takes into

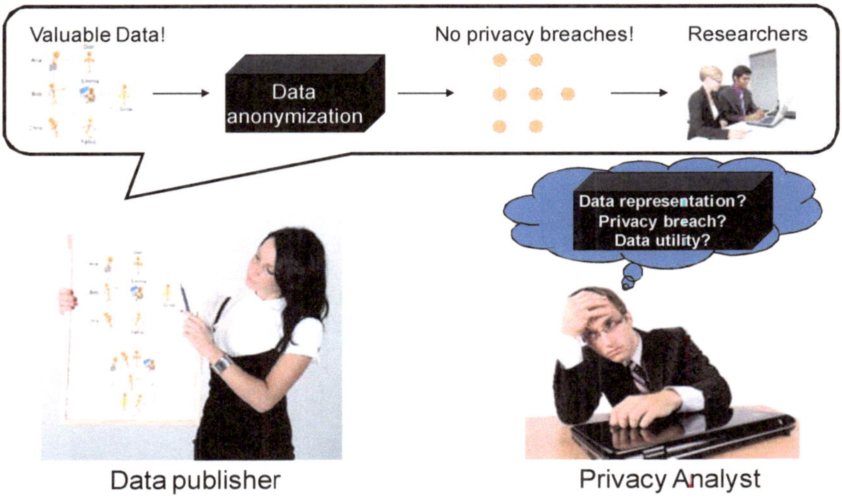

Figure 10.4. Anonymization scenario.

consideration more complex real-world datasets. As discussed earlier, relational data, often represented as a multi-graph, can exhibit rich dependencies between entities. The challenge of sanitizing graph data lies in understanding these dependencies and removing sensitive information which can be inferred by direct or indirect means.

One way in which data providers can sanitize data is by anonymization. Figure 10.4 shows a typical scenario in which a data owner is interested in providing researchers with valuable data and in order to meet privacy concerns, she consults a privacy analyst before publishing a perturbed version of the data. In the process of anonymizing the data, the identifying information is removed and other attributes are perturbed. Anonymizing techniques have been criticized as often being ad hoc and not providing a principled way of preserving privacy. There are no guarantees that an adversary would not be able to come up with an attack which uses background information and properties of the data, such as node attributes and observed links, to infer the private information of users. Another way of sanitizing data is by providing a private mechanism for accessing the data, such as allowing algorithms which are provably privacy-preserving to run on it. Next, we will discuss privacy preservation definitions. Some of these definitions were not developed specifically for network data but we provide examples from the social network domain.

To formalize privacy preservation, Chawla et al. [9] proposed a framework based on the intuitive definition that "our privacy is protected to the extent we

Identifier	Quasi-identifiers			Sensitive
Name	Age	Sex	Zip	Pol. views
Ana	21	F	20740	liberal
Bob	25	M	83222	liberal
Chris	24	M	20742	liberal
Don	29	M	83209	conservative
Emma	24	F	20640	liberal
Fabio	24	M	20760	liberal
Gina	28	F	83230	liberal
Halle	29	F	83201	conservative
Ian	31	M	83220	conservative
John	24	M	20740	liberal

5-anonymity applied to data →

Equiv. class	Quasi-identifiers			Sensitive
	Age	Sex	Zip	Pol. views
C1	[21,24]	*	20***	liberal
C2	[25,31]	*	832**	liberal
C1	[21,24]	*	20***	liberal
C2	[25,31]	*	832**	conservative
C1	[21,24]	*	20***	liberal
C1	[21,24]	*	20***	liberal
C2	[25,31]	*	832**	liberal
C2	[25,31]	*	832**	conservative
C2	[25,31]	*	832**	conservative
C1	[21,24]	*	20***	liberal

Figure 10.5. 5-anonymity applied to data with 10 records.

blend in the crowd." Obviously, with the richness of information in online social network profiles, this is hard to achieve and users are easily identifiable. We will look at a simpler case when a data provider is interested in releasing a dataset with online social network profiles. To give a flavor of existing work, we present four existing privacy preservation approaches which make the definition of "blending in the crowd" more concrete.

3.1 k-anonymity

k-anonymity protection of data is met if the information for each person contained in the data cannot be distinguished from at least $k-1$ other individuals in the data. k-anonymity can be achieved by suppressing and generalizing the attributes of individuals in the data. Suppressing an attribute value means deleting it from the perturbed data. Generalizing an attribute means replacing it with a less specific but semantically consistent value. One can see that suppression is a special case of generalization, and that suppressing all attributes would guarantee k-anonymity. This is why a notion of utility in the data has to be incorporated whenever sanitizing data. The actual objective is to maximize utility by minimizing the amount of generalization and suppression. Achieving k-anonymity by generalization with this objective as a constraint is an NP-hard problem [3]. k-anonymity has been studied mostly for table data, so we begin by presenting its definition using only the nodes V and their attributes $V.A$ i.e., disregarding links and affiliation groups.

DEFINITION 10.10 **k-anonymity**. *A set of records V satisfies k-anonymity if for every tuple $v \in V$ there exist at least $k-1$ other tuples $v_{i_1}, v_{i_2}, ..., v_{i_{k-1}}$ V such that $v_{i_1}.A_q = v_{i_2}.A_q = ... = v_{i_{k-1}}.A_q$ where $A_q \in A$ are the quasi-identifying attributes of the profile.*

Figure 10.5 shows an example of applying 5-anonymity to the data of 10 individuals. The data includes their names, ages, genders and zip codes. The perturbed data meets a 5-anonymity constraint because each individual is indistinguishable from at least 4 other individuals. Here, the assumption is that name is an identifying attribute, therefore it has been suppressed. Three of the attributes, *Age*, *Sex* and *Zip code*, are quasi-identifiers, therefore, they have been generalized. The sensitive attributes remain the same.

k-anonymity provides a clustering of the nodes into equivalence classes such that each node is indistinguishable in its quasi-identifying attributes from some minimum number of other nodes. In the previous example, there were two equivalence classes: class $C1$ of individuals whose age is in the range $[21, 24]$ years and have a zip code $20 * **$, and class $C2$ of individuals whose age is in the range $[25, 31]$ years and have a zip code $832 * *$. Note, however, that these equivalent classes are based on node attributes only, and inside each equivalence class, there may be nodes with different identifying structural properties and edges. This makes it hard to define k-anonymity for nodes in social networks. We discuss some approaches later in Section 4.

k-anonymity ensures that individuals cannot be uniquely identified by a linking attack. However, it does not necessarily prevent sensitive attribute disclosure. Here, we present two possible attacks on k-anonymized data [38]. The first one can occur when there is little diversity in the sensitive attributes inside an equivalence class. In this case, the sensitive attribute of everyone in the equivalence class becomes known with high certainty. For example, if an adversary wants to figure out Ana's political views knowing that her age is 21 and her zip code is 20740, then he can figure out that her record is in equivalence class $C1$. There is no diversity in the sensitive attribute value of equivalence class $C1$, i.e., everyone in $C1$ has liberal political views, therefore, the adversary is able to infer Ana's political views even though he does not know which row corresponds to her. This is known as the *homogeneity attack* [38].

The second problem with k-anonymity is that in the presence of background knowledge, attribute and identity disclosure can still occur. For example, knowing that someone's friends are liberal, makes it highly likely that this person is liberal as well. In our toy example, the knowledge that Gina's friends, Emma and Fabio, belong to equivalence class $C1$ where everyone is liberal, can help an adversary infer with high certainty that Gina is liberal as well. This is known as the *background attack* [38].

There are a number of definitions derived from k-anonymity tailored to structural properties of network data. Some examples of such defintions include *k-degree anonymity* [35], *K-Candidate anonymity* [27], *k-automorphism anonymity* [53], *k-neighborhood anonymity* [51, 47], and *(k,l)-grouping* [13].

We introduce the intuition behind them, together with their definitions in Section 4.1.1 and Section 4.2, privacy mechanisms for networks.

3.2 l-diversity and t-closeness

A privacy definition which alleviates the problem of sensitive attribute disclosure inherent to k-anonymity is l-diversity [38]. As its name suggests, l-diversity ensures that the sensitive attribute values in each equivalence class are diverse.

DEFINITION 10.11 **l-diversity**. *A set of records in an equivalence class C is l-diverse if it contains at least l "well-represented" values for each sensitive attribute. A set of nodes V satisfy l-diversity if every equivalence class $C' \subseteq V$ is l-diverse.*

There are a number of ways to define "well-represented." Some examples include using frequency counts and measuring entropy. However, even in the case of l-diverse data, it is possible to infer sensitive attributes when the sensitive distribution in a class is very different from the overall distribution for the same attribute. If the overall distribution is skewed, then the belief of someone's value may change drastically in the anonymized data (*skewness attack*) [32]. For example, only 30% of the records in Figure 10.5 have conservative political views. However, in equivalence class $C2$ this number becomes 60%, thus the belief that a user is conservative increases for users in $C2$. Another possible attack, known as the *similarity attack* [32], works by looking at equivalent classes which contain very similar sensitive attribute values. For example, if *Age* is a sensitive attribute and an adversary wants to figure out Ana's age knowing that she is in equivalence class $C1$ (based on her *Zip code*), then he would learn that she is between 21 and 24 years old which is a much tighter age range than the range in the whole dataset.

This leads to another privacy definition, t-closeness, which considers the sensitive attribute distribution in each class, and its distance to the overall attribute distribution. The distance can be measured with any similarity score for distributions.

DEFINITION 10.12 **t-closeness**. *A set of records in an equivalence class C is t-close if the distance between the distribution of a sensitive attribute A_s in C and its distribution in V is no more than a threshold t. A set of nodes V satisfy t-closeness if every equivalence class $C' \subseteq V$ is t-close.*

Just like with k-anonymity, sanitizing data to meet either l-diversity or t-closeness comes with a computational complexity burden. There are other privacy definitions of this flavor but they have all been criticized for being ad hoc. While they guarantee syntactic properties of the released data, they come with no privacy semantics [18].

3.3 Differential privacy

The notion of differential privacy was developed as a principled way of defining privacy, so that "the risk to one's privacy [...] should not substantially increase as a result of participating in a database" [17]. This shifts the view on privacy from comparing the prior and posterior beliefs about individuals before and after publishing a database to evaluating the risk incurred by joining a database. It also imposes a guarantee on the data release mechanism rather than on the data itself. Here, the goal is to provide statistical information about the data while preserving the privacy of users in the data. This privacy definition gives guarantees that are independent of the background information and the computational power of the adversary.

Returning to our running example, if the social network data set is released using a differentially private mechanism, this would guarantee that Ana's participation in the social network does not pose a threat to her privacy because the statistics would not look very different without her participation. It *does not* guarantee that one cannot learn sensitive information about Ana using background information but such guarantee is impossible to achieve for any kind of dataset [17].

DEFINITION 10.13 **ϵ-differential privacy**. *A randomized function K satisfies ϵ-differential privacy if for all data sets D_1 and D_2 differing in at most one element, and any subset S of possible outcomes in $Range(K)$,*

$$P(K(D_1) \in S) \leq exp(\epsilon) \times P(K(D_2) \in S). \tag{10.1}$$

Here, one can think of a profile in the social network as being an element, and V being the data set, thus $D_1 \subseteq V$ and $D_2 \subseteq V$. The randomized function K can be thought of as an algorithm which returns a random variable, possibly with some noise. When developing a differentially private algorithm, one has to keep in mind the utility of the data and incorporate the desired knowledge in the algorithm. $Range(K)$ is the output range of algorithm K. A common way of achieving ϵ-differential privacy is by adding random noise to the query answer.

One type of algorithm that has been proven to be differentially private is a *count* query to which one adds Laplacian noise [20]. For example, if the count query is K =*"How many people are younger than 22?"*, then the output range of the query is $Range(K) = \{1, ..., n\}$ where n is the size of the social network. The count query is considered a low-sensitivity query because it has a sensitivity of $\Delta K = 1$ for any D_1 and D_2 differing in one element. Sensitivity is defined as

$$\Delta K = \max_{D_1, D_2} ||K(D_1) - K(D_2)|| \tag{10.2}$$

for any D_1 and D_2 which differ in at most one element. Note that this query has the same sensitivity not only for our specific data but for any data in this format. The Laplacian noise, which is added to the answer, is related to the sensitivity of the query.

A $mean$ query, such as $K =$ *"What is the average age of people in the social network?"*, has an even lower sensitivity for large data sets because removing any profile from the social network would change the output of the query by at most $\Delta K = max(age)/n$. There are also queries, such as $median$ queries, which have high sensitivity and require different techniques for generating noise.

A similar and somewhat weaker definition of differential privacy is the one of (ϵ, δ)-differential privacy which was developed to deal with very unlikely outputs of K [19].

DEFINITION 10.14 **(ϵ,δ)-differential privacy**. *A randomized function K satisfies ϵ-differential privacy if for all data sets D_1 and D_2 differing in at most one element, and any subset S of possible outcomes in $Range(K)$,*

$$P(K(D_1) \in S) \leq exp(\epsilon) \times P(K(D_2) \in S) + \delta. \tag{10.3}$$

Generally, ϵ and δ are considered to be very small numbers and are picked according to different considerations, such as the size of the database.

4. Privacy-preserving mechanisms

So far, we have discussed existing notions of privacy preservation related to the user profiles, mostly ignoring the structural properties of the social network. Next, we discuss how privacy preservation can be achieved considering the network structure: the links between users E_v, and affiliation links E_h to affiliation groups of users H. First, we present existing privacy mechanisms for social networks in Section 4.1. Section 4.2 includes overview of the mechanisms for affiliation networks. Finally, we describe research which considers both types of networks in Section 4.3. Except for the privacy mechanisms based on differential privacy, each mechanism was developed to counterattack a specific adversarial attack and background knowledge which we also present.

4.1 Privacy mechanisms for social networks

The majority of research in this area considers anonymization which strips off all the personal attributes from user profiles but keeps some of the structure coming from the social links between users [4, 26, 27, 35, 51, 53]. We describe this research in Section 4.1.1. In Section 4.1.2, we mention approaches to anonymizing data which consider that there is utility in keeping both attribute and structural information [8, 49].

4.1.1 Anonymizing network structure. One naive way of anonymizing a social network is by removing all the attributes of the profiles, and leaving only the social link structure. This creates an anonymized graph which is isomorphic to the original graph. The intuition behind this approach is that if there are no identifying profile attributes, then attribute and identity disclosures cannot occur, and thus the privacy of users is preserved. Contrary to the intuition, this not only removes a lot of important information but it also does not guarantee the privacy of users. Two types of attacks have been proposed which show that identity and social link disclosures would occur when it is possible to identify a subgraph in the released graph in which all the node identities are known [4]. The *active attack* assumes that an adversary can insert accounts in the network before the data release, and the *passive attack* assumes that a number of friends can collude and share their linking patterns after the data release.

In the active attack an adversary creates k accounts and links them randomly, then he creates a particular pattern of links to a set of m other users that he is interested to monitor. The goal is to learn whether any two of the monitored nodes have links between them. When the data is released, the adversary can efficiently identify the subgraph of nodes corresponding to his k accounts with provably high probability. Then he can recover the identity of the monitored m nodes and the links between them which leads to social link disclosure for all $\binom{m}{2}$ pairs of nodes. With as few as $k = \Theta(\log n))$ accounts, an adversary can recover the links between as many as $m = \Theta(\log^2 n)$ nodes in an arbitrary graph of size n. The passive attack works in a similar manner. It assumes that the exact time point of the released data snapshot is known and that there are k colluding users who have a record of what their links were at that time point.

Another type of structural background information that has been explored is similar in spirit to the linking attack mentioned in Section 2. The existence of an auxiliary social network in which the identity of users is known can help an adversary identify nodes in a target social network [41]. Starting from a set of users which form a clique both in the target and the auxiliary networks, an adversary expands the matching by finding the most likely nodes that correspond to each other in the two networks by using structural information, such as number of user friends (node degree), and number of common neighbors. To validate this attack, it has been shown that the discovered matches sometimes correspond to matches found using descriptive user attributes such as username and location in the social networks of Twitter and Flickr [41].

Structural privacy. Starting from the idea that certain subgraphs in the social network are unique, researchers have studied the mechanism of protecting individuals from identity disclosure when an adversary has *background information about the graph structure* around a node of interest [26, 27, 35, 48, 51, 53]. Each node has structural properties (subgraph signature) that are the same as the ones of a small set of other nodes in the graph, called a candidate set for this node [27]. Knowing the true structural properties of a node, an adversary may be able to discover the identity of that node in the anonymized network. Structure queries can be posed to the network to discover nodes with specific subgraph signatures.

Looking at the immediate one-hop neighbors, each node has a star-shaped subgraph in which the size of the subgraph is equal to the degree of the node plus one. With the assumption that identity disclosure can occur based on a node's degree, the degree becomes an identifying attribute that a data provider would like to hide. In our toy network (Figure 10.1), Ana and Don would be in each other's candidate sets because they both have degree 2; Emma, Gina and Fabio appear in the same candidate set for either of the three nodes; Bob and Chris are uniquely identifiable because they are the only ones in the network with degrees four and one, respectively. The notion of *k-degree anonymity* [35] was formulated to protect individuals from an adversary who has background information of user's node degrees. It states that each node should have the same degree as at least $k-1$ other nodes in the anonymized network.

Adding the links between the one-hop neighbors of a node, sometimes referred to as the 1.5-hop neighborhood, creates a richer structural signature. Based on this, Ana and Don still have the same subgraph signature, and so do Emma and Fabio. However, Gina has a unique signature and is easily identifiable by an adversary who has knowledge of her true 1.5-hop neighborhood structure. Zhou and Pei [51] formalize the desired property to protect individuals from this type of attack. A graph satisfies *k-neighborhood anonymity* if every node in the network has a 1.5-hop neighborhood graph isomorphic to the 1.5-hop neighborhood graph of at least $k-1$ other nodes. The name of this property was given by Wu et al. [47].

In our example, Ana and Don become uniquely identifiable once we look at their 2-hop neighborhoods. Emma and Fabio have isomorphic signatures regardless of the size of the neighborhood for which the adversary has background information. This leads to the most general privacy preservation definitions of *k-candidate anonymity* [27] and k-automorphism anonymity [53].

DEFINITION 10.15 K**-Candidate anonymity**. *An anonymized graph satisfies K-Candidate Anonymity with respect to a structural query Q if there is a set of at least K nodes which match Q, and the likelihood of every candidate for a node in this set with respect to Q is less than or equal to $1/k$.*

K-Candidate anonymity [27], considers the structural anonymity of users given a particular structural query, i.e., a subgraph signature. Hay et al. define three types of structural queries, vertex refinement queries, subgraph queries and hub fingerprint queries [27, 26]. Zou et al. [53] assume a much more powerful adversary who has knowledge of any subgraph signature of a target individual. They propose the notion of *k-automorphism anonymity* to fend off such an adversary.

DEFINITION 10.16 **k-automorphism anonymity**. *An anonymized graph is k-automorphic if every node in the graph has the same subgraph signature (of arbitrary size) as at least $k-1$ other graph nodes, and the likelihood of every candidate for that node is less than or equal to $1/k$.*

Anonymization. The anonymization strategies for social network structure fall into four main categories:

- **Edge modification.** Since complete removal of the links to keep structural properties private would yield a disconnected graph, edge modification techniques propose edge addition and deletion to meet desired constraints. Liu and Terzi anonymize the network degree sequence to meet k-degree anonymity [35]. This is easy to achieve for low-degree nodes because the degree distribution in social networks often follows a power law. For each distinguishable higher-degree node, where distinguishable is defined as a degree for which there are less than k nodes with that degree, the anonymization algorithm increases its degree artificially so that it becomes indistinguishable from at least $k-1$ other nodes. The objective function of the algorithm is to minimize the number of edge additions and deletions. We discuss another edge modification algorithm [51] with a similar objective but a stronger privacy guarantee in Section 4.1.2. Zou et al. [53] propose an edge modification algorithm that achieves k-automorphism anonymity.

- **Randomization.** Anonymization by randomization can be seen as a special case of anonymization by edge modification. It refers to a mechanism which alters the graph structure by removing and adding edges at random, and preserves the total number of edges. Hay et al. [27] show that if this is performed uniformly at random, then it fails to keep important graph metrics of real-world networks. Ying and Wu [48] propose *spectrum-preserving randomization* to address this loss of utility. The graph's spectral properties are the set of eigenvalues of the graph's adjacency matrix to which important graph properties are related. Preserving this spectrum guides the choice of random edges to be added and deleted. However, the impact of this approach on privacy is unclear.

  Two recent studies have presented algorithms for reconstructing randomized networks [44, 46]. Wu et al. [46] take a low rank approximation approach and apply it to a randomized network structure, such that accurate topological features can be recovered. They show that in practice reconstruction may not pose a larger threat to privacy than randomization because the original network is more similar to the randomized network than to the reconstructed network. Vuokko and Terzi [44] consider reconstruction mechanisms for networks where randomization has been applied both to the structure and attributes of the nodes. They identify cases in which reconstruction can be achieved in polynomial time. The effect of both reconstruction strategies on privacy has not been assessed.

- **Network generalization**. One way to alleviate an attack based on structural background information is by publishing the aggregate information about the structural properties of the nodes [26]. In particular, one can partition the nodes and keep the density information inside and between parts of the partition. Nodes in each partition have the same structural properties, so that an adversary coming with a background knowledge is not able to distinguish between these nodes. In practice, sampling from the anonymized network model creates networks which keep many of the structural properties of the original network, such as degree distribution, path length distribution and transitivity. Network generalization strategies for other network types are discussed in Section 4.1.2 [8, 49] and Section 4.3 [6].

- **Differentially private mechanisms**. Differentially private mechanisms refer to algorithms which guarantee that individuals are protected under the definition of differential privacy (see Section 3.3). Hay et al. [24] propose an efficient algorithm which allows the public release of one of the most commonly studied network properties, degree distribution, while guaranteeing differential privacy. The algorithm involves a post-processing step on the differentially private output, which ensures a more accurate result. The empirical analysis on real-world and synthetic networks shows that the resulting degree-distribution estimate exhibits low bias and variance, and can be used for accurate analysis of power-law distributions, commonly occurring in networks.

4.1.2 Anonymizing user attributes and network structure. So far, we have discussed anonymization techniques which perturb the structure of the network but do not consider attributes of the nodes, such as gender, age, nationality, etc. However, providing the (perturbed) structure of social networks is often not sufficient for the purposes of the researchers who study them. In another line of privacy research, the assumption is that anonymized data will have utility only if it contains both structural properties and node attributes.

Anonymization. Zhou and Pei [51] assume that each node has one attribute which they call a label. They show that achieving k-neighborhood anonymity is NP-hard and propose a greedy *edge modification* and *label generalization* algorithm. The algorithm extracts the 1.5-neighborhood signatures for all nodes in the graph and represents them concisely using *DFS trees*. Then it clusters the signatures and anonymizes the ones in each cluster to achieve k-neighborhood anonymity. The objective function of the algorithm is similar to the one of Liu and Terzi [35], the minimization of the number of edge additions.

Zheleva and Getoor [49] study the problem of social link disclosure in graphs with multiplex relations. The assumption is that an adversary has an accurate statistical model for predicting sensitive relationships if given the attributes of nodes and edges in the original data, therefore attributes have to be perturbed in the released data. They propose anonymization by generalization of the data as a two-step process. In the first step, nodes are treated as a table of records, and their attributes are anonymized to guarantee the privacy of users, for example, to meet one of the privacy definitions described earlier. Using k-anonymity, this creates a partition of the network nodes into equivalence classes. In the second step, the structure of the network is partially preserved by keeping aggregate structural information inside and between the equivalence classes.

Campan and Truta [8] also take a network generalization approach to the process of anonymizing a social network. Their greedy algorithm optimizes a utility function using the attribute and structural information simultaneously rather than as a two-step process. They introduce a structural information loss measure, and adopt an existing measure of attribute information loss. The anonymization algorithm can be adjusted to preserve more of the structural information of the network or the nodes' attribute values.

4.2 Privacy mechanisms for affiliation networks

Next, we concentrate on affiliation networks and discuss privacy-preserving techniques developed specifically for this type of network. The affiliation network is represented as a bipartite graph with two types of nodes V and H, and the affiliation links between them E_h. Figure 10.6 shows an illustration of this graph where on the left-hand side there are users, and on the right-hand side there are movies that the users rated. The affiliation links have a weight corresponding to the movie ratings for each user, on a scale from 1 to 5.

Netflix, an online movie rental company, set up a competition aimed at improving their movie recommendation systems. They released a dataset with around 100 million dated ratings from 480 thousand randomly-chosen Netflix customers. To protect customer privacy, each customer id has been replaced with a randomly-assigned id. However, this naive anonymization was found to be vulnerable under a linking attack [40]. Using the dates of user ratings and matching the records released by $Netflix$ and user profiles in $IMDB$, an online movie database, Narayanan and Shmatikov [40] were able to achieve identity and sensitive attribute disclosure for some of the users in the Netflix dataset.

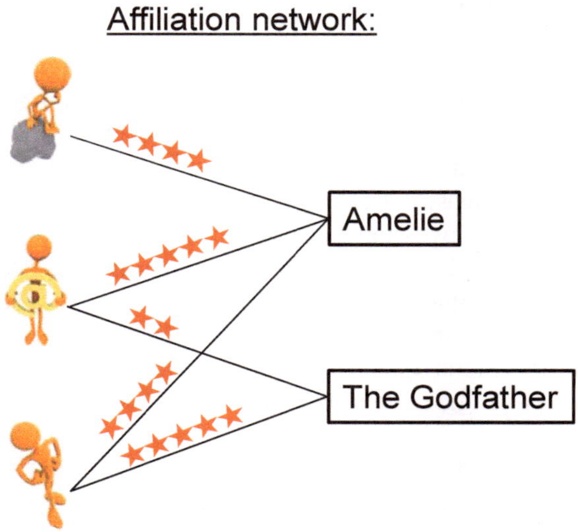

Figure 10.6. An affiliation network as a bipartite graph between three users and two movies. The affiliation links show the ratings that users gave to the movies on a scale from 1 to 5.

A related problem is the problem of releasing a search query graph in which user information is contained in the affiliation links between search engine queries and clicked website URLs [30]. In particular, there is a bipartite graph of (query,URL) pairs.Here, the links have a weight corresponding to the number of users who posed a particular query and clicked on the particular URL. In addition, there are links between queries with a weight equal to the number of users who posed the first query and then reformulated it into the second query. Each query also has counts of the number of times the query was posed to the search engine. The utility in such data is in using it for learning better search ranking algorithms. Figure 10.7(a) shows an example a user-query graph. Figure 10.7(b) shows its reformulation into a search query graph where individual users are not represented explicitly but only as aggregate numbers.

4.2.1 Anonymization. Two types of privacy mechanisms for affiliation networks have been studied in the research literature:

- **Network generalization**. Cormode et al. [13] propose a privacy definition for affiliation networks, *(k,l)-grouping*, tailored to prevent sensitive affiliation link disclosure. The authors make the assumption that affiliation links can be predicted based on node attributes and the structure of the network. They show why existing table anonymization techniques fail to preserve the structural properties of the network, and propose a greedy anonymization algorithm which keeps the structure intact but

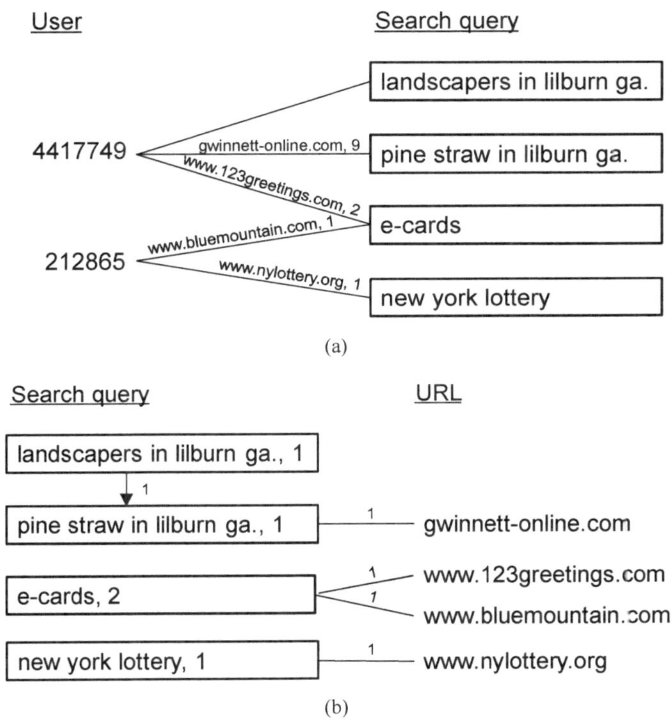

Figure 10.7. a) *User-query graph* representing the users, their queries, the websites they clicked on and the ranking of each website, and b) its reformulation into a *search query graph.*

generalizes node attributes. The algorithm requires that each node is indistinguishable from at least $k-1$ other nodes in terms of node properties, and each affiliation group is indistinguishable from at least $l-1$ other affiliation groups, the basis of (k,l)-grouping. The utility is in being able to answer accurately aggregate queries about users and affiliation groups.

- **Differentially private mechanisms.** A private mechanism for a recommender system has been developed specifically for the movie recommendation setting [39]. The system works by providing differentially private mechanisms for computing counts, rating averages per movie and per user, and the movie-movie covariances in the data. These statistics are sufficient for computing distances based on k-nearest neighbor for predicting the ratings associated with new affiliation links. Using the statistics released by the mechanism, the algorithm performs with an accuracy comparable to the one in the original data.

  Korolova et al. [30] have proposed an (ϵ,δ)-differentially private algorithm which allows the publication of a search query graph for this purpose. Here the search logs are the database, and pairs of databases D_1 and D_2 are considered to differ in one element when one database excludes the search logs of exactly one user. The algorithm keeps only a limited number of queries and clicks for each user and allows for two types of functions on the graph which are sufficient for evaluating ranking algorithms. The first function gives a search query and its noisy count if it exceeds a pre-specified threshold. The second function publishes the noisy weight of the (query,URL) link for the top URLs for each query which was safe to publish according to the first function.

4.3 Privacy mechanisms for social and affiliation networks

There has not been much research on the privacy implications of the interplay between social and affiliation networks. It is obvious that they inherit all the privacy issues discussed so far for either type of network. What is not so obvious is that the complex dependencies these networks create can allow an adversary to learn private information in intricate ways. In particular, one can use the social environment of users to learn private information about them. One type of attack, which we call an *attribute inference attack*, assumes that an attribute is sensitive only for a subset of the users in the network and that the other users in the network are willing to publish it publicly [50]. The analogy in real-world social networks is the existence of private and public profiles. The attack works by creating a statistical model for predicting the sensitive attribute using the publicly available information and applying that model to predict the users with private profiles. In its basic form, the attack assumes that besides the network structure, the only user attributes that are available are the sensitive attribute value for the public profiles. Naturally, using other profile attributes can create even more powerful statistical models, as Lindamood et al. show [33]. An adversary succeeds when he can recover the sensitive attribute values for a subset of the nodes with high probability.

By taking into account all social and affiliation links, often declared publicly in online social networks, the model can use link-based classification techniques. Link-based classification breaks the assumption that data comprises of independent and identically distributed (iid) nodes and it can take advantage of autocorrelation, the property that attributes of linked objects often correlated with each other. For example, political affiliations of friends tend to be similar, students tend to be friends with other students, etc. A comprehensive survey of models for link-based classification can be found in the work by Sen et al. [42]. The results of Zheleva and Getoor [50] suggest that link-based classification can predict sensitive attributes with high accuracy using information about online social groups, and that social groups have a higher potential for leaking personal information than friendship links.

4.3.1 Anonymization. Bhagat et al. [6] consider attacks for sensitive social link disclosure in social and affiliation networks, to which they refer as *rich interaction graphs*. Two nodes participating in the same group is also considered as a sensitive social link between the two users. Bhagat et al. represent the social and affiliation networks as a bipartite graph, in which one type of nodes are the users and the other type of nodes are affiliation groups. Social links are represented as affiliation groups of size two.

They propose two types of network generalization techniques to prevent social link disclosure. The first technique, a *uniform list approach*, keeps the structure intact, in a manner similar to (k, l)-groupings [13]. It divides nodes into classes of size m ensuring that each node's interactions fall on nodes of different classes. Each class is split into label lists of size k, thus ensuring that the probability of a link between two users (through a social link or a common affiliation group) is at most $1/k$. If the adversary has a background knowledge of the identities of r of the nodes and k is equal to m, then this probability becomes $1/(k-r)$. The second technique, a *partitioning approach*, also divides the nodes into classes of size m so that each node's interactions fall on nodes of different classes. However, it does not keep the original network structure, and publishes only the number of edges between partitions. The probability of a link between two users is guaranteed to be at most $1/m$ with or without background knowledge. The utility of the anonymized graph is in allowing accurate structural and attribute analysis of the graph.

5. Related literature

Research on privacy in online social networks is a very young field which discovers and addresses some of the challenges of preserving the privacy of individuals in an interconnected world [4, 6, 8, 26, 27, 31, 30, 33, 35, 41, 48, 50, 49, 51, 53]. However, privacy research has a longer history in the data mining, database and security communities. For example, privacy-preserving data mining aims at creating data mining algorithms and systems which take into consideration the sensitive content of the data [28, 2]. Chen et al. [10] provide a comprehensive, recent survey of the field of privacy-preserving data publishing. The database and security communities have studied interactive and non-interactive mechanisms for sharing potentially sensitive data [17]. Most of this research assumes that there are one or more data owners who would like to provide data access to third parties while meeting privacy constraints. In contrast, access to data in online social networks is often freely available, and users can specify their personal privacy preferences. Addressing the new privacy challenges in this area is an active area of research [29]. The unexpected threats of freely publishing personal data online is exemplified by a number of researchers [1, 33, 41, 50]. boyd points out many privacy concerns and ethical issues, related to the analysis of large online social network data [15]. Measuring the privacy of social network users and enabling them to personalize their online privacy preferences has also been the focus of recent work [36, 21]. Privacy in dynamic social networks has also received recent attention [7, 53].

6. Conclusion

Here, we presented the possible privacy breaches in online social networks, together with existing privacy definitions and mechanisms for preserving user privacy. While initial steps have been taken in understanding and overcoming some of the challenges of preserving privacy online, many open problems remain. In particular, some exciting new directions include studying the effect of different types of privacy disclosures on each other, privacy-preserving techniques that prevent sensitive attribute disclosure in networks, a comparison between existing anonymization techniques in terms of utility, and privacy-preserving techniques that meet the individual privacy expectations of online social network users rather than privacy definitions imposed by a data publisher or an online service provider.

Acknowledgments

The authors would like to thank Liliana Mihalkova, Daozheng Chen and the anonymous reviewers for the useful feedback, and Arkady Yerukhimovich for a fruitful discussion on differential privacy. Some of the images included in Figure 10.3 and Figure 10.4 were taken from Wikimedia Commons and FreeDigitalPhotos.net. The cartoon characters in Figure 10.1 and Figure 10.6 are from www.lumaxart.com. This book chapter was supported in part by NSF Grant #0746930.

References

[1] A. Acquisti and R. Gross. Predicting social security numbers from public data. In *PNAS*, 2009.

[2] C. C. Aggarwal and P. S. Yu. *Privacy-Preserving Data Mining: Models and Algorithms*. Springer, 2008.

[3] G. Aggarwal, T. Feder, K. Kenthapadi, R. Motwani, R. Panigrahy, D. Thomas, and A. Zhu. Approximation algorithms for k-anonimity. *JPT*, Nov. 2005.

[4] L. Backstrom, C. Dwork, and J. Kleinberg. Wherefore art thou r3579x: anonymized social networks, hidden patterns, and struct. steganography. In *WWW*, 2007.

[5] M. Barbaro and T. Zeller. A face is exposed for aol searcher no. 4417749. *New York Times*, August 2006.

[6] S. Bhagat, G. Cormode, B. Krishnamurthy, and D. Srivastava. Class-based graph anonymization for social network data. In *VLDB*, 2009.

[7] S. Bhagat, G. Cormode, B. Krishnamurthy, and D. Srivastava. Privacy in dynamic social networks. In *WWW Poster*, 2010.

[8] A. Campan and T. M. Truta. A clustering approach for data and structural anonymity in social networks. *PinKDD*, 2008.

[9] S. Chawla, C. Dwork, F. Mcsherry, A. Smith, and H. Wee. Toward privacy in public databases. In *TCC*, 2005.

[10] B.-C. Chen, D. Kifer, K. LeFevre, and A. Machanavajjhala. Privacy-preserving data publishing. *Foundations and trends in databases*, 2(1–2):1–167, 2009.

[11] D. R. Choffnes, J. Duch, D. Malmgren, R. Guimera, F. E. Bustamante, and L. Amaral. Swarmscreen: Privacy through plausible deniability in p2p systems tech. Technical Report NWU-EECS-09-04, Department of EECS, Northwestern University, June 2009.

[12] K. Clarkson, K. Liu, and E. Terzi. Towards identity anonymization in social networks. In P.Yu, J. Han, and C. Faloutsos, editors, *Link Mining: Models Algorithms and Applications*. Springer, 2010, in press.

[13] G. Cormode, D. Srivastava, T. Yu, and Q. Zhang. Anonymizing bipartite graph data using safe groupings. In *VLDB*, 2008.

[14] C. Cortes, D. Pregibon, and C. Volinsky. Communities of interest. In *IDA*, 2001.

[15] danah boyd. Privacy and publicity in the context of big data. In *WWW Invited Talk*, 2010. Available at `http://www.danah.org/papers/talks/2010/WWW2010.html`.

[16] S. Das, Ěmer Egecioglu, and A. E. Abbadi. Anonymizing weighted social network graphs. In *ICDE*, 2010.

[17] C. Dwork. Differential privacy. In *ICALP*, 2006.

[18] C. Dwork. An ad omnia approach to defining and achieving private data analysis. *PinKDD*, 4890:1–13, 2007.

[19] C. Dwork, K. Kenthapadi, F. McSherry, I. Mironov, and M. Naor. Our data, ourselves: privacy via distributed noise generation. In *EUROCRYPT*, 2006.

[20] C. Dwork, F. McSherry, K. Nissim, and A. Smith. Calibrating noise to sensitivity in private data analysis. In *TCC*, 2005.

[21] L. Fang and K. LeFevre. Privacy wizards for social networking sites. In *WWW*, 2010.

[22] L. Getoor and C. P. Diehl. Link mining: a survey. *SIGKDD Explorations*, 7(2):3–12, December 2005.

[23] L. Getoor and B. Taskar, editors. *Introduction to statistical relational learning*. MIT Press, 2007.

[24] M. Hay, C. Li, G. Miklau, and D. Jensen. Accurate estimation of the degree distribution of private networks. In *ICDM*, 2009.

[25] M. Hay, G. Miklau, and D. Jensen. Enabling accurate analysis of private network data. In F. Bonchi and E. Ferrari, editors, *Privacy-Aware Knowledge Discovery: Novel Applications and New Techniques*. Chapman & Hall/CRC Press, 2010, in press.

[26] M. Hay, G. Miklau, D. Jensen, and D. Towsley. Resisting structural identification in anonymized social networks. In *VLDB*, August 2008.

[27] M. Hay, G. Miklau, D. Jensen, P. Weis, and S. Srivastava. Anonymizing social networks. Technical report, University of Massachusetts, Amherst, March 2007.

[28] Y. Z. J. Vaidya, C. Clifton. *Privacy Preserving Data Mining*. Springer, 2006.

[29] J. M. Kleinberg. Challenges in mining social network data: processes, privacy, and paradoxes. In *KDD*, pages 4–5, 2007.

[30] A. Korolova, K. Kenthapadi, N. Mishra, and A. Ntoulas. Releasing search queries and clicks privately. In *WWW*, 2009.

[31] A. Korolova, R. Motwani, S. U. Nabar, and Y. Xu. Link privacy in social networks. In *CIKM*, 2008.

[32] N. Li, T. Li, and S. Venkatasubramanian. t-closeness: Privacy beyond k-anonymity and l-diversity. In *ICDE*, 2007.

[33] J. Lindamood, R. Heatherly, M. Kantarcioglu, and B. Thuraisingham. Inferring private information using social network data. In *WWW Poster*, 2009.

[34] K. Liu, K. Das, T. Grandison, and H. Kargupta. Privacy-preserving data analysis on graphs and social networks. In H. Kargupta, J. Han, P. Yu, R. Motwani, and V. Kumar, editors, *Next Generation of Data Mining*, chapter 21, pages 419–437. Chapman & Hall/CRC, 2008.

[35] K. Liu and E. Terzi. Towards identity anonymization on graphs. In *SIGMOD*, 2008.

[36] K. Liu and E. Terzi. A framework for computing the privacy scores of users in online social networks. In *ICDM*, 2009.

[37] L. Liu, J. Wang, J. Liu, and J. Zhang. Privacy preservation in social networks with sensitive edge weights. In *SDM*, 2009.

[38] A. Machanavajjhala, J. Gehrke, D. Kifer, and M. Venkitasubramaniam. l-diversity: Privacy beyond k-anonymity. In *ICDE*, 2006.

[39] F. McSherry and I. Mironov. Differentially private recommender systems: building privacy into the netflix prize contenders. In *KDD*, 2009.

[40] A. Narayanan and V. Shmatikov. Robust de-anonymization of large sparse datasets. *Security and Privacy*, 2008.

[41] A. Narayanan and V. Shmatikov. De-anonymizing social networks. In *Security and Privacy*, 2009.

[42] P. Sen, G. M. Namata, M. Bilgic, L. Getoor, B. Gallagher, and T. Eliassi-Rad. Collective classification in network data. *AI Magazine*, 29(3):93–106, 2008.

[43] L. Sweeney. Achieving k-anonymity privacy protection using generalization and suppression. *International Journal of Uncertainty*, 10(5):571–588, 2002.

[44] N. Vuokko and E. Terzi. Reconstructing randomized social networks. In *SDM*, 2010.

[45] G. Wondracek, T. Holz, E. Kirda, and C. Kruegel. A practical attack to de-anonymize social network users. In *Security and Privacy*, 2010.

[46] L. Wu, X. Ying, and X. Wu. Reconstruction of randomized graph via low rank approximation. In *SDM*, 2010.

[47] X. Wu, X. Ying, K. Liu, and L. Chen. A survey of algorithms for privacy-preserving social network analysis. In C. Aggarwal and H. Wang, editors, *Managing and Mining Graph Data*. Kluwer Academic Publishers, 2009.

[48] X. Ying and X. Wu. Randomizing social networks: a spectrum preserving approach. In *SDM*, 2008.

[49] E. Zheleva and L. Getoor. Preserving the privacy of sensitive relationships in graph data. *PinKDD*, 2007.

[50] E. Zheleva and L. Getoor. To join or not to join: the illusion of privacy in social networks with mixed public and private user profiles. In *WWW*, 2009.

[51] B. Zhou and J. Pei. Preserving privacy in social networks against neighborhood attacks. In *ICDE*, 2008.

[52] B. Zhou, J. Pei, and W.-S. Luk. A brief survey on anonymization techniques for privacy preserving publishing of social network data. *SIGKDD Explorations*, 10(2), 2009.

[53] L. Zou, L. Chen, and M. T. Ozsu. K-automorphism: A general framework for privacy preserving network publication. In *VLDB*, 2008.

Chapter 11

VISUALIZING SOCIAL NETWORKS

Carlos D. Correa
University of California, Davis
correac@cs.ucdavis.edu

Kwan-Liu Ma
University of Calfornia, Davis
ma@cs.ucdavis.edu

Abstract With today's ubiquity and popularity of social network applications, the ability to analyze and understand large networks in an efficient manner becomes critically important. However, as networks become larger and more complex, reasoning about social dynamics via simple statistics is not a feasible option. To overcome these limitations, we can rely on visual metaphors. Visualization nowadays is no longer a passive process that produces images from a set of numbers. Recent years have witnessed a convergence of social network analytics and visualization, coupled with interaction, that is changing the way analysts understand and characterize social networks. In this chapter, we discuss the main goal of visualization and how different metaphors are aimed towards elucidating different aspects of social networks, such as structure and semantics. We also describe a number of methods where analytics and visualization are interwoven towards providing a better comprehension of social structure and dynamics.

Keywords: Information visualization, visual analytics, semantic filtering, centrality

1. Introduction

Visualization is becoming an important tool to gain insight on the structure and dynamics of complex social networks. Since the inception of sociograms, it was soon recognized that understanding social networks by looking at a list of statistics was impractical. To this end, a multitude of visual representations have been proposed. The vast majority of these metaphors are, not surprisingly, variations of the sociogram, where actors in a network are represented with graphical elements and links are represented as lines between these elements. This representation is easy to understand and provides detailed information about the actual relations modeled in the data. Graph drawing software, often at the core of visualization algorithms, has evolved from software of academic interest to widely spread interactive applications. Now, online social networking sites provide their own or third-party interactive visualizations for casual users to explore portions of their networks. These include tools for music discovery such as liveplasma (liveplasma.com), musicovery (musicovery.com), Lastfm's widget galleries (lastfm.com), tools for visualizing and generating maps of people's own circle of friends, such as a myriad of facebook applications (facebook.com), lastfm's friend sociomap (lastfm.com) and generic visualization sites such as IBM's Many Eyes (manyeyes.alphaworks.ibm.com/). But there has been an explosion of tools that incorporate analysis and visualization, such as Pajek, JUNG, Tulip, visone, among others, as surveyed by Freeman [13], Klovdahl [25] and Brandes et al. [5].

Many of these tools are designed for graph analysis in general, and often combine node-link diagrams with standard statistic visualizations, such as scatterplots and histograms. Although these structural visualizations remain popular, today's technology has made the visualizations more sophisticated, spanning other dimensions beyond the graph structure of the networks, such as semantic and temporal dimensions, essential for understanding social dynamics, and have become interactive, allowing users to form hypotheses and validate inferences both analytically and visually.

We witness today a convergence of analytics and visualization, glued together with interaction. Traditional pipelines where analysis is often a preprocessing step and visualization a presentation tool are being replaced by an iterative approach, where visualization contrasts both raw data and a large, complex set of derived quantities from automated analysis. An analyst gains insight on the social structure while interacting with these visualizations, clustering and filtering the data in the search of more appropriate analytic tools, whose results are fed back into the visualization process, and so on.

In this chapter, we present a taxonomy of visualizations for social networks, based on the type of insight provided to the analyst, such as structural, semantic or statistical. We then describe the current trend of combining analytics with visualization and provide two example techniques. In the first one, semantic and structural filtering are coupled with novel visualizations to understand both the structure and dynamics of social networks. In the second example, centrality analysis not only provides interesting statistics on the network, but is also actively exploited to support novel views and filters not envisioned in the previous generation of visualization tools.

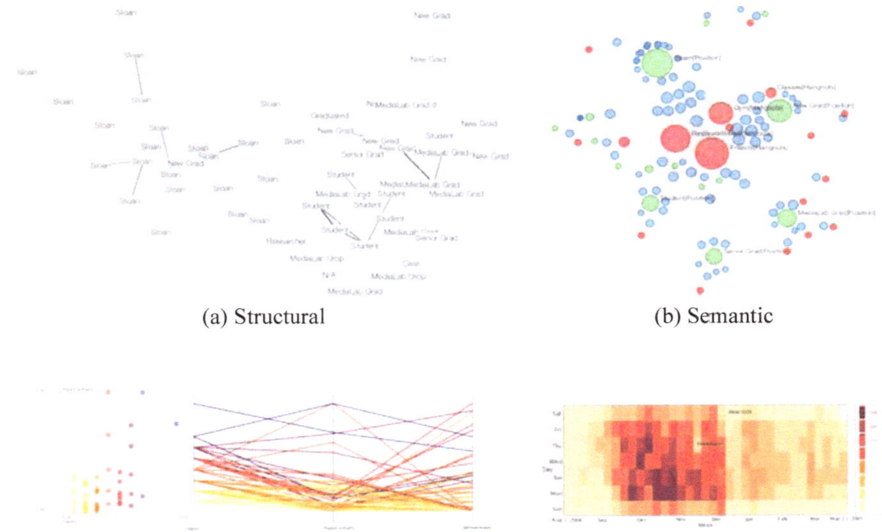

(a) Structural (b) Semantic

(c) Statistical (d) Temporal

Figure 11.1. Example of different types of visualization (a) Structural, typically a node-link diagram. (b) Semantic, where nodes and links can represent different aspects of the social network. (c) Statistical, useful for depicting the distribution of social network metrics and (d) Temporal, a particular case of a semantic diagram that uses time as the main attribute.

2. A Taxonomy of Visualizations

We can classify the visualization of social networks in four main groups, depending on the main focus of the predominant visual task for which the visualization metaphor is envisioned. These are: *structural*, the most common representation thus far, *semantic*, which emphasizes the meaning of the entities and relationships over their structure, *temporal* and *statistical*.

2.1 Structural Visualization

A structural visualization of the social networks focuses precisely on that, its structure. The structure can be thought of as the topology of a graph that represents the actors and relationships in a social network. There are two predominant approaches to structural visualization: node-link diagrams and matrix-oriented methods. While node-link diagrams are easy to interpret and depict explicitly the links between nodes, matrix-oriented representations usually make a better use of limited display area, critical for today's availability of visualizations in a multitude of devices. In the recent years, we have seen efforts to combine the best of the two types into a series of hybrid representations.

2.1.1 The value of network layout in visualization. The purpose of a visualization is to allow users to gain insight on the complexity of social dynamics. Therefore, an aspect such as the layout of network elements must be evaluated with respect to its value toward that goal. Numerous layout algorithms have been proposed, each of them with its strengths and weaknesses. In general, we can highlight a number of high level properties that a layout must satisfy: (1) The positioning of nodes and links in a diagram should facilitate the *readability* of the network. (2) The positioning of nodes should help uncover any inherent *clusterability* of the network, i.e., if a certain group of nodes is considered to be a cluster, the user should be able to extract that information from the layout, and (3), the position of nodes should result in a trustworthy representation of the social network, or, in layman terms, the visualization should not lie [40].

To satisfy these high-level properties, layout algorithms are often formulated in terms of low-level properties. The most widely property is the proximity of nodes, which simply states that if two nodes are highly interconnected, they should appear together. This has been the basis for force-directed methods, as described below. On the other hand, readability is often achieved by ensuring minimal overlap between nodes and edge crossings. Social networks, in particular, suffer greatly from readability, since the power law that governs their structure dictates that most edges occur between a few central nodes and a very large number of not-so-central nodes. Current unsupervised algorithms fail to provide a readable graph and result in an uninformative "hair ball".

For completeness, we summarize some of the most representative layout algorithms, but we do not intend it to be a thorough survey. For a survey, refer to [20, 15].

2.1.2 Node-link Diagrams. As pointed out by Freeman, the sociogram has become a de facto standard for visualizing social networks [13]. In such a representation, actors are represented as nodes, taking geometric forms, and relationships are represented using lines between these forms. Different properties of the network can be encoded visually via geometric properties, such as color, shape, size and thickness.

One of the current challenges in social network visualization is the placement or layout of these nodes in an effective way. For simple structures, simple aesthetic choices can be made to provide an insightful image of the social network. In fact, the first visualizations of social networks were drawn by hand. However, as social networks grow in complexity and size, finding a good layout becomes increasingly challenging. For this reason, graph layout algorithms research has a significant impact on the development of social network visualizations.

Property-based Layouts. The simplest layout of a social network assigns the value of a node property as a location in a coordinate system. This layout is simple to compute and helps discover patterns in the distribution of that property along the network, but it may obscure its global structure. This method was recently used by Aris and Shneiderman as the layout for semantic substrates [1], described later on as a semantic visualization

Due to their simplicity, radial layouts are popular, where nodes are placed in a circle and links are drawn as secant lines through the circle. Namata et al. combine radial and other layouts to provide visual feedback to the user [30]. Nonetheless, radial layouts do not necessarily convey the structure of the network, and, when edges are drawn in such a layout, clutter overcomes the visualization. To improve the readability of radial layouts, Holten bundles related edges together, according to a hierarchical structure in the network [21].

An improvement of the radial layout is the *target sociograms*, as introduced by Northway [32], which uses a a property, typically a centrality measure, as a radius. In this sociogram, nodes are arranged in concentric circles, so that most important nodes are drawn near the center of the circles, while peripheral nodes are drawn in the outer circles [13]. This technique has been embodied successfully in *visone*, a system for visual analysis of social networks, using a variety of network centralities [8] and generalized for graph layout by Brandes et al. [6].

Force-directed and Energy-based Layouts. A force-directed layout draws analogies from a physical structure of rods and springs connecting spheres with the links and nodes in a network. Forces are designed to satisfy low-level properties that guarantee minimal overlap of nodes and proximity of related nodes. For example, attractive forces are often defined between any pair of connected nodes, while repulsive forces are defined between all pairs of nodes. The equilibrium state of such a system of forces results in the "optimal" placement of nodes under that definition. As an alternative to compute the layout as displacements of nodes, one can iteratively update the location of nodes to minimize an energy function directly. This energy function is formulated to satisfy the aesthetic criteria of good graph layouts. A comprehensive survey of these methods appears on Brandes et al. [4].

Although widely used, and easy to implement, force-directed layouts suffer from two main limitations. On one hand, they are expensive to compute, since the time to compute grows cubically with the number of nodes in the network. This makes them impractical even for simple real-life social networks, in the order of only thousands of nodes. On the other hand, maybe more critically, a force directed layout often results in a "hairball" for most moderately sized networks, due to the power law distribution. Brandes and Pich presented an experimental study that shows that multidimensional scaling approaches to graph layout can satisfy aesthetic properties better than force-directed placement [7].

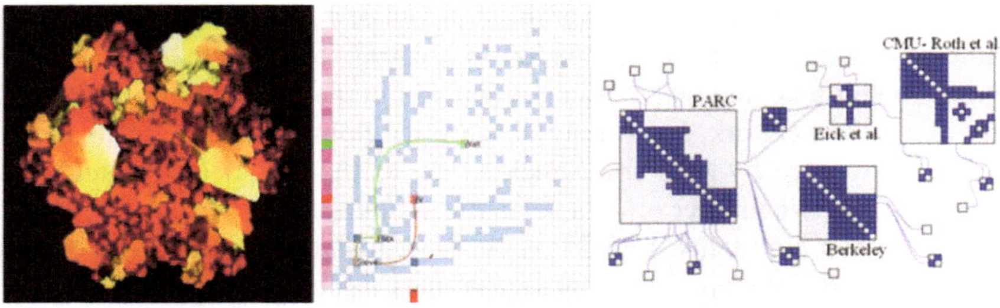

(a) Rapid graph layout [29] (b) Path Visualization [36] (c) Node-trix visualization. [19]

Figure 11.2. Hybrid visualization spaces. (a) Rapid layout of a large network using space filling curves (b) Hybrid path diagram and matrix representation that improves both readability and scalability of the visualization. (c) Node-trix visualization combines a node-link diagram with an adjacency matrix to improve the readability of dense sub-networks

Spectral layouts. This type of algorithms are based on spectral algebra on key matrices that can be extracted from the social structure. It was shown that the eigenvectors of certain matrices can be used as lower dimensional, typically 2D, embeddings of the graph. The most widely application of this technique uses the eigenvectors of the adjacency matrix. In other cases, the eigenvectors of the Laplacian matrix are used as the embedding coordinates [26].

2.1.3 Matrix-oriented Techniques. Matrix-oriented techniques are visualization metaphors designed to represent a social network via an explicit display of its adjacency or incidence matrix. In this visualization, each link is represented as a grid location with cartesian coordinates corresponding to the nodes in the network. Color and opacity are often used to represent important structural or semantic quantities. Consequently, a visual representation of the adjacency matrix is much more compact than a node-link diagram and overlap free, since each link is represented without overlap.

One of the challenges with this matrix representation is enabling the users to visually identify local and global structures in the network. In general, this depends on the way the nodes are ordered along the axes of the matrix view. When the order of nodes is arbitrary, the matrix view may not exhibit the clustering present in the data. Reordering of a matrix is a complex combinatorial problem, and depends on a given objective function. In general, if we follow the high-level desired properties of a good network visualization, it should retain clusters in close proximity. This problem has been addressed as a form of clustering, and formulated in techniques such as generalized blockmodeling [11].

2.1.4 Hybrid Techniques. Node-link diagrams are easy to interpret when compared to adjacency matrix diagrams, but the latter are usually more effective to show overall structure where the network is dense. This observation has led to a number of hybrid techniques, which combine matrix-oriented techniques with node-link diagrams in an attempt to overcome the issues associated with each of them.

Muelder and Ma present a rapid graph layout to depict large networks in a constrained screen space [29]. To this end, a hybrid approach is proposed, where nodes are first positioned in 2D space along a space-filling curve. The position of a node along the curve is determined via a clustering analysis to ensure the close proximity of related nodes. An example is shown in Figure 11.2(a).

Adjacency matrices are often difficult to read. For example, it becomes difficult to follow paths between two actors of interest without effort. Shen and Ma solve this problem with a hybrid matrix, where a basic layer depicts an adjacency graph, while enabling path navigation on a different layer. Using transportation maps as metaphors, this visualization shows paths between multiple pairs of nodes in a readable manner [36]. An example is shown in Figure 11.2(b), which depicts the paths between a few nodes of interest in the friendship network of a hi-tech firm.

Henry and Fekete propose Mat-Link, a hybrid representation that introduces explicit links over more traditional adjacency matrix representations [18]. Henry et al. take this idea further in *Node-Trix*, a hybrid that represents small dense communities within a social network as an adjacency matrix, and connects these within a node-link diagram [19]. This methodology avoids the issues associated with displaying dense networks using links, but retains the readability of the connections among clusters of nodes.

2.2 Semantic and Temporal Visualization

Structural visualizations, although unify the depiction of both overviews and detail information, are less effective when the social network becomes large. Node-link diagrams become rapidly cluttered and algorithmic layouts often result in "hairballs", as highly connected nodes tend to concentrate in the center of the display. For this reason, recent approaches have focused on a different aspect of social networks: semantics. Instead of highlighting the explicit relationships found in the data, these represent high level attributes and connections of actors and links, either as specified explicitly in the data, or implicitly inferred from cross-referencing external sources.

2.2.1 Ontology-based Visualization. One such semantic visualization is the use of ontologies to represent the types of actors and relationships in a social network. An example is Ontovis, where a typical node-link diagram is enhanced with a high-level graphical representation of the ontology [38]. An ontology is a graph whose nodes represent node types and links represent types of representations. Once an ontology is known, either given explicitly or extracted from the data itself, a social network can be represented implicitly by the relationships in this graph. The goal in this type of visualization is not necessarily to discover the structural properties of the network, but rather the distribution of attributes of nodes and links.

Although it does not rely on an onthology, Wattenberg's PivotGraph has a similar goal. Instead of using nodes and links to represent structural information, a PivotGraph summarizes node attributes and their relationships. Using a pivot table as an interaction metaphor, this visualization proves effective to explore multivariate graphs [46]. Another type of visualization that relies on the meaning of actors and links are semantic substrates, as proposed by Aris and Shneiderman [1]. A semantic substrate is a spatial layout of the network where the position of nodes depends on the values of a given node attribute. Multiple semantic substrates can be displayed simultaneously and connected together depending on the values of certain links of interest. Because the placement of the nodes no longer follows the structure of the network, but the actual values of node attributes, it is a more appropriate metaphor for semantic queries. Aris and Shneiderman report successful uses of this approach in the study of legal precedent data, which forms a network of legal court cases from 1978 to 2005 regarding 'regulatory takings', linked whenever a given court case cites another.

2.2.2 Temporal Visualization. A special type of semantic information that has captured the attention of social network visualization researchers is time. Since social interaction is a time-dependent phenomenon, it is only natural to represent the temporal dimension using visual means. Nonetheless, the visualization of dynamic networks has not been explored in depth. One can argue that one of the reasons for this lack of treatment is that handling the temporal dimension from a structural point of view alone is limited and insufficient. A semantic approach, as the ones suggested above, seems more appropriate. However, time as a dimension deserves a treatment different from other data-specific node attributes. One of the difficulties to represent time is a shortage of dimensions to depict a dynamic network in a 2D display. As an alternative, one can represent time along precisely a temporal dimension. Moody et al. considers two types of such dynamic visualizations: flipbooks, where nodes remain static while the edges vary over time, and movies, where nodes are allowed to move as the relationships change [28].

Shen et al. present Mobivis, which enhances an ontology-based visualization with an interactive timechart [37]. This timechart is a pixel-oriented metaphor that incorporates temporal information of actors in a network. One of

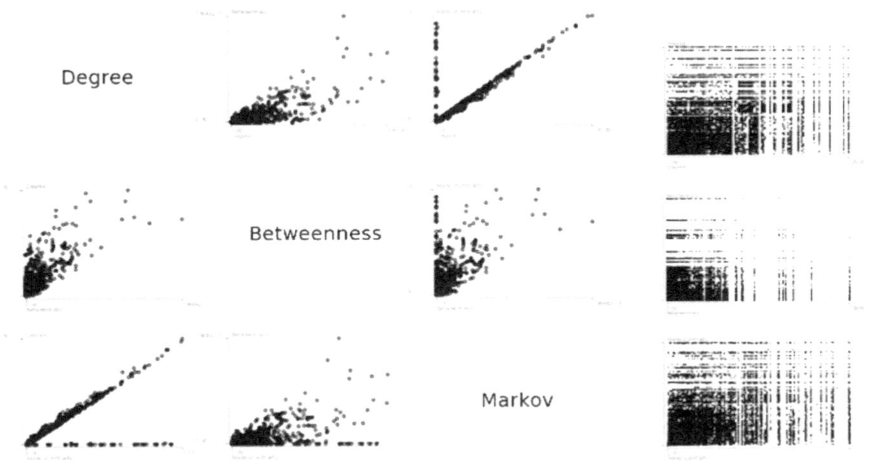

Figure 11.3. Statistical Visualization of the Kazaa social network. Left: scatterplot matrix of three centrality metrics. Right: Edge correlation plots of the same metrics.

the challenges when designing temporal visualizations is the incorporation of the possibly disparate scales and variable granularity of the temporal data. Mobivis addresses this problem via interactive filtering and multiscale timecharts.

Viegas et al. propose PostHistory, which helps visualize the dynamic social network that arises from email exchanges [44]. The visualization combines a pixel-oriented technique, similar to the timechart in Mobivis, which shows both relevance and quantity of emails over time using color and size, respectively. Simultaneously, a visualization displays the inferred social network of email contacts in an ego-centric hierarchical fashion. Because the actual structure of links are not represented explicitly, these visualizations do not suffer from clutter and can be quite effective for dynamic networks.

One can also think of dynamic social networks as the connection between actors and events. This observation has led to approaches such as the one described by Kang et al., where a bipartite graph describes the dynamic changes in participation of a number of actors in different events over time [24].

2.3 Statistical Visualization

An important aspect of visualization is the interplay between analytical and visual tools to gain insight. This is at the core of visual analytics. For this reason, analysts often explore summary visualizations to understand the distributions of variables of interest. These variables often correspond to network statistics that represent the structure of the network, such as degree, centrality and the clustering coefficient. While the first two describe the importance across the network, the latter metric indicates how clusterable are the nodes in a network.

A way to understand these distributions is via visual summaries, such as histograms. Additional insight can be gained through the analysis of the joint distribution between two variables, typically via scatterplots, where points are mapped in a cartesian coordinate system depending on the values of two variables of interest. This approach, although widely used and practical, is limited to two-dimensional joint distributions. In general, network statistics form an N-dimensional space, where a node or an edge is an observation, and each variable corresponds to a attribute or metric. Visualizing such space is thus difficult. Here we highlight two common approaches to the problem. Scatter plot matrices, such as the one depicted in Figure 11.3, shows the joint distribution of all pairs of variables in the N-dimensional space. Each location ij shows the joint distribution of variables i and j, in this case degree, betweenness and Markov centrality. A closer look at this visualization helps us see a seemingly high correlation between Markov centrality and degree, skewed only by a series of outliers with low degree but high centrality. These outliers, however, do not affect the correlation between betweenness centrality and degree.

Koschützki and Schreiber used a scatter plot matrix of common centrality metrics, such as closeness, betweenness and degree, to understand the distribution of importance in a biological network [27]. Dwyer et al. also perform a similar analysis on a scatterplot matrix of centralities for social networks. Another way of representing pairwise joint-distributions is via parallel coordinates. In this case, each data point can be represented as a set of line segments, whose endpoints are the values of each of the variables. Dwyer et al. followed this approach in their visual analysis of network centralities [12].

In the scope of social networks, scatter plots are also useful in representing edge correlations. In this case, one can think of a point in the 2D space as representing an edge, whose x coordinate is the value of a given property of one of the nodes connected to the edge and the y coordinate the value of the same property of the node at the other end of the edge. This technique was explored by Kahng et al. to study the betweenness centrality correlation in a social network [23].

3. The Convergence of Visualization, Interaction and Analytics

Recent years have witnessed an increased effort to combine automated data analysis with visualization tools. This has been possible thanks to the proliferation of consumer-grade workstations capable of complex computations and interactive display of large graphical data.

Visualization and Analysis. More often than not, visualization has been described as the last stage of a long analytic process. But this is changing. Recently, Perer and Shneiderman argued that a tight integration of social network statistics and visualization is necessary for effective exploration of social networks [34], while Bertini et al. have proposed a novel visual analytics framework where visualization and data mining are no longer ends of a pipeline, but are interwoven [2].

Clustering is an aspect of visualization where visualization and analysis converge. As mentioned above, cluster analysis of a social network drives the matrix ordering for an effective adjacency matrix visual representation. The same can be said about node-link diagrams. Noack found that modularity, a popular measure of clusterings, is in fact an energy model minimized in force-directed layouts [31]. This has important implications for visualization, as quality metrics of the visual appearance of a layout directly quantifies the quality of a clustering, useful for analysis, and vice versa. Shi et al. use hierarchical clustering and summarization to visualize large social networks [39]. Extracting a hierarchical structure out of a network has thus clear advantages for visualization. For example, Holten has shown that bundling the edges of a hierarchy leads to more readable visualizations [21]. Systems such as *Viszter* [16] and *Social Action* [33] enhance the visualization with an explicit representation of communities, enabling the analyst to discover groups and interconnections at a glance.

Visualization and Interaction. With today's computational capabilities, visualization has taken a more active role. Pike et al. argue that the interactive manipulation of a visual interface is indeed the analytic discourse, and thus they cannot be thought of as separate entities [35]. This idea has become the driving force in the visualization of online social networks, fueled by the popularity of sites such as Facebook and Flickr. But the needs of such systems are different than analytic tools, and have some common properties: (1) *They feature ego-centric views*. The basic visualization space is no longer the entire network, but the visual elements are now arranged in relation to a given context. This has been formalized by van Ham and Perer as a bottom-up methodology called "search and expand on demand" [42], where visualizations are produced for individual queries rather than the whole. A similar approach is taken by Vizster, a visualization tool for online social networks [17]. In bottom-up approaches queries become manipulations of the different interaction tools, such as expansion and contraction of the local context on demand. This has become a popular device for interacting with large social networks, as embodied in tools such as touchgraph (touchgraph.com). Other tools change the space to reflect this ego-centric view. For example, *lastfm's* friends sociomap (http://qed-portal.com/last_fm/) uses a terrain metaphor to generate views of the local circle of friends of their users. Height in this terrain

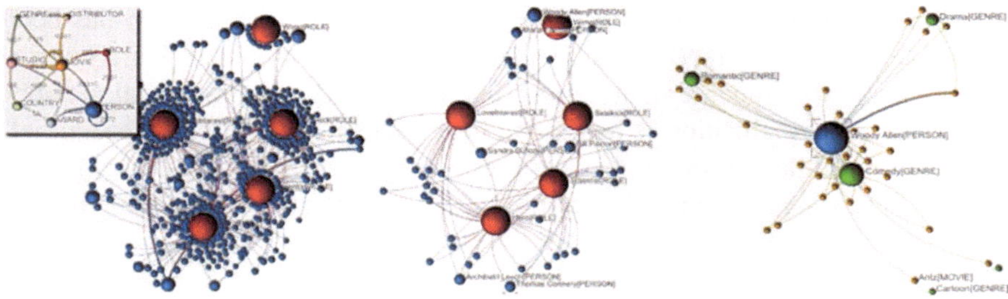

(a) (b) (c)

Figure 11.4. Semantic filtering of a movie social network [38].

indicates the musical compatibility with others. (2) *They are playful.* Online social network tools are primarily designed to help discover people and make sense of structures of community. For this reason, many of these tools are highly interactive and usually playful. The need for interactivity justifies the use of practices often deemed as inefficient when generating a static, passive visualization. For example, force-directed and energy-based layouts are commonly used. Tools such as Viszter and Touchgraph (touchgraph.com) rely on force-directed layouts to represent the local structure of the network and enable *interaction* to expand or contract the network on demand. Fidg't, a tool for visualizing online networks, uses a magnet metaphor where members of a network gravitate towards each other if they share tastes. Dragging nodes around the visualization spaces lets users identify community structures depending on the way the layout changes over time. (3) *They are dynamic.* Social networks are inherently dynamic and their structure changes constantly as the network evolves. PostHistory and Social Fragments are examples where the visualization and interaction take time as the main dimension [45]. An emerging solution to dealing with the size and temporal complexity of social networks is interaction. Via interactive manipulations, one can change the space and visual representations without limiting the knowledge that can be extracted from these views.

There are two other aspects where visualization, analysis and interaction converge. On one hand, structural and semantic filtering involves a continuous loop of analysis and visualization, where insight is obtained by refining visual representations of simplified and filtered data. On the other hand, the analysis of centrality and importance allows visualization practitioners to design and test novel representations and interactive techniques for visual exploration of social networks.

3.1 Structural and Semantic Filtering with Ontologies

Common in current visualization tools is the depiction of global structure as an overview of a network. Interactive tools often allow the analyst to filter data in an attempt to overcome the issues associated with clutter and overlap. An example of such a filter is the removal of nodes and edges that are not important. This results in an abstract network that retains only key actors in a network. In more complex networks, this abstraction may filter some actors that can be considered important along different key attributes, often dependent on the data and the task at hand. To overcome this limitation, Shen et al. propose a series of structural and semantic abstractions based on an ontology representation of the data [38]. The ontology associates a specific type to nodes and links that can be used to obtain a higher level of abstraction. The authors compute a structural metric, based on this ontology, that specifies the disparity of links of a given node. This disparity, measured in terms of the connectivity variance of nodes of a given type, indicates whether a particular node has weak or strong links to a certain type or other nodes of the same type. In addition, analysts can interact directly with the ontology to highlight or remove nodes and edges of a certain type. Unlike a purely structural approach, this integrated method of interaction proves more scalable as networks become increasingly complex.

An example is shown in Figure 11.4 for a movie network, a heterogeneous data set that links actors, directors, movies, genres and roles, among other types. The ontology, depicted in Figure 11.4(a), shows the relationships between the different node types. In this case, a person is represented in blue, a movie in orange and a role in red. The size of the node indicates its disparity. Figure 11.4(a) also shows the resulting visualization of a semantic query that selects all the people who have played any of the roles of hero, scientist, love interest, sidekick and wimp. Even at such a small scale, clutter makes the visualization difficult to read. A structural filtering follows, as depicted in Figure 11.4(b), which removes nodes of degree 1 and duplicate paths. Now we see individual actors, such as Woody Allen, who has played three different roles. This insight prompts the analyst to explore a different dimension of the network, the movies where he has taken these roles and their corresponding genre. This is achieved via interaction with the ontology graph, selecting the corresponding node types. The resulting visualization is shown in Figure 11.4(c).

3.2 Centrality-based Visual Discovery and Exploration

A node centrality is a measure of the importance of a node, from a structural point of view. Metrics such as degree, betweenness, closeness and Eigenvector centralities provide a ranking of the nodes in terms of the number of connections, shortest paths or length of random walks [14, 3, 4].

A rather simplistic approach is to filter nodes based on their centrality. The use of color and size has been exploited to highlight important nodes in the visualization. Other techniques are more aggressive, and define the layout of nodes in terms of centrality. For example, Brandes et al. generalize the target sociogram using centrality metrics, so that central nodes are positioned at the interior of concentric nodes and peripheral nodes in the outer regions [6].

Another approach is to measure the centrality of edges. Analogous to nodes, edges can be ranked in terms of the importance of nodes connected to them, the number of shortest paths that go through them, or their probability of appearing in a number of random walks through the network. van Ham and Wattenberg use edge centralities to simplify complex networks. The visual representation is reduced to the minimum spanning tree of edge betweenness [41]. A similar approach is followed by Jia et al. [22], who use the maximum spanning tree instead. Clearly, each approach highlights different structures from a network that are valid for analysis and understanding. However, because some edge centralities, such as edge betweenness, are not necessarily robust, it is not surprising that results vary when applied to real-world social networks. Although edge centralities highlight important intra-cluster and inter-cluster relationships in star-shaped graphs, they often misrepresent the interior of clusters in dense parts of the networks.

Recently, we have provided a more robust approach, based on node centrality derivatives. A centrality derivative defines the sensitivity of a node's importance to the importance of all other nodes. By measuring the influence of a node onto all others, we can extract information that may be important to the user. For example, we have applied this technique to discover hidden links in a social network. A hidden link occurs when two nodes influence mutually to a great extent, but are not connected directly. This type of relationship often occurs between cluster centers or representatives. As an example, we applied this technique to a synthetic data set that "hides" the structure of a social network as what seems to be two disparate groups. We define a centrality metric derivative as a matrix S whose elements (i, j) are defined as:

$$s_{ij} = \frac{\partial C(v_i)}{\partial t_j} \tag{11.1}$$

where $C(v_i)$ is the centrality of vertex v_i and t_j is a parametrization variable of node j, such as degree. This definition assumes that centrality metric can be defined as a continuous function in terms of t. This is not the case for many metrics, such as degree and betweenness, which are obtained as a sum of edges or shortest paths. However, a certain subset of centralities, such as those based on random walks, assume that the network can be represented as an auxiliary matrix M, and the centrality as a function of such matrix. For example, Eigenvector centralities are obtained as a closed solution of the eigenvalue problem $M\mathbf{x} = \lambda\mathbf{x}$. In general, the centrality of a node v_i can be expressed as a function of the matrix M:

$$C(v_i) = f(M)|_{v_i} \tag{11.2}$$

And, as long as f is differentiable with respect to a simple parameterization t (which is the case of the Eigenvector centralities and its many variants), C is also differentiable with respect to that variable. Using the chain rule:

$$\frac{\partial C_E(v_i)}{\partial t_j} = \frac{\partial f}{\partial M}\frac{\partial M}{\partial t_j} \tag{11.3}$$

where t_j is an independent variable of a node. In our experiments, we use $t_j = \sum_k A_{kj}$ as the degree of a node, where A is the adjacency matrix. In general, the matrix M can take the form of the adjacency matrix, such as the case of Eigenvector centralities, an stochastic version of it, like in PageRank or the Laplacian matrix, useful for finding low dimensional embeddings of the network.

This process of differentiation results in a dense matrix S that encodes the influence between all pairs of nodes. Analyzing the sign and magnitude of this influence helps us extract meaningful groups. It was noted that largest magnitude derivatives often occur *between* cluster centers while small magnitude derivatives occur *within* clusters. A leaf node in a cluster has a little influence on the cluster center regarding its centrality. However, a peer of the cluster center, which in all likelihood is another cluster center, has the ability to influence it greatly [9].

We also found that thresholding the matrix of influence in terms of magnitude for all non-edge pairs helps us identify hidden links in a network. Figure 11.5 shows a synthetic data set simulating the formation of a social network via phone calls. In this data set, there is a hidden structure that occurs when four people decided to switch phones, creating two identities [43]. This phenomenon is very common, and computational models often contains multiple instances of otherwise individuals in the real world. Traditional approaches to this problem fail to recognize this relationship. In our case, as shown in Figure 11.5(a), a node-link diagram results in the familiar "hairball" and fails to provide hints of the structure, except for an apparent concentration of nodes along three centers (where edges are more dense). After applying centrality derivatives, we can simplify the network by choosing only the edges with the highest derivative magnitude. The result is shown in Figure 11.5(b). Now we can see a clear structure of clusters. In addition, we highlight the non-edge pairs of nodes with the highest derivatives, as shown in the grayed areas. The corresponding nodes that form these pairs (highlighted in gray), happen to correspond to the same persons. A visualization that creates this implicit link,

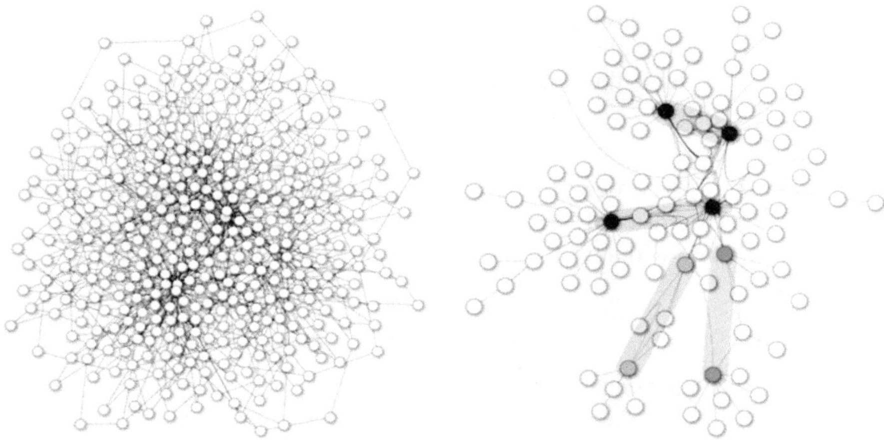

Figure 11.5. Discovering hidden links on a social network. Left: A synthetic social network containing a hidden structure is visualized using a force-directed layout. A grouping of nodes at the interior of the network is obscured by "hairball". Right: After applying a centrality-based analysis, we discover strong links between cluster centers that are not linked directly. These pairings reveal the hidden structure in the network.

which is not explicit in the data set, helps us make assessments of the network with more confidence. We can now think of this subnetwork as a collection of four clusters, each of them centered at these node pairs [10].

4. Summary

Social network applications are clearly driving several areas of information visualization research. In the past, visualization had a very passive role, relegated to the presentation of an overview of the network and the result of time-consuming, often unsupervised analysis. Now, visualization and interaction have a more active role. Not only do we see new and sophisticated ways of displaying network data, using unique combinations of analytical processes, such as centrality analysis and community identification, but also we see the visual analytics process as an interactive, iterative approach. Even when analysis fails, a visual study of a social network could bring analysts' attention to regions that are seemingly unimportant, but may be salient for the task at hand.

The convergence of analysis tools such as centrality and clustering analysis and interactive techniques have led to powerful visualization solutions. Unlike early systems, more focused towards the structural drawing of such a network, current visualization tools offer unprecedented views of the network, with the ability to filter and group nodes along sophisticated metrics such as random-walk based centralities. Semantic clustering and filtering allows analysts to navigate through the large multi-dimensional data associated with social networks. A node-link diagram is no longer a faithful representation of the raw data, often providing little insight due to clutter and overlap, but becomes a useful and effective "slice" through a multi-dimensional data set. Linked views are also becoming commonplace. We do not rely on the often misguided interpretation that force-directed node layouts provide us, but we have at our disposal a wealth of semantic and statistical views that help us understand the structure of social networks in different spaces.

The dynamic aspect of social networks remains a challenge. As pointed out numerous times by visualization researchers, traditional graphs and diagrams fail to convey temporal changes in a social network. New, more effective representations of time, beyond animations and time sliders, are required if we are to understand how social networks form and evolve.

References

[1] Aleks Aris and Ben Shneiderman. Designing semantic substrates for visual network exploration. *Information Visualization*, 6(4):281–300, 2007.

[2] Enrico Bertini and Denis Lalanne. Surveying the complementary role of automatic data analysis and visualization in knowledge discovery. In *VAKD '09: Proceedings of the ACM SIGKDD Workshop on Visual Analytics and Knowledge Discovery*, pages 12–20, New York, NY, USA, 2009. ACM.

[3] Philip Bonacich. Factoring and weighting approaches to status scores and clique identification. *J. of Mathematical Sociology*, 2(1):113–120, 1972.

[4] Ulrik Brandes. Drawing on physical analogies. pages 71–86, 2001.

[5] Ulrik Brandes, Patrick Kenis, Jörg Raab, Volker Schneider, and Dorothea Wagner. Explorations into the visualization of policy networks. *Journal of Theoretical Politics*, 11(11):75–106, 1998.

[6] Ulrik Brandes, Patrick Kenis, and Dorothea Wagner. Communicating centrality in policy network drawings. *IEEE Transactions on Visualization and Computer Graphics*, 9(2):241–253, 2003.

[7] Ulrik Brandes and Christian Pich. An experimental study on distance-based graph drawing. pages 218–229, 2009.

[8] Ulrik Brandes and Dorothea Wagner. Visone - analysis and visualization of social networks. In *Graph Drawing Software*, pages 321–340. Springer-Verlag, 2003.

[9] Carlos D. Correa, Tarik Crnovrsanin, Kwan-Liu Ma, and Kimberly Keeton. The derivatives of centrality and their applications in visualizing social networks. Technical report, Computer Science, CSE-2009-5, University of California at Davis, 2009.

[10] Tarik Crnovrsanin, Carlos D. Correa, and Kwan-Liu Ma. Social network discovery based on sensitivity analysis. In *ASONAM '09: Proceedings of the 2009 International Conference on Advances in Social Network Analysis and Mining*, pages 107–112, Washington, DC, USA, 2009. IEEE Computer Society.

[11] Patrick Doreian, Vladimir Batagelj, Anuska Ferligoj, and Mark Granovetter. *Generalized Blockmodeling (Structural Analysis in the Social Sciences)*. Cambridge University Press, New York, NY, USA, 2004.

[12] Tim Dwyer, Seok-Hee Hong, Dirk Koschützki, Falk Schreiber, and Kai Xu. Visual analysis of network centralities. In *APVis '06: Proceedings of the 2006 Asia-Pacific Symposium on Information Visualisation*, pages 189–197, Darlinghurst, Australia, Australia, 2006. Australian Computer Society, Inc.

[13] Linton Freeman. Visualizing social networks. *Journal of Social Structure*, 1(1), 2000.

[14] Linton C Freeman. Centrality in social networks: Conceptual clarification. *Social Networks*, Vol. 1, No. 3(3):215 –239, 1979.

[15] Stefan Hachul and Michael Jünger. An experimental comparison of fast algorithms for drawing general large graphs. In *In Proc. Graph Drawing*, pages 235–250. Springer-Verlag, 2005.

[16] Jeffrey Heer and Danah Boyd. Vizster: Visualizing online social networks. In *INFOVIS '05: Proceedings of the Proceedings of the 2005 IEEE Symposium on Information Visualization*, page 5, Washington, DC, USA, 2005. IEEE Computer Society.

[17] Jeffrey Heer and Danah Boyd. Vizster: Visualizing online social networks. In *Proc. IEEE Symposium on Information Visualization*, page 5, 2005.

[18] Nathalie Henry and Jean-Daniel Fekete. Matlink: enhanced matrix visualization for analyzing social networks. In *INTERACT'07: Proceedings of the 11th IFIP TC 13 international conference on Human-computer interaction*, pages 288–302, Berlin, Heidelberg, 2007. Springer-Verlag.

[19] Nathalie Henry, Jean-Daniel Fekete, and Michael J. McGuffin. Nodetrix: a hybrid visualization of social networks. *IEEE Transactions on Visualization and Computer Graphics*, 13(6):1302–1309, 2007.

[20] Ivan Herman, Guy Melançon, and M. Scott Marshall. Graph visualization and navigation in information visualization: A survey. *IEEE Transactions on Visualization and Computer Graphics*, 6(1):24–43, 2000.

[21] Danny Holten. Hierarchical edge bundles: Visualization of adjacency relations in hierarchical data. *IEEE Transactions on Visualization and Computer Graphics*, 12(5):741–748, 2006.

[22] Yuntao Jia, Jared Hoberock, Michael Garland, and John Hart. On the visualization of social and other scale-free networks. *IEEE Transactions on Visualization and Computer Graphics*, 14:1285–1292, 2008.

[23] Goh Oh Kahng, E. Oh, B. Kahng, and D. Kim. Betweenness centrality correlation in social networks. *Phys. Rev. E*, 67:01710–1, 2003.

[24] Hyunmo Kang, Lise Getoor, and Lisa Singh. Visual analysis of dynamic group membership in temporal social networks. *SIGKDD Explor. Newsl.*, 9(2):13–21, 2007.

[25] Alden S. Klovdahl. A note on images of networks. *Social Networks*, 3(3):197 – 214, 1981.

[26] Yehuda Koren. On spectral graph drawing. In *Proc. 9th Inter. Computing and Combinatorics Conference (COCOONÕ03), LNCS 2697*, pages 496–508. Springer-Verlag, 2002.

[27] D. Koschützki and F. Schreiber. Comparison of centralities for biological networks. In *Proc German Conf Bioinformatics (GCB'04)*, pages 199–2006, 2004.

[28] James Moody, Daniel Mc Farland, and Skye Bender-deMoll. Dynamic network visualization. *American Journal of Sociology*, 110(4):1206–1241, 2005.

[29] Chris Muelder and Kwan-Liu Ma. Rapid graph layout using space filling curves. *IEEE Transactions on Visualization and Computer Graphics*, 14(6):1301–1308, 2008.

[30] Galileo Mark Namata, Brian Staats, Lise Getoor, and Ben Shneiderman. A dual-view approach to interactive network visualization. In *CIKM '07: Proceedings of the sixteenth ACM conference on Conference on information and knowledge management*, pages 939–942, New York, NY, USA, 2007. ACM.

[31] Andreas Noack. Modularity clustering is force-directed layout. *CoRR*, abs/0807.4052, 2008.

[32] M. L. A Northway. Method for depicting social relationships obtained by sociometric testing. sociometry. 3(2), 1940.

[33] Adam Perer and Ben Shneiderman. Balancing systematic and flexible exploration of social networks. *IEEE Transactions on Visualization and Computer Graphics*, 12(5):693–700, 2006.

[34] Adam Perer and Ben Shneiderman. Integrating statistics and visualization: case studies of gaining clarity during exploratory data analysis. In *CHI '08: Proc. SIGCHI conference on Human factors in computing systems*, pages 265–274, 2008.

[35] William A. Pike, John Stasko, Remco Chang and Theresa A. O'Connell. The Science of Interaction. In *Information Visualization*, 8(4):263–274, 2009.

[36] Zeqian Shen and Kwan-Liu Ma. Path visualization for adjacency matrices. In *EuroVis*, pages 83–90, 2007.

[37] Zeqian Shen and Kwan-Liu Ma. Mobivis: A visualization system for exploring mobile data. In *PacificVis*, pages 175–182, 2008.

[38] Zeqian Shen, Kwan-Liu Ma, and Tina Eliassi-Rad. Visual analysis of large heterogeneous social networks by semantic and structural abstraction. *IEEE Transactions on Visualization and Computer Graphics*, 12(6):1427–1439, 2006.

[39] Lei Shi, Nan Cao, Shixia Liu, Weihong Qian, Li Tan, Guodong Wang, Jimeng Sun, and Ching-Yung Lin. Himap: Adaptive visualization of large-scale online social networks. In *PACIFICVIS '09: Proceedings of the 2009 IEEE Pacific Visualization Symposium*, pages 41–48, Washington, DC, USA, 2009. IEEE Computer Society.

[40] Edward R. Tufte. *The visual display of quantitative information.* Graphics Press, Cheshire, CT, USA, 1986.

[41] F. van Ham and M. Wattenberg. Centrality based visualization of small world graphs. *Computer Graphics Forum*, 27(3):975–982, 2008.

[42] Frank van Ham and Adam Perer. Search, Show Context, Expand on Demand: Supporting large graph exploration with degree-of-interest. *IEEE Transactions on Visualization and Computer Graphics*, 15(6):953–960, 2009.

[43] VAST_Challenge. IEEE VAST 2008 challenge. http://www.cs.umd.edu/hcil/vastchallenge08/, 2008.

[44] Fernanda B. Viégas, Danah Boyd, David H. Nguyen, Jeffrey Potter, and Judith Donath. Digital artifacts for remembering and storytelling: Posthistory and social network fragments. In *HICSS '04: Proceedings of the Proceedings of the 37th Annual Hawaii International Conference on System Sciences (HICSS'04) - Track 4*, page 40109.1, Washington, DC, USA, 2004. IEEE Computer Society.

[45] Fernanda B. Vi?gas, Danah Boyd, David H. Nguyen, Jeffrey Potter, and Judith Donath. Digital artifacts for remembering and storytelling: Posthistory and social network fragments. *Hawaii International Conference on System Sciences*, 4:40109a, 2004.

[46] Martin Wattenberg. Visual exploration of multivariate graphs. In *CHI '06: Proceedings of the SIGCHI conference on Human Factors in computing systems*, pages 811–819, New York, NY, USA, 2006. ACM.

Chapter 12

DATA MINING IN SOCIAL MEDIA

Geoffrey Barbier
Arizona State University
gbarbier@asu.edu

Huan Liu
Arizona State University
huan.liu@asu.edu

Abstract The rise of online social media is providing a wealth of social network data. Data mining techniques provide researchers and practitioners the tools needed to analyze large, complex, and frequently changing social media data. This chapter introduces the basics of data mining, reviews social media, discusses how to mine social media data, and highlights some illustrative examples with an emphasis on social networking sites and blogs.

Keywords: data mining, social media, data representation, social computing, social networks, social networking sites, blogs, blogosphere, event maps

1. Introduction

Data mining, as a young field, has been spearheading research and development of methods and algorithms handling huge amounts of data in solving real-world problems. Much like traditional miners extract precious metals from earth and ore, data miners seek to extract meaningful information from a data set that is not readily apparent and not always easily obtainable. With the ubiquitous use of social media via the internet, an unprecedented amount of data is available and of interest to many fields of study including sociology, business, psychology, entertainment, politics, news, and other cultural aspects of societies. Applying data mining to social media can yield interesting perspectives on human behavior and human interaction. Data mining can be used in conjunction with social media to better understand the opinions people have about a subject, identify groups of people amongst the masses of a population, study group changes over time, find influential people, or even recommend a product or activity to an individual.

The elections during 2008 marked an unprecedented use of social media in a United States presidential campaign. Social media sites including YouTube[1] and Facebook[2] played a significant role in raising funds and getting candidates' messages to voters [51]. Researchers at the Massachusetts Institute of Technology, Center for Collective Intelligence, mined blog data to show correlations between the amount of social media used by candidates and the winner of the 2008 presidential campaign [24]. This powerful example underscores the potential for data mining social media data to predict outcomes at a national level. Data mining social media can also yield personal and corporate benefits. In another example, researchers developed a Group Recommendation System (GRS) for Facebook users using hierarchical clustering and decision tree data mining methods [7]. The GRS matches users, based on their Facebook profiles, with Facebook groups the users are likely to join by applying data mining methods to Facebook groups and their members.

Applying data mining techniques to social media data has gained increasing attention with the significant rise of online social media in recent years. Social media data have three characteristics that pose challenges for researchers: the data are *large*, *noisy*, and *dynamic*. In order to overcome these challenges, data mining techniques are used by researchers to reveal insights into social media data that would not be possible otherwise. This chapter introduces the basics of data mining, reviews social media, discusses how to mine social media data, and highlights some illustrative examples, paving the way for addressing research issues and exploring novel data mining applications.

2. Data Mining in a Nutshell

One definition of data mining is identifying novel and actionable patterns in data. Data mining is also known as Knowledge Discovery from Data (KDD) [28] or Knowledge Discovery in Databases, also abbreviated as KDD [47]. Data mining is related to machine learning, information retrieval, statistics, databases, and even data visualization [43]. One formal definition for data mining is found in Princeton University's WordNet[3] where data mining is defined as:

> "data processing using sophisticated data search capabilities and statistical algorithms to discover patterns and correlations in large preexisting databases; a way to discover new meaning in data"

---

[1] http://www.youtube.com/

[2] http://www.facebook.com/

[3] http://wordnet.princeton.edu/

The key idea behind data mining is finding *new* information in a data set that is hidden or latent[4]. Data mining can help people better understand large sets of data.

Supervised and unsupervised algorithms are used to identify the hidden patterns in data. Supervised approaches depend on some a-priori knowledge of the data (e.g. class labels). Unsupervised algorithms are used to characterize data without any prior instruction as to what kinds of patterns will be discovered by the algorithm. The variety of work accomplished to date pertaining to data mining of online social media data is accomplished with some version of either supervised or unsupervised learning algorithms. Determining whether a supervised or an unsupervised approach would be best depends on the data set and the particular question being investigated. Data sets can be generalized into three types: data with labels, data without labels, and data with only a small portion of labels.

Classification is a common supervised approach and is appropriate when the data set has labels or a small portion of the data has labels. Classification algorithms begin with a set of training data which includes class labels for each data element. The algorithm learns from the training data and builds a model that will automatically categorize new data elements into one of the distinct classes provided with the training data. Classification rules and decision trees are examples of supervised classification techniques.

Clustering is a common unsupervised data mining technique that is useful when confronting data sets without labels. Unlike classification algorithms, clustering algorithms do not depend on labeled training data to develop a model. Instead, clustering algorithms determine which elements in the data set are similar to each other based on the similarity of the data elements. Similarity can be defined as euclidian distance for some numerical data sets but often in data associated with social media, cluster techniques must be able to deal with text. In this case, clustering techniques use keywords that are represented as a vector (to represent a document) and the cosine similarity measure is used to distinguish how similar one vector (data element) is to another.

In addition to classification and clustering methods, there are a variety of mining techniques detailed in several textbooks [28, 56, 69], including association rules, Bayesian classification algorithms, rule-based classifiers, support vector machines, text mining, link analysis, and multi-relational data mining. Additional references of specific data mining topics can be found in [3, 18, 43, 47].

[4]Data mining approaches employ statistical based algorithms, data mining differs from statistics in that the primary focus of common statistics is to organize and summarize information [25] versus identifying hidden patterns.

3. Social Media

We start describing social media beginning with a definition produced from a social media source, Wikipedia[5]. It defines social media as follows:

> "media designed to be disseminated through social interaction, created using highly accessible and scalable publishing techniques. Social media uses Internet and web-based technologies to transform broadcast media monologues (one to many) into social media dialogues (many to many). It supports the democratization of knowledge and information, transforming people from content consumers into content producers."

In [33] Kaplan and Haenlein define Social media as:

> "a group of Internet-based applications that build on the ideological and technological foundations of Web 2.0, and that allow the creation and exchange of User Generated Content."

Mining social media is one type of social computing. Social computing is *"any type of computing application in which software serves as an intermediary or a focus for a social relation"* [53]. Social computing includes applications used for interpersonal communication [53] as well as applications and research activities related to "computational social studies [65]" or "social behavior [15]". Social Media[6] [7] refers to a variety of information services used collaboratively by many people placed into the subcategories shown in Table 12.1.

Table 12.1. Common Social Media Subcategories

Category	Examples
Blogs	Blogger, LiveJournal, WordPress
Microblogs	Twitter, GoogleBuzz
Opinion mining	Epinions, Yelp
Photo and video Sharing	Flickr, YouTube
Social bookmarking	Delicious, StumbleUpon
Social networking sites	Facebook, LinkedIn, MySpace, Orkut
Social news	Digg, Slashdot
Wikis	Scholarpedia, Wikihow, Wikipedia, Event maps

With traditional media such as newspaper, radio, and television, communication is almost entirely one-way, originating from the media source or ad-

[5] http://en.wikipedia.org/wiki/Social_media

[6] Some researchers distinguish between social media and social networks [36].

[7] Social media can also be classified based on social presence/media richness and self-presentation/self-disclosure into six categories: collaborative projects, blogs, social networking sites, content communities, virtual social worlds, and virtual game worlds [33].

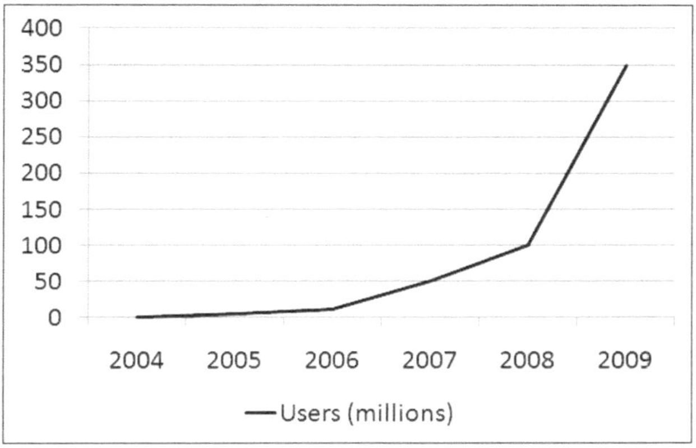

Figure 12.1. Total Facebook Users per Year

vertiser to the masses of media consumers. Web 2.0 technologies and contemporary online social media changed the scene moving from one-way communication driven by media providers to where now almost anyone can publish written, audio, or video content to the masses. This many-to-many media environment is significantly changing the way business communicate with their customers [32, 64] and provides drastically unprecedented opportunities for individuals to communicate with extremely large numbers of people at an extremely low cost. The many-to-many relationships present online and manifest through social media are digitized data sets of social networks on a scale never seen before. The resulting data provides rich opportunities for sociology [44, 14] and new insights to consumer behavior and marketing [65] amongst a host of related applications to similar fields.

The rise and popularity of social media is astounding. For example, consider the popular social networking site Facebook. During the first six years of operation Facebook reached over 400 million active users. [8] Figure 12.1 [9] illustrates the exponential growth of Facebook during its first six years. Facebook is ranked 2nd in the world for internet sites based on the amount of daily internet traffic to the site. [10]

The widespread use of social media is not limited to one geographic region of the world. Orkut, a popular social networking site operated by Google[11] has a majority of users from outside the United States[12] and the use of social

[8] http://www.facebook.com/press/info.php?timeline

[9] Figure produced with data found at http://www.facebook.com/press/info.php?timeline.

[10] Ranked according to http://www.alexa.com/topsites/global, April 2010.

[11] http://www.google.com/

[12] http://www.orkut.com/MembersAll

media among internet users is now mainstream in many parts of the world including countries Europe, Asia, Africa, South America, and the Middle East[13]; even well known organizations such as the United Nations are turning to social media to help accomplish parts of its mission[14]. Social media is also driving significant changes in business and companies have to decide on their strategies for keeping pace with this new media [32].

4. Motivations for Data Mining in Social Media

The data available via social media can give us insights into social networks and societies that were not previously possible in both scale and extent. This digital media can transcend the physical world boundaries to study human relationships [44] and help measure popular social and political sentiment attributed to regional populations without explicit surveys [39, 52, 63]. Social media effectively records viral marketing trends and is the ideal source to study to better understand and leverage influence mechanisms [21]. However, it is extremely difficult to gain useful information from social media data without applying data mining technologies due to unique challenges.

Data mining techniques can help effectively deal with the three main challenges with social media data. First, social media data sets are *large*, consider the 400 million Facebook users as an example. Without automated information processing for analyzing social media, social network data analytics becomes an unattainable in any reasonable amount of time. Second, social media data sets can be *noisy*. For example, spam blogs or "splogs" are abundant in the blogosphere, as well as excessive trivial tweets in Twitter. Third, data from online social media is *dynamic*, frequent changes and updates over short periods of time are not only common but an important dimension to consider in dealing with social media data. Wikis are modified and created, friend networks ebb and flow, and new blogs are routinely published. Other data sets may contain some of the challenges present in social media but usually not all at once. For example, the set of traditional web pages create a data set that is a large and noisy but, compared to social media data, is not nearly as dynamic.

Social media enables massive production of free-form and interactive data. Consider microblog posts, chat messages, and blog comments as examples. Another aspect of social media data is its relational nature that can complicate analysis. However, relational attributes are not a new problem for data mining. Some data mining techniques have been designed specifically to identify patterns and rules based relational attributes [28]. Data mining leverages tech-

[13] http://www.alexa.com/topsites/countries

[14] http://malariaenvoy.com/tabid/61/Default.aspx?udt_373_param_detail=109

niques developed for other problem domains and allows us to apply techniques to social media data without having to start from scratch.

Data mining can help researchers and practitioners overcome these challenges. Applying data mining techniques to large social media data sets has the potential to continue to improve search results for everyday search engines, realize specialized target marketing for businesses, help psychologist study behavior, provide new insights into social structure for sociologists, personalize web services for consumers, and even help detect and prevent spam for all of us [17, 36]. Additionally, the open access to data provides researches with unprecedented amounts of information to improve performance and optimize data mining techniques. The advancement of the data mining field itself relies on large data sets and social media is an ideal data source in the frontier of data mining for developing and testing new data mining techniques for academic and corporate data mining researchers [17].

5. Data Mining Methods for Social Media

Applying data mining methods to social media is relatively new compared to other areas of study related to social network analytics when you consider the work in social network analysis that dates back to the 1930s [67]. However, applications that apply data mining techniques developed by industry and academia are already being used commercially. For example, Samepoint[15], a "Social Media Analytics" company, provides services to mine and monitor social media to provide clients information about how goods and services perceived and discussed through social media. Researchers in other organizations have applied text mining algorithms and disease propagation models to blogs to develop approaches for better understanding how information moves through the blogosphere [26].

Data mining techniques can be applied to social media to understand data better and to make use of data for research and business purposes. Representative areas include community or group detection [7, 60, 70], information diffusion [26], influence propagation [1, 2, 4, 63], topic detection and monitoring [16, 52], individual behavior analysis [8, 44, 48], group behavior analysis [59, 23], and of course, marketing research for businesses [21].

The remainder of this chapter first discusses the issue of data representation for mining social media, next introduces key components of mining social media, and presents some illustrative examples in terms of social networking sites and the blogosphere.

[15] http://www.samepoint.biz/

5.1 Data Representation

Similar to other social network data, it is common to use a graph representation to study social media data sets. A graph consists of a set containing vertexes (nodes) and edges (links). Individuals are typically represented as the nodes in the graph. Relationships or associations between individuals (nodes) are represented as the links in the graph. The graph representation is natural for data extracted from social networking sites where individuals create a social network of friends, classmates, or business associates. Less apparent is how the graph structure is applied to blogs, wikis, opinion mining, and similar types of online social media [16]

In the case of blogs, one graph representation has blogs as the nodes and can be considered a "blog network" and another graph representation has blog posts as the nodes and can be considered a "post network" [1]. Edges in a blog post network are formed when when a blog post references another blog post. Other approaches used to represent blog networks account for people, relationships, content, and time simultaneously - named internet OnLine Analytical Processing (iOLAP) [16]. Wikis can be considered from the perspective of representing authors as nodes and edges are formed when the authors contribute to an article. Alternatively, the wiki topic entries can be represented as nodes and references to related topics entries can be represented as links in a graph [48] or with nodes representing both topics and users and collaborations and affiliations are represented as links [31].

The graph representation enables the application of classic mathematical graph theory [13], traditional social network analysis methods, and work on mining graph data [3]. However, the potentially large size of a graph used to represent social media can present challenges for automated processing as limits on computer memory and processing speeds are maximized and often surpassed when trying to deal with large social media data sets [3, 42, 58]. Other challenges to applying automated processes to enable data mining in social media include identifying and dealing with spam [1, 4], the variety of formats used in the same social media subcategory, and constantly changing content and structure [42].

Representing online social media data as graphs enables leveraging work done with graphs related to influence propagation, community detection, and link prediction. Influence propagation models consider the graph structure characteristics such as which nodes have centrality characteristics and which nodes form bridges in the graph etc. Influence propagation through online so-

[16]Although not traditionally considered social media, a large amount of citation data is available that can be mined for interesting relationships between documents. A graph can represent relationships between documents where a node represents the document and an edge is present when a document cites another document [27].

cial media is a popular research topic, [6, 19, 20, 26, 35, 57]. The purpose of community detection is to discover the community structure in the graph. Applying link analysis algorithms to social media data can detect groups that are not readily apparent [36]. Link prediction is the ability to predict when new relationships will form is known as the link prediction problem [46].

5.2 Data Mining - A Process

No matter what type of social media under study, there are a few basic items that are important to consider to ensure that the most meaningful results are possible. Each type of social media and each data mining purpose applied to social media may require a unique approaches and algorithms to produce a data mining benefit. Different data sets and data questions require different types of tools. If it is known how the data should be organized, a classification tool might be appropriate. If you understand what the data is about but cannot ascertain trends and patterns in the data, a clustering tool may be best.

The problem itself may determine the best approach. There is no substitute for understanding the data as much as possible before applying data mining techniques, and second, understanding the different data mining tools that are available. For the former, subject matter experts might be needed to help better understand the data set. To better understand the different data mining tools available there are a host of data mining and machine learning texts and resources that are available to provide very detailed information about a variety of specific data mining algorithms and techniques.

Once you understand the problem and select an appropriate data mining approach, consider any preprocessing that needs to be done. It may also be necessary to apply a methodical procedure for creating a more sparse data set to enable reasonable processing times. Preprocessing should include consideration for anonymization and appropriate mechanism for protecting privacy. Although social media includes vast quantities of publicly available data, it is important to ensure individual rights and social media site copyrights are protected. The impact of spam needs to be considered along with the temporal representation.

In addition to preprocessing, it is important to consider the impact of time. Depending on the question and the research you may get very different results at one time compared to another. Although the time component is an obvious consideration for some areas such as topic detection, influence propagation, and network growth, less apparent is the impact of time on community detection, group behavior, and marketing. What defines a community at one point in time can be significantly different at another point in time. Group behavior and interests will change over time, and what was selling to individuals or groups today may not be popular tomorrow.

With data represented as a graph, the work begins with a select number of nodes, known as seeds. Graphs are traversed beginning with the set of seeds and as the link structure from the seed nodes is exploited, data is collected and the structure itself is also analyzed. Using the link structure to extend from the seed set and gather new information is known as crawling the network. The application and algorithms that are implemented as a crawler[17] must successfully deal with the challenges present in dynamic social media networks such as format changes, restricted sites, and structure errors (invalid links). As the crawler discovers new information, it stores the new information in a repository for further analysis later. As link information is located, the crawler updates information about the network structure.

Some social media sites such as Technorati, Facebook, and Twitter provide Application Programmer Interfaces (APIs) which allow crawler applications to directly interface with the data sources. However, these sites usually limit the number of API transactions per day depending on the affiliation the API user has with the site. For some sites, it is possible to collect data (crawl) without using APIs. Given the vast size of the social media data available, it may be necessary to limit the amount of data the crawler collects. Once the crawler has collected the data, some postprocessing might be needed to validate and clean up the data. Traditional social network analysis techniques [67] can be applied such as centrality measures and group structure studies. In many cases, additional data will also be associated with a node or a link opening opportunities for more sophisticated methods to consider the deeper semantics that can be brought to light with text and data mining techniques.

We now focus on two specific types of social media data in order to further illustrate how data mining techniques are applied to social media. The two areas are Social Networking Sites and Blogs. Both these areas are characterized by dynamic and rich data sources. Both areas offer potential value to the broader scientific community as well as businesses.

5.3 Social Networking Sites: Illustrative Examples

A social networking site like Facebook or LinkedIn consists of connected users with unique profiles. Users can link to friends and colleagues and can share news, photos, videos, favorite links etc. Users customize their profiles depending on individual preferences but some common information might include relationship status, birthday, an e-mail address, and hometown. Users have options to decide how much information they include in their profile and who has access to it. The amount of information available via a social networking site has raised privacy concerns and is a related societal issue [12].

[17]A crawler is synonymous in this context with spider.

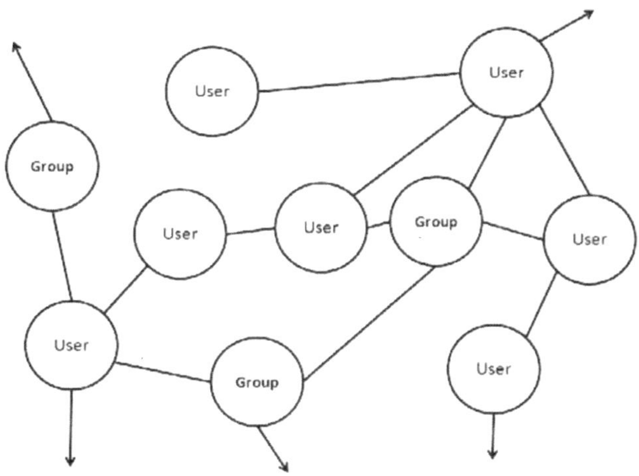

Figure 12.2. Hypothetical graph structure diagram for a typical social networking site. Note links between user nodes and group nodes. Arrows indicate links to larger portions of the graph.

It is important to protect personal privacy when working with social network data. Recent publications highlight the need to protect privacy as it has been shown that even anonymizing this type of data can still reveal personal information when advanced data analysis techniques are used [12, 45]. Privacy settings also can limit the ability of data mining applications to consider every piece of information in a social network. However, some nefarious techniques can be employed to usurp privacy settings [12].

Social networking sites provide excellent sources of data for studying collaboration relationships, group structure, and who-talks-to-whom. The most common graph structure based on a social networking site is intuitive; users are represented as nodes and their relationships are represented as links. Users can link to group nodes as well. Figure12.2 depicts a hypothetical graph representing a portion of a social networking site network. The driving factors for data mining social networking sites is the *"unique opportunity to understand the impact of a person's position in the network on everything from their tastes to their moods to their health."* [45]. The most common data mining applications related to social networking sites include:

- Group detection - One of the most popular applications of data mining to social networking sites is finding and identifying a group. In general, group detection applied to social networking sites is based on analyzing the structure of the network and finding individuals that associate more with each other than with other users. Understanding what groups an individual belongs to can help lead to insights about the individual such as what activities, goods, and services, an individual might be interested in. Group detection can also yields interesting perspectives about the social networking site itself, such as how many different groups are using the social networking site. Although many social networking sites support explicit groups, implicit groups are present in social networking sites as well. Implicit groups are not always apparent. This presents a challenge for identifying whether or not a group exists. Also known as "community detection," group detection has been approached using a various strategies including node-centric, group-centric, network-centric, and hierarchy-centric [3]. The large number of persons participating in social network sites severely limits the ability to detect groups without computational processes.

Latent groups that exist in a friendship network are not always easy to distinguish. There are often more "social dimensions [59]" in a friend network than just one. For example, a user's friendship network may include *family members*, *classmates*, and *co-workers* in the same network. A clustering approach, such as modularity maximization, can be used to detect these subgroups. Modularity maximization permits nodes to belong to more than one group [61]. Principle Modularity Maximization (PMM) is one commonly used approach to account for multiple dimensions by projecting data onto principal vectors and then using clustering algorithms (e.g., k-means) to determine community assignment. In the case of the example, although the friendship network of the user is a group, the subgroups of *family members*, *classmates*, and *co-workers* can be partitioned out using modularity maximization by detecting these subgroups in the user's friendship network because these subgroups interact more with each other than with other members of the friendship network.

- Group profiling - Once a group is found, the next logical question to ask is 'What is this group about' (i.e., the group profile) [62]? The ability to automatically profile a group is useful for a variety purposes ranging from purely scientific interests to specific marketing of goods, services, and ideas [21, 51, 64]. With millions of groups present in online social media, it is not practical to attempt to answer the question for each group manually.

  Advanced data mining techniques are proposed to account for changes in the group profile over time by defining a topic taxonomy [60]. The initial topic taxonomy is adapted from a general taxonomy or generated by human experts. Identifying and tracking changes using the topic taxonomy can yield insights into how group values changes as well as provide a mechanism for identifying similar groups amongst the otherwise intractable amount of social network data. To accomplish this, the list of topics representing a group is organized into a tree. The parent-child relationships in the topic tree define a taxonomy for the group. This tree, when considered as a classifier, can be compared with alternative tree structures to identify the most accurate classifier for a particular group. Over time, the taxonomy is adapted using a top-down approach by comparing the current tree against possible alternative tree structures, finding the best alternative tree, and updating the topic taxonomy with information from the best alternative tree. As group interests change over time, the initial tree is updated to reflect a the most current taxonomy that represents the group. Group taxonomies can be compared to identify similar groups and contrasted to study differences between groups. For example, a group interested in **cooking** may have tags such as *dinner*, *ingredients*, *recipes*, *menu*, *kitchen tips*, *appetizers*, and *main course*. However, over time the same group could become interested in **catering** which could introduce meaningful tags to the group such as *wedding*, *party*, *events*, and *celebration*. The changes in descriptive tags represents a change in the group profile (i.e., the subtle shift from cooking to include catering) that could be tracked using the topic taxonomy approach.

- Recommendation systems - A recommendation system analyzes social networking data and recommends new friends or new groups to a user. The ability to recommend group membership to an individual is advantageous for a group that would like to have additional members and can be helpful to an individual who is looking to find other individuals or a group of people with similar interests or goals. Again, large numbers of individuals and groups make this an almost impossible task without an automated system. Additionally, group characteristics change over time. For those reasons, data mining algorithms drive the inherent recommendations made to users. From the moment a user profile is entered into a social networking site, the site provides suggestions to expand the user's social network. Much of the appeal of social networking sites is a direct result of the automated recommendations which allow a user to rapidly create and expand an online social network with relatively little effort on the user's part.

  One implementation of a recommendation system serves as a good example. Recommendations are based on user profile data and a user's associated link structure which can be used to provide suggestions to users about which group to join [7]. The first step is to identify features of the profile that best match a group member to a particular group. Next, group members are clustered to identify the most representative members of the group. Finally, a decision tree is created based on the members with the most representative profiles. Profile information can also be mined with data from other sources to recommend events a user may find interesting or useful [34]. Hypothetically, perhaps a user's profile includes information about *alpine skiing*. The profile information could be used to recommend a new *alpine skiing* or *winter sport* group.

Social networking sites have been widely adopted and contain a variety of interesting data on scale that is unprecedented to previous social network data sets. Some users are using social networking sites for regular interpersonal communication while abandoning more traditional communication mechanisms such as e-mail [51]. The mass migration to, and continued use of, social networking sites is creating an almost innumerable amount of data that can only be analyzed practically using data mining techniques.

5.4 The Blogosphere: Illustrative Examples

Web logs or "blogs" are user published journals available on the web[18]. Blogs entries, known as posts, cover a variety of subjects from personal logs to professional journalism reporting on current events. In some cases blogs are considered more accurate than traditional one-to-many news media sources [29]. Blogs are typically open to the public and provide a mechanism for readers to comment on the specific post. The set of all blogs and blog posts is referred to as the blogosphere. Earlier in Data Representation, we describe two common graph structure representations used to represent blog networks, *blog networks* and *post networks*. Lakshamanan and Oberhofer highlight clustering, matrix factorization, and ranking as the three most commonly used techniques for data mining in the blogosphere [42]. Applying data mining technologies to analyze blogs and blog posts is pursued for a variety of purposes.

General information and statistics about the blogosphere are readily available[19]. However, the general statistics do not provide the insights and information that are possible using data mining techniques. With over 100 million blogs, data mining methods provide the most promising prospects for finding latent information in the blogosphere. Without data mining methods only a small fraction of the blogosphere could be effectively analyzed. Gathering data from the blogosphere can be accomplished with a crawler or by accessing repositories[20] [21] of blog data. Using a crawler to collect data begins with a relatively small number of seed sites related to the research area and expand-

[18]Video logs or "vlogs" are similar to blogs but use video as the media versus text compositions.

[19]http://www.blogpulse.com/

[20]http://technorati.com/

[21]http://spinn3r.com/

ing from the seed sites to additional sites and from the additional sites to new sites and so on. Depending on the specific research topic, relying on large data repositories can save the time required to crawl but can leave a data miner beholden to rationing[22] and open questions about whether or not the repository contains the most pertinent and up-to-date posts. The most common data mining applications related to the blogosphere include:

- Blog classfication - A straightforward use of data mining related to the blogosphere is the automated classification of blogs themselves [9, 5, 50]. The ability to automatically organize blogs by topic aids blog search applications and and results can also help focus other blog-related social network analytic purposes in one area of the blogosphere. With thousands upon thousands of blogs available to choose from, it is not practical to try to categorize blog sites manually.

  Bai et al [9] developed a "Folksonomy and Support Vector Machine" to automatically classify blog posts with descriptive words (tags). The approach preprocesses a blog post to remove superfluous text and information. The remaining text is compared to a candidate tag database and the best tags are assigned to the blog post using SVM [54] classifiers. Each potential tag has a tag agent (SVM classifier) that is developed using examples of previously tagged blog posts. A new blog post is automatically tagged by a tag agent if the new blog posts is classified positively by a particular tag agent. For example, suppose there are three tag agents that will determine (each independently) whether or not a new blog post, call it x, should be tagged with *recreation*, *work*, and/or *education*. The tag agent for *recreation* determines that x should not be tagged with *recreation*. Next the remaining two tag agents process the new blog post. The tag agent for *work* and the tag agent for *education* both determine their tags apply. The resulting tags (classifcation) for x are *work* and *education*.

- Identifying influential nodes - "A blogger is influential if he/she has the capacity to affect the behavior of fellow bloggers [1]." Understanding how information is disseminated through the blogosphere can provide interesting insights for businesses or any other entity seeking to spread information about a product, service, or topic as fast as possible. The benefit of being able to identify influential bloggers, blogs, or blog posts is that marketing efforts for goods and services could be focussed on points of influence that are most likely to gain support for a topic, product, or message. One challenge is that there are a very large number

[22] Some repositories limit the number of data requests on a daily basis

of bloggers and blog posts. Another challenge is understanding what factors determine influence.

A significant amount of work has been done to develop propagation models and measurement approaches [26, 41, 55] Researchers studying one particular blog topic in the blogosphere can leverage data mining applications to identify influential bloggers. Often influence is only considered from a structural perspective (i.e. the node with the most inlinks is most influential). A model that combines graph based and content based approaches is a more viable technique for identifying influential blogs [1]. The approach, called iFinder [1], considers influence as a combination of four measures: recognition, activity generation, novelty, and eloquence. Recognition is simply measured by counting the inlinks to a blog post. Activity generation is measured by how many comments a blog post receives. Novelty consists of the outlinks and the influence value of the blog posts at the end of the out link (an outlink that points to a influential blog posts decreases the novelty of the blog post under consideraton). Eloquence is an approximated by the length of the blog post. These four factors combine to generate an influence vector for each blog post. The vectors are compared to determine which posts are most influential.

- Topic detection and change - Like other online social medium data, blog content changes over time. New posts are added, new topics are discussed, opinions change, and new communities develop and mature. Understanding what topics are popular in the blogosphere can provide insights into product sales, political views, and future social attention areas [40]. However, new topics are not easily detected amongst the vast amount of blog posts. Additionally, blog sites are updated daily with new information and topics that were popular a few days ago may superseded by a new topic. Applying data mining techniques to blogs can help detect topic trends and changes [49].

  Early work accomplished by Moon and colleagues [49] proposes a three pronged approach to identifying and tracking popular topics in the blogosphere. Using a Bernoulli presence-based model, words are identified that likely represent popular issues. Next blog sites with a high indegree are considered preferred sources of popular topics. Finally, the results are compared to other data sets in order to determine validity. Although additional work needs to be done in this area, leveraging text processing algorithms and techniques such as Latent Dirichlet Allocation [11] will likely yield new and exciting capabilities for researchers and practitioners.

LDA is also used in the foundation of an approach to identify "opinion leaders" [1]. An opinion leader is a blogger that publishes new ideas. Although opinion leaders are influential, not all influential bloggers are opinion leaders. The key differences is that the opinion leader introduces *new* topics. A cosine similarity measure is used to differentiate how similar a blog post is to other blog posts. Thus, detecting when a new topic is introduced when the difference in the measures is significant.

- Sentiment analysis - How people feel about a topic (e.g., their sentiment) can be just as important as identifying the topic itself. Blogs can be classified into categories, influential blogs can be highlighted, and new topics can be detected. It is also possible to ascertain opinions, or sentiment, from the blogosphere using data mining techniques. This is not an easy task as language is filled with ambiguities and there are many different opinions. However, some interesting work has been done and progress is being made in this area.

  Researchers at the University of Maryland have developed an application called *BlogVox*, to retrieve opinions from the blogosphere about a given topic [30]. After pre-processing to remove spam and superfluous information, *BlogVox* uses a SVM to determine whether or not a blog post expresses an opinion. This differs from topic detection in that the data miner is interested in how people feel about a particular topic versus the topic itself.

  Interesting data mining work to ascertain public sentiment has also been done with data from a microblog. Researchers in the United Kingdom used Twitter[23] data to inform prediction model markets [52]. Their approach also implements a SVM-based algorithm used to analyze microblog messages about a particular topic in order to forecast public sentiment. In particular, the method was applied to microblog messages about an influenza pandemic and the results were compared with prediction market data from an independent source. Their work suggests that social media data can be used as a "proxy" for pubic opinion.

Data mining in the blogosphere is an interesting area replete with new challenges. Without data mining technologies, these challenges could hardly be accomplished because of the overwhelming size of the blogosphere. This area is likely to see more and more attention as blog usage increases quickly around the world.

[23] http://twitter.com/

6. Related Efforts

There are two multi-disciplinary research areas very closely related to data mining in social media: digital ethnography and netnography. Additionally, an emerging social media application area, *event maps*, has a variety of uses and can benefit from data mining, as cell phone usage increases globally and portable computing and communication devices become more and more advanced and accessible [22].

6.1 Ethnography and Netnography

Princeton's wordnet[24] defines ethnography as *"anthropology that provides scientific description of individual human societies."* Kozinets [37] coined the word "netnography" to describe conducting online market research based on ethnography.

Kansas State University offers a graduate level *Digital Ethnography* class based on the work of Professor Michael Wesch. Dr. Wesch and his students are studying how digital culture is evolving on YouTube. Specifically, digital ethnography can provide a better understanding of the context of social media data and the implications for present and future data mining applications. For example, in 2008, the group at Kansas State University reported that over 50% of YouTube users are between 18-24 [68]. This type of information can further inform data mining results of detecting a new community, topic detection on via a specific social medium or even a better understanding of what data might be available from a particular social media site in the future as culture, use, and demographics change over time. Ethnography can also help inform thinking about important data mining issues such as authenticity. Whether or not users are honest with what they include or contribute to online social media is an issue that data miners should consider when analyzing large data sets derived from online social media sources.

The netnography methodology is applied to study cultures and communities based on computer-mediated communications [10]. Researchers have applied netnography to study several areas including cosmetic surgery and coffee consumers [10, 38]. The approach to netnography is founded in direct observations but it is conceivable that data mining techniques could be applied to netnography studies.

Both digital Ethnography and Netnography can help provide useful insights to data miners exploring social media. Ultimately applying data mining to social media is about understanding data about people online which is at the heart of digital ethnogoraphy and netnography research.

---

[24] http://wordnetweb.princeton.edu/perl/webwn?s=ethnography

6.2 Event Maps

An *event map* is a social media application which could be viewed as an extension to a wiki combined with a blog. Event maps take advantage of what has become known as *crowd sourcing*. In order to collect information about an event or a set of related events, individuals in the crowd associated with the event update a maps with information reports relevant to the affair. Reports can be generated and disseminated directly to a web-based application, through e-mail, text messaging, and even via social media sites such as micro-blog subscriptions. Geographically correlated markers identify the location of an information report related to the event on a map. Event maps can also be used to help disseminate information during a crisis and are sometimes referred to as *crisis maps*. Individual needs such as water, food, and blankets can be aggregated and tracked over time.

A crisis map framework developed by the Ushahidi[25] organization has been applied to a variety of situations including: wildlife tracking, crime in Atlanta (Georgia, USA), elections in India, H1N1 flu, medical supplies in Kenya, activities in Afghanistan, and the 2010 earthquake in Haiti. After the devastating earthquake that occurred on January 12, 2010, a variety of sources submitted incident reports to the Haiti crisis map implemented by the Ushahidi volunteer group [26].

Event maps can also combine information form other social and traditional media sources. Applications leveraging crowd source information are likely to continue to rise in popularity. Data mining social media data generated from event maps will allow researchers to better understand human behavior but more importantly it will enable people to make better decisions relative to an event and help leaders to respond to human needs in a crisis.

7. Conclusions

There exist ample opportunities for collaboration between computer scientists, social scientists, and other interested disciplines to use data mining technologies and techniques to reveal patterns in online social media data that would not otherwise be visible. However, there are some challenges that need to be addressed. As scientists seek to conduct new research to advance data mining in social media, open sources of social media data for researchers would enable researchers to validate published work. Tools and and policies need to be developed to ensure privacy integrity will be maintained regardless of how the data is aggregated and analyzed [45]. Protecting privacy is likely to remain a challenge for data mining in social media [45]. Although some work

[25] http://www.ushahidi.com

[26] http://haiti.ushahidi.com

has been done to develop technologies that help protect privacy yet still permit the application in data mining [66] and researchers are investing both privacy and security issues surrounding social media [12], more work needs to be done to ensure privacy and security can be maintained in the long term.

Perhaps the most important areas that need to be addressed is longitudinal studies that can be used to inform and validate not only new data mining technologies, methodologies, and applications but also can help enlighten our understanding of social media itself from a broader perspective. Understand the limits of data mining is important to anyone applying data mining to social media. For example, what are the limits of influence propagation? How is influence defined and how can these findings be validated? Access to datasets that can be used by more than one research team would help with validation and also help move technology forward [45].

Researchers are also working to address the challenges associated with large social media data [58], changing network structure [46], etc. Despite these challenges, the power of online social media evidenced by its impact on national elections, business and marketing, and society itself will continue to be significant motivating factor for mining online social media data as valuable information source for gaining a deeper understanding about people.

In 1994 Doug Schuler stated [53]:

> "The social nature of software is inescapable."

Never has the social nature of software been more evident than today with the world-wide ubiquitous use of social media. Data mining social media can reveal insights into the social nature of human beings and is poised to help us change the way we see society as a whole and as individuals.

Harvesting information from the data rich environment of online social media in all of its forms is a topic studied by many groups. Market researchers, psychologists, sociologist, ethnographers, businesses, and politicians all can gain useful insights into human behavior via a variety of social networks by applying data mining techniques to online social media. Data mining offers a variety of approaches that can be applied to social media. The perspective data mining brings can yield information from online social networks that may not be obvious or attainable otherwise. It is important to understand as much as possible about the data set in order to select the right data mining approach.

Politics, technology, business, and other social areas are likely to be impacted by blogging for the foreseeable future [29]. Data mining technologies will help quantify and provide meaningful insights. As the number of social media users continues to grow, we will likely continue to see significant changes in the way we communicate and share information and we will continue to look to data mining to provide us with the empowering ability to look deeper into these large data sets in a more meaningful way. Social networking sites, blogs, and other online social media services provide a digital record of social behavior from a variety of perspectives providing the ultimate data source for social network analytics and related applications.

Acknowledgements

The authors recognize the positive dialogue with all of the researchers in Arizona State University's Data Mining and Machine Learning Laboratory that continually help motivate and inspire their thinking about data mining in social media. The second author would like to acknowledge the grants by AFOSR (FA95500810132) and NSF (#0812551) on social computing and data mining. The views expressed in this chapter are solely attributed to the authors and do not represent the opinions or policies of any of the funding agencies.

References

[1] N. Agarwal and H. Liu. *Modeling and Data Mining in Blogosphere*, volume 1 of *Synthesis Lectures on Data Mining and Knowledge Discovery*. Morgan and Claypool, 2009.

[2] N. Agarwal, H. Liu, S. Subramanya, J. Salerno, and P. Yu. Connecting sparsely distributed similar bloggers. pages 11 –20, dec. 2009.

[3] C. C. Aggarwal and H. Wang, editors. *Managing and Mining Graph Data*. Springer, 2009.

[4] P. K. Akshay Java and T. Oates. Modeling the spread of influence on the blogosphere. Technical Report UMBC TR-CS-06-03, Universtiy of Maryland Baltimore County, 1000 Hilltop Circle Baltimore, MD, USA, March 2006.

[5] A. Ammari and V. Zharkova. Combining tag cloud learning with svm classification to achieve intelligent search for relevant blog articles. In *1st International Workshop on Mining Social Media (MSM09-CAEPIA09)*, 2009.

[6] A. Anagnostopoulos, R. Kumar, and M. Mahdian. Influence and correlation in social networks. In *Proceeding of the 14th ACM SIGKDD international conference on Knowledge discovery and data mining*, pages 7–15, New York, NY, USA, 2008. ACM.

[7] E.-A. Baatarjav, S. Phithakkitnukoon, and R. Dantu. Group recommendation system for facebook. pages 211–219, 2010.

[8] L. Backstrom, C. Dwork, and J. Kleinberg. Wherefore art thou r3579x?: Anonymized social networks, hidden patterns, and structural steganography. In *Proceedings of the 16th international conference on World Wide Web*, pages 181–190, New York, NY, USA, 2007. ACM.

[9] R. Bai, X. Wang, and J. Liao. Folksonomy for the blogosphere: Blog identification and classification. volume 3, pages 631 –635, 31 2009-april 2 2009.

[10] R. Beckmann, C. Suzanne, and R. Langer. Netnography: Rich insights from online research. *Insights@CBS*, pages 1–4, September 2005. Published as a supplement to Insights@CBS, nr. 14, 6. September 2005: . http://frontpage.cbs.dk/insights/670005.shtml.

[11] D. M. Blei, A. Y. Ng, and M. I. Jordan. Latent dirichlet allocation. *Journal of Machine Learning Research*, 3:993–1022, 2003.

[12] J. Bonneau, J. Anderson, and G. Danezis. Prying data out of a social network. pages 249 –254, july 2009.

[13] C. T. Butts. Revisiting the foundation of network analysis. *Science*, 325:414–416, July 2009.

[14] S.-K. Chai. Social computing: An opportunity for mathematical sociologists. *The Mathematical Sociologist*, 12(2), 2008-9.

[15] S.-K. Chai, J. J. Salerno, and P. L. Mabry, editors. *Advances in Social Computing*, Lecture Notes in Computer Science. Third International Conference on Social Computing, Behavorial Modeling, and Prediction, SBP 2010, Springer, March 2010.

[16] Y. Chi, S. Zhu, K. Hino, Y. Gong, and Y. Zhang. iolap: A framework for analyzing the internet, social networks, and other networked data. *Multimedia, IEEE Transactions on*, 11(3):372 –382, april 2009.

[17] J. C. Cortizo, F. M. Carrero, J. M. Gomez, B. Monsalve, and P. Puertas. Introduction to mining social media. In F. M. Carrero, J. M. Gomez, B. Monsalve, P. Puertas, and J. C. a. Cortizo, editors, *Proceedings of the 1st International Workshop on Mining Social Media*, pages 1–3, 2009.

[18] E. Cox. *Fuzzy Modeling and Genetic Algorithms for Data Mining and Exploration*. Elsevier/Morgan Kaufmann, Amsterdam, 2005.

[19] D. Crandall, D. Cosley, D. Huttenlocher, J. Kleinberg, and S. Suri. Feedback effects between similarity and social influence in online communities. In *Proceeding of the 14th ACM SIGKDD international conference on Knowledge discovery and data mining*, pages 160–168, New York, NY, USA, 2008. ACM.

[20] R. da Cunha Recuero. Information flows and social capital in weblogs: a case study in the brazilian blogosphere. In *Proceedings of the nineteenth ACM conference on Hypertext and hypermedia*, pages 97–106, New York, NY, USA, 2008. ACM.

[21] P. Domingos and M. Richardson. Mining the network value of customers. In *Proceedings of the seventh ACM SIGKDD international conference*

on Knowledge discovery and data mining, pages 57–66, New York, NY, USA, 2001. ACM.

[22] N. Eagle, A. Pentland, and D. Lazer. Mobile phone data for inferring social network structure. In H. Liu, J. J. Salerno, and M. J. Young, editors, *Social Computing, Behavioral Modeling, and Prediction*, Computer Science, pages 79–88. Springer, April 2008.

[23] C. Faloutsos, J. Han, and P. S. Yu., editors. *Link Mining: Models, Algorithms and Applications*. 2010.

[24] P. Gloor, J. Krauss, S. Nann, K. Fischbach, and D. Schoder. Web science 2.0: Identifying trends through semantic social network analysis. volume 4, pages 215 –222, aug. 2009.

[25] F. Gravetter and L. Wallnau. *Essentials of Statistics for the Behavioral Sciences*. Wadsworth, Belmont, 2002.

[26] D. Gruhl, R. Guha, D. Liben-Nowell, and A. Tomkins. Information diffusion through blogspace. In *Proceedings of the 13th International Conference on World Wide Web*, pages 491–501, New York, NY, USA, 2004. ACM.

[27] M. Hamdaqa and A. Hamou-Lhadj. Citation analysis: An approach for facilitating the understanding and the analysis of regulatory compliance documents. pages 278 –283, april 2009.

[28] J. Han. *Data Mining Concepts and Techniques*. Morgan Kaufmann, San Diego, 2006.

[29] D. Hughes and R. Kellman. Blogging's global impact and the future of blogging. Blog, October 2009. Accessed March 24, 2010.

[30] A. Java. *Mining social media communities and content*. PhD thesis, Catonsville, MD, USA, 2008. Adviser-Finin, Timothy W.

[31] W. Jun, J. Xin, and W. Yun-peng. An empirical study of knowledge collaboration networks in virtual community: Based on wiki. pages 1092 –1097, sept. 2009.

[32] G. C. Kane, R. G. Fichman, J. Gallaugher, and J. Glasier. Community relations 2.0. *Harvard Business Review*, 87(11):45–50, November 2009.

[33] A. M. Kaplan and M. Haenlein. Users of the world, unite! the challenges and opportunities of social media. *Business Horizons*, 53(1):59–68, Jan 2009.

[34] M. Kayaalp, T. Ozyer, and S. Ozyer. A collaborative and content based event recommendation system integrated with data collection scrapers and services at a social networking site. In *Social Network Analysis and Mining, 2009. ASONAM '09. International Conference on Advances in*, pages 113 –118, july 2009.

[35] E. Kim and S. Han. An analytical way to find influencers on social networks and validate their effects in disseminating social games. In *Social Network Analysis and Mining, 2009. ASONAM '09. International Conference on Advances in*, pages 41 –46, july 2009.

[36] I. King, J. Li, and K. T. Chan. A brief survey of computational approaches in social computing. In *IJCNN'09: Proceedings of the 2009 international joint conference on Neural Networks*, pages 2699–2706, Piscataway, NJ, USA, 2009. IEEE Press.

[37] R. V. Kozinets. I want to believe: A netnography of the x-philes' subculture of consumption. *Advances in Consumer Research*, 24:470–475, 1997.

[38] R. V. Kozinets. The field behind the screen: Using netnography for marketing research in online communities. *Journal of Marketing Research*, 39(1):61–72, February 2002.

[39] S. Kumar, N. Agarwal, M. Lim, and H. Liu. Mapping socio-cultural dynamics in indonesian blogosphere. In *Proceedings of the Third International Conference on Computational Cultural Dynamics (ICCCD 2009)*, 2009.

[40] S. Kumar, R. Zafarani, M. Abbasi, G. Barbier, and H. Liu. Convergence of influential bloggers for topic discovery in the blogosphere. In S. K. Chai, J. Salerno, and P. Mabry, editors, *Social Computing and Behavior Modeling*, volume 6007 of *Lectures Notes in Computer Science*, pages 406–412, Springer, 2010.

[41] Y.-S. Kwon, S.-W. Kim, S. Park, S.-H. Lim, and J. B. Lee. The information diffusion model in the blog world. In *SNA-KDD '09: Proceedings of the 3rd Workshop on Social Network Mining and Analysis*, pages 1–9, New York, NY, USA, 2009. ACM.

[42] G. Lakshmanan and M. Oberhofer. Knowledge discovery in the blogosphere: Approaches and challenges. *Internet Computing, IEEE*, 14(2):24 –32, march-april 2010.

[43] D. Larose. *Discovering Knowledge in Data.* Wiley-Interscience, New York, 2005.

[44] H. Lauw, J. C. Shafer, R. Agrawal, and A. Ntoulas. Homophily in the digital world: A livejournal case study. *Internet Computing, IEEE*, 14(2):15 –23, march-april 2010.

[45] D. Lazer, A. Pentland, L. Adamic, S. Aral, A.-L. Barabasi, D. Brewer, N. Christakis, N. Contractor, J. Fowler, M. Gutmann, T. Jebara, G. King, M. Macy, D. Roy, and M. V. Alstyne. Computational social science. *Science*, 323:721–723, 2009.

[46] D. Liben-Nowell and J. Kleinberg. The link prediction problem for social networks. In *CIKM '03: Proceedings of the twelfth international conference on Information and knowledge management*, pages 556–559, New York, NY, USA, 2004. ACM.

[47] B. Liu. *Web Data Mining: Exploring Hyperlinks, Contents, and Usage Data*. Springer, Berlin, 2006.

[48] Z. Liu and L. Liu. Complex network property analysis of knowledge cooperation networks. pages 544 –547, may 2009.

[49] I.-C. Moon, Y.-M. Kim, H.-J. Lee, and A. Oh. Temporal issue trend identifications in blogs. volume 4, pages 619 –626, aug. 2009.

[50] F. M. R. Pardo and A. P. Padilla. Detecting blogs independently from the language and content. In *1st International Workshop on Mining Social Media (MSM09-CAEPIA09)*, 2009.

[51] E. Qualman. *Socialnomics*. Knopf Books for Young Readers, New York, 2009.

[52] J. Ritterman, M. Osborne, and E. Klein. Using prediction markets and twitter to predict swine flu pandemic. In F. M. Carrero, J. M. Gomez, B. Monsalve, P. Puertas, and J. C. a. Cortizo, editors, *Proceedings of the 1st International Workshop on Mining Social Media*, pages 9–17, 2009.

[53] D. Schuler. Social computing. *Commun. ACM*, 37(1):28–29, 1994.

[54] I. Steinwart. *Support Vector Machines*. Westview, Boulder, 2008.

[55] A. Stewart, L. Chen, R. Paiu, and W. Nejdl. Discovering information diffusion paths from blogosphere for online advertising. In *ADKDD '07: Proceedings of the 1st international workshop on Data mining and audience intelligence for advertising*, pages 46–54, New York, NY, USA, 2007. ACM.

[56] P.-N. Tan. *Introduction to Data Mining*. Pearson Addison Wesley, San Francisco, 2006.

[57] J. Tang, J. Sun, C. Wang, and Z. Yang. Social influence analysis in large-scale networks. In *KDD '09: Proceedings of the 15th ACM SIGKDD international conference on Knowledge discovery and data mining*, pages 807–816, New York, NY, USA, 2009. ACM.

[58] L. Tang and H. Liu. Scalable learning of collective behavior based on sparse social dimensions. In *CIKM '09: Proceeding of the 18th ACM conference on Information and knowledge management*, pages 1107–1116, New York, NY, USA, 2009. ACM.

[59] L. Tang and H. Liu. Toward collective behavior prediction via social dimension extraction. *Intelligent Systems, IEEE*, PP(99):1 –1, 2010.

[60] L. Tang, H. Liu, J. Zhang, N. Agarwal, and J. J. Salerno. Topic taxonomy adaptation for group profiling. *ACM Trans. Knowl. Discov. Data*, 1(4):1–28, January 2008.

[61] L. Tang, X. Wang, and H. Liu. Uncovering groups via heterogeneous interaction analysis. In *Data Mining, 2009. ICDM '09. Ninth IEEE International Conference on*, pages 503 –512, 6-9 2009.

[62] L. Tang, X. Wang, and H. Liu. Understanding emerging social structures — a group profiling approach. Technical report, School of Computing, Informatics, and Decision Systems Engineering, Arizona State University, 2010.

[63] B. Ulicny, M. Kokar, and C. Matheus. Metrics for monitoring a social-political blogosphere: A malaysian case study. *Internet Computing, IEEE*, 14(2):34 –44, march-april 2010.

[64] G. Vaynerchuk. *Crush It!: Why Now Is the Time to Cash in on Your Passion*. HarperCollins, 10 East 53rd Street, New York, NY 10022, 1st edition, 2009.

[65] F.-Y. Wang, K. M. Carley, D. Zeng, and W. Mao. Social computing: From social informatics to social intelligence. *Intelligent Systems, IEEE*, 22(2):79 –83, March-April 2007.

[66] J. Wang, Y. Luo, Y. Zhao, and J. Le. A survey on privacy preserving data mining. pages 111 –114, april 2009.

[67] S. Wasserman and K. Faust. *Social Network Analysis: Methods and Applications*. Cambridge University Press, 1994.

[68] M. Wesch. An anthropological introduction to youtube. Presentation at the Library of Congress/Electronic, June 2008. Contributors include and The Digital Ethnography Working Group at Kansas State University; Accessed on 22 Mar 2010.

[69] I. Witten and E. Frank. *Data Mining*. Morgan Kaufman, San Francisco, 2005.

[70] D. Zhou, I. Councill, H. Zha, and C. Giles. Discovering temporal communities from social network documents. In *Seventh IEEE International Conference on Data Mining*, pages 745 –750, Oct. 2007.

Chapter 13

TEXT MINING IN SOCIAL NETWORKS

Charu C. Aggarwal
IBM T. J. Watson Research Center
Hawthorne, NY 10532, USA
charu@us.ibm.com

Haixun Wang
Microsoft Research Asia
Beijing, China 100190
haixunw@microsoft.com

Abstract Social networks are rich in various kinds of contents such as text and multimedia. The ability to apply text mining algorithms effectively in the context of text data is critical for a wide variety of applications. Social networks require text mining algorithms for a wide variety of applications such as keyword search, classification, and clustering. While search and classification are well known applications for a wide variety of scenarios, social networks have a much richer structure both in terms of text and links. Much of the work in the area uses either purely the text content or purely the linkage structure. However, many recent algorithms use a combination of linkage and content information for mining purposes. In many cases, it turns out that the use of a combination of linkage and content information provides much more effective results than a system which is based purely on either of the two. This paper provides a survey of such algorithms, and the advantages observed by using such algorithms in different scenarios. We also present avenues for future research in this area.

Keywords: Text Mining, Social Networks

1. Introduction

Social networks are typically rich in text, because of a wide variety of methods by which users can contribute text content to the network. For example, typical social networks such as *Facebook* allow the creation of various text content such as wall posts, comments, and links to blog and web pages. Emails between different users can also be expressed as social networks, which can be mined for a variety of applications. For example, the well known *Enron email database* is often used in order to mine interesting connections between the different characters in the underlying database. Using interesting linkages within email and newsgroup databases in addition to the content [5, 8] often leads to qualitatively more effective results.

Social networks are rich in text, and therefore it is useful to design text mining tools for a wide variety of applications. While a variety of search and mining algorithms have been developed in the literature for text applications, social networks provide a special challenge, because the linkage structure provides guidance for mining in a variety of applications. Some examples of applications in which such guidance is available are as follows:

- **Keyword Search:** In the problem of keyword search, we specify a set of keywords, which are used to determine social network nodes which are relevant to a given query. In the problem of keyword search, we use both the content and the linkage behavior in order to perform the search. The broad idea is that text documents containing similar keywords are often linked together. Therefore, it is often useful to determine closely connected clusters of nodes in the social network which contain specific keywords. This problem is also related to the problem of *expertise search* [34] in social networks, in which we wish to determine the individuals in the social network with a particular kind of expertise. The problem is expertise search is discussed in detail in Chapter 8 of the book.

- **Classification:** In the problem of classification, the nodes in the social network are associated with labels. These labeled nodes are then used for classification purposes. A variety of algorithms are available for classification of text from content only. However, the presence of links often provides useful hints for the purpose of classification. For example, label propagation techniques can be combined with content-based classification in order to provide more effective results. This chapter discusses a number of such algorithms.

- **Clustering:** In the problem of clustering, we would like to determine sets of nodes which have similar content for the purposes of clustering. The linkage structure can also play a very useful role during such a clustering process. In many applications, linkage and content [53] can be combined together for the purposes of classification. This results in clustering which is of much better quality.

- **Linkage-based Cross Domain Learning:** Social networks contain a large amount of linked information between different kinds of objects such as text articles, tags, posts, images, and videos. This linkage information can be used in order to transfer knowledge across different kinds of links. We refer to this class of methods as *transfer learning*.

A common characteristic of the above problems is that they are defined in the content space, and are extensively studied by the text mining community. However, social networks can be considered linked networks, and therefore links can be used to enhance each of the above problems. It is important to note that these problems are not just defined in the context of social networks, but have also been studied *more generally* in the context of any linked network such as the World Wide Web. In fact, most of the earlier research on these problems has been performed more generally in the context of the web, which is also an example of a content-based linked network. Thus, this chapter deals more generally with the problem of combining text content analysis with link analysis; it applies *more generally* to a variety of web domains *including* social networks. Some of these problems also arise in the context of the XML domain, which can also be considered a content-based linked graph. For example, the problem of keyword search has been studied extensively in the context of the XML domain; however the techniques are quite useful for content and link-based keyword search even in the social network domain. Many of the techniques which are designed in these different domains are applicable to one another. We have included the study of this class of methods in this book because of its significant importance to the problem of social network analysis.

The linkage information in social networks also provides interesting hints, which can be adapted for problems such as transfer learning. In transfer learning, we attempt to use the knowledge which is learned in one domain to another domain with the use of bridges (or mappings) between different domains. These bridges may be in the form of similar class structure across the domains, dictionaries which define mappings between attributes (as in cross-lingual learning), or links in network based repositories. The links in a social network provide good bridging information which can be leveraged for the learning process [40]. In this chapter, we will provide a key overview of some of the techniques which are often utilized for linkage-based cross-domain learning.

The chapter is organized as follows. The next section will discuss algorithms for keyword search. In section 3, we will discuss algorithms for classification. Section 4 will discuss algorithms for clustering. Section 5 will study the problem of *transfer-learning*, as it relates to the social network domain. Section 6 contains the conclusions and summary.

2. Keyword Search

Keyword search provides a simple but user-friendly interface for information retrieval on the Web. It also proves to be an effective method for accessing structured data. Since many real life data sets are structured as tables, trees and graphs, keyword search over such data has become increasingly important and has attracted much research interest in both the database and the IR communities.

A social network may be considered as a massive graph, in which each node may contain a large amount of text data. We note that many informal forms of social networks such as blogs or paper-citation graphs also contain a large amount of text graph. Many of these graphs do not have any privacy restrictions in order to implement an effective search process. We would like to determine small groups of link-connected nodes which are related to a particular set of keywords. Even though keyword search is defined with respect to the text inside the nodes, we note that the linkage structure also plays an important role in determining the appropriate set of nodes. It is well known the text in linked entities such as the web are related, when the corresponding objects are linked. Thus, by finding groups of closely connected nodes which share keywords, it is generally possible to determine the qualitatively effective nodes. The problem is also related to that of *expertise location* [34] in social networks, in which we would like to determine groups of closely connected individuals with a particular kind of expertise. The problem of expertise search is discussed in detail in Chapter 8 of this book.

Because the underlying data assumes a graph structure, keyword search becomes much more complex than traditional keyword search over documents. The challenges lie in three aspects:

- **Query semantics**: Keyword search over a set of text documents has very clear semantics: A document satisfies a keyword query if it contains every keyword in the query. In our case, the entire dataset is often considered as a single graph, so the algorithms must work on a finer granularity and return subgraphs as answers. We must decide what subgraphs are qualified as answers. The qualification of a subgraph as a valid answer depends both upon the content in the document and the underlying linkage structure.

- **Ranking strategy**: For a given keyword query, it is likely that many subgraphs will satisfy the query, based on the query semantics in use. However, each subgraph has its own underlying graph structure, with subtle semantics that makes it different from other subgraphs that satisfy the query. Thus, we must take the graph structure into consideration and design ranking strategies that find most meaningful and relevant answers. This is not the case for content-based keyword search in which content-based objective functions can be defined in order to quantify the objective function.

- **Query efficiency**: Many real life graphs are extremely large. A major challenge for keyword search over graph data is query efficiency, which, to a large extent, hinges on the semantics of the query and the ranking strategy. Clearly, the ability to perform efficient search depends upon our ability to perform an effective traversal of the underlying graph structure.

2.1 Query Semantics and Answer Ranking

A query consists of a set of keywords $Q = \{k_1, k_2, \cdots, k_n\}$. We must first define what is a qualified answer to Q, and the goodness (the score) of the answer.

For tree structures such as XML, under the most common semantics, the goal is to find the *smallest* subtrees that contain the keywords. There are different ways to interpret the notion of *smallest*. Several algorithms [51, 27, 50] are based on the SLCA (smallest lowest common ancestor) semantics, which requires that an answer (a least common ancestor of nodes that contain all the keywords) does not have any descendent that is also an answer. XRank [21] adopts a different query semantics for keyword search. In XRank, answers consist of substrees that contain at least one occurrence of all of the query keywords, after excluding the sub-nodes that already contain all of the query keywords. Thus, the set of answers based on the SLCA semantics is a subset of answers qualified for XRank.

We can use similar semantics for keyword search over graphs. For this purpose, the answer must first form trees (embedded in the graph). In many graph search algorithms, including BANKS [7], the bidirectional algorithm [29], and BLINKS [23], a response or an answer to a keyword query is a minimal rooted tree T embedded in the graph that contains at least one node from each S_i, where S_i is the set of nodes that match the keyword k_i.

Next, we must define a measure for the "goodness" of each answer. An answer tree T is good if it is meaningful to the query, and the meaning of T lies in the tree structure, or more specifically, how the keyword nodes are connected through paths in T. The goodness measure adopted by BANKS and the bidirectional algorithm is as follows. An answer tree T is decomposed into edges and nodes, and score of T is the combined score of the edges and nodes of T. Specifically, each edge has a pre-defined weight, and default to 1. Given an answer tree T, for each keyword k_i, we use $s(T, k_i)$ to represent the sum of the edge weights on the path from the root of T to the leaf containing keyword k_i. Thus, the aggregated edge score is $E = \sum_i^n s(T, k_i)$. The nodes, on the other hand, are scored by their global importance or prestige, which is usually based on PageRank [10] random walk. Let N denote the aggregated score of nodes that contain keywords. The combined score of an answer tree is given by $s(T) = EN^\lambda$ where λ helps adjust the importance of edge and node scores [7, 29].

Query semantics and ranking strategies used in BLINKS [23] are similar to those of BANKS [7] and the bidirectional search [29]. But instead of using a measure such as $S(T) = EN^\lambda$ to find top-K answers, BLINKS requires that each of the top-K answer has a different root node, or in other words, for all answer trees rooted at the same node, only the one with the highest score is considered for top-K. This semantics guards against the case where a "hub" pointing to many nodes containing query keywords becomes the root for a huge number of answers. These answers overlap and each carries very little additional information from the rest. Given an answer (which is the best, or one of the best, at its root), users can always choose to further examine other answers with this root [23].

Unlike most keyword search on graph data approaches [7, 29, 23], ObjectRank [6] does not return answer trees or subgraphs containing keywords in the query, instead, for ObjectRank, an answer is simply a node that has high authority on the keywords in the query. Hence, a node that does not even contain a particular keyword in the query may still qualify as an answer as long as enough authority on that keyword has flown into that node (Imagine a node that represents a paper which does not contain keyword *OLAP*, but many important papers that contain keyword *OLAP* reference that paper, which makes it an authority on the topic of *OLAP*). To control the flow of authority in the graph, ObjectRank models *labeled* graphs: Each node u has a label $\lambda(u)$ and contains a set of keywords, and each edge e from u to v has a label $\lambda(e)$ that represents a relationship between u and v. For example, a node may be labeled as a *paper*, or a *movie*, and it contains keywords that describe the paper or the movie; a directed edge from a paper node to another paper node may have a label *cites*, etc. A keyword that a node contains directly gives the node certain authority on that keyword, and the authority flows to other nodes through edges connecting them. The amount or the rate of the outflow of authority from keyword nodes to other nodes is determined by the types of the edges which represent different semantic connections.

2.2 Keyword search over XML and relational data

Keyword search on XML data [19, 15, 21, 31] is a simpler problem than on schema-free graphs. In some cases, documents in social networks are expressed as XML documents as well. Therefore, it is interesting to explore this particular case.

XML data is mostly tree structured, where each node only has a single incoming path. This property has significant impact on query semantics and answer ranking, and it also provides great optimization opportunities in algorithm design [51].

It is straightforward to find subtrees that contain all the keywords. Let L_i be the set of nodes in the XML document that contain keyword k_i. If we pick one node n_i from each L_i, and form a subtree from these nodes, then the subtree will contain all the keywords. Thus, an answer to the query can be represented by $lca(n_1, \cdots, n_n)$, the lowest common ancestor of nodes $n_1, \cdots, n_n$ in the tree, where $n_i \in L_i$.

A keyword query may find a large number of answers, but they are not all equal due to the differences in the way they are embedded in the nested XML structure. Many approaches for keyword search on XML data, including XRank [21] and XSEarch [15], present a ranking method. A ranking mechanism takes into consideration several factors. For instance, more specific answers should be ranked higher than less specific answers. Both SLCA and the semantics adopted by XRank signify this consideration. Furthermore, keywords in an answer should appear *close* to each other, and closeness is interpreted as the the semantic distance defined over the XML embedded structure.

For relational data, SQL is the de-facto query language for accessing relational data. However, to use SQL, one must have knowledge about the schema of the relational data. This has become a hindrance for potential users to access tremendous amount of relational data.

Keyword search is a good alternative due to its ease of use. The challenges of applying keyword search on relational data come from the fact that in a relational database, information about a single entity is usually divided among several tables. This is resulted from the normalization principle, which is the design methodology of relational database schema.

Thus, to find entities that are relevant to a keyword query, the search algorithm has to join data from multiple tables. If we represent each table as a node, and each foreign key relationship as an edge between two nodes, then we obtain a graph, which allows us to convert the current problem to the problem of keyword search over graphs. However, there is the possibility of self-joins: that is, a table may contain a foreign key that references itself. More generally, there might be cycles in the graph, which means the size of the join is only limited by the size of the data. To avoid this problem, the search algorithm may adopt an upper bound to restrict the number of joins [28].

Two most well-known keyword search algorithm for relational data are DBXplorer [4] and DISCOVER [28]. They adopted new physical database design (including sophisticated indexing methods) to speed up keyword search over relational databases. Qin et al [41], instead, introduced a method that takes full advantage of the power of RDBMS and uses SQL to perform keyword search on relational data.

2.3 Keyword search over graph data

Keyword search over large, schema-free graphs faces the challenge of how to efficiently explore the graph structure and find subgraphs that contain all the keywords in the query. To measure the "goodness" of an answer, most approaches score each edge and node, and then aggregate the scores over the subgraph as a goodness measure [7, 29, 23]. Usually, an edge is scored by the strength of the connection, and a node is scored by its importance based on a PageRank like mechanism.

Graph keyword search algorithms can be classified into two categories. Algorithms in the first category finds matching subgraphs by exploring the graph link by link, without using any index of the graph. Representative algorithms in this category include BANKS [7] and the bidirectional search algorithm [29]. One drawback of these approaches is that they explore the graph blindly as they do not have a global picture of the graph structure, nor do they know the keyword distribution in the graph. Algorithms in the other category are index-based [23], and the index is used to guide the graph exploration, and support "forward-jumps" in the search.

2.3.1 Graph Exploration by Backward Search. Many keyword search algorithms try to find trees embedded in the graph so that similar query semantics for keyword search over XML data can be used. Thus, the problem is how to construct an embedded tree from keyword nodes in the graph. In the absence of any index that can provide graph connectivity information beyond a single hop, BANKS [7] answers a keyword query by exploring the graph starting from the nodes containing at least one query keyword – such nodes can be identified easily through an inverted-list index. This approach naturally leads to a *backward search* algorithm, which works as follows.

1 At any point during the backward search, let E_i denote the set of nodes that we know can reach query keyword k_i; we call E_i the *cluster* for k_i.

2 Initially, E_i starts out as the set of nodes O_i that directly contain k_i; we call this initial set the *cluster origin* and its member nodes *keyword nodes*.

3 In each search step, we choose an incoming edge to one of previously visited nodes (say v), and then follow that edge *backward* to visit its source node (say u); any E_i containing v now expands to include u as

well. Once a node is visited, all its incoming edges become known to the search and available for choice by a future step.

4 We have discovered an answer root x if, for each cluster E_i, either $x \in E_i$ or x has an edge to some node in E_i.

BANKS uses the following two strategies for choosing what nodes to visit next. For convenience, we define the distance from a node n to a set of nodes N to be the shortest distance from n to any node in N.

1 ***Equi-distance expansion in each cluster***: This strategy decides which node to visit for expanding a keyword. Intuitively, the algorithm expands a cluster by visiting nodes in order of increasing distance from the cluster origin. Formally, the node u to visit next for cluster E_i (by following edge $u \rightarrow v$ backward, for some $v \in E_i$) is the node with the shortest distance (among all nodes not in E_i) to O_i.

2 ***Distance-balanced expansion across clusters***: This strategy decides the frontier of which keyword will be expanded. Intuitively, the algorithm attempts to balance the distance between each cluster's origin to its frontier across all clusters. Specifically, let (u, E_i) be the node-cluster pair such that $u \notin E_i$ and the distance from u to O_i is the shortest possible. The cluster to expand next is E_i.

He et al. [23] investigated the optimality of the above two strategies introduced by BANKS [7]. They proved the following result with regard to the first strategy, *equi-distance expansion of each cluster* (the complete proof can be found in [24]):

THEOREM 13.1 *An optimal backward search algorithm must follow the strategy of equi-distance expansion in each cluster.*

However, the investigation [23] showed that the second strategy, *distance-balanced expansion across clusters*, is not optimal and may lead to poor performance on certain graphs. Figure 13.1 shows one such example. Suppose that $\{k_1\}$ and $\{k_2\}$ are the two cluster origins. There are many nodes that can reach k_1 through edges with a small weight (1), but only one edge into k_2 with a large weight (100). With distance-balanced expansion across clusters, we would not expand the k_2 cluster along this edge until we have visited all nodes within distance 100 to k_1. It would have been unnecessary to visit many of these nodes had the algorithm chosen to expand the k_2 cluster earlier.

2.3.2 Graph Exploration by Bidirectional Search. To address the problem shown in Figure 13.1, Kacholia et al. [29] proposed a *bidirectional search* algorithm, which has the option of exploring the graph by following

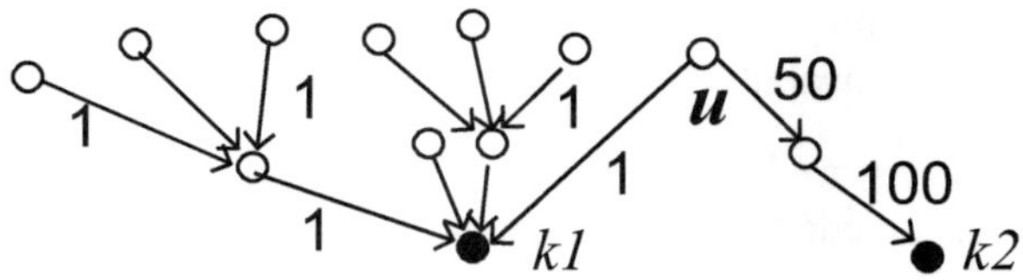

Figure 13.1. Distance-balanced expansion across clusters may perform poorly.

forward edges as well. The rationale is that, for example, in Figure 13.1, if the algorithm is allowed to explore forward from node u towards k_2, we can identify u as an answer root much faster.

To control the order of expansion, the bidirectional search algorithm prioritizes nodes by heuristic *activation factors* (roughly speaking, PageRank with decay), which intuitively estimate how likely nodes can be roots of answer trees. In the bidirectional search algorithm, nodes matching keywords are added to the iterator with an initial activation factor computed as:

$$a_{u,i} = \frac{nodePrestige(u)}{|S_i|}, \forall u \in S_i \qquad (13.1)$$

where S_i is the set of nodes that match keyword i. Thus, nodes of high prestige will have a higher priority for expansion. But if a keyword matches a large number of nodes, the nodes will have a lower priority. The activation factor is spread from keyword nodes to other nodes. Each node v spreads a fraction μ of the received activation to its neighbors, and retains the remaining $1 - \mu$ fraction.

As a result, keyword search in Figure 13.1 can be performed more efficiently. The bidirectional search will start from the keyword nodes (dark solid nodes). Since keyword node k_1 has a large fanout, all the nodes pointing to k_1 (including node u) will receive a small amount of activation. On the other hand, the node pointing to k_2 will receive most of the activation of k_2, which then spreads to node u. Thus, node u becomes the most activated node, which happens to be the root of the answer tree.

While this strategy is shown to perform well in multiple scenarios, it is difficult to provide any worst-case performance guarantee. The reason is that activation factors are heuristic measures derived from general graph topology and parts of the graph already visited. They do not accurately reflect the likelihood of reaching keyword nodes through an unexplored region of the graph within a reasonable distance. In other words, without additional connectivity information, forward expansion may be just as aimless as backward expansion [23].

2.3.3 Index-based Graph Exploration. The effectiveness of forward and backward expansions hinges on the structure of the graph and the distribution of keywords in the graph. However, both forward and backward expansions explore the graph link by link, which means the search algorithms do not have knowledge of either the structure of the graph nor the distribution of keywords in the graph. If we create an index structure to store the keyword reachability information in advance, we can avoid aimless exploration on the graph and improve the performance of keyword search. BLINKS [23] is designed based on this intuition.

BLINKS makes two contributions: First, it proposes a new, *cost-balanced* strategy for controlling expansion across clusters, with a provable bound on its worst-case performance. Second, it uses indexing to support forward jumps in search. Indexing enables it to determine whether a node can reach a keyword and what the shortest distance is, thereby eliminating the uncertainty and inefficiency of step-by-step forward expansion.

Cost-balanced expansion across clusters. Intuitively, BLINKS attempts to balance the number of accessed nodes (i.e., the search cost) for expanding each cluster. Formally, the cluster E_i to expand next is the cluster with the smallest cardinality.

This strategy is intended to be combined with the equi-distance strategy for expansion within clusters: First, BLINKS chooses the smallest cluster to expand, then it chooses the node with the shortest distance to this cluster's origin to expand.

To establish the optimality of an algorithm A employing these two expansion strategies, let us consider an optimal "oracle" backward search algorithm P. As shown in Theorem 13.1, P must also do equi-distance expansion within each cluster. The additional assumption here is that P "magically" knows the right amount of expansion for each cluster such that the total number of nodes visited by P is minimized. Obviously, P is better than the best practical backward search algorithm we can hope for. Although A does not have the advantage of the oracle algorithm, BLINKS gives the following theorem (the complete proof can be found in [24]) which shows that A is m-optimal, where m is the number of query keywords. Since most queries in practice contain very few keywords, the cost of A is usually within a constant factor of the optimal algorithm.

THEOREM 13.2 *The number of nodes accessed by A is no more than m times the number of nodes accessed by P, where m is the number of query keywords.*

Index-based Forward Jump. The BLINKS algorithm [23] leverages the new search strategy (*equi-distance* plus *cost-balanced* expansions) as well as indexing to achieve good query performance. The index structure consists of two parts.

- **Keyword-node lists** L_{KN}. BLINKS pre-computes, for each keyword, the shortest distances from every node to the keyword (or, more precisely, to any node containing this keyword) in the data graph. For a keyword w, $L_{KN}(w)$ denotes the list of nodes that can reach keyword w, and these nodes are ordered by their distances to w. In addition to other information used for reconstructing the answer, each entry in the list has two fields $(dist, node)$, where $dist$ is the shortest distance between $node$ and a node containing w.

- **Node-keywordmap** M_{NK}. BLINKS pre-computes, for each node u, the shortest graph distance from u to every keyword, and organize this information in a hash table. Given a node u and a keyword w, $M_{NK}(u, w)$ returns the shortest distance from u to w, or ∞ if u cannot reach any node that contains w. In fact, the information in M_{NK} can be derived from L_{KN}. The purpose of introducing M_{NK} is to reduce the linear time search over L_{KN} for the shortest distance between u and w to $O(1)$ time search over M_{NK}.

The search algorithm can be regarded as index-assisted backward and forward expansion. Given a keyword query $Q = \{k_1, \cdots, k_n\}$, for backward expansion, BLINKS uses a cursor to traverse each keyword-node list $L_{KN}(k_i)$. By construction, the list gives the equi-distance expansion order in each cluster. Across clusters, BLINKS picks a cursor to expand next in a round-robin manner, which implements cost-balanced expansion among clusters. These two together ensure optimal backward search. For forward expansion, BLINKS uses the node-keyword map M_{NK} in a direct fashion. Whenever BLINKS visits a node, it looks up its distance to other keywords. Using this information, it can immediately determine if the root of an answer is found.

The index L_{KN} and M_{NK} are defined over the entire graph. Each of them contains as many as $N \times K$ entries, where N is the number of nodes, and K is the number of distinct keywords in the graph. In many applications, K is on the same scale as the number of nodes, so the space complexity of the index comes to $O(N^2)$, which is clearly infeasible for large graphs. To solve this problem, BLINKS partitions the graph into multiple blocks, and the L_{KN} and M_{NK} index for each block, as well as an additional index structure to assist graph exploration across blocks.

2.3.4 The ObjectRank Algorithm. Instead of returning sub-graphs that contain all the keywords, ObjectRank [6] applies authority-based ranking to keyword search on labeled graphs, and returns nodes having high authority with respect to all keywords. To certain extent, ObjectRank is similar to BLINKS [23], whose query semantics prescribes that all top-K answer trees have different root nodes. Still, BLINKS returns sub-graphs as answers.

Recall that the bidirectional search algorithm [29] assigns activation factors to nodes in the graph to guide keyword search. Activation factors originate at nodes containing the keywords and propagate to other nodes. For each keyword node u, its activation factor is weighted by $nodePrestige(u)$ (Eq. 13.1), which reflects the importance or authority of node u. Kacholia et al. [29] did not elaborate on how to derive $nodePrestige(u)$. Furthermore, since graph edges in [29] are all the same, to spread the activation factor from a node u, it simply divides u's activation factor by u's fanout.

Similar to the activation factor, in ObjectRank [6], authority originates at nodes containing the keywords and flows to other nodes. Furthermore, nodes and edges in the graphs are labeled, giving graph connections semantics that controls the amount or the rate of the authority flow between two nodes.

Specifically, ObjectRank assumes a labeled graph G is associated with some predetermined schema information. The schema information decides the rate of authority transfer from a node labeled u_G, through an edge labeled e_G, and to a node labeled v_G. For example, authority transfers at a fixed rate from a *person* to a *paper* through an edge labeled *authoring*, and at another fixed rate from a *paper* to a *person* through an edge labeled *authoring*. The two rates are potentially different, indicating that authority may flow at a different rate backward and forward. The schema information, or the rate of authority transfer, is determined by domain experts, or by a trial and error process.

To compute node authority with regard to every keyword, ObjectRank computes the following:

- **Rates of authority transfer through graph edges.** For every edge $e = (u \rightarrow v)$, ObjectRank creates a forward authority transfer edge $e^f = (u \rightarrow v)$ and a backward authority transfer edge $e^b = (v \rightarrow u)$. Specifically, the authority transfer edges e^f and e^b are annotated with rates $\alpha(e^f)$ and $\alpha(e^b)$:

$$\alpha(e^f) = \begin{cases} \frac{\alpha(e^f_G)}{OutDeg(u,e^f_G)} & \text{if } OutDeg(u, e^f_G) > 0 \\ 0 & \text{if } OutDeg(u, e^f_G) = 0 \end{cases} \quad (13.2)$$

  where $\alpha(e^f_G)$ denotes the fixed authority transfer rate given by the schema, and $OutDeg(u, e^f_G)$ denotes the number of outgoing nodes from u, of type e^f_G. The authority transfer rate $\alpha(e^b)$ is defined similarly.

- **Node authorities.** ObjectRank can be regarded as an extension to PageRank [10]. For each node v, ObjectRank assigns a global authority denoted by $ObjectRank^G(v)$ that is independent of the keyword query. The global $ObjectRank^G$ is calculated using the random surfer model, which is similar to PageRank. In addition, for each keyword w and each node v, ObjectRank integrates authority transfer rates in Eq 13.2 with PageRank to calculate a keyword-specific ranking $ObjectRank^w(v)$:

$$ObjectRank^w(v) = d \times \sum_{e=(u \rightarrow v) or (v \rightarrow u)} \alpha(e) \times ObjectRank^w(u) + \frac{1-d}{|S(w)|} \tag{13.3}$$

where $S(w)$ is s the set of nodes that contain the keyword w, and d is the damping factor that determines the portion of ObjectRank that a node transfers to its neighbours as opposed to keeping to itself [10]. The final ranking of a node v is the combination combination of $ObjectRank^G(v)$ and $ObjectRank^w(v)$.

3. Classification Algorithms

The problem of classification has been widely studied in the text mining literature. Some common algorithms which are often used for content-based text classification are the Naive Bayes classifier [36], TFIDF classifier [30] and Probabilistic Indexing classifier [20] respectively. A common tool kit used for classification is Rainbow [37], which contains a variety of different classifiers. Most of the classification algorithms directly use the text content in order to relate the content in the document to the class label.

In the context of social networks, we assume that the nodes in the social network are associated with labels, and each node may contain a certain amount of text content. In the case of social networks, a number of additional challenges arise in the context of text classification. These challenges are as follows:

- Social networks contain a much larger and non-standard vocabulary, as compared to more standard collections such as news collections. This is because of the greater diversity in authorship both in terms of the number and style of different authors.

- The labels in social networks may often be quite sparse. In many cases, some of the label values may be unknown. Thus, social network data is often much more noisy than other standard text collections.

- A particularly useful property of social networks is that they may contain links which can be used in order to guide the classification process. Such links can be very helpful in determining how the labels may be propagated between the different nodes. While pure link-based classification [44, 46, 48] is a well known technique which works effectively in a variety of scenarios, the use of content can greatly improve the effectiveness of the classification process.

The earliest work on combining linkage and content information for classification was discussed in [13]. This technique was designed in the context of the web, though the general idea can be easily extended to the case of social networks. In this paper, a hypertext categorization method was proposed, which uses the content and labels of neighboring web pages for the classification process. When the labels of all the nearest neighbors are available, then a Bayesian method can be adapted easily for classification purposes. Just as the presence of a word in a document can be considered a Bayesian feature for a text classifier, the presence of a link between the target page, and a page (for which the label is known) can be considered a feature for the classifier. The real challenge arises when the labels of all the nearest neighbors are not available. In such cases, a relaxation labeling method is proposed in order to perform the classification. Two methods have been proposed in this work:

- **Completely Supervised Case of Radius one Enhanced Linkage Analysis:** In this case, it is assumed that all the neighboring class labels are known. In such a case, a Bayesian approach is utilized in order to treat the labels on the nearest neighbors as features for classification purposes. In this case, the linkage information is the sole information which is used for classification purposes.

- **When the class labels of the nearest neighbors are not known:** In this case, an iterative approach is used for combining text and linkage based classification. Rather than using the pre-defined labels (which are not available), we perform a first labeling of the neighboring documents with the use of document content. These labels are then used to classify the label of the target document, with the use of *both* the local text and the class labels of the neighbors. This approach is used iteratively for re-defining the labels of both the target document and its neighbors until convergence is achieved.

The conclusion from the work in [13] is that a combination of text and linkage based classification always improves the accuracy of a text classifier. Even when none of the neighbors of the document have known classes, it seemed to be always beneficial to add link information to the classification process. When the class labels of all the neighbors are known, then the advantages of using the scheme seem to be quite significant.

An additional idea in the paper is that of the use of *bridges* in order to further improve the classification accuracy. The core idea in the use of a bridge is the use of *2-hop* propagation for link-based classification. The results with the use of such an approach are somewhat mixed, as the accuracy seems to reduce with an increasing number of hops. The work in [13] shows results on a number of different kinds of data sets such as the *Reuters database*, *US patent database*, and *Yahoo!*. We note that the *Reuters database* contains the least amount of noise, and pure text classifiers can do a good job. On the other hand, the *US patent database* and the *Yahoo! database* contain an increasing amount of noise which reduces the accuracy of text classifiers. An interesting observation in [13] was that a scheme which simply absorbed the neighbor text into the current document performed *significantly worse* than a scheme which was based on pure text-based classification. This is because there are often significant cross-boundary linkages between topics, and such linkages are able to confuse the classifier.

A second method which has been used for text and link based classification is the utilization of the graph regularization approach for text and link based classification [46]. The work presents a risk minimization formulation for learning from both text and graph structures. This is motivated by the problem of collective inference for hypertext document categorization. More details on the approach may be found in [46]. While much of the work in this paper as well as the earlier work in [13] is defined in the context of web data, this is also naturally applicable to the case of social networks which can be considered an interlinked set of nodes containing text content.

There is also some work which deals explicitly with social-network like text interactions. A classic example of this is a set of emails which are exchange between one or more different users. Typically, the emails in a particular "thread" may be considered to be linked based on the structure of the thread. Alternatively, the exchanges in the email between the different users correspond to the links between the different emails. An important problem which arises in the context of email classification is that of the classification of *speech acts* in email. Some examples of speech acts in email could be *request*, *deliver*, *commit*, and *propose*. One method for performing the classification is to use purely the *content* of the email for classification purposes [16]. An important observation in later work is that successive email exchanges between different users can be considered links, which can be utilized for more effective classification. This is because the speech acts in different emails may not be independent of one another, but may significantly influence each other. For example, an email asking for a "request" for a meeting may be followed by one which "commits" to a meeting.

The work in [11] proposes a method for collective classification, which tries to model the relationships between different kinds of acts in the form of a graphical stricture. The links in this graphical structure are leveraged in order to improve the effectiveness of the classification process. The work in [11] proposes an iterative collective classification algorithm. This algorithm us closely related to the implementation of a Dependency Network [25]. Dependency networks are probabilistic graphical models in which the full joint distribution of the network is approximated with a set of conditional distributions that can be learned independently. These probability distributions are calculated for each node given its parent nodes. In the context of an email network, the email messages are the nodes, and the dependencies are the threads which relate the different nodes. The work in [11] shows that the use of linkage analysis provides a much more effective classification analysis, because the class labels between the different nodes are naturally connected by their corresponding linkages.

4. Clustering Algorithms

The problem of clustering arises quite often in the context of node clustering of social networks. The problem of network clustering is closely related to the traditional problem of graph partitioning [32], which tries to isolated groups of nodes which are closely connected to one another. The problem of graph partitioning is NP-hard and often does not scale very well to large networks. The Kerninghan-Lin algorithm [32] uses an iterative approach in which we start off with a feasible partitioning and repeatedly interchange the nodes between the partitions in order to improve the quality of the clustering. We note that that this approach requires random access to the nodes and edges in the underlying graph. This can be a considerable challenge for large-scale social networks which are stored on disk. When the social-network is stored on disk, the random access to the disk makes the underlying algorithms quite inefficient. Some recent work has designed methods for link-based clustering in massive networks [9, 12, 14, 33], though these methods are not specifically designed for the case of disk-resident data. Such methods are typically designed for problems such as community detection [39, 38] and information network clustering [9, 33]. These methods are often more sensitive to the evolution of the underlying network, which is quite common in social networks because of the constant addition and deletion of users from the network. Some recent work [2] has also been proposed for clustering graph streams, which are common representations of different kinds of edge-based activity in social network analysis.

The work discussed above uses only the structure of the network for the clustering process. A natural question arises, as to whether one can improve the quality of clustering by using the text content in the nodes of the social network. The problem of clustering has been widely studied by the text mining community. A variety of text clustering algorithms have been proposed by the data mining and text mining community [3, 18, 42], which use a number of variants of traditional clustering algorithms for multi-dimensional data. Most of these methods are variants of the k-means method in which we start off with a set of k seeds and build the clusters iteratively around these seeds. The seeds and cluster membership are iteratively defined with respect to each other, until we converge to an effective solution. Some of these methods are also applicable to the case of *dynamic text data*, as is the case with social networks. In particular, the methods in [3, 47] can be used in order to cluster text data streams. These methods are designed on the basis of k-means methods which can use non-iterative variants of the k-means methods for clustering streams. Such techniques can be useful for the dynamic scenarios which can arise in the context of social networks. However, these algorithms tend to be at the other end of the spectrum in terms of preserving only content information and no linkage information. Ideally, we would like to use clustering algorithms which preserve both content and linkage information.

The work in [53] proposes a method which can perform the clustering with the use of both content and structure information. Specifically the method constructs a new graph which takes into account both the structure and attribute information. Such a graph has two kinds of edges: *structure edges* from the original graph, and *attribute edges*, which are based on the nature of the attributes in the different nodes. A random walk approach is used over this graph in order to define the underlying clusters. Each edge is associated with a weight, which is used in order to control the probability of the random walk across the different nodes. These weights are updated during an iterative process, and the clusters and the weights are successively used in order to refine each other. It has been shown in [53] that the weights and the clusters will naturally converge, as the clustering process progresses. While the technique is applied to multi-relational attributes, it can also used in a limited way for text attributes, especially when a limited subset of keywords is used. It has been shown in [53] how the method can be used in the context of blog and bibliographic networks, when a number of relational and keyword-based attributes are also utilized for the clustering process. It has been shown in [53] that the combination of structural and attribute information can be used for a more effective clustering process.

A method for leveraging both content and linkage information in the clustering process has been proposed in [43]. While the work in [43] addresses the problem of topic modeling rather than clustering, this process also provides a generative model, which can be used for the purpose of a soft clustering of the documents. A graphical model was proposed to describe a multi-layered generative model. At the top layer of this model, a multivariate Markov Random Field for topic distribution random variables for each document is defined. This is useful for modeling the dependency relationships among documents over the network structure. At the bottom layer, the traditional topic model is used in order to model the generation of text for each document. Thus, the combination of the two layers provides a way to model the relationships of the text and the structure with one another. Methods are proposed to decide the topic structure, as well as the number of topics. The method essentially uses an LDA model in order to construct a topic space, in which the clustering can be performed. This model uses both structure and content information for the modeling process. It has been shown in [43] that this integrated approach is much more useful than an approach which relies purely on the content of underlying documents. In general, model-based clustering methods are very effective, because of being able to model different kinds of data by introducing different model parameters. Another model-based method which has specifically been proposed in the context of social networks is discussed in [22]. The main idea in this method is the use of a latent position cluster model, in which the probability of a tie between two nodes depends on the distance between them in an implicit Euclidean social space, and the location of these nodes in the latent social space which is defined with the use of a mixture of cluster-based distributions. The method in [22] is general enough to incorporate different kinds of attributes in the clustering process. For example, one can associated linkage-behavior and keyword-behavior with different kinds of attributes and apply this approach in order to design an effective clustering. While the work in [22] has specifically not been used with the use of text-based content, the techniques proposed are quite applicable to this scenario, because of the approach used in the paper, which can embed arbitrary data in arbitrary Euclidean social spaces. We note that such latent-space approaches are useful not just for the problem of clustering, but as a tool which can be used for *representation* of the network in an Euclidean space, which is more amenable to data mining problems. A more general piece of work on the latent-space approach may be found in [26].

A major challenge which arises in the context of social networks is that many such networks are heterogeneous, and this makes it difficult to design algorithms which can determine the distances between the nodes in a more robust way. For example, bibliographic networks are classic examples of heterogeneous networks. Such networks contain different kinds of nodes corresponding to authors, keywords, conferences or papers. In general, information networks are a more generalized notion of social networks, which may contain nodes which correspond not just to actors, but also to other kinds of entities which are related to actors. Such networks are far more challenging to cluster as compared to the vanilla social network scenario, because the different kinds of entities may contain different objects such as text, images, and links. A major challenge in the field is to design unified clustering methods which can integrate different kinds of content in the clustering process.

5. Transfer Learning in Heterogeneous Networks

A closely related problem in this domain is that of *transfer learning.* Our discussion in this chapter has so far focussed on how content can be used in order to enhance the effectiveness of typical problems such as clustering or classification in the context of social networks. In this section, we will study how the link in an information network can be used in order to perform cross-domain learning in traditional data mining problems such as clustering and classification. The primary idea in transfer learning is that data mining problems have varying levels of difficulty in different domains either because of lack of data availability or representational issues, and it is often useful to *transfer* the knowledge from one domain to another with the use of mappings. The links in social networks can be used in order to define such mappings. A general survey of transfer-learning methods may be found in [40].

Many social networks contain *heterogeneous content*, such as text, media and images. In particular, text is a common content in such networks. For example, many social media such as *Flickr* contain images which are annotated with keywords. The problem of transfer learning is motivated by the fact that different kinds of content may be more or less challenging for the learning process. This is because different amounts of training data may be available to a user in different domains. For example, it is relatively easy to obtain training data for text content, as well as mapping the features to different classes. This may however not be quite as true in the case of the image domain in which there may be fewer standardized collections. Therefore, a natural approach is to use either the *links in the social network between text and images* or the *implicit links* in terms of annotations as a mapping for the transfer learning process. Such links can be used as a bridge to learn the underlying mapping, and use it for the problem of classification.

A similar observation applies to the case of cross-lingual classification problems. This is because different amounts of training data is available for the documents in different languages. A lot of labeled text content may be available for content in the english language. On the other hand, this may not be the case for other languages such as chinese web pages. However, there may often be a number of links between the documents in the different languages. Such links can be used in order to learn the mappings and use it for the classification process.

A tremendous amount of text-to-image mapping information exists in the form of tag information in social media sites such as *Flickr*. It has been shown in [17], that such information can be effectively leveraged for transfer-learning. The key idea is to construct a mapping between the text and the images with the use of the tags, and then use PLSA in order to construct a latent space which can be used for the transfer process. It has been shown in [17] that such an approach can be used very effectively for transfer learning. A related work [54] discusses how to create connections between images and text with the use of tag data. It shows how such links can be used more effectively for the classification process. These techniques have also been exploited for the problem of image clustering [52]. The work in [52] collects annotated image data from the social web, and uses it in order to construct a text to image mapping. The algorithm is referred to as aPLSA (Annotated Probabilistic Latent Semantic Analysis). The key idea is to unify two different kinds of latent semantic analysis in order to create a bridge between the text and images. The first kind of technique performs PLSA analysis on the target images, which are converted to an image instance-to-feature co-occurrence matrix. The second kind of PLSA is applied to the annotated image data from social Web, which is converted into a text-to-image feature co-occurrence matrix. In order to unify those two separate PLSA models, these two steps are done simultaneously with common latent variables used as a bridge linking them. It has been shown in [52] that such a bridging approach leads to much better clustering results. Clustering is a useful tool for web-based or social-network based image search. Such search results are often hindered by polysemy in textual collections, in which the same work may mean multiple things. For example, the word "jaguar" could either refer to an animal or a car. In such cases, the results of the query are ambiguous as well. A major motivation for clustering is that such ambiguities can be more effectively resolved. In particular when textual features are associated with images, and these are used simultaneously [35] for the clustering process, the overall result is much more effective. Some of the available techniques in the literature use spectral clustering on the distance matrix built from a multi-modal feature set (containing both text and image information) in order to get a better feature representation. The improved quality of the representation leads to much better clustering results. Furthermore, when the number of images is very small, traditional clustering algorithms do not work very well either. This approach does not work too well, when only a small amount of data is available on the association between image and text. A different work in [52] treats this as a heterogeneous transfer learning problem by leveraging social annotation information from sites such as *Flickr*. Such sites contain a lot of information in the form of feedback from different users. The auxiliary data is used in order to improve the quality of the underlying latent representation and the corresponding clustering process in work discussed in [52]. In general, social networks provide tremendous information about the data of different types, which can be leveraged in order to enable an effective learning process across the different domains. This area is still in its infancy, and it is expected that future research will lead to further advances in such linkage-based techniques.

6. Conclusions and Summary

In this chapter, we presented a variety of content-based mining algorithms, which combine text and links in order to design more effective methods for a wide variety of problems such as search, clustering, and classification. In many data domains, links encode a tremendous amount of semantic information which can be leveraged in order to improve the effectiveness of a variety of different algorithms. A number of challenges remain for this particular problem domain. These challenges are as follows:

- Many of the techniques are not designed to be scalable for massive data sets. This may be a challenge, because many network data sets are inherently massive in nature.

- The techniques need to be designed for dynamic data sets. This is especially important because the content and links in a social network are highly dynamic. Therefore, it is important to be able to quickly re-adjust the models in order to take into account the changing characteristics of the underlying data.

- Many of the techniques are designed for homogeneous networks in which the nodes are of a single type. Many of the networks are inherently heterogeneous, in which the nodes may be of different types. For example, social networks contain nodes corresponding to individuals, their posts, their blogs, and the use of such other content. The ability to use such information in the knowledge discovery process can be an advantage in many scenarios.

A considerable research opportunity also exists in the area of transfer learning. Transfer learning methods are dependent upon the ability to define *bridges* or *mappings* between different domains for the learning process. The links in a social network can be leveraged in order to define such bridges. There has been some recent work in leveraging the text annotations in social media for the problem of transfer learning of images. Research in this area is still in its infancy, and considerable scope exists to improve both the effectiveness and the efficiency of the underlying algorithms.

Acknowledgements

Research was sponsored by the Army Research Laboratory and was accomplished under Cooperative Agreement Number W911NF-09-2-0053. The views and conclusions contained in this document are those of the authors and should not be interpreted as representing the official policies, either expressed or implied, of the Army Research Laboratory or the U.S. Government. The U.S. Government is authorized to reproduce and distribute reprints for Government purposes notwithstanding any copyright notation here on.

References

[1] C. C. Aggarwal, H. Wang (ed.) Managing and Mining Graph Data, *Springer*, 2010.

[2] C. C. Aggarwal, Y. Zhao, P. Yu. On Clustering Graph streams, *SIAM Conference on Data Mining*, 2010.

[3] C. C. Aggarwal, P. S. Yu. A Framework for Clustering Massive Text and Categorical Data Streams, *SIAM Conference on Data Mining*, 2006.

[4] S. Agrawal, S. Chaudhuri, G. Das. DBXplorer: A system for keyword-based search over relational databases. *ICDE Conference*, 2002.

[5] R. Agrawal, S. Rajagopalan, R. Srikant, Y. Xu. Mining Newsgroups using Networks arising from Social Behavior. *WWW Conference*, 2003.

[6] A. Balmin, V. Hristidis, and Y. Papakonstantinou. ObjectRank: Authority-based keyword search in databases. In *VLDB*, pages 564–575, 2004.

[7] G. Bhalotia, C. Nakhe, A. Hulgeri, S. Chakrabarti, S. Sudarshan. Keyword searching and browsing in databases using BANKS. *ICDE Conference*, 2002.

[8] C. Bird, A. Gourley, P. Devanbabu, M. Gertz, A. Swaminathan. Mining Email Social Networks, *MSR*, 2006.

[9] D. Bortner, J. Han. Progressive Clustering of Networks Using Structure-Connected Order of Traversal, *ICDE Conference*, 2010.

[10] S. Brin and L. Page. The anatomy of a large-scale hypertextual Web search engine. *Computer networks and ISDN systems*, 30(1-7):107–117, 1998.

[11] V. Carvalho, W. Cohen. On the Collective Classification of Email "Speech Acts", *ACM SIGIR Conference*, 2005.

[12] D. Chakrabarti, R. Kumar, A. Tomkins. Evolutionary clustering. *KDD Conference*, 2006.

[13] S. Chakrabarti, B. Dom, P. Indyk. Enhanced Hypertext Categorization using Hyperlinks, *ACM SIGMOD Conference*, 1998.

[14] Y. Chi, X. Song, D. Zhou, K. Hino, B. L. Tseng. Evolutionary spectral clustering by incorporating temporal smoothness. *ACM KDD Conference*, 2007.

[15] S. Cohen, J. Mamou, Y. Kanza, Y. Sagiv. XSEarch: A semantic search engine for XML. *VLDB Conference*, 2003.

[16] W. Cohen, V. Carvalho, T. Mitchell, Learning to Classify Email into ÂŞSpeech ActsÂŤ. *Conference on Empirical Methods in Natural Language Processing*, 2004.

[17] W. Dai, Y. Chen, G. Xue, Q. Yang, Y. Yu. Translated Learning: Transfer Learning across different Feature Spaces. *NIPS Conference*, 2008.

[18] D. R. Cutting, J. O. Pedersen, D. R. Karger, J. W. Tukey. Scatter/Gather: A Cluster-based Approach to Browsing Large Document Collections, *ACM SIGIR Conference*, 1992.

[19] D. Florescu, D. Kossmann, and I. Manolescu. Integrating keyword search into XML query processing. *Comput. Networks*, 33(1-6):119–135, 2000.

[20] N. Fuhr, C. Buckley. Probabilistic Document Indexing from Relevance Feedback Data. *SIGIR Conference*, pages 45–61, 1990.

[21] L. Guo, F. Shao, C. Botev, J. Shanmugasundaram. XRANK: ranked keyword search over XML documents. *ACM SIGMOD Conference*, pages 16–27, 2003.

[22] M. Handcock, A Raftery, J. Tantrum. Model-based Clustering for Social Networks. *Journal of the Royal Statistical Society*, 170(2), pp. 301–354, 2007.

[23] H. He, H. Wang, J. Yang, P. S. Yu. BLINKS: Ranked keyword searches on graphs. *SIGMOD Conference*, 2007.

[24] H. He, H. Wang, J. Yang, and P. S. Yu. BLINKS: Ranked keyword searches on graphs. Technical report, Duke CS Department, 2007.

[25] D. Heckerman, D. Chickering, C. Meek, R. Rounthwaite, C. Kadie. Dependency networks for inference, collaborative filtering and data visualization. *Journal of Machine Learning Research*, 1, pp. 49–75, 2000.

[26] P. Hoff, A. Raftery, M. Handcock. Latent Space Approaches to Social Network Analysis, *Technical Report No. 399*, University of Washington at Seattle, 2001.

[27] V. Hristidis, N. Koudas, Y. Papakonstantinou, D. Srivastava. Keyword proximity search in XML trees. *IEEE Transactions on Knowledge and Data Engineering*, 18(4):525–539, 2006.

[28] V. Hristidis, Y. Papakonstantinou. Discover: Keyword search in relational databases. *VLDB Conference*, 2002.

[29] V. Kacholia, S. Pandit, S. Chakrabarti, S. Sudarshan, R. Desai, H. Karambelkar. Bidirectional expansion for keyword search on graph databases. *VLDB Conference*, 2005.

[30] T. Joachims. A Probabilistic Analysis of the Rocchio Algorithm with TFIDF for Text Categorization. *ICML Conference*, pages 143–151, 1997.

[31] R. Kaushik, R. Krishnamurthy, J. F. Naughton, and R. Ramakrishnan. On the integration of structure indexes and inverted lists. In *SIGMOD*, pages 779–790, 2004.

[32] B. W. Kernighan, S. Lin, An efficient heuristic procedure for partitioning graphs. *Bell Systems Technical Journal* (49) pp. 291ÂŰ-307, 1970.

[33] M. S. Kim, J. Han. A Particle-and-Density Based Evolutionary Clustering Method for Dynamic Networks. *PVLDB*, 2(1): pp. 622–633, 2009.

[34] T. Lappas, K. Liu, E. Terzi. Finding a Team of Experts in Social Networks. *ACM KDD Conference*, 2009.

[35] N. Loeff, C. O. Alm, D. A. Forsyth. Discriminating image senses by clustering with multimodal features. *ACL Conference*, pp. 547ÂŰ-554, 2006.

[36] M. Maron. Automatic Indexing: An Experimental Inquiry. *J. ACM*, 8(3), pages 404-417, 1961.

[37] A. McCallum. Bow: A Toolkit for Statistical Language Modeling, Text Retrieval, Classification and Clustering. *http://www.cs.cmu.edu/ mccallum/bow*, 1996.

[38] N. Mishra, R. Schreiber, I. Stanton, R. E. Tarjan, Finding Strongly-Knit Clusters in Social Networks, *Internet Mathematics*, 2009.

[39] M. E. J. Newman, Fast algorithm for detecting community structure in networks, *Phys. Rev.* E 69, 066133, 2004.

[40] S.J. Pan, Q. Yang. A Survey on Transfer Learning, *IEEE Transactions on Knowledge and Data Engineering*, October 2009.

[41] L. Qin, J.-X. Yu, L. Chang. Keyword search in databases: The power of RDBMS. *SIGMOD Conference*, 2009.

[42] H. Schutze, C. Silverstein, Projections for Efficient Document Clustering, *ACM SIGIR Conference*, 1992.

[43] Y. Sun, J. Han, J. Gao, Y. Yu, iTopicModel: Information Network-Integrated Topic Modeling. *ICDM Conference*, 2009.

[44] B. Taskar, P. Abbeel, and D. Koller. Discriminative probabilistic models for relational data. In *UAI*, pages 485–492, 2002.

[45] Y. Yang. An evaluation of statistical approaches to text categorization. *Inf. Retr.*, 1(1-2):69–90, 1999.

[46] T. Zhang, A. Popescul, and B. Dom. Linear prediction models with graph regularization for web-page categorization. In *KDD*, pages 821–826, 2006.

[47] S. Zhong. Efficient Streaming Text Clustering, *Neural Networks*, 18 (5–6), pp. 790–798, 2005.

[48] D. Zhou, J. Huang, and B. Schölkopf. Learning from labeled and unlabeled data on a directed graph. In *ICML*, pages 1036–1043, 2005.

[49] H. Wang, C. Aggarwal. A Survey of Algorithms for Keyword Search on Graph Data. appears as a chapter in *Managing and Mining Graph Data, Springer*, 2010.

[50] Y. Xu, Y. Papakonstantinou. Efficient LCA based keyword search in XML data. *EDBT Conference*, 2008.

[51] Y. Xu, Y.Papakonstantinou. Efficient keyword search for smallest LCAs in XML databases. *ACM SIGMOD Conference*, 2005.

[52] Q. Yang, D. Chen, G.-R. Xue, W. Dai, Y. Yu. Heterogeneous Transfer Learning for Image Clustering vis the Social Web. *ACL*, 2009.

[53] Y. Zhou, H. Cheng, and J. X. Yu. Graph clustering based on structural/attribute similarities. *PVLDB*, 2(1):718–729, 2009.

[54] Y. Zhu, S. J. Pan, Y. Chen, G.-R. Xue, Q. Yang, Y. Yu. Heterogeneous Transfer Learning for Image Classification. *AAAI*, 2010.

Chapter 14

INTEGRATING SENSORS AND SOCIAL NETWORKS

Charu C. Aggarwal
IBM T. J. Watson Research Center
Hawthorne, NY 10532, USA
charu@us.ibm.com

Tarek Abdelzaher
University of Illinois at Urbana Champaign
Urbana, IL, USA
zaher@cs.uiuc.edu

Abstract A number of sensor applications in recent years collect data which can be directly associated with human interactions. Some examples of such applications include GPS applications on mobile devices, accelerometers, or location sensors designed to track human and vehicular traffic. Such data lends itself to a variety of rich applications in which one can use the sensor data in order to model the underlying relationships and interactions. It also leads to a number of challenges, since such data may often be private, and it is important to be able to perform the mining process without violating the privacy of the users. In this chapter, we provide a broad survey of the work in this important and rapidly emerging field. We also discuss the key problems which arise in the context of this important field and the corresponding solutions.

Keywords: Sensor Networks, Social Sensors

1. Introduction

Social networks have become extremely popular in recent years, because of numerous online social networks such as *Facebook*, *LinkedIn* and *MySpace*.

In addition, many chat applications can also be modeled as social networks. Social networks provide a rich and flexible platform for performing the mining process with different kinds of data such as text, images, audio and video. Therefore, a tremendous amount of research has been performed in recent years on mining such data in the context of social networks [25, 40, 43, 56]. In particular, it has been observed that the use of a combination of linkage structure and different kinds of data can be a very powerful tool for mining purposes [65, 68]. The work in [65, 68] discusses how one can combine the text in social networks with the linkage structure in order to implement more effective classification models. Other recent work [38] uses the linkage structure in image data in order to perform more effective mining and search in information networks. Therefore, it is natural to explore whether sensor data processing can be tightly integrated with social network construction and analysis. Most of the afore-mentioned data types on a social network are static and change slowly over time. On the other hand, sensors collect vast amounts of data which need to be stored and processed in real time. There are a couple of important drivers for integrating sensor and social networks:

- One driver for integrating sensors and social networks is to allow the actors in the social network to both publish their data and subscribe to each other's data either directly, or indirectly after discovery of useful information from such data. The idea is that such collaborative sharing on a social network can increase real-time awareness of different users about each other, and provide unprecedented information and understanding about global behavior of different actors in the social network. The vision of integrating sensor processing with the real world was first proposed in [67].

- A second driver for integrating sensors and social networks is to better understand or measure the aggregate behavior of self-selected communities or the external environment in which these communities function. Examples may include understanding traffic conditions in a city, understanding environmental pollution levels, or measuring obesity trends. Sensors in the possession of large numbers of individuals enable exploiting the crowd for massively distributed data collection and processing. Recent literature reports on several efforts that exploit individuals for data collection and processing purposes such as collection of vehicular GPS trajectories as a way for developing street maps [34], collectively locating items of interest using cell-phone reports, such as mapping speed traps using the Trapster application [76], use of massive human input to translate documents [55], and the development of protein folding games that use competition among players to implement the equivalent of global optimization algorithms [14].

The above trends are enabled by the emergence of large-scale data collection opportunities, brought about by the proliferation of sensing devices of every-day use such as cell-phones, piedometers, smart energy meters, fuel consumption sensors (standardized in modern vehicles), and GPS navigators. The proliferation of many sensors in the possession of the common individual creates an unprecedented potential for building services that leverage massive amounts data collected from willing participants, or involving such participants as elements of distributed computing applications. Social networks, in a sensor-rich world, have become inherently multi-modal data sources, because of the richness of the data collection process in the context of the network structure. In recent years, sensor data collection techniques and services have been integrated into many kinds of social networks. These services have caused a computational paradigm shift, known as *crowd-sourcing* [15], referring to the involvement of the general population in data collection and processing. Crowd-sourcing, arguably pioneered by programs such as SETI, has become remarkably successful recently due to increased networking, mobile connectivity and geo-tagging [1]. Some examples of integration of social and sensor networks are as follows:

- The *Google Latitude* application [69] collects mobile position data of uses, and shares this data among different users. The sharing of such data among users can lead to significant events of interest. For example, proximity alerts may be triggered when two linked users are within geographical proximity of one another. This may itself trigger changes in the user-behavior patterns, and therefore the underlying sensor values. This is generally true of many applications, the data on one sensor can influence data in the other sensors.

- The *City Sense application* [70] collects sensor data extracted from fixed sensors, GPS-enabled cell phones and cabs in order to determine where the people are, and then carries this information to clients who subscribe to this information. The information can also be delivered to clients with mobile devices. This kind of social networking application provides a "sense" as to where the people in the city are, and can be used in order to effectively plan activities. A similar project, referred to as *WikiCity*, [13] developed at MIT, uses the mobile data collected from cell phones in order to determine the spatial trends in a city, and which the social streets might be.

- This general approach of collecting individual location data from mobile phones can also be used in order to generate interesting business decisions. For example, the project *MacroSense* [73] analyzes customer location behaviors, in order to determine individuals which behave in a similar way to a given target. The application is able to perform real time recommendations, personalization and discovery from real time location data.

- *Automotive Tracking Application:* A number of real-time automotive tracking applications determine the important points of congestion in the city by pooling GPS data from the vehicles in the city. This can be used by other drivers in order to avoid points of congestion in the city. In many applications, such objects may have implicit links among them. For example, in a military application, the different vehicles may have links depending upon their unit membership or other related data.

  Another related application is that of sharing of bike track paths by different users [53]. The problem of finding bike routes is naturally a trial-and-error process in terms of finding paths which are safe and enjoyable. The work in [53] designs *Biketastic*, which uses GPS-based sensing on a mobile phone application in order to create a platform which enables rich sharing of biker experiences with one another. The microphone and the accelerometer embedded on the phone are sampled to infer route noise level and roughness. The speed can also be inferred directly from the GPS sensing abilities of the mobile phone. The platform combines this rich sensor data with mapping and visualization in order to provide an intuitive and visual interface for sharing information about the bike routes.

- *Animal Tracking:* In its most general interpretation, an actor in a social network need not necessary be a person, but can be any living entity such as an animal. Recently, animal tracking data is collected with the use of radio-frequency identifiers. A number of social links may exist between the different animals such as group membership, or family membership. It is extremely useful to utilize the sensor information in order to predict linkage information and vice-versa. A recent project called *MoveBank* [71] has made tremendous advances in collecting such data sets. We note that a similar approach may be used for commercial product-tracking applications, though social networking applications are generally relevant to living entities, which are most typically people.

Social sensors provide numerous research challenges from the perspective of analysis.

- Since the collected data typically contains sensitive personal data (eg. location data), it is extremely important to use privacy-sensitive techniques [28, 52] in order to perform the analysis. A recent technique called *PoolView* [28] designs privacy-sensitive techniques for collecting and using mobile sensor data.

- The volume of data collected can be very large. For example, in a mobile application, one may track the location information of millions of users simultaneously. Therefore, it is useful to be able to design techniques which can compress and efficiently process the large amounts of collected data.
- Many of the applications require *dynamic* and *real time* responses. For example, applications which trigger alerts are typically time-sensitive and the responses may be real-time. The real-time challenges of such applications are quite challenging, considering the large number of sensors which are tracked at a given time.

This chapter is organized as follows. Section 2 briefly discusses some key technological advances which have occurred in recent years, which have enabled the design of such dynamic and embedded applications. Section 3 introduces techniques for social network modeling from dynamic links which are naturally created by the sensor-based scenario. Section 4 discusses a broad overview of the key system design questions which arise in these different contexts. One of the important issues discussed in this section is privacy, which is discussed in even greater detail in a later section. Section 5 discusses the database design issues which are essential for scalability. Section 6 discusses some important privacy issues which arise in the context of social networks with embedded sensors. Section 7 introduces some of the key applications associated with integrated social and sensor networks. Section 8 discusses the conclusions and research directions.

2. Sensors and Social Networks: Technological Enablers

A number of recent technological advances in hardware and software have enabled the integration of sensors and social networks. One such key technological advance is the development is small mobile sensors which can collect a variety of user-specific information such as audio or video. Many of the applications discussed are based on *user-location.* Such location can easily be computed with the use of mobile GPS-enabled devices. For example, most of the recent smart-phones typically have such GPS technology embedded inside them. Some examples of such mobile sensor devices may be found in [45, 42].

Sensors typically collect large amounts of data, which must be continuously stored and processed. Furthermore, since the number of users in a social network can be very large, this leads to natural scalability challenges for the storage and processing of the underlying streams. For example, many naive solutions such as the centralized storage and processing of the raw streams are not very practical, because of the large number of streams which are continuously received. In order to deal with this issue, a number of recent hardware and software advances have turned out to be very useful.

- *Development of Fast Stream Processing Platforms:* A number of fast stream processing platforms, such as the IBM System S platform [72] have been developed in recent years, which are capable of storing and processing large volumes of streams in real time. This is a very useful capability from the perspective of typical cyber-physical applications which need a high level of scalability for real-time processing.

- *Development of Stream Synopsis Algorithms and Software:* Since the volume of the data collected is very large, it often cannot be collected explicitly. This leads to the need for designing algorithms and methods for stream synopsis construction [2]. A detailed discussion of a variety of methods (such as sketches, wavelets and histograms) which are used for stream synopsis construction and analysis is provided in [2].

- *Increased Bandwidth:* Since sensor transmission often requires large wireless bandwidth, especially when the data is in the form of audio or video streams, it is critical to be able to transmit large amounts of data in real time. The increases in available bandwidth in recent years, have made such real time applications a reality.

- *Increased Storage:* In spite of the recently designed techniques for compressing the data, the storage challenges for stream processing continue to be a challenge. Recent years have seen tremendous advances in hardware, which allow much greater storage, than was previously possible.

In addition, the development of miniaturized sensors and batteries have allowed their use and deployment in a number of different social settings. For example, the development of miniaturized sensors, which can be embedded within individual attire can be helpful in a wide variety of scenarios [42, 31, 18, 19]. For example, the spec mote is an extremely small sensor device, which can be embedded in the clothing of a user, while remaining quite unobtrusive.

In addition, the sensing abilities of such devices have also increased considerably in recent years. For example, the *sociometer* [18, 19] is a small wearable device, which can measure the following kinds of interactions:

- Detection of people nearby

- Motion information and accelerometers

- Microphone for speech information

In addition, the device has the flexibility to allow for the addition of other kinds of sensors such as GPS sensors and light sensors. The ability to pack larger and larger amounts of functionality into small and unobtrusive devices has been a recent innovation, which has encouraged the development of an ever-increasing number of social-centered applications. The aim of collecting a large number of such interactive behaviors is to be able to effectively model interactions, between different users, and then model the dynamics of the interaction with the use of the collected information.

3. Dynamic Modeling of Social Networks

In the case of an explicitly linked social network, the relationships between different entities are quite clear, and therefore the dynamics of the interaction can be modeled relatively easily. However, in the case of a sensor network, the links between different entities may or may not be available depending upon the application. For example, the *Google Latitude* application allows for explicit links between different agents. On the other hand, in many social applications [19], the links and communities between different agents may need to be derived based on their location and behavior. In such cases, the structure of the social network itself and the underlying communities [20, 21] can be derived directly from the details of the underlying interaction. This is a challenging problem, especially when the number of agents are large, and the number of interactions between them is even larger and dynamically evolving.

Many sensing platforms such as those discussed in [18], yield sensor data which is varied, and is of a multi-modal nature. For example, the data could contain information about interactions, speech or location. It is useful to be able analyze such data in order to summarize the interactions and make inferences about the underlying interactions. Such multi-modal data can also be leveraged in order to make predictions about the nature of the underlying activities and the corresponding social interactions. This also provides a virtual technique to perform link inferences in the underlying network.

For example, the collection of activity sensing data is not very useful, unless it can be leveraged to summarize the nature of the activities among the different participants. For example,in the case of the techniques discussed in [19], the IR transceiver is used to determine which people are in proximity of one another. However, this cannot necessarily be used in order to determine whether the corresponding people are interacting with another. A knowledge of such interactions can be determined with the use of *speech segmentation* techniques in which it is determined which participants are interacting with one another. The speech portions are segmented out of the ambient noise, and then segmented into conversations. The knowledge of such face-to-face interactions can be used to build dynamic and virtual links among the different participants.

We note that a dynamically linked social network can be modeled in two different ways:

- The network can be modeled as a group of dynamic interacting agents. The stochastic properties of these agents can be captured with the use of hidden markov models in order to characterize various kinds of behaviors. This is the approach used for community modeling as discussed in [12, 21].

- The interactions of the participants can be modeled as links which are continuously created or destroyed depending upon the nature of the underlying interactions. as a graph stream, in which the nodes represent the participants, and the edges represent the interactions among these different participants. Recently, a number of analytical techniques have been designed in order to determine useful knowledge-based patterns in graph streams [4]. These include methods for dynamically determining shortest-paths, connectivity, communities or other topological characteristics of the underlying network.

The inherently dynamic nature of such interactions in an evolving and dynamic social network leads to a number of interesting challenges from the perspective of social network analysis. Some examples of such challenges are discussed below.

(1) Determination of dynamic communities in graph streams: Communities are defined as dense regions of the social network in which the participants frequently interact with one another over time. Such communities in a dynamically evolving social network can be determined by using agent-based stochastic analysis or link-based graph stream analysis. Methods for modeling such a social network as a group of dynamically evolving agents are discussed in [12, 21]. In these techniques, a hidden markov model is used in conjunction with an influence matrix in order to model the evolving social network.

A second approach is to model the underlying face-to-face interactions as dynamic links. This creates an inherently dynamic network scenario in which the structure of the communities may continuously evolve over time. Therefore, a key challenge is to determine such communities in dynamic networks, when the clustering patterns may change significantly over time. Methods for determining evolving clusters and communities in networks have been discussed in [6, 7, 17, 57]. Graph streams pose a special challenge because of the rapid nature of the incoming edges, and their use for determination of evolving communities.

(2) Mining Structural Patterns in Time-Evolving Social Networks: Aside from the common problem of community detection, another interesting problem is that of mining structural patterns of different kinds in time evolving graphs. Some common methods for finding such patterns typically use matrix and tensor-based tools, which are comprehensively described in a tutorial in [27]. Common problems in time-evolving graphs include those of frequent pattern determination, outlier detection, proximity tracking [58], and subgraph change detection [46].

(3) Modeling spatio-temporal dynamics: Many of the approaches discussed above model the dynamics of the interactions as dynamic links. While this provides greater generality, it does not capture the spatio-temporal nature of the underlying agents. For example, the data received in a GPS application often contains spatio-temporal information such as the positions of different agents, and their underlying interactions. Therefore, an interesting and important challenge is to model the aggregate spatio-temporal dynamics in order to determine the underlying patterns and clusters. Such spatio-temporal dynamics can be used in order to make interesting *spatial predictions* such as future regions of activity or congestions. For example, methods for determining clusters and communities from such mobile applications have been discussed in [44].

Ad discussed earlier, the determination of dynamic interactions requires the real-time modeling of face-to-face interactions, which can sometimes be sensitive information. This also leads to numerous privacy challenges, especially since the interactions between the participants may be considered personal information. A number of privacy-sensitive approaches for face-to-face activity modeling and conversation segmentation have been discussed in [61–64]. We will discuss more details on privacy-issues in a later section of this chapter.

4. System Design and Architectural Challenges

The aforementioned monitoring and social computing opportunities present a need for a new architecture that encourages data sharing and efficiently utilizes data contributed by users. The architecture should allow individuals, organizations, research institutions, and policy makers to deploy applications that monitor, investigate, or clarify aspects of *socio-physical* phenomena; processes that interact with the physical world, whose state depends on the behavior of humans in the loop.

An architecture for social data collection should facilitate distillation of concise actionable information from significant amounts of raw data contributed by a variety of sources, to inform high-level user decisions. Such an architecture would typically consist of components that support (i) privacy-preserving sensor data collection, (ii) data model construction, and (iii) real-time decision services. For example, in an application that helps drivers improve their vehicular fuel-efficiency, data collection might involve upload of fuel consumption data and context from the vehicle's on-board diagnostics (OBD-II) interface and related sensors; a model might relate the total fuel consumption for a vehicle on a road segment as a function of readily available parameters (such as average road speed, degree of congestion, incline, and vehicle weight); the decision support service might provide navigation assistance to find the most fuel-efficient route to a given destination (as opposed to a fastest or shortest route). Below, we elaborate on the above functions.

4.1 Privacy-preserving data collection

In a grassroots application that is not managed by a globally trusted authority, an interesting challenge becomes ensuring the privacy of data shared. Anonymity is not a sufficient solution because the data themselves (such as GPS traces) may reveal the identity of the owner even if shared anonymously. One interesting direction is to allow individuals to "lie" about their data in a way that protects their privacy, but without degrading application quality. For example, in a traffic speed monitoring application reconstruction of community statistics of interest (such as average traffic speed on different streets) should remain accurate, despite use of perturbed data ("lies" about actual speed of individual vehicles) as input to the reconstruction process. This is possible thanks to deconvolution techniques that recover the statistical distribution of the original signals, given the statistical distribution of perturbed data and the statistical distribution of noise. Solutions to this and related problems can be found in literature on privacy-preserving statistics [5]. Recently, special emphasis was given to perturbing time-series data [28], since sensor data typically comprise a correlated series of samples of some continuous phenomenon. Perturbing time-series data is challenging because correlations among nearby samples can be exploited to breach privacy. Recent results demonstrate that the frequency spectrum of the perturbation signal must substantially overlap with the frequency spectrum of the original data time-series for the latter to be effectively concealed [28]. Generalizations to perturbation of correlated multi-dimensional time-series data were proposed in [52]. The main challenge addressed in this work was to account for the fact that data shared by different sensors are usually not independent. For example, temperature and location data can be correlated, allowing an attacker to make inferences that breach privacy by exploiting cross-sensor correlations.

A related interesting problem is that of perturbation (i.e., noise) energy allocation. Given a perturbation signal of a particular energy budget (dictated perhaps by reconstruction accuracy requirements), how to allocate this energy budget across the frequency spectrum to optimally conceal an original data signal? A recent technique defines privacy as the amount of mutual information between the original and perturbed signals. Optimality is defined as perturbation that minimizes the upper bound on such (leaked) mutual information. The technique describes how optimal perturbation is computed, and demonstrates the fundamental trade-off between the bound on information leak (privacy) and the bound on reconstruction accuracy [51].

4.2 Generalized Model Construction

Many initial participatory sensing applications, such as those giving rise to the above privacy concerns, were concerned with computing community statistics out of individual private measurements. The approach inherently assumes richly-sampled, low-dimensional data, where many low-dimensional measurements (e.g., measurements of velocity) are redundantly obtained by individuals measuring the same variable (e.g., speed of traffic on the same street). Only then can good statistics be computed. Many systems, however, do not adhere to the above model. Instead, data are often high-dimensional, and hence sampling of the high-dimensional space is often sparse. The more interesting question becomes how to generalize from high-dimensional, sparsely-sampled data to cover the entire input data space? For instance, consider a fuel-efficient navigation example, where it is desired to compute the most fuel-efficient route between arbitrary source and destination points, for an arbitrary vehicle and driver. What are the most important generalizable predictors of fuel efficiency of current car models driven on modern streets? A large number of predictors may exist that pertain to parameters of the cars, the streets and the drivers. These inputs may be static (e.g., car weight and frontal area) or dynamic (e.g., traveled road speed and degree of congestion). In many cases, the space is only sparsely sampled, especially in conditions of sparse deployment of the participatory sensing service. It is very difficult to predict *a priori* which parameters will be more telling. More importantly, the key predictors might differ depending on other parameters. For example, it could be that the key predictors of fuel efficiency for hybrid cars and gas-fueled cars are different. It is the responsibility of the model construction services to offer not only a general mechanism for applications to build good models quickly from the data collected, but also a mechanism for identifying the scope within which different predictors are dominant. A single "one-side-fits-all" prediction model, computed from all available data, is not going to be accurate. Similarly computing a model for each special case (e.g., a model for each type of car) is not going to be useful because, as stated above, the sampling is sparse. Hence, it is key to be able to generalize from experiences of some types of vehicles to predictions of others. Recent work combined data mining techniques based on regression cubes and sampling cubes to address the model generalization problem for sparse, high-dimensional data [32].

4.3 Real-time Decision Services

Ultimately, a generalized model, such as that described above, may be used as an input to an application-specific optimization algorithm that outputs some *decisions* for users in response to user queries. For example, estimates of fuel consumption on different roads on a map can be input to Dijkstra's algorithm to find the minimum fuel route between points specified by the user. This route constitutes a decision output. Hence, support for real-time stream processing and decision updates must be provided as part of the social sensing architecture.

A key property of real-time decision services is the involvement of humans in the loop. A significant challenge is therefore to design appropriate user interfaces. End-user devices will act as data custodians who collect, store, and share user data. The level at which these custodians interact with the user, as well as the nature of interactions, pose significant research problems with respect to minimizing inconvenience to the user while engaging the user appropriately. Context sensing, collaborative learning, persuasion, and modeling of socio-sensing systems (with humans in the loop) become important problems. Participation incentives, role assignment, and engagement of users in modeling and network learning become important application design criteria that motivate fundamental research on game theoretic, statistical, machine learning, and economic paradigms for application design.

4.4 Recruitment Issues

The quality of the social experience gained from a sensor-based framework is dependent on the ability to recruit high quality participants for sensor collection and sharing. The work in [54] observes that the process of recruiting volunteers for participatory sensing campaigns is analogous to recruiting volunteers or employees in non-virtual environments. This similarity is used in order to create a 3-stage process for recruitment:

- **Qualifier:** This refers to the fact that the participants must meet minimum requirements such as availability and reputation.

- **Assessment:** Once participants that meet minimum requirements are found, the recruitment system then determines which candidates are most appropriate based on both diversity and coverage.

- **Progress Review:** Once the sensing process starts, the recruitment system must check participants' coverage and data collection reputation to determine if they are consistent with their base profile. This check can occur periodically, and if the similarity of profiles is below a threshold, this is used as a feedback to an additional recruitment process.

4.5 Other Architectural Challenges

Proper design of the above system components gives rise to other important challenges that must be solved in order to enable development and deployment of successful mobile sensing applications that adequately meet user needs. The following relates challenges described in a recent NSF-sponsored report on social sensing [77].

From the application perspective, mobile sensing applications depend significantly on social factors (user adoption, peer pressure, social norms, social networks, etc) as well as the nature of physical phenomena being monitored or controlled. Exciting interdisciplinary research challenges exist in describing the properties of distributed socio-physical applications. For example, what are the dynamics of information propagation in such systems? What are closed-loop properties of interaction involving social and physical phenomena? What are some fundamental bounds on capacity, delivery speed, and evolution of socio-sensing systems? Answering such questions is fundamental to informed design and performance analysis of sensing applications involving crowd-sourcing.

From the underlying physical network perspective, mobile sensing applications herald an era where many network clients are embedded devices. This motivates the investigation of a network architecture, where the main goal from networking shifts from offering a mere communication medium to offering *information distillation services*. These services bridge the gap between myriads of heterogeneous data feeds and the high-level human decision needs. In a network posed as an information service (as opposed to a communication medium), challenges include division of responsibilities between the end-device (e.g., phone) and network; paradigms for data collection on mobile devices, architectural support for data management, search, and mining; scalability to large-scale real-time information input and retrieval; improved context-awareness; support for predictability; and investigation of network and end-system support for reduction of cognitive overload of the information consumer. Other challenges in the design of network protocols for mobile sensing include energy management, integration of network storage, personalized search and retrieval, support for collaborative sensing, and exploitation of a rich realm of options in information transfer modalities and timing, including deferred information sharing and delay-tolerant communication.

While several social sensing applications are already deployed, exciting research opportunities remain in order to help understand their emergent behavior, optimize their performance, redesign the networks on which they run, and provide guarantees to the user, such as those on bounding unwanted information leakage.

5. Database Representation: Issues and Challenges

A number of database challenges naturally arise in such massive real time applications. For example, it is often the case that millions of streams may be collected simultaneously. It is useful to compress, process and store these streams in real-time. Furthermore,

such compression techniques need to be real-time in order to enable effective processing. In this section, we briefly review some stream compression and processing techniques which may be useful for such applications. In recent years a number of *synopsis structures* have been developed, which can be used in conjunction with a variety of mining and query processing techniques [30]. Some key synopsis methods include those of sampling, wavelets, sketches and histograms. The key challenges which arise in the context of synopsis construction of data streams are as follows:

Broad Applicability: The synopsis structure is typically used as an intermediate representation, which should be usable for a variety of analytical scenarios in the context of social networking applications.

One-pass constraint: The one-pass constraint is critical to synopsis construction algorithms, especially when the volume of the incoming data is large. This is especially true for a social networking application in which millions of sensors are simultaneously transmitting data.

Time and Space Efficiency: Since data streams have a very large volume, it is essential to create the synopsis in a time- and space-efficient way. In this sense, some of the probabilistic techniques such as sketches are extremely effective for counting-based applications, since they require constant-space for provable probabilistic accuracy. In other words, the time- and space-efficiency depends only upon the accuracy of the approach rather than the length of the data stream.

Data Stream Evolution: Since the incoming stream patterns may evolve over time, a synopsis structure which is constructed from the overall behavior of the data stream is not quite as effective as one which uses recent history. Consequently, it is often more effective to create synopsis structures which either work with sliding windows, or use some decay-based approach in order to weight the data stream points.

One key characteristic of many of the above methods is that while they work effectively in the 1-dimensional case, they often lose their effectiveness in the multi-dimensional case either because of data sparsity or because of inter-attribute correlations. The multi-dimensional case is especially for the social networking scenario, because millions of streams may be collected and processed at a given time. Next, we will discuss the broad classes of techniques which are used for synopsis construction in data streams. Each of these techniques have their own advantages in different scenarios, and we will take care to provide an overview of the different array of methods which are used for synopsis construction in data streams. The broad techniques which are used for synopsis construction in data streams are as follows:

Reservoir Sampling: Sampling methods are widely used for traditional database applications, and are extremely popular because of their broad applicability across a wide array of tasks in data streams. A further advantage of sampling methods is that unlike many other synopsis construction methods, they maintain their inter-attribute correlations across samples of the data. It is also often possible to use probabilistic inequalities in order to bound the effectiveness of a variety of applications with sampling methods.

However, a key problem in extending sampling methods to the data stream scenario, is that one does not know the total number of data points to be sampled in advance. Rather, one must maintain the sample in a dynamic way over the entire course of the computation. A method called reservoir sampling was first proposed in [59], which maintains such a sample dynamically. This technique was originally proposed in the context of one-pass access of data from magnetic-storage devices. However, the techniques also naturally extend to the data stream scenario.

Let us consider the case, where we wish to obtain an unbiased sample of size n from the data stream. In order to initialize the approach, we simply add the first n points from the stream to the reservoir. Subsequently, when the $(t+1)$th point is received, it is added to the reservoir with probability $n/(t+1)$. When the data point is added to the reservoir, it replaces a random point from the reservoir. It can be shown that this simple approach maintains the uniform sampling distribution from the data stream. We note that the uniform sampling approach may not be very effective in cases where the data stream evolves significantly. In such cases, one may either choose to generate the stream sample over a sliding window, or use a decay-based approach in order to bias the sample. An approach for sliding window computation over data streams is discussed in [48].

A second approach [3] uses biased decay functions in order to construct synopsis from data streams. It has been shown in [3] that the problem is extremely difficult for arbitrary decay functions. In such cases, there is no known solution to the problem. However, it is possible to design very simple algorithms for some important classes of decay functions. One of these classes of decay functions is the *exponential decay function*. The exponential decay function is extremely important because of its *memory less property*, which guarantees that the future treatment of a data point is independent of the past data points which have arrived. An interesting result is that by making simple implementation modifications to the algorithm of [59] in terms of modifying the probabilities of insertion and deletion, it is possible to construct a robust algorithm for this problem. It has been shown in [3] that the approach is quite effective in practice, especially when there is significant evolution of the underlying data stream.

While sampling has several advantages in terms of simplicity and preservation of multi-dimensional correlations, it loses its effectiveness in the presence of data sparsity. For example, a query which contains very few data points is unlikely to be accurate with the use of a sampling approach. However, this is a general problem with most techniques which are effective at counting frequent elements, but are not quite as effective at counting rare or distinct elements in the data stream.

Sketches: Sketches use some properties of random sampling in order to perform counting tasks in data streams. Sketches are most useful when the *domain size* of a data stream is very large. In such cases, the number of possible distinct elements become very large, and it is no longer possible to track them in space-constrained scenarios. There are two broad classes of sketches: *projection based* and *hash based*. We will discuss each of them in turn.

Projection based sketches are constructed on the broad idea of random projection [39]. The most well known projection-based sketch is the AMS sketch [10, 11], which we will discuss below. It has been shown in [39], that by by randomly sampling subspaces from multi-dimensional data, it is possible to compute ϵ-accurate projections of the data with high probability. This broad idea can easily be extended to the massive domain case, by viewing each distinct item as a dimension, and the counts on these items as the corresponding values. The main problem is that the vector for performing the projection cannot be maintained explicitly since the length of such a vector would be of the same size as the number of distinct elements. In fact, since the sketch-based method is most relevant in the distinct element scenario, such an approach defeats the purpose of keeping a synopsis structure in the first place.

Let us assume that the random projection is performed using k sketch vectors, and r_i^j represents the jth vector for the ith item in the domain being tracked. In order to achieve the goal of efficient synopsis construction, we store the random vectors implicitly in the form of a seed, and this can be used to dynamically generate the vector. The main idea discussed in [35] is that it is possible to generate random vectors with a seed of size $O(\log(N))$, provided that one is willing to work with the restriction that $r_i^j \in \{-1, +1\}$ should be 4-wise independent. The sketch is computed by adding r_i^j to the jth component of the sketch for the ith item. In the event that the incoming item has frequency f, we add the value $f \cdot r_i^j$. Let us assume that there are a total of k sketch components which are denoted by $(s_1 \ldots s_k)$. Some key properties of the pseudo-random number generator approach and the sketch representation are as follows:

- A given component r_i^j can be generated in poly-logarithmic time from the seed. The time for generating the seed is poly-logarithmic in the domain size of the underlying data.

- A variety of approximate aggregate functions on the original data can be computed using the sketches.

Some example of functions which can be computed from the sketch components are as follows:

- **Dot Product of two streams:** If $(s_1 \ldots s_k)$ be the sketches from one stream, and $(t_1 \ldots t_k)$ be the sketches from the other stream, then $s_j \cdot t_j$ is a random variable whose expected value of the dot product.

- **Second Moment:** If $(s_1 \ldots s_k)$ be the sketch components for a data stream, it can be shown that the expected value of s_j^2 is the second moment. Furthermore, by using Chernoff bounds, it can be shown that by selecting the median of $O(\log(1/\delta))$ averages of $O(1/\epsilon^2)$ copies of $s_j \cdot t_j$, it is possible to guarantee the accuracy of the approximation to within $1 \pm \epsilon$ with probability at least $1 - \delta$.

- **Frequent Items:** The frequency of the ith item in the data stream is computed by by multiplying the sketch component s_j by r_i^j. However, this estimation is accurate only for the case of frequent items, since the error is estimation is proportional to the overall frequency of the items in the data stream.

More details of computations which one can perform with the AMS sketch are discussed in [10, 11].

The second kind of sketch which is used for counting is the *count-min* sketch [26]. The count-min sketch is based upon the concept of hashing, and uses $k = \ln(1/\delta)$ pairwise-independent hash functions, which hash onto integers in the range $(0 \ldots e/\epsilon)$. For each incoming item, the k hash functions are applied and the frequency count is incremented by 1. In the event that the incoming item has frequency f, then the corresponding frequency count is incremented by f. Note that by hashing an item into the k cells, we are ensuring that we maintain an overestimate on the corresponding frequency. It can be shown that the minimum of these cells provides the ϵ-accurate estimate to the frequency with probability at least $1 - \delta$. It has been shown in [26] that the method can also be naturally extended to other problems such as finding the dot product or the second-order moments. The count-min sketch is typically more effective for problems such as frequency-estimation of individual items than the projection-based AMS sketch. However, the AMS sketch is more effective for problems such as second-moment estimation.

Wavelet Decomposition: Another widely known synopsis representation in data stream computation is that of the wavelet representation. One of the most widely used representations is the *Haar Wavelet*. We will discuss this technique in detail in this section. This technique is particularly simple to implement, and is widely used in the literature for hierarchical decomposition and summarization. The basic idea in the wavelet technique is to create a decomposition of the data characteristics into a set of wavelet functions and basis

Granularity (Order k)	Averages Φ values	DWT Coefficients ψ values
$k = 4$	(8, 6, 2, 3, 4, 6, 6, 5)	-
$k = 3$	(7, 2.5, 5, 5.5)	(1, -0.5,-1, 0.5)
$k = 2$	(4.75, 5.25)	(2.25, -0.25)
$k = 1$	(5)	(-0.25)

Table 14.1. An Example of Wavelet Coefficient Computation

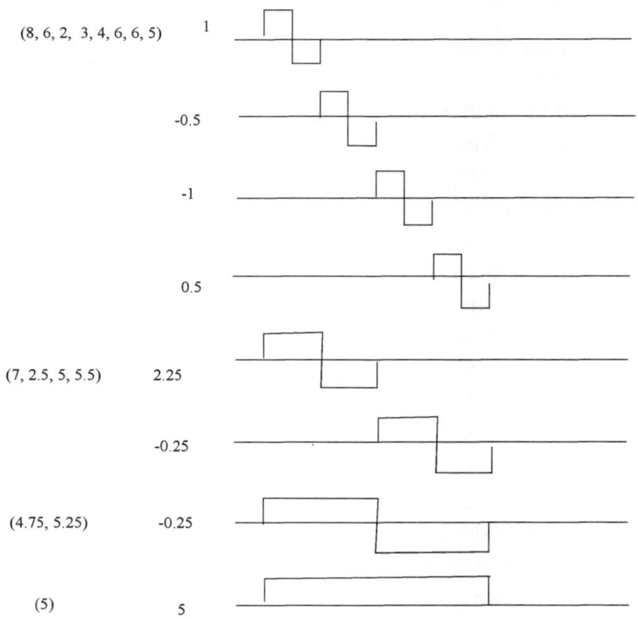

Figure 14.1. Illustration of the Wavelet Decomposition

functions. The property of the wavelet method is that the higher order coefficients of the decomposition illustrate the broad trends in the data, whereas the more localized trends are captured by the lower order coefficients.

We assume for ease in description that the length q of the series is a power of 2. This is without loss of generality, because it is always possible to decompose a series into segments, each of which has a length that is a power of two. The Haar Wavelet decomposition defines 2^{k-1} coefficients of order k. Each of these 2^{k-1} coefficients corresponds to a contiguous portion of the time series of length $q/2^{k-1}$. The ith of these 2^{k-1} coefficients corresponds to the segment in the series starting from position $(i-1) \cdot q/2^{k-1}+1$ to position $i * q/2^{k-1}$. Let us denote this coefficient by ψ_k^i and the corresponding time series segment by S_k^i. At the same time, let us define the average value of the first half of the S_k^i by a_k^i and the second half by b_k^i. Then, the value of ψ_k^i is given by $(a_k^i - b_k^i)/2$. More formally, if Φ_k^i denote the average value of the S_k^i, then the value of ψ_k^i can be defined recursively as follows:

$$\psi_k^i = (\Phi_{k+1}^{2\cdot i-1} - \Phi_{k+1}^{2\cdot i})/2 \tag{14.1}$$

The set of Haar coefficients is defined by the Ψ_k^i coefficients of order 1 to $\log_2(q)$. In addition, the global average Φ_1^1 is required for the purpose of perfect reconstruction. We note that the coefficients of different order provide an understanding of the major trends in the data at a particular level of granularity. For example, the coefficient ψ_k^i is half the quantity by which the first half of the segment S_k^i is larger than the second half of the same segment. Since larger values of k correspond to geometrically reducing segment sizes, one can obtain an understanding of the basic trends at different levels of granularity. We note that this definition of the Haar wavelet makes it very easy to compute by a sequence of averaging and differencing operations. In Table 14.1, we have illustrated how the wavelet coefficients are computed for the case of the sequence $(8, 6, 2, 3, 4, 6, 6, 5)$. This decomposition is illustrated in graphical form in Figure 14.1. We also note that each value can be represented as a sum of $\log_2(8) = 3$ linear decomposition components. In general, the entire decomposition may be represented as a tree of depth 3, which represents the hierarchical decomposition of the entire series. This is also referred to as the *error tree*. In Figure 14.2, we have illustrated the error tree for the wavelet decomposition illustrated in Table 14.1. The nodes in the tree contain the values of the wavelet coefficients, except for a special *super-root* node which contains the series average. This super-root node is not necessary if we are only considering the relative values in the series, or the series values have been normalized so that the average is already zero. We further note that the number of wavelet coefficients in this series is 8, which is also the length of the original series. The original series has been replicated just below the error-tree in Figure 14.2, and it can be reconstructed by adding or subtracting the values in the nodes

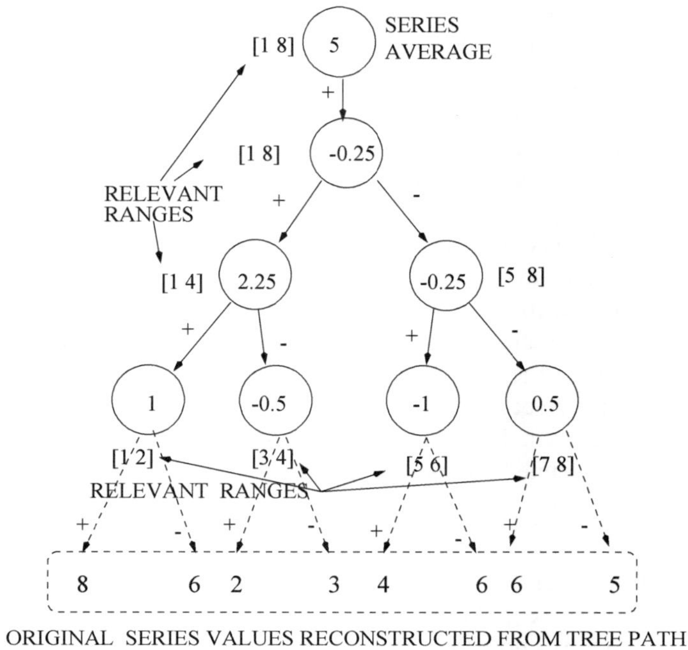

Figure 14.2. The Error Tree from the Wavelet Decomposition

along the path leading to that value. We note that each coefficient in a node should be added, if we use the left branch below it to reach to the series values. Otherwise, it should be subtracted. This natural decomposition means that an entire contiguous range along the series can be reconstructed by using only the portion of the error-tree which is relevant to it. Furthermore, we only need to retain those coefficients whose values are significantly large, and therefore affect the values of the underlying series. In general, we would like to minimize the reconstruction error by retaining only a fixed number of coefficients, as defined by the space constraints.

While wavelet decomposition is easy to perform for multi-dimensional data sets, it is much more challenging for the case of data streams. This is because data streams impose a one-pass constraint on the wavelet construction process. A variety of one-pass algorithms for wavelet construction are discussed in [30].

Histograms: The technique of histogram construction is closely related to that of wavelets. In histograms the data is binned into a number of intervals along an attribute. For any given query, the counts from the bins can be utilized for query resolution. A simple representation of the histogram method would simply partition the data into equi-depth or equi-width intervals. The main inaccuracy with the use of histograms is that the distribution of data points within a bucket is not retained, and is therefore assumed to be uniform. This causes inaccuracy because of extrapolation at the query boundaries. A natural choice is to use an equal number of counts in each bucket. This minimizes the error variation across different buckets. However, in the case of data streams, the boundaries to be used for equi-depth histogram construction are not known a-priori. We further note that the design of equi-depth buckets is exactly the problem of quantile estimation, since the equi-depth partitions define the quantiles in the data. Another choice of histogram construction is that of minimizing the variance of frequency variances of different values in the bucket. This ensures that the uniform distribution assumption is approximately held, when extrapolating the frequencies of the buckets at the two ends of a query. Such histograms are referred to as V-optimal histograms. Algorithms for V-optimal histogram construction are proposed in [36, 37]. A more detailed discussion of several algorithms for histogram construction may be found in [2].

6. Privacy Issues

Social sensing offers interesting new challenges pertaining to privacy assurances on data. General research on privacy typically focuses on electronic communication as opposed to ramifications of increasing sensory instrumentation in a socio-physical world. In contrast, traditional embedded systems research typically considers computing systems that interact with physical and engineering artifacts and belong to the same trust domain. A need arises to bridge the gap in privacy research by formulating and solving privacy-motivated research challenges in the emerging social sensing systems, where users interact in the context of social networks with embedded sensing devices in the physical world.

Sharing sensor data creates new opportunities for loss of privacy (and new privacy attacks) that exploit physical-side channels or a priori known information about the physical environment. Research is needed on both privacy *specification* and *enforcement* to put such specification and enforcement on solid analytic foundations, much like specification and enforcement of safety requirements of high-confidence software.

Specification calls for new physical privacy specification interfaces that are easy to understand and use for the non-expert. *Enforcement* calls for two complementary types of privacy mechanisms; (i) *protection mechanisms from involuntary physical exposure*, and (ii) *control of voluntary information sharing*. The former enforce *physical privacy*. They are needed to prevent "side-channel" attacks that exploit physical and spatio-temporal properties, characteristic of embedded sensing systems, to make inferences regarding private information. Control of voluntary information sharing must facilitate privacy-preserving exchange of time-series data. A predominant use of data in social sensing applications is for aggregation purposes such as computing statistical information from many sources. Mathematically-based data perturbation and anonymization schemes are needed to hide user data but allow fusion operations on perturbed or partial data to return correct results to a high degree of approximation.

While privacy-preserving statistics and privacy-preserving data mining are mature fields with a significant amount of prior research, sharing of sensor data offers the additional challenge of dealing with *correlated multi-dimensional time-series data* represented by sensory data streams. Correlations within and across sensor data streams and the spatio-temporal context of data offer new opportunities for privacy attacks. The challenge is to perturb a user's sequence of data values such that (i) the individual data items and their trend (i.e., their changes with time) cannot be estimated without large error, whereas (ii) the distribution of the data aggregation results at any point in time is estimated with high accuracy. For instance, in a health-and-fitness social sensing application, it may be desired to find the average weight loss trend of those on a particular diet or exercise routine as well as the distribution of weight loss as a function of time on the diet. This is to be accomplished without being able to reconstruct any individual's weight and weight trend without significant error.

Examples of data perturbation techniques can be found in [9, 8, 16]. The general idea is to add random noise with a known distribution to the user's data, after which a reconstruction algorithm is used to estimate the distribution of the original data. Early approaches relied on adding independent random noise. These approaches were shown to be inadequate. For example, a special technique based on random matrix theory has been proposed in [24] to recover the user data with high accuracy. Later approaches considered hiding individual data values collected from different private parties, taking into account that data from different individuals may be correlated [23]. However, they do not make assumptions on the model describing the *evolution* of data values from a given party over time, which can be used to jeopardize privacy of data streams. Perturbation techniques must specifically consider the data evolution model to prevent attacks that extract regularities in correlated data such as spectral filtering [24] and Principal Component Analysis (PCA) [23].

In work discussed earlier in this chapter [28], it was shown that privacy of time-series data can be preserved if the noise used to perturb the data is itself generated from a process that approximately models the measured phenomenon. For instance, in the weight watchers example, we may have an intuitive feel for the time scales and ranges of weight evolution when humans gain or lose weight. Hence, a noise model can be constructed that exports realistic-looking parameters for both the direction and time-constant of weight changes. The resulting perturbed stream can be aggregated with that of others in the community. Since the distributions of noise model parameters are statistically known, it is possible to estimate the sum, average and distribution of added noise (of the entire community) as a function of time. Subtracting that known average noise time series from the sum of perturbed community curves will thus yield the true community trend. The distribution of community data at a given time can similarly be estimated (using deconvolution methods) since the distribution of noise (i.e., data from virtual users) is known. The estimate improves with community size.

The approach preserves individual user privacy while allowing accurate reconstruction of community statistics. Several research questions arise that require additional work. For example, what is a good upper bound on the reconstruction error of the data aggregation result as a function of the noise statistics introduced to perturb the individual inputs? What are noise generation techniques that minimize the former error (to achieve accurate aggregation results) while maximizing the noise (for privacy)? How to ensure that data of individual data streams cannot be inferred from the perturbed signal? What are some bounds on minimum error in reconstruction of individual data streams? What noise generation techniques maximize such error for privacy? Privacy challenges further include the investigation of attack models involving corrupt noise models (e.g., ones that attempt to deceive non-expert users into using perturbation techniques that do not achieve adequate privacy protection), malicious clients (e.g., ones that do not follow the correct perturbation schemes or send bogus data), and repeated server queries (e.g., to infer additional information about evolution of client data from incremental differences in query responses). For example, given that it is fundamentally impossible to tell if a user is sharing a properly perturbed version of their real weight or just some random value, what fractions of malicious users can be accommodated without significantly affecting reconstruction accuracy of community statistics? Can damage imposed by a single user be bounded using outlier detection techniques that exclude obviously malicious users? How does the accuracy of outlier detection depend on the scale of allowable perturbation? In general, how to quantify the tradeoff between privacy and robustness to malicious user data? How tolerant is the perturbation scheme to collusion among users that aims to bias community statistics? Importantly, how does the *time-series* nature of data affect answers to the above questions compared to previous solutions to similar problems in other contexts (e.g., in relational databases)?

Furthermore, how can the above perturbation techniques, defense solutions, and bounds be extended to the sharing of multiple correlated data streams, or data streams with related context? For example, consider a social sensing application where users share vehicular GPS data to compute traffic speed statistics in a city. In this case, in order to compute the statistics correctly as a function of time and location, each vehicle's speed must be shared together with its current GPS location and time of day. Perturbing the speed alone does not help privacy if the correct location of the user must be revealed at all times. What is needed is a perturbation and reconstruction technique that allows a user to “lie" about their speed, location, and time of day, altogether, in a manner that makes it impossible to reconstruct their true values, yet allow an aggregation service to average out the added multi-dimensional noise and accurately map the true aggregate traffic speed as a function of actual time and space. This problem is related to the more general concern of privacy-preserving classification [60, 66], except that it is applied to the challenging case of aggregates of time-series data. Preliminary work shows that the problem is solvable. Understanding the relation between multi-dimensional error bounds on reconstruction accuracy and bounds on privacy, together with optimal perturbation algorithms in the sense of minimizing the former while maximizing the latter, remains an open research problem.

7. Sensors and Social Networks: Applications

In this section, we will discuss a number of recent applications which have been designed in the context of sensors and social networks. Many of these applications are related to storage and processing of mobile data which is continuously collected over time. Such mobile data can be used in order to provide real time knowledge of the different users to one another, trigger alerts, provide an understanding of social trends, and enable a variety of other applications. In this section, we will discuss a number of social-centric applications, which have been developed in recent years. These include specific systems which have been designed by companies such as Google, Microsoft, and SenseNetworks, as well as a number of generic applications, which have not yet been fully commercialized.

7.1 The Google Latitude Application

The Google Latitude Application uses GPS data which is collected from Google map users on mobile cell phones. It is also possible to collect more approximate data with the use of cell phone tower location data (in case the mobile phones are not GPS enabled), or with the use of IP addresses of a computer which is logged into the personalized google page called *iGoogle*. The Latitude application enables the creation of *virtual friends*, who are essentially other users that carry the same location-enabled device, or use other devices such as personal computers which can transmit approximate location data such as IP-addresses. A number of other applications which enabled by the Google Latitude master application are as follows:

- **Location Alerts:** The application allows the triggering of alerts when someone is near their latitude friends. The alerts are triggered only when something interesting is being done. This is done on the basis of both time and location. For example, an alert could be triggered when two friends are at a routine place, but an unusual time. Alternatively, it could be triggered when two friends are at a routine time but unusual place.

- **Public Location Badge:** It is possible to post one's location directly on blog or social network. This in turn increases the visibility of one's information to other users of the site.

- **Use with Chat Applications:** The mobile location can also be used in conjunction with the *Google Talk* application which allows users to chat with one another. Users who are chatting with one another can see each other's location with the use the embedded latitude functionality.

It is clear that all of the above techniques change the nature and dynamics of social interactions between users. For example, the triggering of alerts can itself lead to a changed pattern of interaction among the different users. The ability to mine the dynamics of such interactions is a useful and challenging task for a variety of applications.

While *Google Latitude* is perhaps the most well known application, it is by no means the only one. A number of recent applications have been designed which can track mobile devices on the internet through GPS tracking. Some of these applications have been designed purely for the purpose of tracking a device which might be lost, whereas others involve more complex social interactions. Any software and hardware combination which enables this has the potential to be used for social sensing applications. Some examples of such applications are as follows:

- **Navizon Application:** This application [74] uses GPS in order to allow social interactions between people with mobile phones. It allows the tracking of mobile friends, coverage of particular areas, and trails followed by a particular user.

- **iLocalis Application:** This application [75] is currently designed only for particular mobile platforms such as the iPhone, and it allows the tracking of family and friends. In addition, it is also designed for corporate applications in which a group of mobile employees may be tracked using the web. Once friendship links have been set up, the application is capable of sending a message to the friends of a particular user, when they are nearby.

7.2 The Citysense and Macrosense Applications

The Citysense and Macrosense applications both collect real-time data from a variety of GPS-enabled cell phones, cell phone tower triangulation, and GPS-enabled cabs. The two applications share a number of similarities in terms of the underlying methodology, but they have different features which are targeted towards different kinds of audiences. We describe them below:

7.2.1 CitySense Application.

The citysense application is designed for the broad consumer base which carries mobile cell phones. The Citysense application is designed to track important trends in the behavior of people in the city. For example, the application has been deployed in San Francisco, and it can show the busiest spots in the city on a mobile map.

The CitySense application also has a social networking version of a collaborative filtering application. The application stores the personal history of each user, and it can use this personal history in order to determine where other similar users might be. Thus, this can provide recommendations to users about possible places to visit based on their past interests.

A very similar application is the WikiCity project [13] which collects real time information with the use of GPS and mobile devices. These are then used to collect the location patterns of users, and their use in a variety of neighborhoods.

7.2.2 MacroSense Application.

The MacroSense application is similar in terms of the data it collects and kind of functionality it provides; however it is focussed towards the commercial segment in predicting consumer behavior. The application can predict the behavior of customers based on their location profile and behavior. The application can predict what a particular customer may like next. The broad idea is to segment and cluster customers into marketing groups based on their behavior, and use this information in order to make predictions. For example, the popularity of a product with users who are most like the target can be used for predictive purposes. Thus, this approach is somewhat like collaborative filtering, except that it uses the behavior of customers rather than their feedback. The effectiveness of particular behaviors which predict the interests are also used. This analysis can be performed in real time, which provides great value in terms of predictive interactions. The analytics can also be used in order to predict group influences for the behaviors of the underlying subjects.

7.3 Green GPS

Green GPS [32] is a participatory sensing navigation service that allows drivers to find the most fuel-efficient routes for their vehicles between arbitrary end-points. Green GPS relies on data collected by individuals from their vehicles as well as on mathematical models to compute fuel efficient routes.

The most fuel efficient route may depend on the vehicle and may be different from the shortest or fastest route. For example, a fast route that uses a freeway may consume more fuel because fuel consumption increases non-linearly with speed. Similarly, the shortest route that traverses busy city streets may be suboptimal because of downtown traffic.

The service exploits measurements of standard vehicular sensor interfaces that give access to most gauges and engine instrumentation. Vehicles that have been sold in the United States after 1996 are mandatorily equipped with a sensing subsystem called the On-Board Diagnostic (OBD-II) system. The OBD-II is a diagnostic system that monitors the health of the automobile using sensors that measure approximately 100 different engine parameters. Examples of monitored measurements include fuel consumption, engine RPM, coolant temperature and vehicle speed.

To build its fuel efficiency models, Green GPS utilizes a vehicle's OBD-II system and a typical scanner tool in conjunction with a participatory sensing framework. The team is collecting data from vehicles driven by research participants to determine what factors influence fuel consumption. The data collected by the participants is driving the creation of a mathematical model that enable computing fuel consumption of different cars on different road segments. Early studies have shown that a 13% reduction in consumer gas consumption is possible over the shortest path and 6% over the fastest path.

7.4 Microsoft SensorMap

Most of the applications discussed above are based on location data, which is automatically collected based on user behavior. The SensorMap project [49] at Microsoft allows for a more general framework in which users can *choose to publish any kind of sensor data*, with the understanding that such shared knowledge can lead to interesting inferences from the data sets. For example, the sensor data published by a user could be their location information, audio or video feeds, or text which is typed on a keyboard. The goal of the SensorMap project is to store and index the data in a way such that it is efficiently searchable. The application also allows users to index and cache data, so that users can issue spatio-temporal queries on the shared data.

The SensorMap project is part of the SenseWeb project, which allows sharing and exploring of sensor streams over geo-centric interfaces. A number of key design challenges for managing such sensor streams have been discussed in [47]. Other key challenges, which are associated with issues such as the privacy issues involved with continuously collecting and using the sensors which are only intermittently available is discussed in [41].

7.5 Animal and Object Tracking Applications

While social networks are generally defined for the case of people, a similar analysis can be applied to the case of online tracking of animals. For example, animals which are drawn from the same community or family may be considered to have implicit links among them. Such links can be utilized for the perspective of detailed understanding of how community and family membership affects geographical patterns. Such information can be very useful for a variety of applications, such as building disease propagation models among animals. This general idea can also be extended to applications which are outside the domain of social networks. For example, commercial products can be tracked with the use of RFID tags. The products may have implicit links among them which correspond to shared batches or processes during the production and transportation process. Such tracking data can be used in conjunction with linkage analysis in order to determine the causality and origin of tainted products. It can also be used to track the current location of other products which may be tainted.

7.6 Participatory Sensing for Real-Time Services

A variety of *participatory sensing techniques* can be used for enabling real-time services. In participatory sensing, users agree to allow data about them to be transmitted in order to enable a variety of services which are enabled in real time. We note that the main challenges to participatory sensing include the *privacy-issues* associated with such sensing techniques. Therefore participatory sensing is usually utilized only for applications which are *real-time* and *time-critical*; in many cases such services may involve emergencies or health-care applications. Some examples are as follows:

- **Vehicular Participatory Sensing:** In vehicular participatory sensing, a variety of sensor data from vehicles such as mobile location, or other vehicular performance parameters may be continuously transmitted to users over time. Such data may be shared with other users *in the aggregate* in order to preserve privacy. This is the social aspect of such applications, since they enable useful individual decisions based on global patterns of behavior. In addition, vehicular participatory sensing may be used in order to enable quick responses in case of emergencies involving the vehicle operation.

- **Elderly Healthcare:** The ability to carry such devices allows its use for a variety of healthcare applications involving the elderly. For example, elderly patients can use this in order to call for care when necessary. Similarly, such sensing devices can be utilized for a variety of safety and health-care related applications.

8. Future Challenges and Research Directions

In this chapter, we examined the emerging area of integrating sensors and social networks. Such applications have become more commonplace in recent years because of new technologies which allow the embedding of small and unobtrusive sensors in clothing. The main challenges of using such technologies are as follows:

- Such applications are often implemented on a very large scale. In such cases, the database scalability issues continue to be a challenge. While new advances in stream processing have encouraged the development of effective techniques for data compression and mining, mobile applications continue to be a challenge because of the fact that *both* the *number* of streams and rate of data collection may be extremely large.

- A major challenge in sensor-based social networking are the privacy issues inherent in the underlying applications. For example, individuals may not be willing to disclose their locations [33] in order to enable applications such as proximity alerts. In many cases, such constraints can greatly reduce the functionality of such applications. A major challenge in such applications is to provide individual hard guarantees on their privacy level, so that they become more willing to share their real time information.

- The architectural challenges for such systems continue to be quite extensive. For example, the use of centralized processing methods for such large systems does not scale well. Therefore, new methods [47, 49] have moved away from the centralized architecture for stream collection and processing.

The future challenges of such research include the development of new algorithms for large scale data collection, processing and storage. Some advancements [2, 47, 49] have already been made in this direction.

Acknowledgements

Research was sponsored by the Army Research Laboratory and was accomplished under Cooperative Agreement Number W911NF-09-2-0053. The views and conclusions contained in this document are those of the authors and should not be interpreted as representing the official policies, either expressed or implied, of the Army Research Laboratory or the U.S. Government. The U.S. Government is authorized to reproduce and distribute reprints for Government purposes notwithstanding any copyright notation here on.

References

[1] T. Abdelzaher, Y. Anokwa, P. Boda, J. Burke, D. Estrin, L. Guibas, A. Kansal, S. Madden, J. Reich. Mobiscopes for Human Spaces. *IEEE Pervasive*, 6 (2), pp. 20-29, April 2007.

[2] C. C. Aggarwal (ed.) Data Streams: Models and Algorithms, *Springer*, 2007.

[3] C. C. Aggarwal. On Biased Reservoir Sampling in the presence of Stream Evolution. *VLDB Conference*, 2006.

[4] C. C. Aggarwal, H. Wang (ed.) Managing and Mining Graph Data, *Springer*, 2010.

[5] C. C Aggarwal, P. Yu (ed.) Privacy-Preserving Data Mining: Models and Algorithms, *Springer*, 2008.

[6] C. C. Aggarwal, P. S. Yu. Online Analysis of Community Evolution in Data Streams, *SIAM Conference on Data Mining*, 2005.

[7] C. C. Aggarwal, Y. Zhao, P. Yu. On Clustering Graph streams, *SIAM Conference on Data Mining*, 2010.

[8] D. Agrawal and C. C. Aggarwal. On the design and quantification of privacy preserving data mining algorithms. In *Proceedings of the 20th ACM SIGMOD Symposium on Principles of Database Systems*, pages 247–255, 2001.

[9] R. Agrawal and R. Srikant. Privacy preserving data mining. In *Proceedings of the ACM SIGMOD Conference on Management of Data*, pages 439–450, Dallas, TX, May 2000.

[10] N. Alon, P. Gibbons, Y. Matias, M. Szegedy. Tracking Joins and Self-Joins in Limited Storage. *ACM PODS Conference*, 1999.

[11] Alon N., Matias Y., Szegedy M. (The Space Complexity of Approximating Frequency Moments. *ACM STOC Conference*, pp. 20–29, 1996.

[12] C. Asavathiratham, The lnfluence Model: A Tractable Representation for the Dynamics of Networked Markov Chains, *TR, Dept. of EECS, MIT*, Cambridge, 2000.

[13] F. Calabrese, K. Kloeckl, C. Ratti. Wikicity: Real-Time Urban Environments. *IEEE Pervasive Computing*, 6(3), 52-53, 2007. http://senseable.mit.edu/wikicity/rome/

[14] A. Beberg and V. S. Pande. Folding@home: lessons from eight years of distributed computing. *IEEE International Parallel and Distributed Processing Symposium*, pp. 1-8, 2009

[15] D. Brabham. Crowdsourcing as a model for problem solving: An introduction and cases. *The Journal of Research into New Media Technologies*, 14(1), pp. 75-90, 2008.

[16] A. Evfimievski, J. Gehrke, and R. Srikant. Limiting privacy breaches in privacy preserving data mining. In *Proceedings of the SIGMOD/PODS Conference*, pages 211–222, 2003.

[17] D. Chakrabarti, R. Kumar, A. Tomkins. Evolutionary clustering. *KDD Conference*, 2006.

[18] T. Choudhury A. Pentland. The Sociometer: A Wearable Device for Understanding Human Networks. *International Sunbelt Social Network Conference*, February 2003.

[19] T. Choudhury, A. Pentland. Sensing and Modeling Human Networks using the Sociometer, *International Conference on Wearable Computing*, 2003.

[20] T. Choudhury, A. Pentland. Characterizing Social Networks using the Sociometer. *North American Association of Computational Social and Organizational Science*, 2004.

[21] T. Choudhury, B. Clarkson, S. Basu, A. Pentland. Learning Communities: Connectivity and Dynamics of Interacting Agents. *International Joint Conference on Neural Networks*, 2003.

[22] T. Choudhury, M. Philipose, D. Wyatt, J. Lester. Towards Activity Databases: Using Sensors and Statistical Models to Summarize People's Lives. *IEEE Data Engineering Bulletin*, Vol. 29 No. 1, March 2006.

[23] Z. Huang, W. Du, and B. Chen. Deriving private information from randomized data. In *Proceedings of the 2005 ACM SIGMOD Conference*, pages 37–48, Baltimore, MD, June 2005.

[24] H. Kargutpa, S. Datta, Q. Wang, and K. Sivakumar. On the privacy preserving properties of random data perturbation techniques. In *Proceedings of the IEEE International Conference on Data Mining*, pages 99–106, 2003.

[25] A. Clauset, M. E. J. Newman, C. Moore. Finding community structure in very large networks. *Phys. Rev. E 70, 066111*, 2004.

[26] G. Cormode, S. Muthukrishnan. An Improved Data Stream Summary: The Count-Min Sketch and its Applications. *LATIN*, pp. 29–38, 2004.

[27] C. Faloutsos, T. Kolda, J. Sun. Mining Large Time-Evolving Data using Matrix and Tensor Tools, *ICDM Conference*, 2007.

[28] R. K. Ganti, N. Pham, Y.-E. Tsai, T. F. Abdelzaher. PoolView: Stream Privacy in Grassroots Participatory Sensing, *SenSys*, 2008.

[29] R. K. Ganti, Y.-E. Tsai, T. F. Abdelzaher. SenseWorld: Towards Cyber-Physical Social Networks. *IPSN*, pp. 563-564, 2008.

[30] M. Garofalakis, J. Gehrke, R. Rastogi. Querying and mining data streams: you only get one look (a tutorial). *SIGMOD Conference*, 2002.

[31] R. K. Ganti, P. Jayachandran, T. F. Abdelzaher, J. A. Stankovic, SATIRE: A Software Architecture for Smart AtTIRE. *Mobisys*, 2006.

[32] Raghu Ganti, Nam Pham, Hossein Ahmadi, Saurabh Nangia, Tarek Abdelzaher. GreenGPS: A Participatory Sensing Fuel-Efficient Maps Application. *Mobisys*, San Francisco, CA, June 2010.

[33] B. Gedik, L. Liu. Location Privacy in Mobile Systems: A Personalized Anonymization Model. *ICDCS Conference*, 2005.

[34] T. Guo, K. Iwamura, and M. Koga. Towards high accuracy road maps generation from massive GPS traces data. *Proc. of IGARSS*, pp. 667-670, 2007.

[35] P. Indyk. Stable Distributions, Pseudorandom Generators, Embeddings and Data Stream Computation. *IEEE FOCS*, 2000.

[36] Y. Ioannidis, V. Poosala. Balancing Histogram Optimality and Practicality for Query Set Size Estimation. *ACM SIGMOD Conference*, 1995.

[37] H. Jagadish, N. Koudas, S. Muthukrishnan, V. Poosala, K. Sevcik, T. Suel. Optimal Histograms with Quality Guarantees. *VLDB Conference*, 1998.

[38] Y. Jing, S. Baluja. Pagerank for product image search. *WWW Conference*, pages 307–316, 2008.

[39] W. Johnson W., J. Lindenstrauss. Extensions of Lipshitz mapping onto Hilbert Space. *Contemporary Mathematics*, Vol 26, pp. 189–206, 1984.

[40] R. Kumar, P. Raghavan, S. Rajagopalan, A. Tomkins. Trawling the web for emerging cyber-communities. *WWW Conference*, 1999.

[41] A. Krause, E. Horvitz, A. Kansal, F. Zhao. Toward Community Sensing. *IPSN*, pp. 481–492, 2008.

[42] M. Laibowitz, N.-W. Gong, J. A. Paradiso, Wearable Sensing for Dynamic Management of Dense Ubiquitous Media. *BSN*, 2009.

[43] J. Leskovec, K. J. Lang, A. Dasgupta, M. W. Mahoney. Statistical properties of community structure in large social and information networks. *WWW Conference*, 2008.

[44] Y. Li, J. Han, J. Yang. Clustering Moving Objects, *ACM KDD Conference*, 2004.

[45] J. Lifton, M. Feldmeier, Y. Ono, C. Lewis, J. A. Paradiso. A platform for ubiquitous sensor deployment in occupational and domestic environments. *IPSN*, 2007.

[46] Z. Liu, J. Xu Yu, Y. Ke, X. Lin, L. Chen. Spotting Significant Changing Subgraphs in Evolving Graphs, *ICDM Conference*, 2008.

[47] L. Luo, A. Kansal, S. Nath, F. Zhao. Sharing and exploring sensor streams over geocentric interfaces, *ACM SIGSPATIAL international conference on Advances in geographic information systems*, 2008.

[48] S. Babcock, M. Datar, R. Motwani. Sampling from a Moving Window over Streaming Data. *SIAM Symposium on Discrete Algorithms (SODA)*, 2002.

[49] S. Nath, J. Liu, F, Zhao. SensorMap for Wide-Area Sensor Webs. *IEEE Computer*, 40(7): 90-93, 2008.

[50] M. Newman. Finding community structure in networks using the eigenvectors of matrices. *Physical Review E*, 2006.

[51] N. Pham, T. Abdelzaher, S. Nath. On Bounding Data Stream Privacy in Distributed Cyber-physical Systems, *IEEE International Conference on Sensor Networks, Ubiquitous, and Trustworthy Computing (IEEE SUTC)*, Newport Beach, CA, June, 2010.

[52] N. Pham, R. K. Ganti, Y. S. Uddin, S. Nath, T. Abdelzaher, Privacy preserving Reconstruction of Multidimensional Data Maps in Vehicular Participatory Sensing, *EWSN*, 2010.

[53] S. Reddy, K. Shilton, G. Denisov, C. Cenizal, D. Estrin, M. B. Srivastava. Biketastic: sensing and mapping for better biking. *CHI*, pp. 1817–1820, 2010.

[54] S. Reddy, D. Estrin, M. B. Srivastava. Recruitment Framework for Participatory Sensing Data Collections.*Pervasive*, pp. 138–155, 2010.

[55] M. Romaine, J. Richardson. State of the Translation Industry. *Translation Industry Report*, My Gengo, 2009.

[56] V. Satuluri, S. Parthasarathy. Scalable graph clustering using stochastic flows: Applications to community discovery. *KDD Conference*, 2009.

[57] J. Sun, S. Papadimitriou, P. Yu, C. Faloutsos. Graphscope: Parameter-free Mining of Large Time-Evolving Graphs, *KDD Conference*, 2007.

[58] H. Tong, S. Papadimitriou, P. Yu, C. Faloutsos. Proximity-Tracking on Time-Evolving Bipartite Graphs, *SDM Conference*, 2008.

[59] J. S. Vitter. Random Sampling with a Reservoir. *ACM Transactions on Mathematical Software*, Vol 11(1), pp. 37–57, 1985.

[60] Z. Yang, S. Zhong, and R. N. Wright. Privacy-preserving classification without loss of accuracy. In *Proceedings of the Fifth SIAM International Conference on Data Mining*, pages 92–102, 2005.

[61] D. Wyatt, T. Choudhury, J. Bilmes. Creating Social Network Models from Sensor Data, *NIPS Network Workshop*, 2007.

[62] D. Wyatt, T. Choudhury, J. Bilmes. Conversation Detection and Speaker Segmentation in Privacy Sensitive Situated Speech Data. *Proceedings of Interspeech*, 2007.

[63] D. Wyatt, T. Choudhury, H. Kautz. Capturing Spontaneous Conversation and Social Dynamics: A Privacy-Sensitive Data Collection Effort. *International Conference on Acoustics, Speech, and Signal Processing (ICASSP)*, 2007.

[64] D. Wyatt, T. Choudhury, J. Bilmes. Learning Hidden Curved Exponential Random Graph Models to Infer Face-to-Face Interaction Networks from Situated Speech Data. *Proceedings of AAAI*, 2008.

[65] T. Zhang, A. Popescul, and B. Dom. Linear prediction models with graph regularization for web-page categorization. In *KDD*, pages 821–826, 2006.

[66] N. Zhang, S. Wang, and W. Zhao. A new scheme on privacy-preserving data classification. In *KDD '05: Proceedings of the eleventh ACM SIGKDD international conference on Knowledge discovery in data mining*, pages 374–383, New York, NY, USA, 2005. ACM.

[67] F. Zhao, L. Guibas. *Wireless Sensor Networks: An Information Processing Approach*, Morgan Kaufmann, 2004.

[68] Y. Zhou, H. Cheng, and J. X. Yu. Graph clustering based on structural/attribute similarities. *PVLDB*, 2(1):718–729, 2009.

[69] http://latitude.google.com

[70] http://www.citysense.com

[71] http://www.movebank.org

[72] http://www-01.ibm.com/software/data/infosphere/streams/

[73] http://www.sensenetworks.com/macrosense.php

[74] http://www.navizon.com

[75] http://ilocalis.com

[76] http://www.trapster.com

[77] National Science Foundation Workshop Report on Future Directions in Networked Sensing Systems: Fundamentals and Applications, The Westin Arlington Gateway, Arlington, VA, November 12-13, 2009.

Chapter 15

MULTIMEDIA INFORMATION NETWORKS IN SOCIAL MEDIA

Liangliang Cao, GuoJun Qi, Shen-Fu Tsai,
Min-Hsuan Tsai, Andrey Del Pozo, Thomas S. Huang
Beckman Institute and Coordinated Science Lab
Department of ECE, University of Illinois at Urbana-Champaign
{cao4,qi4,stsai8,mtsai2,delpozo2,huang}@ifp.illinois.edu

Xuemei Zhang and Suk Hwan Lim
Multimedia Interaction and Understanding Lab
HP Labs, Palo Alto, CA
{xuemei.zhang,suk-hwan.lim}@hp.com

Abstract The popularity of personal digital cameras and online photo/video sharing community has lead to an explosion of multimedia information. Unlike traditional multimedia data, many new multimedia datasets are organized in a structural way, incorporating rich information such as semantic ontology, social interaction, community media, geographical maps, in addition to the multimedia contents by themselves. Studies of such structured multimedia data have resulted in a new research area, which is referred to as *Multimedia Information Networks*. Multimedia information networks are closely related to social networks, but especially focus on understanding the topics and semantics of the multimedia files in the context of network structure. This chapter reviews different categories of recent systems related to multimedia information networks, summarizes the popular inference methods used in recent works, and discusses the applications related to multimedia information networks. We also discuss a wide range of topics including public datasets, related industrial systems, and potential future research directions in this field.

Keywords: Multimedia Information Networks, Social Media, Personal Photo Albums, Ontology, Geographical Annotation

1. Introduction

A multimedia information network is a structured multimedia collection, where multimedia documents, such as images and videos are conceptually represented by nodes, that are connected by links. These links correspond to either actual hyperlinks in social and web networks, or logical relationships between the nodes which are implicitly defined by different kinds of relationships, meta-information such as user identifiers, location information or tags. The recent popularity of research in this area is due to the rapid increase in online web content such as web images and the popularity of online communities. For example, Flickr and Facebook host billions of images, which are linked to each other by virtue of actual hyperlinks or their relationships to users, groups, and tags. The resulting network structure contains rich semantic information, such as semantic ontologies, social relationships, and meta-information. It has become an interesting challenge to explore the interplay between the network structure and the rich content information in multimedia information networks. Such network structure and semantic knowledge can be used to convert the content into useful knowledge for a variety of tasks. Thus, the network structure plays a critical role in the conversion process, which is so essential to leveraging the knowledge inherent in the information network. An appropriate recent quote by John Munsell is as follows:
"If the content is king, then the conversion is queen"

Multimedia information networks can be viewed as a marriage of multimedia content and social networks. However, it conveys much richer information than either of the two could express as a stand-alone entity, because of the hidden information which is stored in the interplay between the two entities. In order to understand multimedia information networks, we must consider not only the visual features for each node, but also explore the network structure associated with them. In recent years, there has been a lot of work in this area, and this has begun to create a critical mass of new research in this area.

Although it has become a popular research topic in recent years, the subject of multimedia information networks is still in its infancy. This chapter provides an overview of recent developments in the field of multimedia information networks. Our aim is to provide an understanding and motivation of the key problems and techniques in this field, though it is hard to be exhaustive, given the extraordinarily wide coverage of this area. The chapter also provides the citations to the key literature in the field, for a reader that is interested in a detailed understanding.

It is important to note that the link structures of multimedia information networks are primarily logical, and are created by logical commonality in features, and relationships between different entities in the network. This chapter will describe the different kinds of logical link structures which can be created in an information network, in addition to the natural hyperlinks which are often present in a social network and web environment. We also study the *methodological techniques* for exploiting the interplay between content and network structure. The chapter is correspondingly divided into two parts:

- In the first part, we summarize four categories of popular (logical) link structures in Multimedia Information Networks: semantic ontologies, community media, personal photograph albums, and geographical locations. For each link type, we review some typical methods together with their applications.

- In the second part of the chapter, we discuss some specific problems and techniques in this field: data sets and industrial systems, inference methods, and future directions.

At a more detailed level, the chapter is organized as follows. In section 2, we discuss the derivation of links from semantics. In section 3, we discuss the derivation of links from community media. In section 4, we discuss the networks which are created by the linkage of personal photograph albums. In section 5, we discuss the networks created by the linkage of geographical information. In section 6, we discuss the common inference methods which are used for mining such networks. In section 7, we discuss data sets and industrial systems. Section 8 contains the conclusions, summary and future directions.

2. Links from Semantics: Ontology-based Learning

Ontology plays a pivotal role for representing concepts that we are concerned with and their relations. Ontology would contain whatever human knowledge pertaining to the domain of interests that could help better process and analysis of visual data and textual cues.

In [18], an ontology was constructed by hand to facilitate personal photo album management. In [106], the authors worked on image retrieval for animal domain. They extracted scientific lassification information available in Wikipedia pages as their animal domain ontology. Next, in order to build textual ontology, they parsed relevant Wikipedia sections and found important keywords including concepts and relations. Finally, the relations in the ontology are further cross-verified via "is-a" relations in animal ontology.

In the case of ontology for more general subjects, Wikipedia and WordNet are two important knowledge bases. Wikipedia stores knowledge of generic terms and name entities in its countless articles. This results in difficulty in automatic and systematic knowledge extraction, while WordNet provides a lot of relational information between generic terms. The YAGO system developed in [101] bridges these two and provides a comprehensive ontology covering many generic subjects in daily life.

There have been some works focusing on hierarchical classification and retrieval. In [64], the ontology is more general as it exploits "is-a" and "part-of" relations and is in general a graph. In the resulting graph, each edge e is associated with a binary classifier which computes conditional likelihood given the previous concept. Because the graph may not be a tree, there may be multiple paths from the root concept to any target concept. Each path p is pessimistically associated with the minimum of the conditional likelihoods associated with all edges on the path. The marginal likelihood of any target concept is then optimistically set as the maximum of all path likelihoods from root to the target concept. Similarly for ImageNet constructed in [25], the "tree-max classifier" that propagates maximum of all descendant concept likelihoods one level up was proposed to estimate individual concept likelihood in the tree-structured ontology. In [126], the authors investigated the effects of combining label estimates of classifiers trained at various levels, as well as possibilities of transferring concept models to neighboring concepts like sibling concepts to address small sample problem. A more sophisticated hierarchical classification proposed in [11] is to encode the path from root concept to target concept by a fix-length binary vector and then treat it as a multilabel classification problem.

Effectively modeling structured concepts has become a critical ingredient for retrieving and searching multimedia data on the Web. Many sophisticated models have been proposed to recognize a wide range of multimedia concepts from our everyday lives to many specific domains, which lead to a collection of multimedia model warehouses such as Large-Scale Concept for Multimedia (LSCOM) [76] and 101 semantic concepts in multimedia [99]. To model the ontology, some researchers employ a flat correlative concept structure [81][77], while others try to build hierarchical structures based on semantic correlations [114] [27] [64].

3. Links from Community Media

The primary concept governing community media is that users play the central role in retrieving, indexing and mining media content. The basic idea is quite different from a traditional content-centric multimedia system. The web sites providing community media are not solely operated by the the owners but by millions of amateur users who provide, share, edit and index these media content. In this section, we will review recent research advancements in community media systems from two aspects: (1) retrieval and indexing system for community media based on user-contributed tags, and (2) community media recommendations by mining user ratings on media content.

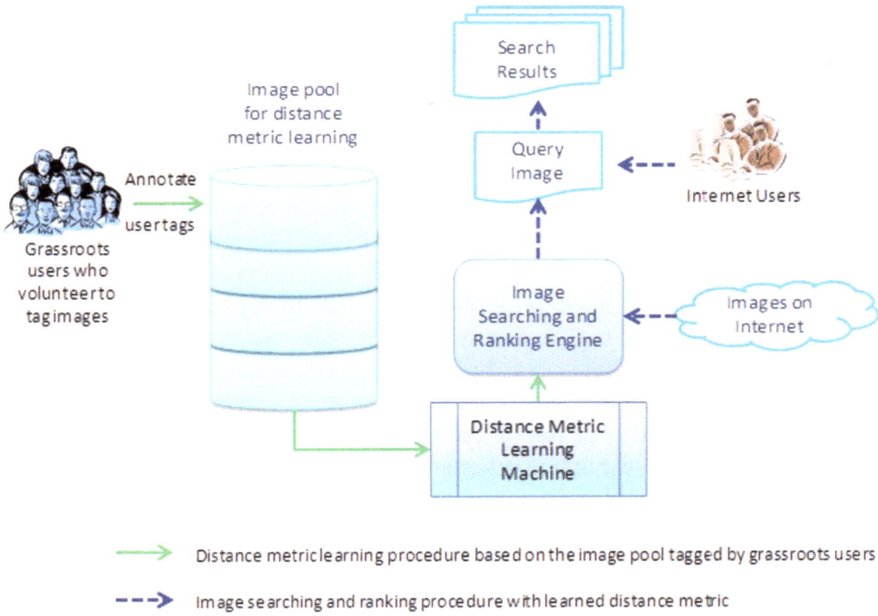

Figure 15.1. The distance metric is mined from the visual content of images together with the tags annotated by the grassroots users. The learned distance metric then is applied to retrieve images on the Internet by ranking their relevances to the query.

3.1 Retrieval Systems for Community Media

Recent advances in internet speed and easy-to-use user interfaces provided by some web companies, such as Flickr, Corbis and Facebook, have significantly promoted image sharing, exchange and propagation among user. Meanwhile, the infrastructures of image-sharing social networks make it an easy task for users to attach tags to images. These huge amount of user tags enable the fine understanding of the associated images and provide many research opportunities to boost image search and retrieval performance. On the other hand, the user tags somehow reflect the users' intentions and subjectivities and therefore can be leveraged to build a user-driven image search system.

To develop a reliable retrieval system for community media based on these user contributed tags, two basic problems must be resolved. First of all, the user tags are often quite noisy or even semantically meaningless [21]. More specifically, the user tags are known to be ambiguous, limited in terms of completeness, and overly personalized [32] [65]. This is not surprising because of the uncontrolled nature of social tagging and the diversity of knowledge and cultural background of the users [55]. To guarantee a satisfactory retrieval performance, tag denoising methods are required to refine these tags before they can be used for retrieval and indexing. Some examples of tag denoising methods are described below.

The work in [103] proposes to construct an intermediate concept space from user tags which can be used as a medium to infer and detect more generic concepts of interest in the future. The work in [112] proposes a probabilistic framework to resolve ambiguous tags which are likely to occur but appear in different contexts with the help of human effort. There also exist many tag suggestion methods [4] [69] [98] [115] which help users annotate community media with most informative tags, and avoid meaningless or low-quality tags. For all these methods, tag suggestion systems are involved to actively guide users to provide high-quality tags based on tags co-occurrence relations.

Secondly, the tags associated with an image are generally in a random order without any importance or relevance information, which limits the effectiveness of these tags in search and other applications. To overcome this problem, [59] proposes a tag ranking scheme that aims to automatically rank the tags associated with a given image according to their relevance to the image content. This tag ranking system estimates the initial relevance scores for the tags based on probability density estimations, and followed by a random walk over a tag similarity graph in order to refine the relevance scores. Another method was proposed in [55] that learns tag relevance by accumulating votes from visually similar neighbors. Treated as tag frequency, this learned tag relevance is seamlessly embedded into tag-based social image retrieval paradigms.

Many efforts have been made on developing the multimedia retrieval systems by mining the user tags. As a typical social image retrieval system illustrated in Figure 15.1, a distance metric is mined from these web images and their associated user tags, which can be directly applied to retrieve web images in a content-based image retrieval paradigm [83]. In [109], Wang et al. propose a novel attempt at model-free image annotation, which is a data-driven approach that annotates images by mining their search results based on user tags and surrounding text. Since no training data set is required, their approach enables annotating with unlimited vocabulary and is highly scalable and robust to outliers.

3.2 Recommendation Systems for Community Media

The problem of developing recommendation systems for community media has attracted considerable attention. This is because of the popularity of Web 2.0 applications, such as Flickr, Youtube and Facebook. Users give their own comments and ratings on multimedia items, such as images, amateur videos and movies. However, only a small portion of the multimedia items have been rated and thus the available user ratings are quite sparse. Therefore, an automatic recommendation system is desired to be able to predict users' ratings on multimedia items, so that they can easily find the interesting images, videos and movies from shared multimedia contents.

Recommendation systems measure the user interest in given items or products to provide personalized recommendations based on user taste [39] [6]. It becomes more and more important to enhance user experience and loyalty by providing them with the most appropriate products in e-commerce web sites (such as Amazon, eBay , Netflix, TiVo and Yahoo). Thus, there are many advantages in designing a user-satisfied recommendation system.

Currently, existing recommendation systems can be categorized into two different types. The content-based approach [1] creates a profile for each user or product which depicts its nature. User profiles can be described by their historical rating records on movies, personal information (such as their age, gender, or occupation) and their movie types of interest. Meanwhile, movie profiles can be represented by other features, such as their titles, release date, and movie genres (e.g., action, adventure, animation, comedy). The obtained profiles allow programs to quantify the associations between users and products.

The other popular recommendation systems rely only on the past user ratings on products with no need to create explicit profiles. This method is known as collaborative filtering (CF) [31], and it analyzes relationships between users and interdependencies among products. In other words, it aims at predicting a user rating based on user ratings on the same set of multimedia items. The only information used in CF is the historical behavior of users, such as their previous transactions or the way they rate products. The CF method can also be cast as two primary approaches - the neighborhood approach and latent factor models. Neighborhood methods compute the relationships between users [38] [9] [85] or items [26] [56] [93] or combination thereof [108] to predict the preference of a user to a product. On the other hand, latent factor models transform both users and items into the same latent factor space and measure their interactions in this space directly. The most representative methods of latent factor models are singular value decomposition (SVD) [80]. Evaluations on recommendation systems suggest that SVD methods have gained state-of-the-art performance among many other methods [80].

Some public data sets are available for comparison purpose among different recommendation systems. Among them, the most exciting and popular one is the Netflix data set for movie recommendation[1]. The Netflix data set contains more than 100 million ratings on nearly 18 thousand movie titles from over 480,000 randomly-sampled customers. These user ratings were collected be-

[1] http://www.netflixprize.com

tween October 1998 and December 2005, and they are able to represent the user trend and preference during this period. The ratings are given on a scale from 1 to 5 stars. The date of each rating as well as the title and year of release for each movie are provided. No other data, such as customer or movie information, were employed to compute Cinematch's accuracy values used in this contest. In addition to the training data set, a qualifying test set is provided with over 2.8 million customer-movie pairs and the rating dates. These pairs were selected from the most recent ratings from a subset of the same customers in the training data set, over a subset of the same movies.[2]

4. Network of Personal Photo Albums

The proliferation of high quality and modestly priced digital cameras has resulted in an explosion of personal digital photo collections in the past ten years. It is not uncommon for a home user to take thousands of digital photos each year. These images are largely unlabeled, and often have minimal organization done by the user. Managing, accessing, and making use of this collection has become a challenging task.

The majority of current work on image annotation and organization makes use of photo collections available on the web, such as those from Flickr, Facebook, or Wiki pages. This provide many insights that are also applicable to personal collections. However, personal collections also have some distinctive properties, that are very different from professional or web collections. We will discuss research works that address the issues related to each of these unique aspects of personal photo collections.

4.1 Actor-Centric Nature of Personal Collections

Both identity of people and number of people in photos are important cues to users in how they remember, describe, and search personal photos [72]. There is a large body of research on face recognition. The accuracy of state-of-the-art face recognition algorithms under controlled-capture situation are reasonably high[68], although accuracy can vary significantly for different persons and data-sets. While accuracy under uncontrolled capture may not be sufficient for fully-automatic annotation, it can be a baseline for very efficient semi-automatic annotation. Personal collections are usually dominated by a small number of subjects. Therefore, with an intelligent user interfaces, it is possible

---

[2]Netflix offered a Grand Prize with $1,000,000 and Progress Prizes with $50,000. On September 2009, Netflix announced the latest Grand Prize winner as team BellKor's Pragmatic Chaos [52]. This result achieves a root mean squared error (RMSE) of 0.8567 on the test subset - a 10.06% improvement over the Cinematch's score on the test subset. The latter uses straightforward statistical linear models with data conditioning. The next Grand Prize winner will have to improve RMSE by at least 10% compared to BellKor's Pragmatic Chaos algorithm.

to achieve 80% recall rate and near 100% precision with minimal amount of user input, such as a few seconds of simple drag-and-drop merging of similar clusters [122].

Subjects in personal photos within a collection are usually related by family ties or friendships. Discovering and understanding the relationship among identified people in personal collections has significant application impact. Sharing of personal photos on social networking sites such as Facebook makes it possible to discover relations beyond an individual's collection. Recent work by Wu et al [113] took advantage of face clustering technology in order to discover social relationships of subjects in personal photo collections. Co-occurrence of identified faces as well as inter-face distances (inferred from in-image distance and typical human face size) are used to calculate link strength between any two identified persons. In such cases, social clusters as well as social importance of individuals can be calculated.

Relationship analysis of subjects in personal photos can be used to improve facial annotation. Gallagher et al [29] exploits pairwise connections between frequent faces in personal photo collections in order to build up prior probabilities of groups of faces appearing in a single image. This information is used to identify individuals from ambiguously-labeled group shots. While the emphasis of this chapter is not on relationship analysis, it shows one of the many potential values in modeling relationships between people in personal photo collections.

4.2 Quality Issues in Personal Collections

The transition to digital photography encouraged much more trial-and-error in consumer photo capture. People often take a number of photos of the same subjects in sequence in the hope of picking out an ideal one later. This habit contributed to the increasing collection size of personal photos. Effective near-duplicate detection is highly useful both in browsing and in creation of photo-based products such as photo-books.

Near-duplicate detection can be done with a variety of approaches, each with different trade-offs in accuracy and efficiency. Detection methods based on global features such as color histograms are fast but are likely to introduce false-positives when two photos with very different contents have similar colors, so they are often used in combination with other methods, or as a pre-filter step [43]. Detection based on structural features are less prone to confusion, at a much higher computational cost [20, 121]. A hybrid approach [102] combines time, color, and local structural information in a cascade framework so that more "expensive" calculations are only done when necessary.

After duplicate clusters are identified, selection, ranking, or mashing of the duplicate photos are usually called for in consumer applications. Selection in a duplicate set can be done by image quality or image appeal [94], or by how well an image represents the cluster [20]. Since duplicates in a personal collection are usually taken with the same camera at the same scene from slightly different viewpoints, it is also possible to combine the images in the duplicate set to form a new composite image that is a “bigger and better" representation of the scene [97].

4.3 Time and Location Themes in Personal Collections

Personal collections are generally captured using a small number of cameras with time stamp (and sometimes GPS information). Typically, users store these photos in folders labeled with time and event information [49]. Event and location information are also among the top cues people remember and use when searching for photos [72]. Due to the availability and importance of time and location information for personal collections, both cues are used in photo clustering and annotation work for personal photos.

Time clustering is one of the fastest and most effective method in organizing personal photos into meaningful groups. It can be done with a simple K-means clustering algorithm [62] or with more sophisticated multi-scale approach [22], or by identifying “bursts” of photo taken with roughly the same rate [33]. Time clustering is often used in combination with image content similarity. In addition to being an informative cue of event grouping, time cues can also be used to limit image similarity calculations to images within a certain time interval, therefore reducing the computation load for content-based clustering [102].

Location information is another key element in event clustering of personal photos. Naaman et al. [74] used both time and location information to create a photo organization system. A location clustering and naming algorithm is used to assign location tags to each photo using GPS information extracted from photo EXIF headers. Cao et al [17] showed that even without GPS tags in EXIF headers, it is possible to generate location tags with usable accuracy when combining image features with existing textual tags. These results indicate the feasibility and usefulness of location identification in personal collection analysis.

4.4 Content Overlap in Personal Collections

For personal photos, users often know more about the content than what can be inferred from a single image, such as who took the picture, who was standing nearby, what happened before/after that moment, and what other objects go together with the objects visible in the image. Looking beyond a single photo can often make a big difference in the annotation accuracy of personal collections.

Annotation of a collection instead of individual photos is one way to take advantage of the photo-to-photo correlation in personal collections. Cao et al [14] used conditional random fields to model correlations of different photos in a sub-collection to annotate photos by scene type and also annotate sub-collections by event type. This work made good use of the inherent event-based organization and strong inter-photo correlations that are characteristic of personal collections to improve image collection annotation.

In the work by Gallagher et al [29], face appearance and co-appearance frequencies within personal collections are used to build up prior probabilities of groups of faces appearing in a single image, and this in turn is used to disambiguate personal labels for individual photos. This is an example of using the correlation of photos within a collection to improve individual photo annotation.

One can also go beyond the personal collection itself, and use photos in web collections and their associated labels to improve personal photo annotation. Liu et al. [61] learns images corresponding to concepts from enormous images and their surrounding text on the web. The links between concepts and visual features are transferred from the Internet to personal photo collections together with concepts hierarchies provided by WordNet(http://wordnet.princeton.edu/), the latter giving "subclass-of" relation between concept in order to decide the negative training images for a certain concept – if concept "pool" has descendants(subclasses) "natatorium", "cistern", "lido", and "sink", then images irrelevant to "pool" will be those surrounded by text that do not contain any of these subclasses. In a word, both concept-to-image link and subclass-of link between concepts are collected and utilized to train the image retrieval system.

Correlations among keywords, visually similar images, and closely time-stamped images usually provide much implicit human knowledge for annotation. Roughly speaking, visually similar photos are supposed to have correlated annotations, and semantically close keywords are usually used to describe largely overlapping sets of images. Motivated by these ideas, Jia et al. [42] proposed to propagate correlations of these three domains around to improve the final annotation, where initial keyword correlation is obtained from Google in a statistical way. After steady-state keyword and visual correlation graphs are obtained based on their initial values and annotation of the images, they are used together with the temporal correlation graph to get the final annotation.

5. Network of Geographical Information

Geographical information is often represented in the form of a longitude-latitude pair in order to represent the locations where the images are taken. In recent years, the use of geographical information has become more and more popular. With advances in low-cost GPS chips, cell phones and cameras have become equipped with GPS receivers, and thus are able to record the locations while taking pictures. Many online communities, such as Flickr and Google Earth, allow users to specify the location of their shared images either manually through placement on a map or automatically using image meta-data embedded in the image files. At the end of 2009, there have been approximately 100 million geo-tagged images in Flickr, and millions of new images continue to be added each month.

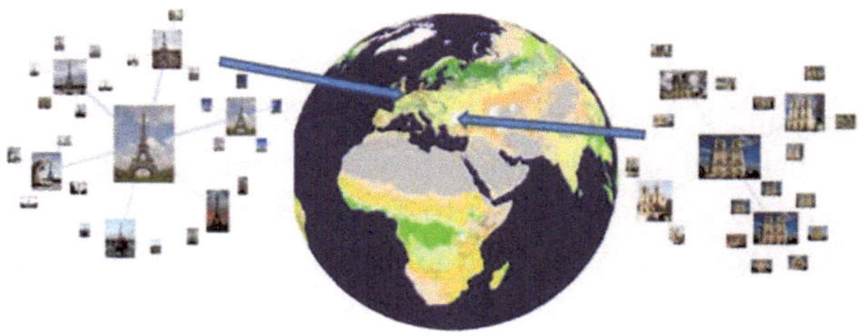

Figure 15.2. GPS Network

Given the geographical information associated with images, we can easily construct a network by grouping images taken from neighboring regions. Figure 15.2 illustrates such a network. The network shows that the visual information may be correlated with GPS positions. This makes it possible to infer the image semantics with geographical information, or to estimate the geographical information from visual content. By exploring the rich media such as user tags, satellite images and wikipedia knowledge, we can leverage the visual and geographical information for many novel applications.

Geographical annotation provides a rich source of information which can link millions of images based on the similarity from geographical measures. There has been a growing body of work in visual research community investigating geographical information for image understanding [73] [2] [16] [118] [45] [119] [47] [71] [84] [63] [95] [12]. One line of research utilizes geographical information for better understanding of the image semantics. Another line of research is devoted to estimating the geographical information from general images.

5.1 Semantic Annotation

Naaman et al. [73] proposed a system to suggest candidate identity labels based on the meta-data of a photo including its time stamp and location. The system explores the information of events and locations, and the co-occurrence statistics of people. However, image analysis techniques are not used in the system.

After Naaman's work, more recent lines of research aim to understand semantics from both visual information and geographical collections. Joshi and Luo [45] propose to explore Geographical Information Systems (GIS) databases using a given geographical location. They use descriptions of small local neighborhoods to form bags of geo-tags as their representation. The associations of Geo-tags and visual features are learned to infer the event/activity labels such as "beach" or "wedding". The authors demonstrate that the context of geographical location is a strong cue for visual event/activity recognition. Yu and Luo [118] propose another way to leverage nonvisual contexts such as location and time stamps. Their approach learns from rough location (e.g., states in the US) and time (e.g., seasons) information, which can be obtained through picture metadata automatically. Both visual and nonvisual context information are fused using a probabilistic graphical model to improve the accuracy of object region recognition. In [63], the authors explore satellite images corresponding to picture location data and investigate their novel uses to recognize the picture-taking environment. The satellite image functions as a third eye above the object. This satellite information is combined with classical vision-based event detection methods. Luo *et al.* [63] employed both color- and structure-based visual vocabularies for characterizing ground and satellite images, respectively. The fusion of the complementary views (photo and satellite) achieves significant performance improvement over the ground view baseline.

5.2 Geographical Estimation

The previous section discusses research relevant to understanding the semantics better using geographical information. An interesting question of a different nature is whether we can use the visual information to estimate the geographical locations even when they are not provided. As evidenced by the success of Google Earth, there is great need for such geographic information from users. Many web users have high interests in not only the places they live but also other interesting places around the world. Geographic annotation is also desirable when reviewing travel and vacation images. For example, when a user becomes interested in a nice photo, he or she may want to know where exactly it is. Moreover, if a user plans to visit a place, he or she may want to find out the points of interest nearby. Recent studies suggest that geo-tags expand the context that can be employed for image content analysis by adding extra information about the subject or environment of the image.

Hays and Efros [37] were among the first to consider the problem of estimating the location of a single image using only its visual content. They collected millions of geo-tagged Flickr images. By using a comprehensive set of visual features, they employed nearest neighbor search in the reference set in order to locate the image. Results show that the approach is able to locate about a quarter of the images (from a test data set) to within approximately 750 km of their true location.

Motivated by [37], Gallagher et al. [30] incorporate textual tags to estimate the geographical locations of images. Their results show that textual tags perform better than visual content but they perform better in combination than either alone. Cao et al. [16] also recognizes the effectiveness of tags in estimating the geolocations. Similar to [30], they combine tags with visual information for annotation, however, they propose a novel model named logistic canonical correlation regression which explores the canonical correlations between geographical locations, visual content and community tags. Unlike [37], they argue that it is difficult to estimate the exact location at which a photo was taken and propose to estimate only the coarse location. A mean-shift based approach is employed to spatially cluster all the images into several hundreds of regions, and then estimate the most likely region for each image. The experimental results show that inference of the coarse location will lead to both meaningful and accurate annotations.

Similar to Cao et al. [16], Crandall et al. [23] only estimate the approximate location of a novel photo. Using SVM classifiers, a novel image is again geo-located by assigning it to the best cluster based on its visual content and annotations. At the landmark scale, both the text annotations and visual content perform better than chance while at the metropolitan scale, only the text annotations perform better than chance. Since landmarks are the most interesting locations, such geo-tagged images have potential to produce tourist maps using geographical annotation techniques [19]. In a recent research work [123] supported by Google, Zhen et al. focused on the landmark recognition. They build a web-scale landmark recognition engine named "Tour the world" using 20 million GPS-tagged photos of landmarks together with online tour guide web pages. The experiments demonstrate that the engine can deliver satisfactory recognition performance with high efficiency. However, it is still an open question whether it is possible to recognize non-landmark locations reliably.

5.3 Other Applications

In addition to the research works discussed above, there are other interesting directions. Agarwal et al. [3] develop an exciting system with a 500 core cluster which matches and reconstructs three dimensional scenes from an extremely large number of photographs collected from Flickr. The results show that three dimensional reconstruction algorithms can scale with the size of the problem and the amount of available computation. Ji et al. [41] and Wang et al. [110] consider the problem of mining geographical information from web blogs and forums together with images. Quack et al. [84] develop a system for linking images from community photo collections to relevant Wikipedia articles. Cao et al. [12] propose to build a tourism recommendation system using web photos with GPS information.

6. Inference Methods

Inference is a central problem in Multimedia information networks. Since it is impossible to overview all the inferences algorithms, next we will discuss some issues which we believe are important with general interests.

6.1 Discriminative vs. Generative Models

Discriminative and generative models are two groups of machine learning algorithms with different ways of learning models from data. Given input x and their label y, generative models aim to learn the joint distribution $P(x, y) = P(x|y)P(y)$. In contrast, discriminative classifiers model the posterior $P(y|x)$ directly, or learn a direct map from inputs x to class labels. Examples of generative models are naive Bayes, Bayesian Network, GMM, HMM, and many graphical models. Discriminative models include logistic regression, SVM, Boosting, and Conditional Random Fields. Generally speaking, when there are enough training samples, discriminative models lead to more accurate classification results than generative models [78]. This is verified by the dominating success of discriminative models in web image retrieval and annotation systems [75] [81]. However, in recent years, there has been a renaissance of generative models for a wide range of multimedia information network applications. Based on our understanding, generative models share the following advantages which make them attractive in many application domains

- Generative models can generate more intuitive interpretation of data samples. Generative models provide an estimation of density functions, from which we can easily determine the marginal distribution in different scenarios. Starting from the $P(x, y)$, we can obtain the conditional distribution $P(x|y)$ and thus obtain the representative samples for each class. Moreover, we can employ the latent topic models [3] [40] to explore the multinomial distributions of coherent factors.

- Generative models can easily handle the missing value problem. In a multimedia information network, it is common that some attributes of a data sample are missing. Generative model can handle such samples easily by using Expectation-Maximization (EM) algorithms to estimate missing values. In contrast, discriminative models usually have to neglect such samples.

- With generative models, it is possible to incorporate network structure with the model. For example, [13] proposes to model the photo correlations using both visual similarity and the temporal coherence, and construct a network for label propagation. Another example lies in network regularized topic model [67], which combines the topic model with a harmonic regularizer based on social network structure. It has been shown that generative models are flexible, and can handle multi-modal information embedded in the information network, which is preferable in many situations.

6.2 Graph-based Inference: Ranking, Clustering and Semi-supervised Learning

An information network can also be represented as a graph, in which nodes are connected by social network or other links. One of the most famous graph-based learning algorithm is PageRank [79], which has led to a revolution in web searching engines since 1998. The main idea of PageRank is to view a link from one page to another as an endorsement of the landing page. The more links point to a page, the more likely it is relevant. In theory, PageRank is closely related the power method

$$\mathbf{b}^{t+1} = \frac{\mathbf{A}\mathbf{b}^t}{||\mathbf{A}\mathbf{b}^t||},$$

where $\mathbf{b}$ will converge to the eigenvector of matrix $\mathbf{A}$. Power method is one of the most efficient ways of finding the dominant eigenvector. In recently years, there has been much effort in speeding up the computation of PageRank [46, 35, 66] and robustness to web spam [7][34]. Bharat and Mihaila proposed the Hilltop algorithm [7], which selects webpages as "good expert" for certain queries, and generates query-dependent authority scores. With a similar motivation, Haveliwala presented Topic-Sensitive Page Rank (TSPR), which computes a set of topic-sensitive PageRank scores for pages using the topics of query keywords [36]. At the query time, TSPR uses linear combination of these scores to generate context-specific importance scores for pages [36].

Like other algorithms such as HITS [51] and SALSA [54], classic PageRank builds the adjacency matrix based on the hyperlinks between web documents. Hyperlinks on the web can be easily added or deleted by web content creators and the PageRank result can be affected by web spammers who purposely create a large number of hyperlinks such as link farms and exchanges. Some researchers proposed to build the adjacent matrix from other types of information, including language models [53], page structural information [10], user browsing history [60], and image local patches [44].

Another popular iterative algorithm is also related to the power method. In [124], Zhou et al. proposes to combine partial labels $\mathbf{y}$ to estimate the score π of each document:

$$\pi^{t+1} = \alpha \mathbf{A} \pi^t + (1 - \alpha)\mathbf{y} \tag{15.1}$$

A similar idea is also developed by Zhu *et al.*[125], where the value of π on labeled samples are fixed as $\mathbf{y}$ and the resulted method corresponds to the harmonic solution of the un-normalized Laplacian computation on the graph.

The idea of [124] [125] is especially useful for the image tagging problem. When the user-provided tags are noisy and not complete, equation (15.1) can be used to refine the tag and propagate the existing labels to the unlabeled images. Rui et al. generalized label propagation methods to a bipartite graph reinforcement model [88]. Liu et al. proposed a similar approach that aims to automatically rank the tags associated with a given image according to their relevance to the image content [58]. In [120], Zha et al. considered the problem of suggesting queries for joint text and image search.

The graph-based ranking approaches also motivate the research of summarizing photo collections, which often contain too many photos for the users to view in a short time. An intuitive solution is to cluster the entire collection before ranking. This can speed up the ranking algorithms and alleviate the computational burden. In [48], the authors cluster the images before ranking in order to obtain representative images or landmarks from Flickr photos. However, a statistical clustering algorithm often fails to distinguish different semantic groups and does not always improve the retrieval results [105]. In [15], Cao et al. proposes to consider ranking and clustering tasks *simultaneously*. By ranking the images in a structural fashion, [15] designed the RankCompete algorithm, which discovers the diverse structure embedded in photo collections, and ranks the images according to their similarity among local neighborhoods instead of across the entire photo collection.

Graph-related representations are also widely used in many manifold learning algorithms [87] [116]. These algorithms first construct the graph based on neighborhood similarity, and then project the high dimensional feature vectors into another space which keeps the graph structure.

6.3 Online Learning

Online learning is a classical area of research which can be traced back to Rosenblatt's work on the perceptron algorithm for linear discriminant functions [86]. Since then, many excellent online learners have been proposed. Some examples include the Winnow family of algorithms [57] and the milestone backpropagation (BP) [90] learning method on Artificial Neural Networks.

In this section, we briefly review some existing online learning algorithms that have been widely used to tackle large scale problems, with an emphasis on multimedia analysis in practice. Our discussion in this section includes a general online learning framework and the corresponding theoretical analysis of the worst case bound on total loss between the online algorithm and their offline counterparts. In the context of the general online learning framework, we will instantiate it with some concrete examples of online learners, including binary classifiers, multi-label classifiers, conditional random fields [92], metric learning and PCA (principal component analysis). These online algorithms have been applied to practical large scale multimedia analysis and related fields and have achieved promising success both in terms of efficiency and effectiveness.

6.3.1 A General Framework for Online Learning. Given a sequence of trials $\mathcal{S} = \{(x_i, y_i)|i = 1, \cdots, \ell\}$, online learning algorithms dynamically maintain a sequence of parameters $\{\theta_t\}$ over a hypothesis space $\mathcal{H}$ for $t = 1, \cdots, \ell$. Before trial t, the model with parameter θ_t is learned from the data in the past trials $\{(x_i, y_i)|i = 1, \cdots, t-1\}$. After the tth trial (x_t, y_t), the parameter θ_t is updated according to rules that gives a new model in $\mathcal{H}$. In general, the model observes a new instance x_t and makes a prediction $\hat{y}(x_t, \theta_t)$ on it. Then the new parameter θ_{t+1} is obtained, depending on the true outcome y_t, the prediction $\hat{y}(x_t, \theta_t)$ and the learning rate η.

To design a proper updating rule, two criteria should be obeyed [50][82].

- Conservativeness. It ought to preserve the old knowledge that has already existed in the current model, because this knowledge has the rich historical information about previous trials;

- Correctiveness. The performance of the model should be improved on the new trial(s).

Following this idea, the new model parameter θ_{t+1} is updated by minimizing an objective function

$$F(\theta_{t+1}) = d(\theta_{t+1}, \theta_t) + \eta_t L(y_t, \hat{y}_t(x_t, \theta_{t+1})) \tag{15.2}$$

where d is a distance measure between two parameterized models with θ_{t+1} and θ_t. L is a loss function between the true outcome y_t and the prediction $\hat{y}_t$, and η_t is the learning rate.

There are many options for the distance measure d. For example, when $\mathcal{H}$ is a hypothesis space consisting of linear predictors, θ_t is a weighting vector. Then d can be a squared Euclidean distance or the relative entropy if θ_t is a probability vector (i.e., each entry of θ_t is nonnegative and the sum of all entries is equal to 1). Notice that the latter choice of the relative entropy indicates that the distance measure d needs not to satisfy the triangle inequality. On the other hand, the loss function L also has many variant forms, depending on the specific problems of interests. Take the example of the aforementioned linear predictors, L can be the squared loss between y_t and $\hat{y}_t$ for regression problems, or the $0/1$ loss for the classification problems. By choosing different d and L, different online learners can be defined. In the next section, we introduce some online learners that have already been proposed in the literature.

6.3.2 Some Examples of Online Learners. We illustrate some examples of recently developed online learners to help illustrate the principles discussed above in a more concrete way.

Multi-Label Classifier: The multi-label classifier was proposed in [82]. In this work, the Kullback-Leibler divergence was used as d in (15.2), and a submanifold $\mathcal{H}$ satisfying multi-label constraints set by the current trial t is formed which acts as the loss function in (15.2). Mathematically, the new model is solved by minimizing

$$D_{KL}(p^{t+1}(y|x_t)||p^t(y|x_t)) + \infty(p^{t+1} \in \mathcal{H}) \tag{15.3}$$

where $\infty(p^{t+1} \notin \mathcal{H})$ is ∞ if $p^{t+1} \notin \mathcal{H}$, otherwise it is 0. D_{KL} is the kullback-leibler divergence.

Adaptive Support Vector Machine Another example of an online learner for binary classification problem is given in [117]. In this work, the squared Euclidean distance between the parameters of two successive linear models w_{t+1} and w_t was used as d and the hinge loss on the new trial (x_t, y_t) served as L in (15.2). Hence, the new parameter w_{t+1} was solved by minimizing the following

$$||w_{t+1} - w_t||_2^2 + \eta_t(1 - y_t w_{t+1} \cdot x_t)_+ \tag{15.4}$$

where $(a)_+ = \max(0, a)$ and $||\cdot||_2$ is the l_2 norm for a vector.

Metric Learning Besides the online learners that involve a sequence of single training examples represented by (x_t, y_t), the work in [24] proposed another form of online learner which updates a metric model with a pair of examples $(x_t^{(1)}, x_t^{(2)}, d_t)$, where d_t is the target distance metric for learning at trial t. In their method, the Bregman-divergence over the positive definite convex cone is used to measure the progress between two successive metric models parameterized by Mahalonobis matrix M_{t+1} and M_t. Meanwhile, the squared loss between the prediction $\hat{d}_t = (x_t^{(1)} - x_t^{(2)})^T M_{t+1}(x_t^{(1)} - x_t^{(2)})$ and the target d_t was used to measure the correctiveness of new model on trial t. Formally, M_{t+1} was computed by minimizing

$$D_{ld}(M_{t+1}, M_t) + \eta_t(\hat{d}_t - d_t)^2 \tag{15.5}$$

where D_{ld} is the Bregman distance between two positive definite matrices.

Besides the above concrete examples, many other online learners have been proposed recently. Some examples are the online PCA algorithm in [111], a new stochastic gradient method for SVM [96] and CRF (conditional random fields) [92]. These online learners follow the main idea in (15.2) but may use some approximations to update the model instead of exactly minimizing it.

7. Discussion of Data Sets and Industrial Systems

Multimedia search has been a popular research topic for more than a decade now. However, for a long time most of the systems were constructed under the assumption of modest amounts of data [89], [107]. In recent years, the popularity of online photo sharing communities, web based infrastructures for such photo-centric social network development and the concurrent development of image search engines has enabled the collection of data sets of an extraordinary scale. For example, Flickr hosted more than 4 billion photographs at the end of 2009, while Facebook hosted more than 15 billion photographs. The easy availability of such data sets on the web has also made it much easier to crawl, store and search such data collections. For example, researchers have been able to create data sets with several million images with the use of very straightforward crawlers. For example, Torralba et al. [104] have collected 80 Million tiny images in 2008. The easy availability of such massive data sets has changed perspectives both from a research and industrial point of view.

On the other hand, it is laborious to annotate such large data sets. Thus, in scenarios where some level of annotation is required, the research continues to be limited to data sets of relatively small size. For example, the Corel image dataset includes only 68K images, while the recently popular Caltech 101[28] dataset owns less than 60 images for most concepts. To overcome this difficulty, two effective approaches are employed to obtain rich annotations. The first approach is to develop an open annotation tool so that the researchers in the field can contribute the labels. Russell et al. in MIT have built such an open annotation interface named "LabelMe" [91], which has earned 111,000 object-level annotations on 30,000 images. The second approach is to employ the Amazon Mechanical Turk as the platform for annotation, where internet users contribute labels based on the instructions. Since many internet users treat the labeling process as an enjoyable task, it is possible to achieve this goal at low cost. Sorokin and Forsyth are the first to employ the Amazon Mechanical Turk for image annotation [100]. More recently, with the aid of the Amazon Mechanical Turk, Deng et al. [25] are able to build a much larger dataset named ImageNet with about 10 million images and 15,000 synsets.

Despite the increasing research interests on social networks, there is no public image data set that contains both image and network structure. However, we can crawl network information from Flickr, Youtube, Facebook, or even Wikipedia. Mislove et al. have built such a network database [70] with no image involved. It will be interesting to enrich such network data sets with visual information.

Motivated in part by the success in academia, more and more industrial systems have begun to take multimedia information into account when developing search engines. Although none of the major search engines (e.g., Google, Microsoft Bing Search) utilized visual feature before 2008, nowadays there have been quite a few attempts to develop large scale visual search systems. TwitPic was launched to allow users to post pictures to follow Twitter posts. Tiltomo was developed to search the Flickr dataset based on tags and similar themes. Tineye and GazoPa allow users to provide their own pictures and find similar peers in the internet. Such similar image searching functions have also been supported by Google Image and Bing Image. Moreover, Google has built a beta version of "Swirl" search, which organizes the image search results into groups by hierarchically clustering the visual features. In addition, more and more companies have targeted the searching problem on the mobile platform, and quite a few systems have been developed including Google Goggles, kooaba, snaptell, etc. Another group of companies focus on vertical visual search, which considers a specific segment of visual search, for example, Paperboy considers on searching news articles or books, while Plink focuses on art works search. Table 15.1 summarizes these industrial systems. Although these industrial engines are not mature enough and only index a small portion of the photos all over the internet, the quality of search has continued to improve over time. It also provides an excellent testbed for evaluating new techniques in multimedia applications.

Table 15.1. Summary of industrial systems on multimedia search systems.

Name	Website
Google Image	http://images.google.com/
Bing Image	http://www.bing.com/images/
TwitPic	http://twitpic.com/
Tiltomo	http://www.tiltomo.com/
Tineye	https://www.tineye.com/
GazoPa	http://www.gazopa.com/
Google Swirl	http://image-swirl.googlelabs.com/
Google Goggles	http://www.google.com/mobile/goggles/♯landmark
kooaba	http://www.kooaba.com/
snaptell	http://www.snaptell.com/
Paperboy	http://www.paperboytool.com/
Plink	http://www.plinkart.com/

In summary, we are witnessing a new age when large scale data sets replace the small ones, and when multimedia search engines begin to take shape.

We can expect that the research on multimedia systems will obtain significant advances in the next decade.

8. Discussion of Future Directions

It is usually difficult to judge which research direction is most important or will become more popular, especially in an area as fast evolving as multimedia information networks. However, in this paper we still make a few audacious estimations, with the hope of not being 100% correct, but reflecting some thoughts we wish to be useful for the audience.

8.1 Content-based Recommendation and Advertisements

A key factor in the fast development of social network and multimedia retrieval lies in the success of web companies such as Flickr, Facebook, Google, etc. For these companies, the most important source of their revenue lies in online advertisements. We can expect that new advertisement techniques will earn wide market recognition and will receive considerable research attention.

Content based recognition and recommendation systems have the potential of locating users' interests, and connecting advertisement providers with their potential customers. This task is challenging because we need to take into account not only the semantics of web multimedia, but also user information such as friends, groups, and viewing history.

The obstruction of content-based research is also closely related to its advantages: since this task is strongly motivated by business profits, the success of recommendation and advertisement system is highly affected by the evolved business model. It is possible that an elegant research algorithm might not be as successful in the field of business.

8.2 Multimedia Information Networks via Cloud Computing

The explosion of multimedia data has made it impossible for single PCs or small computer clusters to store, index, or understand real multimedia information networks. In the United Kingdom, there are about 4.2 million surveillance cameras. This means that there is one surveillance camera for every 14 residents. On the other hand, both videos and photos have become prevalent on popular websites such as Youtube and Facebook. Facebook has collected the largest photo bank in history. Specifically, as of the end of 2009, it has 15 billion photographs, and is increasing at the rate of 220 million new photographs per week. It has become a serious challenge to manage or process such an overwhelming number of multimedia files. Fortunately, we are entering the era of "cloud computing", which provides the potential of processing huge multimedia data and building large-scale intelligent interface to help us understand and manage the media content.

Cloud computing describes the new computing interface whereby details are abstracted from the users who no longer have need of, expertise in, or control over the technology infrastructure "in the cloud" that supports them. Cloud computing system includes a huge data storage center and compute cycles nearby. It constitutes a front ends for users to submit their jobs using a service-based approach, which is naturally abstracted into a logical framework for computation. It incorporates multiple geographically distributed sites where the sites might be constructed with different structure and services. From a developer's viewpoint, cloud computing also reduces development efforts. For example, the MapReduce programming paradigm in cloud computing provides a unified and intuitive framework for job parallelization (using *Map* and *Reduce* paradigms), and is much easier to use than the classical parallel message passing interface (MPI), which would be required to achieve equivalent results. In the past few years, many successful cloud computing systems have been constructed, such Amazon EC2, Google App, IBM SmarterPlanet, and Microsoft Windows Azure.

Despite the fast development of cloud computing systems, most of the current research efforts are spent on designing high performance distributed computing systems and infrastructures for distributed databases. While some work has recently been performed on using cloud computing for pattern recognition and machine learning, these methods are not well suited for multimedia data analysis. This is because multimedia data analysis techniques have a number of natural challenges which are not addressed by the current work. Specifically, the challenges are as follows:

- *Fast indexing techniques*: Unlike text features which can be effectively retrieved using inverted index, multimedia data usually involves high dimensional features. How to design a fast indexing scheme is crucial for large scale applications. Many researchers have worked on locality sensitive hashing (LSH) [5]. However, LSH is not efficient enough for extremely high dimensional features. Moreover, LSH for optimal performance costs much more space than classical index structures such as the KD-tree. Another possible approach is to create a large dictionary for visual features, for which the inverted index can be applied as well as text words. The limitation of such approaches is that a lot of information is lost during the quantization step. Many questions in the indexing domain remain open in terms of both effectivness and efficiency.

- *Effective metric learning and feature selection*: The difficulty of multimedia search lies in the gap between low level feature and high level semantics. How to learn the effective feature for different tasks is among the most important problems in the field of multimedia. The problem of learning distance metrics for low level features is also a crucial problem. In the new era of massive online multimedia data, cloud computing is expected to do a better job by exploring large datasets and associated rich network structure.

Acknowledgement

This research was supported in part by HP Innovation Research Program, and in part by the Army Research Laboratory and was accomplished under Cooperative Agreement Number W911NF-09-2-0053. The views and conclusions contained in this document are those of the authors and should not be interpreted as representing the official policies, either expressed or implied, of the Army Research Laboratory or the U.S. Government. The U.S. Government is authorized to reproduce and distribute reprints for Government purposes notwithstanding any copyright notation here on. Liangliang Cao is supported in part by CSE fellowship in University of Illinois at Urbana-Champaign. S. F. Tsai is supported in part by HP Innovation Research Program and the National Science Council, Taiwan, R.O.C. under contract NSC-095-SAF-I-564-035-TMS.

References

[1] G. Adomavicius and A. Tuzhilin. Toward the next generation of recommender systems: A survey of the state-of-the-art and possible extensions. *IEEE Transactions on Knowledge and Data Engineering*, 17(6), 2005.

[2] M. Agarwal and K. Konolige. Real-time localization in outdoor environments using stereo vision and inexpensive GPS. In *International Conference on Pattern Recognition*, 2006.

[3] S. Agarwal, N. Snavely, I. Simon, S. M. Seitz, and R. Szeliski. Building rome in a day. In *International Conference on Computer Vision*, 2009.

[4] M. Ames and M. Naaman. Why we tag: Motivations for annotation in mobile and online media. In *Proc. of the SIGCHI conference on Human factors in computing systems*, 2007.

[5] A. Andoni and P. Indyk. Near-optimal hashing algorithms for approximate nearest neighbor in high dimensions. *Communications of the ACM*, 51(1):117–122, 2008.

[6] R. M. Bell, Y. Koren, and C. Volinsky. Modeling relationships at multiple scales to improve accuracy of large recommender systems. In *ACM SIGKDD Internal Conference on Knowledge Discovery and Data Mining*, August 2007.

[7] K. Bharat and G. Mihaila. Hilltop: A search engine based on expert documents. In *Proc. of the 9th International WWW Conference*, 2000.

[8] D. Blei, A. Ng, and M. Jordan. Latent dirichlet allocation. *Journal of Machine Learning Research*, 3:993–1022, 2003.

[9] J. S. Breese, D. Heckerman, and C. Kadie. Empirical analysis of predictive algorithms for collaborative filtering. In *Proc. of UAI*, 1998.

[10] D. Cai, S. Yu, J. Wen, and W. Ma. VIPS: a visionbased page segmentation algorithm. *Microsoft Technical Report (MSR-TR-2003-79)*, 2003.

[11] L. Cai and T. Hofmann. Hierarchical document categorization with support vector machines. In *CIKM '04: Proceedings of the thirteenth ACM international conference on Information and knowledge management*, pages 78–87, New York, NY, USA, 2004. ACM.

[12] L. Cao, J. Luo, A. Gallagher, X. Jin, J. Han, and T. Huang. A worldwide tourism recommendation system based on geotagged web photos. In *International Conference on Acoustics, Speech, and Signal Processing (ICASSP)*, 2010.

[13] L. Cao, J. Luo, and T. Huang. Annotating photo collections by label propagation according to multiple similarity cues. In *ACM Conference on Multimedia*, 2008.

[14] L. Cao, J. Luo, H. Kautz, and T. S. Huang. Annotating Collections of Photos Using Hierarchical Event and Scene Models. In *IEEE Proceedings Computer Vision and Pattern Recognition*, 2008.

[15] L. Cao, A. D. Pozo, X. Jin, J. Luo, J. Han, and T. S. Huang. RankCompete: Simultaneous ranking and clustering of web photos. *World Wide Web(WWW)*, 2010.

[16] L. Cao, J. Yu, J. Luo, and T. Huang. Enhancing semantic and geographic annotation of web images via logistic canonical correlation regression. In *Proceedings of the seventeen ACM international conference on Multimedia*, pages 125–134, 2009.

[17] L. Cao, J. Yu, J. Luo, and T. S. Huang. Enhancing Semantic and Geographic Annotation of Web Images via Logistic Canonical Correlation Regression. In *Proceedings of the 17th ACM international conference on Multimedia*, pages 125–134. ACM Press, 2009.

[18] Y. Chai, X.-Y. Zhu, and J. Jia. Ontoalbum: An ontology based digital photo management system. In A. C. Campilho and M. S. Kamel, editors, *ICIAR*, volume 5112 of *Lecture Notes in Computer Science*, pages 263–270. Springer, 2008.

[19] W. Chen, A. Battestini, N. Gelfand, and V. Setlur. Visual summaries of popular landmarks from community photo collections. In *ACM international conference on Multimedia*, pages 789–792, 2009.

[20] W.-T. Chu and C.-H. Lin. Automatic Selection of Representative Photo and Smart Thumbnailing Using Near-Duplicate Detection. In *Proceedings of the 16th ACM international conference on Multimedia*, pages 829–832. ACM Press, 2008.

[21] T.-S. Chua, J. Tang, R. Hong, H. Li, Z. Luo, and Y. Zheng. Nus-wide: A real-world web image database from national university of singapore. In *Proc. of ACM International Conference on Image and Video Retrieval*, 2009.

[22] M. Cooper, J. Foote, A. Girgensohn, and L. Wilcox. Temporal event clustering for digital photo collections. *ACM Transactions on Multimedia Computing, Communications, and Applications*, 1(3):269–288, 2005.

[23] D. Crandall, L. Backstrom, D. Huttenlocher, and J. Kleinberg. Mapping the world's photos. In *International conference on World wide web*, pages 761–770, 2009.

[24] J. V. Davis, B. Kulis, P. Jain, S. Sra, and I. S. Dhillon. Information-theoretic metric learning. In *Proc. of International Conference on Machine Learning*, 2007.

[25] J. Deng, W. Dong, R. Socher, L.-J. Li, K. Li, and L. Fei-Fei. Imagenet: A large-scale hierarchical image database. *Computer Vision and Pattern Recognition*, 2009.

[26] M. Deshpande and G. Karypis. Item-based top-n recommendation algorithms. *ACM Transactions on Information Systems*, 22(1):143–177, January.

[27] J. Fan, Y. Gao, and H. Luo. Hierarchical classification for automatic image annotation. In *Proc. Of ACM SIGIR*. ACM, 2007.

[28] L. Fei-Fei, R. Fergus, and P. Perona. Learning Generative Visual Models from Few Training Examples: An Incremental Bayesian Approach Tested on 101 Object Categories. *CVPR workshop*, pages 178–178, 2004.

[29] A. Gallagher and T. Chen. Using group prior to identify people in consumer images. In *Proc. CVPR SLAM workshop*, 2007.

[30] A. Gallagher, D. Joshi, J. Yu, and J. Luo. Geo-location Inference from Image Content and User Tags.

[31] D. Goldberg, D. Nichols, B. M. Oki, and D. Terry. Using collaborative filtering to weave an information tapestry. *Communications of the ACM*, pages 61–70, 1992.

[32] S. A. Golder and B. A. Huberman. Usage patterns of collzaborative tagging systems. *Jour. Information Science*, 32(2):198–208, 2006.

[33] A. Graham, H. Garcia-molina, A. Paepcke, and T. Winograd. Time as essence for photo browsing through personal digital libraries. In *In Pro-*

ceedings of the second ACM/IEEE-CS Joint Conference on Digital libraries, pages 326–335. ACM Press, 2002.

[34] Z. Gyongyi, H. Garcia-Molina, and J. Pedersen. Combating web spam with trustrank. In *Proceedings of the Thirtieth international conference on Very large data bases-Volume 30*, page 587, 2004.

[35] T. Haveliwala. Efficient Computation of PageRank. *Stanford Technical Report*, 1999.

[36] T. Haveliwala. Topic-sensitive pagerank: A context-sensitive ranking algorithm for web search. *IEEE transactions on knowledge and data engineering*, pages 784–796, 2003.

[37] J. Hays and A. A. Efros. Im2gps: estimating geographic information from a single image. In *IEEE Conference on Computer Vision and Pattern Recognition*, 2008.

[38] J. L. Herlocker, J. A. Konstan, A. Borchers, and J. Riedl. An algorithmic framework for performing collaborative filtering. In *Proceedings of the annual international ACM SIGIR conference on Research and development in information retrieval*, 1999.

[39] J. L. Herlocker, J. A. Konstan, L. G. Terveen, and J. T. Riedl. Evaluating collaborative filtering recommender systems. *ACM Transactions on Information Systems*, 22(1), January.

[40] T. Hofmann. Probabilistic latent semantic analysis. *Conference on Uncertainty in Artificial Intelligence*, 1999.

[41] R. Ji, X. Xie, H. Yao, and W.-Y. Ma. Mining city landmarks from blogs by graph modeling. In *ACM International Conference on Multimedia*, 2009.

[42] J. Jia, N. Yu, and X.-S. Hua. Annotating personal albums via web mining. In *ACM International Conference on Multimedia*, pages 459–468, 2008.

[43] Y. Jing and S. Baluja. PageRank for Product Image Search. In *Proceedings of WWW 2008*, pages 307–316. ACM Press, 2008.

[44] Y. Jing and S. Baluja. Pagerank for product image search. In *Proceedings of the 17th international conference on World wide web*, 2008.

[45] D. Joshi and J. Luo. Inferring generic places based on visual content and bag of geotags. In *ACM Conference on Content-based Image and Video Retrieval*, 2008.

[46] S. Kamvar, T. Haveliwala, C. Manning, and G. Golub. Exploiting the block structure of the web for computing pagerank. In *Proc of 12th International World Wide Web Conference*, 2003.

[47] L. Kennedy, M. Naaman, S. Ahern, R. Nair, and T. Rattenbury. How flickr helps us make sense of the world: Context and content in community-contributed media collections. In *ACM Conference on Multimedia*, 2007.

[48] L. S. Kennedy and M. Naaman. Generating diverse and representative image search results for landmarks. In *Proceeding of the 17th international conference on World Wide Web (WWW)*, pages 297–306, 2008.

[49] D. S. Kirk, A. J. Sellen, C. Rother, and K. R. Wood. Understanding photowork. In *In Proc. CHI 2006, ACM Press*, pages 761–770. ACM Press, 2006.

[50] J. Kivinen and M. K. Warmuth. Exponentiated gradient versus gradient descent for linear predictors. Technical Report UCSC-CRL-94-16, Baskin Center for Computer Engineering and Information Sciences, University of California, Santa Cruz, June 1994.

[51] J. Kleinberg. Authoritative sources in a hyperlinked environment. *Journal of the ACM (JACM)*, 46(5):604–632, 1999.

[52] Y. Koren. The bellkor solution to the netflix grand prize. Technical report, Netflix, Inc, August 2009.

[53] O. Kurland and L. Lee. PageRank without hyperlinks: Structural reranking using links induced by language models. In *Proceedings of international ACM SIGIR conference on Research and development in information retrieval*, page 313. ACM, 2005.

[54] R. Lempel and S. Moran. The stochastic approach for link-structure analysis (salsa) and the tkc effect. *ACM Transactions on Information Systems*, 33(1-6):387–401, 2000.

[55] X. Li, C. G. Snoek, and M. Worring. Learning tag relevance by neighbor voting for social image retrieval. In *MIR '08: Proceeding of the 1st ACM international conference on Multimedia information retrieval*, 2008.

[56] G. Linden, B. Smith, and J. York. Amazon.com recommendations: Item-to-item collaborative filtering. *IEEE Internet Computing*, 2003.

[57] N. Littlestone. *Mistake Bounds and Logarithmic Linear-threshold Learning Algorithms*. Phd thesis, University of California Santa Cruz, 1989.

[58] D. Liu, X. Hua, L. Yang, M. Wang, and H. Zhang. Tag ranking. In *Proceedings of international conference on World Wide Web*, pages 351–360, 2009.

[59] D. Liu, X.-S. Hua, L. Yang, M. Wang, and H.-J. Zhang. Tag ranking. In *Proc. of international conference on World Wide Web*, 2009.

[60] Y. Liu, B. Gao, T.-Y. Liu, Y. Zhang, Z. Ma, S. He, and H. Li. Browserank: letting web users vote for page importance. In *International ACM SIGIR conference on Research and development in information retrieval*, pages 451–458, 2008.

[61] Y. Liu, D. Xu, I. Tsang, and J. Luo. Using large-scale web data to facilitate textual query based retrieval of consumer photos. In *Proceedings of*

the seventeen ACM international conference on Multimedia, pages 55–64. ACM, 2009.

[62] A. C. Loui and A. E. Savakis. Automatic Image Event Segmentation and Quality Screening for Albuming Applications. In *IEEE International Conference on Multimedia and Expo*, pages 1125–1128.

[63] J. Luo, J. Yu, D. Joshi, and W. Hao. Event recognition: viewing the world with a third eye. In *ACM International Conference on Multimedia*, pages 1071–1080, 2008.

[64] M. Marszalek and C. Schmid. Semantic hierarchies for visual object recognition. *Computer Vision and Pattern Recognition, 2007. CVPR '07. IEEE Conference on*, pages 1–7, June 2007.

[65] K. Matusiak. Towards user-centered indexing in digital image collections. *OCLC Systems and Services*, 22(4):283–298, 2006.

[66] F. McSherry. A uniform approach to accelerated PageRank computation. In *international conference on World Wide Web*, page 582, 2005.

[67] Q. Mei, D. Cai, D. Zhang, and C. Zhai. Topic modeling with network regularization. 2008.

[68] K. Messer, J. Kittler, M. Sadeghi, M. Hamouz, A. Kostin, F. Cardinaux, S. Marcel, S. Bengio, C. Sanderson, J. Czyz, L. Vandendorpe, C. McCool, S. Lowther, S. Sridharan, V. Chandran, R. Parades, E. Vidal, L. Bai, L. Shen, Y. Wang, Y.-H. Chiang, H.-C. Liu, Y.-P. Hung, A. Heinrichs, M. Muller, A. Tewes, Z. Wang, F. Xue, Y. Ma, Q. Yang, C. Fang, X. Ding, S. Lucey, R. Goss, and H. Schneiderman. Face Authentication Test on the BANCA Database. In *Proceedings of the International Conference on Pattern Recognition*, volume 4, pages 523–532. ACM Press, 2004.

[69] G. Mishne. Autotag: A collaborative approach to automated tag assignment for weblog posts. In *Proc. of the 15th international conference on World Wide Web*, 2006.

[70] A. Mislove, H. S. Koppula, K. P. Gummadi, P. Druschel, and B. Bhattacharjee. Online social network dataset.

[71] M. Naaman. *Leveraging geo-referenced digital photographs*. PhD thesis, Stanford University, 2005.

[72] M. Naaman, S. Harada, and Q. Wang. Context Data in Geo-Referenced Digital Photo Collections. In *Proceedings of the 12th ACM international conference on Multimedia*, pages 196–203. ACM Press, 2004.

[73] M. Naaman, Y. Song, A. Paepcke, and H. Garcia-Molina. Automatic organization for digital photographs with geographic coordinates. In *International Conference on Digital Libraries*, volume 7, pages 53–62, 2004.

[74] M. Naaman, Y. J. Song, A. Paepcke, and H. Garcia-Molina. Automatic Organization for Digital Photographs with Geographic Coordinates. In

Proceedings of the 4th ACM/IEEE Joint Conference on Digital Libraries, pages 53–62.

[75] M. Naphade, L. Kennedy, J. Kender, S. Chang, J. Smith, P. Over, and A. Hauptmann. A light scale concept ontology for multimedia understanding for TRECVID 2005. *IBM Research Report RC23612 (W0505-104)*, 2005.

[76] M. Naphade, J. R. Smith, J. Tesic, S.-F. Chang, W. Hsu, L. Kennedy, A. Hauptmann, and J. Curtis. Large-scale concept ontology for multimedia. *IEEE Multimedia Magazine*, 13(3), 2006.

[77] A. Natsev, A. Haubold, J. Tesic, L. Xie, and R. Yan. Semantic concept-based query expansion and re-ranking for multimedia retrieval. In *Proc. of the 14th annual ACM international conference on Multimedia*, Augusberg, Germany, 2007. ACM.

[78] A. Ng and M. Jordan. On discriminative vs. generative classifiers: A comparison of logistic regression and naive bayes. In *Advances in Neural Information Processing Systems*, 2002.

[79] L. Page, S. Brin, R. Motwani, and T. Winograd. The pagerank citation ranking: Bringing order to the web. *Stanford Digital Libraries Working Paper*, 1998.

[80] A. Paterek. Improving regularized singular value decomposition for collaborative filtering. In *Proc. of KDD Cup and Workshop*, August 2007.

[81] G.-J. Qi, X.-S. Hua, Y. Rui, J. Tang, T. Mei, and H.-J. Zhang. Correlative multi-label video annotation. In *Proc. of the 14th annual ACM international conference on Multimedia*, Augusberg, Germany, 2007. ACM.

[82] G.-J. Qi, X.-S. Hua, Y. Rui, J. Tang, and H.-J. Zhang. Two-dimensional multi-label active learning with an efficient online adaptation model for image classification. *IEEE Transactions on Pattern Analysis and Machine Intelligence*, 31(10):1880–1897, October 2009.

[83] G.-J. Qi, X.-S. Hua, and H.-J. Zhang. Learning semantic distance from community-tagged media collection. In *Proc. of ACM International Conference on Multimedia*, 2009.

[84] T. Quack, B. Leibe, and L. Van Gool. World-scale mining of objects and events from community photo collections. *ACM Conference on Image and Video Retrieval*, pages 47–56, 2008.

[85] P. Resnick, N. Iacovou, M. Suchak, P. Bergstrom, and J. Riedl. Grouplens: An open architecture for collaborative filtering of netnews. In *Proc. of ACM CSCW*, 1994.

[86] F. Rosenblatt. *Principles of Neurodynamics: Perceptrons and the Theory of Brain Mechanisms*. Spartan Books, Washington, D.C., 1962.

[87] S. Roweis and L. Saul. Nonlinear dimensionality reduction by locally linear embedding. *Science*, 290, 2000.

[88] X. Rui, M. Li, Z. Li, W.-Y. Ma, and N. Yu. Bipartite graph reinforcement model for web image annotation. In *ACM international conference on Multimedia*, pages 585–594, 2007.

[89] Y. Rui, T. Huang, and S.-F. Chang. Image retrieval: current techniques, promising directions, and open issues. *J. Visual Comm. and Image Representation*, 10:39–62, 1999.

[90] D. Rumelhart, G. Hinton, and R. Williams. *Parallel Data Processing*, volume 1, chapter Learning Internal Representation by Error Propagation, pages 318–362. The M.I.T. Press, Cambridge, MA, 1986.

[91] B. Russell, A. Torralba, K. Murphy, and W. Freeman. Labelme: a database and web-based tool for image annotationŤ,. *Intl. Journal of Computer Vision*, 2008.

[92] a. N. N. S. S. V. N. Vishwanathan, M. Schmidt, and K. Murphy. Accelerated training conditional random fields with stochastic gradient methods. In *Proceedings of Internatioanl Conference on Machine Learning*, 2006.

[93] B. Sarwar, G. Karypis, J. Konstan, and J. Riedl. Item-based collaborative filtering recommendation algorithms. In *Proc. of WWW*, 2001.

[94] A. E. Savakis, S. P. Etz, and A. C. Loui. Evaluation of Image Appeal in Consumer Photography. In *Proceedings of SPIE Human Vision and Electronic Imaging V*, 2000.

[95] G. Schindler, P. Krishnamurthy, R. Lublinerman, Y. Liu, and F. Dellaert. Detecting and matching repeated patterns for automatic geo-tagging in urban environments. In *IEEE Conference on Computer Vision and Pattern Recognition*, volume 2008, 2008.

[96] S. Shalev-Shwartz, Y. Singer, and N. Srebro. Pegasos: Primal estimated sub-gradient solver for svm. In *Proceedings of Internatioanl Conference on Machine Learning*, 2007.

[97] A. Sibiryakov. Photo-collection representation based on viewpoint clustering. In *Proceedings of SPIE Electronic Imaging and Multimedia Technology V*, volume 6833, 2007.

[98] B. Sigurbjorsnsson and B. van Zwol. Flickr tag recommendation based on collective knowledge. In *Proc. of the 17th international conference on World Wide Web*, 2008.

[99] C. G. M. Snoek, M. Worring, J. C. v. Gemert, J.-M. Geusebroek, and A. W. M. Smeulders. The challenge problem for automated detection of 101 semantic concepts in multimedia. In *Proc. of the 14th annual ACM international conference on Multimedia*, Santa Barbara, CA, USA, 2006. ACM.

[100] A. Sorokin and D. Forsyth. tility data annotation with amazon mechanical turk. *First IEEE Workshop on Internet Vision*, 2008.

[101] F. Suchanek, G. Kasneci, and G. Weikum. YAGO: A core of semantic knowledge - unifying WordNet and Wikipedia. In C. L. Williamson, M. E. Zurko, and P. J. Patel-Schneider, Peter F. Shenoy, editors, *16th International World Wide Web Conference (WWW 2007)*, pages 697–706, Banff, Canada, 2007. ACM.

[102] F. Tang and Y. Gao. Fast Near Duplicate Detection for Personal Image Collections. In *Proceedings of the 17th ACM international conference on Multimedia*. ACM Press, 2009.

[103] J. Tang, S. Yan, R. Hong, G.-J. Qi, and T.-S. Chua. Inferring semantic concepts from community-contributed images and noisy tags. In *Proc. of ACM International Conference on Multimedia*, 2009.

[104] A. Torralba, R. Fergus, and W. T. Freeman. 80 million tiny images: a large dataset for non-parametric object and scene recognition. *IEEE Transactions on Pattern Analysis and Machine Intelligence*, 30(11):1955–1970, 2009.

[105] E. Voorhees. The cluster hypothesis revisited. *ACM SIGIR Conference*, 1985.

[106] H. Wang, X. Jiang, L.-T. Chia, and A.-H. Tan. Wikipedia2onto — adding wikipedia semantics to web image retrieval. In *WebSci'09: Society On-Line*, 2009.

[107] J. Wang, J. Li, and G. Wiederhold. SIMPLIcity: Semantics-sensitive integrated matching for picture libraries. *IEEE Trans. Pattern Analysis and Machine Intelligence*, 23(9):947–963, 1999.

[108] J. Wang, A. P. D. Vries, and M. J. T. Reinders. Unifying user-based and item-based collaborative filtering approaches by similarity fusion. In *Proceedings of SIGIR*, 2006.

[109] X.-J. Wang, L. Zhang, X. Li, and W.-Y. Ma. Annotating images by mining image search results. *IEEE Transactions on Pattern Analysis and Machine Intelligence*, 30(11):1919–1932, 2008.

[110] Y. Wang, J. Yang, W. Lai, R. Cai, L. Zhang, and W. Ma. Exploring traversal strategy for efficient web forum crawlingg. In *Proceedings of SIGIR*, 2008.

[111] M. K. Warmuth and D. Kuzmin. Randomized online pca algorithms with regret bounds that are logarithmic in the dimension. *Journal of Machine Learnign Research*, 9:2287–2320, October 2008.

[112] Q. Weinberger, M. Slaney, and R. V. Zwol. Resolving tag ambiguity. In *Proc. of International ACM Conference on Multimedia*, 2008.

[113] P. Wu and D. Tretter. Close & Closer: Social Cluster and Closeness from Photo Collections. In *Proceedings of the 17th ACM international conference on Multimedia*. ACM Press, 2009.

[114] Y. Wu, B. Tseng, and J. Smith. Ontology-based multi-classification learning for video concept detection. In *Proc. Of IEEE Int. Conference on Multimedia and Expo*. IEEE, 2004.

[115] Z. Xu, Y. Fu, J. Mao, and D. Su. Towards the semantic web: Collaborative tag suggestions. In *Collaborative Web Tagging Workshop at WWW 2006*, 2006.

[116] S. Yan, D. Xu, B. Zhang, H. Zhang, Q. Yang, and S. Lin. Graph embedding and extensions: A general framework for dimensionality reduction. *IEEE Transactions on Pattern Analysis and Machine Intelligence*, 29(1):40, 2007.

[117] J. Yang, R. Yan, and A. Hauptmann. Cross-domain video concept detection using adaptive svms. In *ACM Conference on Multimedia*, 2007.

[118] J. Yu and J. Luo. Leveraging probabilistic season and location context models for scene understanding. In *International conference on Content-based image and video retrieval*, pages 169–178, 2008.

[119] J. Yuan, J. Luo, and Y. Wu. Mining compositional features for boosting. In *IEEE Conference on Computer Vision and Pattern Recognition*, 2008.

[120] Z.-J. Zha, L. Yang, T. Mei, M. Wang, and Z. Wang. Visual query suggestion. In *ACM international conference on Multimedia*, 2009.

[121] D.-Q. Zhang and S.-F. Chang. Detecting Image Near-Duplicate by Stochastic Attribute Relational Graph Matching with Learning. In *Proceedings of the 12th ACM international conference on Multimedia*. ACM Press, 2004.

[122] T. Zhang, J. Xiao, D. Wen, and X. Ding. Face Based Image Navigation and Search. In *Proceedings of the 17th ACM international conference on Multimedia*, pages 597–600. ACM Press, 2009.

[123] Y. Zheng, M. Zhao, Y. Song, H. Adam, U. Buddemeier, A. Bissacco, F. Brucher, T. Chua, and H. Neven. Tour the World: building a web-scale landmark recognition engine. *IEEE Conference on Computer Vision and Pattern Recognition*, 2009.

[124] D. Zhou, O. Bousquet, T. Lal, J. Weston, and B. Scholkopf. Learning with local and global consistency. *Advances in Neural Information Processing Systems (NIPS)*, 16:321–328, 2004.

[125] X. Zhu, J. Laerty, and Z. Ghahramani. Semi-supervised learning: From Gaussian fields to Gaussian processes. *ICML*, 2003.

[126] A. Zweig and D. Weinshall. Exploiting object hierarchy: Combining models from different category levels. In *ICCV*, pages 1–8, 2007.

Chapter 16

AN OVERVIEW OF SOCIAL TAGGING AND APPLICATIONS

Manish Gupta
University of Illinois at Urbana Champaign
gupta58@illinois.edu

Rui Li
University of Illinois at Urbana Champaign
ruili1@illinois.edu

Zhijun Yin
University of Illinois at Urbana Champaign
zyin3@illinois.edu

Jiawei Han
University of Illinois at Urbana Champaign
hanj@cs.uiuc.edu

Abstract Social tagging on online portals has become a trend now. It has emerged as one of the best ways of associating metadata with web objects. With the increase in the kinds of web objects becoming available, collaborative tagging of such objects is also developing along new dimensions. This popularity has led to a vast literature on social tagging. In this survey paper, we would like to summarize different techniques employed to study various aspects of tagging. Broadly, we would discuss about properties of tag streams, tagging models, tag semantics, generating recommendations using tags, visualizations of tags, applications of tags, integration of different tagging systems and problems associated with tagging usage. We would discuss topics like why people tag, what influences the choice of tags, how to model the tagging process, kinds of tags, different power laws observed in tagging domain, how tags are created and how to choose the right tags for recommendation. Metadata generated in the form of tags can be efficiently used to improve web search, for web object classification, for generating ontologies, for enhanced browsing etc. We would discuss these applications and conclude with thoughts on future work in the area.

Keywords: Social tagging, bookmarking, tagging, social indexing, social classification, collaborative tagging, folksonomy, folk classification, ethnoclassification, distributed classification, folk taxonomy

1. Introduction

Social tagging became popular with the launch of a variety of media-based social networking sites like Delicious and Flickr. This is because such sites support both social interaction, and the presence of rich media objects which can be tagged during such interactions. Since then, different social systems have been built that support tagging of a variety of resources. Given a particular web object or resource, tagging is a process where a user assigns a tag to an object. On Delicious, a user can assign tags to a particular bookmarked URL. On Flickr, users can tag photos uploaded by them or by others. Whereas Delicious allows each user to have her personal set of tags per URL, Flickr has a single set of tags for any photo. On blogging sites like Blogger, Wordpress, Livejournal, blog authors can add tags to their posts. On micro-blogging sites like Twitter, hash tags are used within the tweet text itself. On social networking sites like Facebook, Orkut, etc., users often annotate parts of the photos. Users can also provide tagging information in other forms like marking something as "Like" on Facebook. Upcoming event sites can allow users to comment on and tag events. Recently, tripletags (tags of the format namespace:key=value (e.g., geo:lat=53.1234) are becoming popular. Such a syntax can improve the usability of tags to a large extent. Using rel-tags[1], a page can indicate that the destination of that hyperlink is an author-designated tag for the current page. Rel-tags have been used by various implementation sites to tag blogs, music, links, news articles, events, listings, etc. Citation websites have tags attached to publication entries. Cataloging sites like LibraryThing and Shelfari allow users to tag books. Social news sites like Digg, SlashDot allow users to attach tags to news stories. Yelp, CitySearch and other such business/product reviews sites allow users to attach their reviews and other users to select tags to rate reviews too. Multimedia objects like podcasts, live casts, videos and music can also be tagged on sites like Youtube, imeem, Metacafe, etc. On Yahoo! Answers, you can tag an answer as positive or negative depending on how helpful it was. Tags are often used to collect such binary or multi-valued ratings or

[1]http://microformats.org/wiki/rel-tag

categorical decisions from users. Tags are omni-present on the web. But what led to the emergence of tagging based systems? As we shall see in this section, tags are a better way of generating metadata and prevent problems associated with fixed taxonomies in social systems.

1.1 Problems with Metadata Generation and Fixed Taxonomies

Different web portals focus on sharing of different types of objects like images, news articles, bookmarks, etc. Often to enrich the context related to these objects and thereby support more applications like search, metadata needs to be associated with these objects. However, manual metadata creation is costly in terms of time and effort [35]. Also, vocabulary of this metadata may be completely different from that of system designer or content producers or taxonomy creators or eventual users. Besides associating metadata to the objects, building a taxonomy for these social sharing systems may be useful in classifying and organizing the objects. But fixed static taxonomies are rigid, conservative, and centralized [41]. Items do not always fit exactly inside one and only one category. Hierarchical classifications are influenced by the cataloguer's view of the world and, as a consequence, are affected by subjectivity and cultural bias. Rigid hierarchical classification schemes cannot easily keep up with an increasing and evolving corpus of items. Social systems need to hire expert cataloguers who can use same thinking and vocabulory as users and can build taxonomies which can be stable over time. Once such a hierarchy is created, the object creators can be asked to assign a fixed category to the object, in the hierarchy. This can induce "post activation analysis paralysis" [21] into the user. By their very nature, hierarchies tend to establish only one consistent authoritative structured vision. This implies a loss of precision, erases difference of expression, and does not take into account the variety of user needs and views.

1.2 Folksonomies as a Solution

Folksonomies and social tagging help in preventing these problems and hence provide a simpler, cheaper and a more natural way of organizing web objects. A folksonomy (folk (people) + taxis (classification) + nomos (management)) is a user-generated classification, emerging through bottom-up consensus. The term was coined by Thomas Vander Wal in the AIfIA mailing list to mean the wide-spreading practice of collaborative categorization using freely chosen keywords by a group of people cooperating spontaneously. A folksonomy can be defined as a collection of a set of users, set of tags, set of resources or objects, and a ternary relation between users, tags and resources with a time dimension [12]. Unlike formal taxonomies, folksonomies have no explicitly defined relationship between terms. All terms belong to a flat namespace, i.e., there is no hierarchy. Since users themselves tag the objects, folksonomies directly reflect the vocabulary of users [41]. Hence, a folksonomy is a simple, emergent and iterative system. It helps create the most popular way of organizing objects referred to as desire lines[2]. Apart from this, tagging provides no barriers to entry or cooperation and hence involves low cognitive cost. Tagging helps users get immediate feedback. This feedback loop leads to a form of asymmetric communication between users through metadata. The users of a system negotiate the meaning of the terms in the folksonomy, whether purposefully or not, through their individual choices of tags to describe objects for themselves. Further, folksonomies are inclusive, i.e., they include terms related to popular topics and also terms related to long tail topics. With appropriate browsing support, interlinking related tag sets is wonderful for finding things unexpectedly in a general area.

In summary, folksonomies are a trade-off between traditional structured centralized classification and no classification or metadata at all. Their advantage over traditional top-down classification is their capability of matching user needs and language, not their precision. Building, maintaining, and enforcing a sound controlled vocabulary is often too expensive in terms of development time and presents a steep learning curve to the user to learn the classification scheme. In other words, folksonomies are better than nothing, when traditional classification is not viable.

1.3 Outline

In this survey paper, we present a systematic detailed study of tagging literature. We first list different user motivations and different ways of tagging web objects in Section 2. There have been a lot of generative models proposed to understand the process of tagging. We present a summary of such models in Section 3. Section 4 describes various parameters for tagging system design. In Section 5, we present a summarization of work done on analysis of tagging distributions, identification of tag semantics, expressive power of tags versus keywords. Appropriate rendering of tags can provide useful information to users. Different visualization schemes like tag clouds have been explored to support browsing on web portals. We present some works related to such visualization studies in Section 6. When a user wishes to attach tags to an object, the system can recommend some tags to the user. A user can select one of those tags or come up with a new one. In Section 7, we discuss different ways of generating tag recommendations. In Section 8, we describe different applications for which tags can be used. An integration of such folksonomies can

[2] http://www.adaptivepath.com/blog/2009/10/27/desire-lines-the-metaphor-that-keeps-on-giving/

help in solving the problem of sparsity of tags associated with Web objects. We describe some works about integration of different folksonomies in Section 9. Usage of tags involves a lot of problems like sparsity, ambiguities and canonicalization. We list these problems in Section 10. Finally, we conclude with thoughts on future work in Section 11.

2. Tags: Why and What?

Since 2005, there have been works describing why people tag and what the tags mean. We briefly summarize such works [1, 34, 16, 61, 7, 21, 48, 35, 27, 17] below. We provide a detailed classification of user tagging motivations and also list different kinds of tags in this section.

2.1 Different User Tagging Motivations

- **Future Retrieval:** Users can tag objects aiming at ease of future retrieval of the objects by themselves or by others. Tags may also be used to incite an activity or act as reminders to oneself or others (e.g., the "to read" tag). These descriptive tags are exceptionally helpful in providing metadata about objects that have no other tags associated.

- **Contribution and Sharing:** Tags can be used to describe the resource and also to add the resource to conceptual clusters or refined categories for the value of either known or unknown audience.

- **Attract Attention:** Popular tags can be exploited to get people to look at one's own resources.

- **Play and Competition:** Tags can be based on an internal or external set of rules. In some cases, the system devises the rules such as the ESP Game's incentive to tag what others might also tag. In others, groups develop their own rules to engage in the system such as when groups seek out all items with a particular feature and tag their existence.

- **Self Presentation (Self Referential Tags):** Tags can be used to write a user's own identity into the system as a way of leaving their mark on a particular resource. E.g., the "seen live" tag in Last.FM marks an individual's identity or personal relation to the resource. Another example are tags beginning with "my" like "mystuff".

- **Opinion Expression:** Tags can convey value judgments that users wish to share with others (e.g., the "elitist" tag in Yahoo!'s Podcast system is utilized by some users to convey an opinion). Sometimes people tag simply to gain reputation in the community.

- **Task Organization:** Tags can also be used for task organization e.g., "toread", "jobsearch", "gtd" (got to do), "todo".
- **Social Signalling:** Tags can be used to communicate contextual information about the object to others.
- **Money:** Some sites like Squidoo and Amazon Mechanical Turk pay users for creating tags.
- **Technological Ease:** Some people tag because the current technology makes it easy to upload resources with tags to the web. E.g. drag-and-drop approach for attaching labels to identify people in photos. The latest photo browser commercial packages, such as Adobe Photoshop Album, adopted similar methods to support easy labeling of photos. With 'Phonetags'[3], a listener hears a song on the radio, uses her cell phone to text back to a website with tags and star ratings. Later, returning to the website, the user can type in her phone number and see the songs she had bookmarked.

2.2 Kinds of Tags

- **Content-Based Tags:** They can be used to identify the actual content of the resource. E.g., Autos, Honda Odyssey, batman, open source, Lucene.
- **Context-Based Tags:** Context-based tags provide the context of an object in which the object was created or saved, e.g., tags describing locations and time such as San Francisco, Golden Gate Bridge, and 2005-10-19.
- **Attribute Tags:** Tags that are inherent attributes of an object but may not be able to be derived from the content directly, e.g., author of a piece of content such as Jeremy's Blog and Clay Shirky. Such tags can be used to identify what or who the resource is about. Tags can also be used to identify qualities or characteristics of the resource (e.g., scary, funny, stupid, inspirational).
- **Ownership Tags:** Such tags identify who owns the resource.
- **Subjective Tags:** Tags that express user's opinion and emotion, e.g., funny or cool. They can be used to help evaluate an object recommendation (item qualities). They are basically put with a motivation of self-expression.

[3] http://www.spencerkiser.com/geoPhoneTag/

- **Organizational Tags:** Tags that identify personal stuff, e.g., mypaper or mywork, and tags that serve as a reminder of certain tasks such as to-read or to-review. This type of tags is usually not useful for global tag aggregation with other users' tags. These tags are intrinsically time-sensitive. They suggest an active engagement with the text, in which the user is linking the perceived subject matter with a specific task or a specific set of interests.

- **Purpose Tags:** These tags denote non-content specific functions that relate to an information seeking task of users (e.g., learn about LaTeX, get recommendations for music, translate text).

- **Factual Tags:** They identify facts about an object such as people, places, or concepts. These are the tags that most people would agree to apply to a given object. Factual tags help to describe objects and also help to find related objects. Content-based, context-based and objective, attribute tags can be considered as factual tags. Factual tags are generally useful for learning and finding tasks.

- **Personal Tags:** Such tags have an intended audience of the tag applier themselves. They are most often used to organize a user's objects (item ownership, self-reference, task organization).

- **Self-referential tags:** They are tags to resources that refer to themselves. e.g., Flickr's "sometaithurts"[4] - for "so meta it hurts" is a collection of images regarding Flickr, and people using Flickr. The earliest image is of someone discussing social software, and then subsequent users have posted screenshots of that picture within Flickr, and other similarly self-referential images.

- **Tag Bundles:** This is the tagging of tags that results in the creation of hierarchical folksonomies. Many taggers on Delicious have chosen to tag URLs with other URLs, such as the base web address for the server. For example, a C# programming tutorial might be tagged with the URL http://www.microsoft.com.

2.3 Categorizers Versus Describers

Taggers can be divided into two main types [29]: categorizers and describers. Categorizer users are the ones who apply tags such that the objects are easier to find later for personal use. They have their own vocabulary. Sets in Delicious is a perfect example of metadata by categorizers. On the other

[4] http://www.flickr.com/photos/tags/sometaithurts/

hand, describer users tag objects such that they are easier to be searched by others. Often tags to a single object would contain many synonyms. Vocabulary of a describer is much larger compared to an average categorizer. But a categorizer has her own limited personal vocabulary and subjective tags. ESP game is a perfect example of metadata creation by describers. Categorizers and describers can be identified using these intuitions:

- The more the number of tags that were only used once by a user, the higher the probability that the user is a describer.
- The faster the tagging vocabulary increases, the more likely it is that the person is a describer.
- A categorizer tends to achieve tag entropy that is as low as possible because he tries to "encode" her resources in a good and balanced way.

These intuitions can be formalized as metrics like tag ratio (ratio between tags and resources), orphaned tags (proportion of tags which annotate only a small amount of resources) and tag entropy (reflects the effectiveness of the encoding process of tagging).

2.4 Linguistic Classification of Tags

Based on linguistics, tags can be classified as follows [56].

- Functional: Tags that describe the function of an object. (e.g., weapon)
- Functional collocation: These are defined by function but in addition, they have to be collected in a place (and/or time). (e.g., furniture, tableware)
- Origin collocation: Tags that describe why things are together? (e.g., garbage, contents, dishes (as in "dirty dishes" after a meal)).
- Function and origin: Tags that describe why an object is present, what is the purpose, or where did it come from. (e.g., "Michelangelo" and "medieval" on an image of a painting by Michelangelo)
- Taxonomic: They are words that can help in classifying the object into an appropriate category. (e.g., "Animalia" or "Chordata" tag to an image of a heron)
- Adjective: They describe the object that denotes the resource. (e.g., "red", "great", "beautiful", "funny")
- Verb: These are action words. (e.g., "explore", "todo", "jumping")
- Proper name: Most of the tags are of this category. (e.g., "New Zealand", "Manhattan bridge")

2.5 Game-based Tagging

In the ESP game, the players cannot see each other's guesses. The aim is to enter the same word as your partner in the shortest possible time. Peekaboom takes the ESP Game to the next level. Unlike the ESP Game, it is asymmetrical. To start, one user is shown an image and the other sees an empty blank space. The first user is given a word related to the image, and the aim is to communicate that word to the other player by revealing portions of the image. So if the word is "eye" and the image is a face, you reveal the eye to your partner. But the real aim here is to build a better image search engine: one that could identify individual items within an image. PhotoPlay[13] is a computer game designed to be played by three to four players around a horizontal display. The goal for each player is to build words related to any of the four photos on the display by selecting from a 7x7 grid of letter tiles. All these games, help in tagging the resources.

Problems with Game-Based Tagging

Game-based tagging mechanisms may not provide high quality tags [30]. Maximizing your scores in the game means sacrificing a lot of valuable semantics. People tend to write very general properties of an image rather than telling about the specifics or details of the image. E.g., colors are great for matching, but often are not the most critical or valuable aspects of the image. The labels chosen by people trying to maximize their matches with an anonymous partner are not necessarily the most "robust and descriptive" labels. They are the easiest labels, the most superficial labels, the labels that maximize the speed of a match rather than the quality of the descriptor. In addition, they are words that are devoid of context or depth of knowledge. Tagging for your own retrieval is different than tagging for retrieval by people you know and even more different than tagging for retrieval in a completely uncontextualized environment.

3. Tag Generation Models

In order to describe, understand and analyze tags and tagging systems, various tag generation models have been proposed. These models study various factors that influence the generation of a tag, such as the previous tags suggested by others, users' background knowledge, content of the resources and the community influences. In this section, we present different models which have been proposed in the literature, and discuss advantages and disadvantages of these models.

3.1 Polya Urn Generation Model

Intuitively, the first factor that influences the choice of tags is the previous tag assignments. The amount of effort required to tag items may affect an individual's decision to use tags. Using suggested tags rather than one's own requires less effort. Pirolli and Card's theory of information foraging [40] suggests greater adoption of suggested tags because people adapt their behavior to optimize the information/effort ratio. Users cost-tune their archives by spending the least amount of effort needed to build up enough structure to support fast retrieval of their most useful resources. Based on this intuition, various models based on the stochastic Polya urn process have been proposed.

3.1.1 Basic Polya Urn Model. Golder and Huberman [16] propose a model based on a variation of the stochastic Polya urn model where the urn initially contains two balls, one red and one black. In each step of the simulation, a ball is selected from the urn and then it is put back together with a second ball of the same color. After a large number of draws the fraction of the balls with the same color stabilizes but the fractions converge to random limits in each run of the simulation.

This model successfully captures that previously assigned tags are more likely to be selected again. However, this basic model fails to capture that new tags will also be added into the system. So several extensions of this model have been proposed later.

3.1.2 Yule-Simon Model. Yule-Simon model [50] assumes that at each simulation step a new tag is invented and added to the tag stream with a low probability of p. This leads to a linear growth of the distinct tags with respect to time and not to the typical continuous, but declining growth. Yule-Simon model can be described as follows. At each discrete time step one appends a word to the text: with probability p the appended word is a new word, that has never occurred before, while with probability $1-p$ the word is copied from the existing text, choosing it with a probability proportional to its current frequency of occurrence. This simple process produces frequency-rank distributions with a power law tail whose exponent is given by $a = 1 - p$.

Cattuto et al. [10] study the temporal evolution of the global vocabulary size, i.e., the number of distinct tags in the entire system, as well as the evolution of local vocabularies, that is, the growth of the number of distinct tags used in the context of a given resource or user. They find that the number N of distinct tags present in the system is $N(T) \propto T^{\gamma}$, with $\gamma < 1$. The rate at which new tags appear at time T scales as $T^{\gamma-1}$, i.e., new tags appear less and less frequently, with the invention rate of new tags monotonically decreasing very slowly towards zero. This sub-linear growth is generally referred to as Heaps' law.

3.1.3 Yule-Simon Model with Long Term Memory. Cattuto et al. [11] propose a further variation of the Simon model. It takes the order of the tags in the stream into account. Like the previous models, it simulates the imitation of previous tag assignments but instead of imitating all previous tag assignments with the same probability it introduces a kind of long-term memory. Their model can be stated as follows: the process by which users of a collaborative tagging system associate tags to resources can be regarded as the construction of a "text", built one step at a time by adding "words" (i.e., tags) to a text initially comprised of n_0 words. This process is meant to model the behavior of an effective average user in the context identified by a specific tag. At a time step t, a new word may be invented with probability p and appended to the text, while with probability $1 - p$ one word is copied from the existing text, going back in time by x steps with a probability that decays as a power law, $Q_t(x) = a(t)/(x + \tau)$. $a(t)$ is a normalization factor and τ is the characteristic time-scale over which the recently added words have comparable probabilities. Note that $Q_t(x)$ returns a power law distribution of the probabilities. This Yule-Simon model with long term memory successfully reproduces the characteristic slope of the frequency-rank distribution of co-occurrence tag streams but it fails to explain the distribution in resource tag streams as well as the decaying growth of the set of distinct tags because it leads to a linear growth.

3.1.4 Information Value Based Model. Halpin et al. [18] present a model which does not only simulate the imitation of previous tag assignments but it also selects tags based on their information value. The information value of a tag is 1 if it can be used for only selecting appropriate resources. A tag has an information value of 0 if it either leads to the selection of no or all resources in a tagging system. They empirically estimate the information value of a tag by retrieving the number of webpages that are returned by a search in Delicious with the tag. Besides of the selection based on the information value, the model also simulates the imitation of previous tag assignments using the Polya urn model. They model tag selection as a linear combination of information value and preferential attachment models. Probability of a tag x being reinforced or added can be expressed as $P(x) = \lambda \times P(I(x)) + (1 - \lambda) \times P(a) \times P(o) \times P(\frac{R(x)}{\sum R(x)})$ where λ is used to weigh the factors. $P(a)$ is the probability of a user committing a tagging action at any time t. $P(n)$ determines the number n of tags a user is likely to add at once based on the distribution of the number of tags a given user employs in a single tagging action. An old tag is reinforced with constant probability $P(o)$. If the old tag is added, it is added with a probability $\frac{R(x)}{\sum R(i)}$ where $R(x)$ is the number of times that particular previous tag x has been chosen in the past and $\sum R(i)$ is the sum of all previous tags. Overall, the proposed model leads to a plain power law distribution of the tag frequencies and to a linear growth of the set of distinct tags. It thus only partially reproduces the frequency-rank distributions in co-occurrence and resource tag streams and it is not successful in reproducing the decaying tag growth.

3.1.5 Fine-tuning by Adding More Parameters.

Klaas et al. [12] present the following model: The simulation of a tag stream always starts with an empty stream. Then, in each step of the simulation, with probability I (0.6-0.9) one of the previous tag assignments is imitated. With probability BK, the user selects an appropriate tag from her background knowledge about the resource. It corresponds to selecting an appropriate natural language word from the active vocabulary of the user. Each word t has been assigned a certain probability with which it gets selected, which corresponds to the probability with which t occurs in the Web corpus. The parameter n represents the number of popular tags a user has access to. In case of simulating resource streams, n will correspond to the number of popular tags shown. (e.g., n = 7 for Delicious). In case of co-occurrence streams n will be larger because the union of the popular tags of all resources that are aggregated in the co-occurrence stream will be depicted over time. Furthermore, the parameter h can be used for restricting the number of previous tag assignments which are used for determining the n most popular tags. The probability of selecting the concrete tag t from the n tags is then proportional to how often t was used during the last h tag assignments. Using these parameters, the authors describe a model that reproduces frequency rank for both tag co-occurrence and resource streams and also simulates the tag vocabulary growth well.

3.2 Language Model

The content of resource would affect generation of tags. Hence, tagging process can also be simulated using a language model like the latent Dirichlet allocation model [6]. Tagging is a real-world experiment in the evolution of a simple language [7]. Zhou et al. [63] propose a probabilistic generative model for generation of document content as well as associated tags. This helps in simultaneous topical analysis of terms, documents and users. Their user content annotation model can be explained as follows. For document content, each observed term ω in document d is generated from the source x (each document d maps one-to-one to a source x). Then from the conditional probability distribution on x, a topic z is drawn. Given the topic z, ω is finally generated from the conditional probability distribution on the topic z. For document tags, similarly, each observed tag word ω for document d is generated by user x. Specific to this user, there is a conditional probability distribution of topics, from which a topic z is then chosen. This hidden variable of topic again finally generates ω in the tag.

Figure 16.1 shows the user content annotation model using the plate notation.

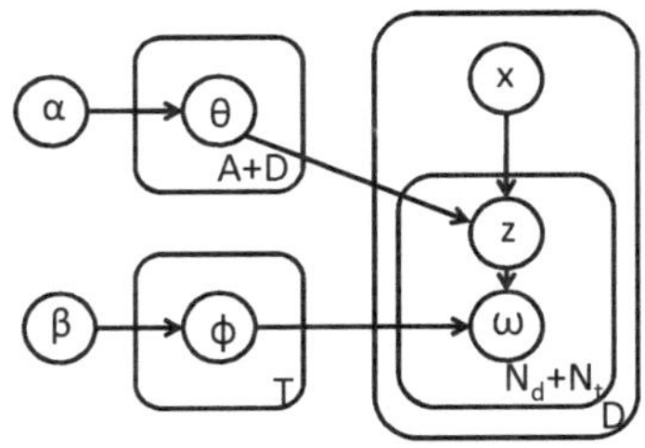

Figure 16.1. User content annotation model

Unknown distributions θ and ϕ can be learnt using EM. But EM can lead to local maxima or may be expensive. Hence, they use Gibbs sampling. Rather than the parameters, the posteriors are evaluated. Posteriors include: $P(d, z \mid w)$ and $P(x, z \mid w)$ alongwith $P(d \mid z)$, $P(x \mid z)$, $P(z \mid w)$. Number of topics are determined using the perplexity measure.

3.3 Other Influence Factors

Besides above models, researchers [48, 34] have also observed that there are other factors which are likely to influence how people apply the tags.

Sen et al. [48] mention three factors that influence people's personal tendency (their preferences and beliefs) to apply tags: (1) their past tagging behaviors, (2) community influence of the tagging behavior of other members, and (3) tag selection algorithm that chooses which tags to display. New users have an initial personal tendency based on their experiences with other tagging systems, their comfort with technology, their interests and knowledge. Personal tendency evolves as people interact with the tagging system. Figure 16.2 shows how these factors affect the tagging behaviour.

Experiments with Movielens dataset reveal the following. Once a user has applied three or more tags, the average cosine similarity for the nth tag application is more than 0.83. Moreover, similarity of a tag application to the user's past tags continues to rise as users add more tags. Besides reusing tag classes, users also reuse individual tags from their vocabulary. Community influence on a user's first tag is stronger for users who have seen more tags. The tag selection algorithm influences the distribution of tag classes (subjective, factual, and personal).

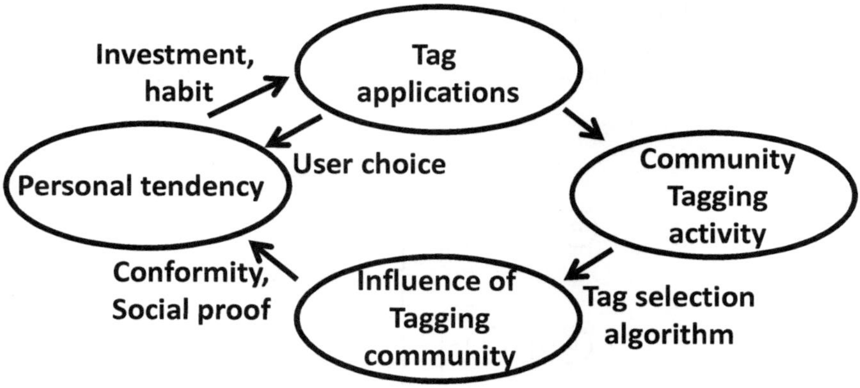

Figure 16.2. Factors affecting tagging behavior

The community influence on tag selection in Flickr has been studied by Marlow et al. [34]. One feature of the contact network is a user's ability to easily follow the photos being uploaded by their friends. This provides a continuous awareness of the photographic activity of their Flickr contacts, and by transitivity, a constant exposure to tagging practices. Do these relationships affect the formation of tag vocabularies, or are individuals guided by other stimuli? They find that the random users are much more likely to have a smaller overlap in common tags, while contacts are more distributed, and have a higher overall mean. This result shows a relationship between social affiliation and tag vocabulary formation and use even though the photos may be of completely different subject matter. This commonality could arise from similar descriptive tags (e.g., bright, contrast, black and white, or other photo features), similar content (photos taken on the same vacation), or similar subjects (co-occurring friends and family), each suggesting different modes of diffusion.

Apart from the different aspects mentioned above, user tagging behaviors can be largely dictated by the forms of contribution allowed and the personal and social motivations for adding input to the system [34].

4. Tagging System Design

What are the different parameters that should be considered when designing a social tagging system? In this section, we present the some design parameters [48, 34].

- **Tag Sharing:** What are the different privacy levels supported by the system for sharing? (public, private, groups).

- **Tag Selection/Tagging Support:** This includes tag recommendation algorithm used, number of recommendations shown, meta information shown. Different categories are a. blind tagging, where a tagging user cannot view tags assigned to the same resource by other users while tagging (e.g., Delicious) b. viewable tagging, where the user can see the tags already associated with a resource (e.g., Yahoo! Podcasts) c. suggestive tagging, where the system suggests possible tags to the user (e.g., Yahoo! MyWeb2.0). The implication of suggested tagging may be a quicker convergence to a folksonomy. In other words, a suggestive system may help consolidate the tag usage for a resource, or in the system, much faster than a blind tagging system would. As for viewable tagging, implications may be overweighting certain tags that were associated with the resource first, even if they would not have arisen otherwise.

- **Item Ownership/Tagging Rights:** Tagging system could allow only owner to tag (Technorati) or anyone (Amazon) or may support different levels of permissions for people to tag (Flickr). Figure 16.3 from [19] shows some examples. The system can specify who may remove a tag, whether no one (e.g., Yahoo! Podcasts), anyone (e.g., Odeo), the tag creator (e.g., Last.fm) or the resource owner (e.g., Flickr). Tags that are assigned to a photo may be radically divergent depending on whether the tagging is performed by the photographers, their friends, or strangers looking at their photos.

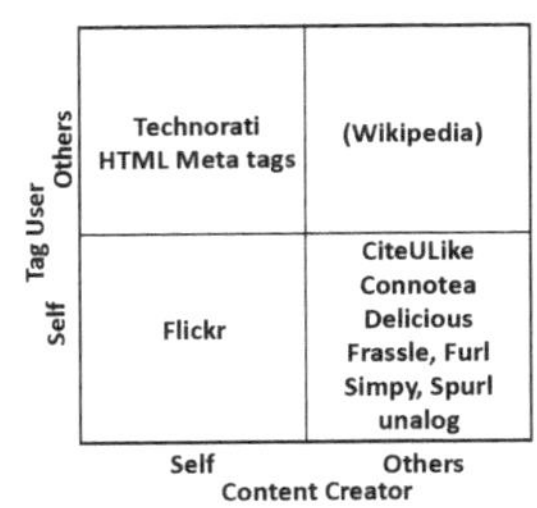

Figure 16.3. Tagging Rights

- **Tag Scope/Tag Aggregation:** Tag scope could be broad or narrow. System with broad tag scope follows a bag model and may allow for a multiplicity of tags for the same resource (<user, item, tag> maintained e.g Delicious). System with narrow tag scope follows a set model approach and asks all users to collectively tag an individual resource, thus denying any repetition (<item, tag> maintained e.g., Technorati, Flickr). In the case that a bag model is being used, the system has the ability to use aggregate statistics for a given resource to present users with the collective opinions of the taggers; thus accurately finding relationships between users, tags, and resources.

- **Tag Format:** Some tagging systems may support multi-word tags, tag normalization and other metadata like notes in Delicious.
- **Type of Object:** An object to be tagged can be web page, bibliographic material, video, image, user etc. Tags given to textual resources may differ from tags for resources/objects with no such textual representation, like images or audio.
- **Source of Material:** Resources to be tagged can be supplied by the participants (e.g., YouTube, Flickr, Technorati, Upcoming), by the system (e.g., ESP game, Last.fm, Yahoo! Podcasts), or, alternatively, a system can be open for tagging of any web resource (e.g., Delicious, Yahoo! MyWeb2.0).
- **Resource Connectivity:** Resources in the system can be linked to each other independent of the user tags. Connectivity can be roughly categorized as linked, grouped or none. E.g., web pages are connected by directed links; Flickr photos can be assigned to groups; and events in Upcoming have connections based on the time, city and venue associated with the event. Implications for resultant tags and usefulness may include convergence on similar tags for connected resources.
- **Social Connectivity:** Some systems allow users within the system to be linked together. Like resource connectivity, social connectivity can also be defined as linked, grouped, or none. Many other dimensions are present in social networks, e.g., whether links are typed (like in Flickr's contacts/friends model) and whether links are directed, where a connection between users is not necessarily symmetric (in Flickr, for example, none of the link types is symmetric). Implications of social connectivity include the adoption of localized folksonomies based on social structure in the system.
- **User Incentives:** Users may tag just for socialization, money, for fun while playing etc. as mentioned in section 2.

5. Tag analysis

To better understand social tagging data, a lot of research has been done in analyzing a variety of properties of social tagging data, such as how tags are distributed and their hidden semantics. In the following subsections we present some major analysis and results.

5.1 Tagging Distributions

Researchers began their study with analyzing tags distribution in tagging systems. They found that most of them are power law distributions, which is one of prominent features of a social tagging system.

5.1.1 Tagging System Vocabulary. As has been noted by different studies on a variety of datasets, total number of distinct tags in the system with respect to time follows a power law. However, recent studies have shown that this vocabulary growth is somewhat sublinear.

5.1.2 Resource's Tag Growth. For a single resource over time, vocabulary growth for tags also follows power law with exponent 2/3 [10]. Frequency-rank distribution of tag streams also follows a power law [12]. For some web-pages tagged on Delicious, tag frequency (sorted) versus tag rank for a web page is a decreasing graph with a sudden drop between rank 7 and 10 [12]. This may be due to an artifact of the user interface of Delicious. The graph of probability distribution of number of tags contained in a posting versus the number of tags displays an initial exponential decay with typical number of tags as 3-4 and then becomes a power law tail with exponent as high as -3.5 [10].

Researchers have also observed convergence of the tag distributions. In [18], Halpin et al. observe that majority of sites reach their peak popularity, the highest frequency of tagging in a given time period, within 10 days of being saved on Delicious (67% in the data set of Golder and Huberman [16]) though some sites are rediscovered by users (about 17% in their data set), suggesting stability in most sites but some degree of burstiness in the dynamics that could lead to a cyclical relationship to stability characteristic of chaotic systems. They also plot KL divergence between the tag frequency distributions for a resource versus the time. The curve drops very steeply. For almost all resources the curve reaches zero at about the same time. In the beginning few weeks, curve is quite steep and slowly becomes gentle as time progresses. Golder and Huberman also find that the proportion of frequencies of tags within a given site stabilizes over time.

Cattuto et al. [10] have shown the variation of the probability distribution of the vocabulary growth exponent γ for resources, as a function of their rank. The curve for the 1000 top-ranked (most bookmarked) resources closely fits a Gaussian curve at $\gamma \approx 0.71$. This indicates that highly bookmarked resources share a characteristic law of growth. On computing the distribution P(γ) for less and less popular resources, the peak shifts towards higher values of γ and the growth behavior becomes more and more linear.

Wetzker et al. [57] also show that most popular URLs disappear after peaking. They also point out that some of the tags can peak periodically, e.g., Christmas.

5.1.3 User Tag Vocabulary Growth. There are also studies that focus on tags applied by a specific user. Golder and Huberman [16] show that certain users' sets of distinct tags grow linearly as new resources are added. But Marlow et al. [34] find that for many users, such as those with few distinct tags in the graph, distinct tag growth declines over time, indicating either agreement on the tag vocabulary, or diminishing returns on their usage. In some cases, new tags are added consistently as photos are uploaded, suggesting a supply of fresh vocabulary and constant incentive for using tags. Sometimes only a few tags are used initially with a sudden growth spurt later on, suggesting that the user either discovered tags or found new incentives for using them.

5.2 Identifying Tag Semantics

Intuitively, tags as user generated classification labels are semantically meaningful. So, research has been done for exploring the semantics of tags. These research works include three aspects: (1) Identifying similar tags, (2) mapping tags to taxonomies, and (3) extracting certain types of tags.

5.2.1 Analysis of Pairwise Relationships between Tags. In order to measure similarity of tags beyond words, researchers proposed various models to explore tags' similarity. Most of them are based on a simple assumption that tags that are similar may be used to tag the same resources, and similar resource would be tagged by similar tags. Therefore, inter tag correlation graph (tag as nodes, edges between two tags if they co-occur, weight on edge = cosine distance measure using number of times a tag was used) can be built for a tagging system. An analysis of the structural properties of such tag graphs may provide important insights into how people tag and how semantic structures emerge in distributed folksonomies. A simple approach would be measuring tags similarity based on the number of common web pages tagged by them. In section 7, we show how analysis of co-occurrence of tags can be used to generate tag recommendations.

5.2.2 Extracting Ontology from Tags. Another line of research for identifying semantics of tags is mapping tags to an existing ontology. Being able to automatically classify tags into semantic categories allows us to understand better the way users annotate media objects and to build tools for viewing and browsing the media objects. The simplest approach is based on string matching. Sigurbjörnsson et al. [49] map Flickr tags onto WordNet semantic categories using straight forward string matching between Flickr tags and WordNet lemmas. They found that 51.8% of the tags in Flickr can be assigned a semantic category using this mapping. To better assign tags to a category, content of resources associated with a given tag could be used. Overell et al. [38] designed a system to auto-classify tags using Wikipedia and Open

Directory. They used structural patterns like categories and templates that can be extracted from resource metadata to classify Flickr tags. They built a classifier to classify Wikipedia articles into eleven semantic categories (act, animal, artifact, food, group, location, object, person, plant, substance and time). They map Flickr tags to Wikipedia articles using anchor texts in Wikipedia. Since they have classified Wikipedia articles, Flickr tags can be categorized using the same classification. They classify things as what, where and when. They show that by deploying ClassTag they can improve the classified portion of the Flickr vocabulary by 115%. Considering the full volume of Flickr tags, i.e., taking tag frequency into account, they show that with ClassTag nearly 70% of Flickr tags can be classified. Figure 16.4 shows an overview of their system. Figure 16.5 shows the classification of Flickr tags.

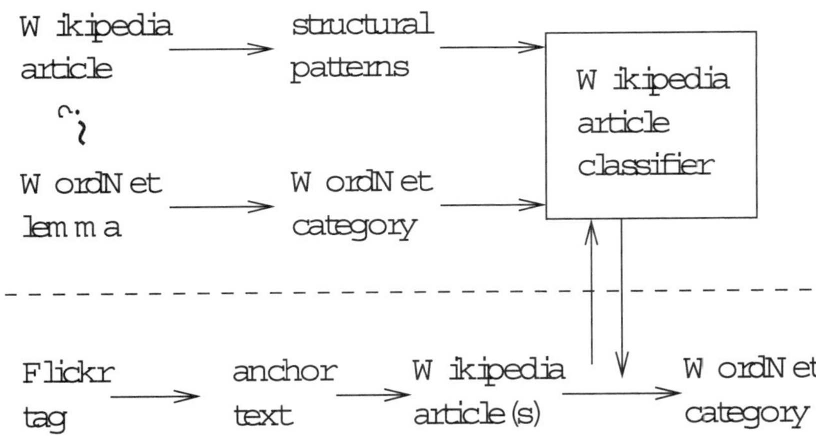

Figure 16.4. Overview of the ClassTag system

5.2.3 Extracting Place and Event Semantics. Tags also contain specific information, such as locations or events. Rattenbury et al. [43] study the problem of extracting place and event semantics for Flickr tags. They analyze two methods inspired by burst-analysis techniques (popular in signal processing) and one novel method: Scale-structure Identification. The location, l_p, (consisting of latitude-longitude coordinates) associated with photo p generally marks where the photo was taken; but sometimes marks the location of the photographed object. The time, t_p, associated with photo p generally marks the photo capture time; but occasionally refers to the time the photo was uploaded to Flickr. They aim to determine, for each tag in the dataset, whether

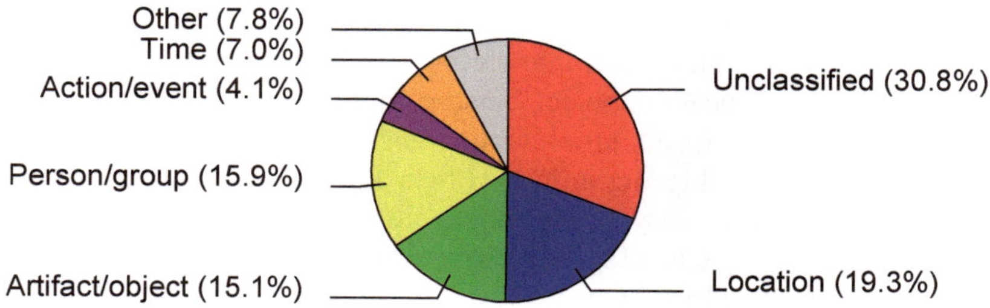

Figure 16.5. Classification of Flickr tags using ClassTag system

the tag represents an event (or place). The intuition behind the various methods they present is that an event (or place) refers to a specific segment of time (or region in space). The number of usage occurrences for an event tag should be much higher in a small segment of time than the number of usage occurrences of that tag outside the segment. The scale of the segment is one factor that these methods must address; the other factor is calculating whether the number of usage occurrences within the segment is significantly different from the number outside the segment. The Scale-structure Identification method performs a significance test that depends on multiple scales simultaneously and does not rely on apriori defined time segments. The key intuition is: if tag x is an event then the points in T_x, the time usage distribution, should appear as a single cluster at many scales. Interesting clusters are the ones with low entropy. For place identification, L_x is used rather than T_x. Periodic events have strong clusters, at multiple scales, that are evenly spaced apart in time. Practically, because tags occur in bursts, a periodic tag should exhibit at least three strong clusters (to rule out tags that just happened to occur in two strong temporal clusters but are not truly periodic). Overall, their approach has a high precision however a large proportion of tags remain unclassified.

5.3 Tags Versus Keywords

To identify the potential of tags in being helpful for search, there have been works that compare tags with keywords. As shown in Figure 16.6, given a web document, the "most important" words (both wrt tf as well as $tf \times idf$) of the document are generally covered by the vocabulary of user-generated tags [32]. This means that the set of user-generated tags has the comparable expression capability as the plain English words for web documents. Li et al. [32] found that most of the missed keywords are misspelled words or words invented by users, and usually cannot be found in dictionary.

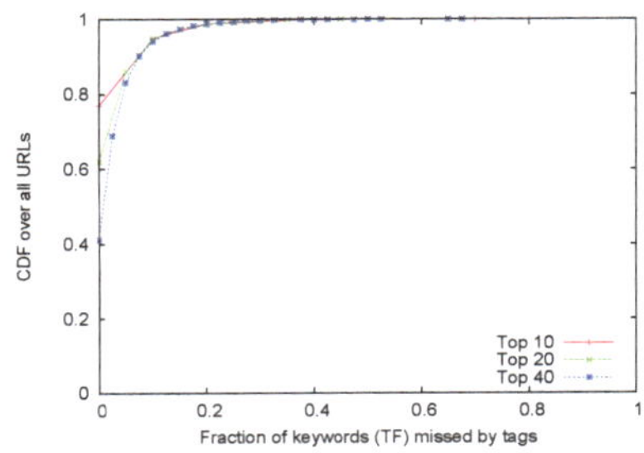

Figure 16.6. Tag coverage for important keywords

Further, they define tag match ratio $e(T, U)$ for tag set T associated with a URL U as ratio of weights of the tags of a particular URL that can be matched by the document. $e(T, U) = \frac{\sum_{k|t_k \in U} w(t_k)}{\sum_i w(t_i)}$. Here, $w(t)$ is the weight of tag t, i.e., the frequency of tag t in the data set. The tag match ratio represents the ratio of important tags of a URL matched by the document. Figure 16.7 shows the distribution of tag match ratio for URLs in their Delicious dataset.

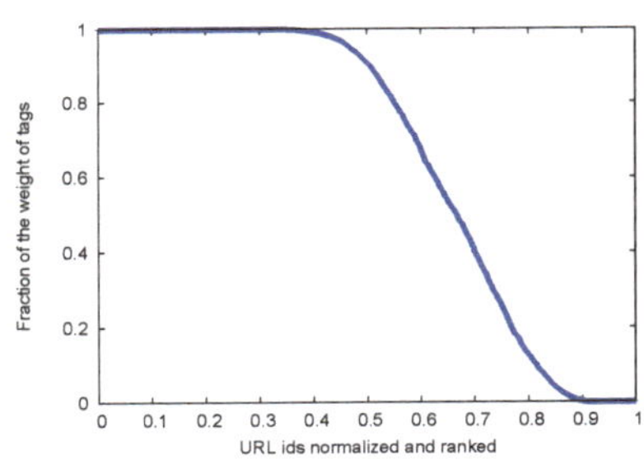

Figure 16.7. Distribution of the tag match ratio

Besides this, tags often have much more expressive power. For example, consider the Google home page. It does not mention the phrase "search engine" anywhere. But "searchengine" can be found as a tag against the bookmarked URL http://www.google.com/ig on Delicious.

6. Visualization of Tags

Social tagging is one of the most important forms of user generated content. Appropriate rendering of tags can provide useful information to users. Tag clouds have been explored to support browsing on web portals, and various tag selection methods for tag clouds have been developed. Much work has been done to identify hierarchy of tags in the tag cloud construction. Visualization schemes stress on display formats and evolutionary aspect of tag clouds, etc. We review these in this section.

6.1 Tag Clouds for Browsing/Search

Tag cloud, a visual depiction of user-generated tags, is used to facilitate browsing and search process of the tags. Sinclair and Cardew-Hall [51] discuss situations when using tag clouds is better than doing search. They conducted an experiment, giving participants the option of using a tag cloud or a traditional search interface to answer various questions. They found that participants preferred the search interface if the information need is specific while they preferred the tag cloud if the information-seeking task was more general. It is partly because tags are good at broad categorization, as opposed to specific characterization of content. In total, the number of questions answered using the tag cloud was greater than those answered using the search box. The tag cloud provides a visual summary of the contents of the database. A number of participants commented that tag clouds gave them an idea of where to begin their information seeking. The tag cloud helps the information seeker to get familiar with the domain and allows more focused queries based on the information gained from browsing. It appears that scanning the tag cloud requires less cognitive load than formulating specific query terms.

Tag clouds have their disadvantages too. First, tag clouds obscure useful information by being skewed towards what is popular. Second, answering a question using the tag cloud required more queries per question than the search box. Third, many of the participants commented that the tag cloud did not allow them to narrow their search enough to answer the given questions. On average, roughly half of the articles in the dataset remain inaccessible from the tag cloud. Most tagging systems mitigate this by including tag links when viewing individual articles, thus exposing some of the less popular tags. However, this is not necessarily useful when someone is seeking specific information.

Millen et al. [36] did experiments on Dogear system where clicking a tag leads to a view of bookmarks that are associated with that tag. They found that the most frequent way to browse bookmarks is by clicking on another person's name, followed by browsing bookmarks by selecting a specific tag from the system-wide tag cloud. It is considerably less common for a user to select a tag from another user's tag cloud and very less chances of using more advanced browsing of tag intersections.

6.2 Tag Selection for Tag Clouds

Since there is only limited display space for tags in tag clouds, how to select the appropriate tags is a challenging task. Hassan-Montero and Herrero-

Solana [20] describe a system for bi-dimensional visualization of tag clouds. Tag selection is based on usefulness as determined by: (1) its capacity to represent each resource as compared to other tags assigned to the same resource, (2) the volume of covered resources as compared to other tags, (3) its capacity to cover these resources less covered by other tags. Semantic relationships among tags are defined in terms of their similarity, quantified by means of the Jaccard coefficient. K-means clustering is then applied on tag similarity matrix, with an apriori chosen number of clusters and a fixed number of selected relevant tags. They apply Multidimensional Scaling, using Pearson's correlation as the similarity function, on a tag-to-tag correlation matrix. MDS creates a bi-dimensional space, which is then visualized through a fish-eye system. Alphabetical-based schemes are useful for know-item searching, i.e., when user knows previously what tag she is looking for, such as when user browses her personal tag cloud. They propose a tag cloud layout based on the assumption that clustering techniques can improve tag clouds' browsing experience. The display method is similar to traditional tag cloud layout, with the difference that tags are grouped with semantically similar tags, and likewise clusters of tags are displayed near semantically similar clusters. Similar tags are horizontally neighbors, whereas similar clusters are vertically neighbors. Clustering offers more coherent visual distribution of tags than traditional alphabetical arrangements, allowing to differentiate among main topics in tag cloud, as well as to infer semantic knowledge from the neighbors' relationships.

Begelman et al. [4] propose a clustering algorithm to find strongly related tags. The algorithm is based on counting the number of co-occurrences of any pair of tags and a cut-off point is determined when the co-occurrence count is significant enough to be used. To determine this cutoff point, they start from the tail on the right end and seek the point where the first derivative of the count has its first high peak (that is when the second derivative goes from positive to negative) and check if the peak was high enough. This results in a sparse matrix that represents tags, so that the value of each element is the similarity of the two tags. Using this definition of similarity, they design an inter-tag correlation network graph. They then cluster this graph using spectral bisection and modularity function.

6.3 Tag Hierarchy Generation

Beyond the flat structure of tags, hierarchical structure also exists in the tagging space. Caro et al. [9] present the tagFlake system, which supports semantically informed navigation within a tag cloud. The system organizes tags extracted from textual content in hierarchical organizations, suitable for navigation, visualization, classification and tracking. It extracts the most significant tag/terms from text documents and maps them onto a hierarchy in such a way that descendant terms are contextually dependent on their ancestors within the given corpus of documents. This provides tagFlake with a mechanism for enabling navigation within the tag space and for classification of the text documents based on the contextual structure captured by the generated hierarchy.

Li et al. [31] present Effective Large Scale Annotation Browser (ELSABer), to browse large-scale social annotation data. ELSABer helps the users browse a huge number of annotations in a semantic, hierarchical and efficient way. ELSABer has the following features: (1) the semantic relations between annotations are explored for browsing of similar resources; (2) the hierarchical relations between annotations are constructed for browsing in a top-down fashion; (3) the distribution of social annotations is studied for efficient browsing. The hierarchy structure is determined by a decision tree with the features including tag coverage, URL intersection rate, inverse-coverage rate, etc.

6.4 Tag Clouds Display Format

Tags clouds can be displayed in different formats. Bielenberg and Zacher [5] have proposed circular clouds, as opposed to the typical rectangular layout, where the most heavily weighted tags appear closer to the center. Font size and distance to the center represent the importance of a tag, but distance between tags does not represent their similarity.

Owen and Lemire [26] present models and algorithms to improve the display of tag clouds that consist of in-line HTML, as well as algorithms that use nested tables to achieve a more general two-dimensional layout in which tag relationships are considered. Since the font size of a displayed tag is usually used to show the relative importance or frequency of the tag, a typical tag cloud contains large and small text interspersed. A consequence is wasteful white space. To handle the space waste problem, the authors propose the classic electronic design automation (EDA) algorithm, min-cut placement, for area minimization and clustering in tag clouds. For the large clumps of white space, the solution is a hybrid of the classic Knuth-Plass algorithm for text justification, and a book-placement exercise considered by Skiena. The resulting tag clouds are visually improved and tighter.

6.5 Tag Evolution Visualization

Other than the text information, tags usually have the time dimension. To visualize the tag evolution process is an interesting topic. Dubinko et al. [15] consider the problem of visualizing the evolution of tags within Flickr. An animation provided via Flash in a web browser allows the user to observe and interact with the interesting tags as they evolve over time. The visualization is made up of two interchangeable metaphors - the ‘river’ and the ‘waterfall’.

The visualization provides a view of temporal evolution, with a large amount of surface data easily visible at each timestep. It allows the user to interact with the presentation in order to drill down into any particular result. It remains "situated" in the sense that the user is always aware of the current point of time being presented, and it provides random access into the time stream so that the user can reposition the current time as necessary. There are two novel contributions in their algorithm. The first is a solution to an interval covering problem that allows any timescale to be expressed efficiently as a combination of a small number of pre-defined timescales that have been pre-computed and saved in the "index" structure. The second contribution is an extension of work on score aggregation allowing data from the small number of pre-computed timescales to be efficiently merged to produce the optimal solution without needing to consume all the available data. The resulting visualization is available at Taglines[5]. In some cases, the user may seek data points that are particularly anomalous, while in other cases it may be data points that are highly persistent or that manifest a particular pattern. The authors focus on one particular notion of "interesting" data: the tags during a particular period of time that are most representative for that time period. That is, the tags that show a significantly increased likelihood of occurring inside the time period, compared to outside.

Russel [44] has proposed Cloudalicious[6], a tool to study the evolution of the tag cloud over time. Cloudalicious takes a request for a URL, downloads the tagging data from Delicious, and then graphs the collective users tagging activity over time. The y-axis shows the relative weights of the most popular tags for that URL. As the lines on the graph move from left to right, they show signs of stabilization. This pattern can be interpreted as the collective opinion of the users. Diagonal lines are the most interesting elements of these graphs as they suggest that the users doing the tagging have changed the words used to describe the site.

6.6 Popular Tag Cloud Demos

Some demos for visualizing tags are also available on the Web. Grafolicious[7] produces graphs illustrating when and how many times a URL has been bookmarked in Delicious. HubLog[8] gives a graph of related tags connected with the given tags. Although these demos gave a vivid picture of social annotations in different aspects, their goals are not to help users to browse an-

[5] http://research.yahoo.com/taglines
[6] http://cloudalicio.us/tagcloud.php
[7] http://www.neuroticWeb.com/recursos/del.icio.us-graphs/
[8] http://hublog.hubmed.org/tags/visualisation

notations effectively. PhaseTwo[9] aims at creating visually pleasant tag clouds, by presenting tags in the form of seemingly random collections of circles with varying sizes: the size of the circle denotes its frequency. Delicious also provides its own tag cloud view[10]. Tag.alicio.us[11] operates as a tag filter, retrieving links from Delicious according to tag and time constraints (e.g., tags from this hour, today, or this week). Extisp.icio.us[12] displays a random scattering of a given user's tags, sized according to the number of times that the user has reused each tag, and Facetious[13] was a reworking of the Delicious database, which made use of faceted classification, grouping tags under headings such as "by place" (Iraq, USA, Australia), "by technology" (blog, wiki, website) and "by attribute" (red, cool, retro). Tag clouds have also been integrated inside maps for displaying tags having geographical information, such as pictures taken at a given location.

7. Tag Recommendations

The tagging system can recommend some tags to a user, and the user can select one of those tags or come up with a new one. Tag recommendation is not only useful to improve user experience, but also makes rich annotation available. There have been many studies on tag recommendation. Tags can be recommended based on their quality, co-occurrence, mutual information and object features.

7.1 Using Tag Quality

Tag quality can guide the tag recommendation process. The tag quality can be evaluated by facet coverage and popularity, and those tags of high quality are used for recommendation. Xu et al. [61] propose a set of criteria for tag quality and then propose a collaborative tag suggestion algorithm using these criteria to discover the high-quality tags. A good tag combination should include multiple facets of the tagged objects. The number of tags for identifying an object should be minimized, and the number of objects identified by the tag combination should be small. Note that personally used organizational tags are less likely to be shared by different users. Thus, they should be excluded from tag recommendations. The proposed algorithm employs a goodness measure for tags derived from collective user authorities to combat spam. The goodness measure is iteratively adjusted by a reward-penalty algorithm, which also in-

[9]http://phasetwo.org/post/a-better-tag-cloud.html
[10]http://del.icio.us/tag/
[11]http://planetozh.com/blog/2004/10/tagalicious-a-way-to-integrate-delicious/
[12]http://kevan.org/extispicious
[13]http://www.siderean.com/delicious/facetious.jsp

corporates other sources of tags, e.g., content-based auto-generated tags. The algorithm favors tags that are used by a large number of people, and minimizes the overlap of concepts among the suggested tags to allow for high coverage of multiple facets and honors the high correlation among tags.

7.2 Using Tag Co-occurrences

One important criterion used for tag recommendation is tag co-occurrence. Those tags co-occurring with the existing tags of the object are used for recommendation. Sigurbjörnsson and Zwol [49] present four strategies to recommend tags. These include two co-ocurrence based strategies: Jaccard similarity and an asymmetric measure $P(t_j \mid t_i) = \frac{|t_i \bigcap t_j|}{|t_i|}$. Tag Aggregation and promotion strategies are based on voting or weighted voting based on co-occurrence count. Given a set of user-defined tags U on an object O, they want to rank candidate tags C that can be recommended for object O based on co-occurrence counts of u and c such that $u \in U$ and $c \in C$. From the tag frequency distribution, they learned that both the head and the tail of the power law would probably not contain good tags for recommendation. Considered that user-defined tags with very low collection frequency are less reliable than tags with higher collection frequency, those tags for which the statistics are more stable were promoted. They compute promotion score for a (u, c) pair by using stability of tag u, descriptiveness of tag c and rank of tag c wrt tag u. These are in turn defined using system parameters k_s, k_d and k_r.

$stability(u) = \frac{k_s}{k_s + abs(k_s - log(|u|))}$ where $|u|$ is the collection frequency of user defined tag u.

Tags with very high frequency are likely to be too general for individual photos.

$descriptive(c) = \frac{k_d}{k_d + abs(k_d - log(|c|))}$

The rank $rank(u, c)$ of a candidate tag c for tag u is $\frac{k_r}{k_r + r - 1}$ where r is position of tag c for a tag u. The promotion score can be defined as follows:

$$promotion(u, c) = rank(u, c) \times stability(u) \times descriptive(c)$$

Tag score is finally computed as follows:

$$score(c) = \sum_{u \in U} vote(u, c) \times promotion(u, c)$$

Here vote(u,c) is 1 if tags u and c co-occur, else 0. Tag frequency distribution follows a perfect power law, and the mid section of this power law contained the most interesting candidates for tag recommendation. They found that locations, artifacts and objects have a relatively high acceptance ratio (user acceptance of the recommended tag). However, people, groups and unclassified tags (tags that do not appear in WordNet) have relatively low acceptance ratio.

7.3 Using Mutual Information between Words, Documents and Tags

Mutual information is another criterion for tag recommendation. Song et al. [52] treat the tagged training documents as triplets of (words, documents, tags), and represent them as two bipartite graphs, which are partitioned into clusters by Spectral Recursive Embedding (SRE) and using Lanczos algorithm for symmetric low rank approximation for the weighted adjacency matrix for the bipartite graphs. Tags in each topical cluster are ranked by a novel ranking algorithm. A two-way Poisson Mixture Model (PMM) is proposed to model the document distribution into mixture components within each cluster and aggregate words into word clusters simultaneously. During the online recommendation stage, given a document vector, its posterior probabilities of classes are first calculated. Then based on the joint probabilities of the tags and the document, tags are recommended for this document based on their within-cluster ranking. The efficiency of the Poisson mixture model helps to make recommendations in linear-time in practice. Within a cluster, node ranking is defined by $Rank_i = exp(-\frac{1}{r(i)^2})$ for $r(i) \neq 0$ where $r(i) = np_i \times log(nr_i)$. N-Precision ($np_i$) of a node i is the weighted sum of its edges that connect to the nodes within the same cluster, divided by the total sum of edge weights in that cluster. N-recall (Nr_i)=edges associated with node i/edges associated with node i within the same cluster.

7.4 Using Object Features

Tag recommendation can also be performed using object features. E.g., the extracted content features from the images can be helpful in tag recommendation. In [33], Liu et al. propose a tag ranking scheme to automatically rank the tags associated with a given image according to their relevance to the image content. To estimate the tag relevance to the images, the authors first get the initial tag relevance scores based on probability density estimation, and then apply a random walk on a tag similarity graph to refine the scores. Since all the tags have been ranked according to their relevance to the image, for each uploaded image, they find the K nearest neighbors based on low-level visual features, and then the top ranked tags of the K neighboring images are collected and recommended to the user. In [58], Wu et al. model the tag recommendation as a learning task that considers multi-modality including tag co-occurrence and visual correlation. The visual correlation scores are derived from Visual language model (VLM), which is adopted to model the content of the tags in visual domain. The optimal combination of these ranking features is learned by the Rankboost algorithm.

8. Applications of Tags

In this section, we would describe different applications for which tags have been used. Social tagging can be useful in the areas including indexing, search, taxonomy generation, clustering, classification, social interest discovery, etc.

8.1 Indexing

Tags can be useful for indexing sites faster. Users bookmark sites launched by their friends or colleagues before a search engine bot can find them. Tags are also useful in deeper indexing. Many pages bookmarked are deep into sites and sometimes not easily linked to by others, found via bad or nonexistent site navigation or linked to from external pages. Carmel et al. [8] claim that by appropriately weighting the tags according to their estimated quality, search effectiveness can be significantly improved. They propose a novel framework for bookmark (a triple of document d, user u, tag t) weighting that estimates the effectiveness of bookmarks for IR tasks as fundamental entities in social bookmarking systems.

8.2 Search

Tags have been found useful for web search, personalized search and enterprise search. Tags offer multiple descriptions of a given resource, which potentially increases the likelihood that searcher and tagger find a common language and thus using tags, retrieval effectiveness may be enhanced. Social bookmarking can provide search data not currently provided by other sources.

Heymann et al. [23] analyze posts to Delicious: how many bookmarks exist (about 115M), how fast is it growing, and how active are the URLs being posted (quite active). They observe the following. (1) Pages posted to Delicious are often recently modified. (2) Approximately 12.5% of URLs posted by users are new, unindexed pages. (3) Roughly 9% of results for search queries are URLs present in Delicious. (4) While some users are more prolific than others, the top 10% of users only account for 56% of posts. (5) 30-40% of URLs and approximately one in eight domains posted were not previously in Delicious. (6) Popular query terms and tags overlap significantly (though tags and query terms are not correlated). (7) Most tags were deemed relevant and objective by users. (8) Approximately 120000 URLs are posted to Delicious each day. (9) There are roughly 115M public posts, coinciding with about 30-50M unique URLs. (10) Tags are present in the pagetext of 50% of the pages they annotate and in the titles of 16% of the pages they annotate. (11) Domains are often highly correlated with particular tags and vice versa.

Similarly, Heckner et al. [21] found out using a survey that Flickr and Youtube users perceive tags as helpful for IR, and show a certain tendency

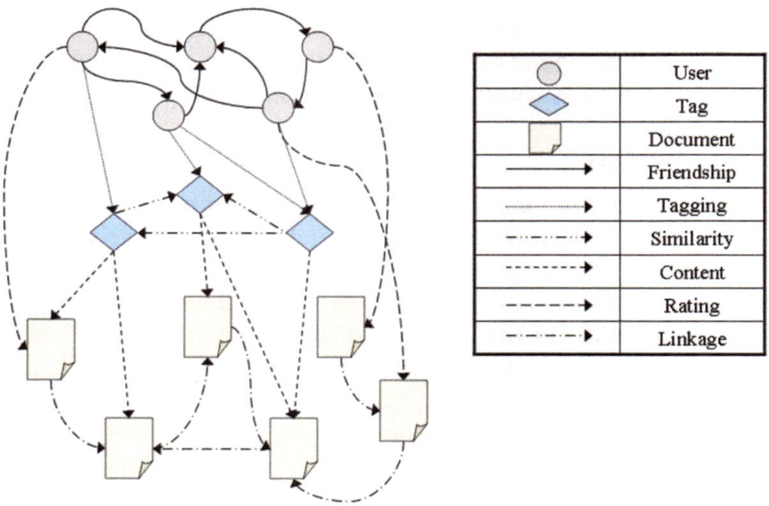

Figure 16.8. Social network model

towards searching other collections rather than their own collections. Users reveal that Flickr search often leads to better precision and recall for pictures compared to Google search. They also point out that Flickr search is quite specific whereas with Google search you get more wild cards you don't expect based on the information on a page rather than just the tags on a photo.

8.2.1 Semantic Query Expansion. Schenkel et al. [45] develop an incremental top-k algorithm for answering queries of the form $Q(u, q_1, q_2, ..., q_n)$ where u is the user and $q_1, q_2, ..., q_n$ are the query keywords. The algorithm performs two-dimensional expansions: social expansion considers the strength of relations among users, and semantic expansion considers the relatedness of different tags. It is based on principles of threshold algorithms, and folds friends and related tags into the search space in an incremental on-demand manner.

Figure 16.8 shows their social network model that incorporates both social and semantic relationships. In contrast with standard IR model, the content-based score of a document is additionally user-specific, i.e., it depends on the social context of the query initiator.

They present an algorithm, ContextMerge, to efficiently evaluate the top-k matches for a query, using the social context score.

ContextMerge makes use of information that is available in social tagging systems, namely lists of documents tagged by a user and number of documents tagged with tags. It incrementally builds social frequencies by considering users that are related to the querying user in descending order of friendship similarity, computes upper and lower bounds for the social score from these frequencies, and stops the execution as soon as it can be guaranteed that the best k documents have been identified.

8.2.2 Enhanced Similarity Measure. Estimating similarity between a query and a web page is important to the web search problem. Tags provided by web users provide different perspectives and so are usually good summaries of the corresponding web pages and provide a new metadata for the similarity calculation between a query and a web page. Furthermore, similar tags are used to tag similar web pages. Semantics of tags can be measured and enhanced similarity measure between queries and tags can be formulated.

Wu et al. [59] show how emergent semantics can be statistically derived from the social annotations. They propose to use a probabilistic generative model to model the user's annotation behavior and to automatically derive the emergent semantics of the tags. Synonymous tags are grouped together and highly ambiguous tags are identified and separated. The three entities (user, resource, tag) are represented in the same multi-dimensional vector space called the conceptual space. They extend the bigram separable mixture model to a tripartite probabilistic model to obtain the emergent semantics contained in the social annotations data. Furthermore, they apply the derived emergent semantics to discover and search shared web bookmarks. They provide a basic search model that deals with queries that are a single tag and rank semantic related resources without considering personalized information of the user. They also extend this basic model for personalized search and to support complicated queries (where a complicated query is a boolean combination of tags and other words appearing in the resources.

Bao et al. [2] also observe that the social annotations can benefit web search in this aspect. They proposed SocialSimRank (SSR) which calculates the similarity between social annotations and web queries. Preliminary experimental results show that SSR can find the latent semantic association between queries and annotations.

8.2.3 Enhanced Static Ranking. Estimating the quality of a web page is also important to the web search problem. The amount of annotations assigned to a page indicates its popularity and indicates its quality in some sense. In order to explore social tags for measuring the quality of web pages, researchers have exploited the tagging graph.

Hotho et al. [24] present a formal model and a new search algorithm for folksonomies, called FolkRank, that exploits the structure of the folksonomy. The FolkRank ranking scheme is then used to generate personalized rankings of the items in a folksonomy, and to recommend users, tags and resources. The social network graph is defined as a tripartite graph of resources, users and tags as nodes where the edges are the relationships between resources and tags, tags and users, and users and resources. Adapted PageRank is then defined as $\vec{w} = \alpha\vec{w} + \beta A\vec{w} + \gamma\vec{p}$ where $\alpha + \beta + \gamma = 1$. The FolkRank algorithm computes a topic-specific ranking in a folksonomy as follows:

- The preference vector $\vec{p}$ is used to determine the topic. It may have any distribution of weights, as long as $||\vec{w}||_1 = ||\vec{p}||_1$ holds. Typically a single entry or a small set of entries is set to a high value, and the remaining weight is equally distributed over the other entries. Since the structure of the folksonomies is symmetric, we can define a topic by assigning a high value to either one or more tags and/or one or more users and/or one or more resources.

- Let $\vec{w_0}$ be the fixed point with $\beta = 1$

- Let $\vec{w_1}$ be the fixed point with $\beta < 1$

- $\vec{w} = \vec{w_1} - \vec{w_0}$ is the final weight vector.

Thus, they compute the winners and losers of the mutual reinforcement of resources when a user preference is given, compared to the baseline without a preference vector. The resulting weight $w[x]$ of an element x of the folksonomy is called the FolkRank of x. They observed that Adapted PageRank ranking contains many globally frequent tags, while the FolkRank ranking provides more personal tags.

Bao et al. [2] also propose a novel algorithm, SocialPageRank (SPR) to measure the popularity of web pages using social annotations. The algorithm also utilize the social tagging graph. The intuition behind the algorithm is the mutual enhancement relation among popular web pages, up-to-date web users and hot social annotations. SocialPageRank (SPR) captures the popularity of web pages and successfully measures the quality (popularity) of a web page from the web users' perspective.

8.2.4 Personalized Search. Furthermore, personal tags are naturally good resources for describing a person's interests. So personal search could be enhanced via exploring personal tags. Xu et al. [60] present a framework in which the rank of a web page is decided not only by the term matching between the query and the web page's content but also by the topic matching between the user's interests and the web page's topics.

The personalized search is conducted by ranking the web pages using two guidelines, term matching and topic matching. When a user u issues a query q, a web page p is ranked not only by the term similarity between q and p but also by the topic similarity between u and p. Three properties of folksonomy are studied for the topic space estimation:

(1) The categorization property. Many of the social annotations are subject descriptor keywords at various levels of specificity. The selection of proper annotations for a web page is somewhat a classification of the web page to the categories represented by the annotations.

(2) The keyword property. Annotations can be seen as good keywords for describing the respective web pages from various aspects.

(3) The structure property. In folksonomy systems, users' bookmarking actions form a cross link structure between the users and the web pages. They model the structure using a user-web page bipartite graph.

When a user u issues a query q, two search processes begin, a term matching process and a topic matching process. The term matching process calculates the similarity between q and each web page to generate a user unrelated ranked document list. The topic matching process calculates the topic similarity between u and each web page to generate a user related ranked document list. Then a merge operation is conducted to generate a final ranked document list based on the two sub ranked document lists. They adopt ranking aggregation to implement the merge operation by $r(u, q, p) = \gamma.r_{term}(q, p) + (1 - \gamma).r_{topic}(u, p)$

Topic space selection is done using (1) social annotations as topics (2) ODP categories as topics (3) interest and topic adjusting via bipartite collaborative link structure.

8.2.5 Intranet (Enterprise) Search. Dmitriev et al. [14] show how user annotations can be used to improve the quality of intranet (enterprise) search. They propose two ways to obtain user annotations, using explicit and implicit feedback, and show how they can be integrated into a search engine.

One way to obtain annotations is to let users explicitly enter annotations for the pages they browse. The implicit method of obtaining annotations is to use the queries users submit to the search engine as annotations for pages users click on. They propose several strategies to determine which pages are relevant to the query, i.e., which pages to attach an annotation to, based on clickthrough data associated with the query. There are different ways of getting feedback using this method. For every click record, the first strategy produces a (URL, Annotation) pair, where Annotation is the QueryString. This strategy is simple to implement, and gives a large number of annotations. A second strategy only produces a (URL, Annotation) pair for a click record which is the last record in a session. Annotation is still the QueryString. A query chain is a time-ordered sequence of queries, executed over a short period of time. The assumption behind using query chains is that all subsequent queries in the chain are actually refinements of the original query. The third strategy, similar to the first one, produces a (URL, Annotation) pair for every click record, but Annotation now is the concatenation of all QueryStrings from the corresponding query chain. Finally, the fourth strategy produces a (URL, Annotation) pair for a click record which is the last record in the last session in a query chain, and Annotation is, again, the concatenation of QueryStrings from the corresponding query chain.

Compared to the baseline system (search engine without annotations), they obtained around 14% improvement in accuracy when using explicit annotations and around 9.3% performance improvement when using implicit annotations.

8.3 Taxonomy Generation

Tags can be organized in hierarchical taxonomy structure based on their semantic meanings. In this part, we introduce two methods to generate the taxonomy structure.

8.3.1 Using Centrality in Tag Similarity Graph. Heymann and Garcia-Molina [22] provide an algorithm to convert a large corpus of tags into a navigable hierarchical taxonomy. Their greedy algorithm extracts a hierarchical taxonomy using graph centrality in a tag similarity graph. It starts with a single node tree and then it adds each tag to the tree in the decreasing order of tag centrality in the similarity graph. It decides the location of each candidate tag by its similarity to every node currently present in the tree. The candidate tag is then either added as a child of the most similar node if its similarity to that node is greater than some threshold, or it is added to the root node if there does not currently exist a good parent for that node. Furthermore, they describe some features that can help to establish hierarchical relationships: (1) density (#annotated objects/#objects) (2) overlap (#shared annotated objects/ #annotated objects) (3) distribution of specificity in the graph that describes the detail level of tags in the system (4) agreement between users on which tags are appropriate for a given subject.

8.3.2 Using Association Rule Mining. Schmitz et al. [46] discuss how association rule mining can be adopted to analyze and structure folksonomies, and how the results can be used for ontology learning and supporting emergent semantics. Since folksonomies provide a three-dimensional dataset (users, tags, and resources) instead of a usual two-dimensional one (items and transactions), they present first a systematic overview of projecting a folksonomy onto a two-dimensional structure. They determine the set of objects, i.e., the set on which the support will be counted by a permutation P on the set 1, 2, 3. To induce an ontology from Flickr tags, Schmitz et al. [47] follow this approach. Term x potentially subsumes term y if: $P(x \mid y >= t)$ and $P(y \mid x < t), D_x >= D_{min}, D_y >= D_{min}, U_x >= U_{min}, U_y >= U_{min}$ where: t is the co-occurrence threshold, D_x is the # of documents in which term x occurs, and must be greater than a minimum value D_{min}, and U_x is the # of users that use x in at least one image annotation, and must be greater than a minimum value U_{min}.

Once the co-occurrence statistics are calculated, candidate term pairs are selected using the specified constraints. A graph of possible parent-child relationships is then built, and the co-occurrence of nodes with ascendants that are logically above their parent is filtered out. For a given term x and two potential parent terms p_{x_i} and p_{x_j}, if p_{x_i} is also a potential parent term of p_{x_j} then p_{x_i} is removed from the list of potential parent terms for term x. At the same time, the co-occurrence of terms x, p_{x_i} and p_{x_j} in the given relationships indicates both that the $x \Rightarrow p_{x_j}$ relationship is more likely than simple co-occurrence might indicate, and similarly that the $p_{x_i} \Rightarrow p_{x_j}$ relationship should be reinforced. Weights of each of these relationships are incremented accordingly. Finally, they consider each leaf in the tree and choose the best path up to a root, given the (reinforced) co-occurrence weights for potential parents of each node, and coalesce the paths into trees. They use this induced taxonomy to improve search by inferring parent terms for images with child terms.

8.4 Public Library Cataloging

Folksonomies have the potential to help public library catalogues by enabling clients to store, maintain and organize items of interest in the catalogue [54]. Spiteri et al. [54] acquired tags over a thirty-day period from the daily tag logs of three folksonomy sites: Delicious, Furl and Technorati. The tags were evaluated against Section 6[14] (choice and form of terms) of the National Information Standards Organization (NISO) guidelines for the construction of controlled vocabularies. This evaluation revealed that the folksonomy tags correspond closely to the NISO guidelines that pertain to the types of concepts expressed by the tags, the predominance of single tags, the predominance of nouns and the use of recognized spelling. Potential problem areas in the structure of the tags pertain to the inconsistent use of the singular and plural form of count nouns, and the incidence of ambiguous tags in the form of homographs and unqualified abbreviations or acronyms. If library catalogues decide to incorporate folksonomies, they could provide clear guidelines

[14] http://www.niso.org/publications/tr/tr02.pdf

to address these noted weaknesses, as well as links to external dictionaries and references sources such as Wikipedia to help clients disambiguate homographs and to determine if the full or abbreviated forms of tags would be preferable.

8.5 Clustering and Classification

Tags can be used as the additional features for both clustering and classification.

8.5.1 K-means Clustering in an Extended Vector Space Model. Ramage et al. [42] explore the use of tags in K-means clustering in an extended vector space model that includes tags as well as page text. They also provide a novel generative clustering algorithm based on latent Dirichlet allocation that jointly models text and tags. They examine five ways to model a document with a bag of words B_w and a bag of tags B_t as a vector V : Words Only, Tags Only, Words + Tags, Tags as Words Times n (vector V is represented as $B_w \cup (B_t * n)$ and vocabulary is $W \cup T$), Tags as New Words (word#computer is different from tag#computer). They evaluate the models by comparing their output to an established web directory. They find that the naive inclusion of tagging data improves cluster quality versus page text alone, but a more principled inclusion can substantially improve the quality of all models with a statistically significant absolute F-score increase of 4%. The generative model outperforms K-means with another 8% F-score increase.

8.5.2 Classification of Blog Entries. Brooks and Montanez [7] analyze the effectiveness of tags for classifying blog entries by gathering the top 350 tags from Technorati and measuring the similarity of all articles that share a tag. They find that tags are useful for grouping articles into broad categories, but less effective in indicating the particular content of an article. They show that automatically extracting highly relevant words can produce a more focused categorization of articles. They also show that clustering algorithms can be used to reconstruct a topical hierarchy among tags. They conclude that tagging does manage to group articles into categories, but that there is room for improvement.

8.5.3 Web Object Classification. Yin et al. [62] cast the web object classification problem as an optimization problem on a graph of objects and tags. They then propose an efficient algorithm which not only utilizes social tags as enriched semantic features for the objects, but also infers the categories of unlabeled objects from both homogeneous and heterogeneous labeled objects, through the implicit connection of social tags.

Let C be a category set, $c_1, c_2, ..., c_k$. Every object u and every tag v is a vertex in the graph $G(u, v \in V)$. If an object u is associated with a tag v, there will be an edge between u and v, denoted as $(u, v) \in E$. V consists of four types of vertices: V_S is a set of objects of type S. V_T^l is a set of labeled objects of type T. V_T^u is a set of unlabeled objects of type T. V_{tag} is a set of tags. The problem of web object classification can then be defined as the problem of assigning category weights to each vertex in the graph.

They propose that: (1) Category assignment of a vertex in V_S should not deviate much from its original label. (2) Category assignment of the vertex in V_T^l should remain the same with its original label if it is fully trustable. Even if it is not, it should not deviate too much. (3) Category of the vertex in V_T^u should take the prior knowledge into consideration if there is any. (4) Category assignment of any vertex in graph G should be as consistent as possible to the categories of its neighbors. Using these properties, they write an objective function. By minimizing the above objective function, the optimal class distribution can be found.

8.6 Social Interesting Discovery

Tags represent common wisdom, so it can be useful for social interest discovery. Li et al. [32] propose that human users tend to use descriptive tags to annotate the contents that they are interested in. User-generated tags are consistent with the web content they are attached to, while more concise and closer to the understanding and judgements of human users about the content.

They have developed an Internet Social Interest Discovery system, ISID, to discover the common user interests and cluster users and their saved URLs by different interest topics.

The aggregated user tags of a URL embrace different human judgments on the same subjects of the URL. This property is not possessed by the keywords of their referring web pages. Tags carrying the variation of human judgments reflects the different aspects of the same subjects. More importantly, it helps to identify the social interests in more finer granularity.

Their evaluation results show that: (1) the URLs' contents within a ISID cluster have noticeably higher similarity than that of the contents of URLs across different clusters, and (2) nearly 90% of all users have their social interests discovered by the ISID system.

ISID architecture provides the following functions. (1) Find topics of interests: For a given set of bookmark posts, find all topics of interests. Each topic of interests is a set of tags with the number of their co-occurrences exceeding a given threshold. ISID uses association rules algorithms to identify the frequent tag patterns for the posts. (2) Clustering: For each topic of interests, find all the URLs and the users such that those users have labeled each of the URLs with all the tags in the topic. For each topic, a user cluster and a URL cluster are generated. (3) Indexing: Import the topics of interests and their user and URL clusters into an indexing system for application queries.

They find that the tag-based cosine similarity is quite close to keyword based cosine similarity, indicating that tags really capture the main concepts of documents. Also their results are significantly different from those of [3]. With the tags of blog data, Bateman et al. [3], found that the average pairwise cosine similarity of the articles in tag-based clusters is only a little higher than that of randomly clustered articles, while much lower than that of articles clustered with high $tf \times idf$ key words. However, evaluation by Li et al. [32] shows that tag-based clustering is highly accurate. The reason of this difference is that the clustering of articles in [3] is based on single tags, while topic clustering in [32] is based on multiple co-occurring tags.

8.7 Enhanced Browsing

Social tagging results into a list of weighted tags associated with every resource. Zubiaga et al. [64] suggest alternative navigation ways using social tags: pivot browsing (moving through an information space by choosing a reference point to browse, e.g., pivoting on a tag allows to look for related tags; pivoting on a particular user), popularity driven navigation (sometimes a user would like to get documents that are popular for a known tag, e.g., retrieving only the documents where a tag has been top weighted), and filtering (social tagging allows to separate the stuff you do not want from the stuff you do want, e.g., gathering documents containing a tag but excluding another one). Currently, Wikipedia supports these navigation methods: search engine, category-driven navigation, link-driven navigation.

The tag cloud (or tag index) supports easy social navigation in that each of the tags is clickable; clicking a tag leads to a view of bookmarks that are associated with that tag. Tag clouds are either system-wide, or specific to one user, depending on the current view. Millen and Feinberg [36] study tag browsing on Dogear system. They point out that there is considerable browsing of the bookmark space by other people, other tags (everyone) and other people's tags. These results suggest widespread curiosity about what others are bookmarking. The most frequent way to browse bookmarks is by clicking on another person's name, followed by browsing bookmarks by selecting a specific tag from the system-wide tag cloud. During the trial period, 89% of individuals (2291 of 2579) clicked on URLs that had been bookmarked by another person. 74% of the total pages visited (32596 of 44144) were bookmarked by someone else. This provides considerable evidence that the Dogear service is supporting a high degree of social navigation.

9. Integration

There exist a large number of folksonomies dealing with similar type of objects. As a result, different folksonomies have different tags for the same object. An integration of such folksonomies can help in solving the problem of sparsity of tags associated with Web objects. Integration of folksonomies can help in creating richer user profiles. Some work has been done to integrate these taxonomies by tag co-occurrence analysis and clustering. We discuss such efforts in this section.

9.1 Integration using Tag Co-occurrence Analysis and Clustering

Specia and Motta [53] tackle the problem of integrating folksonomies. They present an approach to minimize the problems of ambiguity, lack of synonymy and discrepancies in granularity by making explicit the semantics behind the tag space in social annotation systems. Using data collected from Delicious and Flickr, they use co-occurrence analysis and clustering techniques to construct meaningful groups of tags that correspond to concepts in an ontology. By exploiting external resources, such as Wikipedia, WordNet, and semantic web ontologies, meaningful relationships can be established between such tag groups.

Figure 16.9 shows the system pipeline.

To establish relationships between tags within each cluster and to refine clusters, they use the following procedure.

(1) Post each possible pair of tags within the cluster to the semantic web search engine in order to retrieve ontologies that contain both tags. All combinations of pairs are tried, since it is not possible to know within which pairs a relation holds (look for matches with labels and identifiers).

(2) If any of the tags is not found by the search engine, consider that they can be acronyms, misspellings or variations of known terms, and look for them in additional resources like wikipedia or Google spell correction.

(3) If the two tags (or the corresponding terms selected from Wikipedia or Google) are not found together by the semantic web search engine, consider them not to be related and eliminate the pair from that cluster if they are not (possibly) related to any other tags, that is, all the combinations of pairs of tags must be searched.

(4) Conversely, if ontologies are found containing the two tags: (a) Check whether the tags were correctly mapped into elements of the ontologies. Tags can refer to the following elements: concepts, instances, or properties. (b) Retrieve information about the tags in each of the ontologies: the type of tag (concept, instance, property), its parents (up to three levels) if it is a concept or an instance, and its domain and range or value if it is a property.

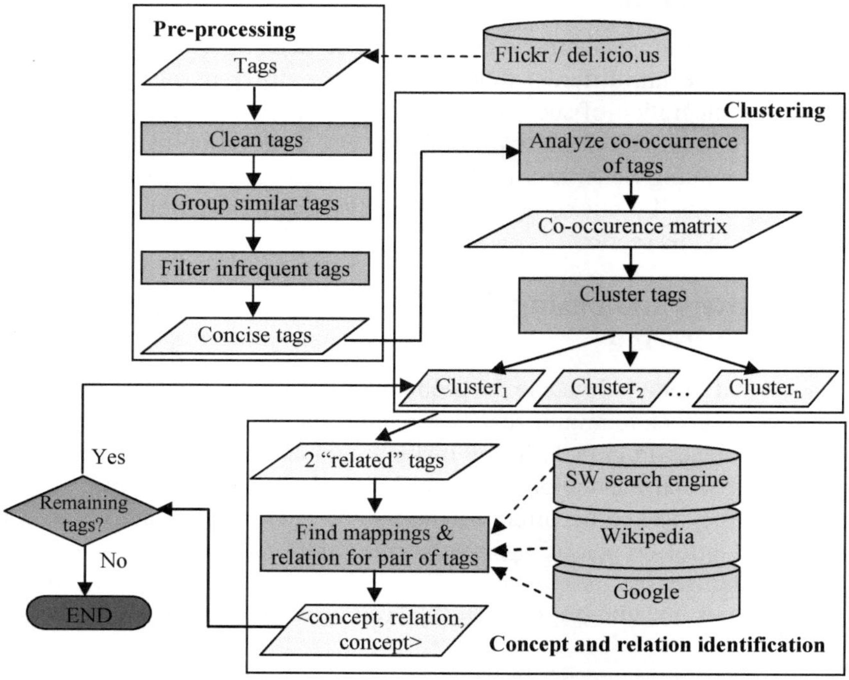

Figure 16.9. Integration system architecture

(5) For each pair of tags for which the semantic web search engine retrieved information, investigate possible relationships between them: (a) A tag is an ancestor of the other. (b) A tag is the range or the value of one of the properties of the other tag. (c) Both tags have the same direct parent. (d) Both tags have the same ancestors, at the same level. (e) Both tags have the same ancestors, at different levels.

9.2 TAGMAS: Federated Tagging System

Iturrioz et al. [25] propose the TAGMAS (TAG Management System) architecture: a federation system that supplies a uniform view of tagged resources distributed across a range of Web2.0 platforms. The TAGMAS system addresses the problem that users do not have consistent view of their resources or a single query end-point with which to search them. The TAGMAS architecture is based on a tagging ontology that provides a homogeneous representation of tags and tagging events. By aggregating user tagging events that span multiple sites, such as Flickr and Delicious, it is possible to query TAGMAS using

SPARQL[15], enabling users to find resources distributed across many sites by their tags, the date when tagged, which site they were tagged in. This declarative query is gradually transformed into a set of distinct invocations where the specificities of each folkserver (data model, location or envelop protocol) is considered. The results are then transported back where details about the envelop protocol or location are gradually removed till raw resources matching the query are rendered to the user which ignore where the resource is located. This heterogeneity stems from four main sources, mainly, the data model, the API model, the enveloped model (REST, XML-RPC or SOAP) and the site place.

Applications of their system include automatic tag creation (which permit to create desktop-specific tags), folksonomy loading (which permit to import a folksonomy from a folkserver), resource annotation (where a resource can be annotated along loaded folksonomies) and resource searching (where tag-based filtering is used to locate resources regardless of where the resource is held). This facility is parameterized for the folkservers whose folksonomy has been downloaded into the desktop.

9.3 Correlating User Profiles from Different Folksonomies

Szomszor et al. [55] compare user tag-clouds from multiple folksonomies to: (1) show how they tend to overlap, regardless of the focus of the folksonomy (2) demonstrate how this comparison helps finding and aligning the user's separate identities, and (3) show that cross-linking distributed user tag-clouds enriches users profiles. During this process, they find that significant user interests are often reflected in multiple Web2.0 profiles, even though they may operate over different domains. However, due to the free-form nature of tagging, some correlations are lost, a problem they address through the implementation and evaluation of a user tag filtering architecture.

Out of the 84851 distinct Delicious tags, and 149529 distinct Flickr tags, 28550 are used in both systems. To measure the alignment between two user tag clouds, they measure the frequency of tags common to Delicious and Flickr. As users tag more resources in Flickr and Delicious, their intersection frequency will increase. Therefore, this increases the confidence that two correlated profiles in Delicious and Flickr refer to the same individual as their total intersection frequency increases.

---

[15] http://www.w3.org/TR/rdf-sparql-query/

10. Tagging problems

Though tags are useful, exploiting them for different applications is not easy. Tags suffer from problems like spamming, canonicalization and ambiguity issues. Other problems such as sparsity, no consensus, etc. are also critical. In this section, we discuss these problems and suggest solutions described in the literature.

10.1 Spamming

Spammers can mis-tag resources to promote their own interests. Wetzker et al. [57] have observed such phenomena where a single user labeled a large number of bookmarks with the same tags all referring to the same blog site. They have also observed a phenomenon where users upload thousands of bookmarks within minutes and rarely actively contribute again. They characterize the spammers as possessing these properties: very high activity, tagging objects belonging to a few domains, high tagging rate per resource, and bulk posts. To detect such spamming, they propose a new concept called diffusion of attention which helps to reduce the influence of spam on the distribution of tags without the actual need of filtering. They define the attention a tag achieves in a certain period of time as the number of users using the tag in this period. The diffusion for a tag is then given as the number of users that assign this tag for the first time. This measures the importance of an item by its capability to attract new users while putting all users on an equal footage. Every user's influence is therefore limited and a trend can only be created by user groups.

Koutrika et al. [28] study the problem of spamming extensively. How many malicious users can a tagging system tolerate before results significantly degrade? What types of tagging systems are more vulnerable to malicious attacks? What would be the effort and the impact of employing a trusted moderator to find bad postings? Can a system automatically protect itself from spam, for instance, by exploiting user tag patterns? In a quest for answers to these questions, they introduce a framework for modeling tagging systems and user tagging behavior. The framework combines legitimate and malicious tags. This model can study a range of user tagging behaviors, including the level of moderation and the extent of spam tags, and compare different query answering and spam protection schemes. They describe a variety of query schemes and moderator strategies to counter tag spam. Particularly, they introduce a social relevance ranking method for tag search results that takes into account how often a user's postings coincide with others' postings in order to determine their "reliability". They define a metric for quantifying the "spam impact" on results. They compare the various schemes under different models for malicious user behavior. They try to understand the weaknesses of existing systems and the magnitude of the tag spam problem. They also make predictions about which schemes will be more useful and which malicious behaviors will be more disruptive in practice.

10.2 Canonicalization and Ambiguities

Ambiguity arises in folksonomies because different users apply terms to documents in different ways. Acronyms can also lead to ambiguities. Users often combine multiple words as a single tag, without spaces, e.g., 'vertigovideostillsbbc' on Flickr. Currently, tags are generally defined as single words or compound words, which means that information can be lost during the tagging process. Single-word tags lose the information that would generally be encoded in the word order of a phrase. There is no synonym or homonym control in folksonomies. Different word forms, plural and singular, are also often both present. Folksonomies provide no formal guidelines for the choice and form of tags, such as the use of compound headings, punctuation, word order. In addition, the different expertise and purposes of tagging participants may result in tags that use various levels of abstraction to describe a resource.

Guy and Tonkin [17] point out the existence of useless tags due to misspellings, bad encoding like an unlikely compound word grouping (e.g., TimBernersLee); tags that do not follow convention in issues such as case and number; personal tags that are without meaning to the wider community (e.g., mydog); single use tags that appear only once in the database (e.g., billybobsdog), symbols used in tags. Conventions have become popular, such as dates represented according to the ISO standard (e.g., 20051201 for "1st December, 2005") and the use of the year as a tag. One wildly popular convention is geotagging, a simple method of encoding latitude and longitude within a single tag; this represented over 2% of the total tags sampled on Flickr. A common source of "misspelt" tags was in the transcoding of other alphabets or characters.

Zubiaga [64] suggests a solution to the canonicalization problem. To merge all forms of the same tag, the system can rely on a method like that by Librarything. This site allows users to define relations between tags, indicating that some of them have the same meaning. In his blog entry, Lars Pind [39] has suggested various ways to solve canonicalization problem, including the following: (1) suggest tags for user, (2) find synonyms automatically, (3) help user use the same tags that others use, (4) infer hierarchy from the tags, and (5) make it easy to adjust tags on old content. Quintarelli [41] mentions that the system can have a correlation feature that, given a tag, shows related tags, i.e., tags that people have used in conjunction with the given tag to describe the same item. Guy and Tonkin [17] suggest educating the users, simple errorchecking in systems when tags are entered by users, making tag suggestions (synonyms, expansion of acronyms etc.) when users submit resources (e.g., using Scrumptious, a recent Firefox extension, offers popular tags from Delicious for every URL). They also suggest creation of discussion tools through which users can share reasons for tagging things in a certain way. More understanding of who is submitting certain tags could possibly alter personal rating of posts by other users.

10.3 Other Problems

There are many other problems related to social tagging, including sparsity, no consensus and search inefficiency. Sparsity is related to the annotation coverage of the data set. Bao et al. [2] point out that certain pages may not be tagged at all. Users do not generally associate tags to newly emerging web pages or web pages that can be accessed easily from hub pages, or uninteresting web pages. Noll et al. [37] observe that the amount of new information provided by metadata (tags, anchor text, search keywords) is comparatively low. All three types of data stay below 6% novelty for about 90% of documents. Search keywords dominate tags which in turn dominate anchor text words. Tags are generally more diverse than anchor texts. On one hand, this result suggests that tags are noisier than anchor texts and therefore potentially less useful. On the other hand, the diversity of tags could be an advantage since it might capture information and meanings that anchor texts miss.

Halpin et al. [18] point that users may not reach a consensus over the appropriate set of tags for a resource leading to an unstable system. As Golder and Huberman [16] suggest, changes in the stability of such patterns might indicate that groups of users are migrating away from a particular consensus on how to characterize a site and its content or negotiating the changing meaning of that site. Quintarelli [41] points out that tags have no hierarchy. Folksonomies are a flat space of keywords. Folksonomies have a very low findability quotient. They are great for serendipity and browsing but not aimed at a targeted approach or search. Tags do not scale well if you are looking for specific targeted items.

11. Conclusion and Future Directions

In this work, we surveyed social tagging with respect to different aspects. We discussed different user motivations and different ways of tagging web objects. We presented a summary of the various tag generation models. We analyzed different tagging system parameters and tagging distributions. We then summarized ways of identifying tag semantics, ways of visualizing tags using tag clouds and ways of recommending tags to users. We presented a variety of applications for which tags have been used. Further, we discussed ways of integrating different folksonomies and problems related to the usage of tags.

Tags are taking on a new meaning as other forms of media like microblogs are gaining popularity. Below we mention a few aspects which can be a part of future research.

11.1 Analysis

Most current research on tagging analysis focus on one single tag stream itself. However, as the type of user generated content evolves, tags may be different and related to different kinds of user generated data, such as microblogs and query logs. For example, How does tag growth differ in microblogs versus that for bookmarks and images. Tagging models for microblogs can be quite different from other tagging models. E.g., certain tags reach a peak on twitter quite unexpectedly. These tags don't relate to any specific events. Such varying degree of social influence when a pseudo event happens hasn't been captured by any of the tagging models, yet.

11.2 Improving System Design

Current tagging systems only support a type of tags and researchers have developed mechanisms to extract hierarchical structures (ontology) from this flat tagging space. Systems can provide more functionality like hierarchical tags, say (programming/java), multi-word tags. A tagging system can also support a tag discussion forum where users can debate about the appropriateness of a tag for a resource. Structured tags can also be supported, i.e., allow people to tag different portions of a web page with different tags and assign key=value pairs rather than just "values". E.g., person="Mahatma Gandhi", location="Porbandar", year="1869", event="birth". By adding more such functionality into the system, we can expect that a more meaningful semantic structure could be extracted.

11.3 Personalized Tag Recommendations

Is the user a describer or organizer? What is the context? Is she tagging on sets in Flickr or just photos in the photostream (i.e. context within the tagging site itself)? Based on her history, what is the probability that she would choose a new tag? What are the words used in her previous tags, words used in her social friends' tags? Given some tags tied to a resource, we can identify whether users prefer to repeat tags for this resource or do they like to put on new tags. Using this we can vary the tag history window size shown with the resource. Apart from tag recommendation, a recommendation system can also recommend related resources once a user selects a particular tag.

11.4 More Applications

There are also interesting applications which are worth exploring. E.g., (1) Tagging support for desktop systems using online tags. (2) Geographical/demographical analysis of users' sentiments based on the tags they apply to products launched at a particular location. (3) Mashups by integrating resources with same/similar tags. (4) Establishing website trustworthiness based on what percent of the keywords mentioned in the <meta> tag are actual tags for web page bookmarks. (5) Summary generation using tags with NLP. (6) Intent detection and behavioral targeting based on user history of tags.

11.5 Dealing With Problems

Sparsity, canonicalization, ambiguities in tags still remain as open problems. More work needs to be done to come up with solutions to effectively deal with them. Also, certain tags get outdated. E.g., a camera model may be marked as 'best camera'. But after two years, it no longer remains the 'best camera'. How can we clean up such kind of tag rot? Similarly, tags that haven't been repeated by another user within a time window, can be considered as personal tags and can be removed from public view.

References

[1] Morgan Ames and Mor Naaman. Why we tag: Motivations for annotation in mobile and online media. In *Conference on Human Factors in Computing Systems, CHI 2007*, Sam Jose, CA, April 2007.

[2] Shenghua Bao, Guirong Xue, Xiaoyuan Wu, Yong Yu, Ben Fei, and Zhong Su. Optimizing web search using social annotations. In *WWW '07: Proceedings of the 16th international conference on World Wide Web*, pages 501–510, New York, NY, USA, 2007. ACM.

[3] Scott Bateman, Christopher Brooks, Gordon Mccalla, and Peter Brusilovsky. Applying collaborative tagging to e-learning. In *Proceedings of the 16th International World Wide Web Conference (WWW2007)*, 2007.

[4] Grigory Begelman, Philipp Keller, and Frank Smadja. Automated tag clustering: Improving search and exploration in the tag space, 2006.

[5] K. Bielenberg. Groups in Social Software: Utilizing Tagging to Integrate Individual Contexts for Social Navigation. Master's thesis, 2005.

[6] David M. Blei, Andrew Y. Ng, and Michael I. Jordan. Latent dirichlet allocation. *J. Mach. Learn. Res.*, 3:993–1022, 2003.

[7] Christopher H. Brooks and Nancy Montanez. Improved annotation of the blogosphere via autotagging and hierarchical clustering. In *WWW '06:*

Proceedings of the 15th international conference on World Wide Web, pages 625–632, New York, NY, USA, 2006. ACM Press.

[8] David Carmel, Haggai Roitman, and Elad Yom-Tov. Who tags the tags?: a framework for bookmark weighting. In *CIKM '09: Proceeding of the 18th ACM conference on Information and knowledge management*, pages 1577–1580, New York, NY, USA, 2009. ACM.

[9] Luigi Di Caro, K. Selçuk Candan, and Maria Luisa Sapino. Using tagflake for condensing navigable tag hierarchies from tag clouds. In Ying Li, Bing Liu, and Sunita Sarawagi, editors, *KDD*, pages 1069–1072. ACM, 2008.

[10] Ciro Cattuto, Andrea Baldassarri, Vito D. P. Servedio, and Vittorio Loreto. Vocabulary growth in collaborative tagging systems, Apr 2007.

[11] Ciro Cattuto, Vittorio Loreto, and Luciano Pietronero. Semiotic dynamics and collaborative tagging. *Proceedings of the National Academy of Sciences (PNAS)*, 104(5):1461–1464, January 2007.

[12] Klaas Dellschaft and Steffen Staab. An epistemic dynamic model for tagging systems. In *HT '08: Proceedings of the nineteenth ACM conference on Hypertext and hypermedia*, pages 71–80, New York, NY, USA, 2008. ACM.

[13] Nicholas Diakopoulos and Patrick Chiu. Photoplay: A collocated collaborative photo tagging game on a horizontal display. preprint (2007) available at http://www.fxpal.com/publications/FXPAL-PR-07-414.pdf.

[14] Pavel A. Dmitriev, Nadav Eiron, Marcus Fontoura, and Eugene Shekita. Using annotations in enterprise search. In *WWW '06: Proceedings of the 15th international conference on World Wide Web*, pages 811–817, New York, NY, USA, 2006. ACM.

[15] Micah Dubinko, Ravi Kumar, Joseph Magnani, Jasmine Novak, Prabhakar Raghavan, and Andrew Tomkins. Visualizing tags over time. In *WWW '06: Proceedings of the 15th international conference on World Wide Web*, pages 193–202, New York, NY, USA, 2006. ACM Press.

[16] Scott Golder and Bernardo A. Huberman. The structure of collaborative tagging systems, Aug 2005.

[17] Marieke Guy and Emma Tonkin. Folksonomies: Tidying up tags? *D-Lib Magazine*, 12, Jan 2006.

[18] Harry Halpin, Valentin Robu, and Hana Shepherd. The complex dynamics of collaborative tagging. In *WWW '07: Proceedings of the 16th international conference on World Wide Web*, pages 211–220, New York, NY, USA, 2007. ACM.

[19] Tony Hammond, Timo Hannay, Ben Lund, and Joanna Scott. Social bookmarking tools (i): A general review. *D-Lib Magazine*, 11(4), April 2005.

[20] Y. Hassan-Montero and V. Herrero-Solana. Improving tag-clouds as visual information retrieval interfaces. In *InScit2006: International Conference on Multidisciplinary Information Sciences and Technologies*, 2006.

[21] M. Heckner, M. Heilemann, and C. Wolff. Personal information management vs. resource sharing: Towards a model of information behaviour in social tagging systems. In *Int'l AAAI Conference on Weblogs and Social Media (ICWSM)*, San Jose, CA, USA, May 2009.

[22] Paul Heymann and Hector Garcia-Molina. Collaborative creation of communal hierarchical taxonomies in social tagging systems. Technical Report 2006-10, Stanford University, April 2006.

[23] Paul Heymann, Georgia Koutrika, and Hector Garcia-Molina. Can social bookmarking improve web search? In *WSDM '08: Proceedings of the international conference on Web search and web data mining*, pages 195–206, New York, NY, USA, 2008. ACM.

[24] Andreas Hotho, Robert Jäschke, Christoph Schmitz, and Gerd Stumme. Information retrieval in folksonomies: Search and ranking. *The Semantic Web: Research and Applications*, pages 411–426, 2006.

[25] Jon Iturrioz, Oscar Diaz, and Cristobal Arellano. Towards federated web2.0 sites: The tagmas approach. In *Tagging and Metadata for Social Information Organization Workshop, WWW07*, 2007.

[26] Owen Kaser and Daniel Lemire. Tag-cloud drawing: Algorithms for cloud visualization, May 2007.

[27] Margaret E. I. Kipp and Grant D. Campbell. Patterns and inconsistencies in collaborative tagging systems : An examination of tagging practices. In *Annual General Meeting of the American Society for Information Science and Technology*. American Society for Information Science and Technology, November 2006.

[28] Georgia Koutrika, Frans A. Effendi, Zolt'n Gyöngyi, Paul Heymann, and Hector G. Molina. Combating spam in tagging systems: An evaluation. *ACM Trans. Web*, 2(4):1–34, 2008.

[29] Christian Körner. Understanding the motivation behind tagging. ACM Student Research Competition - Hypertext 2009, July 2009.

[30] Liz Lawley. social consequences of social tagging. Web article, 2005.

[31] Rui Li, Shenghua Bao, Yong Yu, Ben Fei, and Zhong Su. Towards effective browsing of large scale social annotations. In *WWW '07: Proceedings of the 16th international conference on World Wide Web*, pages 943–952, New York, NY, USA, 2007. ACM.

[32] Xin Li, Lei Guo, and Yihong E. Zhao. Tag-based social interest discovery. In *WWW '08: Proceeding of the 17th international conference on World Wide Web*, pages 675–684, New York, NY, USA, 2008. ACM.

[33] Dong Liu, Xian S. Hua, Linjun Yang, Meng Wang, and Hong J. Zhang. Tag ranking. In *WWW '09: Proceedings of the 18th international conference on World wide web*, pages 351–360, New York, NY, USA, April 2009. ACM.

[34] Cameron Marlow, Mor Naaman, Danah Boyd, and Marc Davis. Ht06, tagging paper, taxonomy, flickr, academic article, toread. In *HYPERTEXT '06: Proceedings of the seventeenth conference on Hypertext and hypermedia*, pages 31–40, New York, NY, USA, 2006. ACM.

[35] A. Mathes. Folksonomies - cooperative classification and communication through shared metadata. *Computer Mediated Communication*, December 2004.

[36] David R. Millen and Jonathan Feinberg. Using social tagging to improve social navigation. In *Workshop on the Social Navigation and Community based Adaptation Technologies*, 2006.

[37] Michael G. Noll and Christoph Meinel. The metadata triumvirate: Social annotations, anchor texts and search queries. *WI/IAT '08: Web Intelligence and Intelligent Agent Technology, IEEE/WIC/ACM International Conference on*, 1:640–647, 2008.

[38] Simon Overell, Börkur Sigurbjörnsson, and Roelof van Zwol. Classifying tags using open content resources. In *WSDM '09: Proceedings of the Second ACM International Conference on Web Search and Data Mining*, pages 64–73, New York, NY, USA, 2009. ACM.

[39] Lars Pind. Folksonomies: How we can improve the tags. Web article, 2005.

[40] Peter Pirolli. Rational analyses of information foraging on the web. *Cognitive Science*, 29(3):343–373, 2005.

[41] Emanuele Quintarelli. Folksonomies: power to the people.

[42] Daniel Ramage, Paul Heymann, Christopher D. Manning, and Hector G. Molina. Clustering the tagged web. In *WSDM '09: Proceedings of the Second ACM International Conference on Web Search and Data Mining*, pages 54–63, New York, NY, USA, 2009. ACM.

[43] Tye Rattenbury, Nathaniel Good, and Mor Naaman. Towards automatic extraction of event and place semantics from flickr tags. In *SIRIR '07: Proceedings of the 30th annual international ACM SIGIR conference on Research and development in information retrieval*, pages 103–110, New York, NY, USA, 2007. ACM Press.

[44] Terrell Russell. cloudalicious: folksonomy over time. In *JCDL '06: Proceedings of the 6th ACM/IEEE-CS joint conference on Digital libraries*, pages 364–364, New York, NY, USA, 2006. ACM.

[45] Ralf Schenkel, Tom Crecelius, Mouna Kacimi, Sebastian Michel, Thomas Neumann, Josiane X. Parreira, and Gerhard Weikum. Efficient top-k querying over social-tagging networks. In *SIGIR '08: Proceedings of the 31st annual international ACM SIGIR conference on Research and development in information retrieval*, pages 523–530, New York, NY, USA, 2008. ACM.

[46] Christoph Schmitz, Andreas Hotho, Robert Jäschke, and Gerd Stumme. Mining association rules in folksonomies. In *Data Science and Classification*, pages 261– 270. Springer, 2006.

[47] Patrick Schmitz. Inducing ontology from flickr tags. In *WWW 2006WWW 2006, May 22Ű26, 2006, Edinburgh, UK*. IW3C2, 2006.

[48] Shilad Sen, Shyong K. Lam, Al Mamunur Rashid, Dan Cosley, Dan Frankowski, Jeremy Osterhouse, F. Maxwell Harper, and John Riedl. tagging, communities, vocabulary, evolution. In *CSCW '06: Proceedings of the 2006 20th anniversary conference on Computer supported cooperative work*, pages 181–190, New York, NY, USA, November 2006. ACM.

[49] Börkur Sigurbjörnsson and Roelof van Zwol. Flickr tag recommendation based on collective knowledge. In *WWW '08: Proceeding of the 17th International Conference on World Wide Web*, pages 327–336, New York, NY, USA, 2008. ACM.

[50] Herbert A. Simon. On a class of skew distribution functions. *Biometrika*, 42(3/4):425–440, 1955.

[51] James Sinclair and Michael Cardew-Hall. The folksonomy tag cloud: when is it useful? *J. Inf. Sci.*, 34(1):15–29, 2008.

[52] Yang Song, Ziming Zhuang, Huajing Li, Qiankun Zhao, Jia Li, Wang C. Lee, and C. Lee Giles. Real-time automatic tag recommendation. In *SIGIR '08: Proceedings of the 31st annual international ACM SIGIR conference on Research and development in information retrieval*, pages 515–522, New York, NY, USA, 2008. ACM.

[53] Lucia Specia and Enrico Motta. Integrating folksonomies with the semantic web. In *ESWC '07: Proceedings of the 4th European conference on The Semantic Web*, pages 624–639, Berlin, Heidelberg, 2007. Springer-Verlag.

[54] Louise F. Spiteri. Structure and form of folksonomy tags: The road to the public library catalogue. *Webology*, 4(2, Artikel 41), 2007.

[55] Martin Szomszor, Ivan Cantador, and Harith Alani. Correlating user profiles from multiple folksonomies. In *ACM Confrence on Hypertext and Hypermedia*, June 2008.

[56] Csaba Veres. The language of folksonomies: What tags reveal about user classification. In *Natural Language Processing and Information Systems*, volume 3999/2006 of *Lecture Notes in Computer Science*, pages 58–69, Berlin / Heidelberg, July 2006. Springer.

[57] Robert Wetzker, Carsten Zimmermann, and Christian Bauckhage. Analyzing social bookmarking systems: A del.icio.us cookbook. In *Proceedings of the ECAI 2008 Mining Social Data Workshop*, pages 26–30. IOS Press, 2008.

[58] Lei Wu, Linjun Yang, Nenghai Yu, and Xian S. Hua. Learning to tag. In *WWW '09: Proceedings of the 18th international conference on World wide web*, pages 361–370, New York, NY, USA, 2009. ACM.

[59] X. Wu, L. Zhang, and Y. Yu. Exploring social annotations for the semantic web. In *Proc. of the 15th International Conference on World Wide Web (WWW'06)*, 2006.

[60] Shengliang Xu, Shenghua Bao, Ben Fei, Zhong Su, and Yong Yu. Exploring folksonomy for personalized search. In *SIGIR '08: Proceedings of the 31st annual international ACM SIGIR conference on Research and development in information retrieval*, pages 155–162, New York, NY, USA, 2008. ACM.

[61] Zhichen Xu, Yun Fu, Jianchang Mao, and Difu Su. Towards the semantic web: Collaborative tag suggestions. In *WWW2006: Proceedings of the Collaborative Web Tagging Workshop*, Edinburgh, Scotland, 2006.

[62] Zhijun Yin, Rui Li, Qiaozhu Mei, and Jiawei Han. Exploring social tagging graph for web object classification. In *KDD '09: Proceedings of the 15th ACM SIGKDD international conference on Knowledge discovery and data mining*, pages 957–966, New York, NY, USA, 2009. ACM.

[63] Ding Zhou, Jiang Bian, Shuyi Zheng, Hongyuan Zha, and C. Lee Giles. Exploring social annotations for information retrieval. In *WWW '08: Proceeding of the 17th international conference on World Wide Web*, pages 715–724, New York, NY, USA, 2008. ACM.

[64] Arkaitz Zubiaga. Enhancing navigation on wikipedia with social tags. In *Wikimania '09*, 2009.

Index

K-Candidate Anonymity, 294
ϵ-Differential Privacy, 291
k-Automorphism Anonymity, 295
k-anonymity, 288
l-diversity, 290
t-closeness, 290
(ϵ,δ)-Differential Privacy, 292
ArnetMiner, 235
BANKS, 357
BLINKS, 357
BlogVox, 343
CONNEX, 235
City Sense Application, 381
DBXplorer, 359
DISCOVER, 359
FacetNet, 97
Google Latitude Application, 381
HITS Algorithm, 223
ImageNet, 416
NetClus Algorithm, 98
NetExpert System, 233
ObjectRank Algorithm, 364
PageRank Algorithm, 222
PoolView, 382
SAGE, 235
SPUD, 235
SimRank, 252
TAGMAS, 486
Trapster, 380
WikiCity, 381
WordNet, 415
XRank, 359
XSEarch, 359
YAGO system, 415

Adamic/Adar, 53
Adsorption for Node Classification, 134
Advertising in Online Social Networks, 206
Affliation Link Disclosure, 284
Affliation Link Disclosure with Confidence, 285
Agglomerative Algorithms, 87
Animal Tracking with Social Sensors, 382
Anonymization in Social Networks, 277
Anonymizing Network Structure, 292
Anonymizing Networks with User-Attributes, 296
Answer Ranking, 357
attribute Disclosure, 282
Attribute Disclosure with Confidence, 282
Attribute Inference Attack, 300
Authorities, 223
Autocorrelation and Influence, 197
Automotive Tracking with Social Sensors, 382

Backward Search, 360
Bayesian Probabilistic Models for Link Prediction, 259
Belief Propagation for Expertise Location, 225
Bidirectional Search, 361
Blog Classification, 341
Blogosphere, 327, 340
Blogs, 327, 334, 340
Bookmarking, 448
Burstiness of Activity, 23
Bursty Additions, 36

Cascade Model, 201
Categorizer Tags, 453
Centrality and Visualization, 319
Centrality Measures, 180
Chance-Constrained Link Prediction, 256
Change Detection in Blogs, 342
Class Skew in Link Prediction, 254
Classification, 354
Classification Models for Link Prediction, 253
Cloud Computing in Social Media, 434
Clustering, 56, 354
Clustering in Social Networks, 80
Clustering with Text and Links, 369
Co-citation Regularity, 118
Co-reference Resolution Query, 281
Coarsening Algorithms for Clustering, 90
Collaborative Filtering, 65
Collaborative Tagging, 448
Collective Classification, 368
Common Neighbors, 53
Community Discovery, 80
Community Discovery in Directed Networks, 98

Community Discovery in Dynamic Networks, 95
Community Media, 415
Community Structure, 27
Community Tracing, 156
Commute Times, 50, 58
Computer Vision, 64
Conductance, 85
Constant and Oscillating Connected Components, 34
Content-based Community Discovery, 100
Crowd-sourcing, 381

Data Mining in Social Media, 328
Data Representation in Social Media, 334
Data Sets for Social Network Analysis, 24, 68
De-duplication with Link Prediction, 244
Degree Centrality, 180
Densification Power Law, 32
Describer Tags, 453
Diameter of Social Networks, 20
Diameter-plot, 33
Differential Privacy, 291
Diffusion Influence Model, 200
Disclosure in Social Networks, 277
Dynamic Community Discovery, 386
Dynamic Modeling of Social Networks, 385
Dynamic Probabilistic Models, 162
Dynamic Social Networks, 149
Dynamic Unweighted Graphs, 32
Dynamic Weighted Graphs, 36

Edge Betweenness, 180
Edge Labeling, 143
Edge Measures for Influence, 178
Edge Weights Power Law, 28
Eigenvalue Power Law, 27
Email Classification, 368
Energy-based Layout, 311
Entropy Plots, 23
Ethnography, 344
Event Maps, 345
Event Semantics from Tags, 465
Evolution of Social Networks and Link Prediction, 246
Existence Query, 281
Existential Test of Social Influence, 188
Expert Location via Referrals, 233
Expert Location with Score Propagation, 218
Expert Location without Graph Constraints, 218
Expert Score Propagation, 224
Expert Team Formation, 218
Expertise Location, 216
Exponential Kernel, 268

Feature Construction for Link Prediction, 247
Federated Tagging System, 486
Folksonomy, 448, 449
Force-directed Layout, 311
Friendship Drift and Influence, 196

Game-based Tagging, 455
Gelling Plot, 33
Geographical Annotation, 413, 424
Girvan-Newman Algorithm, 87
Graph Clustering for Node Classification, 142
Graph Labeling, 115
Graph Regularization, 132, 368
Graph-based Inference, 428
Group Profiling, 338
Grouping Behavior and Influence Analysis, 198

Harmonic Functions, 54, 63
Heavy-tailed Degree Distribution, 26
Heavy-tailed Distributions, 22
Heterogeneous Networks, 97
HITS Algorithm, 46, 223
Hitting Time, 249
Hitting Times, 50, 58
Homophily, 183
Homophily for Node Classification, 118
Hubs, 223
Hybrid Techniques, 312

Identity Disclosure, 281
Incremental Community Tracing, 156
Independent Cascade Model, 234
Inference in Multimedia Information Networks, 427
Influence and Autocorrelation, 197
Influence and Friendship Drift, 196
Influence Maximization, 200
Influence Statistics, 178
Influential Blog Discovery, 206
Influential Bloggers, 341
Influential Node Selection, 234
Information Value based Model for Tagging, 457
Information Visualization, 307
Iterative Formulation for Classification, 130

Jaccard Coefficient, 53

Katz Centrality, 181
Katz Measure, 249
Kernel Approach to Link Prediction, 257
Kernel Feature Conjunction, 251
Kernighan-Lin Algorithm, 86
Kernighan-Lin Objective, 85
Keyword Search, 354, 356
Keyword Search over Graph Data, 360
Keyword Search over XML and Relational Data, 358
Kronecker Kernels, 258

Label Propagation, 129
Label Summarization, 144
Language Model for Tagging, 458
Language Models for Expert Location, 219
Laplacian, 124
Laplacian Kernels, 268
Latent Communities, 162
Laws of Social Network Evolution, 17, 167
Leaders in Social Networks, 206
Linear Algebraic Methods for Link Prediction, 267
Linear Threshold Model, 234
Linguistic Classification of Tags, 454
Link Prediction, 66, 244
Links from Community Media, 416
Links from Semantics, 415
Local Classifiers, 124
Local Probabilistic Model, 244
Local Probabilistic Models for Link Prediction, 259

Map-Reduce Framework for Node Classification, 138
Mapping Query, 281
Marketing with Influence Analysis, 200
Markov Clustering, 91
Matrix-oriented Techniques, 312
Maximizing the Spread of Influence, 204, 233
MDL for Community Discovery, 96
Medial Measures, 182
Mercer Kernels, 258
Metadata Generation, 449
Metric Labeling for Node Classification, 140
Microblogs, 332
Minimum Description Length (MDL), 96
Modularity, 86
Monitoring Latent Communities, 162
Multi-step Propagation for Expertise Location, 226
Multimedia Information Networks, 413

Netnography, 344
Network Generalization, 296
Network of Geographical Information, 423
Network of Personal Photo Albums, 420
Node Centrality, 182
Node Classification, 115, 117
Node Neighborhood based Features, 247
Node-link Diagrams, 310

Online Learning in Multimedia Information Networks, 429
Ontology-based Learning, 415
Ontology-based Visualization, 313
Opinion Leaders, 207, 343
Opinion Mining, 334
Oscillating Connected Components, 34

Page Rank, 46, 222
Personal Photo Albums, 413
Personalized Page Rank, 49, 60
Personalized Search in Tagging, 478
Place Extraction from Tags, 465
Polya Urn Generation Model, 456
Power Laws, 17, 22
Preferential Attachment, 251
Principal Eigenvalue over Time, 36
Privacy Breaches, 280
Privacy in Social Networks, 277
Privacy Issues with Social Sensors, 388
Probabilistic Relational Models for Link Prediction, 264
Propagation Models, 342

Query Semantics, 356

Radial Centrality Measures, 181
Random Walks, 45
Random Walks for Node Classification, 127
Real-time Decision Services with Social Sensors, 389
Recommendation Systems for Community Media, 418
Reconstruction Mechanisms for Randomized Networks, 295
Record Linkage with Link Prediction, 244
Relational Bayesian Network for Link Prediction, 266
Relational Markov Networks, 266
Relational Models for Link Prediction, 264
Relationship Analysis in Photo Albums, 421
Rendezvous Approach to Label Propagation, 131
Retrieval Systems for Community Media, 417
Rooted Pagerank, 250

SALSA, 47
Scalability of Node Classification, 136
Scientific Classification in Wikipedia, 415
Self-similar Weight Additions, 36
Semantic Annotation, 425
Semantic Filtering, 307
Semantic Ontologies, 415
Semantic Query Expansion with Tagging, 476
Semantic Visualization, 313
Semi-supervised Learning, 53
Sensors and Social Networks, 379
Sentiment Analysis, 343
Shingling, 93
Shrinking Diameter, 32
Shuffle Test for Social Influence, 188
Simrank, 49, 60
Small Diameter, 26
Smoothly Evolving Communities, 160
Snapshot Power Laws, 29

Social Action Tracking, 190
Social Classification, 448
Social Data Collection with Sensors, 387
Social Indexing, 448
Social Link Disclosure, 283
Social Link Disclosure with Confidence, 283
Social Media, 327, 413
Social Network Evolution, 18, 149
Social Network Streams, 154
Social Sensors, 379
Social Similarity and Influence, 183
Social Tagging, 448
Sociograms, 311
Sociometer, 384
Spamming in Tags, 488
Spatio-temporal Modeling of Social Networks, 387
Spec Mote, 384
Spectral Algorithms, 89
Spectral Clustering in Dynamic Networks, 97
Spectral Partitioning for Labeling, 141
Speech Segmentation from Social Interactions, 385
Static Properties of Social Networks, 26
Static Unweighted Graphs, 26
Static Weighted Graphs, 27
Statistical Properties of Social Networks, 17
Statistical Visualization, 315
Structural Holes, 182
Structural Privacy, 293
Structural Visualization, 309
Supervised Classification for Link Prediction, 246

Tag Ambiguity, 489
Tag Analysis, 462
Tag Canonicalization, 489
Tag Clouds, 468
Tag Clouds Display Format, 470
Tag Evolution Visualization, 470
Tag Generation Models, 455
Tag Growth, 463
Tag Hierarchy Generation, 469
Tag Recommendations, 472
Tag Selection, 468
Tag Visualization, 467
Tagging Distributions, 463
Tagging Motivations, 451
Tagging Problems, 488
Tagging Rights, 461
Tagging System Design, 460
Tagging System Vocabulary, 463
Tags versus Keywords, 466
Team Formation, 216
Temporal Smoothness, 160
Temporal Visualization, 313
Text Analysis, 64, 353
Text Mining in Social Networks, 353
Tie Strength, 178
Time and Location Themes in Multimedia Information Networks, 422
Topical Change Detection in Blogs, 342
Topical Factor Graph, 186
Transfer Learning in Networks, 371
Triadic Closure, 179
Triangle Power Law, 27

User-Attribute and Network Structure Anonymization, 296

Vertex Feature Aggregation, 251
Viewpoint Neighborhoods, 94
Viral Marketing, 200
Visual Analytics, 307
Visualization of Social Networks, 307
Visualization of Tags, 467

Weak Ties, 179
Webspam, 66
Weight Power Law, 28
Weighted Principal Eigenvalue over Time, 38
Wikis, 334

Yule-Simon Model, 456